CURRICULUM DESIGN

THE OPEN UNIVERSITY
FACULTY OF EDUCATIONAL STUDIES

The Curriculum Design and Development Course Team

Robert Bell
Dennis Briggs
Sheila Dale
Robert Glaister
Michael Golby
Jane Greenwald
Alan Harris
Donald Holms
Margaret Johnson
Martin Lawn
Ken Little
Robert McCormick
John Miller
Caroline Pick
William Prescott (Chairman)
Diana Roantree
David Seligman
Ruth West
Heather Young

Consultants

Clem Adelman (University of East Anglia)
Ray Bolam (University of Bristol)
Keri Davies (University of Stirling)
John Elliott (University of East Anglia)
Philip Gammage (University of Bristol)
Eric Hoyle (University of Bristol)
David Jenkins (University of East Anglia)
Denis Lawton (London Institute of Education)
Barry MacDonald (University of East Anglia)
Harry McMahon (New University of Ulster)
Dudley Plunkett (University of Southampton)
Richard Pring (London Institute of Education)
John Reynolds (University of Lancaster)
Peter Scrimshaw (Homerton College of Education)
Malcolm Skilbeck (New University of Ulster)
Hugh Sockett (New University of Ulster)
Rob Walker (University of East Anglia)

Curriculum Design

Edited by
Michael Golby, Jane Greenwald
Ruth West
at The Open University

CROOM HELM LONDON
in association with
THE OPEN UNIVERSITY PRESS 1975

Croom Helm Ltd, Provident House, Burrell Row,
Beckenham, Kent BR3 1AT
Croom Helm Australia, PO Box 391,
Manuka, ACT 2603, Australia

Reprinted 1976, 1977, 1978, 1979, 1981, 1982 and 1983

ISBN 0-85664-218-5

Printed and bound in Great Britain by
Redwood Burn Limited
Trowbridge, Wiltshire.

CONTENTS

FOREWORD

Two companion volumes of readings, *Curriculum Design* and *Curriculum Innovation,* have been prepared for the course, Curriculum Design and Development (E203), offered by the Faculty of Educational Studies at the Open University.

Curriculum Design is in two parts: Perspectives on the Curriculum, and Issues in Curriculum Design. Among the issues discussed are objectives for the whole curriculum, curriculum organisation, approaches to planning, and curriculum evaluation. *Curriculum Innovation* includes the following sections: styles of curriculum development, curriculum development at national and local levels, innovation and the school, innovation and the teacher, and strategies of innovation.

The Readers form one component of the course, which also includes correspondence texts, radio and television programmes, personal tuition and a number of prescribed texts. In order to avoid duplication we have deliberately excluded from the Readers any material which will appear in one of the other components of the course. This accounts for the non-appearance of some familiar names which might otherwise be expected to appear in such readers.

The Editors wish to acknowledge the help of the consultants to the course team in compiling these Readers.

INTRODUCTION

It is only four years ago that the Open University first began production of a course in the curriculum area, and, as part of the project, produced a Reader called *The Curriculum: Context, Design and Development* (R. Hooper, Oliver and Boyd, Edinburgh, 1971). But during those four years the whole nature and scope of curriculum studies have changed with alarming rapidity. It is perhaps not too dramatic to claim that during these years 'curriculum' has genuinely become a study in its own right, as distinct from a rather vague dimension of educational theory in general. Formerly the area was characterised by discrete contributions from philosophers, psychologists, sociologists and historians, all of whom brought their own discipline to bear on specific questions about specific aspects of curriculum design. Now, specialists like Professor Malcolm Skilbeck are making a convincing case for a study of curriculum issues which transcends individual disciplines, and which demands new modes of enquiry and assessment, and new intellectual perspectives.

The first part of this Reader is intended to illustrate ways in which curriculum theory has developed in this direction; but it is not intended to be a coherent historical survey of the field, nor can it claim to be a balanced selection from theorists of current influence. Either task would have demanded a much larger book; and in any case our final choice of papers (as explained in the Foreword) had to be determined primarily by the needs of students pursuing a particular course of study. For this reason it seems useful here to clarify the lines of thought developed in the first part of that course, so that other readers can appreciate the context in which our selection of papers was made.

In the first place, we wished to make the point that 'curriculum' is not an easy word to define, and that curriculum *issues* spread far wider than one might suspect. An actual situation was explored where a curriculum innovator (R. S. Mackenzie) encountered a wide range of political problems as well as problems which might be thought more intrinsic to the formulation of aims, methods, content (and so on) of a particular school curriculum.

The nature of curriculum issues is then explored systematically, and the following question pursued in some depth. In what ways must curriculum design take into account:

(a) *political, moral and social ideologies* (how is and how should the nature of a curriculum be influenced by the values of the society in which it functions?)
(b) *the nature of knowledge itself* (what epistemological considerations

can help us to decide what 'subjects' to teach and in what 'sequence' to teach them? how can one select, from the whole range of human knowledge, what to teach?)

(c) *the social context of the curriculum* (how do educational institutions interact with other institutions, and with society in general?)

(d) *the ways in which children learn and develop* (what can we learn from the psychology of learning and development about the best ways to teach and to structure the curriculum? what can we derive from psychology in terms of new insights into desirable curriculum objectives?)

(e) *styles of developing the curriculum* (how can those involved in education initiate desirable changes?)

In pursuit of these questions, students are referred to seminar writings in books and educational journals, and the purpose of Part 1 of the Reader is mainly to provide the student with the most important of these writings.

We need not apologise for starting with a work of fiction. *The Saber-tooth Curriculum* is a satire based on the observation that curriculum designers are always behind the times because they do not understand how to adapt education to social change. All the most important and basic questions are sharply illustrated; and these are picked up and developed in the readings which follow.

In some cases it has been possible to summarise major debates of the last decade. For example, Michael F. D. Young exercised considerable influence by redefining the whole nature of the sociology of education, and by exploring the educational implication of a phenomenological approach to knowledge. These implications seemed to be of radical importance, but the claims of Young and his followers were received sceptically by analytical philosphers, whose objections are represented here by Richard Pring's paper, 'Knowledge out of Control'. It was not, however, possible in the space available to do justice to the range of current debates on 'forms of thought', and therefore in the area of epistemology we have had to be content with two 'classics' by Dewey and Phenix; though further developments are represented in Part 2 of this Reader.

Elsewhere, papers are included because they illustrate significant approaches to the development of curriculum theory. For example, a highly individualistic paper by David Jenkins illustrates a trend in the direction of the use of metaphor to illuminate education issues – a quite different sort of approach from the coolly analytical style of Hirst and Peters, or from the visionary pleading of Paulo Freire.

We hope that despite the inevitably fragmentary nature of the selection, even in isolation from the Open University course, it will serve to illustrate the most important recent developments in the curriculum field.

The texts have been reproduced with their original spelling and punctuation, though the use of quotation marks and the treatment of headings have been standardised throughout. Obvious misprints have been corrected. Numbered notes have been put at the end of each chapter (renumbered sequentially if necessary), followed by any further references. Asterisked notes are at the foot of the page, and a small number of these have been omitted where they refer to deleted material. Editorial omissions or interpolations are indicated by the use of square brackets. The editors' introductions to each chapter are set in italic type.

Part 1 Perspectives on the Curriculum

1. THE SABER-TOOTH CURRICULUM

Harold Benjamin

From *The Saber-tooth Curriculum* by J. A. Peddiwell. Foreword by Harold Benjamin. Copyright 1939 by McGraw-Hill Inc. Used with permission of McGraw-Hill Book Company (New York).

This is a chapter from a famous satire on curriculum published in the United States in 1939. It tells the story of a prehistoric tribe which decided to introduce systematic education for its children. The curriculum was specifically designed to meet particular survival needs in the local environment and so included such subjects as saber-tooth-tiger-scaring with fire. But the climate of the region changes and the saber-tooth tigers perish. Attempts to change the curriculum to meet new survival needs encounter stern opposition.

The first great educational theorist and practitioner of whom my imagination has any record was a man of Chellean times whose full name was *New-Fist-Hammer-Maker* but whom, for convenience, I shall hereafter call *New-Fist.*

New-Fist was a doer, in spite of the fact that there was little in his environment with which to do anything very complex. You have undoubtedly heard of the pear-shaped, chipped-stone tool which archeologists call the *coup-de-poing* or fist hammer. New-Fist gained his name and a considerable local prestige by producing one of these artifacts in a less rough and more useful form than any previously known to his tribe. His hunting clubs were generally superior weapons, moreover, and his fire-using techniques were patterns of simplicity and precision. He knew how to do things his community needed to have done, and he had the energy and will to go ahead and do them. By virtue of these characteristics he was an educated man.

New-Fist was also a thinker. Then, as now, there were few lengths to which men would not go to avoid the labor and pain of thought. More readily than his fellows, New-Fist pushed himself beyond those lengths to the point where cerebration was inevitable. The same quality of intelligence which led him into the socially approved activity of producing a superior artifact also led him to engage in the socially disapproved practice of thinking. When other men gorged themselves on the proceeds of a successful hunt and vegetated in dull stupor for many hours thereafter, New-Fist ate a little less heartily, slept a little less stupidly, and arose a little earlier than his comrades to sit by the fire and think. He would stare moodily at the flickering flames and wonder about various parts of his environment until he finally got to the point where he became strongly dissatisfied with the accustomed ways of his tribe. He began to catch glimpses of ways in which life might be made better for himself, his family, and his group. By virtue of this development, he became a dangerous man.

This was the background that made this doer and thinker hit upon the concept of a conscious, systematic education. The immediate stimulus which put him directly into the practice of education came from watching his children at play. He saw these children at the cave entrance before the fire engaged in activity with bones and sticks and brightly colored pebbles. He noted that they seemed to have no purpose in their play beyond immediate pleasure in the activity itself. He compared their activity with that of the grown-up members of the tribe. The children played for fun; the adults worked for security and enrichment of their lives. The children dealt with bones, sticks and pebbles; the adults dealt with food, shelter, and clothing. The children protected themselves from boredom; the adults protected themselves from danger.

'If I could only get these children to do the things that will give more and better food, shelter, clothing, and security,' thought New-Fist, 'I would be helping this tribe to have a better life. When the children became grown, they would have more meat to eat, more skins to keep them warm, better caves in which to sleep, and less danger from the striped death with the curving teeth that walks these trails by night.'

Having set up an educational goal, New-Fist proceeded to construct a curriculum for teaching that goal. 'What things must we tribesmen know how to do in order to live with full bellies, warm backs, and minds free from fear?' he asked himself.

To answer this question, he ran various activities over in his mind. 'We have to catch fish with our bare hands in the pool far up the creek beyond that big bend,' he said to himself. 'We have to catch fish with our bare hands in the pool right at the bend. We have to catch them in the same way in the pool just this side of the bend. And so we catch them in the next pool and the next and the next. Always we catch them with our bare hands.'

Thus New-Fist discovered the first subject of the first curriculum – fish-grabbing-with-the-bare-hands.

'Also we club the little woolly horses,' he continued with his analysis. 'We club them along the bank of the creek where they come down to drink. We club them in the thickets where they lie down to sleep. We club them in the upland meadow where they graze. Wherever we find them we club them.'

So woolly-horse-clubbing was seen to be the second main subject in the curriculum.

'And finally, we drive away the saber-tooth tigers with fire,' New-Fist went on in his thinking. 'We drive them from the mouth of our caves with fire. We drive them from our trail with burning branches. We have firebrands to drive them from our drinking hole. Always we have to drive them away, and always we drive them with fire.'

Thus was discovered the third subject – saber-tooth-tiger-scaring-with-fire.

Having developed a curriculum, New-Fist took his children with him as he went about his activities. He gave them an opportunity to practice these three subjects. The children liked to learn. It was more fun for them to engage in these purposeful activities than to play with colored stones just for the fun of it. They learned the new activities well, and so the educational system was a success.

As New-Fist's children grew older, it was plain to see that they had an advantage in good and safe living over other children who had never been educated systematically. Some of the more intelligent members of the tribe began to do as New-Fist had done, and the teaching of fish-grabbing, horse-clubbing, and tiger-scaring came more and more to be accepted as the heart of real education.

For a long time, however, there were certain more conservative members of the tribe who resisted the new, formal educational system on religious grounds. 'The Great Mystery who speaks in thunder and moves in lightning', they announced impressively, 'the Great Mystery who gives men life and takes it from them as he wills – if that Great Mystery had wanted children to practice fish-grabbing, horse-clubbing, and tiger-scaring before they were grown up, he would have taught them these activities himself by implanting in their natures instincts for fish-grabbing, horse-clubbing, and tiger-scaring. New-Fist is not only impious to attempt something the Great Mystery never intended to have done; he is also a damned fool for trying to change human nature.'

Whereupon approximately half of these critics took up the solemn chant, 'If you oppose the will of the Great Mystery, you must die,' and the remainder sang derisively in unison, 'You can't change human nature.'

Being an educational statesman as well as an educational administrator and theorist, New-Fist replied politely to both arguments. To the more theologically minded, he said that, as a matter of fact, the Great Mystery had ordered this new work done, that he even did the work himself by causing children to want to learn, that children could not learn by themselves without divine aid, that they could not learn at all except through the power of the Great Mystery, and that nobody could really understand the will of the Great Mystery concerning fish, horses, and saber-tooth tigers unless he had been well grounded in the three fundamental subjects of the New-Fist school. To the human-nature-cannot-be-changed shouters, New-Fist pointed out the fact that paleolithic culture had attained its high level by changes in human nature and that it seemed almost unpatriotic to deny the very process which had made the community great.

'I know you, my fellow tribesmen,' the pioneer educator ended his argument gravely, 'I know you as humble and devoted servants of the Great Mystery. I know that you would not for one moment consciously oppose yourselves to his will. I know you as intelligent and loyal citizens of this great cave-realm, and I know that your pure and noble patriotism will not permit you to do anything which will block the development of that most cave-realmish of all our institutions – the paleolithic educational system. Now that you understand the true nature and purpose of this institution, I am serenely confident that there are no reasonable lengths to which you will not go in its defense and its support.'

By this appeal the forces of conservatism were won over to the side of the new school, and in due time everybody who was anybody in the community knew that the heart of good education lay in the three subjects of fish-grabbing, horse-clubbing, and tiger-scaring. New-Fist and his contemporaries grew old and were gathered by the Great Mystery to the Land of the Sunset far down the creek. Other men followed their educational ways more and more, until at last all the children of the tribe were practiced systematically in the three fundamentals. Thus the tribe prospered and was happy in the possession of adequate meat, skins, and security.

It is to be supposed that all would have gone well forever with this good educational system if conditions of life in that community had remained forever the same. But conditions changed, and life which had once been so safe and happy in the cave-realm valley became insecure and disturbing.

A new ice age was approaching in that part of the world. A great glacier came down from the neighboring mountain range to the north. Year after year it crept closer and closer to the headwaters of the creek which ran through the tribe's valley, until at length it reached the stream and began to melt into the water. Dirt and gravel which the glacier had collected on its long journey were dropped into the creek. The water grew muddy. What had once been a crystal-clear stream in which one could see easily to the bottom was now a milky stream into which one could not see at all.

At once the life of the community was changed in one very important respect. It was no longer possible to catch fish with the bare hands. The fish could not be seen in the muddy water. For some years, moreover, the fish in this creek had been getting more timid, agile, and intelligent. The stupid, clumsy, brave fish, of which originally there had been a great many, had been caught with the bare hands for fish generation after fish generation, until only fish of superior intelligence and agility were left. These smart fish, hiding in the muddy water under the newly deposited glacial boulders, eluded the hands of the most expertly trained fish-grabbers. Those tribesmen who had studied advanced fish-grabbing in the secondary school could do no better than their less well-educated fellows who had taken only an elementary course in the subject, and even the university graduates with majors in ichthyology were baffled by the problem. No matter how good a man's fish-grabbing education had been, he could not grab fish when he could not find fish to grab.

The melting waters of the approaching ice sheet also made the country wetter. The ground became marshy far back from the banks of the creek. The stupid woolly horses, standing only five or six hands high and running on four-toed front feet and three-toed hind feet, although admirable objects for clubbing, had one dangerous characteristic. They were ambitious. They all wanted to learn to run on their middle toes. They all had visions of becoming powerful and aggressive animals instead of little and timid ones. They dreamed of a far-distant day when some of their descendants would be sixteen hands high, weigh more than half a ton, and be able to pitch their would-be riders into the dirt. They knew they could never attain these goals in a wet, marshy country, so they all went east to the dry, open plains, far from the paleolithic hunting grounds. Their places were taken by little antelopes who came down with the ice sheet and were so shy and speedy and had so keen a scent for danger that no one could approach them closely enough to club them.

The best-trained horse-clubbers of the tribe went out day after day and employed the most efficient techniques taught in the school, but day after day they returned empty-handed. A horse-clubbing education of the highest type could get no results when there were no horses to club.

Finally, to complete the disruption of paleolithic life and education, the new dampness in the air gave the saber-tooth tigers pneumonia, a disease to which these animals were peculiarly susceptible and to which most of them succumbed. A few moth-eaten specimens crept south to the desert, it is true, but they were pitifully few and weak representatives of a once numerous and powerful race.

So there were no more tigers to scare in the paleolithic community, and the best tiger-scaring techniques became only academic exercises, good in themselves, perhaps, but not necessary for tribal security. Yet this danger to the people was lost only to be replaced by another and even greater danger, for with the advancing ice sheet came ferocious glacial bears which were not afraid of fire, which walked the trails by day as well as by night, and which could not be driven away by the most advanced methods developed in the tiger-scaring courses of the schools.

The community was now in a very difficult situation. There was no fish or meat for food, no hides for clothing, and no security from the hairy death that walked the trails day and night. Adjustment to this difficulty had to be made at once if the tribe was not to become extinct.

Fortunately for the tribe, however, there were men in it of the old New-Fist breed, men who had the ability to do and the daring to think. One of them stood by the muddy stream, his stomach contracting with hunger pains, longing for some way to get a fish to eat. Again and again he had tried the old fish-grabbing technique that day, hoping desperately that at last it might work, but now in black despair he finally rejected all that he had learned in the schools and looked about him for some new way to get fish from that stream. There were stout but slender vines hanging from trees along the bank. He pulled them down and began to fasten them together more or less aimlessly. As he worked, the vision of what he might do to satisfy his hunger and that of his crying children back in the cave grew clearer. His black despair lightened a little. He worked more rapidly and intelligently. At last he had it – a net, a crude seine. He called a companion and explained the device. The two men took the net into the water, into pool after pool, and in one hour they caught more fish – intelligent fish in muddy water – than the whole tribe could have caught in a day under the best fish-grabbing conditions.

Another intelligent member of the tribe wandered hungrily through the woods where once the stupid little horses had abounded but where now only the elusive antelope could be seen. He had tried the horse-clubbing technique on the antelope until he was fully convinced of its futility. He knew that one would starve who relied on school learning to get him meat in those woods. Thus it was that he too, like the fish-net inventor, was finally impelled by hunger to new ways. He bent a strong, springy young tree over an antelope trail, hung a noosed vine therefrom, and fastened the whole device in so ingenious a fashion that the passing animal would release a trigger and be snared neatly when the tree jerked upright. By setting a line of these snares, he was able in one night to secure more meat and skins than a dozen horse-clubbers in the old days had secured in a week.

A third tribesman, determined to meet the problem of the ferocious bears, also forgot what he had been taught in school and began to think in direct and radical fashion. Finally, as a result of this thinking, he dug a deep pit in a bear trail, covered it with branches in such a way that a bear would walk out on it unsuspectingly, fall through to the bottom, and remain trapped until the tribesmen could come up and despatch him with sticks and stones at their leisure. The inventor showed his friends how to dig and camouflage other pits until all the trails around the community were furnished with them. Thus the tribe had even more security than before and in addition had the great additional store of meat and skins which they secured from the captured bears.

As the knowledge of these new inventions spread, all the members of the tribe were engaged in familiarizing themselves with the new ways of living. Men worked hard at making fish nets, setting antelope snares, and digging bear pits. The tribe was busy and prosperous.

There were a few thoughtful men who asked questions as they worked. Some of them even criticized the schools.

'These new activities of net-making and operating, snare-setting, and pit-digging are indispensable to modern existence,' they said. 'Why can't they be taught in school?'

The safe and sober majority had a quick reply to this naive question. 'School!' they snorted derisively. 'You aren't in school now. You are out here in the dirt working to preserve the life and happiness of the tribe.

What have these practical activities got to do with schools? You're not saying lessons now. You'd better forget your lessons and your academic ideals of fish-grabbing, horse-clubbing, and tiger-scaring if you want to eat, keep warm, and have some measure of security from sudden death.'

The radicals persisted a little in their questioning. 'Fishnet-making and using, antelope-snare construction and operation, and bear-catching and killing,' they pointed out, 'require intelligence and skills – things we claim to develop in schools. They are also activities we need to know. Why can't the schools teach them?'

But most of the tribe, and particularly the wise old men who controlled the school, smiled indulgently at this suggestion. 'That wouldn't be *education*,' they said gently.

'But why wouldn't it be?' asked the radicals.

'Because it would be mere training,' explained the old men patiently. 'With all the intricate details of fish-grabbing, horse-clubbing, and tiger-scaring – the standard cultural subjects – the school curriculum is too crowded now. We can't add these fads and frills of net-making, antelope-snaring, and – of all things – bear-killing. Why, at the very thought, the body of the great New-Fist, founder of our paleolithic education system, would turn over in its burial cairn. What we need to do is to give our young people a more thorough grounding in the fundamentals. Even the graduates of the secondary schools don't know the art of fish-grabbing in any complete sense nowadays, they swing their horse clubs awkwardly too, and as for the old science of tiger-scaring – well, even the teachers seem to lack the real flair for the subject which we oldsters got in our teens and never forgot.'

'But, damn it,' exploded one of the radicals, 'how can any person with good sense be interested in such useless activities? What is the point of trying to catch fish with the bare hands when it just can't be done any more? How can a boy learn to club horses when there are no horses left to club? And why in hell should children try to scare tigers with fire when the tigers are dead and gone?'

'Don't be foolish,' said the wise old men, smiling most kindly smiles. 'We don't teach fish-grabbing to grab fish; we teach it to develop a generalized agility which can never be developed by mere training. We don't teach horse-clubbing to club horses; we teach it to develop a generalized strength in the learner which he can never get from so prosaic and specialized a thing as antelope-snare-setting. We don't teach tiger-scaring to scare tigers; we teach it for the purpose of giving that noble courage which carries over into all the affairs of life and which can never come from so base an activity as bear-killing.'

All the radicals were silenced by this statement, all except the one who was most radical of all. He felt abashed, it is true, but he was so radical that he made one last protest.

'But – but anyway,' he suggested, 'you will have to admit that times have changed. Couldn't you please *try* these other more-up-to-date activities? Maybe they have *some* educational value after all?'

Even the man's fellow radicals felt that this was going a little too far.

The wise old men were indignant. Their kindly smiles faded. 'If you had any education yourself,' they said severely, 'you would know that the essence of true education is timelessness. It is something that endures through changing conditions like a solid rock standing squarely and firmly in the middle of a raging torrent. You must know that there are some eternal verities, and the saber-tooth curriculum is one of them!'

2. CLASSIC AND ROMANTIC IN THE CURRICULUM LANDSCAPE

David Jenkins

Source: Reading from Unit 6 of *The Curriculum: Context, Design and Development, Open University Press, 1972* (revised 1975).

Taking 'landscape' (rather more specifically than 'field') as his metaphor, David Jenkins analyses distinctions between 'classic' and 'romantic' in approaches to curriculum design. This analysis emphasises taste *and* judgement *but does not ignore the link between aesthetic responses to the curriculum on the one hand, and perceptual frameworks derived from the social sciences on the other.*

The purpose of this analysis is to pose a number of current 'dilemmas' in the curriculum debate against the broader dichotomy of classic and romantic traditions in education. Professor Skilbeck has analysed this dichotomy in terms of a number of binary pairs.[1] The concepts in the left-hand column exemplify the concerns of a classic tradition, the concepts in the right-hand column those of a romantic tradition:

(1)	Standards	against	Expression
(2)	Structure	against	Style
(3)	Unity	against	Diversity
(4)	Excellence	against	Excellences
(5)	Rationality	against	Experience
(6)	Culture	against	Sub-cultures

But first I need to establish my chosen metaphor, which is the curriculum as landscape. The intention is to press the landscape metaphor in the direction of the classic/romantic analysis and see what insights it generates.

My text for the day is borrowed from Anthony Ashley, Third Earl of Shaftesbury, who opposes the 'horrid graces of the wilderness' and the 'formal mockery of princely gardens':

> . . . even the rude rocks, the mossy caverns, the irregular unwrought grottos and broken falls of water, with all the horrid graces of the wilderness itself . . . appear with a magnificence beyond the formal mockery of princely gardens.[2]

Since the Dartmouth Seminar and the publication of John Dixon's *Growth through English*[3] the word 'growth' has had a central (and some say questionable) importance to English teachers working on the ideological frontiers of the subject. The ramifications of the metaphor take us back towards particular models of learning and suggest a related set of infinitives for teaching (to cultivate? to nurture?).

But why does the prospect of comparing landscape and curriculum appear initially attractive? Firstly, I suggest, because it raises issues of taste and judgement. Teachers sometimes feel hounded by the means/ends rationalism of much that passes for curriculum theory, and I want to offer an initial reassurance. It also offers the freedom of a new vocabulary. I am sure I shall end up talking about the *gothic curriculum,* the *neo-curriculum* and the *formal curriculum garden.* But to do so would arguably not involve a radical departure from the way in which we already use language if we assent to an ideology of 'growth'. The problem can be formulated more prosaically. Have we an adequate language by which different teaching strategies and curriculum styles can be articulated?

The second reason for taking the opposition in landscape between the 'wilderness' and the 'princely gardens' for our metaphor is that it raises the issue of human intervention in the landscape, which tends to remain singularly obscured by the general concept of 'growth'. Also, the scale is right. Landscapes are natural, but they can be organised. The concept of intervention raises several issues. Growth towards what – the princely gardens or the horrid graces of the wilderness?

The third reason for taking the metaphor of the landscape is that it will allow the dichotomy of curriculum between romantic and classic traditions to be argued out. It will enable me to draw a number of implications from Malcolm Skilbeck's analysis.

Fourthly, it seems to me that there is a suggestive link here between aesthetic responses and perceptual frameworks in the social sciences, a point of comparison returned to recently by Richard Hoggart.[4] Howard Becker could have been referring to landscape when he asserted that everything is seen from *somebody's* perspective. Robin Blackburn declares that such *points of view* frequently embrace value positions:

> All the bourgeois social sciences declare their ambition to become 'value-neutral' sciences. Once theories are thoroughly cleansed of all 'value judgements' it is believed that they will be governed only by the wholesome discipline of objective facts. The predictable consequence of this attempted purge of values is to orient theory and research towards certain crude over-abstracted value notions masquerading as scientific concepts.[5]

Metaphors can perhaps probe more deeply if the object of the comparison has attracted an intellectual history in its own right. Metaphors themselves may conceal value positions.

Fifthly, the concept of a landscape reminds us that the perceiving figures are themselves Barbara Hepworth-like 'figures *within* a landscape'. They see not a cartographer's view but a locational one[6] divisible into background, middle distance and foreground. In the same way as an aesthetic response is conditioned by distance, so in curriculum theory there may be different levels of analysis, variously appropriate to different people in different situations.

The present purpose, then, is to articulate a classic and a romantic tradition, and to use the concepts employed as exploratory tools in analysing a current curriculum dilemma. We will refer from time to time to our landscape metaphor, hoping that its usefulness will go beyond surface decoration to the structure of the argument. It may be convenient to begin by taking a look at the classic tradition.

Although I don't want my text for the day to prejudge the issues involved, Shaftesbury's phrase – 'the mockery of princely gardens' – is a suggestive one. It is suggestive for two reasons: it raises the issue of the distributive element in curriculum (the gardens are for 'princes') and it invites the question of precisely what is involved in the term 'mockery' (does life imitate art?). The classic tradition takes a certain view of knowledge, and identifies how it is to be produced and by whom it is to be consumed. It may be briefly described as a number of focal concerns within education.

(1) An emphasis on standards of performance

What the learner is to aspire to is clearly delineated. To this extent it offers support for the notion of external examinations[7] in so far as these embody the concern for public standards. The standards are objective and apply even to aesthetic areas, within which appropriate rules incorporating 'good taste' can be generated. It may be worth puzzling whether some school subjects have relative difficulty in establishing the criteria by which performances reach an acceptable standard.

(2) An emphasis on structure

Structure is again a concept suggesting objective organisation, as its standards are not dependent upon the preferences of individuals. Structure gives rise to a sense of form. Recently this argument has entered the curriculum debate through a re-emphasis on the structure and syntax of individual disciplines of knowledge.[8] There have been several results of this concern, including the following:

(a) Boundary maintenance. A tendency for scholars to defend the traditional notions within which concerns for one's subject tend to be expressed.

(b) A process of self-renewal within individual subjects or disciplines. This has focused around the quest for key concepts, key generalisations, methodological issues (how to proceed from raw data to conclusion) and truth tests or validation procedures. (The truth conditions for propositions encountered in the social sciences may be different from the truth conditions for propositions encountered in the expressive arts.)

It is less clear how a rigid view of structure (itself linked to a view that knowledge is a public commodity) is connected with the activity of inquiry. The difficulty occurs precisely because inquiry is itself a 'structuring' activity, seeking to understand and organise experience. At times the frameworks of teachers and taught appear to be on a collision path. Harold Rosen has commented upon the 'desperate mimickry' when pupils try to acquire superficial features of the teacher's langauge.[9] But if we push the notion of inquiry itself beyond a superficial level, we end up explicitly or implicitly with some kind of inquiry *models* (e.g. ways of finding out that are relatively established and not unconnected with the structure of disciplines).

(3) An emphasis on unity

At a simple level this involves the belief that knowledge accords easily with action, that educated persons think like men of action and act like men of thought. The style is one within which contradictions, tensions and ambiguities are absent. Its supreme assertion is Aristotle's belief that absence of moral effort is a symptom of virtue. The curriculum reflects this unity (the tidiness of the *seven liberal arts,* etc.). The difficulties of espousing this classic view of curriculum relate ultimately to cultural pluralism. Smith, Stanley and Shores' *Fundamentals of Curriculum Development* analyses the possible contemporary usefulness of the notion of a cultural 'core', but ends up suggesting something of a quest.[10] The core *contains* contradictions, tensions and ambiguities. Education is for uncertainty, if not an apprenticeship in desolation.

(4) An emphasis on excellence

The notion of excellence, historically, leans back towards the Greek 'upbringing'. It emphasises quality and reputation, and its standards are consistent and objective. There is some indication that the concept in a modified form is becoming increasingly fashionable within the curriculum debate following Broudy, Smith and Burnett's *Democracy and Excellence in American Secondary Education.*[11]

(5) An emphasis on rationality

It is perhaps in this area that the current revival of classicism is most marked, and where the humanities teacher feels a particular uncertainty. In John Wilson's *Education and the Concept of Mental Health,* even mental health appears ultimately to be reduced to rationality. Wilson's work for the Farmington Trust attempts the same kind of exercise for moral education, 'operationalising' the concept into a number of discrete 'moral behaviours' ('Phil', 'Dik', 'Emp' and all that 'Krat').[12] Other fashionable areas in which rationality is currently being re-emphasized are curriculum theory itself (Tyler's 'rational curriculum planning')[13] and systems analysis, based on a hard distinction between means and ends.[14] It may be worth noting that the whole issue of the prespecification of educational objectives arises from the 'demands' of a rational design model. Such schemes are pushed back too infrequently towards the necessary appraisal of their 'models of man'.

(6) An emphasis on culture

Within the classic tradition this ultimately means an emphasis on the high culture, the 'princely' gardens. The whole concept of curriculum development, as conventionally understood, appears to deny one of the basic assumptions of the classic tradition, that culture depends upon a settled conceptual apparatus, stable 'expectations', and a community of outlook.[15]

In all classic traditions cultural change is something that occurs, if at all, out at the frontiers and stems from the influence of the centre. The implication is that the centre doesn't need it. The model is a 'centre-peripheral' one, based on the need to 'civilise' the 'outposts'. (In passing, it may be interesting to ask how many of the Schools Council curriculum development projects have unconsciously adopted this model.)[16]

So much for this quick analysis of salient features within a classic tradition, and I hope I did not give the impression that I find it wholly unattractive. But before we adjudicate its concerns within their own terms, we must discover what alternatives are available within a romantic tradition. In accordance with our somewhat extreme 'text for the day' we now turn to the 'horrid graces of the wilderness'. Anthony Ashley himself, of course, was articulating a shift in taste from the formal eighteenth-century garden to the cult of the picturesque and the whole 'machinery' of the gothic; an interesting guide through this area of aesthetic history is Christopher Hussey's *The Picturesque: Studies in a Point of View.*[17]

The romantic alternatives are presented as starkly contrasting, leaving the reader to make his own choice or resolution (at this point, the exponents of the classic tradition hold up a prompt-card that reads: 'Do not adjust your mental set; there is a temporary fault in the picture.')

(1) For 'standards read 'expression'

Expression is emphasised precisely because it is a supremely individualist virtue. At one extreme, the question whether any particular expression reaches a 'standard' is dismissed as irrelevant. It is not that the expression should or should not reach a standard. Rather the notion of expression has actually replaced the notion of standard. English teaching is currently very sympathetic towards this shift in emphasis. John Dixon's *Growth through English* depicts the teacher as incomplete, himself struggling for growth.[18]

He makes visible to the pupils his own self-testing and self-exposure. Peter Cox and Malcolm Ross, outlining the ideology of the Schools Council *Arts and the Adolescent Project,* emphasise the pupil's need for a rich, full, expressive life. Access to this full expressive life is a matter of 'enthusiasm' depending on 'the personality of the teacher'. An emphasis on expression often appears to be based on a questionable set of minimum assumptions about the kind of learning that leads to performance. How many invitations to 'creative writing' in such books as *English through Experience,*[19] are set up within a naïve stimulus-response theory?

(2) For 'structure' read 'style'[20]

The 'horrid graces of the wilderness' gave us the gloomy landscapes of Claude of Lorraine and Salvator Rosa. The equivalent poetical output departed from conventional notions of form in favour of immediacy, at best 'local poetry' embellished with historical retrospection and incidental meditation. Contemporary pop culture reflects this return to the notion of style, coupled with the realisation that, properly understood, style is personal (not to be confused with 'decorum' which defines 'appropriate' behaviour in the classic framework.) To emulate anybody else is to lay oneself open to criticism. Style demands 'doing one's thing'. In passing it is interesting to observe this notion of style nudging into morality, which is seen by Peter McPhail (Director of the Schools Council *Moral Education Project*) as involving a particular inter-personal style, labelled 'considerate'. In this respect the Schools Council *Moral Education Project* contrasts with that of the Farmington Trust.

(3) For 'unity' read 'diversity'

The romantic tradition does not just accept diversity, it exalts and glorifies it. If the curriculum is seeking a way to celebrate this diversity in people and ideas, it may begin with what James Macdonald calls an assertion of its 'moral commitment to freedom'.[21] Burke's *Of our Ideas of the Sublime and Beautiful*[22] emphasises this diversity in relation to landscape; its light and shade, its massively rugged forms, juxtaposed contrasts and restlessly moving clouds. It is difficult to view the many *landscape with banditi* produced at this time without responding to the sense of awe and tragic destiny as nature overwhelms man with her own moods. The figures are not reassuring to those whose image of man is confined to *homo sapiens.*

The notion of diversity within curriculum thinking has been sensitively explored by Basil Bernstein. It is interesting to ask how much of the analysis in *Open Schools, Open Society?* relates ultimately to the classic/romantic dichotomy.[23] Curriculum builders could well learn one important lesson from the gothic, i.e., the need to allow emotion to be an integral part of the impact. Similarly solving curriculum problems may be as much an intuitive process involving empathy and feel for the human situation under which the curriculum is implemented, as a purely rational process.[24] How much did our own schooling exhibit a recognition of the diverseness of individuals?

(4) For 'excellence' read 'excellences'

The romantic tradition places a great significance on the plural form. It emphasises a variety of channels, a variety of practices, a variety of behaviours, a variety of styles. One implication is the unlikelihood of implausibility of an overarching theory. The alternative is a return to the concrete.[25] The dichotomy is particularly clear in literature, and not just as a distinction between craft and criticism. Aristotle's propositions are typically universal ('this is the nature of tragedy in general'). Contrast Wordsworth's refusal to intellectualise experience:

> . . . I cannot paint
> What then I was. The sounding cataract
> Haunted me like a passion: the tall rock,
> The mountain, and the deep and gloomy wood,
> Their colours and their forms, were then
> to me
> An appetite; a feeling and love,
> That had no need of a remoter charm,
> By thought supplied . . .
>
> *Lines composed a few miles above Tintern Abbey*

(5) For 'rationality' read 'experience'[26]

The preference for experience over against rationalism is based on the view that experience *itself* is somehow elusive, refusing to be subdued to rules and generalities. In an extreme form the argument would deny that the basis upon which 'meanings' become available to a person reflecting on his own experience is through a public system of symbols. At least one philosopher of knowledge has postulated a 'realm of meaning' embracing what Michael Polanyi calls 'personal knowledge' and Martin Buber the 'I – thou' relation.[27] Philip Phenix calls this realm *synoetics* signifying 'relational insight' or 'direct awareness'.[28] Phenix's solution is to identify this as one discrete 'realm' within a number of distinct 'realms' of meaning.[29] It may be worth asking how much 'direct awareness' contributes, and in what way, to other forms of understanding. Neither is it too clear what are the curriculum implications of the different positions one could take on this issue.

The same dichotomy between 'rationality' and 'experience' is explored by Lindblom in his article 'The Science of Muddling Through'.[30] Lindblom offers alternative models of decision-making. The 'root' model is 'rational-comprehensive' and the 'branch' model 'successive-limited'. He suggests that instead of pursuing the 'ideal' rational model, decision-takers could concentrate usefully on improving their understanding of, and control over, the constituents of the 'branch' model.

Root and Branch Models

Rational-Comprehensive (Root)	*Successive-Limited (Branch)*
(1a) Clarification of values or objectives distinct from and usually prerequisite to empirical analysis of alternative policies.	(1b) Selection of values, goals and empirical analysis of the needed action are not distinct from one another but are closely intertwined.[31]
(2a) Policy formulation is therefore approached through means/ends analysis: first the ends are isolated, then the means to achieve them are sought.	(2b) Since means and ends are not distinct, means/ends analysis is often inappropriate or limited.
(3a) The test of a 'good' policy is that it can be shown to be the most appropriate means to desired ends.	(3b) The test of a 'good' policy is typically that various analysts find themselves agreeing on a policy (without their agreeing that it is the most appropriate means to an agreed objective).
(4a) Analysis is comprehensive: every important relevant factor is taken into account.	(4b) Analysis is drastically limited: (i) Important outcomes are neglected. (ii) Important alternative potential policies are neglected. (iii) Important affected values are neglected.
(5a) Theory is often heavily relied on.	(5b) A succession of comparisons greatly reduces or eliminates reliance on theory.

It may be interesting to wonder to what extent Tyler's 'rational curriculum plan' can be equated with Lindblom's left-hand column. Those finding the rational-comprehensive model attractive still have to face problems associated with its realisation in practice. There is also a suggestive link back to Joseph Schwab's paper. How would one identify Schwab's *practical arts* in relation to Lindblom's model? What style of decision-making would it involve?

(6) For 'culture' read 'sub-cultures'

One critical issue within this shift in emphasis is the extent to which the youth sub-culture should itself underpin a significant part of the school curriculum. Certainly the recognition of a diversity of sub-cultures undermines a view of the teacher as cultural mediator within a culture conservation/preservation mode.[32] The English teacher will recognise that one spin-off from this area of uncertainty is the need to rethink the role of a literary critic (and consequently some of the conventional teaching tasks of the English lesson). George Watson poses the issue succinctly in *Literary Critics*[33] when he says that the critic as middleman may be a feature of a decadent civilisation – an implicit denial of the possibility of a self-explaining culture.

The new rhetoric of English criticism celebrates the dilemma, the cultural uncertainty. Its key concepts are words like 'ambiguity', 'irony', and 'tension'. The fabric of language itself reflects the diversity of the culture. But we must recognise that a critical language poor in technical terms is likely to be value-charged. This dilemma has been insufficiently faced by the Schools Council/Nuffield Humanities Curriculum Project[34] in its suggestions for treating literature as evidence.

NOTES

1. Lecture given to a curriculum theory seminar at Keele by Malcolm Skilbeck in 1971.
2. This quotation from Shaftesbury's *Moralists, Characteristics II*, 125 is reprinted in R. L. Brett (1951), *The Third Earl of Shaftesbury: a Study in Eighteenth-century Literary Theory*, Hutchinson's University Library, p. 144.
3. See J. Dixon (1969 and revised edition) *Growth through English: A Report based on the Dartmouth Seminar 1966*, Oxford University Press.
4. In 'The literary imagination and the study of society', a paper given to the sociology section of the British Association at Leeds in 1967, Hoggart asks how a creative writer's way of arriving at 'truth' compares with that of a social scientist. 'Social insight' arises from a writer 'holding in his imagination' an enormous amount of material. The writer makes his 'significant explorations' not by conscious controlled aggregation, but by 'imaginative power'. Hoggart scorns the 'hard-nosed unimaginativeness' that claims to be 'value-free'. In social science and in literary criticism, he says, we are acting most intelligently when we face valuations, not when we evade them.
5. See R. Blackburn (1969), 'A brief guide to bourgeois ideology', in *Student Power*, A. Cockburn and R. Blackburn (eds.), Penguin, p. 205. See also A. W. Gouldner (1970), 'Anti-minotaur: the myth of a value-free sociology', in *The Relevance of Sociology*, J. D. Douglas (ed.), Appleton-Century-Crofts.
6. This may have an interesting reflection on the increasing tendency to research education through a methodology of participant observation, itself reflecting Schwab's appeal for an eclectic approach. See R. Weiss (1968), 'Issues in Holistic Research', in *Institutions and the Person: Essays Presented to Everett C. Hughes*, H. Becker, B. Gear, D. Riesman and R. Weiss (eds.), Aldine; see also H. Becker (1958), 'Problems of Inference and Proof in Participant Observation', in *American Sociological Review*, vol. 23, No. 6, December 1958. An interesting general book using 'humanistic' rather than 'scientific' models of man is S. Bruyn (1966), *Human Perspective in Sociology: the Methodology of Participant Observation*, Prentice-Hall.
7. See J. Gardner, 'Education as a sorting-out process', In this paper Gardner relates the notion of 'objective standards' to the control function that education performs as a 'selective mechanism' for society.
8. See especially J. S. Bruner (1960), *The Process of Education*, Harvard University

Press; A. A. Bellack (1964), 'The Structure of Knowledge and the Structure of Curriculum', in *Reassessment of the Curriculum,* D. Huebner (ed.), Teachers College Press, Columbia University; and C. Ford and L. Pugno (eds.) (1964), *The Structure of Knowledge and the Curriculum,* Rand McNally. There has been a tendency for specialists to work out the implications of the concept within particular disciplines. See, for example, E. S. Johnson (1962), 'The Concept of Structure in the Social Sciences', in *Educational Record,* 43, July 1962. Richard Jones has argued cogently, however, in R. Jones (1970), *Fantasy and Feeling in Education,* University of London Press, that an over-emphasis on cognitive structures in such courses as the Education Development Centre's social studies project 'Man: a Course of Study' could impoverish the affective responses that teachers would play for intuitively were it not for the 'schema' presented.

9. See H. Rosen (1969), 'A Language Policy Across the Curriculum', in *Language, the Learner, and the School,* D. Barnes, J. Britton, H. Rosen and the LATE (eds.), Penguin Education.
10. See B. O. Smith, W. O. Stanley and J. H. Shores (1957 revised edition), *Fundamentals of Curriculum Development,* Harcourt, Brace and World.
11. See H. S. Broudy, B. O. Smith and J. R. Burnett (1964), *Democracy and Excellence in American Secondary Education,* Rand McNally.
12. See J. Wilson, N. Williams and B. Sugarman (1967), *Introduction to Moral Education,* Penguin. Alan Harris takes a closer look at this approach to moral education in Unit 8.
13. See R. W. Tyler (1971), *Basic Principles of Curriculum and Instruction,* University of Chicago Press.
14. An interesting analysis of means and ends is given by H. Hugh Sockett (1972), 'Curriculum Aims and Objectives: Taking a Means to an End', in *Proceedings of the Philosophy of Education Society,* January 1972.
15. See R. Irvine Smith (1966), 'Curriculum Reform' in *New Society,* 12 May 1966. Irvine Smith argues that the curriculum has become an object of social policy precisely because of cultural instability: 'The state of knowledge and the nature of society are both changing rapidly, too rapidly for the curriculum to keep pace.'
16. This kind of issue is approached perceptively in an unpublished paper: 'Geography 14–18: a framework for development', by John Reynolds, of the Schools Council Geography 14–18 Project.
17. See C. Hussey (1927), *The Picturesque: Studies in a Point of View,* Putnam.
18. See J. Dixon (1969 and revised edition), *Growth through English: A Report based on the Dartmouth Seminar 1966,* Oxford University Press. This may, in fact, be nothing more than an interesting reinterpretation of the role of the teacher as a 'competence model'. The term 'competence model' is an important one in the debate. For a broadly 'classic' view of competence models. . . See the evaluation report on the Education Development Center social studies project 'Man: a Course of Study'; see J. P. Hanley, D. K. Whitla, E. W. Moo and A. S. Walter (1970), *Curiosity, Competence, Community,* Education Development Center. The teacher's cognitive style is at stake, and he must help pupils to realise that 'external' bodies of knowledge and intellectual systems can be internalised in a way that allows pupils to build up generative rules to explain the world and themselves. A more 'romantic' approach is taken by Joseph Schwab in J. Schwab (1969), *College Curriculum and Student Protest,* University of Chicago Press. The teacher represents an equivocal culture. He does not defend evident failures but vivifies the need to put pressing questions.
19. See A. W. Rowe and P. Emmens (1963–7), *English through Experience Books 1–5,* Blond Educational.
20. This choice is developed by Elliot Eisner as his 'second dilemma' in E. W. Eisner (1971), 'Persistent Dilemmas in Curriculum Decision-making' in *Confronting*

Curriculum Reform, E. W. Eisner (ed)., Little, Brown: 'Yet the goal of balance in curriculum is not without a lusty competitor . . . as Harold Benjamin called it, the cultivation of idiosyncracy' (p. 167).

21. See J. B. Macdonald (1971), 'Responsible Curriculum Development', in *Confronting Curriculum Reform,* E. W. Eisner, (ed.), Little, Brown, pp. 121–2, where Macdonald argues the romantic case, espousing what he calls 'aesthetic rationality' as against 'technological rationality'.

    Curriculum development is always evaluative thinking, not objective theoretical thought. Thus, as Levi-Strauss says about the humanities, we deal with metaphors, not cause-effect chains. . . A curriculum ought to be a vehicle for the unfolding of alternatives, with a many-valued focus; not the result of the elimination of alternatives or a single-valued point to be arrived at.

    See also J. B. Macdonald (1967), 'An example of disciplined curriculum thinking in *Theory into Practice,* vol. VI, No. 4, October 1967. There is a link between James Macdonald and the Goldsmith's College Curriculum Laboratory (Macdonald spent a year there as visiting professor). Readers familiar with the Curriculum Laboratory will be able to judge for themselves how much of the ideology of its journal *Ideas,* or for that matter of C. James (1968), *Young Lives at Stake: Changing Priorities in Secondary Education,* Collins, could be labelled 'romantic'.

22. See E. Burke (1958), *A Philosophical Enquiry into the Origin of our Ideas of the Sublime and Beautiful,* Routledge and Kegan Paul.

23. See B. Bernstein (1967), 'Open schools, open society?' in *New Society,* 10, 14, September 1967.

24. See in this context R. Harrison and R. Hopkins (1970), 'The Design of Cross-Cultural Training: An alternative to the University Model', in *The Planning of Change,* W. G. Bennis, K. D. Benne and R. Chin (eds.), Holt, Rinehart and Winston. The authors analyse the educational problems of the Peace Corps by contrasting the traditional goals of university education with the divergent goals of overseas education. They list appropriate meta-goals for cross-cultural training in a way that acknowledges the emotional element in real situations. Problem solving is less a 'rational' process, more a 'social' process involving empathy and communication.

25. The argument tends to reappear in a bastardised version that centres around the belief that the 'Newsom child' ought to be 'good with his hands'. Is it *central* to the folk wisdom of 'romantic' teaching that every child is excellent at something?

26. This is reflected in the debate about aims and objectives in education. An emphasis on experience would be relatively favourable towards an 'intuitive' approach using implicit aims, or placing an emphasis on 'procedural principles' rather than closely defined goals that somehow precede educational programmes. Two articles that probe 'rational curriculum planning' in its extreme means/ends formulation are R. S. Peters (1963 2nd edition), 'Must an Educator have an Aim?' in *Authority, Responsibility and Education,* R. S. Peters (ed.), Allen and Unwin; and E. W. Eisner (1967), 'Educational Objectives: Help or Hindrance?' in *School Review* LXXV, Autumn 1967. For the operational approach in its extreme formulation see W. French (1957), *Behavioural Goals and General Education in High School,* Russell Sage. 'Experience' is itself a critical term.

    One of the key questions investigated by the Symposium on Operationalism (1945) was whether experience itself is 'ultimate', subject to immediate intuition, or whether it is itself a proper construct for operational definition; see the introduction to H. Feigl (1945), 'Symposium on Operationism', in *The Psychological Review,* vol. 52, No. 5, September 1945.

27. Presumably people make personal accommodations between the conflicting claims of the 'other-ness' of other people and the 'us-ness' by which we know them.

28. See the introduction to P. H. Phenix (1964), *Realms of Meaning: a Philosophy of the Curriculum for General Education,* McGraw Hill. The issue is approached from the romantic side by John Dewey in J. Dewey (1956), *The Child and the Curriculum: School and Society,* University of Chicago Press.
29. Phenix has argued further that there is sufficient correspondence between 'realms of meaning' and existing 'disciplines of knowledge' for the disciplines to be the most significant consideration in the selection and organisation of content for the school curriculum. See P. H. Phenix (1962), 'The Disciplines as Curriculum Content', in *Curriculum Crossroads,* A. H. Passow (ed.), Teachers College Press, Columbia University.
30. See C. Lindblom (1964), 'The Science of Muddling Through' in *The Making of Decisions,* W. J. Gore and J. Dyson (eds.), Free Press of Glencoe. See also C. M. Berners-Lee (ed.) (1965), *Models for Decision,* English Universities Press.
31. The different attitudes to the formulation of goals explored by Lindblom's dichotomous models can be traced in P. H. Taylor (1970), *How teachers plan their courses,* NFER. A number of teachers are clearly operating within a successive-limited model and are unable to handle requests for clarification within the framework of the rational-comprehensive model. Another issue raised by Taylor is the tendency for some goal statements to be made almost exclusively in terms of content – see his discussion of geography teaching (p. 21 ff.).
32. See for example the current Penguin *Connexions* series, which echoes and parodies the format and graphics of the youth culture.
33. See G. Watson (1964), *Literary Critics,* Chatto and Windus.
34. See L. Stenhouse (1968), 'The Humanities Curriculum Project', in *Journal of Curriculum Studies,* 1 November 1968.

3. THE SCHOOL AND CULTURAL DEVELOPMENT

Malcolm Skilbeck

Source: The Northern Teacher, Winter 1973.

Professor Skilbeck considers the possible roles of schooling in relation to social and political change. Schools can 'swim with the tide', seek to preserve valued elements from the past, carry on with their own pre-occupations irrespective of the world outside, or attempt to anticipate future social developments and, as far as possible, influence *them. He goes on to consider the last of these possibilities (dubbed 'reconstructionist') as an educational doctrine.*

In this paper I shall be discussing the conception of education known as reconstructionism. Many thinkers holding very different beliefs have entertained this conception, but what unites them is their acceptance that the school has a capacity to facilitate, promote and possibly guide certain forms of social change. It is more accurate to say cultural rather than social change, since the reconstructionists tend to take a comprehensive view of education, and to examine the ways in which it is influenced by and can influence those beliefs, values, attitudes, customs, skills, relationships and so forth for which the term culture is used. Throughout the paper I shall be referring mainly to cultural change, and using the term reconstructionists use to denote those thinkers and practitioners who subscribe to the view that the school can and should take an active part in assessing the worthwhileness of contemporary culture and promoting what it takes to be educationally desirable changes in that culture.

My purpose in discussing the reconstructionist conception of education is to consider how far and in what ways it makes sense to regard an educational system as a significant force for planned change in a particular society.

Periodically, in the history of western educational thought and institutions, groups of reformers have looked to the schools as principal agents of social and political change. At other times, the prevailing view has been that schools have a relatively limited role and they should concentrate their energies on performing this well. It is not necessary to illustrate the latter view as it is enshrined in the typical curriculum of our schools where the transmission of pre-established knowledge and skills is taken for granted. Examples of the former way of thinking include Plato's 'Republic', the view of education held by some of the early Christians, the plans in France and America in the latter part of the eighteenth century for using schools as nation-builders, and, in the twentieth century, the widespread interest amongst the politicians and administrators of the new nations in education as a major facilitator of social development.

A closer inspection of those theories and movements in which education is conceived as one of the primary agencies of cultural development would show that they usually emerge in periods of upheaval, or rapid change. The more limited view of the purpose and function of education characterises more stable situations. The culture development theories appear in countries or regions where there has been, or is impending, a political revolution, or they are systematically related by their authors to serious problems or deficiencies in the societies to which they refer. During the late nineteen twenties and early thirties, in the U.S.A., advocates of the movement in education which came to be known as social reconstructionism justified their radical educational policies by reference to the national economic crisis. In the developing countries, the justification for using education as part of a planned policy of nation building is not dependent on crisis but rather on the supposed capacity of a certain type of educational system to develop skills and attitudes appropriate to a modernised culture.

Thus, we may find examples of the reconstructionist conception of education amongst established societies undergoing major upheaval or crisis, and amongst newly developing states. It is not the purpose of this paper to examine in detail the different forms taken by reconstructionist thinking in different social economic and political situations, but it is worth noting that these settings have been extremely diverse: reconstructionist thinking is to be found amongst democrats and totalitarians, christians and atheists, rationalists and empiricists, conservatives and radicals. When the Napoleonic armies overran the German states, it was the idealist philosopher Fichte who, in his 'Addresses to the German Nation', proposed a far-reaching project of nation-building through a reformed education. In the Soviet Union during the nineteen-thirties, a quite different political system and philosophical approach provided the under-pinning for no less determined attempts to relate education to nation-building. In the present day, practical illustrations of reconstructionism in and through education may be found in the democratic socialist republic of Tanzania, in Israel and in the modernisation programmes launched in Spain and in Portugal in 1969. Evidence of the wide variety of political systems where reconstructionist thinking is influencing education policies is provided by James Coleman in his 'Education and Political Development'.

Rapid and extensive change in values, beliefs and techniques in a culture is, of course, not a new phenomenon; it is one of the declining characteristics of the western industrial state. However, rates of change vary in different societies, for example contemporary Spain and France. Rates of change also vary over what may be quite a short period of time; and there may be widely differing rates of change within particular subsections, such as the educational and the industrial systems. These differing rates of sub-sector change have given rise to the once popular theory of social lag, and to the still common criticism that schools do not adapt themselves rapidly enough to what is loosely called social change. This criticism is a peculiar one in that it is often stated in such a way as to suggest that schools are not really part of society – that society exists 'out there' and schools are over here and something different. The school is a social institution as real as any other, schooling is one social process amongst many others, and there can be no question of schools adjusting themselves to or fitting into society but only of their adjusting and otherwise relating themselves to (and being adjusted and related to) *other* social institutions.

This point is an important one since it affects both our understanding of the school's role and our response to the various demands made on schooling, such as the demand that schooling should be more 'socially relevant'. In answer to this demand we need to know to which other institution and processes schooling is supposed to be made relevant and for what purpose.

The demand for relevance helps to bring out the basic strategies which, it might be supposed, schools can adopt in relation to total cultural change. There are four of these hypothetical strategies. *First,* schools may swim with the tide by identifying basic trends and going with rather than resisting them. *Second,* schools may identify particular elements in the past, and seek to preserve them. *Third,* schools may carry on their work largely ignorant of or indifferent to what is happening in other key sectors of the culture. *Fourth,* schools may look forward, trying to anticipate situations in the future, assessing them for their educational significance, and influencing them through the various limited means at their disposal.

There are, of course, variations in the refinements of these four strategies and I do not want to suggest that every aspect of a school's work could be examined systematically by reference to one or other of them. Nevertheless, by considering them in turn we may be in a better position to understand many of the functions performed by the schools in our midst.

Swimming with the tide is apparently what is envisaged by the advocates of relevance and adjustment. It is a strategy that has the merit of encouraging teachers to find out more about what is happening in their society and ways in which their pupils are responding to the social situation in which they find themselves. There is clearly a sense in which teaching is futile unless its content and methodology reflect these concerns. However, a modern society is highly complex and, if it is a democracy, its values, beliefs and life patterns will be varied and conflicting. Is the school to align itself simply with what presents itself with most clamour and urgency? Even if the school were thought of as an institution whose purpose is to induct the young into the culture, irrespective of consideration of the values of that culture, the task remains of identifying and selecting those parts of the culture which a single institution – the school and a single process, education – could reasonably undertake. Clearly, criteria and objectives are needed. Granted that individual teachers may not spend a lot of time reflecting on these it is nevertheless important that there should be some in the educational system who are doing so. 'Swimming with the tide' only makes educational sense if some educationists are assessing and helping to direct the movements of the tide.

The second strategy, that of selecting elements from the past and seeking to preserve them, does at least recognise that no single social institution, such as a school, can undertake to transmit to the young all that is available for transmission in a culture. Selection and preservation imply criteria and an educative intent. Whose criteria and whose intentions are to prevail? By its nature, preservationism tends to be teacher and parent centred: the teacher decides, the parent influences. What is absent is the expressed interest of the pupils and of groups other than those professionally engaged in education, except insofar as they form themselves into educational pressure groups. Thus, the culture that is selected for transmission may be very distasteful to the young who have to be persuaded, for example by the very workings of the selective system, that it is 'good' for them. It is not surprising that the extrinsic motivations of public examinations should be so powerful in selective secondary schools.

A further point about the preservationist strategy is that it very easily lapses into an intransigence in the face of possibilities different from those which have formed the experience of the conservers. The most striking examples of this intransigence are to be found in secondary education where institutions and their curricula are sanctified because they have proved valuable in serving and sustaining the interests of particular groups. I refer, of course, to selective secondary schools whose functionality in preserving the class interest of those who exercise political and social power in this community and a certain view of the academic life which has been fostered by particular universities, is beyond dispute. The strategy of selected preservation from the past is fundamentally backward looking and uncritical. It tends to ignore emerging experience from other institutions and societies, and adopts and accepts a fixed stand towards matters which should be considered open, viz., the social purposes of education, the interests to be satisfied by educational institutions and processes, and the future which people wish to make for themselves. Of course, it does not follow from treating these issues as open that another type of institution should simply replace selective secondary schools. An experimental approach to this question is vitally important: I only wish at this juncture to draw attention to some of the consequences of adopting a preservationist strategy.

The third possibility which is open to schools in the face of a rapidly changing culture is to carry on their particular pursuits ignorant of or indifferent to these changes. This barely counts as a strategy since it is little more than a policy of inward-looking drift. It has resemblances to the first approach I discussed, namely going with the tide, but it differs in being less self-conscious and in that the designs to which it gives rise are less elaborate and sophisticated. It has resemblances also to the preservationist strategy in that the effect of drift in schooling is to make no mark on and hence to maintain unscathed those forces and interests which are uppermost in the culture.

As the American educational theorist and philosopher, John Dewey, long ago pointed out, a policy of social drift is no educational policy at all. It may emerge as a result of neglect or apathy, which unfortunately not all schools are free from. One way of overcoming the staleness and mindless conservatism that result when schools refuse to examine, reflect upon and appraise the societies in which they are functioning is to introduce a universal programme of inservice education. Apathy and narrowness are natural consequences of isolation and neglect. The teacher who is left alone to 'get on with it' can all too easily continue throughout his career to reproduce the attitudes, techniques and information with which he himself was imbued as a student. By far the most potent and exciting possibility in the James Report and the White Paper is the commitment to universal, life-long inservice education of teachers. Whether the potentiality of this measure is realised in practice depends on the nature of studies teachers undertake, hence the importance of building up strategies of inservice education which will be not only acceptable and meaningful to teachers but will also challenge their settled assumptions and provide them with new perceptions of what is educationally possible and desirable in the future.

The fourth strategy available to schools in the face of a rapidly changing culture to whose needs they are expected to respond, looks to the future. This strategy requires schools to relate their activities essentially to three things. *First,* schools need a set of educational criteria, possibly in the form of objectives, which have been worked through by the school staff and others who can reasonably claim to have a stake in the process. *Second,* the schools need to have formed a clear understanding of the effects of what they have done in the past. *Third,* the schools need to look ahead, anticipating the effects of present trends in culture and relating all of their work explicitly to the assessments they are able to make.

This fourth strategy is essentially that of the reconstructionists, though it takes very different forms in different societies. For example, in totalitarian societies schools have objectives given to them and these objectives are uniform and homogeneous. In the British tradition it is open to the schools to define their own objectives – not in isolation, nor with complete freedom, but with a very wide scope for choice of direction and emphasis.

It may seem odd that one should have to offer reasons favouring a strategy of intelligent analysis, appraisal and forecasting for an educational institution. In so far as these activities of analysis, criticism, anticipation and so forth are all constituent of a rational approach to problem-solving we would expect them to be conspicuous in those institutions in society which have a fundamental and primary educative interest. The process of education is not limited to rational reflection, yet rationality, both as intention of the educator and as a basic condition of the methods and materials he uses, is what distinguishes education from all other forms of guidance, direction and influence.

Schooling and education are, however, often two rather different processes. Schools have education as one of their purposes. This is not their only purpose, nor are they always in a condition to carry out this purpose effectively: providing the conditions for an education are no less important than having a clear conception of the process. Teachers in schools are very well aware of constraints and deficiencies which limit the achievement of desirable educational results. These negative factors are not only objective so far as the teacher is concerned, that is they do not result only from the material limitations, the unsatisfactory work conditions, the reluctance of children to undertake educative activities and so forth. The teacher needs to ask himself whether his own perception of the task suffers from a cramped experience, a refusal to reflect on possibilities and a preference for easy solutions and procedures.

It must be admitted that to expect schools to undertake as complex and arduous a task as analysing the culture and projecting trends and defining educational roles in relation to those trends is unrealistic in the present situation. Apart from the negative factors I have just mentioned, schools have been designed and equipped and their work has been approved, in the light of very limited assumptions and expectations. Were schools to become the kind of nerve centres of an emerging culture that reconstructionists like H. G. Wells in England and H. Rugg and T. Brameld in America envisaged they would have to become very different and they would have to seek social acceptance as different kinds of institutions from what most of them are at present.

It might be concluded, then, from this brief review of strategies, that only the second, conservationism, and the fourth, reconstructionism, will withstand close scrutiny. Reconstructionism is open to the criticism that it makes more substantial demands on schools and teachers than they are equipped to meet. There are other objections, or at least difficulties, which it is not immediately relevant to enter into. For example, the authority of the school, as one social institution and the teachers, as one professional group, to seek to modify the directions of cultural development is by no means clear in a pluralistic society. Another point to bear in mind is the risk of indoctrination where global and holistic approaches to education are being recommended. These difficulties notwithstanding the reconstructionist strategy appears to me to be the most fruitful one can explore, in considering the relationships schools and teachers might develop with their surrounding culture.

No one is in a position to make accurate prognostications of the future main lines of cultural development. The philosopher Karl Popper has demonstrated this in a way which is important to students of cultural processes. He has argued that in modern industrialised society, one of the principal forces influencing all facets of life is knowledge itself. Fresh discoveries through research are characteristic of the growth of knowledge, thus knowledge cannot forecast its own future and as a consequence societies cannot accurately forecast their future. The importance of this argument for my purpose is that it encourages a more tentative and speculative approach to future planning,not that it rules out attempts to anticipate. Popper himself has contributed, both conceptually and empirically, to the advancement of social self knowledge. It is this kind of knowledge that a strategy of educational renewal needs. The focus of this knowledge is contemporary culture, as this is exhibited in the various cultural domains: the arts, sciences, social sciences, the polity, the economy, morals, belief systems, the principal social institutions and the forms of everyday experience.

Except for the last one mentioned, these cultural domains are sometimes treated as remote from the lives of children and their subjective experience. Hence schools, seeking a more relevant curriculum, may be inclined to focus too narrowly on those concerns which are frequently found in courses built on pupil interest, on vocational aspirations, and on local and environmental studies. These approaches may be termed the temptation of subjective experience. More traditional approaches, through the academic disciplines of knowledge, while more objective and fundamental, are by no means the best way of directing the energies of pupils and teachers towards the problems of their present world and of the future. They may be termed the temptation of academic respectability.

In the final section of this paper, I want to raise some of the issues which seem to me central in considering ways in which schools might contribute towards desirable modifications and developments of culture. There are three main aspects of schooling which it is important to consider: the curriculum, internal school organisation, and styles of teaching and learning. All three are crucial but it would unduly extend this paper if I discussed them all, so I shall consider just the first, the curriculum.

Through the curriculum, a map or chart of actual and potential experience is presented to the pupil. Typically, the experience with which he is confronted is structured according to the symbols – and the customs – of the discrete disciplines of knowledge: physical science, history, language, mathematics and so forth. These disciplines have developed and consolidated over time and they express a partial, precise and adult view of aspects of reality. The pupil, by various means, is aided and encouraged to partake of the modes of thought and the conceptual systems which these disciplines have generated and by which they maintain their vitality. The disciplines of knowledge, or indeed any item of activity which it is proposed to include in the curriculum, must be so arranged and presented as to connect with the child's experience, if he is to learn anything. Hence the disciplines are a resource, to be drawn upon, together with other resources, in the construction of school curricula.

How the disciplines and other cultural modes are drawn upon and organised for use in schools is the most fundamental question in curriculum design. Whether these intellectual resources for learning are to have certain effects on the child's perception of this social world and his attitude towards his own and others' roles in that social world depends on the purpose for which curriculum content is selected and the use made of it. For example, history, geography, politics, sociology and morality may be presented as problematic, controversial and many-sided, or as so much settled knowledge to be learnt and reproduced according to the conventions of the essay or the examination paper. A curriculum plan in a school can aim to foster critical, reflective thinking; it can stimulate and provide the opportunities for participation in practical projects by which the community betters itself; and it can encourage pupils to see themselves as the organisers of their own experiences and of their own society. Conversely, a curriculum plan very often in fact produces acquiescent, docile and socially uninvolved people.

A cynic, looking to the future, may well seek to maintain the traditional split, in education, between the creative, responsible, reflective minority, and a majority of followers. Curriculum policy makers, teachers, and all who have an interest in education and in the well-being of the community have a responsibility in actively contributing towards the formation of culture. This is not a task for schools alone, nor is it one which schools should neglect. A radical appraisal of the school curriculum is needed, to see how far in intention or actuality it is fostering the values and understandings of a just and creative society.

Of course, reappraisal of the curriculum is an ongoing task. But we need to ask whether this task is being carried on with the determination and vigour that are needed if schools are to have an effect. The countervailing forces are very powerful. Studies of attitude formation, political values, prejudice, culture participation and the distribution of economic opportunity suggest that the early formative experiences in the home and the neighbourhood, together with the socio-economic background and educational attainments of parents, have a decisive influence which the school can scarcely match. This influence is reinforced in later childhood and adolescence by the effects of television, popular journalism, the leisure industry and, in later years by the work environment.

It does not follow from these studies that schools are helpless or that it is a waste of time to seek through the curriculum to widen understanding and to develop tolerance, sympathy and other virtues of communal life. Rather, the effectiveness of extra school agencies, and the limited achievement of many of the aims earlier generations of educational reformers have held out indicates that different strategies are required. It is not surprising that political and social attitudes seem relatively unaffected by schooling when the schools have not set out resolutely and operationally to modify attitudes, nor that other forces in society exert greater influence when, in so many instances, schools have not sought to understand or to utilise these other forces: television is a notable example of this.

The study and appraisal of contemporary culture, its principal modes and manifestations, its tendencies and possibilities, is a more appropriate curriculum target for schools which wish to prepare children for future living than the snippets and fragments, mostly of a second-hand factual type, which still commonly feature especially in secondary education. This means that teachers require more sociology, social psychology, politics, economics, environmental science, contemporary history and more experience of problem-solving, critical enquiry and creative activity in their training. It may be that these are what could be most appropriately examined in inservice courses of a type where teachers are encouraged to examine their own teaching, to redesign curricula and to relate their work to the systematic analysis of contemporary cultural movements. In these courses, it will be no less important for teachers to come to view themselves as agents of change and renewal and not as transmitters of settled or slowly changing bodies of knowledge. This is a role from which some teachers may shrink, because of the demands it makes. Yet, unless teachers can learn to adopt this role and to take up the challenges that go with it the effectiveness of the school as a means of educating the community will rapidly diminish as other and more persuasive forces take over.

4. Ideology and the Curriculum: the Value Assumptions of System Builders

Fred Inglis

Source: The Journal of Curriculum Studies, vol. 6, No. 1, May 1974.

Fred Inglis analyses three contemporary heresies of curriculum planning: one 'appeals to a model of reason' whose terms derive from 'a coarse authoritarianism'; one derives from a 'hidden policy' of 'liberal non-intervention'; one (illustrated by Bruner's curriculum innovation) is the product of 'the end-of-ideology ideology which marked America in the early sixties'. He goes on to develop the argument that all three heresies fail to generate (or even to accommodate) any concept of 'the complete man', or to 'give our "cultivation of the Soul" historic point and purchase'.

I would like to accomplish the following tasks. First, to offer a rapid description of three styles of thought dominant in powerful institutions in society. Second, to discover how these three styles, or certain of their characteristics, enter the planning of national curricula, and to set out some of their latent contradictions and deficiencies. Third, I would also like to counterpose against what may be called the *public* styles of thought, examples of the teachers' typically *private* styles and characteristics—styles which have a course of different absences and defects. Fourth and last I would like to indicate some points of growth in the private styles, and one or two ways in which privacy may usefully return to public life. Such a return and process of reconnection which it implies, may affect our teaching both in its social relations and its specific content. What I have to say has, I hope, quite practical consequences for the making of a human curriculum.

The first style of thought which dominates curricular and educational planning is directly a product of modern technocracies. It appeals to a model of reason whose terms derive from the course utilitarianism developed for the administration of social welfare in a mass competitive and consumer society. This model defines practical objectives and aims to calculate probable human responses to them. Such models cannot, as I hope to show, answer tests of rationality, but pass themselves off as rational because they answer the criteria of cost, productivity, growth and efficiency as defined by the input-output economists and investment accountants who uphold the systems of planning in Whitehall and the corporations. In the absence of opposition, these criteria now provide the instructional models for the control and evaluation of public knowledge. A condition of the latter day utilitarianism which this style of thought expresses is that society is held to be static, and that the extension of benefits follows from increased economic growth and the elimination of conflict by legislation. The model implies the end of ideology[1] and the eradication of history. It celebrates the complex divisions of labour in a technocracy as offering the best vehicle for social variety, social opportunity, and social progress. In this non-ideological climate the managers preoccupy themselves with questions of means and efficiency; the point is then to work out how best to run a system which so clearly works to create the best of all possible worlds.

The techniques devised on the basis of this model run counter to a strong tradition in educational thinking which has also been vigorously critical of that same specialization, and the industrialism which produced it. Yet the techniques themselves deeply penetrate the official forms of educational thought. It is easy to find operational management manuals which provide curriculum models of this sort[2]:

NEED		PLAN	
Aims	Objectives	Strategies	Tactics
IMPLEMENTATION		REVIEW	
Methods	Techniques	Evaluation	Consolidation

The model is offered in the interest of rationalization. Professor Merritt then applies the model.[3]

> Let us first look at the simple sequence which may be observed in any complete action. Motivation Plan Implementation Review. We may remember the initials: MPIR. There is no action without motivation, no satisfaction without a plan that is then implemented, no satisfactory profit from experience without review. . . It is not enough that a child should have knowledge of his needs, he must be able to weigh one need against another and determine his priorities. To do this, he must first distinguish between his aims and his objectives. His aims are those states of body or mind which he wishes to attain. His objectives are the environmental correlates of those aims. Thus, the satisfaction of hunger may be an aim. A plate of steak might be correlated objective.

It is in the first place much too reductive to describe all human action as impelled by 'need', unless 'need' is to turn out on examination to be a hopelessly elastic and slippery term. The model supposes that all action is intended to bring about the reduction of 'need'. But in what sense can we say that we teach in order to satisfy 'need' – and whose need? The teacher's or the child's? Inasmuch as the term 'need' may be ascribed either to behaviour which follows certain rules *or* to behaviour which has no conscious structure (dreams, psychosis, randomness) it is not clear what connections there are between our needs and our aims and objectives. Indeed it cannot be shown that there are *any* connections between 'need' and 'aim' unless you adopt a theory of such flaccidity as 'all behaviour stems from the need to reduce tensions'.

This disjunction, the product of a vulgar-minded failure to think the application of operational management to education right through, penetrates the model. It seems to derive from the same submerged and universalized theory of homeostasis: that you do something to satisfy your needs and then check that you can do it again. No doubt this model is true for simple forms of locomotor co-ordination. The trouble is that psychologists of learning have then applied the same paradigm to all kinds of situations. In learning we are confronted with obstacles. We overcome them. We feel satisfaction. We do it all again. But how does this routinized behaviour apply to playing football? Or reading a novel? Or talking with our friends? In no sense is that satisfaction usefully to be fitted into the homeostatic or pleasure principle model.[4] It does not follow that the flow chart fits all, or indeed any of the non-repeatable situations which compose most of our lives. But it is characteristic of this thought-form that it predicates *all* human actions as of this type. It derives from modern theories of organization which define efficiency as obtainable by dividing tasks into units – goals, aims, objectives – and arranging these in regular taxonomies. In this way the sorting and control of input, the process of transformation, and the quantification of output can allegedly be scrutinized and regulated. The means are broken down and organized for the optimization (as they say) of the ends. It is held that the school fits this model.

As in many other institutions (including assembly-line plants) the appropriateness of the flow chart model to education may be refuted on three grounds. First, the objectivity of assessment and prediction which is a supreme factor in the effective application of means-end planning is logically impossible to achieve since the teachers are required to *bring about* their own predictions. (The most bitter example of this is the requirement that teachers predict the exact number of 11+ successes which the grammar school can take.) Second, individual actions have no experimental relationship to flow chart rationality. In Alasdair MacIntyre's words,[5] 'Institutions are milieux within which people live their lives'. The terms of the curriculum flow chart are not terms in which any agent would or could explain and give reasons for his actions. It won't do to say that objectives planning just helps people to concentrate when they would normally go ahead without thinking. For it is held to be the *point* of the flow chart that all means are directed towards ends, and that therefore you must follow the arrows in the right order. Some actions, however (especially at school) may *be* their own ends (playing cricket, reading *Jane Eyre*); others may have no ends at all (taking a class of infants for a walk); others again may not at all admit the application of operational analysis (listening to *Cosi fan tutte*[6]) nor the schematic division into a hierarchy of behaviours which it involves. The third and most damaging objection to the planning of a curriculum by this model is that the flow chart is itself irrational. Modern demographic movement and organizations being what they are, all individuals must be substitutable, and all regulations adjusted to the LCM of the participants. Stupid people must be able to take over from clever ones. In spite of the rules, however, the system is always breaking down because the flow of information is sporadic and inaccurate. Consequently, modern organizations require as well as dull or strict adherence to routines, a prompt show of initiative, flexibility, spontaneity and audacity. It is of course logically impossible to supply both, so many people are required to spend much of their time reconciling deep-seated contradictions which curriculum development on this model can only exacerbate. And there's no way out of this dead end by arguing for the free play of individual and curriculum ('idiographic' and 'nomothetic' in the cant). It is, again, the *point* of the flow chart that it moves steadily towards the specific objective and ignores all the attractive eccentricities on the way.

The second style of thought which has so deeply marked curricular planning is of a piece with the 'ideology of no ideology' which is so strong in systems analysis and management techniques. The problems the style poses are more a challenge to the sociology of ignorance than anything else. The stylists in question are the philosophers of education, amongst whom the best known, as well as the most graceful wearers of the style are Richard Peters and Paul Hirst. I do not wish to be misunderstood here. I am considering their work because it is clearly important in its own right; they have done a lot to clear up all sorts of confusions in educational thinking; they have attacked sentimentality and spoken up for a proper and valuable sense of traditional purpose and pieties. But they have also defended without naming it a hidden policy of, so to speak, liberal non-intervention. In their useful primer *The Logic of Education*[7] Hirst and Peters enter what has become a liturgical caveat about the relevance of philosophy to education. Philosophy, they say, '. . . is an activity which is distinguished by its concern with certain types of second-order questions . . . Philosophy, in brief, is concerned with questions about the analysis of concepts and with questions about the grounds of knowledge, beliefs, actions and activities.' It is this latter-day definition of analytic philosophy which permits its authors to leave unexamined certain main validating premisses. Technically they are right; practically, 'second order' permits them to leave out essential questions about the relationship between 'grounds' and morality, and between both these and social structures. When O'Connor[8] declares that 'philosophy is not in the ordinary sense of the phrase a body of knowledge, but rather an activity of criticism or clarification' . . . 'it is not a kind of superior science . . . to answer difficult and important questions about human life,' he joins the others in rendering up contemporary philosophy as the essential adjunct of the rational liberal. And the rational liberal in the absence of any other contender becomes the good man.

These accents, and the vast efforts made in their name in philosophy of education courses, keep in circulation the idea of philosopher as handmaid, practical not purposive, the tidier up of confusions. The idea is strongly criticized by Peter Winch for resting on a *mistake*[9]; it was rejected with patrician scorn by Collingwood[10] as a dereliction of duty thirty-five years ago. His stirring condemnation of a philosophy which denied that a pupil would find in it any guidance for his life, would strike chords in the hearts of Peters and his men. But they have left themselves with no explicit justification for such a response. Instead they leave the way open for 'the adventurers in politics', the desperadoes who are quite happy to see their own apologia set out in these genteel cadences:

> In both senses of the 'public interest' the school is obviously concerned with promoting it; for the training of technicians, typists, and countless other forms of skilled workers necessary to the viability of the economy of an industrialized society. Unless the wheels of industry keep turning the conditions will be absent which will permit any man to pursue a multitude of individual interests. And keeping the wheels of industry turning is a policy that favours no particular sectional interest. This is what leads economists to speak of money spent on schools as a public investment.[11]

Richard Dearden echoes Peters in this when, speaking of 'Values in the Curriculum' he emphasizes that in a 'pluralist' society 'there does remain an . . . acceptable consensus on what is valuable for social competence in our form of life.' 'To begin with, there is the importance of being economically viable . . .' These easy-going statements leave out of account questions as to whether things should be as they are, and further questions about how things came to be that way. The philosophers admit that the conceptual analysis entails moral argument, but they do not pursue the argument and its inevitable tangle with politics, for fear of muddying what they take to be their 'realist' function. To refuse the pursuit, it has been a political platitude to say since *The Theses on Feuerbach*, is to leave things as they are. The main charge against the philosophers is that they have cast themselves as quietist celebrators of the-way-things-are. This comes out most sharply when Paul Hirst speaks[12] of each subject as being defined by an autonomous body of knowledge and a set of concepts peculiar to its nature. Hirst never analyses the inner connections between ideology and the map of knowledge. He provides no account of the *history* of knowledge, of the philosophic analysis which would identify the distributions of knowledge as in part the product of an antecedent and impermanent epistemology,[13] and in part the way things are. For all Hirst has to say about the contingencies and overlapping of the 'forms of knowledge', he puts in circulation a disembodied version of knowledge without history, change, or social and ideological roots. There seems no reason why there should not be more or less than seven forms and many of the forms are themselves porous in a way which is not allowed for by Hirst's map of the 'domains'.[14] What he has to say about 'coming to look at things in a certain way' can only have meaning *if* the education in question looks also at the origins of this process. His education does not. His description of the forms of knowledge is as much an autobiography of willing imprisonment as anything: 'initiation' (Peter's key concept, of course[15]) becomes the process of socialization into a given intellectual identity.[16] There seems then to be no way for new modes of thought to arise (the novel, for instance) nor for individuals to create for themselves radically different intellectual identities – the process so unforgettably described in, say, Keat's or Constable's or Mill's *Collected Letters.* The special aridity of Hirst's argument is brought out in a paper allegedly refuting Hirst, in which the writer[17] paints himself into a corner where he says that literary criticism is a form of knowledge, but painting isn't. So much the worse for the forms of knowledge.

In practising this style of thought, the philosophers do their considerable bit to make more trivial the study of education. I do not mean that they ought to be political scientists, but that although the nature of their philosophic inquiry is irredeemably moral, they sever themselves from its root. The point is not the same as Marcuse's silly objection to Wittgenstein and John Austin, that they described and did not change the world. (They changed it utterly by describing it differently.) The point is that Peters and Hirst do not describe the world sufficiently. They deprive the educational world of its history, ideology, and social origins.

Many comparable omissions and silences occur when one turns to the work of the curriculum builders themselves. (I am referring here to general or liberal studies curricula rather than to specific disciplinary equipment like the Nuffield Science scheme or SMP.) Jerome Bruner's famous and exciting 'Man – a Course of Study' is probably the most influential scheme and it prefigures much of the combined curricular studies in this country, among which the Schools Council Humanities Project is probably the best known. But excitement is not the point. Bruner's scheme, the intentions and plan of which he sets out in *Toward a Theory of Instruction*[18] is crippled on two counts.[19] The scheme sets out a study of man for 10 year olds which moves from simple transformational grammar to the growth of technology and onto the analysis of the role structure of society (yes, it does). Much of this is achieved by the study of alien cultures in the present day – the Bushmen, the Esquimaux. The first, radical absence is of any sense that societies are made and changed by men, that conflicts occur, and that class or ethnic interests are often bitterly at odds. One could never guess from this thrilling, varied, multi-media pack of equipment that men have beliefs, that they fight about them, and that some men dominate other men. The pack is the product of the end-of-ideology ideology which marked America in the early sixties, and which is so strongly present in the two styles of thought already described: the managerial and the philosophic-educational.

Now Bruner is a psychologist. The second main characteristic of his style of thought is his partiality for a specific version of cognitive development. The version would be congenial to managerial thought and to Hirst's 'forms of knowing'. In a transcript from a discussion amongst teachers about a film of Esquimau life shown to children, the consultant psychologist said:

> They learned a lot about technology. On that we're agreed. And they had a good exercise of the cognitive skills involved in concept attainment: focussed observation, identification, categorization, classification, generalization, analytical thought, objectivity, and the rest. Good. They also had a healthy exercise in the emotional skills necessary to support such cognitive activities: control, containment, postponement.[20]

Yet it is not enough to object by saying that Bruner is all cognitive skills and misses out the soul. That is true. What psychologist, in his ready play with cognition and development would ever use the idea of a soul? But the stock response is to add a new section to the pack which takes care of the soul.

This is to commit the classical heresy of modern technocracies. It was J. S. Mill's in the first place, and it has been teachers' since. Their heresy sees correctly that modern scientific thought, with its stress on 'objectivity' and sense-datum empiricism, misses out something. It then supposes that what you do is create a reserve area – 'the culture of the feelings' (Mill's phrase, picked up by David Holbrook) – where you look after that something. The mind is one thing, and thinks, decides, takes actions; the feelings are another, but must be tended. Art and literature serve this purpose and are therefore necessary to keep the plain practical technocrat civilized. Art and the study of the thick texture of its culture then becomes one of the agreeable graces – needful to be sure, but in no sense a dominant mode of thought.

This view of art as an emollient addition to the tough cognitions which really make the world of knowledge and power what it is, is deeply unattractive. What is absent in all three styles of thought is an account of man in his culture which resists these merely contingent splits in his consciousness, and which restores some sense of the interrelation as well as the division of labour; an account which will, in turn, permit us at least an idea of the complete man. The idea has been central to western educational traditions.

Such a call to intellectual action returns us to the first and most central criticism of Bruner's curriculum – it is static. It includes no mention of change or conflict. It has no politics. But of course to profess no politics, to believe in the end-of-ideology, is itself a political and ideological act. This comes out very clearly in a consideration of the Schools Council Humanities pack. The most serious disservice these materials do to education is to eliminate the truth. Their main assumptions are organized by the sociology of mass communications about the central and articulating assumption, that morality is choice, and free choice is displayed and vindicated by the free expression of opinion. That contemporary style of thought – consensus achieved by committee discussion – dominates such curricula.[21] It springs from the liberal supposition that you may choose all your values and ascribe them to the social facts as a function of your existential self. The concept of 'balance', learned painlessly and all the time from *Talkback, 24 Hours, Any Questions?* and all the other forums of instant banality, turns out to mean something more like a balancing act, a nimble dodging along a thread of points of view. If a man says anything, let another man say the opposite. Thus we will discover the 'balanced' position. It is a necessary part of such a curriculum that its contents will be on the whole brief quotations from *New Society* and *The Guardian,* or passages of black-and-white social-realist literature with a distinct bias. The view of rationality as judicious moderation which transpires from the packs, sorts well with English notions of the free agent as freely discussing, moderate and middle-of-the-road, agnostic but humane. The notion of 'balance' as poise, as the clairvoyant goodness of an artist in the full and frightening exercise of his powers, is simply not available. Just as importantly the truth of an argument in the sense of its irrefutability – the truth that it cannot be a matter of choice there is or is not a God, or that England is or is not an unjust country, or that all men have or have not a right to the education they ask for – this sense of truth vanishes in the quest for consensus which is the latent ideology of liberal-minded group discussion. The model of the group is a microcosm of the society, a plural, self-correcting play of minority forces keeping themselves in a state of tensile equilibrium. Once more, the model eliminates change, and conflict as leading to change. It completes the arc of meaning drawn by the flow chartists and the philosophers by confining the terms of discussion to the limits of party politics and the limits of intelligence to the liberal, tax-paying, punctual and orderly voter.

Curriculum theory and practical developments of this kind strengthen the grip of the dominant thought-forms. The training of cognition and the rationalization of learning combine in the mythology of modern technology, the opiate of the intellectuals. The technology creates its own systems, and the construction of systems is its own politics. The point of such systems is to eradicate as far as possible the multiple idiosyncracies and deviances of human behaviour.

Certain sections of the education system – certain ways of teaching, certain subject-matters, certain relationships – have long represented themselves to themselves as resisters of the rationalizer. What these teachers have done who have seen themselves as providing a dissident form of consciousness is cultivate the private soul; they have cherished the unofficial, the sporting, the creative, the poetic and personal. They have created forms of curricula which act as enclosures within public thought-forms and morality and affirm the private, the impromptu, the normal and rhythmic texture of human life.

Within these enclaves, such teaching has made possible alternative relationships which simply by their presence can be seen, consciously or not, as criticizing the official rituals of relationship within schools. It has, for example, long been an acknowledged technique for controlling difficult low-stream boys that teachers take them out of the school on various expeditions whose ideological intention lies somewhere between the Newsom report and *Scouting for Boys.* Taken out of the precise situation of school, and its multiple emphasis on the classroom relationship of teacher and taught, completely other points of human access open up. It is every probationer's experience. 'Why aren't they always like that?' The change makes suddenly possible for the teacher and the pupil alike much deeper penetration of the other's feelings and attitudes. However well advanced (*pace* Basil Bernstein) the change may be from *positional* (sc. 'authoritarian') to *personal* forms of control in the school, the difference between a camping expedition and the progressive project-bound curriculum is obviously enormous. These small outings may have many intentions: a main, simple one is often to get to know a group of difficult, violent, inarticulate children better. Similarly, the intentions of such 'enclave activities' as a school play may be officially far more to do with the corporate, public face of the school than with looking after childish or intimate things. And yet, within the chaos, bloodymindedness, and staff-room or PTA rancour which surrounds the school play, the producer and his colleagues almost always succeed in creating a novel, rich network of relationships which flourishes in a consciously non-curricular way. It is a network of lunch hours and late nights, of unused corners of the school and improbable curricular combinations – electric circuits, dressmaking, *Romeo and Juliet,* brought together in decidedly unintegrated but nonetheless intense, formative ways. These are some of the private and often dissident ways of thinking which importantly resist – are seen by the practitioners as resisting – the implications of more technical planning.

Many of the same points could be made about sport, and its central function as a hinge between official and unofficial cultures in schools.[22]

With a more deliberate defiance, the art and music rooms have long been a refuge for handfuls of a school outlawry, and, in particular, English teaching for the past fifteen or so years has mounted a fragmentary but not ineffective campaign against the public world and some of its blander features. The English teacher's lesson on advertising, on a politician's prose, on school rules, connects with the long and honourable tradition of radical dissidence in his subject matter, literature. Falstaff at the Battle of Shrewsbury, Pip helping the escaped Magwitch on the Essex marshes, Huck Finn lighting out for the territory, all these speak up for the private, the critical, the uncompliant voice which gets relegated hearing in the roll-calls of the objectives.

But, as the foregoing analysis suggests, the cultivation of our own souls has left public life, history, and politics untenanted by teachers. Liberal ideology, which places the individual as the fount of all value, has no point of insertion into systems technology. It stands helpless. For it is not only a defect, it is a principle that liberalism cannot tell us what to do. We choose for ourselves in all circumstances. And yet this inactivity clearly leads to the steady relinquishing of freedoms until it is only in our play and our cultivated leisure[23] that we make a stand and say, 'Here, on this ground, I'm my own man'. What can be salvaged from this refusal to believe, and to act?

Liberalism acknowledges that the freely choosing individual must be rational; this is the clue we need. A necessary part of the scheme of things must be the preservation of reason, especially since its nominal custodians have made such a mess of things. To consider what it is to be rational returns us to the consideration of what it is to be moral and to be good, terms the omission of which has made contemptible and frivolous so much of recent discussions of moral education and of curricular developments. To consider rationality is to reconsider those qualities which we are taught rational men should admire.

Contemporary rationality is largely content with the positivist model which sets up an easy victory for social calculus over social intuitions. Anyone who objects to this version of reason as narrow and disgusting is then branded as a Luddite or clock-turner-back. But vast areas of human and extra-human life have been and are being – quite literally – stripped, burned, and devastated for ever by this kind of reason. It is not reasonable to live in the present way, and moral disgust *is* a reasonable reaction. It is to resist the alleged rationality of the rationalizers with their own key weapon, reasonableness, to talk in this way, and it is the least we may expect of an education system.

Such reasonableness, however, cannot stop there. As I said, to consider what it is reasonable to admire is to debate what we ought to do. It is to inquire into the good. Not, 'be ye therefore rational'; but, 'be ye therefore perfect, as . . .'. The worst office of the styles of thought which I have criticized have been to foreclose any discussion of the moral ends of education. The moral tradition that a man's ends are his own business has been, in the politics of today's world, overdrawn beyond the point of bankruptcy. The present relations of the curriculum and ideology work busily to keep it solvent. Systems analysts, analytic philosophers, cognitive psychologists, and teacher-as-TV chairman combine to recommend the ideal modern man as responsible, sincere, self-aware, puzzled and helpless.

The moral ends are no longer digestible by such a weak stomach. One can hardly suggest in a paragraph or two what the ends might be. But it is at this point that the effort is needed to redefine the affirmations of the private and impromptu in such a way as to give our 'cultivation of the soul' historical point and purchase. It is likely that a large number of teachers feel that present ways of thinking are disastrously not enough to cope with the world. A number, in their different ways, acknowledge and press home the counter-claims of the 'unofficial' styles of thinking. To teach in this way the commonplace lessons of secondary schools – the English teacher on advertising, on *Great Expectations,* or school uniform, the History teacher on Peterloo, the Geography teacher's traffic count and the Music teacher's lesson on the *Pastoral Symphony* or the *Eroica* – is to see how mighty is the force of an alternative map of knowledge and culture. Pressing home these implicit claims is likely to cause conflict, in and out of school. That is a perfectly understandable reason for having softened the pressure. But it is not a rhetorical flourish by now to say that the values of our education have lost substance and honour by avoiding conflict.

The education community could recover some of that lost honour by setting all its members the task of discovering to what extent they are their own men and women.

NOTES

1. The title, of course, of Daniel Bell's now notorious apologia, first published in 1961, just about the moment when the argument became incredible.
2. Quoted from John Merritt, Professor of Educational Studies, The Open University, 'Priorities in curriculum design' in *Journal of the Institute of Education of the Universities of Newcastle-Upon-Tyne and Durham,* Nov. 1970, vol. 22, 110.
3. *The Curriculum, Context, Design and Development* – 'Reading and the Curriculum', R. Hooper ed., Oliver and Boyd for the Open University 1971, pp. 216–231. For a similar enterprise see John F. Kerr's synopsis of the necromancers in Changing the Curriculum, J. F. Kerr (ed.), University of London Press, 1965. First in the field was Ralph Tyler, *Basic Principles of Curriculum and Instruction,* University of Chicago. The other main hornbook in College and Department of Education curriculum courses is Hilda Taba, *Curriculum Development: Theory and Practice,* Harcourt Brace Jovanovich, 1962.
4. I derive here some points from R. S. Peters' *The Concept of Motivation,* Routledge, 1958, pp. 27–52.
5. To whose unpublished paper on rationalization I am immensely in debt.
6. Trying to provide operational justification for this makes it clear, I think, just how limited is the use to which one may put D. R. Krathwohl, B. S. Bloom, and B. B. Masia, *Taxonomy of Education Objectives: the Classification of Educational*

Goals – Handbook II: the Affective Domain, David McKay and Longmans, 1964.

7. Students' Library of Education, Routledge, 1970, pp. 2–3.
8. In *An Introduction to the Philosophy of Education,* 1957, p. 4.
9. In *The Idea of a Social Science,* Routledge, 1967.
10. In *An Autobiography,* Oxford, 1939, pp. 138–9.
11. R. S. Peters, *Ethics and Education,* Allen and Unwin, 1966, p. 170.
12. In 'Liberal Education and the Nature of Knowledge', contributed to *Philosophical Analysis and Education,* R. D. Archambault (ed.), Routledge, 1965, pp. 113–18.
13. Marjorie Grene, in her remarkable *The Knower and the Known,* Faber, 1965, is the text here.
14. Cf. also his contribution 'Educational Theory' to *The Study of Education,* J. W. Tibble (ed.), Students' Library of Education, Routledge, 1966, especially p. 42 and ff.
15. See *Ethics and Education, passim,* but especially pp. 54–55, 259–63. See also Michael Oakeshott in *Rationalism in Politics and Other Essays* (Methuen, 1962).
16. The term is Basil Bernstein's. More than anyone in England Bernstein has unlocked those mysteries, and uncovered the connections between knowledge and power. Not that there's any easy solace for left or right in the revelation.
17. J. Gribble, 'Forms of Knowledge', in *Educational Philosophy and Theory,* 2, I, pp. 3–14, March, 1970.
18. Belknap, Harvard, 1962, pp. 73–102.
19. He concedes, rather crossly, some of his charges in *The Radical Alternative,* Tri-University Project in Elementary Education, New Orleans, 1970.
20. See Richard M. Jones in *Fantasy and Feeling in Education,* University of London, 1968, who quotes the psychologist and proposes the solution criticized here.
21. Cf. also those Schools Council projects and kits: Project for the Integration of the Humanities: Social Education Project; The Arts and the Adolescent; General Studies Project; Moral Education Curriculum Project; the Whole Curriculum for the Middle Years of Schooling.
22. Suggested in my *The Englishness of English Teaching,* Longmans, 1970, p. 180.
23. Which is all that G. H. Bantock would want to make of the English literature he purportedly admires. He rests easily upon the status quo and hands over the creative writing in order that the working class will be kept quiet. See particularly his 'Towards a Theory of Popular Education', *TES* 12th and 19th March, 1971.

5. The Concept and Aims of Education

P. H. Hirst and R. S. Peters

Source: P. H. Hirst and R. S. Peters, *The Logic of Education* (Routledge and Kegan Paul Ltd., London, 1970), pp. 19–28.

This extract illustrates the analytical approach of the most influential British school of the philosophy of education.
Hirst and Peters contrast the concepts of 'curing' and 'educating', and the difference between the two leads to an appraisal of education as 'instruction'. Objections to the notion that education is 'intrinsically good' are considered, and the authors go on to argue that the aim or aims of education are 'intentions formulated at a fair level of generality'.

The concept of 'education'

It might be suggested straightaway that there is a close parallel between educational reasons and medical reasons. In the practice of medicine, though stress is now put on prevention, the doctor is mainly concerned with making people better, or curing them. 'Curing' covers a family of processes, such as surgery, the administration of drugs, and so on, whose principle of unity is the contribution to the end of being better in respect of physical or mental health, just as reforming people covers a family of processes which contribute to making them morally better. Similarly, 'educating' people suggests a family of processes whose principle of unity is the development of desirable qualities in them. So 'educational reasons' would be connected with the development of desirable qualities in people.

There are, however, obvious differences, which spring in part from the nature of the ends with which the doctor and the teacher are respectively concerned. 'Curing' someone, on the one hand, suggests that he has lapsed from some standard which the cure is restoring. 'Education', on the other hand, has no such suggestion. It often consists in putting people in the way of values of which they have never dreamt. Secondly there is a general consensus amongst doctors as to what constitutes physical health as an end, though mental health is more indeterminate. About the end of 'desirable qualities', however, there is no such agreement. That is why there is a lot of talk about aims of education; for in formulating aims of education we are attempting to specify more precisely what qualities we think it most desirable to develop. There is, however, some limitation on what might count as an end in the case of education. For 'education' suggests not only that what develops in someone is valuable but also that it involves the development of knowledge and understanding. Whatever else an educated person is, he is one who has some understanding of something. He is not just a person who has a know-how or knack. There is also the suggestion that this understanding should not be too narrowly specialized.

If this analysis is correct, therefore, teachers who enter the profession because they are concerned about education, would be striving to initiate others into a form of life, which they regard as desirable, in which knowledge and understanding play an important part. The decisions, too, which, as teachers, they take on educational grounds, would be related to the promotion of this general end. Of course there would be great differences amongst them about what constitutes a desirable form of life and some would value some forms of knowledge more than others just as some would place more value on depth and understanding and others on breadth. But at least this general end would give criteria by reference to which decisions taken on educational grounds could be distinguished from decisions taken on personal, economic, or medical grounds. A structure of considerations would also be provided which would render most speculations about unconscious motives unimportant or irrelevant.

The matter however, is not quite as straightforward as this; for 'education' is not quite so straightforward a concept as 'cure' or 'reform'. In particular it is doubtful whether 'education' is always used to designate processes that lead up to a general end in the way in which 'cure' and 'reform' always seem to be used. Doubts can be thrown on this parallel by probing along the lines suggested in Ch. I to see whether any conditions that even begin to look like logically necessary conditions have been provided for the use of the term 'education'. To test this counter-examples have to be produced.

(a) Objections to the desirability condition

Roughly speaking, two types of conditions have been suggested for the use of the term 'education', namely desirability conditions and knowledge conditions. Let us consider first counter-examples to the desirability condition. They are as follows:

(i) We often talk of the educational system of a country without commending what others seem concerned to pass on. This objection can be met by citing the parallel of talking about the moral code of another community or of a sub-culture within our own. Once we understand from our own case how terms such as 'educate' and 'moral' function, we can use them in an external descriptive sort of way as do anthropologists, economists, and the like. As observers we appreciate that, in the moral case, their way of life is valuable to them, and, in the case of an educational system, we appreciate that those, whose system it is, consider that they are passing on what they think valuable. But we, as observers, do not necessarily commend it when we use the word 'moral' or 'educational' to refer to it.

(ii) We can talk of poor education or bad education. This can be met by saying that we are suggesting that the job is being botched or that the values with which it is concerned are not up to much.

(iii) A much more serious objection, however, is that many regard being educated as a bad state to be in. Their objection is not to a particular system of education, but to *any* sort of education. They appreciate that 'education' has something to do with the transmission of knowledge and understanding. Indeed they probably associate it with books and theories. And this is why they are against it; for they think of it either as useless or as corrupting. Of course they bring up their own children, perhaps in traditional skills and folk-lore. But they do not see any connection between what they think valuable and 'education', and have no specific word to differentiate the handing on of what they think valuable from handing on a lot of other things.

This last point suggests one way in which the objection could be met. It could be argued, with some cogency, that people, who think that being educated is a bad state to be in, lack our concept of being educated. Their understanding has not become differentiated to the extent of needing a special word for referring to the passing on of what they do think is valuable. They have a concept of education; for they use the term to refer to what goes on in schools and universities. But they have not *our* concept. The only trouble about this way of dealing with the objection is that people who lack our concept of education are, at the moment, rather numerous. 'We', in this context, are in the main educated people and those who are professionally concerned with education; and 'we' are not in the majority of people who use the word 'education'. So it is doubtful whether the desirability condition of 'education' is a logically necessary condition of the term that is in current use. It stands in this relation to a more specific, differentiated concept that has emerged. This possibility will be considered in more detail later.

Another way, not of really meeting the objection but of accounting for the discrepancies with regard to the desirability condition, is to suggest that the knowledge conditions are the only proper logical conditions, and that the desirability condition is dependent on them. On this view the fundamental notion involved in being educated would be that of having knowledge and understanding. Because knowledge and understanding are valued in our culture, both for their own sake and for what they contribute to technology and to our quality of life generally, being educated has come to be thought of as a highly desirable state to be in – but not by everybody. Whether or not the desirability condition is fulfilled would depend, therefore, upon contingent facts about the attitude of people talking about education to the passing on of knowledge and understanding. The desirability condition, therefore, would not be, properly speaking, a logically necessary condition of the use of the term 'education'. It would rather be a contingent consequence of certain people's valuations.

This way of simplifying the analysis has much to commend it:

(i) It certainly takes care of those who regard education as a bad thing. As, on this view, the connection between education and something that is valued depends only on the contingent fact that people value knowledge and understanding, it is not surprising that simple people or hard-headed practical men are against it. For it seems to serve no useful function in their lives; indeed it may be seen as an influence that is likely to undermine their way of life. If they see that it may help them to run a farm or to cure a disease they may accord a limited value to it, but only of an instrumental type.

(ii) There would be no need to make any elaborate philosophical moves to deal with cases where we speak of education and educational systems without approving or disapproving of what goes on. Education would be, as indeed it is sometimes called, the 'knowledge industry'. We could talk of it in the same way as we talk of any other set of practices that we might or might not think important.

(iii) 'Poor' or 'bad' education would simply mark the efficiency with which knowledge was handed on or the worth of the type of knowledge that was handed on.

This, then, is a most attractive simplification of the analysis. Its main feature, however, is that it puts all the weight of the analysis on the knowledge conditions, and it is questionable whether they are strong enough to support it. They must therefore be tested by counter-examples in the same way as was the desirability condition.

(b) Objections to knowledge conditions

The knowledge conditions, it will be remembered, include both depth and breadth of understanding.

(i) An obvious counter-example would be, therefore, that we often talk of specialized education. This objection could be met by saying that often, when we have multiple conditions, we can withdraw one of them by using a countermanding word. For instance, people talk of knowing things 'intuitively', where 'intuitively' countermands one of the usual conditions of 'knowledge', namely that we have grounds for what we believe. Similarly 'specialized' could be regarded as withdrawing the breadth condition of 'education'.

(ii) We might talk of Spartan education, or of education in some even more primitive tribe, when we know that they had nothing to pass on except simple skills and folk-lore. This objection could, perhaps, be met by saying either that the term was being extended analogically, as when

dogs are spoken of as being 'neurotic', or that the people using the term had not yet developed a differentiated concept of 'education' which takes us back to the type of situation which was encountered about people who think that education is a bad thing. As there are a lot of people who talk in a quite unabashed way about Spartan education, it is difficult to maintain that the knowledge conditions are logically necessary conditions of the term in general use. This point is strengthened by the third objection.

(iii) The case of 'Spartan education' is just one of a wider class of cases. A little etymological research reveals the fact that 'education' is, or has been, used without this conceptual connection which is suggested with knowledge. The Latin word 'educere' was usually, though not always, used of *physical* development. In Silver Latin 'educare' was used of the rearing of plants and animals as well as children. In English the word was originally used just to talk in a very general way about the bringing up of children and animals. In the seventeenth century, for instance, harts were said to delight in woods and places of their first education. The word was often used of animals and birds that were trained by human beings such as hounds and falcons. In the nineteenth century it was even used of silkworms! (See O.E.D.) Nowadays we sometimes use it in this general way as when, for instance, we talk about Spartan education or when we use it of our own forms of training that do not have any close connection with knowledge and understanding. In other words the older usage still survives.

Arguments from etymology, of course, establish very little. At best they provide clues which it may be worth-while to follow up. In this case, for instance, it seems that the word originally had a very generalized meaning. With the coming of industrialism, however, and the increasing demand for knowledge and skill consequent on it, 'education' became increasingly associated with 'schooling' and with the sort of training and instruction that went on in special institutions. This large-scale change, culminating in the development of compulsory schooling for all, may well have brought about such a radical conceptual tightening up that we now only tend to use the word in connection with the development of knowledge and understanding. We distinguish now between 'training' and 'education', whereas previously people did not. We would not now naturally speak of educating animals and we would never speak in this way of plants. But we do speak of training animals and of training roses and other sorts of plants.

These counter-examples to both the desirability condition and the knowledge conditions of 'education' make it very difficult to maintain that an adequate analysis has been given of the concept. It is possible, however, that there is some explanation of these counter-examples. It could be the case, in other words, that the cases that fail to fit the analysis could themselves be linked in some way. If we could get clearer about the principle underlying the counter-examples further light would be shed on the concept of 'education' generally.

(c) Education and the educated man

As a matter of fact there is another etymological point that may put us on the track of the explanation of cases that do not fit the original analysis. A little research in the O.E.D. reveals that the notion of 'educated' as characterising the all-round development of a person morally, intellectually and spiritually only emerged in the nineteenth century. It was also in this century that the distinction between education and training came to be made explicitly. This use was very much connected with instruction by means of which desirable mental qualities were thought to be produced, as well as with the drawing out and development of qualities thought to be potential in a person. The term, however, continued to be used, as it had previously been used, to refer to the rearing and bringing up of children and animals, as well as to the sort of instruction that went on in schools. In other words, though previously to the nineteenth century there had been the ideal of the cultivated person who was the product of elaborate training and instruction, the term 'an educated man' was not the usual one for drawing attention to this ideal. They had the concept but they did not use the word 'educated' quite with these overtones. Education, therefore, was not thought of explicitly as a family of processes which have as their outcome the development of an educated man in the way in which it is now.

Nowadays, especially in educational circles, the concept of an educated man as an ideal has very much taken root. It is natural, therefore, for those working in educational institutions to conceive of what they are doing as being connected with the development of such a person. They have become very sensitive to the difference between working with this ideal in mind and having more limited and specific goals, for which they use the word 'training'. Witness, for instance, the change of nomenclature, following the Robbins Report, from Training Colleges to Colleges of Education. Witness, too, the change from Physical Training to Physical Education. In brief, because of the development of the concept of an 'educated man', the concept of 'education' has become tightened up because of its natural association with the development of such a person. We distinguish between educating people and training them because for us education is no longer compatible with any narrowly conceived enterprise.

Now in the analysis previously given of 'education' as being comparable to 'reform' and 'cure' a connection was assumed between education and the development of an educated man. It was admitted that other people may not have developed this more differentiated type of conceptual structure, but it was maintained that it is important to make these distinctions even if people do not use terms in a specific enough way to mark them out. But it could well be that the older use of 'education' is widespread in which there is no such tight connection between various processes of bringing up and rearing and the development of an educated man. It may well be that many people still use the word 'education' to cover not only any process of instruction, training, etc., that goes on in schools but also less formalized child-rearing practices such as toilet training, getting children to be clean and tidy, and to speak with a nice accent. They may think these achievements desirable, though they have little connection with knowledge and understanding. I do not think, however, that the word is now used, except semi-humorously, to talk about the training of animals, and I have never heard it used to honour the labours of gardeners with their plants. At least the concept has shifted more or less universally in these respects from that of the seventeenth century.

It looks, therefore, as if the concept of 'education' is a very fluid one. At one end of a continuum is the older and undifferentiated concept which refers just to any process of bringing up or rearing in which the connection either with what is desirable or with knowledge is purely contingent. There may be uses which link it just with the development of desirable states without any emphasis on knowledge; there may be uses which pick out the development of knowledge without implying its desirability. The more recent and more specific concept links such processes with the development of states of a person that involve knowledge and understanding in depth and breadth, and also suggests that they are desirable. The analysis of 'education' given at the start of the chapter is of this more differentiated specific concept. It will be with the implications of this more specific concept that we shall be concerned in this book.

Aims of Education

A teacher who enters the profession because he is keen on education, or who makes decisions about teaching on educational grounds, would manifestly not be relying on the earlier undifferentiated concept; for this could provide no grounds whatever for doing anything in particular. How, then, would reasons, deriving from the later more specific concept of 'education', provide guidance? The general injunction to promote desirable states of a person, that involve depth and breadth of understanding, would indicate only a general direction; it would offer no specific guidance.

More specific guidance would have to be obtained by the teacher getting clearer about his aims in educating people. For the function of the formulation of aims is to specify more precisely what one is trying to achieve, one's target in a metaphorical sense. This attempt to specify precise targets also takes over a further suggestion from the context of shooting and throwing, where the concept of 'aim' has its natural home, namely that the end in view is not altogether easy to achieve. Distance and difficulty seem to be endemic to ends that we would characterize as 'aims'. Aims, however, cannot specify states of affairs that it would be manifestly impracticable to bring about. In this respect they differ from 'ideals'. A person can expatiate on his ideals as a teacher without having to raise awkward questions about practicalities. If, on the other hand, he attempts to formulate his aims, he has to have regard to practicalities. He also has to be more specific than he is licensed to be if he is asked about his ideals. An educational ideal, for instance, might be that every child should learn out of the joy of discovery. A teacher's aim, in the same context, might be a more specific and attainable objective such as that every child in his class should be brought to see some point in learning what had to be learnt.

Formulating aims in education must be distinguished from attempting to answer the general question 'What is *the* aim of education?' This is an unhelpful sort of question to ask in this context because the answer must either be a conceptual truth or a persuasive definition. It would be a conceptual truth if it specified an adequate analysis of the general end brought about by processes of education. In other words, if the foregoing analysis of the specific concept of 'education', as the family of processes leading up to desirable states of mind in people involving depth and breadth of understanding, is more or less adequate, then it would be a conceptual truth that the production of this general end is the aim of education. It would be like saying that the aim of reform is to make men better. And to reiterate this would not provide much guidance for the teacher. Suppose, however, that something more concrete were produced as a specification of this general end. Suppose it were said that *the* aim of education is to produce specialized knowledge. Then a stipulative definition would be produced which would have the function of recommending a specific policy. Instead of coming out into the open and saying '*My* aim in educating people is to develop specialists', covert support would be obtained for this policy by trading on the suggestion that pursuing this, and only this end, is consistent with educating people. This, it is true, would help the teacher in giving more specific guidance. But the help would be at the expense of conceptual clarity.

Suppose, then, the teacher attempts to specify *his* aim in educating people or the aims of a particular educational institution. What sort of answer could be given? Roughly speaking any answer which could be a more precise specification of what an educated man is considered to be. Features would be emphasized – e.g. critical thinking, specialized knowledge, autonomy, aesthetic sensitivity – which would be part of the teacher's understanding of what it means to be 'educated'. Content would be given to the general form of 'an educated man' provided by the analysis in terms of desirability and knowledge conditions. Arguments, of course, would have to be produced for emphasizing some desirable qualities rather than others. Indeed this is one important respect in which educating people differs from curing them, to revert to the comparison with medicine. For in education there is as much debate about the ends of education as there is about the methods to be adopted to promote these ends. The same is not true of medicine. There is much more consensus about what constitutes being 'cured' than there is about what constitutes being 'educated'.

It is important to distinguish 'aims of education' in these cases from aims of education when the more general undifferentiated concept of 'education' is being used – e.g. by politicians talking about the educational system. A politician or administrator, in an economic frame of mind, might think of education as the means by which a supply of trained manpower is assured. He might think of education purely in this way and have no regard for the endeavours of educators who might in their turn be impervious to the economist's frame of reference. They might be concerned purely with the development of educated men and women. Of course looking at what goes on in schools and universities from this economic point of view is not *necessarily* antagonistic to being concerned with education in the more specific sense. Indeed a teacher might regard the development of responsible citizens, who have the competence to fulfil some occupational role, as his unifying aim as an educator. For him this civic consciousness might be the hall-mark of an educated person. He might, in his approach, concentrate on getting his pupils technically equipped to do certain jobs, and attempt to make technical skill and knowledge the lynch-pin of a person's depth and breadth of understanding as a citizen.

Similarly a teacher might teach a subject such as science with purely vocational or economic ends in view. He might regard himself just as equipping people for vocations or as serving a national need for trained manpower, without much thought about the development of the individuals concerned, as individuals. He might conceive of what he was doing just as contributing to economic growth. But teaching science with these limited ends in view should be distinguished from educating people. Teaching, as has already been pointed out, is not necessarily educative. On the other hand, though not unmindful of the nation's needs, a teacher might also teach science because he regarded this form of understanding as central to his concept of an educated person. Whether a teacher is educating people or just training them depends, mainly, on his intentions, on how he conceives of what he is trying to bring about [. . .]. When these intentions are formulated at a fair level of generality we call them 'aims'.

It is essential for a teacher to try to get a bit clearer about his aims; for unless he does this he will not have criteria by reference to which he can determine satisfactorily the content and methods of his teaching. Suppose, for instance, that he is a teacher of French. Is his aim simply to enable his pupils to rub along all right during holidays in France? Does he hope that they will eventually be able to write French? Does he envisage the learning of the language as the best way of coming to understand, from the inside, the form of life of another nation? Or is his aim just the non-educational one of getting through an examination that will open the door to a range of occupations? Unless he asks himself questions of this sort he will have no clear guide-lines for determining the content and methods of his teaching. 'Education' implies processes of learning; so how can content and method be combined so that learning will result of the type that is aimed at? And how does this contribute to the outcome of an educated man? How are processes of education to be conceived?

6. Open Education: Assumptions about Children, Learning and Knowledge

Roland S. Barth

Source: David E. Purpel and Maurice Belanger (eds.), *Curriculum and the Cultural Revolution* (McCutchen Publishing Corp., Berkeley, California, 1972), pp. 424–51. Adapted from a chapter in *Open Education and the American School,* copyright 1972 by Roland S. Barth. Reprinted by kind permission of the publisher, Agathon Press, Inc.

Underlying the set of practices that characterise 'open education' are a number of assumptions about children, learning and knowledge. Barth attempts to tease them out and stresses the need for educators who adopt such practices to understand their underlying rationale.

Introduction

In education as in other domains, practice frequently precedes theory. To the extent that practice helps generate theory, this is a healthy and even desirable sequence. To the extent that practice without an accompanying theory is random, disordered, and misunderstood, practice may become weak and even unproductive.

The present practice of what I have chosen to call 'open education' reflects both of these conditions; it is helping to give rise to a coherent educational theory, but at the same time it has been handicapped by the lack of an apparent underlying rationale. Most accounts of open education have been anecdotal and descriptive, painting for the reader a picture of what is happening to the child, to the teacher, and to the curriculum in open classrooms. Reports abound of children making important decisions each day affecting their learning and education, of children posing, solving, and verifying their own problems, of an environment rich in materials and activities, of the teacher no longer in the center ring, but in a role supportive of children's concerns. Yet for all the growing literature on open education, few accounts have attempted anything approaching a systematic analysis of the important assumptions on which these practices are built.*

Endemic to education and to educators is a disposition to search for the new, the different, the flashy, the radical, or the revolutionary. Once an idea of a practice, such as *team teaching, nongrading* or *paraprofessional* has been so labeled by the establishment, teachers and administrators are quick to adopt it. More precisely, educators, who are quick to assimilate new ideas into their cognitive and operational framework, often distort the ideas or practices from the original conception without recognizing either the distortion or the assumptions violated by the distortion. This seems to happen partly because the educator has taken on the verbal abstraction of a new idea without going through a concomitant personal reorientation of attitude and behavior. Vocabulary and rhetoric are easily changed while practices, people, and institutions often remain little affected. If open education is to have a fundamental and purposeful effect on American education, and if changes are to be consciously made, then the important theoretical assumptions underlying these practices need to be exposed and analyzed. Descriptions without analysis will not suffice.

I hope my exposure of some of these assumptions will move advocates of open education further away from the realm of ideology, cult, mystique, or technique (which permits one proponent to say, "If I have to explain it to you, you'll never understand") toward the more rational realm of a coherent theory or philosophy. Until an explanation is offered, most educators will remain puzzled, if fascinated, by open education.

To date, interest in open education and sources of information about it have been limited to England and the United States, where terms such as *free day, integrated day, integrated classroom, informal classroom, development classroom,* and *child-centered classroom* are being used to describe this educational point of view. In England, two particularly important sources of information should be mentioned: The *Plowden Report,* commissioned in 1963 by the British Ministry of Education "to consider primary education in all its aspects, and the transition to secondary education," and the National Froebel Foundation, which publishes pamphlets on a variety of topics related to open education. In the United States, the Education Development Center (EDC) in Newton, Massachusetts, has been the unofficial center for thought, dissemination, and implementation of open education. Within EDC, the Elementary Science Study and, more recently, the Follow Through Program have been the source of numerous published and unpublished materials.

Despite the plethora of information accumulating around open education, there is still virtually no rigorous research concerning its effects on the development of children's thinking, attitudes, and behavior as compared with the effects associated with more traditional forms of education. However, underlying the more or less clearly circumscribed set of practices associated with open education there is, I believe, a set of assumptions.

My purpose here will be to make overt and organize a number of covert assumptions about children's learning and the nature of knowledge, which underlie the practices and utterances of open educators. Classification will be generative; that is, each assumption will be based to some extent on those which have preceded it and will give rise to some extent to those which follow. Though I realize not all of these assumptions would be acceptable to every advocate of open education, they do, I believe, reflect the thinking of most. In fact, I have "tested" these assumptions with over a dozen British primary teachers, headmasters, and inspectors, at an inservice workshop for teachers offered by the Leicestershire Advisory Centre and with a number of American proponents of open education at

EDC and elsewhere. To date, although many qualifications in language have been suggested, there has not been a case where an individual has said of one of the assumptions, "No, that is contrary to what I believe about children's learning."

It should also be made clear that, while I personally share many of these beliefs, these are assumptions which I attribute to open educators. It will not be my purpose to assess their validity or to answer the question, "How does one *know* the practices related with these assumptions are in the interest of children?" I shall not attempt to evaluate open education; rather, my concern will be to uncover and analyze what I see to be its salient features and to point out some of the perplexing questions associated with the assumptions. The format which follows will be a statement of the assumption, a sample of open educators' thinking which both exemplifies and gives rise to the assumption, and my own reactions.

Assumptions about Children's Learning

Motivation

Assumption 1: Children are innately curious and display exploratory behavior quite independent of adult intervention.

> Young children display a natural curiosity about their environment which provokes them to explore and to ask questions.[1]
>
> The child appears to have a strong drive, which shows itself at a very early age, toward activity and the exploration of the environment. . . As far as can be judged, this behavior is autonomous since it occurs when there is no obvious motivation such as hunger.[2]
>
> A little child's motives for learning come, in the first place, from his own nature, from his innate impulse to achieve, to find out, to master his own body and his environment.[3]
>
> The most powerful learning mechanisms available to us are built in biologically rooted mechanisms of search and exploration, relatively separate from the primary biological drives of hunger, sex, and the like.[4]

Assumption 2: Exploratory behavior is self-perpetuating.

> explorations carried on in any consecutive direction can always be turned into a self-rewarding, self-extending, self-multiplying process.[5]

The concept of motivation has always had a prominent place in theories of learning. Since such theories are man-made constructs, it is not surprising to find the intervention of adults commonly associated with the learning of other organisms. The pigeon pecks at the light and the adult human dispenses the pellet or arranges to have the pellet dispensed. The child submits a perfect paper and the adult supplies the A. In these views of motivation we find the adult placing himself in a position of both importance and control with respect to the learning organism. This seems to be a place of some comfort.

Open educators question whether motivation generated and manipulated by the adult results in greater learning or just in increased production. They also question whether the adult's intervention is essential for the child to be motivated and to learn. Thus, the assumption that children are innately curious and predisposed toward exploration and not dependent on adults, for either the initiation or the perpetuation of learning activities, seriously challenges much conventional learning theory and raises some important questions.

The assumptions discussed here about motivation point toward an underlying sense of *trust* in the innate abilities of children, in their capacity to energize and direct their own exploration, and in their wanting to explore and learn. This implies the existence of an inner motivation on the part of the child and a hands off role for the adult.

A closer examination of these assumptions about motivation suggests another component as important as the autonomy of the child's motivation. Motivation is realized only through the relationship of the individual to something outside himself, to other persons or to bits and pieces of the world. That is, one is not motivated in a vacuum; one must have something to be motivated about. The source of motivation resides neither in the child nor in the external world but in the *interaction* of one with the other. It is only through the interaction of the person with what is external to him that motivation comes to exist and to energize learning. One has only to imagine withdrawing all external stimuli from a motivated child to see the importance of the object of exploration as well as the capacity for exploration.

In contrast to the thinking of many educators and psychologists, open educators do not see adults as the unique suppliers of the elements of the external world that will release the child's potential for motivation. The world is there, and children, just by being in and of the world, have their own access to it. They can influence their own motivation and exploration just as much as can the adult. They bring things into the classroom as well as use what is supplied by the teacher.

Motivation, then, which may seem from some of these assumptions to be internal, personal, and autonomous, has an external component over which both adult and child have influence. It remains for open educators to clarify the place of the adult in releasing or activating the child's motivation and to differentiate the child's control from the adult's.

Conditions for Learning

Assumption 3: The child will display natural exploratory behavior if he is not threatened.

> exploratory behavior dominates only in the absence of the more urgent needs.[6]
> Children can think and form concepts, as long as they work at their own level, and are not made to feel that they are failures.[7]

Assumption 4: Confidence in self is highly related to capacity for learning and for making important choices affecting one's learning.

> Perhaps the greatest benefit that time in the infant school gives is confidence in what has been learned. The child's own satisfaction in having really mastered something, whether it be riding a bicycle or telling the time, is important. If the beginnings of school work are only half learned and anxiety ridden, the effects may persist throughout school days. Confidence in the power to learn is vital.[8]

Open educators assume that opportunities to explore, to try and fail in the absence of threat, contribute to a sense of mastery and the development of a child's knowledge. There seems to be some relationship between knowing oneself and self-esteem, and this self-esteem is seen to be crucial for learning. Put more strongly, a strong self-concept on the part of the child is the *sine qua non* of open education; if, and only if, the child respects himself will he be able to be responsible for his own learning. Does this mean that schools are in some fundamental way responsible for fostering self-confidence?

Open educators often think of children's potential for self-directed learning not in terms of "smart", "dumb", "fast", or "slow", but rather along dimensions of self-esteem. If the child feels good about himself – if he is self-confident – then he will be capable of initiating and sustaining his own learning. If he does not have these qualities he will not.

But what is self-esteem? What are the minimum components of self-confidence which would permit one to say a child has it? A circular argument underlies the reasoning here: if a child is capable of making important choices affecting his own learning, he has a strong self-concept and he will be able to make responsible choices. Or looked at in another way, children who are trusted to make choices may develop self-control, but those with self-control are more likely to be trusted to make choices.

Open educators have only touched on children's reasons for making choices. Is choice by the child, *qua* choice, desirable, or only choice out of certain motives? Is the behavior of a child who chooses to swing the pendulum in order to attract the teacher's attention or to wrest the apparatus away from another child as desirable as that of the child whose choice is directed by his desire to explore the relationship between the swing of the pendulum and the length of the string? Are the former child's choices as legitimate, whatever his reasons, as those of the latter?

The important point here is that open educators have not yet considered, let alone established, a relationship between development of self-confidence and the ability to make responsible choices about learning. So far, the two are seen as necessary to one another, but the nature of the relationship remains to be spelled out.

Assumption 5: Active exploration in a rich environment, offering a wide array of manipulative materials facilitates children's learning.

> At every stage of learning children need rich and varied materials. . .[9]
>
> You don't teach children to think; you give them something to think about.[10]
>
> When using any material for the first time, the child will experiment with it, exploring its possibilities.[11]
>
> the interest in *things* is a perfectly real, perfectly independent and autonomous interest which is there just as genuinely as the interest in persons is there in young children. And some children are *only* able to develop humanly by first coming to grips in an exploratory and involved way with the inanimate world.[12]
>
> I hear, and I forget
> I see, and I remember
> I do, and I understand[13]
>
> the child must discover for himself in his own time. He will do this if the relevant material is available to him in sufficient quantity and variety, if he is given many opportunities of handling it and trying it out. . .[14]

Assumption 6: Play is not distinguished from work as the predominant mode of learning in early childhood.

> play is the natural way of learning for all young things.[15]
>
> In play, children gradually develop concepts of causal relationships, the power to discriminate, to make judgements, to analyze and synthesize, to imagine and formulate. We know that play in the sense of "messing about" either with material objects or with other children, and of creating fantasies, is vital to children's learning and therefore vital in school.[16]
>
> The word water is learned quite early, but its full range of suggestions can only be learned through play, through having discovered all the things that water can and cannot do and the words: run, soak, drip, freeze, gurgle, splash, etc., which stand for these things.[17]

Children's learning, like motivation, does not occur in a vacuum. Children play *with* something or someone, they do not just play. Exploratory behavior is of little consequence unless there is something to explore.

The word *play* is often used in schools to distinguish activities from *work* but in many open schools neither term is appropriate; this distinction has all but disappeared and given way to one between involvement and lack of involvement.

Yet perhaps this distinction should not be dismissed quite so easily. There are many activities in which children engage, such as learning to play the piano, which are tedious, laborious, and even painful. Others, such as playing ball, are fun, unrestrained, and carefree for most children. Both may be characterized by active involvement with materials, but they have considerable differences, as any child knows. One appears from the adult point of view to be work and the other play. How, if at all, do open educators account for these differences?

Most would admit that there are vast differences in the nature of activities in which children become involved, but that rewards come from participating in and completing the activity and are not dependent on the ease of the activity. Hence, the labor in learning to play a musical instrument may well be greater than that of playing ball, but so may be the reward. Otherwise, the child would be playing ball, not playing the piano.

One of the problems open educators have had in trying to distinguish between work and play or in trying to eliminate the distinction is that they have not been able to separate the adult's view of what the child does from the child's view. Young children are not conscious of a work-play distinction, but become increasingly aware of one as they go through the grades. It appears to be an adult artifact. Adults have assumed that anything that is productive for children in school is difficult and often painful. If it hurts, there must be something beneficial about it. Conversely, it has been assumed that things that are fun and pleasurable are unproductive and usually take place in "free time" or out of school. It would seem that open educators have some obligations to make the relationship between play and learning clearer.

Assumption 7: Children have both the competence and the right to make significant decisions concerning their own learning.

Assumption 8: Children will be likely to learn if they are given considerable choice in the selection of the materials they wish to work with and in the selection of the questions they wish to pursue with respect to those materials.

Assumption 9: Given the opportunity, children will choose to engage in activities which will be of high interest to them.

Assumption 10: If the child is fully involved in and having fun with an activity, learning is taking place.

> The child is the agent in his own learning.[18]

> children can respond to courteous treatment by adults, and that to a great extent they can be trained to take the initiative in learning, if choices are real and if a rich variety of material is offered them.[19]

> the best materials are ambiguous; they can be used for many purposes.

> By choosing their own uses . . . the children learn on their own terms.[20]
>
> the understanding of a subject, the grasp of its structure, comes . . . . in short, learning comes . . . through a self directed activity of the child, an activity of invention and discovery.[21]
>
> they learn most effectively if they choose what to do from amongst a range of materials . . . [22]
>
> It seemed to me in watching that even when they were not playing things "straight" (i.e., *our* way) they were learning a great deal, and learning things that they could not learn when we were in control.[23]

Central to open education is the question of agency. Who or what will direct the child's explorations and play? What will be the origin of the problems and materials in which he is engaged?

Many open educators eschew any attempt whatsoever to control or manipulate children's behavior. However, in the act of selecting materials for the classroom, the adult does in fact exercise a large measure of control over the direction of the child's learning and exploration. Ideas and concepts emerge out of activity with materials. Control of materials, then, implies control of experience, which in turn implies control of ideas and concepts. By bringing books into the classroom the teacher makes it more likely that children will want to learn how to read. If there were not written words available perhaps they would not. By bringing a telescope into the classroom the teacher increases the likelihood that children will become interested in the stars and planets.

If open educators really wish to free children from all adult controls they may have to let children bring all materials into the classroom themselves. They also may have to abandon the institution of school altogether. It is doubtful that even these measures would eliminate adult control of children's activities. At the same time it is questionable whether complete removal of adult control is desirable. Most children do not have access to a wide range of materials which they might want to explore, nor do they have the time and place that would permit such exploration.

The success of the open classroom would seem to depend not on the abdication of adult control to children, but on a deliberate and conscious sharing of responsibility for learning on the part of child and teacher. The adult, to a large extent, determines the nature of the school environment; the child decides with which of these materials he will work, to which problems he will address himself, for how long, and with whom.

Since the materials for children's learning are so important, criteria for their selection are crucial.[24] The teacher in the open school favors materials that are likely to initiate and sustain interest, exploration, and learning. For five-year-olds he might choose a set of blocks rather than a deck of cards, or a picture book rather than a dictionary. Often his selection is based on a hunch that the materials will be found interesting.

Applied purely, this criterion meets with difficulty. Almost anything might be expected to evoke some interest for some children, some time, be it a scrap of linoleum, a jar of mayonnaise, or a mathematics text. Saying that children will choose to engage in activities which interest them, then, approaches tautological reasoning, for if children are given the chance, what they choose to do is by definition what interests them. Hence, there is a second criterion often used by open educators: the teacher selects materials which in all likelihood will stimulate a child to explore in a productive way, along a productive course toward a productive understanding. But what does *productive* mean? It is commonly held that *any* material which fully stimulates a child's interest is productive and leads to productive learning. To the extent, therefore, that productivity is defined in terms of a child's interest and not the predetermined interests of an adult, this criteria becomes indistinguishable from the previous one.

Thus, we find open educators inconsistent and even somewhat confused on the question of criteria for selection of materials. On the one hand there is confidence that any activity in which the child is fully engaged and interested is productive and will result in learning; on the other, there is an inclination to make distinctions between productive materials. The former implies a trust in children to choose what is best for themselves and the latter suggests that adults know what is best for children. We find democratic and humanistic assumptions about children – that the individual regardless of his age and size is master of his own life and mind – contrasted with doubts that the child always knows what is best. This is an area that needs clarification.

Rather than attempting to gain a consensus somewhere on the spectrum of trust in children, it might be more productive to ask and try to resolve questions of another sort. What should be the division of responsibility in the child's learning between adult and child? What are the kinds of situations in which the older and presumably wiser, more mature adult should prevail, and what are the situations in which the child's judgment should predominate? We need to know, for example, whether the "what am I supposed to do" syndrome of children is a cue for more adult intervention or an expression of need for greater child responsibility. We need to know whether the fact that children study about the things they know and care most about is a cue to give more external direction and control or an argument foı releasing the child to follow his own path. We need to know whether in giving up control over the content of a child's learning by letting him choose what to pursue, adults are not gaining control over his motivation and participation. We need guidelines and statements of priorities to help adults make decisions. We need to know which of these guidelines are generalizable and which are specific to the child and to the situation.

Social Learning

Assumption 11: When two or more children are interested in exploring the same problem or the same materials they will often choose to collaborate in some way.

Assumption 12: When a child learns something which is important to him he will wish to share it with others.

> When children explore for themselves they make discoveries which they want to communicate to their teachers and to other children.[25]

Open educators emphasize the individual: individualized learning, individualized materials, individualized knowledge. There is talk about the interpersonal relation of the child with the teacher, but very little of the relationship of one child to another; yet children come to school together, sit together, work together, eat together, and learn together. Children seem to be seen as individual learners with unique styles, while in fact they are often members of many groups. Is this an inconsistency? What place do other children play in the individual's learning?

The interaction of children within groups has important implications for learning. For instance, children learn to talk, not individually, but through participation in group activities. The development of spoken language is crucial to concept formation. Often children understand one another's problems, interests, and possibilities better than adults do and are able to assist in ways which would be impossible for adults.

Open educators only hint at the place other children play in an individual's learning: each child is seen as a potential resource for another, just as the library, the adult, the classroom materials may be seen as resources for the child's learning. However, the view of the other person as a resource seems to place him in the position of an animate *object,* a place quite inconsistent with the prevailing humanism of open education.

The dynamics among children are essential to any educational rationale. As yet, open educators have not clarified either the meaning for the child or the effect on learning that such interaction might have.

Intellectual Development

Assumption 13: Concept formation proceeds very slowly.

> Learning takes place over time . . . involving what often looks to an adult like mere play or mindless repetitions.[26]

> Piaget was the first to see that the process of forming a concept takes far longer than had been believed, and that much work, seemingly unrelated to the concept, must be done before there is any clue to the direction which the thinking is taking.[27]

> all of us must cross the line between ignorance and insight many times before we truly understand. Little facts, "discoveries" without the

growth of insights are *not* what we should seek to harvest.[28]

A great majority of primary school children can't just be told things . . . they learn basic math concepts much more slowly than adults realize . . . the patterns of abstract thought used must be built up from layer after layer of direct experience . . . seeing, hearing, feeling, smelling.[29]

what I'm speaking for is a laboratory involvement which may be painfully slow, which "doesn't get anywhere". You don't "cover the material" but you spend a good many hours of the week doing something.[30]

What the children know, they know for sure; they have time in which to establish an understanding of extremely basic things.[31]

Assumption 14: Children learn and develop intellectually not only at their own rate, but in their own style.

There is an individual pattern of growth for all living things.[32]

In the last 20 years schools have provided for more individual work as they have increasingly realized how much children of the same age differ in the power of perception and imagery, in their own interests in their span of concentrations.[33]

[school organization] allows for individual differences, but only as those differences show up in one dimension, a rate of progression . . . we should emphasize individual differences in all their qualitative richness.[34]

Assumption 15: Children pass through similar stages of intellectual development . . . each in his own way, and at his own rate and in his own time.

Although children think and reason in different ways, they all pass through certain stages depending on their chronological and mental ages and their experiences.[35]

Children learn by stages and . . . it is no use hurrying them on to later stages before they have mastered earlier ones.[36]

Assumption 16: Intellectual growth and development takes place through a sequence of concrete experiences followed by abstractions.

If you want abstractive learning, then you have to provide something from which the child can abstract.[37]

One of the most important conclusions [of Piaget's research] is that the great majority of primary school children can only learn effectively from concrete situations as lived or described. From these situations children acquire concepts in every area of the curriculum.[38]

in order to establish a conceptual framework, you have to draw away the true nature of the ideas from direct experience.[39]

Assumption 17: Verbal abstractions should follow direct experience with objects and ideas, not precede them or substitute for them.

> In the Garden of Eden, Adam saw the animals before he named them.[40]

> Verbal explanation in advance of understanding based on experience may be an obstacle to learning, and children's knowledge of the right words may conceal from teachers their lack of understanding.[41]

> Students may learn the formal terminologies and expand their useful vocabularies, but we hope they will know what they are talking about first . . . .[42]

> It is part of the ESS approach to avoid introducing the formal names of things and concepts before the reality is understood . . . we feel it is necessary for the student to confront the real world and its physical materials directly, rather than through intermediaries such as textbooks.[43]

> The place for talk about the subject, for verbal discriminations and communication, is late in the phases of learning, not at the beginning, and not all the time; here and there, gathering momentum as interest merits.[44]

The elements of intellectual development emphasized by open educators appear to be the following: children need time to learn; they go through developmental stages; their thinking progresses along a sequence from concrete to abstract.

Open educators question whether the adult is the best judge of how to organize children's time to ensure maximum intellectual development. They argue that until adults know more about how children think and learn, the child is a better judge of his needs with respect to time than is the adult. Children need varying amounts of time – often quite a long time – to develop concepts. They need time to repeat experiences over and over again, such as lighting a bulb with a battery and wire, or measuring volume with a cup. Children's exploration is initiated and directed by materials and interest and facilitated rather than controlled by the clock. In short, time is the servant, not the master, of the child.

The fact that Piaget and others have identified and described stages of intellectual development characteristic of most children has great significance for open education and for the schools. Some educators have responded by trying to accelerate children's passage through the stages, an intention which Piaget has deplored, as have most open educators.

What the stages imply for open educators is not clear. Although Piaget, like open educators, believes that children need materials in order to develop cognitively, there is some difference between his emphasis and theirs. Piaget has children use materials so that he can see what they are thinking. Open educators encourage children to use materials in hopes that certain discoveries will be made. Whereas materials permit Piaget to describe children's thinking, open educators' materials appear instead to prescribe children's thinking. Measuring devices and sand are provided in classroom with the expectation that children will develop the concept of conservation of volume. But does this imply that all children should be required to play with these materials? Is there an optimal or logical sequence of materials which corresponds to the stages of intellectual development?

Open educators distinguish between concrete and abstract; between object and symbol, especially with regard to language acquisition. Piaget's research has demonstrated the immense difference between the thought world of the child and that of the adult – quantitatively and qualitatively. What appears to be conceptual thinking on the part of the child is often verbal association. Consequently, open educators believe that children must go through a physical, kinesthetic experience before they can talk or write about the ideas implicit in the experience. They resist labeling or having children label bits of learning before they have these primary experiences. They feel that if the verbal level of thought is not based on concrete experiences, words may obscure rather than enhance meaning. One can infer a hierarchy of thought and communication that must be negotiated in some order.

What are the practical implications? For instance, how soon after a child has had a primary experience and under what conditions can he verbalize ideas? Is adulthood seen as a period of abstract verbal thinking based on the collected experiences of childhood, or must anyone at any age develop his ideas by moving up and down the hierarchy of experience to abstract verbalization? Is it more desirable for the child to operate from the real to the abstract or move toward the time when he can operate in both modes simultaneously or in alternation? Is the goal a condition where the concrete is no longer necessary?

By holding that intellectual development can be reduced to a sequence of concrete experiences followed by abstractions, open educators ignore an important alternative view – that experience and abstraction, rather than being discrete, ordered, and mutually exclusive in time, occur simultaneously from the moment of first sensory perception – a position that cannot be put aside lightly.

Furthermore, open educators have not yet reconciled their view of learning as unique and idiosyncratic to each individual with the uniformity of thinking, or at least of the development of thinking, implicit in the idea of intellectual stages of development. So far the existence of stages and the flow from concrete to abstract in the development of children's thinking has been of great interest to open educators, but it has not led to a theoretical basis from which decisions about materials and activities can be made.

[Assumptions 18–24 are about evaluation.]

Assumptions about Knowledge

Traditionally, the goals of education have been abbreviated and symbolized by the word *knowledge.* Implicit in the ideas of open education are assumptions that bring into question not only the importance of knowledge *qua* knowledge, but also its meaning for the learner. Rather than an end in itself, knowledge is seen as a vehicle for the development of processes of thinking such as logic, intuition, analysis and hypothesis formation and as a catalyst that facilitates the individual's development toward the ultimate goals of education: self-esteem, dignity, and control over himself and his world.

Assumption 25: The quality of being is more important than the quality of knowing: knowledge is a means of education not its end. The final test of an education is what a man is *not what he* knows.

> More important than knowledge of the fact of science is the experience of having been personally involved in a search for knowledge.[45]
>
> These children are engaged in living, not in becoming those unfortunate trained animals called students or pupils.[46]

Assumption 26: Knowledge is a function of one's personal integration of experience and therefore does not fall into neatly separate categories or "disciplines".

> The particular key which opens a new door for a particular child is not predictable. Therefore our curriculum is not at all to be cut into separate disciplines, fenced off by frontiers of technique and history.[47]
>
> A nine year old who writes an account of an experiment in science which has involved some measurement and calculation, does not think: "Now I am doing English, now science, now mathematics," though all three are involved . . . The classification is of course useful, but its usefulness is limited and it may even be a hindrance . . . . Young children simply do not think this way.[48]
>
> We are striving at present to bring together again, at least on the top levels of education, the different parts of a world which we have allowed to get divided and partitioned; but how much better if we merely made up our minds from the outset always to keep it one, since as one for each of us it begins.[49]
>
> [a good primary school] insists that knowledge does not fall into neatly separate compartments . . . . [50]

Assumption 27: The structure of knowledge is personal and idiosyncratic, and a function of the synthesis of each individual's experience with the world.

The question comes up whether to teach the structure, or to present the child with situations where he is active and creates the structure himself. The goal in education is not to increase the amount of knowledge, but to create the possibilities for a child to invent and discover. When we teach too fast, we keep the child from himself inventing and discovering. Teaching means creating situations where structures can be discovered; it does not mean transmitting structures which may be assimilated at nothing other than a verbal level.[51]

we as scientists would be mistaken to be impressed by the logic and structure of these scientific [chemistry, physics, biology] materials; rather we ought to regard them all as they are seen, experienced, worked on, and evolved by the child and his teacher.[52]

We do not correct any grammatical errors. We write it just as the child says it. Don't attempt to put it grammatically correct, because the child is only going to read what he said . . . he would read "Me is going shopping" even if you wrote "I am going shopping".[53]

Assumption 28: There is no minimum body of knowledge which is essential for everyone to know.

no real core of knowledge exists that is essential for everyone.[54]

"Do you have any standard that you try to get all the children to do by the time they leave you and go on to the junior school?" "Well yes, we do like to send every child to the junior school able to attempt reading."[55]

There is no important body of material in science . . . which for convenient reasons must be learned and learned well. The names and sizes of the planets, or the classification of local mammals to the family level, or the parts of the perfect flower, do not impress us as universal nuggets of science everyone must score up. It is equally true that the so-called methodology of science, with its neat hierarchy of observation, hypothesis testing and so on, is a mythology without appeal.[56]

Assumption 29: It is possible, even likely, that an individual may learn and possess knowledge of a phenomenon and yet be unable to display it publicly. Knowledge resides with the knower, not in its public expression.

Education must reconcile the two modes of thought, the thought which pertains to the public domain and the thought which is personal, private.[57]

Much less is said in the literature of open education about knowledge than about learning. Perhaps this is because knowledge is seen as an integral part of learning rather than a separate entity. Knowledge is not separated from the knower; the emphasis is on the process of interaction between the knower and what he comes to know. The assumptions made by open educators about knowledge raise profound questions for education: Does no knowledge exist outside the idiosyncratic thought of the child? Are there not some things that open educators would prefer children to learn? Is not the knowledge of the spoken and written language, for instance, more desirable than how to pick the lock of an automobile? Can learning take place in an institution where adults have no priorities about what is worthwhile for students to learn?

It is likely that open educators have priorities with respect to knowledge, but for some reason they seem reluctant to make their preferences known. As important as whether adults have or choose to reveal their priorities for children's learning is the fact that children can generally *feel* what it is that adults prefer for them to be doing or learning. In other words, there may well be a "known" which is external to children's idiosyncratic thinking and perhaps even to adults' conscious and deliberate planning, a known that is conveyed to children more subtly than knowledge is conveyed in most schools.

If knowledge is acquired and organized in very personal and idiosyncratic ways, peculiar to each individual, can a statement of *goals* or *objectives* in terms of knowledge or content so common to most educational theories have meaning?

> everyone appears to be working at an individual level, and . . . if you asked the teacher what the aims of this particular lesson were, he wouldn't understand the question.[58]

If a particular lesson is too small a realm for goals to be articulated, do open educators have goals for children with respect to larger questions? If so, they have been reluctant to put them forth.

For someone to say, for example, that "all children shall have an understanding of the causes of the American Civil War" would imply to an open educator that all children will want, be able, and choose to reach this particular understanding through their unique and independent routes at about the same time and, once they have reached it, will have personally structured this understanding in a way similar to that of every other student as well as to that of the adult who posited the understanding. Given the foregoing assumptions about learning, such a notion of congruence of method and content on the part of each student and adult is extremely inconsistent. Open educators' assumptions about knowledge suggest that one cannot predict, let alone predetermine, with any certainty the direction or destination of another's inquiry; it is impossible for one person to pose a question, a problem, or an objective which will be truly significant for another. But because one cannot predict the learning outcome of a child in response to specific subject presentations or experiences does not imply that educators do not have priorities of importance with respect to content and experience or that a child's life in school can be immune from these adult priorities. Learning then, is perhaps best thought of as neither person-centered nor subject-centered but as an interaction of person and subject.

This is not to say that the educator has *no* influence on the direction or content of another's thinking. If a battery, a bulb, and a piece of copper wire are put before a child, he is unlikely to pursue a sequence of thoughts and actions that will lead him to the causes of the Civil War, but he is quite likely to try to light the bulb and in the course of this experience think about what we might call an *electrical circuit.* One cannot, however, be sure that he will "know" what others know about a circuit or come to know it in the way others come to know it. One student might reach the idea of a closed or complete circuit through a diagram on the blackboard or in his head; another might have used batteries, bulbs, and wire or a water and pump model; a third might never reach it at all.

In open educators' assumptions about knowledge there is the belief that one person cannot program or determine either the learning style or what is to be learned for another. One cannot give experiences to another; one can only present opportunities for experience and accept what the student does or does not do with them. This is a devastating realization, for it implies relinquishing the immense control of adults over what the child learns – something which educators have always, perhaps mistakenly, believed they possessed.

The instrument whereby knowledge is thought to be conveyed to students is the curriculum. What do open educators' assumptions about knowledge imply for the concept of curriculum? Is there a place for curriculum in open education? What does the word mean? To the extent that curriculum is seen as that which adults deem important for children to know – that which is broken down from simple to complex in a predetermined trail of adult footprints leading presumably from where the child is to where the adult would have him be (i.e. where the adult is) – open education has no curriculum.

What then do open educators mean when they say "curriculum"? Is an individual's knowledge so personal that another person cannot influence it? For open educators there is both an adult and a child component to curriculum; the adult selects materials – objects, books, water, tubs, etc. which on the basis of experience are known to be likely to stimulate the thinking and exploration of children. Experience also provides information about the kinds of things the child will do and the kind of thinking the child will engage in with these materials and perhaps a guess about the knowledge that will result from this thinking. This is not to say that children are required or even expected to light a bulb when given the materials – they may make a necklace – but making a bulb light is what *most* children do under these circumstances. Why they do it, or who really controls their doing it, are questions that have yet to be explored.

For open educators, then, curriculum is a joint responsibility, guided by the adult through the selection and construction of materials and determined by the child through his individual response to the materials. Curriculum has the quality both of adult initiation and uniformity and of student initiation and diversity. In a real sense, children's own experiences are the subject matter – the content – for their learning. These experiences are good and bad, productive and nonproductive, pleasant and unpleasant. Open educators worry less whether a child has had a particular experience than the quality and meaning for him of the experiences he has had. It is for time and future experience to assess the significance of a student's experience, not the adult.

One must ask another set of questions of open educators' assumptions about knowledge: Where is the source of continuity? What is the organizing principle: the lenses through which children perceive, focus, and organize their experiences? Is there a logical sequence to knowledge or only a psychological sequence? Is learning but a series of discrete, random experiences – a smorgasbord – connected and related only by contiguity in time? Will myriads of personal experiences bounced about within a child's head ultimately settle in organized arrangements that have meaning and relatedness? Can random experiences have meaning without some conceptual framework? Who or what is to provide and to be responsible for the integration and organization of experience? Does this happen naturally?

The means commonly used to organize knowledge in schools are the disciplines: math, science, English, social studies, etc. It is assumed that students' experiences with knowledge so packaged has permitted them to organize the knowledge in corresponding categories in their heads. Open educators question the usefulness and validity of arbitrary distinctions of subjects. But what, if anything, takes the place of the disciplines in organizing experience and knowledge?

A source of great interest in open education in the United States has been the Elementary Science Study. This, I believe, is significant, for it is science that open educators see as providing the theoretical and practical rationale which organizes experience and knowledge.

> Science is not itself the world; it is one reaction to the world. It is on this view of science, and on the view of man which underlies it, that we choose to rest the structure of our growing curriculum.[59]
>
> Science *is* a humanity, and indeed for better or worse, that which today more distinctively stamps all our civilization, as well as shapes our material fate.[60]

It is not the content of science, nor perhaps even the so-called method of science, but rather what might be called the culture of science which provides structure for open educators and for children's learning in open classrooms. The culture of science is nothing less than the self-conscious, deliberate analysis of experience.

Open educators note important similarities between the exploratory behavior, curiosity, search for explanation, and tendency to reconcile beliefs and assumptions with discrepant information of the child-explorer on the one hand, and the behavior of the adult scientist on the other. Indeed some argue that the child is not *like* a scientist but *is* a scientist. If one were to examine the spontaneous interests of young children, one would find them asking questions about what things are, what they are made of, where they came from, and how they work. A great deal of their activity resembles what is commonly regarded as scientific inquiry.

Science, for open educators, then, is not a body of knowledge but a way of thinking, knowing, and being. It is questioning, guessing, trying and failing, and learning by failing. It is pragmatic. Some things work; others do not. It is these qualities of the culture of science to which Isaacs refers when he proposes to "integrate science in its broadest sense, into its proper place in the education of us all."

But is science the only appropriate and desirable way of knowing for young children? Is it only that which can be experienced and learned by the methods of science that is worth knowing? Can scientific methods accommodate all the subjects, feelings, information, and values that are desirable for the enrichment and fulfilment of human life? It is a strange paradox that open education – a very humanistic way of thinking about children, learning, and knowledge – seems to be so dependent on, and possibly restricted by, the culture of science.

Despite the fact that open educators claim not to acknowledge distinctions between subjects or disciplines in the primary schools, they often *act* as if such distinctions existed. Most materials seem to have an explicitness that causes the object to be associated with a discipline. A book is literature; an adding machine, mathematics; a telescope, science. Open classrooms are commonly arranged into "interest tables" or subject corners devoted to math, science, reading, social studies, art, etc. (At a workshop for teachers in Leicestershire a separate *room* was provided for each subject area in which adults were encouraged to explore freely.) Spatial organization by subject area is employed despite the fact that one cannot be certain that a child in the science corner is doing what adults would label *science,* or *math* in the math corner, or *reading* in the reading corner. For when a child is given freedom to explore materials in his own way he is likely to be oblivious to the categories in which adults have placed the materials.

A child playing with a pendulum may be engaged in music by beating time with the swing, or art by making interesting patterns with a sand pendulum, or math by timing the frequency as a function of string length. But the pendulum is placed in the science corner, because the adult sees it as having intrinsic science value. It is puzzling that open educators continue to organize their materials by academic subject, when they see such distinctions as having no meaning for children. We are left with an important and unanswered question: To what extent, and in what ways is it appropriate for the adult to *order* the environment in which the children are exploring and learning?

It is quite clear that the subject science can be explored using the methods of science, but what about the other subjects? If children's exploration is dependent on materials and concrete manipulations are to precede verbal abstractions, how are situations going to be provided in which children may explore when the topic is not appropriate for the child? The means seem to determine the end; only that which is reducible to concrete nonverbal materials can be learned. This is too simple and too narrow a view. It implies that knowledge that can be reduced to and stimulated by materials is inherently more valuable than the knowledge that remains in history, story, or abstraction. This is a value judgement based on expediency, which is hard to accept.

This view, nonetheless, has led to some fresh and ingenious thinking about materials in schools. One could build a huge Greek fluted column and place it in the room. From that material, a child might ask: What is it? What is it used for? Where can I go to see columns? – all questions that would lead him into filmstrips, reading, or trips to see local examples of neoclassical architecture. In other words, although it may be difficult, it is possible to place materials in a classroom that will lead to exploration, by essentially scientific means, of essentially nonscientific content. Open educators are doing more and more to explore and exploit the use of materials and primary experiences to initiate *all* of children's learning. Materials such as math blocks, musical instruments, animals, plants, pictures, and tools are being brought into classrooms, and children are being taken out of the classrooms for ever wider experiences. The limitation of materials as a means of helping children to gain knowledge about themselves and about the world seems now to be more one of space than of ideas. The implications for buildings and environments suitable for children's exploration of the material world present exciting prospects.

Conclusion

What is open education? Why does this term best represent the foregoing assumptions? Open education is a way of thinking about children, learning, and knowledge. It is characterized by openness: doors are ajar, and children come and go; classrooms are open, and children bring objects of interest in and take objects of interest out; space is fluid, not preempted by desks and chairs organized in rows or in any enduring way; a variety of spaces are filled with a variety of materials; children move openly from place to place, from activity to activity; time is open to permit and release rather than constrain or prescribe; and the curriculum is open to choices by adults and children as a function of the interests of children. The curriculum is the dependent variable – dependent on the child – rather than the independent variable upon which the child must depend.

Perhaps most importantly, open education is characterized by an openness of self on the part of children and adults. Persons are openly sensitive to and supportive of other persons, not closed off by anxiety and threat. Feelings are exposed and respected. Teachers are open to the possibilities inherent in children; children are open to the possibilities inherent in other children, in materials, and in themselves. In short, open education implies an environment in which the possibilities for exploration and learning about self and the world are unobstructed.

Open educators assume that children learn by exploring living things, inanimate materials, and quite animate persons, in short by exploring the real world in all its richness and variety. Learning is not distinguished from living, or living from learning.[61]

Knowledge is a goal of open education, and the teacher and school are important means of reaching this goal: but the meaning of knowledge is radically changed. Knowledge is the child's personal capacity to confront and handle new experiences successfully, not the ability to verbalize the adult known on demand. Knowledge is a system of strategies and processes – intellectual, personal, social – that an individual develops for handling the world.

Do the assumptions made by open educators constitute a philosophy of education? The question is perhaps less important than asking what are the historical and philosophical antecedents that are giving open education its distinctive character. There seem to be elements of many other philosophies embodied in the ideas of open education. The philosophy of pragmatism finds expression in open educators' emphasis on the methods and the culture of science: the emphasis of the consequences of an action on subsequent behavior. Open educators' commitment to a child-centered curriculum and child-centered learning and on the material and the social aspects of school life are reminiscent of the progressives' philosophy. Many have even called open education a neoprogressive movement. Certainly open education's emphasis on the cognitive development of the child and on a rich availability of educational materials distinguishes one from the other, but further differences and similarities need to be explored. Finally, open education's emphasis on the child's being of and experiencing the world and learning and growing from these experiences seems to reflect the philosophy of existentialism.

The state of thought surrounding open education is still primitive. The foregoing assumptions are hunches, based largely on impressions, emotional responses, and informal observations in classrooms. The assumptions do not constitute a coherent system or structure. There are inconsistencies and voids; there is little supporting research. Indeed, some of these assumptions – such as assumption 7: "Children have both the right and the competence to make significant decisions concerning their own learning" – are all but impossible to test and validate.

It is my hope that this attempt at articulating open educators' assumptions about learning and knowledge will lead to a more critical and complete explication. However, one cannot lightly push aside the possibility that an effort such as this may prove dangerous. Any attempt to clarify a phenomenon as fundamental and complex as open education introduces a disturbing dilemma: at best such an attempt can be only tentative, incomplete, and subjective; at worst it can be misunderstood, or misused. Furthermore, articulating these assumptions can have the effect of fore-closing and restricting the development within each individual of his *own* thinking about children, learning, and knowledge. In short, there is considerable danger that in attempting to make explicit the assumptions underlying open education one can do more harm than good. As William Hull put it in a personal correspondence in May 1969, "I would prefer that people be fascinated and puzzled than to think they understand something which they don't."

Yet the alternative horn of this dilemma represents in my judgement an even less tenable and responsible position. To do nothing is to perpetuate the mystique, romanticism, and confusion that so envelop open education today. To make no attempt at clarification is to sanction the haphazard and perilous attempts of those who are already trying to adopt the practices and *appearances* of open education with little or no understanding or acceptance of the beliefs about learning that attend those practices.

For some then, to draw attention to these assumptions may terminate interest in open education. All to the good; a well-organized, consistent, authoritarian classroom, for example, probably has a far less harmful influence on children than a sloppy, permissive, and chaotic, though well-intentioned, attempt at an open classroom in which teacher and child must live with contradiction and conflict. For others, awareness of these assumptions may stimulate confidence and competence in their attempts to change what happens to children in school. In any case, this attempt at explication will have been worthwhile if it provokes the educator to become more conscious of, examine, and develop his own assumptions about children, learning and knowledge. When he is sure of what he believes, all will profit.

NOTES

1. Schools Council for the Curriculum and Examinations, *Mathematics in Primary Schools: Curriculum Bulletin No. 1.* (London: Her Majesty's Stationery Office, 1966).
2. *Plowden Report,* p. 17.
3. E. H. Walters, *Activity and Experience in the Infant School* (London: National Froebel Foundation, 1951).
4. David Hawkins, "On Living in Trees", mimeographed (Newton, Mass.: Elementary Science Study) (The Kark Muenzinger Memorial Lecture, delivered at Colorado University, December 1964), reprinted in *The ESS Reader* (Newton, Mass.:

Education Development Center, 1970).

5. Nathan Isaacs et al. *Some Aspects of Piaget's Work* (London: National Froebel Foundation, 1966).
6. Hawkins, "On Living in Trees," p. 9.
7. *Plowden Report,* p. 196.
8. *Plowden Report,* p. 462.
9. *Plowden Report,* p. 196.
10. Roy A. Illsley, "Summer Institute for Teachers, 1966, Cleveland, Ohio, U.S.A.," mimeographed (Newton, Mass.: Elementary Science Study).
11. Beatrice F. Mann, *Learning through Creative Work* (London: National Froebel Foundation, 1962).
12. David Hawkins, "I–Thou–It," *Mathematics Teaching* no. 46 (Spring 1962); also in *The ESS Reader* (Newton, Mass.: Education Development Center, 1970).
13. Many at EDC and the Nuffield Foundation in England are fond of quoting this Chinese proverb.
14. John Blackie, *Inside the Primary School* (London: Her Majesty's Stationery Office, 1967).
15. Friedrich Froebel, *The Education of Man* (1826).
16. *Plowden Report,* p. 193.
17. Blackie, op. cit., p. 32.
18. *Plowden Report,* p. 194.
19. Joseph Featherstone, "A New Kind of Schooling," *The New Republic* 158, no. 9 (March 2, 1968): 12.
20. Joy Schlesinger, "Leicestershire Report: The Classroom Environment," mimeographed (Cambridge, Mass.: Harvard Graduate School of Education, 1965).
21. Hawkins, "I–Thou–It," p. 12.
22. *Plowden Report,* p. 273.
23. Anthony Kallet, "Notes from Leicestershire," mimeographed (Newton, Mass.: Elementary Science Study, 1963).
24. For a further discussion of criteria for selecting materials, see R. S. Barth, "On Selecting Materials for the Classroom", *Childhood Education* 47, no. 6 (March 1971).
25. Schools Council, op. cit., p. xv.
26. Featherstone, op. cit.
27. Z. P. Dienes, *Building Up Mathematics* (London: Hutchinson Educational, 1960).
28. David Hawkins, "Messing About in Science", *Science and Children* 2, no. 5 (February 1965).
29. Ibid.
30. Philip Morrison, "Less May Be More," *American Journal of Physics* 32, no. 6 (June 1964).
31. Featherstone, op. cit., p. 9.
32. Mann, op. cit., p. 2.
33. *Plowden Report,* p. 273.
34. Hawkins, "On Living in Trees," p. 8.
35. Schools Council, op. cit., p. 9.
36. Blackie, op. cit., p. 85.
37. Leonard Sealey, "Education in Leicestershire County," mimeographed (Newton, Mass.: Elementary Science Study, 1963).
38. *Plowden Report,* p. 192.
39. Sealey, "Education in Leicestershire."
40. Open educators are fond of quoting A. N. Whitehead's *Science and the Modern World* (New York: Macmillan Co., 1926).
41. *Plowden Report,* p. 196.
42. *Introduction to the Elementary Science Study* (Newton, Mass.: Education Development Center, 1968).

43. Ibid.
44. Hawkins, "On Living in Trees," p. 12.
45. Benjamin Nichols, "Elementary Science Study: Two Years Later," *ESI Quarterly Report* (Summer-Fall 1965).
46. A. P. French, "Lessons from Leicestershire," *ESI Quarterly Report* (Spring-Summer 1966).
47. Morrison, Philip, "Experiments in the Classroom," *ESI Quarterly Report* (Winter-Spring 1964).
48. Blackie, op. cit., p. 50.
49. Nathan Isaacs, *Early Scientific Trends in Children* (London: National Froebel Foundation, 1958).
50. *Plowden Report,* p. 187.
51. Piaget, quoted in Hawkins, "Living in Trees," p. 11.
52. Morrison, "Experiments."
53. Cazden, op. cit., p. 14.
54. Illsley, "Summer Institute".
55. Cazden, op. cit., p. 15.
56. Morrison, "Tensions".
57. Anthony Kallye, "Unexplored Connexions," mimeographed (Newton, Mass.: Elementary Science Study, 1965).
58. Sealey, "Education in Leicestershire."
59. Morrison, "Experiments."
60. Isaacs, *Early Scientific Trends,* p. 2.
61. Isaacs has used the term *living-learning* to try to capture the essence of open education.

7. Pedagogical Principles Derived from Piaget's Theory: Relevance for Educational Practice

Constance Kamii

Source: Constance Kamii, 'Pedagogical Principles Derived from Piaget's Theory: Relevance for Educational Practice', in Milton Schwebel and Jane Raph (eds.), *Piaget in the Classroom* (Routledge and Kegan Paul, London, 1974), pp. 199–215.

The need for learning to be an active process of knowledge construction, the importance of social interaction in the classroom, and the priority of experience over language are three principles that can be drawn from Piagetian theory. Kamii discusses these principles in relation to current educational theory and practice. The current focus on the teaching of skills and the beliefs that teaching should proceed from the concrete to the abstract neglect important aspects of Piaget's theory.

In this chapter[1] Piagetian pedagogical principles will be compared with theories on which much of current practice in schools appears to be based. The discussion will begin with statements of three main principles together with an elaboration of these statements expressed by Piaget about education (*1935*). It will continue with a focus on several of the current beliefs and practices in education that conflict with Piaget's theory. References to such current thinking will be to the general state of the art, not to the exceptions. A concluding section will consider the role of the teacher.

Basic Pedagogical Principles of Piaget

A first principle drawn from Piaget's theory is the view that learning has to be an active process, because knowledge is a construction from within. Almy et al. (1966), Chittenden (1969), Ginsburg and Opper (1969), and others have all emphasized this point. Duckworth (1964) selected the highlights of the statement Piaget made on education in 1964:

> As far as education is concerned, the chief outcome of this theory of intellectual development is a plea that children be allowed to do their own learning . . . You cannot further understanding in a child simply by talking to him. Good pedagogy must involve presenting the child with situations in which he himself experiments, in the broadest sense of the term – trying things out to see what happens, manipulating symbols, posing questions and seeking his own answers, reconciling what he finds one time with what he finds at another, comparing his findings with those of other children . . . (p. 2).

This statement expresses the major difference between Piaget's theory and the other theories on which current practice in education is based. Teaching is still, by and large, considered a matter of presenting the material to be learned and reinforcing the correct answers that the learner gives back to the teacher. Even when a discovery method is advocated, "discovery" usually means to discover only what the teacher wants to have discovered.

A second principle suggests the importance of social interactions among children in school. Piaget believed strongly that for intellectual development the cooperation among children is as important as the child's cooperation with adults. Without the opportunity to see the relativity of perspectives, the child remains prisoner of his own naturally egocentric point of view. A clash of convictions among children can readily cause an awareness of different points of view. Other children at similar cognitive levels can often help the child more than the adult can to move out of his egocentricity.

Teachers and teacher trainers often advocate committee work and discussions among pupils. However, current theories do not have a clear rationale for deliberately setting up the classroom to encourage children of similar cognitive ability to exchange their views. In practice, social interactions among children are *allowed* more than they are expressly *encouraged* as a means of actively involving children in juxtaposing different points of view.

A third principle points to the priority of intellectual activity based on actual experiences rather than on language. Almy et al. (1966), Duckworth (1964), and Furth (1970), for example, have pointed out that language is important, but not at the expense of thinking. Sinclair and the author (Sinclair and Kamii, 1970) have particularly insisted on the necessity of letting the preoperational child go through one stage after another of giving the "wrong" answers before expecting him to have adult logic and adult language. Sinclair has shown (Chapters 2 and 3) that the child reasons from different systems (e.g., number and space), each of which is correct in itself. We shall return to this point later in the discussion.

Teachers and teacher trainers have made some progress in recognizing the importance of concrete experiences prior to using words, but the emphasis is still on words and the correct answer that the teacher wants. At the preschool level, there is an incredible preoccupation with the teaching of language without coming to grips with how the preoperational child really thinks. In junior high school, youngsters still answer the questions at the end of the chapter by copying the book day after day. A typical question is "Define photosynthesis".

Furth (1970) recently went even further than objecting to educators' overemphasis on empty words. He took a bold and correct stand in saying that the first goal of education must be to teach thinking. He argued that reading is indeed an important tool for learning, but it has unfortunately become the preoccupation of educators to the exclusion of high-operative thinking. Schools of education have made a cliché out of individual differences, but in practice educators still continue to expect all children to learn to read in first grade, whether or not they are interested and/or "ready" for reading.

In order to develop the first principle further, we shall turn to what Piaget himself said about active learning in *Encyclopédie Française* (Piaget, 1935). This early publication is tangible evidence of how incredibly long it takes for research findings to be applied in education, even when the researcher himself sits down to write the pedagogical implications of his research. Much of what Piaget criticized then as being obsolete is still being practised in our schools and advocated in teacher-training institutions.

With regard to active learning, Piaget pointed to Pestalozzi, Froebel, Montessori, Susan Isaacs, and others who had developed "active" methods in the sense of involving actions on things rather than listening to the teacher or looking at books. However, Piaget found various problems with each one of these "active" methods. Many of the objections he raised are still in the vanguard of educational criticism today. For example, Montessori wanted to give to children the materials that would exercise the free, spontaneous activities of the child to develop his intelligence. However, according to Piaget, her materials are based on a psychology that is not only an adult psychology but also an artificial psychology. Making cylinders fit into holes, seriating colors of various shades, discriminating the sounds made with stuffed boxes, etc., may be activities, but they are activities that take place in a limited and artificially limiting environment. Piaget suggested that in trying to free the child from clumsy adult interference, Montessori's work emphasized sensory training rather than the development of intelligence.

What Piaget said about Susan Isaacs' belief in experience is particularly relevant to current issues in early childhood education. Isaacs' school had the greatest collection of possible materials at the children's disposal, and in order to let the children organize their own experiences the teachers abstained from intervening in the children's play. Piaget wrote that in emphasizing the role of experience as the foundation for intellectual development, Isaacs overlooked the importance of the structuring, elaborating, and reasoning processes. The children learned to observe and to reason by playing freely, said Piaget, but nevertheless *some* systematization by the adult would have been helpful. There is, after all, the need for a rational, deductive activity to make sense even in scientific experiments.

In nursery school for privileged, bright children, it is probably sufficient just to let the children have a lot of "experience", because they themselves will give structure to their experience. In a program for the disadvantaged, however, the children need structuring appropriate for them and this requires the teacher to be in genuine contact with the child. Experience alone, no matter how rich or varied, is not sufficient unless the level of the child's development is considered.

Structuring, too, can be excessive. Piaget credited Pestalozzi, a disciple of Rousseau's, with being right in having a school that was a true society, with a sense of cooperation and responsibility among pupils who actively helped each other in their research. However, Piaget criticized Pestalozzi for being preoccupied with the idea of having to proceed from the simple to the complex in all domains of teaching. Therefore, in spite of Pestalozzi's general belief in the importance of the learner's interests and activity, his methods were characterized by schedules, the classification of the content to be taught, exercises for mental gymnastics, and a mania for demonstrations. For Piaget, young children's logic deals sometimes with undifferentiated, global wholes and sometimes with isolated parts. Therefore, we cannot always proceed from the analytic parts that to adults seem simpler than the whole.

To summarize what Piaget said about active methods, he pointed out that the criterion of what makes an "active" method active is not the external actions of the learner. He said, for example, that Socrates used an active method with language and that the characteristic of the Socratic method was to engage the learner in actively constructing his own knowledge. The task of the teacher is to figure out what the learner already knows and how he reasons in order to ask the right question at the right time so that the learner can build his own knowledge.

Piaget is usually believed to have interest only in the child's cognitive development. In 1935, however, he wrote that the goal of education is to adapt the child to the social environment of the adult. In other words, for Piaget, the purpose of education, in a broad sense, is to transform the psychobiological constitution of the child to function in a society that stresses certain social, intellectual, and moral values. The important difference is that, when Piaget talks about the social, intellectual, and moral values of the adult world, he insists that part of society's goals should be not only the transmission of old knowledge and values, but also the creation of new knowledge and values. This point is substantiated by what Piaget said about Rousseau's pedagogy.

Piaget praised Rousseau for believing that the pupil has to reinvent science rather than merely to follow its findings. However, he criticized Rousseau's pedagogy for dissociating the individual from his social milieu. In the traditional school, said Piaget, adults are the source of all morality and all truths. The child merely obeys the adult in the moral realm and recites things in the intellectual realm. In Piaget's opinion, schools must emphasize not obedience but the development of autonomy and co-operation. He criticized Rousseau for believing that a child could learn to be moral without practising moral judgement and moral behavior with other children in school. Just as intelligence can develop only by being actively used, moral behavior, too, can develop only by being actively used in daily living. In today's modern school, "citizenship" is still all too frequently equated with "obedience".

Current Educational Practices

Turning to an examination of current education practices in the light of Piaget's theory, we see two clusters of beliefs and practices: the school's focus on teaching *skills*, and the belief that children move from *concrete experiences* to *abstract thinking.*

The Teaching of Skills

Education has progressed at least to the point of our becoming aware of the futility of teaching encyclopedic facts. In turning away from mere facts to a focus on cognitive progresses, however, educators became preoccupied with the teaching of skills. Skills traditionally have implied motor or mechanical skills, or isolated proficiencies such as typing, penmanship, or swimming. In the modern version of the report card teachers are asked to check whether or not the child has *skills* – arithmetic, visual, auditory, word attack, information-processing, and many others. There may be some justification for delineating these behaviors as skills, but the inclusion of so-called comprehension skills in reading raises questions about how the child understands the written word and whether that process can validly be defined as a skill.

Piaget's biological theory of intelligence states that intelligence is a general coherent framework within which all the parts function. It becomes clear, then, that addition skills, for example, are not mere skills. Although specific training in addition may lead children to rote learning, it is unlikely to contribute to the development of a general cognitive framework in which addition and subtraction processes can be understood, either by themselves or in relationship to each other.

In this connection S. Lai, one of our teachers who taught in our pre-school for two years before teaching a class of first graders referred to as *slow,* reported the following: After teaching these children to read according to an experiential approach, she came to the conclusion that, although the mechanical skills of reading can be taught relatively easily, comprehension of what is read cannot be taught directly. These children, for instance, made little out of a sequence of pictures in the book they were supposed to be reading. They lacked the physical, social, and logico-mathematical framework required for such an understanding.

Furth (1970) insists that meaning in words and pictures is derived not from their figurative aspect but from operative knowing. Education is still preoccupied with the figurative aspects of knowledge. Reading cannot be taught just by teaching the mechanical skills any more than children can be expected to identify with the pictures and become better readers just because the white faces of *Dick and Jane* have been changed to black faces.

Even perceptual discrimination or perceptual skills require more intelligence than educators usually assume. Current practices suffer from not having made the distinction that Piaget made between perception and perceptual activities.

He (Piaget, 1969; Piaget and Inhelder, 1967) emphasized the role of actions in perception. He showed, for example, that recognition of geometric shapes cannot be achieved only by perception, i.e., only by focusing on the immediately given sensory data. This recognition requires perceptual activities, i.e., the moving of the eyes, hands, or feet to center on various points of the particular spatial configuration to construct it actively. What is important in perceptual activities is not the action of moving the eyes or fingers but the active mental construction of the spatial configuration.

Let us assume that the objective to get the child to recognize a square through class actions is an appropriate one. The teacher who is aware of the difference between perception and perceptual activities probably uses haptic perception (the sense of touch) to achieve her goal. This method of teaching is not just the use of many sensory modalities for perception. Visual perception of simple shapes is rather automatic, but haptic exploration presents the child with the need to construct a spatial structure when his visual perception is not permitted, i.e., haptic perception provokes perceptual activity. Sharpening the teacher's theoretical understanding can thus result in very different teaching methods.

The comments suggest that a psychology that focuses on sensory information and motor behavior results in the conceptualization of goals and teaching methods involving skills rather than on the child's entire cognitive framework. In the next section another set of examples will be presented from a different angle to suggest again that a lack of theoretical precision results in the kind of teaching that does not maximize children's chances of developing their intelligence.

Proceeding from the "Concrete" to the "Abstract"

Educators have progressed to the point of realizing that children do not learn by simply being told or having things explained to them verbally. We now recognize the necessity of having concrete experiences first and buying lots of manipulatives from toy companies.

Few people have asked, however, what concrete experiences are, and what abstraction means. Concrete experience usually refers to any direct contact with real objects and events, and abstract thinking generally refers to the use of representation and the so-called higher order concepts. Piaget's conceptualization of experience and abstraction gives guidelines to the teacher as to how to make moment-to-moment decisions in the classroom to develop children's intelligence.

Closely related to the importance of "concrete experience" is the importance attached to "discovery". It is often said that the child learns more through direct experience, and that he learns even more if this experience is discovered rather than being offered. The pedagogical question becomes "Should we design a curriculum in which everything is taught by the discovery method?" Piaget makes a distinction between "discovery" and "invention". His favorite example of "discovery" is Columbus' discovery of America. Columbus did not invent America, he points out. America existed before Columbus discovered it. The airplane, on the other hand, was not discovered it was invented because it did not exist before its invention.

Corresponding to the distinction between discovery and invention is the distinction between how physical knowledge and how logico-mathematical knowledge are constructed. Physical knowledge can be built by discovery, but logico-mathematical knowledge cannot. It can be built only by the child's own invention. For example, by putting a needle in water, the child can discover whether or not the needle floats. By acting on objects, he can thus discover their properties. In logico-mathematical knowledge, on the other hand, the child cannot discover from the objects themselves whether there are more brown beads or more beads in a collection. All logico-mathematical structures have to be invented, or created, by the child's own cognitive activity rather than discovered from the reaction of objects.[2]

An example from our own project will illustrate the importance of the distinction between discovery and invention. One of the many mistakes made during the first year of our project was to concentrate on logico-mathematical knowledge and to overlook physical knowledge. Another thing we did wrongly was to make up many classification kits and select the objects according to how we thought children should sort them easily. For example, we made kits for sorting by color or use (e.g., a red comb, red hairbrush, red clothespin, and red pencil; a pencil, pen, and crayon). Naturally, when the children sorted in ways for which the kit was not intended, the teachers said to them, "That's very nice, BUT . . . can you think of another way?" (i.e., the teacher's way).

In March of the first year half a dozen Piagetian friends arrived to help in the development of our curriculum. They pointed out to us that in logico-mathematical knowledge, when we contradict the child, we only make him unsure of himself, because without the necessary cognitive structure the child has no way of understanding why his way is not right. Particularly in classification, whatever criterion the child selects is right, provided he uses it consistently.

In physical knowledge, in contrast, the child is not made to feel unsure of himself if the object flatly contradicts him. If the child believes that a block will sink when it is put in water and the object contradicts him, he can understand the object's reaction as being part of its nature. We went on to speculate that an emphasis on the teaching of physical knowledge may even give a sense of security and confidence to the children by enabling them to control objects and to predict the regularity of their reactions. We knew that our children lacked initiative and curiosity and speculated that a lot of activities in physical knowledge might increase their curiosity because the objects' reactions were in themselves interesting to all young children.

With this wisdom, we ran our second year with a new group of 4 year olds, and the contrast between the first and second year was dramatic. Our visitors' most frequent comment during the second year was that our children were independent, well organized, active, and full of initiative. We thus found that the theoretical distinction between "discovery" and "invention" made a difference in the way we taught and in the "concrete experiences" children had with objects. When our teachers learned when to let the child discover and how to facilitate "invention" indirectly, our children became more confident about their ability to figure things out. They stopped looking at the teacher's face for approval and relied more on their own ability to think. The inseparable relationship between the child's cognitive development and ego development thus became evident.

Language and the importance of encouraging children to say exactly what they think assume an important place here. First, unless children tell us how they think, we cannot get the diagnostic insights that are essential for diagnostic teaching. Second, children must have sufficient confidence in their own way of experiencing things and their own process of reasoning rather than "learning" through social conformity only. For example, if the child thinks that 8 objects spread out in a top row are "more" than 8 objects clustered together in a bottom row, he must have freedom to say so with confidence, rather than being shaped into reciting the "right" answer. The space occupied is an important consideration in the construction of number, and any attempt to teach numbers must let the child himself work out the relationship between space and number through his own process of reasoning. If the process becomes well structured, the correct conclusion is bound to emerge. Therefore, we must work on the underlying processes, not the answer or the surface behavior.

An experiment involving children taught by S. Engelmann (Kamii and Derman, 1971) showed that in teaching language and thinking, children must be allowed to be honest with themselves. The 6-year-old children who took part in this experiment were taught to conserve weight and volume and to explain specific gravity. In the post-test, they were often found to give the correct answers, but usually in a sing-song fashion, as if they did not understand what they were saying. Teaching methods that are rooted in the child's entire cognitive framework, which is in turn rooted all the way back in sensori-motor intelligence, must encourage him to express *exactly* what he experiences and *exactly* what he believes.

In the teaching of inner-city children, much emphasis is placed on a positive self-concept and the teaching of language. But methods based on mechanistic psychology and the perspective of the adult tend to be too direct and self-defeating. For example, a group of children had just finished drinking their juice. The teacher placed piles of cut-out circles, squares, and triangles on the table. She then gave to one child a sheet of paper on which a circle was drawn with a crayon. The child correctly responded to the teacher's request to "find a shape that's just like your circle and put it right on top of your circle." The next question the teacher asked was "Is the circle you took just as big as the one on your paper?" The child was visibly bothered because she found the teacher's circle to be about 5/16 of an inch smaller than hers all around. When the teacher repeated the question, the child said nothing and pretended not to know. The teacher then told the child that the two were the same size and went on to say, "Now, let's say it together. This (pointing) circle is just as big as this one (pointing) . . . Very good . . . Let's say it again. This circle is just as big as this one."

This is a trivial example, but it serves to illustrate how much children are taught from the adult's perspective. In attempting to teach language and size discrimination, the teacher was also unwittingly teaching other things, such as the message that the "correct" answer always comes from the teacher's head. Without theoretical clarity, good intentions can thus result in experiences that force the adult's perspective. We cannot foster a positive self-image if we do not stop to ask the child what he honestly thinks.

From the preceding comments on concrete experiences we shall turn to what is commonly called "abstraction". Piaget would agree that representation is a kind of abstraction because the child deals with objects and events that are not concrete and present. However, in his terminology and conceptualization, "abstraction" means something quite different and there are two kinds of abstraction: abstraction from the object and abstraction from coordinated actions.

Abstraction from the object takes place in physical knowledge, and abstraction from the child's coordinated actions takes place in logico-mathematical knowledge. Whether or not a needle sinks in water is physical knowledge that can be found by discovery and generalized by empirical generalization. But the notion of specific gravity cannot be discovered empirically or built by empirical generalization. Specific gravity has to be invented by abstraction from the child's own cognitive activity in combination with empirical experience. The conservation of number, too, cannot be discovered by empirical generalization.

If knowledge is simply built from the concrete to the abstract, a 4 year old who has walked all over a particular town such as Ypsilanti would know that he has been in Ypsilanti. But knowledge is not simply built from the concrete to the abstract in the sense of representation, and each child has to construct an entire cognitive structure by abstraction from objects and his own coordinated cognitive activity, so that he will have the framework within which he will be able simultaneously to understand the meaning of terms such as "New Brunswick" and "university" in a spatial, temporal, social, classificatory, seriational, and numerical sense.

From the standpoint of the child's cognitive development, there are thus many kinds of "concrete" experiences and many kinds of "abstraction". As stated in an earlier paper (Kamii, 1970), the teacher who understands these differences will have the guidelines she needs to decide what to teach and how, and what not to teach and why. We shall now elaborate on this point by discussing the role of the teacher in a Piagetian school.

The Role of the Teacher in a Piagetian School

The role of the teacher in a Piagetian school is not one of transmitting ready-made knowledge to children. Her function is to help the child construct his own knowledge by guiding his experiences. In physical knowledge, for example, if the child believes that a block will sink in water, she can encourage him to prove the correctness of this statement. If he predicts that a marble placed on one side of a balance will make that side go down and the other side go up, she does not say, "You are right," but instead says, "Let's find out." She lets the child discover the truth by letting the object give the answer.

In the logico-mathematical realm, the role of the teacher is not to impose and to reinforce the "correct" answer but to strengthen the child's own process of reasoning. For example, rather than trying to teach the conservation of number by empirical generalization, she tries to increase the child's mobility of thought in all realms – in classification, in paperfolding activities, in symbolization, in physical knowledge, etc. Only incidentally and as part of the general development of the entire cognitive structure does she ask questions such as, "Do you think there will still be enough cups for all of us after we wash them?"

The role of the teacher in a Piagetian school is an extremely difficult one because she has constantly to engage in diagnosing each child's emotional state, cognitive level, and interests by carrying a theoretical framework in her head. She also has to strike a delicate balance between exercising her authority and encouraging children to develop their own standards of moral behavior. She can much more easily follow a curriculum guide, put the children through prescribed activities, and use old techniques of discipline.

The teacher in a Piagetian school has to be a highly conscientious and resourceful professional who does not have to have standards that are enforced from the outside. The kind of teacher Piaget would like to have is the kind of adult that a Piagetian school aspires to produce – one who with strong personal standards continues to be a learner throughout his life.

In summary, the pedagogical implications of Piaget's theory suggest the kind of reform that makes learning truly active and encourages social interactions among pupils to cultivate a critical spirit. The teacher in a Piagetian school does not present ready-made knowledge and morality but, rather, provides opportunities for the child to construct his own knowledge and moral standards through his own reasoning. The emphasis of a Piagetian school is definitely on the child's own thinking and judgement, rather than on the use of correct language and adult logic.

Piaget's theory suggests needed reforms for education. Although the theory is radically different from the other theories on which current practices are based, it is also in line with the old clichés of schools of education, e.g., "the whole child," individual differences, the teaching of children to think, the encouraging of initiative and curiosity, and the desirability of intrinsic motivation.

Schools of education alone cannot change the current practices, but, by definition, it is they who have to assume the leadership in changing the state of affairs. Piaget's theory gives more precise guidelines than those that were previously available to translate the old ideals into actual practice. The responsibility of schools of education is particularly heavy because society can no longer afford to perpetuate a system of compulsory attendance in which an enormous number of consumers are literally forced to accept the services that unnecessarily create academic failures, discipline problems, and unemployable dropouts.

NOTES

1. The chapter is part of the Ypsilanti Early Education Program, which was funded under Title III of the Elementary and Secondary Education Act of 1965 (No. 67–042490). The opinions expressed herein, however, do not reflect the position or policy of the funding agency, and no official endorsement by the Office of Education should be inferred. I am grateful to Hermina Sinclair, Rheta DeVries, and Leah Adams for critically reading the chapter.
2. In the discussion that followed the presentation of this chapter, Dr. Sinclair added the following two points about the distinction between physical and logico-mathematical knowledge: (1) The significance of the distinction is that the mode of structuring is different, not just the source of knowledge. (2) Neither physical knowledge nor logico-mathematical knowledge can exist without the other. Pure logic almost exists, but physical knowledge is involved even in the classical example of the child who always found 10 pebbles, whether he counted them from left to right, or from right to left. The fact that pebbles let themselves be ordered is an example of physical knowledge. Physical and logico-mathematical knowledge are thus almost indissociable and are seen more as a continuum than as a dichotomy.

   Piaget often makes a theoretical distinction and turns around to say that the two are in reality indissociable. Assimilation and accommodation, and the figurative and operative aspects of knowledge, are other examples of theoretical distinctions that have to be kept clearly in mind in education, even though they are inseparable in reality. Awareness of the distinction makes a difference in the way we teach.

REFERENCES

Almy, M., Chittenden, E., and Miller, P. *Young children's thinking.* New York: Columbia Teachers College Press, 1966.

Chittenden, E. A. What is learned and what is taught. *Young Children 25* (1969) 12–19.

Duckworth, E. Piaget rediscovered. In R. E. Ripple and V. N. Rockcastle (eds.), *Piaget rediscovered* (a report of the Conference on Cognitive Studies and Curriculum Development). Ithaca, N.Y.: Cornell University School of Education, 1964.

Furth, H.G. *Piaget for teachers,* Englewood Cliffs, N.J.: Prentice-Hall, Inc., 1970.

Ginsburg, H., and Opper, S. *Piaget's theory of intellectual development: An introduction.* Englewood Cliffs, N.J.: Prentice-Hall, Inc., 1969.

Kamii, C. Piaget's theory and specific instruction: A response to Bereiter and Kohlberg. *Interchange 1* (1970), 33–9.

Kamii, C. An application of Piaget's theory to the conceptualization of a preschool curriculum. In R. K. Parker (ed.), *The preschool in action.* Boston: Allyn and Bacon, 1972.

Kamii, C., and Derman, L. The Engelmann approach to teaching logical thinking: Findings from the administration of some Piagetian tasks. In D. R. Green, M. P. Ford, and G. B. Flamer (eds.), *Measurement and Piaget.* New York: McGraw-Hill, 1971.

Piaget, J. Education et instruction. *Encyclopédie Française.* Paris: Librairie Larousse, 1935. Tome XV.

Piaget, J. *The mechanisms of perception.* New York: Basic Books, 1969; London: Routledge and Kegan Paul, 1969.

Piaget, J., and Inhelder, B. *The child's conception of space.* New York: Norton, 1967; London: Routledge and Kegan Paul, 1956.

Sinclair, H., and Kamii, C. Some implications of Piaget's theory for teaching young children, *School Review 78* (1970), 169–183.

8. The Long Revolution
Raymond Williams

Source: R. Williams, *The Long Revolution,* 1961 (Pelican Books, Harmondsworth, 1965), pp. 161–8. Reprinted by permission of the author and Chatto and Windus Ltd.

Nineteenth-century Britain saw a major reorganisation of elementary, secondary and higher education, along lines which are still generally followed today. The revolutionary idea of 'education for all' got its impetus from the rise of an organised working class demanding education, and from the pressures of a changing economy. These economic pressures led to a complex argument about the nature of the curriculum. The curriculum that evolved was a compromise between the public educators, the industrial trainers, and the old humanists – with the industrial trainers predominant. In the twentieth century the public educators' idea of education for all has been extended but the 'shadow of class thinking' remains.

The nineteenth-century achievement is evidently a major reorganization of elementary, secondary, and university education, along lines which in general we still follow. Both in kinds of institution, and in the matter and manner of education, it shows the reorganization of learning by a radically changed society, in which the growth of industry and of democracy were the leading elements, and in terms of change both in the dominant social character and in types of adult work. At no time in England have the effects of these influences on the very concept of education been clearer, but, precisely because this was so, a fundamental argument about the purposes of education was the century's most interesting contribution. Two strands of this argument can be separated: the idea of education for all, and the definition of a liberal education. The former, as we have seen, was fiercely argued, and the history of the century represents the victory of those who, in the early decades, had been a minority. Two major factors can be distinguished: the rise of an organized working class, which demanded education, and the needs of an expanding and changing economy. In practice, these were closely interwoven, in the long debate, and the victory of the reformers rested on three elements: a genuine response to the growth of democracy, as in men like Mill, Carlyle, Ruskin, and Arnold; protective response, the new version of 'moral rescue', very evident in the arguments for the 1870 Education Act in relation to the franchise extensions of 1867 – 'our future masters . . . should at least learn their letters'; and the practical response, perhaps decisive, which led Forster in 1870 to use as his principal argument: 'upon the speedy provision of elementary education depends our industrial prosperity'. In the growth of secondary education this economic argument was even more central.

The democratic and the industrial arguments are both sound, but the great persuasiveness of the latter led to the definition of education in terms of future adult work, with the parallel clause of teaching and required social character – habits of regularity, 'self-discipline', obedience, and trained effort. Such a definition was challenged from two sides, by those with wider sympathies with the general growth of democracy, and by those with an older conception of liberal education, in relation to man's health as a spiritual being. This interesting alliance is broadly that which I traced as a tradition in *Culture and Society,* and the educational argument was always near the centre of this continuing tradition. On the one hand it was argued, by men with widely differing attitudes to the rise of democracy and of working-class organization, that men had a natural human right to be educated, and that any good society depended on governments accepting this principle as their duty. On the other hand, often by men deeply opposed to democracy, it was argued that man's spiritual health depended on a kind of education which was more than a training for some specialized work, a kind variously described as 'liberal', 'humane', or 'cultural'. The great complexity of the general argument, which is still unfinished, can be seen from the fact that the public educators, as we may call the first group, were frequently in alliance with the powerful group which promoted education in terms of training and disciplining the poor, as workers and citizens, while the defenders of 'liberal education' were commonly against both: against the former because liberal education would be vulgarized by extension to the 'masses'; against the latter because liberal education would be destroyed by being turned into a system of specialized and technical training. Yet the public educators inevitably drew on arguments of the defenders of the old 'liberal' education, as a way of preventing universal education being narrowed to a system of pre-industrial instruction. These three groups – the public educators, the industrial trainers, and the old humanists – are still to be distinguished in our own time . . . . . In general, the curriculum which the nineteenth century evolved can be seen as a compromise between all three groups, but with the industrial trainers predominant. The significant case is the long controversy over science and technical education. If we look at the range of scientific discovery between the seventeenth and the end of the nineteenth centuries, it is clear that its importance lies only in part in its transformation of the techniques of production and communication; indeed lies equally in its transformation of man's view of himself and of his world. Yet the decisive educational interpretation of this new knowledge was not in terms of its essential contribution to liberal studies, but in terms of technical training for a particular class of men. The old humanists muddled the issue by claiming a fundamental distinction between their traditional learning and that of the new disciplines, and it was from this kind of thinking that there developed the absurd defensive reaction that all real learning was undertaken without thought of practical advantage. In fact, as the educational history shows, the classical linguistic disciplines were primarily vocational, but these particular vocations had acquired a separate traditional dignity, which was refused to vocations now of equal human relevance. Thus, instead of the new learning broadening a general curriculum, it was neglected, and in the end reluctantly admitted on the grounds that it was of a purely technical kind. The pressure of the industrial trainers eventually prevailed, though not with any general adequacy until the Technical Instruction Act of 1889, and even here, significantly, it was 'instruction' rather than 'education'. This history was damaging both to general education and to the new kinds of vocational training, and yet it was only an exceptional man, such as Huxley, who could see this at the time and consequently argue in the only adequate way: that science must become a part of general education and of liberal culture, and that, as a further provision, there must be an adequate system of specific professional training, in all kinds of scientific and technical work, on the same principle as the further professional training of doctors, lawyers, teachers, artists, and clergy. We can take only a limited satisfaction in the knowledge that the industrial trainers won, inert and stupid as the old humanists were and have continued to be. Huxley was a public educator, in the full sense, and it was only in this tradition that the problem might have been solved.

The shadow of class thinking lies over this as over so much other nineteenth-century educational thinking. The continued relegation of trade and industry to lower social classes, and the desire of successful industrialists that their sons should move into the now largely irrelevant class of gentry, were alike extremely damaging to English education and English life. As at the Reformation, a period of major reconstruction of institutions was undertaken largely without reference to the best learning of the age, and without any successful redefinition of the purposes of education and of the content of a contemporary liberal culture. The beginnings of technical instruction in the Mechanics' Institutes might have developed into a successful redefinition, but again it was the training of a specific class, whereas in fact the new sciences were radical elements in the society as a whole: a society which had changed its economy, which under pressure was changing its institutions, but which, at the centres of power, was refusing to change its ways of thinking. And then to the new working class, the offered isolation of science and technical instruction was largely unacceptable, for it was precisely in the interaction between techniques and their general living that this class was coming to its new consciousness. Politics, in the wide sense of discussing the quality and direction of their living, was excluded from these Institutes, as it was to remain largely excluded from the whole of nineteenth-century education. It was only very slowly, and then only in the sphere of adult education, that the working class, drawing indeed on very old intellectual traditions and on important dissenting elements in the English educational tradition, made its contribution to the modern educational debate. This contribution – the students' choice of subject, the relation of disciplines to actual contemporary living, and the parity of general discussion with expert instruction – remains important, but made little headway in the general educational organization. Like the individual public educators, their time was not yet.

* * * * *

In the twentieth century, the framework inherited from the nineteenth century has been greatly expanded and improved. Elementary education has been redefined as primary education, ending at eleven, and from this definition, since 1944, it has been possible to provide secondary education for all. A greatly expanded system of combined first-grade and second-grade secondary schools has been brought into being, and arrangements for a substantial minority to pass from primary schools into this system, and for a much smaller minority to pass on to higher education, have been if not completely at least effectively established. A large number of third-grade secondary schools, with limited connexions to the minority system, are in process of creation, and vary considerably in quality. In primary education, a notable expansion of the curriculum is perhaps the century's major achievement: it is mainly here that the influence of the public educators has been effective. The universities, if unevenly and at times without clear definition, have expanded their curricula in vitally important ways. It is at the level of secondary education, whether 'grammar' or 'modern', that the essential argument continues, in terms that reveal again the close relationship between curriculum and organization.

In theory, the principles of the public educators have been accepted: that all members of the society have a natural right to be educated, and that any good society depends on governments accepting this principle as a duty. In practice the system is still deeply affected by other principles, as a few examples will show. The continued existence of a network of private education, in the preparatory and public schools, may or may not be socially desirable, but in any case it shows the kind of education, and the necessary level of investment in it, which a particular social group accepts as adequate for itself. The large class, for example, has haunted public education from the beginning: from Lancaster's 1,000 children under one master, through the 60–80 of the urban board schools, to the still common 40–50 of our own day. In the private network, very much smaller classes, and the necessary investment to ensure them, have been accepted as a private duty, in a quite different way from the interpretation of public duty in the national system. Similarly, by the same social group, the necessary minimum level of education of all its members has been set as at least the second-grade school, usually followed by further professional training, whereas the public definition, for the members of other social groups, is at the lower minimum of what is still very much the old third grade. Again, the minimum level, for the limited social group, is set to include subjects which are only available to a minority of the society as a whole. It is not easy to argue that this limited social group has no right to provide the education it thinks fit for its own members, but the contrasts between this and the general provision show very clearly the survival of a familiar kind of class thinking, which has limited the practical execution of a formally accepted public duty. In the analysis of our present educational system, this point is usually neglected in favour of an argument in terms of levels of intelligence, and it is often argued that we face wholly new problems, in the education of the 'masses', because levels of measured intelligence vary so widely. There are problems indeed, but in fact the education of this limited social class has throughout its history had to deal with this same kind of mental variation, and it has been the level of education required by a member of this class, rather than the level thought appropriate to a particular mental measurement, that has in fact governed its organization. If we put the matter in this way, that because a child will be this kind of adult, he must be brought to a given degree of education, we can begin to see the pattern more clearly.

Differences in learning ability obviously exist, but there is great danger in making these into separate and absolute categories. It is right that a child should be taught in a way appropriate to his learning ability, but because this itself depends on his whole development, including not only questions of personal character growth but also questions of his real social environment and the stimulation received from it, too early a division into intellectual grades in part creates the situation which it is offering to meet. The effect of stimulation on intellectual performance has been interestingly described, in our present context, by Professor Vernon:

> 'After 11, in Britain, we do get bigger divergences in environmental stimulation. Children are now at an age when they should be acquiring complex concepts and modes of thought, and the different kinds of schooling provided in grammar, modern and other schools, together with the different intellectual levels of their homes, may well affect their growth. At 15 the majority leave school and enter jobs which do little to exercise their "brains", and their leisure pursuits are mostly non-stimulating. But a privileged minority continue to receive intellectual stimulation to 17, 18, 21 or later, and are more likely to enter jobs where they use their minds, and to indulge in cultural leisure-time pursuits. Hence we would expect, as has been clearly proved, that education during the teens does affect the ultimate adult intelligence level. The man with full secondary and university education has on the average a 12 IQ point advantage over the man who was equally intelligent at 15 but has had no further education since then.'

This is the reality behind the confident use of mental measurement to ratify graded systems of education. To take intelligence as a fixed quantity, from the ordinary thinking of mechanical materialism, is a denial of the realities of growth and of intelligence itself, in the final interest of a particular model of the social system. How else can we explain the very odd principle that has been built into modern English education: that those who are slowest to learn should have the shortest time in which to learn, while those who learn quickly will be able to extend the process for as much as seven years beyond them? This is the reality of 'equality of opportunity', which is a very different thing from real social equality. The truth is that while for children of a particular social class we have a conception, however imperfect, of a required minimum of general education whatever their measured intelligence might be, we have no such conception, or a much lower conception, for the majority of those outside this class. This fact in itself, together with other social processes, magnifies natural inequalities, in a persistent way. For of course there is no absolute correlation between intelligence and membership of a particular occupational group. The mean I.Q. of children of such groups varies, but the differences within groups are greater than those between the groups. And then, if longer education can be bought by a few, and if more favourable learning environments are perpetuated by the social inequality resulting from previous inequalities of real opportunity, natural inequalities are again magnified and take on a direct social relevance. If one is asked, at any point in this process, to 'stop being utopian and consider the hard facts about educating the masses', it is very difficult to be patient. While we shall always be faced with substantial differences in learning ability among all children, we have to face the really hard fact that we are now meeting this problem in a particular way which serves in the end to magnify the differences and then pass them off as a natural order. We can only change this way if we get rid of conscious or unconscious class thinking, and begin considering educational organization in terms of keeping the learning process going for as long as possible, in every life. Instead of the sorting and grading process, natural to a class society, we should regard human learning in a genuinely open way, as the most valuable real resource we have and therefore as something which we should have to produce a special argument to limit rather than a special argument to extend. We will perhaps only get to this when we have learned to think of a genuinely open culture.

9. An Approach to the Study of Curricula as Socially Organized Knowledge[1]

Michael F. D. Young

Source: Michael F. D. Young (ed.), *Knowledge and Control* (Collier-Macmillan, London, 1973).

In this seminal paper Dr. Young reassesses the whole nature of the sorts of interests sociologists should have in education. The argument is highly complex, but its essential features are as follows:

Knowledge is a 'social construct'. Criteria of 'truth' are entirely relative to the social context in which they are believed to be true. Even logic itself is a social construct, and is therefore not to be trusted. This 'relativity' of knowledge should make us suspicious of the sort of 'authority' attributed to any sort of expert, including educationists. Teachers (unwittingly or deliberately) use their 'authority' to exercise control over the learner, to preserve a status quo *(and therefore their own prestige) in a hierarchical social system. So do all others (such as doctors and lawyers) whose professional language helps to distance them from the layman.*

The almost total neglect by sociologists of how knowledge is selected, organized and assessed in educational institutions (or in any other institutions for that matter) hardly needs documenting. Some answers to the question why this happened, and an attempt to show that this neglect arises out of narrow definitions of the major schools of sociological thought (in particular, those stemming from Marx, Weber and Durkheim) rather than out of their inadequacies, may provide a useful perspective from which to suggest the directions in which such work might develop. This paper explicitly does not set out to offer a general theory of culture, or to be a direct contribution to the sociology of knowledge, except to the extent that it raises questions about what might be meant by the notion of knowledge being socially organized or constructed. It has the more limited aim of trying to suggest ways in which questions may be framed about how knowledge is organized and made available in curricula. However, it would be my contention that if such questions became the foci of research in the sociology of education, then we might well see significant advances in the sociology of knowledge in particular, and sociological theory in general. The paper then has four parts:

1. The changing focus of the public debates about education in the last twenty years.
2. A brief examination of the limitations and possibilities of existing

approaches to the sociology of education and the sociology of knowledge in generating either fruitful theories or research in the field of curricula.

3. An outline of some of the possibilities of the Marxist, Weberian and Durkheimian traditions.
4. An elaboration of the implications of the previous sections to suggest a framework and some possible directions for future research.[2]

1.

One can only speculate on the explanations, but it is clearly possible to trace three stages in the public debates on education in England in the last fifteen to twenty years; the foci have been *equality of opportunity* and the *wastage of talent, organization and selection of pupils,* and the *curriculum.* In each case one can distinguish the political, sociological and educational components, and though both of the sets of distinctions are over-simplified and schematic, they do provide a useful context for considering the problems posed in this paper. The latter three distinctions do not refer to the content of issues, but to the groups involved and the way they defined the problems.[3] In the first stage, the facts of educational 'wastage' were documented by the Early Leaving and Crowther Reports (and later by Robbins) and the 'class' nature of the lack of opportunity was demonstrated by Floud and Halsey. Though the sociological research largely complemented the public reports and was tacitly accepted as a basis for an expansionist policy by successive ministers, it also threw up a new set of questions concerning the social nature of selection, and the organization of secondary education in particular. Thus, the second phase of public debate from the midsixties focused on the issues of *selection* and *comprehensive reorganization.* That the debate now became an issue of political conflict is an indication that the policies involved, such as the abolition of selective schools, threatened certain significant and powerful interests in society – particularly the career-grammar, direct-grant and public school staff and the parents of the children who expected to go to such schools. The manifest inefficiency and less well-documented justice of the 11+ [4] made its abolition a convenient political commitment for reformist politicians. This debate was paralleled by an increasing interest by sociologists in all kinds of organizations and the possibility of applying the more general models of 'organization theory' to schools and colleges.[5]

It is only in the last two or three years that the focus of the debate has moved again from *organization* to *curriculum,* and again one can only speculate on the reasons. Four might be worth exploring; the first three particularly, in relation to the kind of projects on curriculum reform sponsored by the Schools Council:

(1) *Government pressure for more and better technologists and scientists*

The origins and implications of this are highly complex and can only be briefly referred to here. Mcpherson (1969), Blaug and Gannicott (1969) and Gorbutt (1970) have all cast doubts on the widely held notions that pupils in secondary schools are 'swinging from science'. This swing has been an 'official' problem, with various 'official' sets of remedies since the publication of the Dainton Report (1968). Gorbutt (1970) draws on the earlier studies and suggests that what has been called the 'swing from' science may be less the product of an identifiable change in the pattern of 'subject' choice by school pupils, and more an indication of how particular interest groups 'use' official statistics.

The failure of sociologists to make explicit the theoretical assumptions underlying contemporary definitions of this problem and the research it has generated is worth considering here. The whole 'subject-choice' and 'swing from science' debate presupposes taking as 'given' the social definitions implicit in our commonsense distinction between 'arts' and 'sciences'. What 'does' and 'does not' count as 'science' depends on the social meaning given to science, which will vary not only historically and cross-culturally but within societies and situationally. The dominant English cultural definitions of science might be characterized as what Habermas (1970) calls 'objectivistic', by which he means that we accept the scientists' claim that they 'apply their method without thought for their guiding interests'. In other words an idea of science has developed in which what is thought of as scientific knowledge is abstracted from the institutional contexts in which it is generated and used. Goodman (1969b) is making a similar point in discussing the implications of alternative social definitions of technology. Once the meanings associated with 'science' and 'technology', and 'pure' and 'applied', are seen as socially determined, not only does it become possible to explore how these social meanings become part of the school context of pupil preference, but a sociological enquiry into the intellectual content of what counts as science becomes possible (King, 1971).

(2) *The commitment to raising the school leaving age*

The implications of this change stem from the obvious if neglected fact that length of educational career is probably the single most important determinant of pupils' curricular experience. Thus for the 50% of pupils who at present leave when school is no longer legally compulsory, by 1973 teachers will be forced to conceive of curricula for a further 'terminal year'.

One development, which can be seen as a possible 'solution' to the 'extra year', has been the extension, to at least one half of all school leavers, of publicly recognized school exams. The extension of 'mode 3' or 'teacher based' exams has introduced a potentially greater flexibility in approach and the possibility of a more critical questioning of existing syllabi. The 'guiding interests' of the examination boards have so far remained outside the field of sociological enquiry. It is possible that such 'interests' may become more 'public' if the various pressures to abolish G.C.E. 'O' level grow.

(3) *Comprehensive amalgamations*

Many of these involve grammar schools which are obliged to receive an unselective pupil intake. Thus teachers who for years have successfully produced good 'A' level results from highly selected groups are now faced with many pupils who appear to neither know how to 'learn' the 'academic knowledge', nor appear to want to. This inevitably poses for teachers quite new problems of finding alternatives.

(4) *Student participation*

It is undeniable that as the demands of students in colleges and universities have moved from the arena of union and leisure activities to discipline and administrative authority and finally to a concern to participate in the planning of the structure and content of courses and their assessment, staff have themselves begun to re-examine the principles that underlay their curricula and which have for so long been taken for granted. It is more rather than less likely that this pressure from the students will increase and extend to the senior forms of the schools. Perhaps the most dramatic demonstration of this trend is the Negro students in the U.S.A. who are demanding courses in black studies.

Again the public debate has taken place on two levels, the 'political' and the 'educational' – though such a distinction is necessarily an oversimplification, and it is not intended to suggest that educational ideas do not have a political content. At the political level the main protagonists have been the Marxist 'left' (Anderson, 1969) and the conservative or Black Paper (Cox and Dyson, 1969a, 1969b) 'right'. The 'left' criticizes contemporary curricula for 'mystifying the students' and 'fragmenting knowledge into compartments'. They also claim that such curricula, by denying students the opportunity to understand society as a 'totality', act as effective agents of social control.* The conservative 'right' criticize progressive teaching methods, unstreaming and the various curricular innovations in English, history, and maths, as well as the expansion of the 'soft' social sciences. In the name of preserving 'our cultural heritage' and providing opportunities for the most able to excel, they seek to conserve the institutional support for the educational tradition they believe in – particularly the public and direct-grant grammar schools. What is significant for the sociology of education is that in spite of attempts, the politics of the

*Considerably more sophisticated versions of this thesis, which are not considered here, have been put forward by French and German social scientists (for instance, H. Lefebvre [1969]).

curriculum have remained outside of Westminster. Apart from compulsory religious instruction, the headmaster or principal's formal autonomy over the curriculum is not questioned. That this autonomy is in practice extremely limited by the control of VIth-form (and therefore lower form) curricula by the universities,* both through their entrance requirements and their domination of all but one of the school examination boards, hardly needs emphasizing. Furthermore any likelihood of the new 'polytechnics' developing alternative sets of criteria is limited by the powerful indirect control (of all degree-based courses) held by universities through their membership of the C.N.A.A. Boards. It becomes apparent that it is the legitimacy of university control, rather than teacher autonomy, that is being upheld.

It is as if by what has been called in another context the 'politics of non-decision making' (Bachrach and Baratz, 1963) through which the range of issues for party political debate are limited, that consideration of the curriculum is avoided[6] except for broad discussions about the need for more scientists. There are sufficient parallels in other contexts to suggest that the avoidance of such discussion is an indication of the interrelationship between the existing organization of knowledge and the distribution of power, the consideration of which might not be comfortable in an era of consensus politics.[7]

The context of the 'educationalists' ' debate about the curriculum has been different and inevitably less contentious. This lack of contentiousness is in stark contrast with the kind of direct confrontation that exists in America between the American academic establishment and its critics (Goodman, Friedenburg, Chomsky, Holt, *et al.*). It is possible that this contrast may in part be accounted for by the different contexts and historical antecedents of the prevailing 'liberal' orthodoxies in each country. The difference is also apparent when we consider some of the issues of the 'educationalists' ' debate in this country; early tracking into the sciences or arts, over-specialization and neglect of applied science in the VIth form, as well as the possibility of introducing new knowledge areas such as the social sciences. On another level, what has been labelled the 'tyranny of subjects' typical of much secondary education has been opposed by suggestions for integrated curricula based on 'themes' and 'topics'.

Three features that have characterized the educationalists' part in this debate should also be mentioned: (1) *The emphasis on secondary curricula.* Virtually all the issues have focused on aspects of secondary school curricula, which have in practice undergone least change; the absence of debate over changes at the primary level would seem to point, paradoxically, to the much greater autonomy of that part of the educational system with

*No direct control is implied here, but rather a process by which teachers legitimate their curricula through their shared assumptions about 'what we all know the universities want'.

the lowest status. (2) *The stream of working papers and proposals of the Schools Council.** (3) *The critiques of the philosophers of education.* Starting from certain *a priori assumptions* about the organization (or forms) of knowledge (Hirst, 1969), their criticisms focus either on new topic-based syllabi which neglect these 'forms of understanding', or on new curricula for the so-called 'less able' or 'Newsom child' which they argue are consciously restricting them from access to those forms of understanding which in the philosopher's sense are 'education'. The problem with this kind of critique is that it appears to be based on an absolutist conception of a set of distinct forms of knowledge which correspond closely to the traditional areas of the academic curriculum and thus justify, rather than examine, what are no more than the socio-historical constructs of a particular time. It is important to stress that it is not 'subjects', which Hirst recognizes as the socially constructed ways that teachers organize knowledge, but forms of understanding, that it is claimed are 'necessarily' distinct. The point I wish to make here is that unless such *necessary* distinctions or intrinsic logics are treated as problematic, philosophical criticism cannot examine the assumptions of academic curricula.

Unlike in the debates on *equality* and *organization,* sociologists, except as political protagonists, have remained silent. We have had virtually no theoretical perspectives or research to suggest explanations of how curricula, which are no less social inventions than political parties or new towns, arise, persist and change, and what the social interests and values involved might be.

2.
A. Sociology of Education and the Curriculum

Having mapped out the context of the debates on the curriculum, let us turn to the sociology of education and consider why its contribution has been so negligible.[8] Sociologists seem to have forgotten, to paraphrase Raymond Williams, that education is not a product like cars and bread, but a selection and organization from the available knowledge at a particular time which involves conscious or unconscious choices. It would seem that it is or should be the central task of the sociology of education to relate these principles of selection and organization that underlie curricula to their institutional and interactional setting in schools and classrooms and to the wider social structure. I want to suggest that we can account for the failure of sociologists to do this by examining on the one hand the ideological and methodological assumptions of the sociologists, and on the other hand the institutional context within which the sociological study of education has developed. However, perhaps as significant a fact as any in accounting for the limited conception of the sociology of education in

*This point will be taken up later in the paper.

Britain has been that in spite of the interest in the field reported by respondents to Carter's recent survey (Carter, 1967), *very few* sociologists have been involved in research in education.

Much British sociology in the late fifties and the sociology of education in particular drew its ideological perspective from Fabian socialism and its methodology from the demographic tradition of Booth and Rowntree. They broadened the notion of poverty from lack of income to lack of education, which was seen as a significant part of working-class life chances. The stark facts of the persistence of inequalities over decades and in spite of an overall expansion do not need repeating, but what is important is that these studies and those such as Douglas and Plowden which followed, in their concern for increasing equality of opportunity, focused primarily on the characteristics of the failures, the early leavers and the drop-outs. By using a model of explanation of working-class school failure which justified reformist social policies, they were unable to examine the socially constructed character of the education that the working-class children failed at – for instance, the peculiar content of the grammar school curriculum for the sixteen-year-old in which pupils are obliged to do up to ten different subjects which bear little relation to each other or to anything else. It would not be doing these studies an injustice to say that they developed primarily from a sociological interest in stratification in the narrow sense rather than education. They were concerned to show how the distribution of life chances through education can be seen as an aspect of the class structure. Inevitably this led to an over-mechanistic conception of 'class' which isolated the 'class' characteristics of individuals from the 'class' content of their educational experience. It may clarify this point by looking at the implicit model more formally as follows:

Assumptions	*Independent variable*	*Dependent variable*
Criteria of educational success – curricula, methods and evaluation. What counts as 'knowledge and knowing' in school	Social characteristics of the success and failure groups	Distribution of success and failure at various stages – stream, 11+, 'O' level, etc.

Though the table illustrates the point in a crude and over-simplified form, it does show that within that framework the content of education is taken as a 'given' and is not subject to sociological enquiry – the 'educational failures' become a sort of 'deviant'.[9] We can usefully reformulate the problem in a similar way to that suggested by Cicourel and Kitsuse (1963a) in their discussion of how 'official statistics' on crime are produced, and ask what are the processes by which rates of educational success and failure come to be produced. We are then led to ask questions about the context and definition of success and how they are legitimized. In other words, the methods of assessment, selection and organization of knowledge and the principles underlying them become our focus of study. The point is important because what is implied is that questions have to be raised about matters that have either not been considered important or have been tacitly accepted as 'given'. How does the education that poor working-class children fail at come to be provided? What are the social assumptions that are implicit in the criteria used in the Crowther Report to delineate a 'second group' who 'should be taught a sensible practicality – moral standards and a wise use of leisure time'? One could raise similar questions about the Newsom Report's 'below average child', and in fact about much educational research. One can see that this kind of reformulation would not have been consistent either with the methods or with the ideology of most British sociological research, particularly that concerned with social class and educational opportunity. A similar point can be made about studies of schools and colleges as 'organizations'. They have either begun with 'models' from 'organizational theory' or have compared schools with mental hospitals and prisons as 'people processing organizations'.[10] In neither case is it recognized that it is not only people but knowledge in the educational institutions that is 'processed', and that unless what is 'knowledge' is to be taken as 'given', it is the interrelation of the two processes of organization that must form the beginning of such studies.[11] An examination of the knowledge teachers have of children and how this influences the knowledge they make available to them would provide one way of tackling this empirically (Keddie, 1970).

Turning to the institutional context, it does seem clear that most of the teaching and published work in the sociology of education has taken place in colleges, institutes and departments of education. It is only very recently that university departments of sociology have offered main options at either B.Sc. or M.Sc. level in this field. Thus sociology of education has developed in institutions devoted to the 'academic' study of education where ten to fifteen years ago it hardly existed. We can pose the question as to how did the new specialists legitimate their contribution to educational studies and justify their particular field of expertise – particularly when the ex-school subject specialists and the philosophers had defined their area of competence as covering the curriculum and pedagogy. Not surprisingly, the sociologists mapped out new unexplored areas. They started from the social context of education, with an emphasis on social class, relationships to the economy, the occupational structure and the family, and moved to the consideration of schools as organizations and pupil subcultures. Through an arbitrary division of labour which had no theoretical basis, this allowed the expansion of sociology of education with the minimum of 'boundary disputes'. Inevitably this is speculation, but it does suggest an explanation of what appears to have been a consensus among sociologists and non-sociologists alike that the curriculum was not a field for sociological research.

Although this discussion has focused on British sociology, the points are equally applicable to the American situation. Functionalist theory, which has been the perspective of the majority of sociologists in the U.S.A., presupposes at a very general level an agreed set of societal values or goals which define both the selection and organization of knowledge in curricula. With one or two notable exceptions,[12] even the best American work in the sociology of education has been concerned with the 'organization' or 'processing' of people (whether pupils or students), and takes the organization of knowledge for granted.[13] It is important to stress that this limitation has also been characteristic of the work of those who have criticized the structural-functionalists.[14] This is of importance as it points to the limitations of the symbolic interactionist perspective. This perspective, derived largely from the ideas of G. H. Mead, has given rise to valuable studies of lawyers, medical students, nurses and others. These studies have raised questions that are not considered by functionalists about the processes of interaction and the situational significance of beliefs and values. However, they have not been able to consider as problematic the knowledge that is made available in such interactions. This would have led to considering the structural contingencies influencing what is defined as legal, medical, nursing or other knowledge, and would inevitably take the research out of the 'situated action' and therefore out of the symbolic interactionist framework.

B. Sociology of Knowledge and the Curriculum

It would have seemed that a field which was concerned with the social conditions influencing the development of knowledge, and with attempts to place ideas in their socio-historical setting, would have seen educational institutions and how knowledge is selected and organized in them as an obvious area for research. However, the main tradition which stems from Marx has been largely restricted to philosophies, political theories and theologies. These comments do not refer to the sociology of knowledge that stems from the phenomenology of Alfred Schutz, until recently totally neglected by sociologists. Schutz treats the institutional definitions or typifications (whether of education, or families or politics) as the intersubjective reality which men have constructed to give meaning to their world; therefore though they are part of the accepted world of everyday life for teachers, mothers and politicians, they can become the objects of sociological enquiry. In other words, if 'knowledge' or 'what is taken for knowledge' is ideal-typical in construction, Schutz is pointing to a study of the 'construction' of subjects, disciplines and syllabi as sets or provinces of meaning which form the basis of the intersubjective understandings of educators. The school curriculum becomes just one of the mechanisms through which knowledge is 'socially distributed'. As Schaffer (1970) suggests, the question 'how do children learn mathematics' presupposes answers to the prior question as to what is the social basis of the 'set of meanings that come to be typified under the term mathematics?'

Three strands, which characterize the more familiar traditions in the sociology of knowledge, indicate not its lack of potential but why the direction it has taken has made its contribution to the sociology of education so insignificant. Firstly, except in the American work on mass media, most writings have either, like Child[15] and Mannheim, been on the border of sociology and epistemology and have been concerned primarily with the existential nature of knowledge, or more recently have been little more than overviews. In both cases, with the exception of Mannheim's essay on 'Conservative Thought' (Mannheim, 1936), substantive empirical research has been eschewed. Secondly, there has been since Marx, a persistent neglect of the cognitive dimension of the categories of thought and how they are socially constrained – studies have been restricted to the values, standards and 'views of the world' of different groups.[16] Thirdly, and most importantly for the issues raised in this paper, the process of transmission, as itself a social condition, has not been studied. If it had, as we shall demonstrate in referring to Bourdieu's comments on Durkheim, the sociology of knowledge would have been inevitably concerned with the curricula through which knowledge is transmitted.

3.

A. The Marxist Tradition

Marx himself wrote very little about education, though a notion of 'polytechnical education' which underlies the educational policy of the 'communist' countries can be found in one of his early speeches.[17] Though Marx does have a theory which at a very general level can account for the changes in men's consciousness or categories of thought in terms of the changing means of production and the social relations they generate, he does not extend this to a systematic analysis of the educational system of his time comparable with his analysis of the economy. The limitations of Marxist theory also relate to its focus on how the knowledge is controlled and legitimized and its neglect of the equally important process of its acquisition. However, Marx's claim that education in a 'capitalist society' is a 'tool of ruling class interest', does direct one to examine the relation between the interest of economically dominant groups and the prevailing ideas of education as 'good' or 'worthwhile' in itself. It follows that the dominant emphasis of the education systems of capitalist societies, which might be described as the competitive concern with exams, grades and degrees, can be seen as one expression of the principles of a market economy (Hellerich, 1970). It is difficult to avoid the view that while these ideas may be true up to a point, they are on such a general level as to make them of limited value as starting points for the analysis of elite curricula. They do not point to explanations of the dynamics and particular configurations of different curricula.

However, the Italian Marxist Antonio Gramsci was more specifically concerned with education, and although only fragments of his work (Gramsci, 1957, 1967) are available in English, his primary concern with both the role of intellectuals (and by implication 'their kind of knowledge') and what he called the cultural hegemony which he saw as imposed on the working classes who are thus prevented from thinking for themselves, is important for any consideration of the content of education. Two aspects of Gramsci's thought that I refer to below are no more than illustrative and do not claim to be necessarily his most important ideas. His deep interest in the role of intellectuals in different kinds of society led him to consider many of the educational distinctions which we take for granted as historical products. They therefore become not 'given' but open to explanation and change. Examples such as 'theory' and 'practice', creation and propagation of knowledge (or in contemporary terms 'teaching' and 'research'), and what he calls the 'laws of scholarship' and the 'limits of scientific research' are all unexamined parts of the framework within which most formal education takes place. The second aspect relates to his distinction between 'common sense' and 'philosophy' in which he sees that some people's common sense becomes formally recognized as philosophy, and other people's does not, depending on their access to certain institutional contexts. This suggests that sociologists should raise the wider question of the relation between school knowledge and commonsense knowledge, of how, as Gramsci suggests, knowledge available to certain groups becomes 'school knowledge' or 'educational' and that available to others does not.

The most interesting recent attempt within a Marxist framework is that of Anderson (1969) in which he attempts to relate the content of the humanities in English academic curricula to the historical development of the class struggle. It is relatively easy and not very helpful to show that the examples of English culture that he takes are not representative and are selected to suit his thesis. However, a more important theoretical weakness is in his claim to a *structural analysis,* which seems unwittingly to exhibit the same flaws as most functional analyses of institutions. It emphasizes the interrelations of existing patterns of culture rather than seeing them as developing through the interaction of competing beliefs and ideas in the context of developing knowledge and a changing institutional setting. This 'structural' analysis allows Anderson to treat cases that do not fit as 'deviant' and not in need of explanation, another parallel with functional theories.

With a neo-Marxist framework, Williams (1961) provides perhaps the most promising and (by sociologists) most neglected approach to the study of the content of education. He distinguishes four distinct sets of educational philosophies or ideologies which rationalize different emphases in the selection of the content of curricula, and relates these to the social position of those who hold them. He then suggests that curricula changes have reflected the relative power of the different groups over the last hundred years. These can conveniently be summarized in the table below. He makes the significant point that the last of the foci was only recognized as legitimate outside the formal educational system. It is paradoxical when one considers the persisting subordinate position of the manual worker, that aspects of the populist educational ideology are now being 'resurrected' not by manual workers but in student demands for participation in the planning of curricula of universities,[18] institutions to which only about 3% of the sons of manual workers ever attain.

Ideology	*Social position*	*Educational policies*
1. Liberal/ conservative	Aristocracy/gentry	Non-vocational – the 'educated' man, an emphasis on character
2. Bourgeois	Merchant and professional classes	Higher vocational and professional courses. Education as access to desired positions
3. Democratic	Radical reformers	Expansionist – 'education for all'
4. Populist/ proletarian	Working classes/ subordinate groups	Student relevance, choice, participation

In placing curricular developments in their historical context, Williams's chapter is original and insightful though inevitably lacking in substantive evidence. It is only regrettable that in the nine intervening years no sociologist has followed it up. Perhaps the greatest weaknesses of the approach are that little attention is given to the changing power relations between the groups which might account for curricular changes, and one is left in doubt as to how the 'democratic' and 'bourgeois' ideologies arise from what would appear to be the same social group. Other attempts have been made to develop more systematically the Marxist concept of ideology for empirical research, though not primarily in the field of education. However, one study which warrants note in the context of this paper is Mills's (1943) early account of the professional ideology of social problem-orientated sociologists in the twenties and thirties. He characterized their 'common thought style' from a content analysis of a wide range of popular texts, and showed the relation of this to their common social origins and professional experience. It is a model study of how to relate complex empirical data to a theoretical perspective in order to show how, in this case, university sociology syllabuses developed at a particular time. It would seem to have relevance as an approach, given the dominating influence of textbooks on secondary education, to a wide range of knowledge areas, particularly in the humanities.

B. The Weberian Contribution

Max Weber's ideas (and not only his writings on bureaucracy) have not been neglected by sociologists of education, for the well-known analyses of the changing function of universities have been based on his ideal-types of the 'expert' and the 'cultivated man'.[19] However, with the exception of Musgrove,[20] the possibilities of his work for posing questions about the selection and organization of knowledge have not been examined. I shall not try here to redress the balance, but refer by way of illustration to his study of Confucian education.[21] Weber identified three characteristics of the education of the Chinese literati (or administrators):

1. An emphasis on propriety and 'bookishness', with a curriculum largely restricted to the learning and memorizing of classical texts.
2. This curriculum was a very narrow selection from the available knowledge in a society where mathematicians, astronomers, scientists, and geographers were not uncommon. However, all these fields of knowledge were classified by the literati as 'vulgar', or perhaps in more contemporary terms 'non-academic'.
3. Entry into the administrative elite was controlled by examinations on this narrow curriculum, so that the 'non-bookish' were for the purposes of the Chinese society of the time 'not educated'.

Weber explains his curriculum selection by relating it to the characteristics of what he called the patrimonial bureaucracy, in which administration was carried out by referring to the classical texts. Any change in curriculum would have undermined the legitimacy of the power of the administration whose skills therefore had to be defined as 'absolute'. As the whole question is secondary to Weber's main interest in comparative religion, we do not get suggestions as to the relationships of those with access to 'non-bookish' knowledge, and the possibility of their forming a competing power group with a radically different definition of education. Drawing on Weber, Wilkinson (1964) has a similar thesis about the classical curriculum of the nineteenth-century English public schools. Both writers are suggesting that curricula are defined in terms of the dominant group's idea of the 'educated man', which directs us back to the question raised implicitly earlier as to what model of the educated man is implicit in the 'worthwhile activities' or 'forms of understanding' of contemporary philosophies of education. Each of these studies, like Ben-David's (1963) interesting comparison of the relative influence of local pressure groups and elite values on American and English university curricula, are limited by the lack of an overall framework for linking the principles of selection of content to the social structure. However, both Weber and Ben-David, as well as a recent symposium on elite education (Wilkinson, 1969), point to the value of comparative studies in suggesting how different definitions of legitimate academic study arise and persist.

C. Durkheim

His specific works on education, apart from the emphasis on the social nature of curricula and pedagogy, are not very helpful, though it is important to remember that these books are collections of his lectures to student teachers and not systematic studies in sociology. The familiar criticisms, which do not need elaborating, are however applicable – firstly, his undifferentiated view of society which blurs the culture/social structure distinction and assumes them to be either synonymous or congruent or functionally related; and secondly, an over-emphasis on the value-component of education which he envisages as having a primarily integrative rather than stratifying and differentiating function. However, recent writers such as Bourdieu (1967) and Bernstein (1967) have focused on Durkheim's work as a whole and suggested that it is his work on religion and primitive classification (Durkheim and Mauss, 1963) leading indirectly to a sociology of knowledge that are of most significance for the sociological study of education. Bourdieu suggests that there is an analogy between Durkheim's account of the social origins of the categories of thought in small-scale societies with the development of thought categories through the process of transmission of culture in the school. Implicit in this process of transmission are criteria of what is topical, and the legitimacy of a hierarchy of 'study objects' becomes built into categories of thought themselves. Bernstein's work will be referred to in more detail later in the paper, but it is worth pointing out that he has extended Durkheim's work in two ways that are important here. He has elaborated the link between social change (mechanical to organic solidarity) and cultural change (the move from collection to integrated type curricula) and secondly, by emphasizing language and the curriculum he has moved the Durkheimian approach to education to the cognitive as well as the evaluative level.

To summarize this section, an attempt has been made to show that sociological research drawing on the Marxist, Weberian and Durkheimian traditions can contribute to a reorientation of the sociology of education that would no longer neglect curricula nor, as Talcott Parsons treats 'power', consider it as an epiphenomenon.

4.

The previous section has, from different points of view, suggested that consideration of the assumptions underlying the selection and organization of knowledge by those in positions of power may be a fruitful perspective for raising sociological questions about curricula. We can make this more explicit by starting with the assumptions that those in positions of power will attempt to define what is to be taken as knowledge, how accessible to different groups any knowledge is, and what are the accepted relationships between different knowledge areas and between those who have access to them and make them available. It is thus the exploration of how these processes happen, since they tend in other than pre-literate societies to take place in and through educational institutions, that should form the focus of a sociology of education. Our understanding of the processes is so rudimentary at present, that it is doubtful if we can postulate any clear links between the organization of knowledge at the level of social structure and the process as it involves teachers in classrooms. However, from these assumptions we can, drawing on Bernstein (1969), pose three interrelated questions about how knowledge is organized in curricula.

(1) The power of some to define what is 'valued' knowledge leads to problems of accounting for how 'stratified' knowledge is and by what criteria. Implicit in this idea of 'stratification of knowledge' is the distinction between the 'prestige' and the 'property' components of stratification. To the former are linked the different social evaluations placed on different knowledge areas,[22] and to the latter are the notions of 'ownership' and freedom (or restriction of access).[23] Thus the 'property' aspect of stratification points to 'knowledge' in use, and the reward structure associated with it. It suggests that in different societies the dominant conception of knowledge may be akin to 'private property', property shared by particular groups, or communally available on the analogy of 'common land'. The analysis which follows implicitly places greater emphasis on the prestige component of the stratification of knowledge. This is in part because the focus of the analysis is on curricula in one society rather than across societies, when it would become easier to conceptualize different definitions of 'knowledge as property'.

(2) The restriction of the accessibility of knowledge areas to different groups, poses the question in relation to curricula as to what is the *scope* of curricula available to different age groups, and more specifically to the social factors influencing the degree and kind of specialization at any age level.

(3) Earlier in the paper I raised the question as to what fields of enquiry were, at different times and in different cultures, embraced by a term like 'science'. More broadly this raises the question of the relation between knowledge areas and between those with access to them.

It may be useful to conceive of these three questions dichotomously and to represent the possible curricular alternative diagrammatically. (See table on opposite page.)

Bernstein's two ideal-type curricula, the 'integrated' and 'collection' types (1969) are shown to include different sub-types in which the stratification and specialization of knowledge is high or low. The conceptual structure implicit in the diagram was suggested by Bernstein (1969, 1970), though he concentrates his analysis primarily on types 4 and 5 and some of their 'variants' on account of their obvious historical significance. While it is not suggested, as some typologists do, that we should expect to find all of the types, it might be valuable to speculate on the conditions that we would expect to give rise to the various types.[24]

The expansion of knowledge, and the access to it, is paralleled by its increasing differentiation. *Empirically* we could no doubt also demonstrate that increasing differentiation is a necessary condition for some groups to be in a position to legitimize 'their knowledge' as superior or of high value. This high value is institutionalized by the creation of formal educational establishments to 'transmit' it to specially selected members of the society. Thus highly-valued knowledge becomes enshrined in the academy or school and provides a standard against which all else that is known is compared. That this description is analogous to the process described by Davis and Moore (1945) when discussing social stratification

Dimensions of the Social Organization of Knowledge in Curricula

How related are the knowledge areas? (openness)

		OPEN		CLOSED	
What is the scope of knowledge areas? (degree of specialization)		NARROW (specialized)	BROAD	NARROW	BROAD (unspecialized)
How stratified are the knowledge areas? (degree of stratification)	HIGH	1	2	5	6
	LOW	3	4	7	8

[alternatives 1–4 represent 'integrated' types and 5–8 represent 'collection' types in Bernstein's terminology]

is not unintended; the limitations of the latter point also to those of the analysis presented above. The important point, made originally by Buckley (1958), is that, though empirically differential social evaluation often follows from increasing differentiation, there is no necessary relationship between the two processes. In other words the pattern of social evaluation must be explained, independently of the process of differentiation, in terms of the restricted access to certain kinds of knowledge and the opportunity for those who have access to them to legitimize their higher status and control their availability.

The framework presented focuses on the principles of organization and selection of knowledge and only implicitly suggests how these are related to the social structure. The sociological assumption is that the most explicit relation between the dominant institutional order and the organization of knowledge will be on the dimension of stratification; moves therefore to 'destratify' or give equal value to different kinds of knowledge, or 'restratify' (moves to legitimize other criteria of evaluation), by posing a threat to the power structure of that 'order', will be resisted. This proposition is made on a very general level to which two qualifications should be made. Firstly, the notion of a dominant institutional order implies that among various economic, political, bureaucratic, cultural and educational interest groups which make up such an order, there is a consensus on the definitions of knowledge which is only likely under certain specific conditions. One would imagine, for example, that business and academic elites would not, except if faced with a common threat, share assumptions in their definitions of knowledge (see for example Thompson, 1970). Secondly, although one can trace historically (Williams, 1961; Birnbaum, 1970), some of the mechanisms of resistance and change, and also explore them in case studies at the organizational and interactional level, we still lack, as was indicated earlier, a way of conceptualizing the relationship between these levels.

Similarly, movements to make the scope of knowledge in a curriculum less restricted (a decrease in specialization), and the relations between knowledge areas more 'open', will also pose threats to the patterns of social relations implicit in the more restricted and less open forms, and likewise will be resisted.[25] It should therefore be possible to account for the persistence of some characteristics, particularly of academic curricula, and the changes of others in terms of whether they involve changes in either the criteria of evaluation of knowledge, or its scope or relations.[26] I want to suggest, therefore, that it may be through this idea of the stratification of knowledge that we can suggest relations between the patterns of dominant values and the distribution of rewards and power, and the organization of knowledge. Such analysis would be necessary both historically and cross-culturally on the societal level[27] and also at different age levels and in different knowledge areas.[28]

Academic curricula in this country involve assumptions that some kinds and areas of knowledge are much more 'worthwhile' than others: that as soon as possible all knowledge should become specialized and with minimum explicit emphasis on the relations between the subjects specialized in and between the specialist teachers involved. It may be useful, therefore, to view curricular changes as involving changing definitions of knowledge along one or more of the dimensions towards a less or more stratified, specialized and open organization of knowledge. Further, that as we assume some patterns of social relations associated with any curriculum, these changes will be resisted in so far as they are perceived to undermine the values, relative power and privileges of the dominant groups involved.

Before looking in more detail at the stratification of knowledge, I should like to indicate by examples the kind of questions that the ideas of scope and openness suggest.[29] First, *scope*: by referring to the degree of specialization, we are by implication concerned with the distribution of resources (pupil and teacher time, resources and materials).[30] This suggests why, in spite of much publicity to the contrary, specialization is so firmly entrenched. Its institutional basis in the schools would seem an important area of sociological enquiry.[31] Let us take as an illustration recent changes in medical and engineering curricula, which bring out the ways in which the characteristics and content of curricula are influenced by the changing values and interests of the controlling groups involved.

One feature that medical and engineering curricula have in common is that those controlling them have recently appeared concerned to introduce a social science component into the courses. In the absence of research, one can only speculate about the changing definitions of socially relevant knowledge involved in this broadening of the curriculum. Conceivably, these changes reflect a change in the position of the engineer and doctor, who both find themselves working increasingly in large organizations isolated from the direct consequences of their work, but still subject to public criticisms of what they do. The significance of this example is to point out the way changes in the social or occupational structure may influence definitions of relevant knowledge and thus curricula.

Turning to the question of *openness;* there are critical research problems here, for the idea of curricula consisting of knowledge areas in 'open' or closed relation to each other presupposes that definitions of knowledge areas or 'subjects' are not problematic. It is important to recognize that 'subjects' or, even as was suggested earlier in this paper, broad fields like 'arts' and 'sciences', though they may be part of educators' taken for granted world, cannot be seen as such by sociologists. However, in order to conceptualize the changing relationships between teachers, some assumptions have to be made, and it may be valuable as an illustration of the utility of the framework to point to some of the differences that are likely to arise from 'integration' in the 'arts' and in the 'sciences'. The characteristic of all teaching of sciences at any level is that however strong loyalties and identification may be (and this is likely to be closely associated with the level of teaching), those teaching do tend to share implicitly or explicitly norms and values which define what science is about, and thus chemistry, physics and biology are at one level 'integrated'. It is not surprising, therefore, that in an area of the academic curriculum not striking for its innovations, the VIth form, both biological and physical sciences are increasingly taught as fully-integrated courses. An indication of the significance of the stratification dimension of knowledge is that the core base of the former is biochemistry and of the latter is mathematics: both high-status knowledge fields among scientists. Evidence of the different situation that arises when attempts to integrate appear to reduce the status of the knowledge is the failure of the general science movement after World War II. Whereas the physicist and biologist share a fairly explicit set of values through being scientists, it is doubtful if being in the 'humanities' has any common meaning for historians, geographers and those in English and foreign languages.* In this case, any movement to 'integration' involves the construction of new values to replace subject identities. It is not surprising that this side of the academic VIth-form curriculum has undergone very little change.

The third question that was raised about the organization of knowledge concerned how far and by what criteria were different knowledge areas *stratified.* I would argue that it is the most important, for it is through this idea that we are led to consider the social basis of different kinds of knowledge and we can begin to raise questions about relations between the power structure and curricula, the access to knowledge and the opportunities to legitimize it as 'superior', and the relation between knowledge and its functions in different kinds of society.

If knowledge is highly stratified there will be a clear distinction between what is taken to count as knowledge, and what is not, on the basis of which processes of selection and exclusion for curricula will take place. It would follow that this type of curricular organization presupposes and serves to legitimate a rigid hierarchy between teacher and taught, for if not, some access to control by the pupils would be implied, and thus the processes of exclusion and selection would become open for modification and change. The degree to which this model characterizes the contemporary university and its implications for student movements would seem worth exploring. A further point is that access to control by pupils or students implies that alternative definitions of knowledge are available to them. It would be useful to examine the conditions under which such alternative definitions were available, and to compare different age groups, and different areas of study.

So taken for granted by most educators is the model referred to in the previous paragraph, that it is difficult to conceive of the possibility of a curriculum based on knowledge which is differentiated but not stratified. That it poses a revolutionary alternative is apparent, when one considers whether the terms teacher, pupil and examination in the sense normally used would have any meaning at all. It suggests that assumptions about the stratification of knowledge are implicit in our ideas of what education 'is' and what teachers 'are'.

As previously suggested, the contemporary British educational system is dominated by academic curricula with a rigid stratification knowledge. It follows that if teachers and children are socialized within an institutionalized structure which legitimates such assumptions, then for teachers, high status (and rewards) will be associated with areas of the curriculum that are (1) formally assessed, (2) taught to the 'ablest' children, (3) taught

*Except in the situation where they all see themselves competing for resources with the scientists.

in homogeneous ability groups of children who show themselves most successful within such curricula.

Two other implications follow which would seem to warrant exploration.

(1) If pupils do identify high-status knowledge as suggested, and assume that the characteristics of 'worthwhile knowledge' to be that it is taught in 'sets', formally examined, and not studied by the 'less able', they could well come to reject curricular and pedagogic innovations which necessarily involve changing definitions of relevant knowledge and teaching methods.

(2) If the criteria of high-status knowledge are associated with the value of the dominant interest groups, particularly the universities, one would expect maximum resistance to any change of the high status of knowledge associated with academic curricula. This, as I shall elaborate on later, is supported by evidence of the Schools Council proposals for curriculum reform. The Council has accepted the existing stratification of knowledge and produces most of its recommendations for reform in the low-status knowledge areas. These are associated with curricula which are for the young and less able and do not undermine the interests of those in positions of power in the social structure.

Let us explore a bit further the idea of knowledge being stratified. It does suggest two kinds of questions to be asked:

(1) In any society, by what criteria are different areas of, kinds of and approaches to knowledge given different social value? Those criteria will inevitably have developed in a particular social and historical context, but, if isolated, may be useful if related to social, political and economic factors in accounting for changes and resistances to changes in curricula.

(2) How can we relate the extent to which knowledge is stratified in different societies, and the kinds of criteria on which such stratification may be based,[32] to characteristics of the social structures?

The first question requires an attempt to postulate some of the common characteristics of academic curricula, and to show how, over a particular historical period, they have become legitimated as of high status by those in positions of power. As suggested earlier, these characteristics are not absolute, but socio-historical constructs, so it is not inappropriate to draw on three strands of thinking which emphasize this. These are, first, the comparative perspective on pre- and post-literate societies (Mead, 1938); secondly, consideration of the consequences of literacy for contemporary culture (Goody and Watt, 1962); and thirdly the way a gradual 'bureaucratization' of the education systems of industrializing societies has led to an increasing emphasis on 'examinations' as the most 'objective' means of assessing (and therefore identifying) 'expert' knowledge (Weber, 1952). Weber discusses the process of what he calls the 'bureaucratic domination of the nature of education'. He implicitly suggests that the major constraint on what counts as knowledge in society will be whether it can be 'objectively assessed'.[33] There is an interesting and not entirely fortuitous parallel with Kelvin's sentiment that 'when you cannot express it in numbers, your knowledge is of a meagre and unsatisfactory kind'[34] in the idea implicit in contemporary education that 'if you cannot examine it, it's not worth knowing'.[35] The way formal examinations place an increasing emphasis on literacy rather than oral expression is raised by Davie (1961), and the implications of the 'literate' character of modern culture brought out by Goody and Watt (1962). They argue that so great is the discontinuity or even the contradictions between the private oral traditions of family and home and the public literate tradition of the school that 'literate skills form one of the major axes of differentiation in industrial societies'. They go on to suggest that reading and writing (which are the activities which occupy most of the timetable of most of those being educated) are inevitably solitary activities, and so a literate culture brings with it an increasing individualization. This individualization is symbolized in its most dramatic form in the various ways in which those being educated are assessed or examined.

In comparing literate and non-literate cultures Goody and Watt suggest that the peculiar characteristics of the former are 'an abstraction which disregards an individual's social experience . . . and a compartmentalization of knowledge which restricts the kind of connections which the individual can establish and ratify with the natural and social world'.[36] The final point they make is how most knowledge in a literate culture is fundamentally at odds with that of daily life and common experience. In discussing the way educational emphases have moved from 'learning' to 'teaching', Mead (1938) brings out a related point, when she links the idea of groups holding some kinds of knowledge as superior and the notion of 'a hierarchical arrangement of cultural views of experience', to the increasing emphasis on changing the beliefs, habits, knowledge, ideas and allegiances that children bring with them to school.

Over-simplifying, we can draw together the main ideas of the previous paragraphs to suggest the dominant characteristics of high-status knowledge, which we will hypothesize as the organizing principles underlying academic curricula. These are literacy, or an emphasis on written as opposed to oral presentation; individualism (or avoidance of group work or co-operativeness),[37] which focuses on how academic work is assessed and is a characteristic of both the 'process' of knowing and the way the 'product' is presented; abstractness of the knowledge and its structuring and compartmentalizing independently of the knowledge of the learner;[38] finally and linked to the former is what I have called the unrelatedness of academic curricula, which refers to the extent to which they are 'at odds' with daily life and common experience.[39]

If status of knowledge is accorded in terms of these criteria, academic curricula would be organized on such principles; in other words they will tend to be abstract, highly literate, individualistic and unrelated to non-school knowledge. It may also be useful as a preliminary way of posing questions to see curricula ranked on these characteristics which then become four dimensions in terms of which knowledge is stratified. Thus one can suggest conditions under which (non-academic) curricula will be organized in terms of oral presentation, group activity and assessment, concreteness of the knowledge involved and its relatedness to non-school knowledge.

One way is to view these characteristics as the specific historical consequences of an education system based on a model of bookish learning for medieval priests which was extended first to lawyers and doctors, and increasingly has come to dominate all education of older age groups in industrial societies (Goodman, 1969a). However, their use of sociologists may be to highlight the unquestioned dimensions of academic curricula – to elaborate – these characteristics can be seen as social definitions of educational value, and thus become problematic in the sense that if they persist it is not because knowledge is in any meaningful way best made available according to the criteria they represent, but because they are conscious or unconscious cultural choices which accord with the values and beliefs of dominant groups at a particular time.[40] It is thus in terms of these choices that educational success and failure are defined. One might speculate that it is not that particular skills and competences are associated with highly-valued occupations because some occupations 'need' recruits with knowledge defined and assessed in this way. Rather it is suggested that any very different cultural choices, or the granting of equal status to sets of cultural choices that reflect variations in terms of the suggested characteristics, would involve a massive redistribution of the labels 'educational' 'success' and 'failure', and thus also a parallel redistribution of rewards in terms of wealth, prestige and power.

Two important limitations of this approach must be mentioned; firstly, not only are the categories highly tentative but they are formal, and no operational rules are suggested with direct relevance to analysing questions of substantive content.[41] Their use in the analysis of texts, syllabi, reports, exam questions 'marking' criteria and the day-to-day activities of the classroom would lead either to narrower but more substantive categories, or their modification, depending on the nature of the research problem posed. Secondly, by its primary emphasis on the social organization and not the social functions of knowledge, this approach does not make explicit that access to certain kinds of knowledge is also potential access to the means of changing the criteria of social evaluation of knowledge itself and therefore to the possibility of creating new knowledge, as well as the means of preserving these criteria. However, changing criteria involve social actions which inevitably are concrete, corporate and related as well as involving oral as well as written communication. Perhaps it is through the disvaluing of social action and the elevation of the value placed on 'knowledge for its own sake' through the separation of knowledge from action, well symbolized by the values implicit in such distinctions as 'pure and applied' and 'theory and practice', that knowledge of social alternatives in our educational system is both restricted and, when available, is perceived as 'alternatives in theory'.[42] However, we can illustrate some more specific ways in which this approach might be useful for a sociology of educational knowledge:

(1) If the relations between the patterns of domination and the organization of knowledge are as have been suggested, one would only expect a reduction in specialization for any particular age group, an increase in inter-subject integration, or a widening of the criteria of social evaluation of knowledge, if they were to follow or be closely dependent on changes in these patterns of domination.[43]

If we assume the absence of such changes we would expect most so-called 'curricular innovations' to be of two kinds:

(a) Those in which existing academic curricula are modified but there is no change in the existing social evaluation of knowledge.[44]

Two examples are the new Nuffield 'O' level science syllabuses and the integrated science projects referred to earlier. A significant research problem would be to examine the influence of the Nuffield sponsors, the Science Masters' Association (now the Association for Science Education, and an organization which has close links with the universities and traditionally an active membership drawn largely from public, direct-grant and grammar schools with large science VIths) and the university advisors, which led to the Nuffield Project being directed, in the first place, to 'O' level, which is taken by a maximum of 30% of pupils, rather than to reforming secondary school science as a whole.

(b) 'Innovations' which disregard the social evaluations implicit in British academic curricula, but are restricted in their availability to less able pupils.

In becoming the major sponsor for such innovations, the Schools Council can be seen as legitimizing the existing organization of knowledge in two ways. Firstly, by taking the assumptions of the academic curricula for granted, the social evaluations of knowledge implicit in such curricula are by implication being assumed to be in some sense 'absolute' and therefore not open to enquiry. Secondly, by creating new courses in 'low status' knowledge areas, and restricting their availability to those who have already 'failed' in terms of academic definitions of knowledge, these failures are seen as individual failures, either of motivation, ability or circumstances, and not failures of the academic system itself. These courses, which explicitly deny pupils access to the kinds of knowledge which are associated with rewards, prestige and power in our society are thus given a kind of legitimacy, which masks the fact that educational success in terms of them would still be defined as 'failure'. The link with teachers' definitions of the raising of the school leaving age as being a problem of social control rather than of intellectual development is not difficult to see.

(2) It should be fruitful to explore the syllabus construction of knowledge practitioners in terms of their efforts to enhance or maintain their academic legitimacy. Some examples worth investigation would be the various professional examining bodies, the attempts to obtain university entrance recognition for new knowledge areas, and the presentation of previously non-degree knowledge areas (particularly technical and administrative fields, art, dance and physical education) as suitable for degree status.[45]

Returning to the second question of this section, which was concerned with how we account for the criteria implicit in the different ways knowledge is stratified, we do not know how relations between the economy and the educational system produce different degrees and kinds of stratification of knowledge. It is possible to trace schematically a set of stages from non-literate societies where educational institutions are not differentiated from other institutions, to feudal type societies where formal education in separate schools is almost entirely restricted to a priestly caste, and, through the church ownership of land, such schools remained largely independent (at least in regard to the curricula) of the economic and political processes of the time. Gradually schools and colleges became increasingly differentiated and dependent on the economies of the societies they were in, when clearly the dominant economic and political orders became the major determinants of the stratification of knowledge. Comparative studies of educational arrangements in developing countries might shed light on these relationships in more detail. One way would be to compare the kinds of knowledge stratification in countries like North Korea where the schools are less separate from the economy and many activities of learning are also activities of production, with systems like our own where in school nothing is 'for real', even in the workshops.

To sum up, then, an attempt has been made to offer a sociological approach to the organization of knowledge in curricula. The inevitably limited and schematic nature of the outline presented together with the total lack of research by sociologists in the field turns us back to the question posed at the beginning of this paper. Why no sociology of the curriculum? Perhaps the organization of knowledge implicit in our own curricula is so much part of our taken for granted world that we are unable to conceive of alternatives. Are we then reluctant to accept that academic curricula and the forms of assessment associated with them are sociological inventions to be explained like men's other inventions, mechanical and sociological?

ACKNOWLEDGEMENTS

I should like to thank my colleagues, Basil Bernstein and Brian Davies for their comments on earlier drafts, and to express my appreciation to them and the other members of the departmental seminar for the valuable discussion that arose out of some of the preliminary ideas in this paper. A similar debt is owed to those graduate students of the department with whom I have benefited from many discussions around the themes of this paper. This extended and revised version owes much to the many hours of discussion I had with Basil Bernstein, whose constructive criticisms I only came to appreciate fully when it came to re-writing. Also I have continued to learn much from my graduate students, in particular, Nell Keddie and Geoff Esland.

NOTES AND REFERENCES

1. The title would imply that we can make statements about curricula in general which when one considers the diversities within even one education system, would seem unwarranted. In effect, the paper focuses largely on what is commonly called the 'academic curriculum' of secondary and higher education in England. The relevance of any of the general ideas presented for infant and junior curricula or the various technical courses available must remain doubtful.
2. These ideas represent a development from a preliminary attempt by the author (Young, 1967) to begin a 'sociology of the curriculum'. Here the analogy between explanations of 'educational failure' and 'deviance' in contemporary sociology is explored in more detail.
3. A detailed historical study of the social composition of the groups involved and the social and political circumstances in which their educational ideas developed and influenced 'educational practice' would make an important contribution to our understanding of the origins, persistence and change of educational ideologies. Banks (1955) and Taylor (1963) are perhaps the only significant attempts to carry out such a study in this country. Each, however, is limited by an implicit conceptual framework which takes 'academic knowledge' as 'given' rather than 'to be explained'.

   The unsatisfactory use of the concept 'educational ideology' in the literature stems in large part from a lack of substantive studies, but in part also from the failure to relate the sets of beliefs, their social contexts and their implications for practical action. Those using the concept have either, like Hoare (1967), Burnett and Palmer (1967) and D. I. Davies (1969), relied on broad 'political' categories without demonstrating that they have any necessary 'educational' implications, or like Brameld (1967) have developed typologies of educational ideas without linking them to either a theory of social change or to the social origins of those who are assumed to have held them. It seems likely that the more limited approach of exploring how 'beliefs' about children implicit in psychological theories become institutionalized and situationally significant in providing 'explanations' for various curricular and pedagogic practices, may be more fruitful (Friedman, 1967; Eastman, 1967; Esland, 1970).
4. This 'inefficiency' refers to the evidence collected or summarized by writers such as Vernon (1957) and Westergaard and Little (1964) concerning the arbitrariness of the 11+ (in terms of predicting future attainment) and the discrepancy between the distribution of opportunity for selective education and the distribution of *measured* intelligence that has been produced by the 11+; in neither case does one find serious counter-claims in the literature. The 'injustice' presupposes that some other administrative technique which would replace the 11+ (e.g. parental 'choice', teacher recommendation, 'flexible grouping in non-selective secondary

schools'), would be both 'less arbitrary' and in some sense 'fairer'. The evidence, such as it is, points to the opposite being as likely an outcome of the change (Floud, 1957; Douglas, 1969; Ford, 1969).

5. The possible explanations of why such studies have focused on 'pupil subcultures' is discussed fully elsewhere (W. B. Davies, 1970; Seaman, 1970). In this context it is perhaps worth pointing out that as in the earlier phase of the educational debate which focused on 'equality' and 'wastage', the sociological definition of the problem complements those of teachers and research sponsors. In this case the problem is one of 'control' of pupils, which leads to a concern to isolate their common characteristics. These are conceptualized as the 'subculture', particularly of the least 'controllable' pupils. Though there is much more in each study, this is the primary emphasis of both Hargreaves (1968) and Lacey (1970).
6. The financing of a new statutory body, the Schools Council, with responsibility for sponsoring curriculum development 'projects', and having specific powers over how secondary school children are examined, is itself an indication of an increasing political concern over the control of educational knowledge. The Schools Council's much-publicized 'autonomy' from the D.E.S., together with the recruitment of 'practising teachers' on to its staff and committees, suggests an attempt to deny that the Schools Council marks anything other than an extension by teachers of their 'traditional' control over the curriculum.
7. This point needs exploring in specific circumstances, but might be illustrated by referring to examples from other kinds of institutions. With regard to the Church, we might consider the Vatican's resistance to allowing celibacy and 'natural law' to be on the agenda of the Bishop's Conference. A similar example was the persistent refusal of those controlling the Anglican Lambeth Conference to allow 'freemasonry' to be discussed. Other examples from political parties would also point to the way legitimate areas of discussion are defined by existing hierarchies.
8. It is ironical that the one outstanding study, which looks at the various social, cultural and institutional factors influencing the organization of knowledge, is by a philosopher, G. E. Davie. His study of curricular change in the nineteenth-century Scottish universities raises many of the issues about selection of content and relation between areas of knowledge that are considered later in the paper (Davie, 1961).
9. The analogy between explanations of 'deviancy' and 'educability which take social class as their independent variable is explored in more detail (Young, 1967). The analogy points to how both explanations rely on similar functionalist presuppositions which, in each case, demonstrate the significance of *social class,* but are unable to account for the process through which this significance is active.
10. For example Swift (1969) and Shipman (1968).
11. One of the few empirical studies to attempt this is Burton Clark's *Open Door College* (1961).
12. See Burton Clark (1960).
13. See Gross, *et al.* (1957).
14. Cicourel and Kitsuse (1963b), Becker, *et al.* (1961, 1969).
15. Child (1943).
16. A useful outline of trends in the sociology of knowledge which implicitly makes this point is given by Bottomore (1956).
17. Blake (1968).
18. The most dramatic example has been the development of demands for black studies courses in the U.S.A.
19. Halsey (1960).
20. Musgrove (1968).
21. Weber (1952).
22. By the use of such terms as 'academic', 'pure', 'theoretical', etc.

23. I am referring here to the secret knowledge that 'professionals' protect as if it was their own.
24. A much more detailed analysis than those yet available, of the genesis of examples of any particular curricular-types, would be a necessary preliminary to such an exercise.
25. It may be possible to examine the whole history of the arguments about secondary school specialization from Crowther (1959) and Petersen (1960) to today in this perspective.
26. An illustration of this is to compare the resistance to the introduction of new knowledge areas for the curriculum for the same age group in different institutions (e.g. the grammar school VIth form and the College of Further Education).
27. The work of Ben-David (1963), Davie (1961) and Rothblatt (1969) is a valuable beginning in this direction.
28. Perhaps the only significant study here is that of Reisman, Gusfield and Gamson (1970 in press).
29. The possible implications of this specialization and the degree of insulation between what is studied as well as of changes are explored in detail by Bernstein (1971).
30. It is a paradox of the English educational system worth exploring, that while those most in need of education get least of it, those with the longest educational careers have curricula of the most limited scope.
31. Studies relating the career structure of teachers in different knowledge areas and the strategies of the various subject-based associations would be one possible way of exploring this question empirically.
32. Ben-David (1963) in comparing university curricula in the U.S.A., U.S.S.R. and U.K., among other countries, shows wide variations in the criteria on which the stratification of knowledge is based in different countries.
33. There are two ways in which Weber's discussion is unsatisfactory, both of which raise important questions for any sociological research on examinations. First he took for granted that process by which some activities are selected as 'worth objective assessment', a prior question to his consideration of the 'effects' of examinations. Secondly the notion of what is meant by the 'objectivity' of examinations is left unexplored. The point touched on briefly elsewhere about the priority given to 'knowledge as product' as opposed to 'knowing as process' is only one aspect of this.
34. Curiously but significantly on the façade of the University of Chicago Social Science Research Building!
35. The fact that non-examined curricula are relegated to 'leisure' courses, liberal and general studies, and courses for the 'less able' is indicative of the implicit validity of this thesis.
36. Goody and Watt, *op. cit.*
37. The term *individualism* is far from satisfactory, as it is ambiguous and has a much wider meaning than is intended here.
38. There are problems in the use of the term 'abstract' because it presupposes some kind of absolute notion of what is 'abstract', and neglects the way in which one can have different 'kinds of abstraction', some of which may be 'labelled' concrete by others using different 'abstraction' criteria. Horton (1967, 1968) explores this question indirectly, but it is an area that sociologists have too readily taken as not requiring research. While 'abstractness' seems to be a satisfactory category for describing academic curricula, the problems raised by Horton mean that as an analytic category it presupposes just those assumptions that one would want to treat as problematic. It may be possible to reconceptualize the problem by treating 'abstractedness' as an 'educators' category' to be explained.
39. See the section earlier on Gramsci for a more detailed consideration of this. The concept *'unrelatedness'* refers to a similar characteristic of formal educational

systems that Henry (1960) calls 'disjunctiveness'. Again we are faced with conceptual problems, not surprisingly since the question of school and non-school knowledge has hardly been considered by sociologists. Similarly (and I am very grateful to Mr. Derek Frampton of Garnett College for pointing this out to me), these categories are unable to deal with professional curricula where the knowledge is undoubtedly of high status, but not on the criteria that have been suggested in this paper.

40. See note 31.

41. For instance, the gradual disappearance of classics (particularly Greek) from most secondary school curricula is not accountable in these terms. Nor specifically is the changing content of school history, geography or English literature.

42. An interesting example of the 'philosophical sleight of hand' required to reach this position appears in an otherwise excellent paper by Rytina and Loomis (1970). After criticizing Marx and Dewey for using *metaphysical* justifications of the truth of what men 'know' in terms of what men 'do', they do likewise in drawing on a *metaphysical* 'out there' in terms of which, they claim, we must check out our theories against our practice.

43. Specific reservations were made earlier about such an all-embracing phrase. Clearly the crucial 'dominating' factor is the limited access to higher education, which enables universities to control secondary school curricula. Limited changes, such as the breakdown of the near monopoly, by university boards, of school examinations, would be important but secondary to this.

44. Most of the discussion of curriculum reform is of this kind. In general the question is asked, given that we know our objectives, how can we more efficiently achieve them? There is an enormous literature in this field which demonstrates the concern of those who have been aptly labelled 'the curriculum mongers'* to create and institutionalize an autonomous discipline 'curriculum studies' with its own so-called 'theory', house journals and professors. Most of the writing, with the exception of parts of Miles (1964), is more informative about the writer's perspectives and beliefs than about school curricula.

45. The activities of the Council for National Academic Awards Boards of Studies would be particularly important to study in terms of the assumptions polytechnic staff have of what these boards will recognize as 'honours degree standard'.

*The term was first suggested by John White (Department of Philosophy, University of London Institute of Education), in an article with that title in *New Society* (March 1969).

10. Knowledge out of Control

Richard Pring

Source: *Education for Teaching* (the journal of the Association of Teachers in Colleges and Departments of Education), Autumn, 1972.

Richard Pring counters the arguments of Michael Young (and his followers) by agreeing that there is a (trivial) sense in which knowledge is 'socially constructed' but by showing that this is not wholly *the case. It can be argued that some aspects of logic, for example, are not 'relative' in the wholesale sense of the phenomenologists, and that their position needs to be clarified considerably before the teacher need abandon his academic 'authority'.*

Institutions and professional bodies control access to their membership. Frequently they do this by setting tests in these matters which they agree to be important. At times, of course, the tests might, to the outsider, seem odd or indeed trivial. But in practice neither oddity nor triviality matter, because these tests and no other provide legitimate access (or 'legitimise' access) to the desired goals; and, in any case, by what standards are oddity or triviality to be judged?

It is a small, and sometimes tempting, step to extend this account to other areas of social activity, especially schooling. We are all familiar with the criticisms of examinations – whether these be the 11+ or 'O' level or 'A' level or university degrees. Some people somewhere say what is to be learnt in order for others to pass these examinations, and (society being what it is) those who have been schooled need to pass these examinations in order to graduate into a socially acceptable (and comfortable) position in life. Thus in the ultimate analysis achievement is determined by those who *decide* what is to count as achievement and who can reinforce their decision through control of the examination system.

Familiar arguments such as these have their equally familiar counter arguments. Thus it might be admitted that *in fact* schooling (and in particular the examinations towards which so much schooling leads) has taken on an institutional life of its own; that *in fact* achievement, in the different areas of approved learning, is that which is decided upon and reinforced by those who play a commanding role in the institution; and that *in fact* the standards that are advocated, passed on, and mastered in school have no validity other than that they are approved of by the teachers and *their* masters. But whatever may *in fact* be the case in some or many schools and to a greater or lesser extent, there remains the belief (and the hope) that such schooling is open to evaluation by standards of appraisal which are 'above' and independent of the particular institutional framework through which one is schooled. Hence the familiar cry that the curriculum should not aim to satisfy an externally imposed set of examinations, but that the examinations themselves should measure what has been judged valuable independently and on educational grounds. Curriculum reform, so it is argued, is achieved through the perception of some educational ideal and the translation of this ideal into curriculum terms. The consequent map of learning is explicable by reference not simply to the biographical details of those who happen to be in power or to the inherited institutional traditions, but also to factors which arise from the necessary structure of knowledge, from standards of validity and criteria of meaning to which all should defer. Whatever might happen *in fact,* there remains the ideal of an education which arises from considerations quite disconnected from power politics and control mechanisms.

But is there such an educational ideal? May it be the case that in ridding oneself of one form of control over what is to account as knowledge, as valid argument, as good writing, as moral behaviour, one simply falls under some other form of control – that in the end all standards are relative to the decisions or choices or even idiosyncrasies of those who are placed in a position of judgement and influence? If this is the case, then the teacher is no longer the way from ignorance to enlightenment, the introduction to a wiser, more valuable way of life; rather is he the spokesman for a particular way of life, the servant of a particular form of control. And the reply of the discerning student to his appreciation of a piece of literature or appraisal of some historical event or explanation of some social phenomenon or exposition, of some religious doctrine is not to attend to the argument in detail, but to dismiss it from the onset as a rationalisation of this or that way of life or of this or that power group within society.

The criticism might be extended further and the educational ideal become paler. For might it not be argued that the very way we have come to organise knowledge, to divide it up into recognisable disciplines, and to train teachers within these disciplines, is itself arbitrary, could have been otherwise, and has little to commend it other than convenience and career prospects? Different subjects, so it is argued, have precisely those boundaries which fellow scholars agree amongst themselves that they should have. Any disagreement amongst scholars is frequently more reminiscent of politics than of scholarship. Philosophers, sociologists, psychologists, etc., jealously guard their respective disciplines, *decide* what is to count as good philosophy, sociology, and psychology, and close their ranks when alternative proposals are made.

This view of knowledge, the removal of its autonomous and sacred character, and its suggested dependence upon social and historical determinants, would seem to gain immediate plausibility from a cursory glance at the development (or simply change?) that historically can be observed within the different forms of thought. Moral and religious beliefs have changed; so have the standards by which we appreciate art and literature; even basic concepts of self-knowledge and appraisal alter in tune with changing social conditions; people have come 'to see things differently', to highlight certain things as important and to relegate others to insignificance. Who then is to say that this belief or that value is preferable to, or more valid than, that one? The criticism is relentless for not even the sciences and mathematics, not even logic itself, escape the accusation of social relativism. There are different schools of science, just as there are different schools of philosophy and of sociology. And ultimately one must *choose* the school of science (or the scientific paradigms); there is no meta-language through which one can debate the relative merits of rival schools or rival paradigms. And changes within science are revolutionary rather than continuous, and thus are to be explained by factors external to science rather than within it.

The social relativism of our thoughts, and its dependence upon those conditions which control our minds as well as our actions are to be observed not only in historical developments but also in comparative studies of other societies. Anthropologists give accounts of quite different ways of conceptualising – of putting into meaningful order – the experiences even of everyday life. It is not, we are told, a better or a worse way of thinking about things. It is simply a different one. At most it is a more or less useful one. Pragmatism is the by-product of relativism.

Where then do we look for understanding in the differentiated structure of human thought? How are we to fathom the *real* explanation of why we hold these beliefs rather than those, or conceptualise our experience in one way rather than another? Above all, what is the way of breaking the control of different systems or forms of thinking – or (more importantly) the control of those who *decide* what is to count as a valid way of thinking?

It may seem likely, if not inevitable, that some further, more accurate, understanding of the way we experience reality and organise that experience will be provided by sociological analysis. After all if the concepts we employ are social constructs, and if the differentiated knowledge claims we make and standards we implicitly appeal to are relative to particular social conditions, what better for an understanding of these standards than to observe their connection with, and determination by, the non-cognitive, non-mental conditions with which they are associated? What better, in other words, than to crown sociology, especially the sociology of knowledge, as the new queen of the sciences?

There are grounds for believing that some of the contributors to the recent symposium, *Knowledge and Control*[1] are making such a claim and that, in the wake of their 'observations' about the social nature of meaning, the social relativity of beliefs and values, the unquestioned change in theoretical and conceptual frameworks through which we gain mastery over even our physical environment, they are throwing suspicion upon the standards of objectivity which teachers, in their respective disciplines, have implicitly believed in and which have sustained their belief in an educational ideal that transcends the institutional and political life in which they inevitably operate. And such a claim has immediate appeal to those students who can now see, in what is claimed to be an education, a sinister form of control by those who represent the system. Subject divisions, for instance, not only 'compartmentalise' and 'fragment' what is indivisible, not only 'reify' what is elusive and mental, they also reflect and perpetuate power groups and systems of control. An integrated curriculum (or code), on the other hand, would reflect the more fluid, personal, unified, and relative nature of our thinking, and would disconnect or at least weaken the control by others, exercised through the accepted disciplines of thinking. At a time when the traditional curriculum in both schools and universities is being questioned, the sociological contribution to the analysis of knowledge has been particularly timely.

There is need, however, to pause a little and to examine a little more precisely what the thesis is that is being put forward. Stated too simply it contains too many paradoxes for easy assimilation. Stated in all its complexity it does not appear quite so radical and devastating to the teacher's ideal as all that. First of all there is an important truth in the affirmed connection between agreed opinion and exercise of control and power. Sitting at the feet of the master is frequently a necessary prerequisite to donning the master's shoes; and all sorts of non-cognitive strategies can be observed for keeping the young disciple on the same cognitive path. Secondly, it is true that concepts are social constructs and would not exist, were it not for some form of social life in which they are 'created' and developed for particular purposes. (Whoever could think otherwise?) Thirdly, there are doubtless important differences in the way different cultures and epochs come to conceptualise, reflect upon, explain, appraise, and justify their experiences, and these differences are inevitably connected with different social conditions, interests, needs, etc. Fourthly, it is undoubtedly the case that most areas of thinking are problematic in the sense that the possibility of further enquiry, further examination should not be ruled out 'a priori'. But from such undisputed observations, what conclusions are being drawn by sociologists or what new perspective is being offered in our understanding of knowledge, its organisation, and its control and management? What consequences should teachers draw if these conclusions and this perspective are correct? Would there, as a result of what is argued, be reason for questioning the contents of their teaching, for reappraising the standards or objectivity implicit within their teaching programmes, and indeed for revising their very teaching role?

That something is being said about the nature of knowledge is clear enough, although the sociology of knowledge need not concern itself with these questions. Some sociologists (read, for example, Gurvitch's recent book *The Social Frameworks of Knowledge*) make a clear distinction between the empirical and theoretical studies of sociology and the 'critical' and epistemological questions of philosophy. Gurvitch even goes on to warn that 'it is essential for the development of the sociology of knowledge that it learn to remain modest and renounce inordinate pretensions'.[2] This is not an appeal for a strict division between philosophers and sociologists (each to their own trade, as it were) but rather for the recognition of the distinction between a philosophical and a sociological question. In pronouncing on the nature of knowledge the contributors to *Knowledge and Control* are of course raising and answering philosophical questions, but most fail to see what sort of questions they are raising, or what is involved in such procedures.

Bernstein, on the other hand, does seem a little clearer. His hypothesis is: 'How a society selects, classifies, distributes, transmits and evaluates the educational knowledge it considers to be public, reflects both the distribution of power and the principles of social control' (p. 47). Bernstein does not raise questions about the 'intrinsic logic of the various forms of public thought' but about the 'forms of their transmission'. Whatever the difficulties raised by the introduction of yet more labels into curriculum discourse – 'collective and integrated codes', 'weak and strong frames' – these are not necessarily of an epistemological kind and it is these latter, epistemological difficulties, with which I am chiefly concerned.

The general thesis implicit within the book that seems to raise important philosophical questions is as follows:

(a) Sociologists of education have *previously* been concerned with the social conditions in which learning takes place, and with the correlation between these conditions and the outcomes of learning; the learning processes themselves and the actual organisation of knowledge have not *previously* been the province of sociologists.

(b) This conception of sociology is too limited, sociology is able to explain either wholly or in part the actual processes of learning and the organisation of knowledge that we have in the curriculum.

(c) This explanation will be empirical, that is, it will be able to show how the organisation of knowledge is determined by certain specifiable social conditions.

(d) Such a theory about the sociology of knowledge has consequences for the conception we have of knowledge and its structure. In particular:

  (i) We do not 'know' the world as it *really* is, but only as mediated through the conceptual framework we have.

  (ii) This framework is a human construction, could have been otherwise, and is relative to such contingencies as particular social structures.

  (iii) The validity of arguments, the truth of statements, and the correct application of concepts to experience, therefore, are to be accepted and explained by reference to the legitimising authorities within a specifiable social group. Different groups could legitimise different standards of validity, truth and correctness. These are causally determined and in no sense absolutely so.

(iv) The understanding or the explanation therefore of the ways in which we structure our thought – the concepts we use, the types of argument we employ, the criteria of truth we refer to – lies solely in establishing the causal connections between these structures and certain social conditions. It would not be an objection to this thesis to say that there are *logical* as opposed to *causal* considerations in the explanation of these structures of thought, because what we accept as a logical connection is itself a structure of thought that can be empirically explained.

(v) As a further extension of this point, the distinction between being rational and being irrational is one that is relative to a particular social context, and therefore can be explained empirically. The 'rational' in our society is, (to quote), 'the dominant legitimising category' – a dogma which itself is open to enquiry.

(vi) As a further extension of this point the distinction between true and false is one that is relative to a particular social context. Thus the statement 'You ought not to steal' is true given certain moral norms, which themselves are explicable in terms of social conditions. There is no rationality therefore in the sense of an appeal to a universal and impersonal standard of truth.

If I have correctly understood the general thesis of these and likeminded sociologists, two broad areas of questions need to be raised before the connection they seek between 'knowledge' and 'control' is in fact made and therefore before teachers, quaking before the prospect of 'socio-historical relativism', need forgo their educational ideal and their instructive role. The first broad area concerns crucial points of clarification. (There are of course many detailed difficulties of clarity.) The second area contains philosophical difficulties that the authors seem unaware of. I shall begin with the questions of clarification.

Firstly, it is not clear how much is being subsumed under the sociological explanation given – whether it be the entire structure of knowledge or simply and in particular the normative or what could be called 'ideological' super-structure. The examples used tend to be statements of a normative kind or descriptions of social processes. And Berger and Luckmann extend the determining influence of society to the content of 'human idealism, with the exception of mathematics and part of the natural science.'[3] In other places, however, (and on occasions quite explicitly so) the analysis is extended to mathematics and scientific statements. But what is meant by saying that these are human constructs? Are they human constructs in *the same sense* as the legal apparatus is a human construct? If not what would be the difference between the two senses? This sort of distinction of course is crucial in clarifying what is meant by 'human construction', in determining the limits of man's constructive powers, and in understanding the various uses of 'objectivity'. But nowhere is it made.

The second point of clarification is whether such phrases as 'conditioned by', 'caused by', 'determined by', 'reflects' are intended to tell the whole story about the structure of knowledge, or only part of it, albeit a major part. Thus there is a trivial sense in which all concepts are social. That is, they embody rules for classifying and individuating experience, and to that extent are publicly accessible. Furthermore, the conceptual framework through which we think could have been different; the distinctions which are embodied in our language could have highlighted some features of experience which have been ignored, and ignored others which have been highlighted. One might say that there is no 'a priori' limit to the *number* of ways in which we might organise our experience. But to say this is *not* to say that there are *no* limits to how we might organise our experience. Thus, firstly, any conceptualising of experience would need to respect fairly basic rules of intelligibility – and one might see one major task of philosophy to be that of making these rules explicit. There is a point beyond which it would make no sense to ask if things could have been conceived otherwise – because one would not know what would count as an answer. For example, it would be inconceivable to organise experience outside a spatio-temporal framework of material objects. Identity and difference would seem to presuppose necessarily such a world. This is a line of argument that could be pressed much further. Secondly, the way in which we do come to discriminate must rest partly upon discriminable features of a relatively stable kind in our experience. Thus one may give a sociological account of why we come to make the distinctions we do; but there must be something about the world which makes these distinctions possible. That we distinguish between cats and dogs may be due to certain social conditions; that we *can* so distinguish has something to do with cats and dogs. The point of clarification therefore concerns the scope of the thesis. From the rather trivial points that all concepts are social and that all reality is mediated through concepts, is it being argued that reality is *nothing but* a social construction, and that there are no other limiting features either in the nature of thought (picked out by philosophy) or in the nature of reality?

Thirdly, there seems little doubt that in talking of the categories of thought being problematic and open to enquiry, these sociologists see the enquiry to be empirical, and the connection therefore between that which is to be explained (or is determined) and that which does the explaining (or determines) to be contingent. Given therefore that the structure of knowledge or consciousness is empirically explicable in terms of social conditions, difficulties arise about the nature of this explanation. What is to be explained is (in Schutz's words) 'social reality'. And the argument requires that, despite it being social reality rather than the world of nature that is being observed and generalised about, the essence of scientific theory is in no way affected, namely, the discovery of 'determinate relations between a set of variables, in terms of which . . . empirically ascertainable regularities can be explained'. There are serious difficulties here about the method of sociology, and the limitations of its pretension to be scientific in any way comparable with that of the natural sciences. In saying that 'x' is determined by 'y', is it meant that there is a causal relation between x and y that can be quantified in some way, and that can be verified? If so, x, the social conditions, will need to be so specified that they might constitute the data of empirical theory. If this is not the sort of explanation of x by y that is in mind, then the proponents of this view may well need to say what sort of empirical explanation it is.

Fourthly, the final point of clarification concerns the theoretical formulation of what is said about knowledge. Put briefly, it would seem that, if all knowledge is explicable in terms of the social conditions with which it is connected, then the claim that this is so might itself be determined by particular social conditions, namely, the institutional framework of certain sociologists with particular biographies from which it emanates. If so, one might ask, why should such a proposal be taken seriously by those who do not share (and on this account need not share) the criteria for valid argument accepted by these sociologists? Mannheim's solution to this problem (to the scepticism to which social and historical 'conditioning' leads) lay in finding 'a formula for translating the results of one (social perspective) into those of the other and to discover a common denominator for these varying perspectivistic insights'. But to talk of such a formula is of course to beg the question. What sense could be made of such a formula, since it too would be socially and historically conditioned?

There are many detailed criticisms that could be raised against the strong claim of the sociologists, in which *all* knowledge is determined by social conditions and in which therefore the differentiation of knowledge is seen to be but a reflection of the social distribution of power – arising from a 'negotiation' between different interests in a sort of power struggle. The general line of argument here would be towards preserving a concept of knowledge that is raised about the level of 'bargaining', and a concept of reality that is not open to *any* sort of definition. I shall therefore introduce difficulties of a fairly general nature.

Firstly, there are difficulties about the very conditions of intelligibility. In one obvious sense all concepts are social; the way in which we conceptualise things does change and is different in some degree from society to society; and to understand a language is to understanding 'a form of life'. Acceptance, however, of these points about concepts does not provide an adequate basis for the conclusions that 'all knowledge is relative', or that truth and validity are 'derived through certain relevances and legitimacies', or that 'these criteria of validity and truth . . . are themselves, in their persistence and change, open to socio-historical relativisation', or that the 'rules of the game change with a shift in interest', or that a critique of knowledge is necessarily a critique of producers of knowledge, or that the 'boundaries (between kinds of knowledge) are *only (sic)* human constructs and can, therefore, be broken'.

The reason I suggested earlier for denying such conclusions to follow from such premises was two-fold, namely, that, firstly in thinking at all there are some general grounds of intelligibility which must be pre-supposed and that, secondly, however great the number of ways in which we *could* conceptualise reality, these will still be limited by the limited features of a finite world on the basis of which discriminations are made and, of course, the limiting features of the person making the discriminations. With reference to the first reason, I pointed out how at least certain general categories of thought connected with the material world must be pre-supposed in order to raise significant questions. One might argue further that the categorical framework in which we address and argue with *persons,* attribute *motives* to them, detect their *intentions,* see them as having *feelings,* attribute *thought and deliberation,* interpret *meanings* (as opposed to observe behaviours) is one which is necessarily pre-supposed – however differently its conceptualisation might vary. Certain criteria of intelligibility must be presupposed for otherwise it would not be possible to recognise something as another's definition of reality. (Alternative definitions of reality presuppose some common understanding of 'reality'.)

Furthermore, where basic canons of rationality are treated as 'problematic' and 'open to enquiry', it is not possible to understand what such an enquiry might consist in. For example, if the principle of contradiction is 'problematic', it would not be possible to engage in an enquiry about it. Any enquiry presupposes that self-contradiction is unintelligible.

The criticism here, then, is that relativist theories, if not formulated in a careful and restricted manner, do raise serious logical problems, not least for the status of the theories themselves. It is necessary to keep distinct questions about the validity of human thought from questions about its genesis; otherwise thought itself becomes totally unintelligible.

To understand any particular state of consciousness in terms of the social context is to deny any explanation in terms of the logical connection between this state of consciousness and some prior state, that is, it denies that there is any development of thought that might be understood in terms of logic of the thought itself. For what seems to be a logical progression itself is to be empirically explained and thereby explained by factors extrinsic to the thought itself. Thus anyone who thinks hard

1. Pedagogy of the Oppressed

Paulo Freire

Source: Paulo Freire, *Pedagogy of the Oppressed,* Ch. 2 (Penguin Books, Harmondsworth, 1970).

Freire develops the contrast between two approaches to education: the banking *concept and the* problem-posing *concept.*

He argues that the former is an insult to human dignity. Students become 'depositories', they are seen as 'adjustable, manageable beings' who are therefore easily 'dominated'.

By contrast, the problem-posing concept respects the individuality of the student. 'Problem-solving education is revolutionary futurity. Hence it is prophetic (and, as such, hopeful), and so corresponds to the historical nature of man.'

The contrast between the approaches is related in particular to education in societies where the bulk of the people are impoverished and politically impotent.

A careful analysis of the teacher-student relationship at any level, inside or outside the school, reveals its fundamentally *narrative* character. This relationship involves a narrating Subject (the teacher) and patient, listening objects (the students). The contents, whether values or empirical dimensions of reality, tend in the process of being narrated to become lifeless and petrified. Education is suffering from narration sickness.

The teacher talks about reality as if it were motionless, static, compartmentalized and predictable. Or else he expounds on a topic completely alien to the existential experience of the students. His task is to 'fill' the students with the contents of his narration – contents which are detached from reality, disconnected from the totality that engendered them and could give them significance. Words are emptied of their concreteness and become a hollow, alienated and alienating verbosity.

The outstanding characteristic of this narrative education, then, is the sonority of words, not their transforming power. 'Four times four is sixteen; the capital of Pará is Belém.' The student records, memorizes and repeats these phrases without perceiving what four times four really means, or realizing the true significance of 'capital' in the affirmation 'the capital of Pará is Belém,' that is, what Belém means for Pará and what Pará means for Brazil.

Narration (with the teacher as narrator) leads the students to memorize mechanically the narrated content. Worse still, it turns them into 'containers', into receptacles to be filled by the teacher. The more completely he fills the receptacles, the better a teacher he is. The more

about a problem and then reaches a conclusion would be in e
believed that this conclusion resulted from the logic of this th
would be explicable in relation to the social condition with
might be empirically correlated.

On the wider level, progress in science would have to be und
not by the valid canons of scientific method which transcend the i
crasies of particular individuals and social contexts, but by re
solely to its genesis and social conditions. There is of course a super
plausible case to be made out for this – the 'particular direction s
has taken bears some relation to the social condition (the consequ
of the armament for space race, for example) and the very scien
theories propounded might bear some relation to non-scientific fact
in the suppression of evidence) but such considerations in no way af
the validity of what is said in science and the possibility of having o
results validated by other scientists, irrespective of their social conditi
Even Kuhn's revolutionary changes from paradigm (referred to by Esla
to illustrate the possibility of total reconstructions) do not stand up to to
close an examination. After all, the followers of Newton and the followe
of Einstein remained on speaking terms.

What then is to be concluded? It is true that the way we come to organise, select, value, and transmit our knowledge is *to some extent* explicable by reference to those who do the organising, selecting, valuing and transmitting. And *to that extent* there is a relationship between what and how we know and those who 'manage' and organise what and how we learn. Not only is it useful to be reminded of this: it would be even more useful to have this connection explored in all its detail and complexity. In such exploration uncomfortable doubts may be raised about the status and value of much that we believe. But the establishment of this connection, although it might stimulate important questions about knowledge, does not itself tell us what counts as knowledge or what constitutes a valid judgement or what is or is not meaningful – for those are not empirical questions. These are limits to what meanings can be negotiated or realities reconstructed, and there seems little ground for turning the classroom into either a market place or a building site.

NOTES

1. Young, M. F. D. (ed.), *Knowledge and Control,* Collier-Macmillan, 1971.
2. Gurvitch, G., *The Social Framework of Knowledge,* Blackwell, 1971, p. 11.
3. Berger, P. H., and Luckmann, T., *The Social Construction of Reality,* Allen Lane, The Penguin Press, 1966, whose influence one author at least acknowledges.

meekly the receptacles permit themselves to be filled, the better students they are.

Education thus becomes an act of depositing, in which the students are depositories and the teacher is the depositor. Instead of communicating, the teacher issues communiqués and 'makes deposits' which the students patiently receive, memorize, and repeat. This is the 'banking' concept of education, in which the scope of action allowed to the students extends only as far as receiving, filing, and storing the deposits. They do, it is true, have the opportunity to become collectors or cataloguers of the things they store. But in the last analysis, it is men themselves who are filed away through the lack of creativity, transformation, and knowledge in this (at best) misguided system. For apart from inquiry, apart from the praxis, men cannot be truly human. Knowledge emerges only through invention and re-invention, through the restless, impatient, continuing, hopeful inquiry men pursue in the world, with the world, and with each other.

In the banking concept of education, knowledge is a gift bestowed by those who consider themselves knowledgeable upon those whom they consider to know nothing. Projecting an absolute ignorance into others, a characteristic of the ideology of oppression, negates education and knowledge as processes of inquiry. The teacher presents himself to his students as their necessary opposite; by considering their ignorance absolute, he justifies his own existence. The students, alienated like the slave in the Hegelian dialectic, accept their ignorance as justifying the teacher's existence – but, unlike the slave, they never discover that they educate the teacher.

The *raison d'être* of libertarian education, on the other hand, lies in its drive towards reconciliation. Education must begin with the solution of the teacher-student contradiction, by reconciling the poles of the contradiction so that both are simultaneously teachers *and* students.

This solution is not (nor can it be) found in the banking concept. On the contrary, banking education maintains and even stimulates the contradiction through the following attitudes and practices, which mirror oppressive society as a whole:

1. The teacher teaches and the students are taught.
2. The teacher knows everything and the students know nothing.
3. The teacher thinks and the students are thought about.
4. The teacher talks and the students listen – meekly.
5. The teacher disciplines and the students are disciplined.
6. The teacher chooses and enforces his choice, and the students comply.
7. The teacher acts and the students have the illusion of acting through the action of the teacher.
8. The teacher chooses the programme content, and the students (who were not consulted) adapt to it.

9. The teacher confuses the authority of knowledge with his own professional authority, which he sets in opposition to the freedom of the students.
10. The teacher is the subject of the learning process, while the pupils are mere objects.

It is not surprising that the banking concept of education regards men as adaptable, manageable beings. The more students work at sorting the deposits entrusted to them, the less they develop the critical consciousness which would result from their intervention in the world as transformers of that world. The more completely they accept the passive role imposed on them, the more they tend to simply adapt to the world as it is and to the fragmented view of reality deposited in them.

The capacity of banking education to minimize or annul the students' creative power and to stimulate their credulity serves the interests of the oppressors, who care neither to have the world revealed nor to see it transformed. The oppressors use their 'humanitarianism' to preserve a profitable situation. Thus they react almost instinctively against any experiment in education which stimulates the critical faculties and is not content with a partial view of reality but is always seeking out the ties which link one point to another and one problem to another.

Indeed, the interest of the oppressors lie in 'changing the consciousness of the oppressed, not the situation which oppresses them' (Simone de Beauvoir in *La Pensée de Droite Aujourd'hui*) for the more the oppressed can be led to adapt to that situation, the more easily they can be dominated. To achieve this end, the oppressors use the banking concept of education in conjunction with a paternalistic social action apparatus, within which the oppressed receive the euphemistic title of 'welfare recipients'. They are treated as individual cases, as marginal men who deviate from the general configuration of a 'good, organized, and just' society. The oppressed are regarded as the pathology of the healthy society, which must therefore adjust these 'incompetent and lazy' folk to its own patterns by changing their mentality. These marginals need to be 'integrated', 'incorporated' into the healthy society that they have 'forsaken'.

The truth is, however, that the oppressed are not marginals, are not men living 'outside' society. They have always been inside – inside the structure which made them 'beings for others'. The solution is not to 'integrate' them into the structure of oppression, but to transform that structure so that they can become 'beings for themselves'. Such transformation, of course, would undermine the oppressors' purposes; hence their utilization of the banking concept of education to avoid the threat of student conscientization.

The banking approach to adult education, for example, will never propose to students that they consider reality critically. It will deal instead with such vital questions as whether Roger gave green grass to the goat, and insist upon the importance of learning that, on the contrary, Roger gave green grass to the rabbit. The 'humanism' of the banking approach masks the effort to turn men into automatons – the very negation of their ontological vocation to be more fully human.

Those who use the banking approach, knowingly or unknowingly (for there are innumerable well-intentioned bank-clerk teachers who do not realize that they are serving only to dehumanize), fail to perceive that the deposits themselves contain contradictions about reality. But, sooner or later, these contradictions may lead formerly passive students to turn against their domestication and the attempt to domesticate reality. They may discover through existential experience that their present way of life is irreconcilable with their vocation to become fully human. They may perceive through their relations with reality that reality is really a *process,* undergoing constant transformation. If men are searchers and their ontological vocation is humanization, sooner or later they may perceive the contradiction in which banking education seeks to maintain them, and then engage themselves in the struggle for their liberation.

But the humanist, revolutionary educator cannot wait for this possibility to materialize. From the outset, his efforts must coincide with those of the students to engage in critical thinking and the quest for mutual humanization. His efforts must be imbued with a profound trust in men and their creative power. To achieve this, he must be a partner of the students in his relations with them.

The banking concept does not admit to such a partnership – and necessarily so. To resolve the teacher-student contradiction, to exchange the role of depositor, prescriber, domesticator, for the role of student among students would be to undermine the power of oppression and to serve the cause of liberation.

Implicit in the banking concept is the assumption of a dichotomy between man and the world: man is merely *in* the world, not *with* the world or with others; man is spectator, not re-creator. In this view, man is not a conscious being (*corpo consciente*); he is rather the possessor of a consciousness; an empty 'mind' passively open to the reception of deposits of reality from the world outside. For example, my desk, my books, my coffee cup, all the objects before me – as bits of the world which surrounds me – would be 'inside' me, exactly as I am inside my study right now. This view makes no distinction between being accessible to consciousness and entering consciousness. The distinction, however, is essential: the objects which surround me are simply accessible to my consciousness, not located within it. I am aware of them, but they are not inside me.

It follows logically from the banking notion of consciousness that the educator's role is to regulate the way the world 'enters into' the students. His task is to organize a process which already happens spontaneously, to 'fill' the students by making deposits of information which he considers constitute true knowledge.[1] And since men 'receive' the world as passive entities, education should make them more passive still, and adapt them to the world. The educated man is the adapted man, because he is more 'fit' for the world. Translated into practice, this concept is well suited for the purposes of the oppressors, whose tranquillity rests on how well men fit the world the oppressors have created, and how little they question it.

The more completely the majority adapt to the purposes which the dominant minority prescribe for them (thereby depriving them of the right to their own purposes), the more easily the minority can continue to prescribe. The theory and practice of banking education serve this end quite efficiently. Verbalistic lessons, reading requirements,[2] the methods for evaluating 'knowledge', the distance between the teacher and the taught, the criteria for promotion: everything in this ready-to-wear approach serves to obviate thinking.

The bank-clerk educator does not realize that there is no true security in his hypertrophied role, that one must seek to live *with* others in solidarity. One cannot impose oneself, nor even merely co-exist with one's students. Solidarity requires true communication, and the concept by which such an educator is guided fears and proscribes communication.

Yet only through communication can human life hold meaning. The teacher's thinking is authenticated only by the authenticity of the students' thinking. The teacher cannot think for his students, nor can he impose his thought on them. Authentic thinking, thinking that is concerned about *reality*, does not take place in ivory-tower isolation, but only in communication. If it is true that thought has meaning only when generated by action upon the world, the subordination of students to teachers becomes impossible.

Because banking education begins with a false understanding of men as objects, it cannot promote the development of what Fromm, in *The Heart of Man*, calls 'biophily', but instead produces its opposite: 'necrophily'.

> While life is characterized by growth in a structured, functional manner, the necrophilous person loves all that does not grow, all that is mechanical. The necrophilous person is driven by the desire to transform the organic into the inorganic, to approach life mechanically, as if all living persons were things. . . . Memory, rather than experience; having, rather than being, is what counts. The necrophilous person can relate to an object – a flower or a person – only if he possesses it; hence a threat to his possession is a threat to himself; if he loses possession he loses contact with the world. . . . He loves control, and in the act of controlling he kills life.

Oppression – overwhelming control – is necrophilic; it is nourished by love of death, not life. The banking concept of education, which serves the interests of oppression, is also necrophilic. Based on a mechanistic, static, naturalistic, spatialized view of consciousness, it transforms students into receiving objects. It attempts to control thinking and action, leads men to adjust to the world, and inhibits their creative power.

When their efforts to act responsibly are frustrated, when they find themselves unable to use their faculties, men suffer. 'This suffering due to impotence is rooted in the very fact that the human equilibrium has been disturbed', says Fromm. But the inability to act which causes men's anguish also causes them to reject their impotence, by attempting

> . . . to restore [their] capacity to act. But can [they], and how? One way is to submit to and identify with a person or group having power. By this symbolic participation in another person's life, [men have] the illusion of acting, when in reality [they] only submit to and become a part of those who act.

Populist manifestations perhaps best exemplify this type of behaviour by the oppressed, who, by identifying with charismatic leaders, come to feel that they themselves are active and effective. The rebellion they express as they emerge in the historical process is motivated by that desire to act effectively. The dominant elites consider the remedy to be more domination and repression, carried out in the name of freedom, order and social peace (the peace of the elites, that is). Thus they can condemn – logically, from their point of view – 'the violence of a strike by workers and [can] call upon the state in the same breath to use violence in putting down the strike' (Niebuhr's *Moral Man and Immoral Society*).

Education as the exercise of domination stimulates the credulity of students, with the ideological intent (often not perceived by educators) of indoctrinating them to adapt to the world of oppression. This accusation is not made in the naïve hope that the dominant elites will thereby simply abandon the practice. Its objective is to call the attention of true humanists to the fact that they cannot use the methods of banking education in the pursuit of liberation, as they would only negate that pursuit itself. Nor may a revolutionary society inherit these methods from an oppressor society. The revolutionary society which practises banking education is either misguided or mistrustful of men. In either event, it is threatened by the spectre of reaction.

Unfortunately, those who espouse the cause of liberation are themselves surrounded and influenced by the climate which generates the banking concept, and often do not perceive its true significance or its dehumanizing power. Paradoxically, then, they utilize this very instrument of alienation in what they consider an effort to liberate. Indeed, some 'revolutionaries' brand as innocents, dreamers, or even reactionaries those who would challenge this educational practice. But one does not liberate men by alienating them. Authentic liberation – the process of humanization – is not another 'deposit' to be made in men. Liberation is a praxis: the action and reflection of men upon their world in order to transform it. Those truly committed to the cause of liberation can accept neither the mechanistic concept of consciousness as an empty vessel to be filled, nor the use of banking methods of domination (propaganda, slogans – deposits) in the name of liberation.

The truly committed must reject the banking concept in its entirety, adopting instead a concept of men as conscious beings, and consciousness as consciousness directed towards the world. They must abandon the educational goal of deposit-making and replace it with the posing of the problems of men in their relations with the world. 'Problem-posing' education, responding to the essence of consciousness – *intentionality* – rejects communiqués and embodies communication. It epitomizes the special characteristic of consciousness: being *conscious of,* not only as intent on objects but as turned in upon itself in a Jasperian 'split' – consciousness as consciousness *of* consciousness.

Liberating education consists in acts of cognition, not transferrals of information. It is a learning situation in which the cognizable object (far from being the end of the cognitive act) intermediates the cognitive actors – teacher on the one hand and students on the other. Accordingly, the practice of problem-posing education first of all demands a resolution of the teacher-student contradiction. Dialogical relations – indispensable to the capacity of cognitive actors to cooperate in perceiving the same cognizable object – are otherwise impossible.

Indeed, problem-posing education, breaking the vertical patterns characteristic of banking education, can fulfill its function of being the practice of freedom only if it can overcome the above contradiction. Through dialogue, the teacher-of-the-students and the students-of-the-teacher cease to exist and a new term emerges: teacher-student with students-teachers. The teacher is no longer merely the one-who-teaches, but one who is himself taught in dialogue with the students, who in their turn while being taught also teach. They become jointly responsible for a process in which all grow. In this process, arguments based on 'authority' are no longer valid; in order to function, authority must be *on the side of* freedom, not *against* it. Here, no one teaches another, nor is anyone self-taught. Men teach each other, mediated by the world, by the cognizable objects which in banking education are 'owned' by the teacher.

The banking concept (with its tendency to dichotomize everything) distinguishes two stages in the action of the educator. During the first, he cognizes a cognizable object while he prepares his lessons in his study or his laboratory; during the second, he expounds to his students on that object. The students are not called upon to know, but to memorize the contents narrated by the teacher. Nor do the students practise any act of cognition, since the object towards which the act should be directed is the property of the teacher rather than a medium evoking the critical reflection of both teacher and students. Hence in the name of the 'preservation of culture and knowledge' we have a system which achieves neither true knowledge nor true culture.

The problem-posing method does not dichotomize the activity of the teacher-student: he is not 'cognitive' at one point and 'narrative' at another. He is always 'cognitive', whether preparing a project or engaging in dialogue with the students. He does not regard cognizable objects as his private property, but as the object of reflection by himself and the students. In this way, the problem-posing educator constantly re-forms his reflections in the reflection of the students. The students – no longer docile listeners – are now critical co-investigators in dialogue with the teacher. The teacher presents the material to the students for their consideration, and re-examines his earlier considerations as the students express their own. The role of the problem-posing educators is to create, together with the students, the conditions under which knowledge at the level of the *doxa* is superseded by true knowledge, at the level of the *logos.*

Whereas banking education anaesthetizes and inhibits creative power, problem-posing education involves a constant unveiling of reality. The former attempts to maintain the submersion of consciousness; the latter strives for the *emergence of* consciousness and *critical intervention* in reality.

Students, as they are increasingly faced with problems relating to themselves in the world and with the world, will feel increasingly challenged and obliged to respond to that challenge. Because they apprehend the challenge as interrelated to other problems within a total context, not as a theoretical question, the resulting comprehension tends to be increasingly critical and thus constantly less alienated. Their response to the challenge evokes new challenges, followed by new understandings; and gradually the students come to regard themselves as committed.

Education as the practice of freedom – as opposed to education as the practice of domination – denies that man is abstract, isolated, independent, and unattached to the world; it also denies that the world exists as a reality apart from men. Authentic reflection considers neither abstract man nor the world without men, but men in their relations with the world. In these relations consciousness and world are simultaneous: consciousness neither precedes the world nor follows it. *'La conscience et le monde sont dormés d'un même coup; extérieur par essence ã la conscience, le monde est, par essence relatif ã elle'*, writes Sartre. In one of our culture circles in Chile, the group was discussing the anthropological concept of culture. In the midst of the discussion, a peasant who by banking standards was completely ignorant said: 'Now I see that without man there is no world.' When the educator responded: 'Let's say, for the sake of argument, that all the men on earth were to die, but that the earth itself remained, together with trees, birds, animals, rivers, seas, the stars . . . wouldn't all this be a world?' 'Oh no,' the peasant replied emphatically. 'There would be no one to say: "This is a world".'

The peasant wished to express the idea that there would be lacking the consciousness of the world which necessarily implies the world of consciousness. 'I' cannot exist without a 'not I'. In turn, the 'not I' depends on that existence. The world which brings consciousness into existence becomes the world *of* that consciousness. Hence the previously cited affirmation of Sartre: *'La conscience et le monde sont dormés d'un même coup.'*

As men, simultaneously reflecting on themselves and on the world, increase the scope of their perception, they begin to direct their observations towards previously inconspicuous phenomena. Husserl writes:

> In perception properly so-called, as an explicit awareness [*Gewahren*], I am turned towards the object, to the paper, for instance. I apprehend it as being this here and now. The apprehension is a singling out, every object having a background in experience. Around and about the paper lie books, pencils, ink-well and so forth, and these in a certain sense are also 'perceived', perceptually there, in the 'field of intuition'; but whilst I was turned towards the paper there was no turning in their direction, nor any apprehending of them, not even in a secondary sense. They appeared and yet were not singled out, were not posited on their own account. Every perception of a thing has such a zone of background intuitions or background awareness, if 'intuiting' already includes the state of being turned towards, and this also is a 'conscious experience', or more briefly a 'consciousness of' all indeed that in point of fact lies in the co-perceived objective background.

That which had existed objectively but had not been perceived in its deeper implications (if indeed it was perceived at all) begins to 'stand out', assuming the character of a problem and therefore of challenge. Thus, men begin to single out elements from their 'background awarenesses' and to reflect upon them. These elements are now objects of men's consideration, and, as such, objects of their action and cognition.

In problem-posing education, men develop their power to perceive critically *the way they exist* in the world *with which* and *in which* they find themselves; they come to see the world not as a static reality, but as a reality in process, in transformation. Although the dialectical relations of men with the world exist independently of how these relations are perceived (or whether or not they are perceived at all), it is also true that the form of action men adopt is to a large extent a function of how they perceive themselves in the world. Hence, the teacher-student and the students-teachers reflect simultaneously on themselves and the world without dichotomizing this reflection from action, and thus establish an authentic form of thought and action.

Once again, the two educational concepts and practices under analysis come into conflict. Banking education (for obvious reasons) attempts, by mythicizing reality, to conceal certain facts which explain the way men exist in the world; problem-posing education sets itself the task of de-mythologizing. Banking education resists dialogue; problem-posing education regards dialogue as indispensable to the act of cognition which unveils reality. Banking education treats students as objects of assistance; problem-posing education makes them critical thinkers. Banking education inhibits creativity and domesticates (although it cannot completely destroy) the *intentionality* of consciousness by isolating consciousness from the world, thereby denying men their ontological and historical vocation of becoming more fully human. Problem-posing education bases itself on creativity and stimulates true reflection and action upon reality, thereby responding to the vocation of men as beings who are authentic only when engaged in inquiry and creative transformation. In sum: banking theory and practice, as immobilizing and fixating forces, fail to acknowledge men as historical beings; problem-posing theory and practice take man's historicity as their starting point.

Problem-posing education affirms men as beings in the process of *becoming* – as unfinished, uncompleted beings in and with a likewise unfinished reality. Indeed, in contrast to other animals who are unfinished, but not historical, men know themselves to be unfinished; they are aware of their incompleteness. In this incompleteness and this awareness lie the very roots of education as an exclusively human manifestation. The unfinished character of men and the transformational character of reality necessitate that education be an ongoing activity.

Education is thus constantly remade in the praxis. In order to *be*, it must *become*. Its 'duration' (in the Bergsonian meaning of the word) is found in the interplay of the opposites *permanence* and *change*. The banking method emphasizes permanence and becomes reactionary; problem-posing education – which accepts neither a 'well-behaved' present nor a predetermined future – roots itself in the dynamic present and becomes revolutionary.

Problem-posing education is revolutionary futurity. Hence it is prophetic (and, as such, hopeful), and so corresponds to the historical nature of man. Thus, it affirms men as beings who transcend themselves, who move forward and look ahead, for whom immobility represents a fatal threat, for whom looking at the past must only be a means of understanding more clearly what and who they are so that they can more wisely build the future. Hence, it identifies with the movement which engages men as beings aware of their incompleteness – an historical movement which has its point of departure, its subjects and its objective.

The point of departure of the movement lies in men themselves. But since men do not exist apart from the world, apart from reality, the movement must begin with the men-world relationship. Accordingly, the point of departure must always be with men in the 'here and now', which constitutes the situation within which they are submerged, from which they emerge, and in which they intervene. Only by starting from this situation – which determines their perception of it – can they begin to move. To do this authentically they must perceive their state not as fated and unalterable, but merely as limiting – and therefore challenging.

Whereas the banking method directly or indirectly reinforces men's fatalistic perception of their situation, the problem-posing method presents this very situation to them as a problem. As the situation becomes the object of their cognition, the naïve or magical perception which produced their fatalism gives way to perception which is able to perceive itself as it perceives reality, and can thus be critically objective about that reality.

A deepened consciousness of their situation leads men to apprehend that situation as an historical reality susceptible of transformation. Resignation gives way to the drive for transformation and inquiry, over which men feel themselves in control. If men, as historical beings necessarily engaged with other men in a movement of inquiry, did not control that movement, it would be (and is) a violation of men's humanity. Any situation in which some men prevent others from engaging in the process of inquiry is one of violence. The means used are not important; to alienate men from their own decision-making is to change them into objects.

This movement of inquiry must be directed towards humanization – man's historical vocation. The pursuits of full humanity, however, cannot be carried out in isolation or individualism, but only in fellowship and solidarity; therefore it cannot unfold in the antagonistic relations between oppressors and oppressed. No one can be authentically human while he prevents others from being so. The attempt *to be more* human, individualistically, leads to *having more,* egotistically: a form of dehumanization. Not that it is not fundamental *to have* in order *to be* human. Precisely because it *is* necessary, some men's *having* must not be allowed to constitute an obstacle to others' *having*, to consolidate the power of the former to crush the latter.

Problem-posing education, as a humanist and liberating praxis, posits as fundamental that men subjected to domination must fight for their emancipation. To that end, it enables teachers and students to become subjects of the educational process by overcoming authoritarianism and an alienating intellectualism; it also enables men to overcome their false perception of reality. The world – no longer something to be described with deceptive words – becomes the object of that transforming action by men which results in their humanization.

Problem-posing education does not and cannot serve the interests of the oppressor. No oppressive order could permit the oppressed to begin to question: Why? While only a revolutionary society can carry out this education in systematic terms, the revolutionary leaders need not take full power before they can employ the method. In the revolutionary process, the leaders cannot utilize the banking method as an interim measure, justified on grounds of expediency, with the intention of *later* behaving in a genuinely revolutionary fashion. They must be revolutionary – that is to say, dialogical – from the outset.

NOTES

1. This concept corresponds to what Sartre calls the 'digestive' or 'nutritive' concept of education, in which knowledge is 'fed' by the teacher to the students to 'fill them out'. See Jean-Paul Sartre, 'Une idée fondamentale de la phénoménologie de Husserl: l'intentionalité', *Situations I.*
2. For example, some teachers specify in their reading lists that a book should be read from pages 10 to 15 – and do this to 'help' their students!

12. The Child and the Curriculum

John Dewey

Source: John Dewey: *Selected Educational Writings*, F. W. Garforth (ed.) (Heinemann, London, 1966).

There are two fundamental factors in education, Dewey states: the immature child on one hand, and on the other the accumulated knowledge and traditions of society embodied in the 'matured experience of the adult'; the educational process consists in the 'due interaction' between them.

But some educational processes can turn this interaction into opposition. Dewey argues that such opposition is unreal, and goes on to develop the argument that the child's 'present experience' and the stored experience of the past each contains the essential elements of the other, they are 'initial and final terms of one reality'. The content of the curriculum should assist in 'freeing the life process for its own most adequate fulfilment'.

Profound differences in theory are never gratuitous or invented. They grow out of conflicting elements in a genuine problem – a problem which is genuine just because the elements, taken as they stand, are conflicting. Any significant problem involves conditions that for the moment contradict each other. Solution comes only by getting away from the meaning of terms that is already fixed upon and coming to see the conditions from another point of view, and hence in a fresh light. But this reconstruction means travail of thought. Easier than thinking with surrender of already formed ideas and detachment from facts already learned, is just to stick by what is already said, looking about for something with which to buttress it against attack.

Thus sects arise; schools of opinion. Each selects that set of conditions that appeal to it; and then erects them into a complete and independent truth, instead of treating them as a factor in a problem, needing adjustment.

The fundamental factors in the educative process are an immature, undeveloped being; and certain social aims, meanings, values incarnate in the matured experience of the adult. The educative process is the due interaction of these forces. Such a conception of each in relation to the other as facilitates completest and freest interaction is the essence of educational theory.

But here comes the effort of thought. It is easier to see the conditions in their separateness, to insist upon one at the expense of the other, to make antagonists of them, than to discover a reality to which each belongs. The easy thing is to seize upon something in the nature of the child, or upon something in the developed consciousness of the adult, and insist upon *that* as the key to the whole problem. When this happens, a really serious practical problem – that of interaction – is transformed into an unreal, and hence insoluble, theoretic problem. Instead of seeing the educative steadily and as a whole, we see conflicting terms. We get the case of the child *vs.* the curriculum; of the individual nature *vs.* social culture. Below all other divisions in pedagogic opinion lies this opposition.

The child lives in a somewhat narrow world of personal contacts. Things hardly come within his experience unless they touch, intimately and obviously, his own well-being, or that of his family and friends. His world is a world of persons with their personal interests, rather than a realm of facts and laws. Not truth, in the sense of conformity to external fact, but affection and sympathy, is its keynote. As against this, the course of study met in the school presents material stretching back indefinitely in time, and extending outward indefinitely into space. The child is taken out of his familiar physical environment, hardly more than a square mile or so in area, into the wide world – yes, and even to the bounds of the solar system. His little span of personal memory and tradition is overlaid with the long centuries of the history of all peoples.

Again, the child's life is an integral, a total one. He passes quickly and readily from one topic to another, as from one spot to another, but is not conscious of transition or break. There is no conscious isolation, hardly conscious distinction. The things that occupy him are held together by the unity of the personal and social interests which his life carries along. Whatever is uppermost in his mind constitutes to him, for the time being, the whole universe. That universe is fluid and fluent; its contents dissolve and re-form with amazing rapidity. But, after all, it is the child's own world. It has the unity and completeness of his own life. He goes to school, and various studies divide and fractionize the world for him. Geography selects, it abstracts and analyzes one set of facts, and from one particular point of view. Arithmetic is another division, grammar another department, and so on indefinitely.

Again, in school each of these subjects is classified. Facts are torn away from their original place in experience and rearranged with reference to some general principle. Classification is not a matter of child experience; things do not come to the individual pigeon-holed. The vital ties of affection, the connecting bonds of activity, hold together the variety of his personal experiences. The adult mind is so familiar with the notion of logically ordered facts that it does not recognize – it cannot realize – the amount of separating and reformulating which the facts of direct experience have to undergo before they can appear as a 'study', or branch of learning. A principle, for the intellect, has had to be distinguished and defined; facts have had to be interpreted in relation to this principle, not as they are in themselves. They have had to be regathered about a new centre which is wholly abstract and ideal. All this means a development of a special intellectual interest. It means ability to view facts impartially and objectively; that is, without reference to their place and meaning in one's own experience. It means capacity to analyze and synthesize. It means highly matured intellectual habits and the command of a definite technique and apparatus of scientific inquiry. The studies as classified are the product, in a word, of the science of the ages, not of the experience of the child.

These apparent deviations and differences between child and curriculum might be almost indefinitely widened. But we have here sufficiently fundamental divergences: first, the narrow but personal world of the child against the impersonal but infinitely extended world of space and time; second, the unity, the single whole-heartedness of the child's life, and the specializations and divisions of the curriculum; third, an abstract principle of logical classification and arrangement, and the practical and emotional bonds of child life.

From these elements of conflict grow up different educational sects. One school fixes its attention upon the importance of the subject-matter of the curriculum as compared with the contents of the child's own experience. It is as if they said: Is life petty, narrow, and crude? Then studies reveal the great, wide universe with all its fullness and complexity of meaning. Is the life of the child egoistic, self-centred, impulsive? Then in these studies is found an objective universe of truth, law, and order. Is his experience confused, vague, uncertain, at the mercy of the moment's caprice and circumstance? Then studies introduce a world arranged on the basis of eternal and general truth; a world where all is measured and defined. Hence the moral: ignore and minimize the child's individual peculiarities, whims, and experiences. They are what we need to get away from. They are to be obscured or eliminated. As educators our work is precisely to substitute for these superficial and casual affairs stable and well-ordered realities; and these are found in studies and lessons.

Subdivide each topic into studies; each study into lessons; each lesson into specific facts and formulae. Let the child proceed step by step to master each one of these separate parts, and at last he will have covered the entire ground. The road which looks so long when viewed in its entirety, is easily travelled, considered as a series of particular steps. Thus emphasis is put upon the logical subdivisions and consecutions of the subject-matter. Problems of instruction are problems of procuring texts giving logical parts and sequences, and of presenting these portions in class in a similar definite and graded way. Subject-matter furnishes the end, and it determines method. The child is simply the immature being who is to be matured; he is the superficial being who is to be deepened; his is narrow experience which is to be widened. It is his to receive, to accept. His part is fulfilled when he is ductile and docile.

Not so, says the other sect. The child is the starting-point, the centre, and the end. His development, his growth, is the ideal. It alone furnishes the standard. To the growth of the child all studies are subservient; they are instruments valued as they serve the needs of growth. Personality, character is more than subject-matter. Not knowledge or information, but self-realization, is the goal. To possess all the world of knowledge and lose one's own self is as awful a fate in education as in religion. Moreover, subject-matter can never be got into the child from without. Learning is active. It involves reaching out of the mind. It involves organic assimilation starting from within. Literally, we must take our stand with the child and our departure from him. It is he and not the subject-matter which determines both quality and quantity of learning.

The only significant method is the method of the mind as it reaches out and assimilates. Subject-matter is but spiritual food, possible nutritive material. It cannot digest itself; it cannot of its own accord turn into bone and muscle and blood. The source of whatever is dead, mechanical, and formal in schools is found precisely in the subordination of the life and experience of the child to the curriculum. It is because of this that 'study' has become a synonym for what is irksome, and a lesson identical with a task.

This fundamental opposition of child and curriculum set up by these two modes of doctrine can be duplicated in a series of other terms. 'Discipline' is the watchword of those who magnify the course of study; 'interest' that of those who blazon 'The Child' upon their banner. The standpoint of the former is logical; that of the latter psychological. The first emphasises the necessity of adequate training and scholarship on the part of the teacher; the latter that of the need of sympathy with the child, and knowledge of his natural instincts. 'Guidance' and 'control' are the catchwords of one school; 'freedom and initiative' of the other. Law is asserted here; spontaneity proclaimed there. The old, the conservation of what has been achieved in the pain and the toil of the ages, is dear to the one; the new, change, progress, wins the affection of the other. Inertness and routine, chaos and anarchism, are accusations bandied back and forth. Neglect of the sacred authority of duty is charged by one side, only to be met by counter-charges of suppression of individuality through tyranical despotism.

Such oppositions are rarely carried to their logical conclusions. Common-sense recoils at the extreme character of these results. They are left to theorists, while common-sense vibrates back and forward in a maze of inconsistent compromise. The need of getting theory and practical common-sense into closer connection suggests a return to our original thesis: that we have here conditions which are necessarily related to each other in the educative process, since this is precisely one of interaction and adjustment.

What, then, is the problem? It is just to get rid of the prejudicial notion that there is some gap in kind (as distinct from degree) between the child's experience and the various forms of subject-matter that make up the course of study. From the side of the child, it is a question of seeing how his experience already contains within itself elements – facts and truths – of just the same sort as those entering into the formulated study; and, what is of more importance, of how it contains within itself the attitudes, the motives, and the interests which have operated in developing and organizing the subject-matter to the plane which it now occupies. From the side of the studies, it is a question of interpreting them as outgrowths of forces operating in the child's life, and of discovering the steps that intervene between the child's present experience and their richer maturity.

Abandon the notion of subject-matter as something fixed and ready-made in itself, outside the child's experience; cease thinking of the child's experience as also something hard and fast; see it as something fluent, embryonic, vital; and we realize that the child and the curriculum are simply two limits which define a single process. Just as two points define a straight line, so the present standpoint of the child and the facts and truths of studies define instruction. It is continuous reconstruction, moving from the child's present experience out into that represented by the organized bodies of truth that we call studies.

On the face of it, the various studies, arithmetic, geography, language, botany, etc., are themselves experience – they are that of the race. They embody the cumulative outcome of the efforts, the strivings, and successes of the human race generation after generation. They present this, not as a mere accumulation, not as a miscellaneous heap of separate bits of experience, but in some organized and systematized way – that is, as reflectively formulated.

Hence, the facts and truths that enter into the child's present experience, and those contained in the subject-matter of studies, are the initial and final terms of one reality. To oppose one to the other is to oppose the infancy and maturity of the same growing life; it is to set the moving tendency and the final result of the same process over against each other; it is to hold that the nature and the destiny of the child war with each other.

If such be the case, the problem of the relation of the child and the curriculum presents itself in this guise: Of what use, educationally speaking, is it to be able to see the end in the beginning? How does it assist us in dealing with the early stages of growth to be able to anticipate its later phases? The studies, as we have agreed, represent the possibilities of development inherent in the child's immediate crude experience. But, after all, they are not parts of that present and immediate life. Why, then, or how, make account of them?

Asking such a question suggests its own answer. To see the outcome is to know in what direction the present experience is moving, provided it move normally and soundly. The far-away point, which is of no significance to us simply as far away, becomes of huge importance the moment we take it as defining a present direction of movement. Taken in this way it is no remote and distant result to be achieved, but a guiding method in dealing with the present. The systematized and defined experience of the adult mind, in other words, is of value to us in interpreting the child's life as it immediately shows itself, and in passing on to guidance or direction.

Let us look for a moment at these two ideas: interpretation and guidance. The child's present experience is in no way self-explanatory. It is not final, but transitional. It is nothing complete in itself, but just a sign or index of certain growth-tendencies. As long as we confine our gaze to what the child here and now puts forth, we are confused and misled. We cannot read its meaning. Extreme depreciations of the child morally and intellectually, and sentimental idealizations of him, have their root in a common fallacy. Both spring from taking stages of a growth or movement as something cut off and fixed. The first fails to see the promise contained in feelings and deeds which, taken by themselves, are unpromising and repellent; the second fails to see that even the most pleasing and beautiful exhibitions are but signs, and that they begin to spoil and rot the moment they are treated as achievements.

What we need is something which will enable us to interpret, to appraise, the elements in the child's present puttings forth and fallings away, his exhibitions of power and weakness, in the light of some larger growth-process in which they have their place. Only in this way can we discriminate. If we isolate the child's present inclinations, purposes, and experiences from the place they occupy and the part they have to perform in a developing experience, all stand upon the same level; all alike are equally good and equally bad. But in the movement of life different elements stand upon different planes of value. Some of the child's deeds are symptoms of a waning tendency; they are survivals in functioning of an organ which has done its part and is passing out of vital use. To give positive attention to such qualities is to arrest development upon a lower level. It is systematically to maintain a rudimentary phase of growth. Other activities are signs of a culminating power and interest; to them applies the maxim of striking while the iron is hot. As regards them, it is perhaps a matter of now or never. Selected, utlized, emphasized, they may mark a turning-point for good in the child's whole career; neglected, an opportunity goes, never to be recalled. Other acts and feelings are prophetic; they represent the dawning of flickering light that will shine steadily only in the far future. As regards them there is little at present to do but give them fair and full chance, waiting for the future for definite direction.

Just as, upon the whole, it was the weakness of the 'old education' that it made invidious comparisons between the immaturity of the child and the maturity of the adult, regarding the former as something to be got away from as soon as possible and as much as possible; so it is the danger of the 'new education' that it regards the child's present powers and interests as something finally significant in themselves. In truth, his learnings and achievements are fluid and moving. They change from day to day and hour to hour.

It will do harm if child-study leave in the popular mind the impression that a child of a given age has a positive equipment of purposes and interests to be cultivated just as they stand. Interests in reality are but attitudes towards possible experiences; they are not achievements; their worth is in the leverage they afford, not in the accomplishment they represent. To take the phenomena presented at a given age as in any way self-explanatory or self-contained is inevitably to result in indulgence and spoiling. Any power, whether of child or adult, is indulged when it is taken on its given and present level in consciousness. Its genuine meaning is in the propulsion it affords towards a higher level. It is just something to do with. Appealing to the interest upon the present plane means excitation; it means playing with a power so as continually to stir it up without directing it towards definite achievement. Continuous initiation, continuous starting of activities that do not arrive, is, for all practical purposes, as bad as the continual repression of initiative in conformity with supposed interests of some more perfect thought or will. It is as if the child were forever tasting and never eating; always having his palate tickled upon the emotional side, but never getting the organic satisfaction that comes only with the digestion of food and transformation of it into working power.

As against such a view, the subject-matter of science and history and art serves to reveal the real child to us. We do not know the meaning either of his tendencies or his performances excepting as we take them as germinating seed, or opening bud, of some fruit to be borne. The whole world of visual nature is all too small an answer to the problem of the meaning of the child's instinct for light and form. The entire science of physics is none too much to interpret adequately to us what is involved in some simple demand of the child for explanation of some casual change that has attracted his attention. The art of Rafael or of Corot is none too much to enable us to value the impulses stirring in the child when he draws and daubs.

So much for the use of the subject-matter in interpretation. Its further employment in direction or guidance is but an expansion of the same thought. To interpret the fact is to see it in its vital movement, to see it in its relation to growth. But to view it as a part of a normal growth is to secure the basis for guiding it. Guidance is not external imposition. *It is freeing the life-process for its own most adequate fulfilment.* What was said about disregard of the child's present experience because of its remoteness from mature experience; and to the sentimental idealization of the child's naïve caprices and performances, may be repeated here with slightly altered phrase. There are those who see no alternative between forcing the child from without, or leaving him entirely alone. Seeing no alternative, some choose one mode, some another. Both fall into the same fundamental error. Both fail to see that development is a definite process, having its own law which can be fulfilled only when adequate and normal conditions are provided. Really to interpret the child's present crude impulses in counting, measuring, and arranging things in rhythmic series, involves mathematical scholarship – a knowledge of the mathematical formulae and relations which have, in the history of the race, grown out of just such crude beginnings. To see the whole history of development which intervenes between these two terms is simply to see what step the child needs to take just here and now; to what use he needs to put his blind impulse in order that it may get clarity and gain force.

If, once more, the 'old education' tended to ignore the dynamic quality, the developing force inherent in the child's present experience, and therefore to assume that direction and control were just matters of arbitrarily putting the child in a given path and compelling him to walk there, the 'new education' is in danger of taking the idea of development in altogether too formal and empty a way. The child is expected to 'develop' this or that fact or truth out of his own mind. He is told to think things out for himself, without being supplied any of the environing conditions which are requisite to start and guide thought. Nothing can be developed from nothing; nothing but the crude can be developed out of the crude – and this is what surely happens when we throw the child back upon his achieved self as a finality, and invite him to spin new truths of nature or of conduct out of that. It is certainly as futile to expect a child to evolve a universe out of his own mere mind as it is for a philosopher to attempt that task. Development does not mean just getting something out of the mind. It is a development of experience and into experience that is really wanted. And this is impossible save as just that educative medium is provided which will enable the powers and interests that have been selected as valuable to function. They must operate, and how they operate will depend almost entirely upon the stimuli which surround them, and the material upon which they exercise themselves. The problem of direction is thus the problem of selecting appropriate stimuli for instincts and impulses which it is desired to employ in the gaining of new experience. What new experiences are desirable, and thus what stimuli are needed it is impossible to tell except as there is some comprehension of the development which is aimed at; except, in a word, as the adult knowledge is drawn upon as revealing the possible career open to the child.

It may be of use to distinguish and to relate to each other the logical and the psychological aspects of experience – the former standing for subject-matter in itself, the latter for it in relation to the child. A psychological statement of experience follows its actual growth; it is historic; it notes steps actually taken, the uncertain and tortuous, as well as the efficient and successful. The logical point of view, on the other hand, assumes that the development has reached a certain positive stage of fulfilment. It neglects the process and considers the outcome. It summarizes and arranges, and thus separates the achieved results from the actual steps by which they were forthcoming in the first instance. We may compare the difference between the logical and the psychological to the difference between the notes which an explorer makes in a new country, blazing a trail and finding his way along as best he may, and the finished map that is constructed after the country has been thoroughly explored. The two are mutually dependent. Without the more or less accidental and devious paths traced by the explorer there would be no facts which could be utilized in the making of the complete and related chart. But no one would get the benefit of the explorer's trip if it was not compared and checked up with similar wanderings undertaken by others; unless the new geographical facts learned, the streams crossed, the mountains climbed, etc., were viewed, not as mere incidents in the journey of the particular traveller, but (quite apart from the individual explorer's life) in relation to other similar facts already known. The map orders individual experiences, connecting them with one another irrespective of the local and temporal circumstances and accidents of their original discovery.

Of what use is this formulated statement of experience? Of what use is the map?

Well, we may first tell what the map is not. The map is not a substitute for a personal experience. The map does not take the place of an actual journey. The logically formulated material of a science or branch of learning, of a study, is no substitute for the having of individual experiences. The mathematical formula for a falling body does not take the place of personal contact and immediate individual experience with the falling thing. But the map, a summary, an arranged and orderly view of previous experiences, serves as a guide to future experience; it gives direction; it facilitates control; it economizes effort, preventing useless wandering, and pointing out the paths which lead most quickly and most certainly to a desired result. Through the map every new traveller may get for his own journey the benefits of the results of others' explorations without the waste of energy and loss of time involved in their wanderings – wanderings which he himself would be obliged to repeat were it not for just the assistance of the objective and generalized record of their performances. That which we call a science of study puts the net product of past experience in the form which makes it most available for the future. It represents a capitalization which may at once be turned to interest. It economizes the workings of the mind in every way. Memory is less taxed because the facts are grouped together about some common principle, instead of being connected solely with the varying incidents of their original discovery. Observation is assisted; we know what to look for and where to look. It is the difference between looking for a needle in a haystack, and searching for a given paper in a well-arranged cabinet. Reasoning is directed, because there is a certain general path or line laid out along which ideas naturally march, instead of moving from one chance association to another.

There is, then, nothing final about a logical rendering of experience. Its value is not contained in itself; its significance is that of standpoint, outlook, method. It intervenes between the more casual, tentative, and roundabout experiences of the past, and more controlled and orderly experiences of the future. It gives past experience in that net form which renders it most available and most significant, most fecund for future experience. The abstractions, generalizations, and classifications which it introduces all have prospective meaning.

The formulated result is then not to be opposed to the process of growth. The logical is not set over against the psychological. The surveyed and arranged result occupies a critical position in the process of growth. It marks a turning-point. It shows how we may get the benefit of past effort in controlling future endeavour. In the largest sense the logical standpoint is itself psychological; it has its meaning as a point in the development of experience, and its justification is in its functioning in the future growth which it ensures.

Hence the need of reinstating into experience the subject-matter of the studies, or branches of learning. It must be restored to the experience from which it has been abstracted. It needs to be *psychologized*; turned over, translated into the immediate and individual experiencing within which it has its origin and significance.

Every study or subject thus has two aspects; one for the scientist as a scientist; the other for the teacher as a teacher. These two aspects are in no sense opposed or conflicting. But neither are they immediately identical. For the scientist, the subject-matter represents simply a given body of truth to be employed in locating new problems, instituting new researches, and carrying them through to a verified outcome. To him the subject-matter of the science is self-contained. He refers various portions of it to each other; he connects new facts with it. He is not, as a scientist, called upon to travel outside its particular bounds; if he does, it is only to get more facts of the same general sort. The problem of the teacher is a different one. As a teacher he is not concerned with adding new facts to the science he teaches; in propounding new hypotheses or in verifying them. He is concerned with the subject-matter of the science as *representing a given stage and phase of the development of experience.* His problem is that of inducing a vital and personal experiencing. Hence, what concerns him, as teacher, is the ways in which that subject may become a part of experience; what there is in the child's present that is usable with reference to it; how such elements are to be used; how his own knowledge of the subject-matter may assist in interpreting the child's needs and doings, and determine the medium in which the child should be placed in order that his growth may be properly directed. He is concerned, not with the subject-matter as such, but with the subject-matter as a related factor in a total and growing experience. Thus to see it is to psychologize it.

It is the failure to keep in mind the double aspect of subject-matter which causes the curriculum and child to be set over against each other as described in our early pages. The subject-matter, just as it is for the scientist, has no direct relationship to the child's present experience. It stands outside of it. The danger here is not a merely theoretical one. We are practically threatened on all sides. Text-book and teacher vie with each other in presenting to the child the subject-matter as it stands to the specialist. Such modification and revision as it undergoes are a mere elimination of certain scientific difficulties, and the general reduction to a lower intellectual level. The material is not translated into life-terms, but is directly offered as a substitute for, or an external annex to, the child's present life.

Three typical evils result: In the first place, the lack of any organic connection with what the child has already seen and felt and loved makes the material purely formal and symbolic. There is a sense in which it is impossible to value too highly the formal and the symbolic. The genuine form, the real symbol, serve as methods in the holding and discovery of truth. They are tools by which the individual pushes out most surely and widely into unexplored areas. They are means by which he brings to bear whatever of reality he has succeeded in gaining in past searchings. But this happens only when the symbol really symbolizes – when it stands for and sums up in shorthand actual experiences which the individual has already gone through. A symbol which is induced from without, which has not been led up to in preliminary activities, is, as we say, a *bare* or *mere* symbol; it is dead and barren. Now, any fact, whether of arithmetic or geography, or grammar, which is not led up to and into out of something which has previously occupied a significant position in the child's life for its own sake, is forced into this position. It is not a reality, but just the sign of a reality which *might* be experienced if certain conditions were fulfilled. But the abrupt presentation of the fact as something known by others, and requiring only to be studied and learned by the child, rules out such conditions of fulfilment. It condemns the fact to be a hieroglyph: it would mean something if one only had the key. The clue being lacking, it remains an idle curiosity, to fret and obstruct the mind, a dead weight to burden it.

The second evil in this external presentation is lack of motivation. There are not only no facts or truths which have been previously felt as such with which to appropriate and assimilate the new, but there is no craving, no need, no demand. When the subject-matter has been psychologized, that is, viewed as an outgrowth of present tendencies and activities, it is easy to locate in the present some obstacle, intellectual, practical, or ethical, which can be handled more adequately if the truth in question be mastered. This need supplies motive for the learning. An end which is the child's own carries him on to possess the means of its accomplishment. But when material is directly supplied in the form of a lesson to be learned as a lesson, the connecting links of need and aim are conspicuous for their absence. What we mean by the mechanical and dead in instruction is a result of this lack of motivation. The organic and vital mean interaction – they mean play of mental demand and material supply.

The third evil is that even the most scientific matter, arranged in most logical fashion, loses this quality, when presented in external, ready-made fashion by the time it gets to the child. It has to undergo some modification in order to shut out some phases too hard to grasp, and to reduce some of the attendant difficulties. What happens? Those things which are most significant to the scientific man, and most valuable in the logic of actual inquiry and classification, drop out. The really thought-provoking character is obscured, and the organizing function disappears. Or, as we commonly say, the child's reasoning powers, the faculty of abstraction and generalization, are not adequately developed. So the subject-matter is evacuated of its logical value, and, though it is what it is only from the logical standpoint, is presented as stuff only for 'memory'. This is the contradiction: the child gets the advantage neither of the adult logical formulation, nor of his own native competencies of apprehension and response. Hence the logic of the child is hampered and mortified, and we are almost fortunate if he does not get actual non-science, flat and commonplace residua of what was gaining scientific vitality a generation or two ago – degenerate reminiscence of what someone else once formulated on the basis of the experience that some further person had, once upon a time, experienced.

The train of evils does not cease. It is all too common for opposed erroneous theories to play straight into each other's hands. Psychological considerations may be slurred or shoved one side; they cannot be crowded out. Put out of the door, they come back through the window. Somehow and somewhere motive must be appealed to, connection must be established between the mind and its material. There is no question of getting along without this bond of connection; the only question is whether it be such as grows out of the material itself in relation to the mind, or be imported and hitched on from some outside source. If the subject-matter of the lessons be such as to have an appropriate place within the expanding consciousness of the child, if it grows out of his own past doings, thinkings, and sufferings, and grows into application in further achievements and receptivities, then no device or trick of method has to be resorted to in order to enlist 'interest'. The psychologized *is* of interest – that is, it is placed in the whole of conscious life so that it shares the worth of that life. But the externally presented material, conceived and generated in standpoints and attitudes remote from the child, and developed in motives alien to him, has no such place of its own. Hence the recourse to adventitious leverage to push it in, to factitious drill to drive it in, to artificial bribe to lure it in.

Three aspects of this recourse to outside ways for giving the subject-matter some psychological meaning may be worth mentioning. Familiarity breeds contempt, but also it breeds something like affection. We get used to the chains we wear, and we miss them when removed. 'Tis an old story that through custom we finally embrace what at first wore a hideous mien. Unpleasant, because meaningless, activities may get agreeable if long enough persisted in. *It is possible for the mind to develop interest in a routine or mechanical procedure, if conditions are continually supplied which demand that mode of operation and preclude any other sort.* I frequently hear dulling devices and empty exercises defended and extolled because 'the children take such an "interest" in them'. Yes, that is the worst of it; the mind, shut out from worthy employ and missing the taste of adequate performance, comes down to the level of that which is left to it to know and do, and perforce takes an interest in a cabined and cramped experience. To find satisfaction in its own exercise is the normal law of mind, and if large and meaningful business for the mind be denied, it tries to content itself with the formal movements that remain to it – and too often succeeds, save in those cases of more intense activity which cannot accommodate themselves, and that make up the unruly and *declassé* of our school product. An interest in the formal apprehension of symbols and in their memorized reproduction becomes in many pupils a substitute for the original and vital interest in reality; and all because, the subject-matter of the course of study being out of relation to the concrete mind of the individual, some substitute bond to hold it in some kind of working relation to the mind must be discovered and elaborated.

The second substitute for living motivation in the subject-matter is that of contrast-effects; the material of the lesson is rendered interesting, if not in itself, at least in contrast with some alternative experience. To learn the lesson is more interesting than to take a scolding, be held up to general ridicule, stay after school, receive degradingly low marks, or fail to be promoted. And very much of what goes by the name of 'discipline', and prides itself upon opposing the doctrines of a soft pedagogy and upon upholding the banner of effort and duty, is nothing more or less than just this appeal to 'interest' in its obverse aspect – to fear, to dislike of various kinds of physical, social, and personal pain. The subject-matter does not appeal; it cannot appeal; it lacks origin and bearing in a growing experience. So the appeal is to the thousand and one outside and irrelevant agencies which may serve to throw, by sheer rebuff and rebound, the mind back upon the material from which it is constantly wandering.

Human nature being what it is, however, it tends to seek its motivation in the agreeable rather than in the disagreeable, in direct pleasure rather than in alternative pain. And so has come up the modern theory and practice of the 'interesting', in the false sense of that term. The material is still left; so far as its own characteristics are concerned, just material externally selected and formulated. It is still just so much geography and arithmetic and grammar study; not so much potentiality of child-experience with regard to language, earth and numbered and measured reality. Hence the difficulty of bringing the mind to bear upon it; hence its repulsiveness; the tendency for attention to wander; for other acts and images to crowd in and expel the lesson. The legitimate way out is to transform the material; to psychologize it – that is, once more, to take it and to develop it within the range and scope of the child's life. But it is easier and simpler to leave it as it is, and then by trick of method to *arouse* interest, to *make* it *interesting;* to cover it with sugar-coating; to conceal its barrenness by intermediate and unrelated material; and finally, as it were, to get the child to swallow and digest the unpalatable morsel while he is enjoying tasting something quite different. But alas for the analogy! Mental assimilation is a matter of consciousness; and if the attention has not been playing upon the actual material, that has not been apprehended, nor worked into the faculty.

How, then, stands the case of Child *vs.* Curriculum? What shall the verdict be? The radical fallacy in the original pleadings with which we set out is the supposition that we have no choice save either to leave the child to his own unguided spontaneity or to inspire direction upon him from without. Action is response; it is adaptation, adjustment. There is no such thing as sheer self-activity possible – because all activity takes place in a medium, in a situation, and with reference to its conditions. But, again, no such thing as imposition of truth from without, as insertion of truth from without, is possible. All depends upon the activity which the mind itself undergoes in responding to what is presented from without. Now, the value of the formulated wealth of knowledge that makes up the course of study is that it may enable the educator *to determine the environment of the child*, and thus by indirection to direct. Its primary value, its primary indication, is for the teacher, not for the child. It says to the teacher: Such and such are the capacities, the fulfilments, in truth and beauty and behaviour, open to these children. Now see to it that day by day the conditions are such that *their own activities* move inevitably in this direction, towards such culmination of themselves. Let the child's nature fulfil its own destiny, revealed to you in whatever of science and art and industry the world now holds its own.

The case is of Child. It is his present powers which are to assert themselves; his present capacities which are to be exercised; his present attitudes which are to be realized. But save as the teacher knows, knows wisely and thoroughly, the race-expression which is embodied in that thing we call the Curriculum, the teacher knows neither what the present power, capacity, or attitude is, nor yet how it is to be asserted, exercised, and realized.

13. Realms of Meaning

P. H. Phenix

Source: P. H. Phenix, *Realms of Meaning* (McGraw-Hill, New York, 1964), Ch. 1.

Phenix argues that a unitary philosophy of curriculum is needed if the individual is to attain an integrated outlook on life. Such a philosophy, he believes, can be developed from the notion that human beings are essentially creatures who have the power to experience meanings. General education is the process of engendering essential meanings.

He goes on to analyse six possible 'realms of meaning' and to indicate the significance of this analysis for curriculum design.

It is not easy to sustain a sense of the whole. Many a person pursues his own limited calling with scarcely a thought for his place in the total drama of civilized endeavor. While he may have a vague notion of the larger context in which his contribution is made, he may never engage in any sustained study and reflection about his relation to the entire pattern of civilization.

This limitation of outlook is evident even in education. All too commonly the teacher teaches a particular subject or unit within a subject without any reference to its relationships to other components of the curriculum. Similarly, the student may study one subject after another with no idea of what his growing fund of knowledge and skill might contribute to an integrated way of life. Students and teachers alike are prone to take the curriculum as they find it, as a traditional sequence of separate elements, without ever inquiring into the comprehensive pattern within which the constituent parts are located.

Since education is the means of perpetuating culture from generation to generation, it is natural that the partiality of outlook endemic in the culture generally would be found also in education. Yet, this consequence need not follow. Indeed, the special office of education is to widen one's view of life, to deepen insight into relationships, and to counteract the provincialism of customary existence – in short, to engender an integrated outlook.

If this integral perspective is to be attained, a philosophy of the curriculum is necessary. By such a philosophy is meant a critically examined, coherent system of ideas by which all the constituent parts of the course of instruction are identified and ordered.

A unitary philosophy of the curriculum is important for many reasons, among which the following four may be cited: First, comprehensive outlook is necessary for all intelligent decisions about what shall be included and excluded from the course of study. If one subject is to be chosen instead of another, it is important to know how the one differs from the other and why the one is to be preferred to the other as a constituent in the complete pattern of the learner's experience and character.

Second, because a person is essentially an organized totality and not just a collection of separate parts, the curriculum ought to have a corresponding organic quality. Since it is one and the same person who undergoes each of the successive experiences in his course of study, the plan of study can best contribute to the person's growth if it is governed by the goal of wholeness for the human being.

Third, society, as well as individual persons, depends upon principles of community; corporate life, like the life of each individual, requires some overall plan. A curriculum planned as a comprehensive design for learning contributes a basis for the growth of community, while an atomized program of studies engenders disintegration in the life of society.

Fourth, a comprehensive concept of the structure of learning gives added significance to each of the component segments of the curriculum. The value of any subject is enhanced by an understanding of its relationship with other subjects, and its distinctive features are best comprehended in the light of its similarities and contrasts with other subjects.

The purpose of the present work is to sketch a view of the curriculum for general education by showing how the desirable scope, content, and arrangement of studies may be derived from certain fundamental considerations about human nature and knowledge. It will be shown that the controlling idea of general education, imparting unity to the pattern of studies, emerges from a philosophy of man and his ways of knowing.

The main line of argument may be summarized as follows:

Human beings are essentially creatures who have the power to experience *meanings*. Distinctively human existence consists in a pattern of meanings. Furthermore, *general education is the process of engendering essential meanings.*

Unfortunately, the pathway to the fulfillment of meaning is never smooth. The human situation is such that mankind is always threatened by forces that destroy meaning. Values, purposes, and understandings are fragile achievements and give way all too readily to attitudes of futility, frustration, and doubt. Meaning is thus lost in an abyss of meaninglessness.

The perennial threat to meaning is intensified under the conditions of modern industrial civilization. Four contributing factors deserve special emphasis. The first is the spirit of criticism and skepticism. This spirit is part of the scientific heritage, but it has also tended to bring the validity of meanings into question. The second factor is the pervasive depersonalization and fragmentation of life caused by the extreme specialization of a complex, interdependent society. The third factor is the sheer mass of cultural products, especially knowledge, which modern man is required to assimilate. The fourth factor is the rapid rate of change in the conditions of life, resulting in a pervasive feeling of impermanence and insecurity.

Since the object of general education is to lead to the fulfillment of human life through the enlargement and deepening of meaning, the modern curriculum should be designed with particular attention to these sources of meaninglessness in contemporary life. That is to say, the curriculum should be planned so as to counteract destructive skepticism, depersonalization and fragmentation, overabundance, and transience.

If education is to be regarded as grounded in the search for meaning, the primary goal of a philosophy of the curriculum is to analyze the nature of meaning. Meaningful experience is of many kinds; there is no single quality that may be designated as the one essence of meaning. Accordingly, we should speak not of meaning as such, but meanings, or of the *realms of meaning.* Hence, a philosophy of the curriculum requires a mapping of the realms of meaning, one in which the various possibilities of significant experience are charted and the various domains of meaning are distinguished and correlated.

Six fundamental patterns of meaning emerge from the analysis of the possible distinctive modes of human understanding. These six patterns may be designated respectively as *symbolics, empirics, esthetics, synnoetics, ethics,* and *synoptics.*

Each realm of meaning and each of its constituent subrealms may be described by reference to its typical methods, leading ideas, and characteristic structures. These features may be exhibited both in their uniqueness for each realm or subrealm and in their relationships and continuities with the other types of meaning. Leaving the details to be elaborated in subsequent chapters, the six realms can be broadly characterized as follows:

The first realm, *symbolics,* comprises ordinary language, mathematics, and various types of nondiscursive symbolic forms, such as gestures, rituals, rhythmic patterns, and the like. These meanings are contained in arbitrary symbolic structures, with socially accepted rules of formation and transformation, created as instruments for the expression and communication of any meaning whatsoever. These symbolic systems in one respect constitute the most fundamental of all the realms of meaning in that they must be employed to express the meanings in each of the other realms.

The second realm, *empirics,* includes the sciences of the physical world, of living things, and of man. These sciences provide factual descriptions, generalizations, and theoretical formulations and explanations which are based upon observation and experimentation in the world of matter, life, mind, and society. They express meanings as probable empirical truths framed in accordance with certain rules of evidence and verification and making use of specified systems of analytic abstraction.

The third realm, *esthetics,* contains the various arts, such as music, the visual arts, the arts of movement, and literature. Meanings in this realm are concerned with the contemplative perception of particular significant things as unique objectifications of ideated subjectivities.

The fourth realm, *synoetics,* embraces what Michael Polanyi calls "personal knowledge" and Martin Buber the "I-Thou" relation. The novel term "synnoetics", which was devised because no existing concept appeared adequate to the type of understanding intended, derives from the Greek *synnoesis,* meaning "meditative thought," and this in turn is compounded of *syn*, meaning "with" or "together", and *noesis*, meaning "cognition". Thus synnoetics signifies "relational insight" or "direct awareness". It is analogous in the sphere of knowing to sympathy in the sphere of feeling. This personal or relational knowledge is concrete, direct, and essential. It may apply to other persons, to oneself, or even to things.

The fifth realm, ethics, includes moral meanings that express obligation rather than fact, perceptual form, or awareness of relation. In contrast to the sciences, which are concerned with abstract cognitive understanding, to the arts, which express idealized esthetic perceptions, and to personal knowledge, which reflects intersubjective understanding, morality has to do with personal conduct that is based on free, responsible, deliberate decision.

The sixth realm, *synoptics,* refers to meanings that are comprehensively integrative. It includes history, religion, and philosophy. These disciplines combine empirical, esthetic, and synnoetic meanings into coherent wholes. Historical interpretation comprises an artful re-creation of the past, in obedience to factual evidence, for the purpose of revealing what man by his deliberate choices has made of himself within the context of his given circumstances. Religion is concerned with ultimate meanings, that is, with meanings from any realm whatsoever, considered from the standpoint of such boundary concepts as the Whole, the Comprehensive, and the Transcendent. Philosophy provides analytic clarification, evaluation, and synthetic coordination of all the other realms through a reflective conceptual interpretation of all possible kinds of meaning in their distinctiveness and in their interrelationships.

The symbolics, which have been placed at one end of the spectrum of meanings, encompass the entire range of meanings because they are the necessary means of expressing all meanings whatever. Similarly, the synoptics, which have been placed at the other end of the spectrum, also gather up the entire range of meanings by virtue of their integrative character. Between these two realms of symbolics and synoptics lie the realms of empirics, esthetics, synnoetics, and ethics as four essentially distinct (though interdependent) dimensions of meaning or modes of significant human relatedness to the world and to existence.

The six realms thus charted provide the foundations for all the meanings that enter into human experience. They are the foundations in the sense that they are the pure and archetypal kinds of meaning that determine the quality of every humanly significant experience. From this viewpoint, any particular meaning can be analyzed as an expression of one of the fundamental meanings or as a combination of two or more of them. In practice, meanings seldom appear in pure and simple form; they are almost always compounded of several of the elemental types.

Despite this complexity in practice, it is useful for purposes of curriculum analysis and construction to distinguish the basic ingredients in all meaning and to order the learning process for general education in the light of these elements.

If the six realms cover the range of possible meanings, they may be regarded as comprising the basic competences that general education should develop in every person. A complete person should be skilled in the use of speech, symbol, and gesture, factually well informed, capable of creating and appreciating objects of esthetic significance, endowed with a rich and disciplined life in relation to self and others, able to make wise decisions and to judge between right and wrong, and possessed of an integral outlook. These are the aims of general education for the development of whole persons.

A curriculum developing the above basic competences is designed to satisfy the essential human need for meaning. Instruction in language, mathematics, science, art, personal relations, morals, history, religion, and philosophy constitutes the educational answer to the destructively critical spirit and to the pervasive modern sense of meaninglessness. Moreover, all of these elements are necessary ingredients in the formation of a mature person.

Because the realms of meaning form an articulated whole, a curriculum based upon them counteracts the fragmentation of experience that is one of the sources of meaninglessness. The various meanings do not merely occupy separate and isolated domains; they are interrelated and complementary, forming parts of a single hierarchical system of meaning. The symbolic and the synoptic fields, especially, serve as binding elements running through the various realms and welding them into a single meaningful pattern.

In addition to decisions about the scope of studies, the planning of the curriculum requires decisions about the ordering of content. With respect to the sequence of studies three factors are of major importance. The first is the previously discussed factor of integrity, which suggests that every student at every stage of his learning career should receive some instruction in all six of the realms of meaning. In this way continuous progress toward wholeness of meaning may best be assured.

The second factor in sequence is the intrinsic logical order of the various kinds of meaning. Clearly the languages, being essential to expression in all the other fields, need special initial emphasis. On the other hand, the synoptic fields, depending upon a substantial fund of other meanings to be integrated, can most profitably be pursued at a later stage in the learner's career. The descriptive sciences may be entered upon with less prior preparation than can the moral disciplines, which gain significance only with the assumption of real responsibility. The esthetic and synnoetic disciplines are intermediate in the degree of experience required for most effective learning. Thus, the logical interrelations of the realms of meaning have some bearing on the optimum sequence of studies.

The third factor in ordering studies is that of human development and maturation. Empirical studies show that the growing person becomes ready for different types of learning at different stages of growth. These levels of preparedness should be taken into account in planning the sequence of instruction.

Beyond the scope and sequence of studies, curriculum making requires principles for the selection and organization of content. Given the enormous volume of knowledge available to be learned, the educator is faced with the task of choosing a minute fraction of this total cultural stock for inclusion in the course of study. It was pointed out above that surfeit of knowledge is one of the causes of frustration and the sense of meaninglessness in the present-day world. If some defensible criteria can be found for reducing the mass of material to assimilable proportions, a major contribution can be made to the quest for meaning.

It will be recalled that another source of meaninglessness is the rapidity of change in modern life, which soon renders much that is learned obsolete. Again, a signal contribution can be made to fulfillment of meaning if curricular content can be selected so as to have a measure of permanence amid pervasive changefulness.

Four principles for the selection and organization of content are suggested as means of ensuring optimum growth in meaning. The first principle is that the content of instruction should be drawn entirely from the fields of disciplined inquiry. The richness of culture and the level of understanding achieved in advanced civilization are due almost entirely to the labors of individual men of genius and of organized communities of specialists. A high level of civilization is the consequence of the dedicated service of persons with special gifts for the benefit of all. Every person is indebted for what he has and is to a great network of skilled inventors, experimenters, artists, seers, scholars, prophets, and saints, who have devoted their special talents to the well-being of all. Nobody, no matter how capable, can make any perceptible progress on his own without dependence on the experts in the various departments of life.

It follows that the teacher should draw upon the specialized disciplines as the most dependable and rewarding resource for instructional materials. While he should seek to make the disciplined materials his own, he should not presume to originate the knowledge to be taught, nor should he expect the fruits of learning to come forth as if by miracle from the shared experience of the students or as the products of common sense.

This term "discipline" is not meant to refer to an unchanging set of established fields of knowledge. New disciplines are regularly coming into being, such as cybernetics, parapsychology, theory of games, astronautics, and the like. New combinations, such as biochemistry and history of science, are forming. Also, many established disciplines are undergoing radical internal transformations: modern physics, music, history, and theology, to mention only a few. In fact, there is scarcely a field of study that is not today different in important respects from what it was only a few decades ago. Hence the present proposal to use materials from the disciplines does not constitute an argument for education to return to a traditional subject-matter curriculum. It simply argues for the exclusive use of materials that have been produced in disciplined communities of inquiry by men of knowledge who possess authority in their fields. Given the developments in disciplined inquiry, the proposal to use knowledge from the disciplines favors a modern rather than a traditional type of curriculum.

The second principle for the selection of content is that from the large resources of material in any given discipline, those items should be chosen that are particularly *representative* of the field as a whole. The only effective solution to the surfeit of knowledge is a drastic progress of simplification. This aim can be achieved by discovering for each discipline those seminal or key ideas that provide clues to the entire discipline. If the content of instruction is carefully chosen and organized so as to emphasize these characteristic features of the disciplines, a relatively small volume of knowledge may suffice to yield effective understanding of a far larger body of material. The use of teaching materials based on representative ideas thus makes possible a radical simplification of the learner's task.

A third and related principle is that content should be chosen so as to exemplify the *methods of inquiry* and the modes of understanding in the disciplines studied. It is more important for the student to become skillful in the ways of knowing than to learn about any particular product of investigation. Knowledge of methods makes it possible for a person to continue learning and to undertake inquiries on his own. Furthermore, the modes of thought are far less transient than are the products of inquiry. Concentration on methods also helps to overcome the other two forms of meaninglessness earlier considered, namely, fragmentation and surfeit of materials. Every discipline is unified by its methods, which are the common source of all the conclusions reached in that field of study. As this common thread, the characteristic modes of thought are induced in the category of representative ideas, which, as indicated above, allow for the simplification of learning.

A fourth principle of selection is that the materials chosen should be such as to arouse *imagination.* Growth in meaning occurs only when the mind of the learner actively assimilates and re-creates the materials of instruction. Ordinary, prosaic, and customary considerations do not excite a vital personal engagement with ideas. One of the qualities of good teaching is the ability to impart a sense of the extraordinary and surprising so that learning becomes a continuous adventure. According to this principle, ordinary life-situations and the solving of everyday problems should not be the basis for curriculum content. The life of meaning is far better served by using materials that tap the deeper levels of experience. Such materials reveal new perspectives on old problems by throwing familiar experiences into fresh combinations and showing old beliefs in novel contexts. Such imaginative use of materials generates habits of thought that enable the student to respond to rapid changes in knowledge and belief with zest instead of dismay and to experience joy in understanding rather than the dead weight of ideas to be absorbed and stored.

Such, in barest outline, is the argument to be elaborated and illustrated in the following pages. This philosophy of the curriculum for general education centers on the idea of *meaning* as the key to distinctively human experience. Hence the processes of teaching and learning are to be guided by reference to the major varieties of meaning. Six fundamental patterns of meaning are found to cover the spectrum of significant human experience, and each of these can be analyzed into constituent disciplines. These domains of understanding comprise sources from which curricular materials are to be drawn. The sequence of studies and the selection of materials is to be based on the logic of the realms of meaning, the psychology of human development, and certain content criteria that minimize the following principal enemies of meaning: destructive skepticism, fragmentation, overabundance, and transience.

In the foregoing summary nothing has been said explicitly about the social factors in the formation of the curriculum. Surely the conditions and needs of society do and ought to play an important part in educational decision making. Why, then, is no specific reference made to these factors in the present analysis? There are three principal reasons.

First, the basic concept of meaning, around which this study is focused, is itself inherently social. Meanings are relational. They are shared. No one can have a significant life in isolation. The community of meaning applies to all the realms without exception. Every pattern of meaning is a shared way of understanding. Hence, a curriculum of general education constructed on the basis of the fundamental patterns of meaning necessarily incorporates the realities and ideals of life in relation to others.

Second, particular social factors are more relevant to the curriculum of specialized education than of general education. The nature of a society is reflected in the character and distribution of its specialized occupations. These functions vary from society to society more than do the qualities of meaning that a person needs in any society to fulfill his being as a person. It follows that particular social needs have less relevance to the curriculum of general education than to the curriculum of specialized education, which is not covered in the present work.

Third, no claim is made that the principles herein recommended provide a complete basis for the construction of the curriculum even of general education. The considerations presented are intended to give only a broad framework within which specific curriculum decisions can be made by taking account of many other factors relating to particular personal and cultural situations. The special needs and resources of the society in which and for which education takes place are among the additional factors pertinent to what is taught in the institutions of learning.

This philosophy of the curriculum for general education is thus intended as a comprehensive but not exhaustive guide to the fulfillment of human existence through education. It may perhaps be regarded as a contribution to what James Harvey Robinson called "the humanizing of knowledge".[1] The fruits of inquiry by professional scholars are largely beyond the comprehension of the layman, even though he may be intelligent and formally well educated. Also this knowledge may appear to have little pertinence to the vital concerns of any except those who are professionally committed to it. There is a great need for the best insights of civilization to be made available to people generally and for its humane significance to be made clear. "Popular culture" need not be mediocre and trivial. Meaning is lost both when knowledge is abstruse and inaccessible and when it is commonplace and superficial. The present philosophy of the curriculum is dedicated to the proposition that the finest treasures of civilization can be so mediated as to become a common inheritance of persons who are seeking to realize their essential humanness.

NOTES

1. See his book by this title, 2d rev. ed., George H. Doran Company, New York, 1926.

Part 2 Issues in Curriculum Design

INTRODUCTION

Section I considers some key issues that confront any attempt to design a whole curriculum. Should the curriculum encourage generalism or specialism? Should there be a common curriculum or different curricula for different categories of student? Should individual interests or cultural tradition determine content?

This section looks at four different prescriptions for the whole curriculum, embodying four different solutions to this set of issues. Hirst argues for a curriculum based on the disciplines of knowledge as represented in seven distinct 'forms of thought'. He believes that the curriculum should develop rationality by initiating all pupils into each of its seven forms. By contrast, Wilson argues for a curriculum based firmly on pupils' individual interests. He values rationality and disciplined thinking as much as Hirst, but believes that they can only truly be developed in pursuit of whatever activities the individual finds intrinsically valuable. Bantock takes issue with Hirst. He argues that many pupils do not have the capacity to benefit from an academic curriculum and therefore he advocates the 'dual curriculum' providing a very different offering for pupils who are not academically minded. Midwinter advocates another type of special curriculum, one firmly rooted in the pupil's local community, which he developed to meet the special needs of pupils in inner city areas. Merson and Campbell analyse the elements of this curriculum and criticise it for its tendency to perpetuate inequality of educational opportunity.

These four models for the design of a whole curriculum are not the only ones, nor necessarily the most influential. They are presented simply to demonstrate that value judgements and moral commitments are involved in selecting objectives for the whole curriculum and that these allow wide differences in patterns of curriculum provision.

Section II looks at issues of curriculum organisation. These issues involve consideration of two factors – the nature of knowledge and the nature of the learning process. Of three common forms of organisation, namely subject organisation, activity-based work and thematic enquiry, organisation into subjects is still the most prevalent. But the subjects of the timetable are often taught without any appreciation of how subject divisions arise or of how an understanding of their underlying structures might make it possible to teach them more effectively. Schwab argues that, although discipline boundaries are often redrawn as our knowledge develops, the underlying structure of a discipline can be taught in a way that enhances understanding of a body of knowledge at the same time as it prepares one to meet changes in that structure.

A radically opposed approach to curriculum organisation is represented by Kilpatrick. His 'project method' is a prototype for an activity-based curriculum.

The pressing issue of curriculum integration raises in new form many of these issues. Analysing this popular notion, Pring shows various proposals for integration to have completely different theoretical underpinnings. James' proposals for a 'fourfold curriculum' embody a pragmatic solution to issues of curriculum organisation, providing for both inter-disciplinary and discipline-based study within a single curriculum. The value of active enquiry and problem-solving is emphasised.

Section III concentrates on an approach to curriculum planning which has had a considerable vogue both in the United States and elsewhere, namely the idea that curricula should be planned through the specification of objectives. While it is true that curricula-making is a purposive activity which may be well or badly done (or even neglected), the precise role that objectives can and ought to play is hotly disputed. Hirst draws attention to the multi-faceted nature of objectives, but maintains that the curriculum must rely on clear objectives of all the relevant kinds for adequate planning. Bloom puts the view that objectives have to be geared to student mastery: his is a plea for objectives that are attainable and not just distant goals. Eisner, an art educator of distinction, broadens the debate by insisting upon the essentially open nature of many sorts of educational encounter. His 'expressive' objectives are designed to facilitate the unpredictable and creative dimension of curricular happenings. Davies illustrates both the difficulties and some techniques for overcoming the difficulties involved in stating general and specific objectives. Macdonald-Ross gives an overview of the whole area of concern. Of particular value is his reassessment of Popham's classic defence of behavioural objectives.

Curriculum evaluation is another area of current debate. Who should evaluate the school curriculum? What is the relationship between examinations, testing and evaluation? What are the most valid methods to be employed? White looks at the logic of the field, stressing the necessary connection between curriculum objectives and evaluation while Cronbach wants to see evaluations as a tool for increasing the efficiency of curriculum towards its stated goals. Parlett relies heavily on the notion that educational situations can only be fully understood (and therefore evaluated) in their own context or, in some sense, 'from the inside'. So the evaluator has to develop techniques akin more to those of the anthropologist than to those of the botanist. Harlen gives an account of her role as an evaluator of a curriculum project. It is a useful exercise to work out the position of Science 5–13 on the central questions raised in this section.

Section V is a case-study of a well-known American curriculum project, 'Man: A Course of Study'. The three extracts in this section are: Bruner's exposition of one of the main theoretical assumptions of the course, namely that "subjects" are most effectively taught through their underlying structure; an extract from a book by Jones, a psycho-analyst whose critique of the course's failure to deploy emotions effectively have been taken into account by recent developments of the course; and an extract from the evaluation report of the project, explaining the sophisticated methodology of the 'comprehensive' evaluation programme and summarising its conclusions.

It is easy to assume that curriculum issues arise only in school situations. This is not so for the simple reason that wherever responsibility for the learning of others is institutionalised then a curriculum appears. This is so, for example, in the training of policemen and women and in the education and training of teachers. In the latter case, which is the subject of Section VI, issues have to be resolved that have a significance, through a knock-on effect, for school curricula. For example, if student teachers specialise in some particular academic subject at college, there is a natural tendency on their part to perpetuate in their careers particular divisions of the school curriculum. Browne discusses the college curriculum in terms of balancing some by now traditional elements. Skilbeck challenges the idea of balance by remarking the paucity of analysis of the "culture" of schooling and its relation to surrounding values. Renshaw challenges some assumptions in college curriculum design, notably the notion that some parts of the curriculum are specifically educative while others are servicing elements. He does this through an analysis of a concept of self-development. Brown summarises some of the rather scanty empirical evidence available to us regarding curriculum design in teacher education and training.

I OBJECTIVES FOR THE WHOLE CURRICULUM

1. THE LOGIC OF THE CURRICULUM

Paul H. Hirst

Source: *Journal of Curriculum Studies,* vol I. No. 2, 1969, pp. 142–58. (Published twice yearly by William Collins Sons and Co. Ltd.) Reprinted by permission in R. Hooper (ed.), *The Curriculum: Context, Design and Development* (Oliver and Boyd, Edinburgh, 1971), pp. 236–50.

In the United Kingdom there are two major curriculum problems which raise a number of philosophical issues – what sort of curriculum are we to have in secondary schools in any age of universal secondary-school provision? What can be done about persistent deficiencies in the grammar school curriculum, particularly the effects of specialisation? Hirst argues that the development of mind has been marked by the progressive differentiation in human consciousness of some seven or eight distinguishable cognitive structures. Thus the acquisition of these different forms of knowledge, different ways of thinking about the world, must be universal objectives for the curriculum. If these forms of knowledge are denied to certain categories of child, for example the 'average' child, then they are being denied certain basic ways of rational development. Secondary curricula must therefore be devised which initiate all children into these distinct cognitive structures. In the grammar-school curriculum Hirst's 'map of knowledge' can be used to avoid the dangers of over-specialisation on one side and over-generalisation on the other.

There are two major curriculum problems that are forcing on us in the U.K. fundamental questionings of a philosophical character. First, there is the question of the curriculum we are to have in secondary schools now that we have universal secondary education. Secondly, there is the persistent problem of the deficiencies of the education provided by our traditional grammar school curriculum,[1] particularly the effects of specialisation. Granted universal secondary education, we have yet to get really to grips with the question of what the objectives are of an education that is so widely spread. Can there in fact be genuinely universal objectives? Irrespective of the kind of institutions that we have, does it make sense to set about trying to achieve the same ends with pupils whose I.Q.'s are about 102, and those whose I.Q.'s are, say, well below 100? Is it that we need different means for different pupils, or must we formulate different, but equally justifiable ends? In fact, what is equality of educational opportunity if you stick to strictly *educational* opportunity? Is it the equal chance to go toward the same goals, so that we need to discover how best to help the less able pupil along the line, or do we recognise quite different goals for the less able and seek to provide them with every facility to pursue these? In fact, how far does it really make sense to talk of educational objectives as alternatives? To begin to get clear on this matter there is, I think, no escaping an examination of the nature of educational objectives and the significance of pursuing different goals.

What is more, we need to know how these objectives are related to each other. Are they simply isolable items of knowledge or skill that can be acquired as one might collect individual pebbles from a beach? Can the objectives we want be quite freely classified and arranged by teachers into any convenient units, so that there is an endless variety of organisations of curricular means to these ends? Or are many of the objectives so closely interrelated to each other that one must necessarily pursue them in logically cohesive groupings? What in other words are the structural or logical features of the objectives we are interested in, features we cannot ignore if our curricula are to be coherent? I suggest then that uncertainties about the secondary school curriculum go deep, and that to help sort matters out we need philosophical aid in two particular respects. We need to understand what is implied in choosing different educational objectives and we need to know what kind of demands educational objectives put on the curriculum plan itself.

Just the same two forms of philosophical aid are needed to help us with the problems of our traditional grammar school curriculum. The principle of specialisation has been the schools' answer to the vast increase in knowledge and its progressive fragmentation into ever narrower and more technical domains. We have allowed, or rather have insisted on, the dropping of subjects from an early age, trusting to the forces of interest, ability, and vocational intention to do a responsible selection job for us. But unfortunately the narrow-minded boffin reared on a restricted diet of science and mathematics from fourteen to fifteen, is now all too common a phenomenon, as also is the arts man, blank in his incomprehension of the scientific outlook. In our worst moments we argue either that this situation doesn't matter, or that it is inevitable, there being some pseudo-justification of a psychological kind for our current practices. You will recall the Crowther Report's fantastic contention that our most able children, and only those who are most able, just do by nature undergo a period of specialist subject-mindedness in their later teens.[2] In our wiser moments we begin to think twice about our selection of educational objectives and our ways of achieving them. What if narrow mindedness is a necessary consequence of our failure to educate a person in certain respects? In that case the remedy is in our own hands. To be clear on this point, an examination of the nature of educational objectives is precisely what we need.

We must also ask, if, with the vast increase in knowledge, the only satisfactory way to limit what is pursued is in fact by selecting some limited areas for specialist treatment. It is at least possible that within the structure of knowledge itself there are other more suitable bases of selection. There is also the problem that at a time when we are so specialist minded in our grammar schools, the old traditional demarcations between the subjects or disciplines from which our young specialists must choose, are themselves being called in question. New subjects are being freely developed in the universities and they are creeping into even the most conservative schools. As a result the whole domain of knowledge seems to be disintegrating into a strange chaos, so that no one person can begin to have any significant map of knowledge as a whole, only a limited grasp of certain particular areas. Certainly, we are failing to communicate an over-all view of the range of intellectual achievements of man, even in that section of our secondary education where we are surest of the positive value of the curriculum. The result is that many of our pupils are not only ignorant of major forms of human understanding, they are intolerant of them, unable to appreciate that they have their appropriate place and value in the life of man. We must then ask the philosophical question whether or not there are within the domain of knowledge demarcatory features in terms of which the domain is intelligible as a whole, and whether or not there are possibilities of significant selection other than that of ruthless specialisation.

Let me then turn to these two important philosophical problems. First, what kind of objectives does education have, and secondly, how are these objectives related to each other – what formal structure have they got? The objectives of education are surely certain developments of the pupil which are achieved in learning, and I suggest that these are all basically connected with the development of a rational mind. This is not to say that education is concerned only with intellectual development, as if, for example emotional development was to be ignored, and knowledge and belief taken to be the only manifestations of mind. Nor is it even to say that education is concerned only with mental development in its widest sense. Rather it is to say that all those forms of development with which education is concerned are related to the pupil's progress in rational understanding. This means that physical education, for instance, is pursued in accordance with a rational appraisal of the place and value of physical activities in human life which we wish the pupil to acquire, that the activities themselves are viewed as those of a developing rational being, not merely an animal, and that they therefore constitute part of the life of a rational person. But to characterise the objectives of education in relation to the development of rationality, is certainly to put at the very centre of what is pursued those forms of knowledge and belief in which we make sense of our experience. It is necessarily by means of knowledge if not by knowledge alone, that fancy gives place to a recognition of fact, that irrational wishes give place to reasonable wants, and that emotional reactions give place to justifiable actions. Thus, although all the possible or justifiable objectives of education are not themselves explicitly developments of mind, it is, I suggest, by their connection with such specific developments that other objectives have their place and their justification in education at all. As I cannot here begin to consider the nature and interrelationship of educational objectives of very different kinds, I shall therefore confine myself to considering what is involved in the achievement of those most central objectives of all, the acquisition of knowledge and rational beliefs, without which the development of rationality in any wider sense is logically impossible.

What then is involved in the acquisition of knowledge? Certainly it involves learning many different concepts, using these in a growing awareness of facts, truths and forms of many kinds, mastering many logical operations and principles, applying the criteria of different types of judgment, and so on. What an exhaustive list of the elements would be, I would not like to say, but what matters for my purpose at the moment is not a complete classification of them in independent categories, so much as a recognition of the kind of achievements that these are. They are, in fact, neither more nor less than the very achievement of mind itself.

Unfortunately our concept of mind is so persistently bedevilled by myths, largely of an empiricist nature, that we all too easily misconceive entirely what is going on in learning to understand and in acquiring knowledge. We have an almost ineradicable conviction that the mind is to be thought of as a room or box into which, via the senses, ideas or images come as ready-made copies of objects or events or facts in the external world. Further, these ideas come into the mind as quite distinct elements of awareness, rather as furniture might be put into a room. The ideas are there in the room, but they are in no sense essentially part of the room. In addition we tend to regard the mind as a kind of machine, designed to carry out certain processes of rational thought on the ideas which the senses convey, thereby building new ideas from what is given, by processes of abstraction, deduction and the like. Thus there is produced new furniture to be housed and stored, within the mind, ready for use when required. Some of us have less effective machinery than others when it comes to reasoning, and practice and exercise are needed to get the best out of what each of us is given. But essentially the processes of rational thought are regarded as natural activities of the mind. On this kind of picture, the acquiring of knowledge and understanding as the objective of education, involves two major tasks: furnishing the mind with the right ideas, and getting the machine working properly.

Now there are many reasons why this kind of account of mind must be totally rejected, three of which are particularly relevant here. First the account does not begin to do justice to what we know about the development of understanding, even at the level of sense-perception. What we see or understand about any situation is not a simple given. It is dependent on those concepts and categories, those basic units of intelligibility, which the mind brings to the situation. The possibility of discriminating elements in our experience at all, necessitates having concepts. To see things is not just to register things for what they are, it is for them to be picked out or articulated in our consciousness. Only by the use of certain concepts is the mind able to discriminate. What the development of understanding involves is, in fact, a progressive differentiation of our experience through the acquisition of new concepts under which it is intelligible. The mind is therefore not a passive recipient of ideas which bring understanding from the external world. It is rather that we achieve understanding through the use of categorical and conceptual apparatus. Having such an apparatus of concepts is a necessary part of what it means to have a mind. Thus the development of a mind involves the achievement of an array of concepts and on this all intelligibility depends. The provision of experience in itself is quite inadequate for developing even the simplest body of concepts, and without these nothing more complex can possibly be achieved.[3]

In the second place, the view I am criticising regards knowledge as something which the mind may or may not possess. Knowledge is not in any sense constitutive of mind. To acquire new knowledge is simply as it were to acquire different furniture or new furniture for a room. To have scientific knowledge as distinct from historical knowledge, is for the furniture to be of one kind rather than another. For the mind itself, nothing turns on this, the room itself remains unchanged; it simply lacks the other type of furniture. In essence minds do not differ in any way by having different knowledge. The real differences between minds are simply in what is naturally given. To acquire one form of knowledge rather than another in no way affects the fundamental characteristics of the mind. Yet surely this will not do. To be without any knowledge at all is to be without mind in any significant sense. Nor is it just that the mind needs some content to work on, as if otherwise its characteristics could not be expressed. The acquisition of knowledge is itself a development of mind and new knowledge means a new development of mind in some sense. Knowledge is not a free-floating possession. It is a characteristic of minds themselves. Thus to fail to acquire knowledge of a certain fundamental kind, is to fail to achieve rational mind in that significant respect. Not all knowledge is of equal importance in the development of rationality of course, yet the fundamental relationship between knowledge and the development of mind is of central educational significance. Nor must we regard knowledge as unrelated to the development of other aspects of mind, an outlook encouraged by the view I am opposing. It is in large measure by acquiring new knowledge that we begin to reconceive our activities and that we come to feel differently about them.

In the third place we must, I suggest, reject the notion that the mind naturally carries out certain mental activities according to the canons of valid reasoning, as if logical principles were laws of psychological functioning. The question of the development of the rational mind is surely not a question of the strengthening or habitualising of certain patterns of mental functioning. It is rather a question of developing a recognition that one's belief and one's arguments, the outcomes of thought, must satisfy important public tests. Tests of rationality are tests to be applied to the *achievements* of one's thought as formulated in propositions, not tests for thought *processes* themselves. To say one has reasoned something out is not to describe a particular sequence of mental occurrences, it is to say that one has achieved in the end a relationship between propositions which satisfies the public criteria necessary for giving reasons. What is more, these standards that define the achievements of reason, are certainly not natural possessions of minds. They have to be learnt, usually by dint of considerable hard work. The development of rationality is, therefore, not dependent on the exercising of particular mental processes, but it is dependent on one's coming to recognise that there are tests of validity for one's arguments and tests of truth for one's beliefs.

But I must turn to the other philosophical question. If the fundamental objectives of education are developments of the rational mind, what formal relationships are there between the various objectives, the concepts, facts, norms, principles, and so on? In spite of an immediate tendency to think of these items of knowledge as detached and isolated from each other, a little reflection quickly suggests this is not the case. It is because the concepts are used in a particular way that any proposition is meaningful. The concepts on which our knowledge is built form distinctive networks of relationships. If we transgress the rules of the relationships which the concepts meaningfully permit, we necessarily produce nonsense. If we talk about magnetic fields being angry, actions being coloured, beauty having weight, or stones being right or wrong we have simply produced conceptual confusions. But not only do we convey meaning by the use of networks of interrelated concepts, meaningful propositions are judged true or false, valid or invalid, by criteria appropriate to the types of propositions. A moral judgment is not validated in the same way as a mathematical theorem, nor a historical explanation in the same way as a theological proposition. There are thus within knowledge a number of distinct types of rational judgment. From considerations of this kind it can be seen that the acquisition of knowledge in any area involves the mastery of an interrelated group of concepts, of operations with these, of particular criteria of truth or validity associated with these concepts, as well as more general criteria of a reasoning common to all areas of knowledge. Indeed, the objectives of education we have been considering are closely related together as elements of distinguishable cognitive structures, each unique in crucial respects.

Looked at this way, the development of mind has been marked by the progressive differentiation in human consciousness of some seven or eight distinguishable cognitive structures, each of which involves the making of a distinctive form of reasoned judgment and is, therefore, a unique expression of man's rationality. This is to say that all knowledge and understanding is logically locatable within a number of domains, within, I suggest, mathematics, the physical sciences, the human sciences and history, literature and the fine arts, morals, religion and philosophy. These would seem to me to be the logically distinct areas, though this division might well be disputed. It is not, of course, that these forms of knowledge are totally separate from each other. That is not what I am saying. Manifestly there are overlaps in the concepts used in the different forms, and there are overlaps in the patterns of valid reasoning. But in respect of the distinctive rational judgments concerned, each structure involves elements which are irreducible to any of the others, singly or in combination. Moral judgments and scientific judgments are different in logical character, needing distinct forms of justification, and that in spite of the fact that these may at times use some of the same concepts and some of the same criteria for reasoning. The objectives with which education is most centrally concerned are thus not isolated ends, but elements within integrated developing structures of understanding. Certainly all the concepts, truths, norms, principles, criteria, all the developments of mind we are interested in, have their appropriate place in relation to these structures, and even those elements which are common to different areas have significance only within these structures.[4]

If what I have said is valid, then the domain of knowledge can be seen to have important structural features, and nothing could be further from the truth than to suggest that that domain is an unintelligible chaos. Knowledge has not disintegrated, it has become more clearly differentiated. It is not even that the traditional medieval map of knowledge has become totally unacceptable, for many of the logical distinctions there made are perfectly valid.[5] It is simply that the development of knowledge necessitates some new lines in the picture, and we are not yet sure of the precise details as to where to put them. We may no longer have a hierarchy of knowledge based on realist metaphysics, but we are not without the important logical distinctions that make it possible for us to see some intelligible pattern in knowledge. We may no longer have a clear grasp of the unity of knowledge, as if it all formed, in the end, one coherent network of harmonious elements. Yet unifying theories are part of the pursuit of the sub-divisions within the areas I have mentioned and there is every reason to hope that we can become much clearer on the relationships between the logically distinct forms that I have distinguished.

Yet what then of the modern transgressions of the old frontiers? Is it not the case that besides the progressive differentiation of say the sciences or historical studies, there are new disciplines or forms of knowledge emerging? Maybe this is so, I see no a priori reason whatever why new forms of knowledge should not arise. But there is, I think, little positive reason to think that this is in fact what is happening. What there are in abundance now, are new interdisciplinary areas of study in which different forms of knowledge are focused on some particular interest, and because of the relations between the forms, what is understood in each discipline is thereby deepened. Such new areas of study do not constitute new areas on a map of knowledge based on the logical distinctions I have mentioned. They are essentially composite, second order constructions, not to be confused with the primary forms of knowledge which I have distinguished on logical grounds. In terms of these primary forms of knowledge, the new areas seem to be exhaustively analysable.

As a final comment on the structure of knowledge, it must be said that the internal logical characteristics of the distinct forms and their relationships to each other, are likely to contain important principles that should govern the teaching of these areas. In some forms certain concepts logically pre-suppose others. That is to say, certain concepts are unintelligible unless other concepts pre-supposed are already understood. Equally, certain areas of knowledge pre-suppose others, parts of the physical sciences, for instance, are plainly unintelligible without a good deal of mathematical knowledge. In general terms the necessary elements of order in learning have been recognised for a long time, but there is a great deal of detailed logical work needed here, which is only now beginning to be done, and it might well transform much of our teaching in due course.[6]

But let me now return to the curriculum problems which led me into these philosophical considerations. What is the bearing of these remarks on the issue of the curricula for universal secondary education? One crucial implication is, I think, plain. If the acquisition of certain fundamental elements of knowledge is necessary to the achievement of the rational mind in some particular respect, then these at any rate cannot but be universal objectives for the curriculum. If the objectives of our education differ for sections of our society so as to ignore any of these elements for some of our pupils, either because they are considered too difficult, or for some reason they are thought less important for these pupils, then we are denying to them certain basic ways of rational development and we have indeed got inequality of educational opportunity of the most far-reaching kind. Our schools may set themselves, and often do, objectives which I have not considered. They may concern themselves with the pursuit of interesting and worthwhile activities of an endless variety, with vocational skills, with many forms of general socialisation and so on. But it is education which I take to be the prime function of the school, and it is only because of the connection these other objectives have with rational development that they have a place in education at all. If once the central objectives of rationality are submerged, or are given up so that these other pursuits take over, then I suggest the school has betrayed its educational trust, no matter how successful it may be in these other respects, and no matter how laudable these other ends may be in themselves. Whatever other principles may govern the curriculum I am arguing that we can have no adequate grounds for forsaking a child's progressive initiation into all the distinctive forms of rationality, until we have done everything in our power to achieve just this. As noted earlier, we are all too ready on psychological grounds to rationalise our present practice. In this case we most often escape our responsibility by a rigid view of human abilities, saying that children just cannot understand these things, by a curious notion of the needs of the pupil in which other needs are of higher priority than the development of rationality, and by a perverted doctrine of the importance of a pupil's present interests.

But if the universality of these objectives is granted, what further can be said about the curriculum? How, for instance, are we to choose the particular elements from the forms of knowledge in order best to obtain our objectives of rationality? One thing must, I am sure, be made plain here. The purpose of the curriculum I am concerned with, is not the production of even embryonic specialists in the different forms of knowledge. Manifestly one can study any subject in different ways, with the emphases on very different parts of the interrelated whole. We do not in this case want pupils to amass a great deal of, say, scientific information, nor do we want a mastery of techniques of investigation. Nor is it a matter of teaching what has everyday usefulness. The point is that the pupil shall begin to think in a distinctive way, and that means acquiring such a hold of those features which most distinctively characterise this form of knowledge, that one's thought is developed into autonomous functioning using the relevant concepts and criteria. This will mean selecting, and then concentrating one's teaching on, the most central and fruitful concepts, forms of explanation, criteria and methods of justification in the area. The idea is that pupils themselves will master the use of the concepts in the right way, and, by formulating and considering truths in the domain, that they will appreciate the features of knowledge of this particular kind, and know the reasons or kinds of evidence on which its truths turn. Manifestly we have not yet begun to discover in any systematic sense what is involved in producing courses of this nature. Our eyes have been far too fixed on the specialist training of the young physicist to find out what is needed in courses in physics that will develop a sympathetic grasp of the cognitive structure of science, an appreciation of what it involves and thereby a recognition of its significance in the rational life. This is not to ask for courses *about*, say, science rather than courses *in* science. It is to ask for courses in science which direct their attention away from the mastery of detail that a specialist requires and towards the mastery of the general and basic elements of the mode of thought.

But can such courses be taken by every pupil? The answer, from what I have argued already, must surely be that it is imperative that we find courses involving these central elements that all pupils can take successfully. I see no adequate grounds for saying this is impossible when we have in fact spent so little of our effort trying to achieve this. Such courses need not be identical for all pupils in spite of their common objectives and a likely high degree of common content. There are many different ways that teachers can use in approaching a particular concept, a particular scientific law or a particular historical explanation. Granted even that one is going to teach precisely the same course to groups of differing ability, there are ways of easing the difficulty. But there are good ways of doing this and bad ways, and we need to distinguish between them. It is all too easy, with the best intentions in the world, to cease to teach the subject to the less able pupil in any significant sense at all. By not really bothering whether or not they have got hold of the concepts and can use them, by being content with memorised statements, by allowing pure repetition of operations, by omitting anything which demands even the briefest unrehearsed argument or justification, we simply evade all the problems and totally fail to develop any significant understanding. However we accommodate ourselves to the less able, it must not be by losing essential concepts, by losing genuine operations with them, by being uncritical of invalid reasoning, and so on.

The necessary elements of knowledge are necessary elements and we cannot evade the implications of that simple tautology, try as we may. Yet there are things we can do. We can reduce the complexities by seeing that the conceptual relations we include are those absolutely essential for our purpose. Every unnecessary element that might befog an explanation can be omitted. We can cut down the extent of sustained argument by carefully analysing the stages that are demanded. We can use every opportunity to emphasise the central core of what is being done, rather than go in for extension and exploration of the ideas and their more complex applications. At least this is how we can set about things in the first place, and in our best teaching we do this already.

But what about the general structure of the secondary curriculum? The logical distinctness of the different forms of knowledge and the close inter-relation of the various elements within a form of a sub-division of it, would seem to suggest that the most rational way in which to develop the distinct modes of understanding, would be by direct organisation of the curriculum in units corresponding to the forms. There is good historical precedent for this as it is precisely what we do to a large extent in the traditional subject curriculum of the grammar school. Such an approach has many obvious merits from a logical point of view, as it is less likely than any other to cause confusion between the concepts and criteria which belong to the different areas, and it enables a thoroughly systematic approach to be made to the development of the form of thought in terms of the concepts to be acquired, the operations involved, and so on. But it has the disadvantages that go with its advantages, for it emphasises the differences between forms of knowledge, and the many important interconnections between them can be forgotten to the impoverishment of them all. Unfortunately too, the subject approach of the grammar school is still associated with very formal teaching methods, though these are not necessarily connected with it, and such an organisation of the curriculum has as a result largely been taken to be unsuitable for less able pupils. It seems to me there is place here for a careful reassessment of the benefits of such a curriculum and for experiment in its wider application with more enlightened teaching methods.

The alternative, of topics approached from different points of view, is necessarily less systematic in the development of understanding it involves, and it does not permit the choice of content to be aimed so directly at central concepts, operations, criteria and other logically distinct features of the various forms of knowledge. Indeed, from the point of view of the general development of rationality, such a curriculum by topics is difficult to handle efficiently and effectively, and, I suggest, hard to justify. Indeed, its central justification is not to be found in the contribution it makes to the development of rationality, but elsewhere, in that a suitable choice of topics can overcome many motivational problems with less able pupils, and much practical and useful information and many useful skills can be acquired easily and efficiently when approached this way. There is here, in fact, a most genuine tension between different principles which must be taken into account when deciding the best curriculum in any one particular case. What must be remembered however, is that whatever curriculum pattern or syllabus pattern is adopted, the elements of learning which pupils are to acquire must find their place in the coherent yet logically distinct cognitive structures which the pupils are slowly mastering. Significant learning cannot be a random business. The more we are aware of the logical relations involved, the more we promote our pupils' mastery of these, the more genuinely effective our teaching will be.

On the traditional grammar school curriculum I need to say little, as indeed all I have just said of the secondary curriculum in general, has particular application here. But I must give direct answers to the specific questions I raised earlier. From what I have said of the significance of knowledge for the development of the rational mind, the narrow-mindedness of so many of our grammar school products is, I think, an inevitable outcome, and a vicious indictment, of the curriculum we use. It is also, I think, a witness to the fact that the courses which pupils drop at 'O' level, however satisfactory they may be for future specialists in these subjects, are not in themselves adequate in achieving any long-standing development of rational thought in these areas, for many pupils. This, I am sure, is primarily a matter of the intention of the courses and the particular content used. We have yet to seriously face the truth that 'doing physics' can mean many different things, each of which has its distinctive values. When we get hold of the fact that any area of knowledge has many distinct elements to it, and that courses can therefore be directed to highlighting quite different features, we might set about producing courses that have greater general educational value in developing rational understanding than those we have at present. It seems to me not only unnecessary, but fundamentally miseducative, both to allow our present specialisation in the curriculum, and to teach many subjects from the start as if all pupils were eventually to become specialists in them. The remedies for our ills in these cases are surely in our hands, and I am afraid at the moment we simply lack the will to effect the cure.

As to the problem of the selection of knowledge that is to be made for inclusion in the curriculum, it seems to me there are clear indications of how this can be done on logical grounds rather than by the ruthless butchery of specialisation. The logically distinct forms of knowledge are comparatively few and not all of them need to be taught all the time; yet serious and sustained attention must be given to all these, and surely none of them should be dismissed for good from the enterprise of education earlier than is absolutely necessary, certainly not at the stage at which we permit this in our schools today. Within any one form of knowledge, the content can be chosen according to the importance of the elements for the development of the form of thought, if this is indeed accepted as a fundamental aim. The aim of specialisation certainly makes the domains of knowledge seem vast and overwhelming, so that one hardly knows what to choose. Yet set oneself rather different objectives, in this case the pursuit of rational understanding in these areas, and I suggest that the enterprise is by no means so unmanageable.

In this paper I have argued that there is, at least to some extent, a map of knowledge, and if so, the logical demarcations it shows cannot but be helpful in providing our pupils with an idea of the range of human understanding, and therefore some perspective of human pursuits. But this does demand that pupils develop to a significant degree the various forms of thought, that they appreciate their distinctive functions and their relationships to each other. We cannot expect pupils to acquire a rational perspective on the lives and affairs of men unless we equip them to achieve this by developing the forms of thought that define that perspective.

Finally, what of the organisation of the curriculum into the traditional subjects? Though I am very concerned about the specialist type of content to these subjects as we now have them, the principle of division between the subjects seems to me to be supremely justified in the education of able pupils. It has the strongest justification in those logical distinctions within knowledge which I have outlined. The sustained discipline, according to the necessary features of the subjects, that this approach demands, is obviously of immense value. More modern organisations of study that are being developed in the universities and are now coming into schools, may have their good points. But achieving the basic modes of thought is a difficult business, and if the newer approaches result in any evasion of the discipline necessary to the development of those forms of thought, then it seems to me they will do us a great disservice in the end.

I have tried in this paper to make one or two general philosophical points and to show their bearing on certain curriculum questions. All I have said must be taken together with considerations of other kinds that I have ignored. I hope I have vindicated my claim that on curriculum matters philosophers have things to say that cannot go unheeded or unexamined in responsible curriculum planning. As I said at the beginning, the practical problems of education must never be left to philosophers to solve, but to ignore what they can contribute to their solution is a sure way to ill-considered judgments. In this area as in so many others, philosophers may not be kings, but I trust I have shown that they cannot with impunity be totally excluded from the conduct of the affairs of state.

NOTES

1. I use this term to denote a kind of curriculum, whether it happens to be implemented in a grammar school, a comprehensive, or public school.
2. *15 to 18*, report of the Central Advisory Council for Education (H.M.S.O. 1959, vol. I, ch. 25). See also A. D. C. Peterson, 'The Myth of "Subject-mindedness" ' (*Universities Quarterly*, June 1960).
3. R. S. Peters, *Ethics and education* (Allen & Unwin, 1966, ch. 2); also W. Kneale, *On having a mind* (Cambridge University Press, 1962).
4. For a further discussion of the distinctions between different forms of knowledge see P. H. Hirst, *Liberation education and the nature of knowledge* in R. D. Archambault (ed.), *Philosophical analysis and education* (Routledge and Kegan Paul, 1965). See also S. Elam (ed.), *Education and the structure of knowledge* (Rand McNally, Chicago, 1964).
5. J. Maritain, *The degrees of knowledge* (G. Bles, 1959, Pt. I).
6. See papers by D. W. Hamlyn and P. H. Hirst in R. S. Peters (ed.), *The concept of education* (Routledge & Kegan Paul, 1967).

2. Curriculum Priorities and the Voluntary Principle

J. P. White

Source: J. P. White, *Towards a Compulsory Curriculum* (Routledge and Kegan Paul, London, 1973), pp. 61–72.

John White argues for the principle that the educational system should establish a basic minimum of achievement that it can expect of all its pupils. He also argues for a certain kind of content in which that minimum should consist. This content would include activities that cannot be understood without participation in them. It would aim to give pupils an understanding of as many different patterns of life as possible and some ability to integrate this knowledge into an actual way of life, based on consideration of both their own and others' interests. For these aims the humanities are more important than the sciences. Within each curriculum area, the basic minimum should be enough to enable a pupil to know whether or not he wants to spend time either contemplating or engaging in work in the area. Once the basic minima of a compulsory curriculum have been established, there should be room for a wide range of voluntary activities – voluntary in the real sense that the pupil would have the chance of opting out of any or all of them.

What overall pattern of a curriculum has emerged from the argument so far? How far are we now any clearer about what the basic minimum achievement expected of any school leaver might be?

While the previous argument has not sought to provide anything like a comprehensive blueprint for a curriculum, it has laid down some guidelines for further elaboration. First, school leavers must be equipped to understand enough about different ways in which they may want to spend their lives to enable them to choose their own version of the Good Life as they see it. This requires an understanding not only of kinds of activities, but also of kinds of ways of life. Each class should be as wide as possible.

Taking kinds of activities first, some of these must be pursued as part of one's education, since no understanding of them is possible without participation. These include speaking one's mother tongue, mathematics, physical science, art and philosophy. While many other activities must be known about, they do not need to be engaged in for this purpose and do not, on this argument at least, find a place in a curriculum. Educationally relevant examples are housecraft, handicraft, foreign languages, games and creative activities in the arts. Teachers should introduce children to activities in the former category not only as options which may be chosen for their own sake, but also in such a way as to open doors to understanding other activities which logically depend on them for their intelligibility. Mathematics and physics, for instance, open the door to an understanding of various types of engineering; the study of literature, to acting or creative writing; one's mother tongue, to innumerable things – from bingo and billiards, to foreign languages, housecraft and other practical activities.

School leavers must also know about as many different ways of life as possible so that their preferred activities may find a place within an overall pattern of life which they choose themselves. They should not be pressed towards any one particular way of life. The study of history is important here in making them aware that there is no natural necessity about the dominant ways of life which people follow in contemporary society. Literature also has a vital role to play in revealing different ways of life. This is over and above its role mentioned in the previous paragraph of helping the pupil towards an understanding of art in general. There is no reason why literature should be only English literature. Philosophy, too, has a place under this heading.

Literature, philosophy and biographical history are also helpful in achieving a second main desideratum in education, over and above a knowledge of different ways of life and ingredients within them: some ability to integrate this knowledge into an actual way of life. This integration must take into account both the individual's own good and others' good. Self-regarding integration must be subordinate to moral integration. Integration of both sorts presupposes practical kinds of understanding not already mentioned like a knowledge of financial, economic, social and political institutions, and a knowledge of the impediments to mental health. This points to new compulsory areas of the curriculum: to an area of socio-economic studies on the one hand and an area of psychological studies on the other. In addition, a comprehensive careers information service is also a *sine qua non.*

The sciences versus the humanities

So much for the main features of the 'basic minimum', at least as regards its breadth. I shall be looking at its depth in a moment. But before doing so, I should like to say something about the relative importance of some of the different subject components of the compulsory curriculum outlined above. These may be divided, very roughly (there are obvious qualifications to make here) into three areas: the natural sciences (physics, mathematics), the humanities (literature and other arts, philosophy, history) and the social sciences. Now several contemporary curriculum theories do not include any hierarchy of curriculum activities: they insist on an initiation into a number of different 'realms of meaning' (Phenix, 1964) or 'forms of knowledge' (Hirst, 1965) – including, for instance, things like physical science, mathematics, the arts, philosophy, the human sciences, even moral knowledge – but are neutral about their relative importance. The theories themselves give no reason for thinking, for instance, that the sciences, natural and social, are any less important than the humanities. But, in fact, they are. Let us first compare the natural sciences with the humanities. This is to return to the 'two cultures' debate of some years ago. An important decision which one ought to make here is whether one is debating the intrinsic worth of these pursuits or their educational worth. On the first issue, there do not seem any reasons, apart from subjective preferences, to rate the natural sciences any lower than the humanities. But educationally speaking they are in one way less important. Suppose we take two secondary-age pupils who, after a broad primary education, specialize for a few years, one in physics, chemistry and mathematics, the other in literature, history and, later, philosophy. Suppose, too, that they never study anything except their specialisms. The humanist would be inadequately educated. He could well have a good appreciation of the larger bearings of his life – of a variety of different ways of life open to him, of the moral considerations in these choices, of the need to integrate his life into a meaningful whole; he would also have some understanding of some particular activities he could pursue for intrinsic or extrinsic reasons; but he would lack an understanding of mathematics and physics and other activities dependent on these, and to this extent his options would be limited. But the scientist would not even be inadequately educated: he could scarcely be said to be educated at all. He would be a man without any general orientation to his life, apart from what he might pick up unreflectingly from his environment – at best, a specialist of genius but trapped within his discipline; at worst, a sophisticated serf.

The humanities have a more central role in the curriculum than the natural sciences, therefore, because they alone enable one to weave together a human life. They are also more important than the social sciences. A young specialist in this area would, again, not be inadequately educated but not educated at all. He might have a good knowledge of different institutions, of means to ends of different kinds – legal, financial, political, psychological – but he would have little understanding of ends themselves – not even how those connected with natural science – except in so far as his study of means itself became an end. He could well learn things about different ways of life, but only the actual ways of life of contemporary societies: he could not contemplate those unreal forms of life which a Shakespeare could construct from his imagination, or those real yet ideal forms which a Burckhardt could reconstruct from his sources.

The problem of depth

Let us turn back to the problem of the 'basic minimum'. We have looked at this in breadth. But in one way the hardest question still remains: what depth of achievement is necessary within each curriculum-area? How much initiation does a pupil require in the arts, say, or mathematics, before he has reached the basic minimum in these areas? To look at a specific example: how much initiation does a pupil require in the arts before he has reached his basic minimum in this particular area? How far does the general argument in this essay help us to answer this?

It does give us some clue. He has to acquire enough understanding of art to enable him to know whether or not he wants to spend time (a) contemplating works of art or (b) engaging in logically higher-order aesthetic activities, like creation or performance. Some achievements would clearly fall short of this – having listened to only one piece of poetry, for instance, while knowing nothing of music or painting at all; others would be as obviously too far above the mark as this would be below it – being able, for instance, to write sensitive critical studies of works of art of many different styles and in many different media. The criterion we want of a basic aesthetic understanding clearly falls somewhere within this range. If we can agree on this much, this would seem to suggest that there is some hope for objective agreement when one turns to details. The pupil will have to be acquainted with many different types of works of art before he builds up, from their criss-crossing similarities and differences, an adequate understanding of what art is. Could any particular art form be left out of his education entirely? Could sculpture, say, be skipped if painting were included, along with literature and music? One test would be whether one could understand anything of the aesthetic interest of works of sculpture simply on the basis of one's acquaintance with other art forms, but without actually seeing any sculpture – perhaps simply from an oral description. Another test would be whether with such a background in the other arts one could pick out the aesthetically relevant features of any first piece of sculpture with which one was presented. Could one? I would be less doubtful about this than about whether one could understand what it was for music to be aesthetically interesting if one had never heard any but knew only about painting, sculpture and architecture. But it would have to be left to experts within the artistic area to work out more detailed priorities of this sort: experts, however, not in isolated specialisms, but men with some understanding of the different arts and what might be called their orders of intelligibility relationships as just exemplified. This applies, too, to such relationships not only between the different major art forms, but also within any particular form itself. I see no reason why experts on aesthetic education should not be able roughly to agree, provided their sympathies were liberal enough, on what criteria of understanding a student would have to meet in order to satisfy conditions (a) and (b) mentioned at the beginning of this paragraph. Rough agreement, within fairly tolerant boundaries, is all that one could reasonably expect here: one should not insist on anything very precise, since understanding is not an all-or-nothing phenomenon but develops by degrees. There is, however, one further guideline here which should help to narrow any area of disagreement. It follows from the insistence on the principles of liberty in this essay that the presumption is that the pupil should be obliged to study as little as possible. The experts should bear this in mind in laying down their minimal criteria of understanding and keep them as unsophisticated as is consonant with the purposes they have in view.

These points apply as much to theoretical disciplines as to the arts. In mathematics, for instance, an acquaintance with the four basic processes, fractions and decimals clearly falls below the minimum. This gives one neither an insight into the fascination of pure mathematics nor an understanding of the application of mathematics in some of the more sophisticated professions. But how far does one have to penetrate through the conceptual hierarchies of different branches of mathematics in order to achieve these? Once again, it is fairly clear what would be too good an achievement: a first degree in the subject, perhaps. But what, roughly speaking, the basic minimum would be is again a question for the experts.

What, though, of knowledge of ways of life and 'integration'? It may seem odd to talk of basic minima here – odder than in mathematics, say, where we are used to examinations for school leavers, which attempt something of this kind. But I see no reason in principle why minima cannot be worked out in these other areas also. As for ways of life, one could see what would show too little understanding – a lack of awareness of any ways of life except those approved in one's local community; and also what would be plainly more than sufficient – an ability to make fine discriminations between all sorts of life-styles. Somewhere between these two extremes will be the minimum understanding for which we are looking. It is true that there are no experts in ways of life as there are in mathematics, although philosophers, sociologists and students of literature each have an interest. Perhaps they may be especially helpful in working out the basic minimum. This may also be true of the even more intractable area of 'integration'. Again, students who had failed to integrate any of their learning in the ways described should be easy enough to recognize. Clearly, too, one should not pitch the requirement very high, since few are going to achieve the maturity that comes through integration while they are still completing their formal education. But school-leavers must at least be aware of what integration is in its different forms; beyond this, they must also provide evidence that they are not only aware of it but see its importance and are beginning to apply it to their own lives. All this, I am aware, is very embryonic. This whole area is one in which, to my knowledge, very little work has yet been done. But there could hardly be a more important topic to which educationists could address themselves.

If experts in different fields can work out basic minima in this way, we can then have a yardstick by which to ensure that every pupil has received an adequate education. This does not necessarily imply a school-leaving examination for everyone, based on these minima. If, for instance, a pupil can solve problems in calculus and the basic minimum in mathematics falls below the level of calculus, this itself is enough to show that he has reached the minimum. This can be generalized for all curriculum areas: work which shows a more advanced understanding than that minimally required is as good a test as any. In many fields it may even well be the best, e.g. where conventional examinations are ill able to discriminate real understanding from learning-off (and are in other well-known ways imperfect). It is surprising, perhaps, that this form of assessment – what might be called "assessment by more advanced understanding' – is not, to my knowledge, widely used. But perhaps it is not so surprising after all, in a society where forms of assessment are seen as competitive devices. For it only makes sense when one's objective is to ensure that those assessed have all reached the same standard rather than to see what is the best that each individual can do. Examinations of the more conventional kind may also, of course, be used to satisfy the first of these objectives, but just when and where they are preferable to assessment by more advanced understanding is a question for more detailed research.

Once one has fixed the basic minima in depth and breadth for the seventeen- or eighteen-year-old school leaver, one can proceed to work out syllabuses at different levels to lead pupils to them. There is no reason to think that any one syllabus will be the best for all children: there may be many routes to the same goal and different syllabuses may suit different children or different teachers (Hirst and Peters, 1970, pp. 69–70). On the other hand, diversity should not be so extreme as to make it impossible, practically speaking, to integrate the work of teachers in any one curriculum area through the different age-groups. The foundations of mathematical understanding laid by the teacher of seven-year-olds must support what is taught to eight-, nine- and ten-year-olds and so on until they reach the basic minimum. If there is no official syllabus extending through this age-range, there must at least be integration at school or individual level, so that the teacher of very young children clearly sees how her work locks in with that of her successors to lead up to the basic minimum. Without this integration, education becomes a hit-and-miss affair. If there is to be no public syllabus, there must at least be some kind of public check that syllabuses are properly integrated through time. The absence of such a check in our present educational system is, in my opinion, one of its most serious faults. What the best forms of public check might be and to what extent they would necessitate controls on the individual teacher's freedom to teach what he wants are again questions for research.

Compulsory and voluntary activities

Basic minima are features of a compulsory curriculum. In discussing which curriculum areas should be compulsory, I have largely concentrated on those activities which are unintelligible without participation. The case for these is unarguable: without participation one can gain no understanding of them and so will be cut off from them as options. But what of those other familiar timetable items – foreign languages, painting, games, cookery, handicraft and so on – about which I may have seemed so far somewhat luke-warm? I have argued that there is not the same reason as before for making them compulsory: they can be understood to some extent without participation. As I stressed, however, there may well be other reasons for insisting on them, although I know of no compelling ones. The onus is on those who wish to make them obligatory to argue their case afresh. This is an important point. It is still taken as read in many quarters, especially in our secondary modern schools, that the average child's education will be largely based on activities like these: this proposition has been indoctrinated into teachers so diligently for seventy odd years that it is now become the unquestioned first axiom of a whole belief system. But it is not at all self-evident. On the contrary: there seems no good reason why any of these activities should be compulsory. This is why their supporters must be challenged at every point to give their reasons.

Suppose, however, that good reasons are not available. It would not follow that these activities should not be taught at all. Not all learning need be compulsory. There is also room for voluntary activities: not optional ones which appear on timetables already, for these are only options within a compulsory framework; but activities which children are free to choose or not choose as they wish: in a voluntary system, opting out of the whole programme is itself an option. The case for a voluntary system running parallel with the compulsory one is that children are not merely educands: they are also persons with their own life to lead. Adult life is typically differentiated into an area of compulsion – the work one has to do, the enforced roles one has to fill – and one of freedom or leisure. Adults can typically choose between many different leisure activities: they earn money which enables them, *inter alia*, and to different degrees, to follow activities of their choice. If this pattern is acceptable for adults, as I believe it is, I see no reason why it should not be so for children. The compulsory curriculum which children might follow would be their equivalent of their parents' paid employment. Beyond this, they should be provided with the material wherewithal, within reason, to follow activities of their choice. There is a strong case here for providing them with institutions where all kinds of voluntary activities can go on, activities, unlike those in the compulsory system, about which children can understand enough to enable them to choose them as options. They will include not only the kind of things mentioned above, but also activities from the compulsory curriculum of which children have some understanding and wish to pursue at greater length.

A pattern for such a voluntary system is, with certain important reservations, the Young Pioneer movement found in eastern Europe. In these countries, compulsory education is in principle in the morning only. Children are left free in the afternoon to join, if they want to, the various Pioneer 'circles' or groups, organized either on the school premises or in Pioneer Houses and Palaces serving several schools. These are elaborate youth centres, housing a great variety of 'circles' which go in for anything from gymnastics to model railways, to keeping pets, practical chemistry and playing the violin.

Eastern Europe is well ahead of us in voluntary education and I believe it has a lot to teach us. This is not to advocate slavish imitation. Voluntary education should not be used as a means of indoctrinating children into a set of political beliefs, as the Young Pioneer movement undoubtedly is. But even here we have something to learn. For the communists mix with indoctrination a great deal of what for us would be worth-while moral education of a practical sort. Habits of co-operativeness and social service, as well as obedience to party and fatherland, are deliberately fostered through group activities.

A voluntary system in this country could find room for all the types of activity whose place in the compulsory curriculum is open to doubt. Children would be able to learn languages if they wanted to; draw, paint, sing, write stories, play instruments; do woodwork, cooking and needlework; play games, swim and do gymnastics; 'contract in' to religious groups. Community service could also find a place here. There would also be room, as in the Soviet system, to pursue all sorts of hobbies, from aeromodelling to building radios. The Newsom Report did well to stress these activities, but unfortunately still within an overall compulsory framework. If we ignore this framework, the voluntary education system I have in mind would be in many ways the realization of the Newsom ideal.

It should also satisfy the libertarians. For the strong point of those who favour maximum freedom is that the child is not simply an adult in the making. He is also a child, with his own life to lead, who should be left free to do what he wants as far as possible.

This means, of course, that once the compulsory part of the school day is over, the child has the right to do nothing, if he wants to; and some people may be horrified at the prospect of millions of children idle and uncontrolled. But there should be no shortage of volunteers. The attractiveness to children of such a voluntary system would be likely to make the real problem how to keep up with the numbers.

No doubt there would be some children who did not want to join in. But provided one made sure they knew what activities were going on – which might mean more active encouragement for the younger than for the older child to attend – I see no reason for obstructing them in their wish not to join.

Many schools are moving in this direction. But too many children are still obliged to do things which they should not be obliged to; and too many lack the facilities and time to do all sorts of things they want to. Our education system needs to be rationalized. The compulsory element in it needs strengthening – to ensure that all children and not only the more able of them gain a thorough understanding of the basic disciplines. And the voluntary element needs not so much to be strengthened, as to be introduced, for we have very little conception of it as yet.

If it were introduced, it might well lead us to challenge another deep-lying assumption. It seems to have been taken as read since state education began a century ago that children should not only begin compulsory school at five, but also spend the whole of the school day, morning and afternoon, in compulsory activities (including options within a compulsory framework). But what are the grounds for this? I know of none. Again, the onus is on those who wish to support such a system to produce their arguments: *prima facia*, it seems morally unjustified, as an unfounded interference with the liberty of the child. In earlier chapters I have tried to indicate what kinds of compulsion can be justified. But I have said nothing about how much of the child's time, both from day to day and from year to year, should be spent this way. It may well be that compulsory activities need only occupy two or three hours a day on average; for all I know – or anyone knows – children may be able to spend the larger part of the day on voluntary activities. This is not a statement of belief. We quite simply have never got round to thinking seriously about this topic. The same is true of what should happen year by year. Is there any good reason why compulsory education should begin at five? Perhaps a better age would be seven. Or should there be very little compulsion on the younger child? Would it be better to leave as much as possible to adolescence? Until much more research has been done on all this and also on the amount of time a child needs, on average, to reach the basic minimum of different areas, we can only continue to grope on in the dark.

REFERENCES

Hirst, P. H. (1965), 'Liberal education and the nature of knowledge', in Archambault, R. D. (ed.), *Philosophical Analysis and Education*, Routledge & Kegan Paul.

Hirst, P. H. and Peters, R. S. (1970), *The Logic of Education*, Routledge & Kegan Paul.

Phenix, P. H. (1964), *Realms of Meaning*, McGraw-Hill, New York.

3. Interests and Education

P. S. Wilson

Source: P. S. Wilson, *Interest and Discipline in Education* (Routledge and Kegan Paul, London, 1971), pp. 67–9, 83–90.

Schooling and education are not necessarily the same thing. Wilson argues that a child's education can proceed only through the pursuit of his own interests, since these reflect his capacity to find intrinsic value in life. His teacher's task must be to sustain him in his efforts to pursue his interests in a disciplined and effective way. To the extent that he is interested in something the child is already engaged in thinking about it in a disciplined way. Such thinking is logically bound to lead him to differentiate the separate forms of disciplined, rational enquiry which some would like to see placed compulsorily at the centre of the curriculum. But these forms of thought are not indissolubly bound to traditional academic disciplines as embodied in school subjects. There is no more justification for compulsory initiation into 'disciplines' in this sense than there is for any other form of discipline not inherent in interests themselves.

A person's interests, dispositional and occurrent, represent his capacity (such as it is) to find intrinsic value in the circumstance of living, and his inclination to pursue or seek such value in terms of feeling and understanding and of activity seems appropriate to its practical point. Such a person's 'education', I believe whether in or out of 'school', consists in whatever helps him to develop this capacity for valuing and this inclination to pursue what is valued. Thus, whatever enables him to appreciate and understand his interest more fully, and to pursue it more actively and effectively, is 'educative'. But this does not mean that teachers, even when they are thinking about 'educating' children rather than just about 'schooling' them, should give assistance in the pursuit of anything and everything which catches the interest of a particular child. Still less does it mean that they should stand aside, or merely 'follow' the child down 'divergent paths'. There is a difference between helping a child to follow an interest *for* himself, and abandoning him to get on with it *by* himself. A merely tolerated child is apt to wonder in the end what his teacher is doing at school at all, if all that he ever hears from that teacher is 'Yes, Billy. On you get with it, then.' Ultimately Billy will be bound to start asking what *teacher* is 'getting on with'. Meanwhile, the interest which he had been casting around for ways of pursuing 'appropriately', founders for lack of help.

There is a constant risk involved in pursuing an interest, since no one can ever say in advance exactly how it is going to turn out. In it, one is not trying to approximate to a norm of action, or in other words to do what the majority of people might agree that one 'needs' to do. It is not a matter of trying to conform to *proven* or *consensual* standards or norms of value. It is more like trying to find out more about what it is which gives value *to* norms, or like *seeking* a measure of value against which to *evaluate* norms. In principle, this is a risky business. There might turn out to *be* precious little value in the direction in which we have taken it to lie. Or, in gaining what is of value in an interest, we might lose other values which previously we had achieved in other directions, or jeopardize the future achievement of further values in store. Just as each new understanding which we gain restructures our entire conceptual grasp of the world in which we live, so each new value which we find or seek, in pursuing an interest, brings about a shift – and sometimes a radical shift – in our entire current *scale* of values. Such changes, although pursued for their interest, are by no means always in *our* interest, let alone in the interest of anyone else. The inherent uncertainty of life's outcomes is what makes possible its interest. It also makes unavoidable its risk. Children, therefore, and perhaps especially children educationally speaking, need constantly the kind of confidence to proceed which comes from receiving effective help. This effective help is the educative function of teachers, and it *includes* the weighing of each risk against its possible gains. [. . .]

A child's interests are already selective. Through them he begins to discriminate intelligible and possibly valuable features of the world. Trying to pursue an interest means always, then, trying to see those features more and more clearly, and in doing so, *trying out* (as it were) their possible value. The child's *educational* need is to be sustained and helped through these trials, so that his interests neither become fixed in some stereotyped form through his inability to see how to develop them further, nor remain at the fleeting level which, by themselves, his own unaided efforts might achieve. But neither on educational nor on any other grounds does the child 'need' to pursue *all* his interests. Indeed, it is only on educational grounds that he 'needs' to pursue *any* of them. There is room, then, for other grounds such as prudence, practicality and morality to be considered, when the selection is being made as to which of his interests should be pursued in school. [. . .]

On this view, whether the actual activities in which pupils are engaged are cookery, gardening, mathematics, cricket, hopscotch, wall-climbing, history or anything else, is of no particular *educational* significance, any more than it is *educationally* significant that it was America, not some other place, which Columbus happened to discover. One might be concerned about pupils' activities on *other* grounds, such as whether they were dangerous, for example, or involved harm to others – and on these grounds one would *have* to exercise some control over the activities and the pupils. It would be absurd, for example, to let a child dash across a busy street in front of traffic merely on the *educational* ground that he was extremely interested in something happening on the other side of the road. Nevertheless, in advance of knowing which activities were interesting to pupils, one could never rule out any activity at all on the grounds that it was inherently *uneducative,* nor could one have any *educational* ground for declaring that there are some things rather than others which all pupils, regardless of their interests, *must* study.

Worthwhile activities

It is at this point, perhaps, that there is some conflict between the view of education which I am describing and that of R. S. Peters, although just how fundamental this conflict may be I am still not altogether sure. (The matter is discussed in Wilson, 1967; Peters, 1967b.)

It is, he says, because some activities rather than others best exemplify or most explicitly embody disciplined, rational inquiry, that we should place these activities compulsorily at the centre of the school curriculum for all. The very fact that we are concerned to give good reasons for a curriculum is itself the best possible reason for getting pupils going on those theoretical pursuits such as science and history in which the different forms of disciplined thought can be seen (by us, at least) in their most highly developed state.

Whenever a teacher or a pupil starts to think seriously about what he is doing (as he must start to think, if he is going to engage in it in a disciplined, educationally worthwhile way), then, argues Peters, he is bound to find himself involved in the sorts of intellectual pursuit of which ultimately (as we, at least, can see) the curriculum of a university is largely constructed. Thus, he says:

> It would be irrational for a person who seriously asks himself the question 'Why do this rather than that?' to close his mind arbitrarily to any form of inquiry which might throw light on the question which he is asking. (1966, pp. 162–3)

Therefore, he argues, if the curriculum of any child's schooling is to be *educationally* justifiable, it must include those intellectual pursuits which we can see as best exemplifying the giving of good reasons for *anything*, even if at first the children themselves, understandably, cannot see them in this way.

If the kind of compulsion which is being envisaged here is logical, or in other words if all that is being said is that *any* serious thought is *logically* bound to take more or less orderly and intelligible forms, then I am not sure that the conflict between what is being said and the principle of 'learning through interest' is a fundamental one. Unfortunately, however, the argument can also be interpreted (White, 1969) as meaning that all pupils must compulsorily be *made* to undertake studies such as science and history seriously – and the compulsion intended here is psychological and perhaps, if necessary, physical. This compulsion, it is argued, has a prudential function, as a prerequisite for the pupils' eventual attainment of a worthwhile way of life. In no other way, the argument runs, could we be sure that *all* pupils would have the opportunity to develop the capacity (eventually) for making rational choices about what they should do when (eventually) the compulsion is lifted. Not before this point (i.e. eventually) would it be rational to free them from external compulsion.

But obviously one aspect of the problem here is to find a *rational* way of deciding what is meant by 'eventually', or in other words of deciding *when* it would be rational for the external compulsion to be withdrawn. Plato, for example, seemed to think that it could not be before the age of about fifty or so that people (and then only a very few people) would be able to make rational choices and, therefore, would be fit to graduate from the ranks of the compelled to join the ranks of the compellers. This, of course, was just Plato's opinion. There is no rational way of *knowing* whether or not a person has become capable of rational choice. One could never be sure on *rational* grounds alone that one's criteria for judging rationality were themselves rational and were being rationally employed.

Further than this, however, from what I have already written it should be plain that there is something very odd about the whole idea of proposing to use physical and psychological sanctions to 'make' pupils undertake certain studies seriously, just as there would be about trying to 'make' them interested in something by such methods. One can compel someone's obedience to a system of social control, but no one can be *psychologically* or *physically* 'made' to submit to the *logical* and *moral* imperatives of disciplined thinking. It would be like standing over someone with a stick or a threat of imprisonment and saying 'Will you or will you not admit that 2 and 2 make 4!' or 'Will you or will you not admit that one should pursue truth!', and continuing in this way until (eventually) he was 'forced' to admit it. It may be an empirical question whether or not, and in what precise circumstances, anyone subjected to such treatment ever *does* subsequently become interested in or start to think seriously about the matters which he has first been, as it were, force-fed. But at least it should be clear that the force-feeding, in itself, does nothing to help the pupils even to *start* to understand or see the intrinsic point of the subject-matter. I cannot see anything *rational* about my trying to force someone to study seriously the things which I take seriously and see as best exemplifying rationality but which he as yet does not. On the face of it, indeed, I would think that such treatment would be at least as likely to close his mind to those things as to open it. To offer him some extrinsic reward for studying or to threaten him with a penalty for not studying might, indeed, be the very thing most likely to convince him that there is no *intrinsically* good reason for such studies, and that the real reason for undertaking them must therefore lie in their contingent utility for getting pleasures and avoiding pains.

Moreover, it is in any case one of the main theses for which I have been arguing that there is no *educational* need to treat pupils in this way, however necessary it may seem at times on grounds of prudence. And, on balance, I think that this argument, rather than such arguments for the compulsory curriculum as those of J. P. White to which I have referred, is supported by the main part of what R. S. Peters has written on the subject. [. . .] What has been shown, I believe, by Peters is that a more or less disciplined understanding of *whatever* a pupil is engaged in is an essential part of what we mean by the educativeness of a situation. His argument, as I see it, is not that children need to be forced to 'study science', for example, because then they will *get to think* rationally. Rather, it seems to me, he is saying that 'studying science' is one of the things which we *mean* by 'thinking rationally'. It would follow, then, that to the extent that a child was engaged in *any* activity in a way which involved trying to think about it rationally, he would thereby *unavoidably* be engaged in thinking about it 'scientifically'. If this were so, then the issue turns on how narrowly or widely one limits or defines the activities which one is prepared to count as being bona fide examples of 'thinking scientifically', 'historically', 'mathematically', 'aesthetically', 'morally', and so on. Differences of definition in this case, however, would be stipulative, not a matter of differences of fundamental principle. An infant school and a university teacher might have differences, for example, about what they were prepared to call 'art'. Both, however, could still agree as to the seriousness, and therefore the more or less disciplined, rational and educative character, of their pupils' thinking.

To me it would seem then that what has been established is that a child does not have to be made to wait until he has studied certain school subjects as defined, say, by university teachers, before he can be adjudged to be (more or less) rational. If he is seriously studying the doing of *anything*, then he is engaged already in trying to be more rational about *it*. If his teacher, in separating out the logically distinct forms of thought which the child is actually developing in this way, finds it helpful to use, or to avoid, labels such as 'science', 'history' and so on, this does not affect the basic issue of principle which is involved, nor should it be allowed in any *further* way to put limits on what the child *must* do if he is to succeed in his activity. If a child is interested to find out more about how his family, for example, or his neighbourhood or school or anything else, got to be the way it is, whether or not one calls this 'studying history' is not the vital issue; and to try to compel him to undertake such inquiries because one considers it vital for him to 'do history', would be a pointless undertaking. What is of fundamental importance educationally is whether or not his inquiries (whatever they are) are being engaged in for their intrinsic interest. What makes his curriculum educationally worthwhile is not the presence on it of any particular school subject, but the presence *in* it of serious thought about *whatever* he is doing.

'Serious thought' means thought for which one is prepared to give one's reasons, up to the point at which there are no more reasons which one can give. At this point one can and should be willing to be instructed, but, educationally speaking, no one can or should try to psychologically or physically *make* one receive that instruction. To see the point of an instruction one has to be trying to do so. One cannot be 'made' to see its point by being instructed to *do* so. The only way in which one could interpret such *unilluminating* instruction ('Do it or else!') would be as a series of commands to be obeyed.

'Disciplines' and 'subjects''

In the present chapter I have tried to explain my view that whereas 'instructing' in the sense of commanding or 'giving orders' which are backed by psychological and physical sanctions has no place at all in educative teaching, instructing in the sense of 'informing' is an integral part of such teaching. It seems to me misguided, then, to try to restrict instruction, as many teachers do, to certain 'compulsory' subjects or to the so-called 'basic skills', while depriving children of educative instruction in other areas. Usually this deprivation is called 'leaving children free to discover', and, apart from 'discovery learning' in mathematics and science, the areas in which children are commonly left to flounder about by themselves in this way are those of the so-called 'practical' and 'creative' activities of 'topics'. Where instruction is unilluminating, naturally enough it must seem to the child to be no more than a stream of arbitrary constraints. On the other hand, when children do find instruction informative, their being given it does not somehow make them less 'free' or in some sense imply that they have been prevented from 'discovering' its significance *for* (as opposed to by) themselves. Logically speaking, one could never 'discover' something which was totally 'unstructured', inchoate, formless – for in a formless experiential flux there would be nothing 'there', so to speak, to 'discover'. Aside from that, however, when pupils *do* grasp the illuminating point of instruction it makes perfectly good sense to say that *they* have thereby been helped to 'discover' or 'find' its relevance or connection with whatever it is which they are trying to do. One of the main values in having a good teacher, I would have thought, is from the child's point of view that with this instructive help interesting activities and experiences do not remain in a *relatively* formless, incoherent, 'unstructured' state.

I am not concerned, therefore, with the relative merits of 'instruction' and 'discovery learning' as *alternative* methods of teaching (Dearden,

1967), since I do not see them *as* alternatives. What seems to me of main importance, rather, is the dependence of *both* of them, if they are to be educative or in other words to help children to make any progress in the pursuit of their interest, on the selection of appropriate subject-matter for study in school. If the teacher is preoccupied, above all else, with getting the children to study certain 'subjects' whether they find them interesting or not, then, where there *is* no interest there will *be* no 'illuminating point' in his instructions, since there will be nothing in the pupils' experience for those instructions to connect with. Similarly, if he abandons explicit instructions in favour of 'discovery materials' intended to get the children going on those subjects by themselves, the children in this case will still not have the faintest idea what it is that they are supposed to be 'discovering'. In neither case can the situation become an educational one. The children's 'practical activities' remain on the undeveloped level of more or less fleeting and pointless amusements or diversions. Little serious thought goes into them, because no effective help is being given about *how* to think about them in a more disciplined and effective way. Where there is *no* intrinsic connection between the teacher's preoccupations and the children's interests, probably the most that the latter will 'discover' is that school is a place where it pays you to *look* as though you're seriously busy, regardless of whether you yourself can see the point of what you're doing or not. Meanwhile the teacher expends *his* effort in securing obedience to his instructions, or attention to his 'discovery materials', generating theoretical pursuits whose practical point may be clear enough to *him*, but could never be clear to the children except in some more or less remote and eventual future.

The content of the particular 'fields of knowledge' (e.g. Hirst, 1967; 1969) as one actually finds it in 'school subjects', is arrived at chiefly, I would think, on the *practical* grounds of its interest to the people engaged in teaching it. What concerns me is that these practical grounds are seldom the pupils' ones. More often they relate, for example, to particular academic traditions and to the examination requirements by means of which teachers test knowledge of those traditions. What I am suggesting is that in many cases the teacher's overprotective attitude towards or preoccupation with his own 'discipline' and his concern with getting pupils to pursue it in the way, eventually, in which he would like (or would have liked) to pursue it himself, is educationally speaking misplaced. To the extent that a child is 'thinking seriously' at all, rather than acting merely on impulse or from liking or for immediate gratification or to please or placate (or annoy) his teacher, then it seems to me that it is *logically* unavoidable that his thinking will come increasingly to take conceptually distinct 'forms'. But these categorial or conceptually distinct 'forms', increasingly explicit in disciplined ways of thinking or 'forms of thought', are not somehow paradigmatically embodied in 'school subjects' or in 'fields of knowledge' as these are found in school curricula. What particular children will think seriously *about* is something which we cannot forecast or preselect with any reliability until we ourselves are taking an interest in and 'thinking seriously' about the practical pursuits of those children. This is something which we scarcely ever do, since the main part of our effort goes into devising 'methods' and 'materials' for getting the children, theoretically at least, to engage in *our* favoured pursuits.

It does not seem to me, then, that we have good grounds for saying that there are *some* activities ('doing' history, science, research, and so on) about which one can 'think seriously' and other activities (e.g. keeping pets, playing hopscotch, cooking, telephoning a friend) about which one cannot really 'think' in an educationally worthwhile way at all. Whether (for economic or other reasons) we call it 'work' or 'play' (Dearden, 1967; Manser, 1967), the 'seriousness' of any activity is shown by one's willingness to try to give reasons for the way in which one is engaging in it, or in other words by the extent to which one can show that one is thinking about it in a more or less disciplined way. For example, the *moral* seriousness of a game (any game), as something to be played 'properly' rather than just 'played about' (or fooled around) *with*, seems to me a far better guarantee that children will be likely to exert themselves in 'serious' thought about it (Wilson, 1968), than that provided by the vocational or economic or other 'good' reasons with which we so often try to persuade children to 'work'.

Practical considerations can be placed first, then, in planning school curricula, without this endangering in any way the disciplined character of pupils' thinking. But the chief practical consideration for the teacher, in my view, should not be his respect for his *own* characteristic style of thinking (nor that of the academic tradition in which he sees *himself* as working), but for the pupil's. The pupil's thinking, too, has a tradition, and, unless the teacher begins his instructive communication with the pupil in a language and in relation to experiences and activities which *already* the pupil understands something of the point of, then no conceptual development and no development of interest will result directly from the encounter. To quote Bernstein again:

> If the culture of the teacher is to become part of the consciousness of the child, then the culture of the child must first be in the consciousness of the teacher. This may mean that the teacher must be able to understand the child's dialect, rather than deliberately attempting to change it. (1970, p. 120)

'*May* mean' is the understatement of the year: this is what it *must* mean. Moreover it must mean that the culture of the teacher, too, must change, at least until it reaches a state in which he is prepared to admit that the child *has* a 'culture', or in other words is something more than a mere barbarian at culture's gates.

REFERENCES

BERNSTEIN, B., 'A critique of the concept of "compensatory education" ' in Rubinstein and Stoneman (ed.), 1970.

DEARDEN, R. F., 'Instruction and learning by discovery' in Peters (ed.), 1967.
DEARDEN, R. F., 'The concept of play' in Peters (ed.), 1967.

HIRST, P. H., 'The logical and psychological aspects of teaching a subject', 1967, in Peters (ed.), 1967.
HIRST, P. H., 'The logic of the curriculum' in *Journal of Curriculum Studies*, vol. I, May 1969.

PETERS, R. S., *Ethics and Education*, London: Allen & Unwin, 1966.
PETERS, R. S., 'In defence of Bingo: a rejoinder' in *British Journal of Educational Studies*, vol. 15, June 1967 (b).

MANSER, A. R., 'Games and family resemblances' in *Philosophy*, vol. 42, July 1967.

WILSON, P. S., 'In defence of Bingo' in *British Journal of Educational Studies*, vol. 15, February, 1967.
WILSON, P. S., 'Review of Dearden, R. F., *The Philosophy of Primary Education*' in *Education for Teaching*, no. 77, Autumn, 1968.

4. Towards a Theory of Popular Education

G. H. Bantock

Source: *The Times Educational Supplement*, 12 and 19 March 1971. Reprinted by permission in R. Hooper (ed.), *The Curriculum: Content, Design and Development* (Oliver and Boyd, Edinburgh, 1971), pp. 215–64.

G. H. Bantock puts forward specific curriculum proposals to provide a satisfactory education for the mass of children for whom the present watered-down academic education is failing. Bantock dissents from the view of Professor Hirst that there is no need for a radically new pattern of the curriculum. Bantock also argues against Hirst's view that all curricula for all children should have as their central objective the development of mind. Instead of a cognitively based curriculum with emphasis on linguistic and abstract forms of thought, Bantock argues that the basis of the curriculum should be more concrete, more practical and 'affective-artistic' in orientation.

Two fundamental and highly intractable educational problems have arisen out of the scientific and technological revolution of the last 200 years, and the industrialization which has accompanied it.

In the education of the meritocracy, which has replaced the old landed aristocracy as the ruling elite, we are faced with the need to find a substitute for the old classical curriculum as the central humanistic and civilizing discipline which in the past penetrated into so many aspects of our social and cultural life.

Only Dr F. R. Leavis has suggested a solution to this problem in pointing to English literature as the civilizing agency, a solution, however, which is necessarily partial and in any case not likely to achieve universal acceptance.

The second problem relates to the need to provide a satisfying education for those children who have entered the schools as a result of the universal provision of education following the 1870 Act, but for whom the watered down academic education we still provide as the core of the curriculum would seem to have failed.

What is common to both is a concern for the content of education, in contrast to controversies which currently distract us and which centre on organization and methodology and thus avoid the fundamental issues about what to teach – and to whom.

Before I proceed I had better explain my title. A theory of education implies the bringing to bear of the various disciplines relevant to education in an attempt to clarify aims and purposes. History, sociology, psychology and philosophy provide us with information or clarification in a variety of ways which can help us in coming to practical decisions about how to educate people. As Professor Hirst has indicated, an educational theory is perhaps best classified as a form of moral knowledge.

By popular, in this context, I intend in the first place a general reference to those children with whom our present schooling would appear to have failed. As a group, they are perhaps most clearly defined in the pages of the Schools Council inquiry *Young School Leavers* (1968). I quote from the introduction:

> 'The intended raising of the school leaving age to 16 . . . means retaining in school for a fifth year of secondary education some 60 per cent more of the age group than now stay on voluntarily. The majority of those affected have an ability for scholastic work which is average or below average. Some will come from homes which will attach small value to extended schooling. For many, vocational motivation will be weak; it will be difficult to gain their interest and sense of relevance; some will actively resent having to study longer in school.'

I would be happy if, in the first place, my suggestions could be applied to approximately the bottom 50 per cent of this group and throughout their secondary school careers, from 11. They will be children of low achievement, probably though not invariably of low I.Q., come from culturally deprived homes, wish to leave school as soon as possible and find themselves employed on leaving in unskilled or semi-skilled jobs. To be more specific still, I am thinking of the bottom stream in small secondary modern schools, in the bottom two or three streams in larger modern and comprehensive schools.

Let me begin by attempting to place what will inevitably be the majority of these children in their historico-sociological setting. This historical dimension is often lacking in our thinking about them. In pre-industrial times there were two broad cultures – that based on literacy for the sophisticated and that based on an oral tradition for the folk. Most of the children I have picked out above will, in terms of cultural background, come from the traditional folk group – dull children from the traditionally sophisticated group are likely to find themselves in the private education sector.

As a help to diagnosing their level of understanding it may be helpful if we seek some clues concerning the traditional nature of folk consciousness. In Professor Owst's *Literature and pulpit in mediaeval England* he quotes with approval Miss Evelyn Underhill's statement that 'It is characteristic of the primitive mind that it finds a difficulty about universals and is most at home with particulars': and Professor Owst adds that the characteristic features of English medieval preaching 'exhibit this same desire to escape as far as possible from the abstract and universal in religion and to be at home in particulars'.

If we then turn to a nineteenth century comment on the peasant consciousness in George Bourne's *Change in the village,* we read:

> '. . . We may say that a modern man's thought goes on habitually at two main levels. On the surface are the subjects of the moment – that endless procession of things seen or heard – which make up the outer world; and here is where intercourse with the old type of villager was easy and agreeable. But below the surface, the modern mind has a habit of interpreting these phenomena by general ideas of abstract principles . . . and into this region of thought the peasant's attention hardly penetrated at all.'

D. H. Lawrence, the one twentieth-century working-class imaginative writer of genius, spoke of his father's generation in these terms:

> 'The colliers were deeply alive instinctively. But . . . they avoided, really, the rational aspect of life. They preferred to take life instinctively and intuitively.'

Lawrence's whole analysis of the working-class consciousness implicit throughout much of his work is, of course, of the deepest significance for my theme. But these evocations drawn partly from the past and partly from an imaginative writer would cut little ice with many were they not uncannily picked up by the findings of a modern empirical sociologist.

In a paper on 'Social class, language and socialization', Professor Bernstein has analysed what he terms 'the two codes employed by English people' and which he refers to respectively as elaborated and restricted. He argues that 'elaborated codes orient their users towards universalistic meaning, whereas restricted codes orient and sensitize their users to particularistic meanings'.

The implication of universalistic he explains is that 'the meanings are less tied to a given context'; where the orders of meaning are particularistic they are 'more context bound' – that is, 'tied to a local relationship and to a local social structure'. Finally, '. . . restricted codes draw upon metaphor whereas elaborated codes draw upon rationality'.

If I am right to place the group of children in whom I am interested among those whose language code is significantly restricted, then both the historical and contemporary evidence points to features of their language usage which can be empirically demonstrated and which must be taken into account in considering the viability of any system of education, such as ours, which conventionally is deeply linguistically oriented.

Our present system of education, indeed, is language oriented not only in the demands that it makes on conceptual development needed for an understanding of the relevant school subjects, but in the very nature of the consciousness which is fundamental to its whole meaning and significance. Fundamental to the culture of the school is the book; and it is astonishing how little we have asked the apparently simple question: 'When we teach people to read, what do we do to them?'

I have attempted to explore this problem in my inaugural lecture at Leicester University, *The implications of literacy*. Briefly, the effect is to introduce a child at an early age into a quite different level of consciousness than that implicit in the early folk tradition. Reading implies a concentrated attempt to translate inanimate shapes on a printed page into significant meaning. Whereas, in face-to-face contact, our voice, gestures, facial expressions, vocal emphases, add meaning, none of these aids are present where the printed word is concerned; our need then is to evoke meaning from something that is essentially inanimate and dead.

As R. G. Collingwood put it in his *Principles of art*: 'The written or printed book is only a series of hints from which the reader then works out for himself the speech gestures which alone have the gift of expression.' Anyone who has had any experience of attempting to teach reading to backward children does not need to be told how fantastically difficult a task some of them find this to be.

Yet it is upon this subtle understanding of printed language that the culture of the school continually makes demands. The school curriculum, it is true, constitutes a watered-down and simplified high culture; but in general its meaning structures become progressively more universalistic as its material becomes increasingly more complex. By nature it is primarily cognitive and even when it involves some degree of affectivity, as in literature, it still necessitates a capacity for highly subtle translation of written symbol into meaning – a meaning both cognitive and affective.

Furthermore, the culture of the school as at present constituted involves delayed satisfaction and a whole set of cultural expectations and requirements which make it not surprising that it is the middle classes rather than the working classes that benefit most easily from it. The working class ethos as, for example, it is defined impressionistically by writers such as Richard Hoggart, contains elements of emotional warmth and a stress on the immediacies of social contact which belie the isolation and intellectualization of the school curriculum. The social conditions of the working classes do not encourage the detachment from immediate contacts which the nature of school subjects imposes.

Since most of the children I have in mind are likely to come from those descendants of the traditional folk, the working classes – if only because such classes contain more members than any other section of the community – and, furthermore, the theory of embourgeoisement has recently become less acceptable and we are less sure than we used to be that gradually working class people are becoming assimilated to middle class habits, the precise nature of working class gregariousness is of paramount importance for my theme – as is the nature of working class expectations and satisfactions.

Clues concerning these will be noted in the predominating nature of mass media communications. The popular culture of television, radio and mass circulation newspaper evokes immediate satisfaction and reveals the vital role of affectivity in its appeal. Advertisements do not stress rationality, but use images evocatively to persuade and cajole.

A typical popular manifestation on the media implies an interest in personality and transmits its meaning as often as not visually (even when the medium is print – our most popular newspapers make excessive use of visual aids for what is primarily a print medium) in ways which imply that visual symbols rather than language is a potent way into the consciousness of the folk. Identification with people and life styles rather than critical assessment is what is invited. It is not surprising when the nature of much of our popular culture is assessed that D. H. Lawrence should have indicated that knowledge for the people must be 'mythical, symbolical, dynamic'.

I believe that this general picture of the level at which the people of whom I am speaking operate, is supported by such psychological insight as we have acquired in recent years into the nature of children's learning. It is first of all reasonable to expect that not all children can be brought to the same level of achievement. It is true that recently the fashionable doctrine has tended to be that even allowing for the observed deficiencies of many children, these are explicable in terms of inhibitory environmental factors which can be compensated for; thus there has been a stress on compensatory education in order to aid deficiencies in conceptualization. Implied has been a near equality of endowment which only inequalities of background have inhibited from full fruition.

Latterly, the claims of heredity have again been put forward and the work of Burt, Eysenck and Jensen has stressed the element of hereditary endowment. Difficult and complicated though the nature–nurture controversy is, the notion of the almost infinite plasticity of human intellectual endowment has suffered a number of blows from which it is not likely to recover. Compensatory education in America especially has been directed to filling in the gaps in achievement in order to equalize opportunity to take advantage of the current curriculum. The current curriculum, however, with its cognitive emphasis seems to remain obstinately beyond the grasp in any meaningful sense, of the children about whom we are talking; results of American compensatory programmes have not on the whole been propitious.

Professor Arthur Jensen, indeed, has made the interesting suggestion on empirical grounds that two different levels of mental functioning exist – one at the conceptual level and one at what he has termed 'the level of associative learning'. This seems to tally uncannily with the impressionistic diagnoses of mental functioning on which I have drawn earlier in this article from my historical sources.

Some evidence for the possibility that many children may remain roughly at Piaget's level of concrete operations at a time when their sophisticated fellows are moving into the abstractions of formal operations may supply further supportive evidence to this picture. Thus, Mr. Roger Hallam has conducted some investigations into children's capacities to grasp historical concepts used in history teaching ('Piaget and the teaching of history', *Educational Research*, vol. 12, no. 1, November 1969). Using Piaget's work on logical thinking as a basis, he has come to the conclusion that:

> 'Whatever stage might have been reached by a particular pupil, the majority of secondary school pupils up to the mental age of 16 years seem to be at the concrete operational level of thought. The syllabuses should therefore be organized to take account of the limitations in pupils' reasoning.'

Hence he points to the need to concentrate, for many pupils, on what he terms concrete history. The need for care in the use of specialist terms is further illustrated in Mr. Douglas Barnes's admirable Penguin paper on education, *Language, the learner and the school* where in his analysis of the language of instruction he also draws attention to the use of language forms which, while not specific to any one subject, are nevertheless of a kind a pupil would be unlikely to encounter in everyday informal speech.

It is true that Dr. Hallam's own work on the use of specialist terms peculiar to history is limited in scope and needs to be followed up by further investigations. It is even more true that we need many more of the sorts of investigations he has mounted into the precise capacity of children to grasp the abstractions peculiar to particular subject areas of the school curriculum; and further, that we need to know a great deal more about what Mr. Barnes refers to as 'the language of secondary education' – school language of a non-specialist kind but peculiar to the classroom. What can be said is that much is misunderstood by children of lesser intelligence. The ability to understand abstractions at different levels and in different conceptual fields is fundamental to the implementation of our present purposes in education and a major reason for thinking some extensive reorientation of our present practices desirable.

I can perhaps illustrate this point and at the same time begin to move towards a more positive statement of the implications of this analysis by considering a statement made by Professor P. H. Hirst in *Working Paper no. 12*, published by the Schools Council, on 'The educational implications of social and economic change'.

There, Professor Hirst explicitly asserts that there is no need for a 'radically new pattern of the curriculum'. He continues:

> 'As I see it, the central objectives of education are developments of mind. . . . No matter what the ability of the child may be, the heart of all his development as a rational being is, I am saying, intellectual. Maybe we shall need very special methods to achieve this development in some cases. Maybe we have still to find the best methods for the majority of people. But let us never lose sight of the intellectual aim upon which so much else, nearly everything else, depends. Secondly, it seems to me that we must get away completely from the idea that linguistic and abstract forms of thought are not for some people.'

This view represents a powerful body of opinion in the educational world and, unlike some such opinions, is backed by some of the best minds working in education. At the same time, it is a view from which I must in many respects dissent. The grounds of dissent will already have been implicit in a good deal of what I have said . . . ; but a brief analysis of Professor Hirst's statements may perhaps help in further clarifying my objections to his position. He deprecates the idea that 'linguistic and abstract forms of thought are not for some people'.

Now, it is perfectly true that linguistic forms of thought must be for everyone above the level of the seriously brain damaged. Language is the characteristic feature of human communication and is, indeed, one of the features in terms of which one can define what it is to be human. Insofar therefore as people are capable of thinking at any level at all in a rational way, language is likely to be the mode through which their thought processes are made manifest. In this trivial sense, then, we may well admit that linguistic forms of thought are for all.

It is the inclusion of the word 'abstract' that causes the difficulty. Abstraction, according to the dictionary, denotes 'the act of considering something as a general quality or characteristic apart from any concrete realities, specific object, or actual instance'. All normal people make use of some abstractions. No one, for instance, is likely to have any difficulty in understanding the sentence 'All chairs are meant to sit upon', where one is considering the general characteristic of chairs apart from any specific instance.

There are, too, certain abstract terms which are sufficiently context-bound to indicate clearly their significance. No one, again, is likely to have much difficulty with the word 'free' in the sentence 'You are free to leave the room'. But what is at issue is not the ability of people to understand and employ abstractions of this sort, but to comprehend complicated abstract arguments on the use of abstractions in contexts which make their precise significance much more difficult to decide upon.

Many school subjects, after all, develop complex patterns of abstractions as an essential part of their logical framework. When terms are used, as in areas like social studies (often thought highly relevant to the 'needs' of less able children) which are also in general usage – terms like 'freedom', 'authority', 'responsibility', 'representative' – it is not surprising that the often highly abstract nature of the discourse is beyond the grasp of many. If, for instance, one utters the sentence 'Freedom is an essential human right', notions of 'freedom' and 'rights' are much more difficult to determine with any degree of precision and the appearance of such sentences in the course of a developing argument is likely to bewilder many.

Clearly one has to go carefully here. I have already . . . pointed to the absence of detailed empirical studies which would guide us in understanding the precise levels of abstraction which in different subject areas children at different ages are likely to be able to encompass.

At the same time, my initial evidence drawn over a long historical period and the particular analysis which Professor Bernstein has given us, make it reasonable to assert that many levels of abstraction are likely to be beyond the capacity of numbers of people and that among those numbers are likely to be included the particular group of children with whom I am specifically concerned in this article.

It is no good persisting in our current ways on the grounds that we just do not know whether some different approach might not enable people to encompass the necessary abstractions determined by the school curriculum. After all, we have tried a watered down 'high culture' for nearly a hundred years – and still not found the way. It is entirely reasonable to make extrapolations from what we already do know and can observe, and to act responsibly on a basis of this.

It would be the more justified if it were possible to provide an alternative curriculum which would avoid the trivialities implicit in much of the vocational and life adjustment work done as a sop to the less able.

The question that faces us is indeed: 'Can we find a syllabus which will be at once demanding but which, based on different principles from the current one, will afford greater opportunities to those who at present show little aptitude for the cognitively based curriculum?' I believe it is, and that its basis should be affective-artistic rather than cognitive-intellectual.

It is interesting in this respect to note that Professor Hirst asserts in the working paper mentioned that 'we must get away from what can be called a retreat into the Arts and practical activities, as being more suitable for the less intellectually able'. His use of the word 'retreat' seems to me highly significant. I will, for the moment, avoid his reference to 'practical activities' and concentrate specifically on his reference to the arts.

I am particularly interested in his view that work in the arts should seem to betoken a 'retreat', as if somehow they constituted an inferior way of looking at the world than that implicit in the more rational subjects. Admittedly, and to be fair to him, Professor Hirst does indicate that 'there is a central place in education for the Arts'; but he proceeds: 'the significance of the Arts is limited and any retreat from the demands of other forms of development in language is to set barriers to the developments open to many children'. Of course, the significance of the arts is limited as, for that matter, is the significance of the sciences; either forms only a segment of the totality of human awareness and understanding. But the use of the word 'retreat' would seem to indicate that Professor Hirst would have serious reservations about regarding the arts as the key to the education of any children.

Put it another way, his persistent emphasis is on the linguistic as the tool of thought rather than on expressive action as the key to emotional discipline. And here I would disagree with him.

Before, however, I proceed to clarify my meaning, it is desirable to summarize what has emerged implicitly from my analysis as relevant to the formulation of a curriculum for these children.

The level to be aimed at must, it would seem, as far as possible, be that of practical common life. This is implicit in the need to be concrete and specific. But it must be practical life without any of the more dismal overtones which the word 'practical' too often conveys. 'Practicality', indeed, does not necessarily imply undertakings of limited vision and imaginative poverty. Practical life at the domestic and work levels is important for these children, but so is the 'practical' life of entertainment and human relationships.

Television, film and the popular press are part of their culture and these, in however poverty stricken a way, make demands on their imagination – as spectators of course, not as participants. Part, too, of the practical world is that of marriage and human relationships and these test at the profoundest and subtlest levels.

It will be necessary then to appeal to 'practicality' not only in the mundane terms of adding up the change, but at levels which can make the most intense demands at the appropriate levels on the individual's personality and imaginative capacities.

Furthermore, the emphasis on the affective which has been implicit in much of the preceding analysis, points to the need for an education of the emotions in ways which our cognitive curriculum sorely neglects. Freud has shown the extent to which our emotional life is fundamental and the arts provide traditional means by which we may seek to come to terms with these emotions.

Finally, the new leisure that may characterize later twentieth century living as a result of the development of automation, means that an element of liberal education is central to any genuine education for these children. Traditionally, a liberal education has implied a leisure class. It is highly possible that we are moving into an era when all will participate in some degree of leisure which it is vitally important that education should help to fill.

The fundamental discipline of the old education, whether elementary or advanced, was the act of reading, the gateway to the inner consciousness, social detachedness and the opportunity to develop rationality. The fundamental discipline of a revised educational system for those who have found the culture of the book almost totally unacceptable is the art of movement with its emphasis on motor skills, communal participation and the opportunity to develop perception and empathy. I refer in the first instance to the particular type of movement education which Rudolph Laban has done so much to develop. Bodily movement is a fundamental characteristic of all human beings, a means through which their affectivity can be expressed: and the development of a kinetic sense is a means of entry into various of the ordered activities of the arts and of the qualities of mind which the practice of the arts demands. (The important role of mind and intellect in art has been persuasively argued by Professor Edgar Wind in *Art and Anarchy*.)

Movement in the disciplined sense intended involves the exploration of space in ways which can afford expression involving inner feelings and the images of human behaviour they evoke. At the same time, as Laban indicated, 'Dance is not to relieve feelings, it is not self-expression. Dance is no longer spontaneous gestures, but deliberate acts.' (All arts involve, at bottom, a making, not simply an outlet; it is this which makes them educative.) Thus, movement, as it merges into dance as a socialized participatory form based on rhythmic repetitions and patterned bodily behaviour becomes an art form, an articulation of gestures.

Music here is clearly relevant, both to respond to and to create in its own right. It is noteworthy that T. R. Fyvel found that music was the one expressive form to which even the most apathetic and bored of his 'insecure offenders' would respond to.

Another route from movement is in mime and drama. Here Dr. V. R. Bruce's *Dance and dance drama in education* provides an admirable introduction to rationale and possibilities. Drama implies the spoken word as well as the written text and these children certainly need practice in ordered and imaginative speech as well as in working from the printed word.

It must be clear that reading and writing must still inevitably form an important part of the work they are to do, though the approach I am suggesting will be a different one; they will arise out of other activities rather than form the central core of their schools' culture. The ability to read and write is a fundamental necessity in the twentieth century, but it needs to be done in terms which are affectively rather than cognitively oriented. Fortunately, Mr. David Holbrook has pointed the way here in his *English for the rejected*, a way where the links with movement, drama and other arts so far mentioned are clearly possible.

Other aspects of movement in a more limited sense merge into design and craft work and art in two or three dimensions. The Schools Council project under the direction of Professor S. J. Eggleston has shown the way forward into new areas of significance where traditional craftwork is linked with the profounder awareness of design. Art has long been part of our normal school syllabus and Herbert Read's *Education through art* which is highly relevant to this curriculum is now nearly 20 years old.

What, however, also need exploiting are possibilities specifically within the characteristic twentieth-century art forms like film, television and radio. Film making and film editing, photography in general, are means through which children can develop iconographic awareness, which are already part of today's cultural consciousness. The use of microphones and tape recorders in the classroom offer opportunities for verbalized projects which again exploit important modern media. The aim where these and the study of television are concerned should be critical as well as creative. What is needed is not only some attempt to induce critical awareness where print is involved (e.g., the study of newspapers) but some awareness of the possibilities of the media which form the background leisure-time activities of the bulk of the population of this country.

Whether this constitutes a 'radically new pattern of the curriculum' is a moot point. It certainly lays the stress in quite different ways than does the current curriculum. At the same time some elements among my suggestions – like art – are to be found extensively taught in schools, others, like film education, are to be found in a few at least. Anything too radically new would fail to attract possible support because of its totally untried nature. There is in nearly all cases I have mentioned, then, a limited body of expertise to be drawn upon. At the same time the fundamental role assigned to movement education supplies the reorientation of attitude necessary.

The approach to consciousness and mind (still the ultimate aim, for it is a fundamental error not to see that, as the arts develop, they inevitably come to involve knowledge and understanding) is through body awareness. This awareness is projected into a variety of kinetic disciplines which combine 'practicality' with imagination, affective expression and discipline and which exploit characteristic twentieth-century cultural forms.

All this at the appropriate levels, together with some emphasis on the physical life, games, outward bound projects, the opportunities which form part of the new physical education, should take up approximately three-fifths of the children's time. The rest of the time would be concerned partly with the domestic life (home management, preparation for marriage which so many parents tend to neglect, some knowledge of human relationships and sex education). This is something which boys and girls should share, though perhaps there should be a greater emphasis for girls. The other area of concern would be the technical, which would exploit especially the boys' interest in some of the mechanical inventions by which they are surrounded.

I am, of course, fully aware of the fact that if able children come to tackle this curriculum, they would accomplish it much better – academically bright children, as is well known, tend to be able all round, and indeed, Miss Marion North has recently shown that there is a good reason to believe that intelligent children have a wider and subtler range of movement than children with a lower I.Q.

Nevertheless, I remain convinced that the specific and concrete nature of the crafts and those arts which arose historically out of the crafts, provides a better route for children whose minds find existence easier to grasp in terms of the concrete and the particular – and who need help in coping with the cultural media which are the prime influences in their lives to an extent which the book is not.

This is not an education for helots, an inferior sop handed out to the inadequate, because it provides an entry into many of the greatest riches of our civilization; the point is, however, that it exists positively on many levels (as the groundling at the Shakespeare play discovered) to an extent that logical and rational thought does not. Half-baked 'ideas', indeed, the off-shoot of an attempted rationality by those ill-equipped to do the necessary thinking, constitute one of the gravest menaces to the future of our civilization.

I hold in fact what might seem to be two somewhat contradictory views. One is that children differ ineluctably in capacity for both intellectual and affective experience – heredity alone sees to that. At the same time, I am equally convinced that many children in our schools (like many people in our society) are grossly and palpably underfunctioning. The crucial question is indeed that of content – of the way to exploit such talents as they have. It is distressing to think, when the problem so clearly lies here, that we have wasted so much time and effort on the futilities of organization, as if justice was not a matter of appropriateness rather than sameness.

5. Curriculum and the EPA Community School
Eric Midwinter

Source: *Projections: an Educational Priority Area at Work,* Eric Midwinter (Ward Lock Educational, 1972), pp. 24–36.

The director of the Liverpool Educational Priority Area Project, Eric Midwinter, argues for a new sort of curriculum in the community school more in keeping with the social role of the community school. This social purpose must become implicit in the curriculum. One of the problems with changing the curriculum is that, because of massive changes in teaching methods over the last twenty years, educationists think that the revolution is over. Much of that revolution has over-emphasised method and done little about changing content. The community-oriented curriculum in the EPA school has three advantages – children will do better in traditional skills because these skills will be geared to their experience; the child is dignified by the curriculum dealing with his world and not evading it for the 'cowsheds of rurality'; parental involvement would be increased. Eric Midwinter concludes by describing the steps that the project has taken to implement a locally-based, community-oriented curriculum.

The underlying national theme of the EPA Project is the community school, recommended in the Plowden Report as being especially needed in educational priority areas. The major task of the project is the pilot testing of approaches in community schooling with a view to suggesting a national policy on the subject. The community school has as many different definitions as there are people opening their mouths on the topic, but most of them tend towards an 'open' as opposed to a 'closed' school, with more intensive usage of plant by the community in the evenings and during holidays and usually some pattern of parental participation in school life. This is surely welcome and the EPA Project has worked hard in these fields. But one might also wonder whether the curriculum needs some reappraisal. There is a danger that the community school will be the same package as before, albeit with the knots and wrapping paper a little easier to untie. Is there, in fact, a case for the community school having a community-oriented curriculum, suited to the aims of community education?

The community school is normally seen as a method of achieving harmony between school and community, but it could go beyond that. As well as providing a means, it could suggest an end. In the EPA the fundamental need is for communal regeneration and for the resolution of the dreadful social ills that beset the inhabitants. Eventually, this should mean some form of self-regeneration as the people involved set about solving these problems. Pouring in palliatives in the form of resources or services from outside is not sufficient; indeed, without the active and vital participation of the local inhabitants such interventionist policies lose much of their point. The transference of social and educational problems to new housing estates emphasizes this. A natural aim for the community school might be the education of children to be the next generation of parents, voters and citizens in the neighbourhood, in the hope that they will conceive of creative responses to the pressing needs of the downtown and other disadvantaged districts.

A negative illustration is provided by the planners' lip-service to consultation. They may knock on the door of a client for rehabilitation or decantation and ask what sort of home and environment is required. What is the unfortunate interviewee to say in answer to this? What, in too many cases, he could say is something like, 'I was never educated to listen to that kind of question nor to articulate responses, technical or creative, to it.' He might well add: 'If you would ask me to repeat the symptoms of the Black Death, recite *Cargoes* or write an essay on the Masai tribe, I should be happy to oblige.' The community school presupposes a social role for education and, in turn, this might equally apply to the curriculum. In educational priority areas, if not elsewhere, the important issues are social and not basically literary or numerary. The school could attempt to help by placing a larger emphasis on social education and a corresponding smaller emphasis on 'academic' education, the inverted commas reminding one that social education can be as intellectually and spiritually rewarding as conventional scholarship.

Herein lies the essential difference between community education and compensatory education. The latter assumes the correctness of a uniform system and merely attempts to lubricate it where, as in EPAs, it seems a trifle inefficient and rusty. This is fine, but the net result is the provision of educational passports out of the area for a few more lucky winners, the ones who, as they say, have the potential to stay on for further education. No one would begrudge them the chance, as long as it is remembered that this does no more than dilute the majority. In 1991, according to the planners, there will be 90,000 people living in the Liverpool EPA; as many again will have been ferried out to the redevelopment estates on the outskirts of the city. The children in our primary schools will by then have children at primary school. Community education in the EPAs needs to give urgent priority to these and their peers elsewhere.

This social purpose must become implicit in the curriculum. One difficulty is that so extensive and successful has been the massive modification of method in the schools over the last twenty years, that many educationists think the educational revolution is past and over. There has not, unhappily, been a similar radicalism in content and wonderfully colourful methodology has disguised the old-hatted sterility of much of the substance of education. The prime example of this is the teaching of French. In the spacious days following the Cobden-Chevalier Treaty, a wing-collared clerk scratching a few words of French was something of an asset for a merchant house trading with the continent. The 1904 Memorandum on Secondary Education sustained the idea and imbued it with its own strange brand of academic respectability. Supported by the recruitment of French graduates, who were blooded by this system and justified on the ludicrous grounds that our halting endeavours to transcribe sentences like 'Summon the postillion, my grandmother's ear-trumpet has been struck by lightning' somehow strengthened international understanding, the confidence trick boomed. French eventually moved into the primary school, presumably to fit children for more energetic construing at the secondary stage. The hardware was moved in. Records, tapes, earphones, language labs and a sizeable load of other technical equipment was deployed, giving the subject a trendy modish air. It became the vogue to teach French and the Plowden Report smiled approvingly. Despite the fact that five times as many people go to Spain as France for their holidays, and that we run the risk of turning out children illiterate in two languages rather than in one, we insist on the most specious grounds on teaching the subject. Princess Margaret opened a primary school in Barrow-in-Furness a year or so back and during her visit to its large French set-up 'at no time', according to the *Guardian*, 'did the children speak a word of English'. Trad meets mod; the outmoded Edwardian discipline is saved by the technological mechanics of today and the whole mixes up to what might be called the *chef d'oeuvre* of irrelevancy.

Most other subjects in some (not, of course, in all) places could similarly be assessed. With the onset of the white-hot technological era, for instance, science has had a face-lift and the jars of Bottogas have been appearing in junior school classrooms. The water-filled milk bottle, containing straws adorned with pieces of plasticine, has replaced watercress on blotting paper and, lo, the scientific salvation of the nation is nigh. Yet it still seems to dwell in the dreary Edwardian world of museum mustiness with its tedious series of wrongly-called 'experiments' on matters resolved a million times over. Tunes change but melodies linger on. Given the massive factor of perpetuation in education, teachers sometimes discover themselves transmitting an artificial heritage – the one, in fact, transmitted to them. There is bric-a-brac of this and that, bits and pieces of history, shreds and patches of geography, dribs and drabs of scripture, bubbles and squeaks of science, odds and sods of maths, poems and stories, a ragbag of shoddy oddments with little meaning outside the school. It's not only remote and sterile, it tends to be backward looking and romanticist. It is romanticist about the dainty, twee Victoriana of poesy and the country. City teachers, for instance, are occasionally heard saying 'some of the children in my class have never seen a cow', as though the cow has some especially bovine godlike quality or as though its modern existence is so delightfully pastoral. All the more praise to the hundreds of city teachers who withstand the heavy pressure of the unwritten conventions of the timetable and struggle manfully to get to grips with the valid educational problems around them. This is the optimistic note. There seems some awareness among headteachers and teachers that the common curricular round might not be admirably suited to the EPA.

It is time to look closely at subjects as such. The lengthy debate between informal and formal protagonists, the former with their heads blinded in the clouds, the latter with their feet clogged on the ground, has been reminiscent of the Lilliputians divided into large-enders and small-enders with no one bothering about the egg itself. Never mind a 'new' approach to maths. Can maths be justified in its own right and, if so, can it be justified for every day of the school year? Even the purported 'integration' of subjects can mislead. What price the 8+ centre of interest on monasticism, hopeful of drawing religious education (the monkish virtues), history (the Middle Ages), geography (Northumberland), English (a day in the life of a monk), and art and craft (drawings and models of monasteries and/or their inmates) into epistemological harmony? This can compound the felony. Having decided on a topic outside, at any reasonable level of accuracy and meaning, the conceptual grasp of the child, one ends with a series of third-hand exercises in support of a theme only open to second-hand consideration.

Many curricular activities are justified in terms of the 'interest motif', but interest is method, not aim. The child assuredly needs to be interested if he is to be educated, but the reverse is not always true. Surely it is the task of the teacher to make dull old ditchwater sparkle like champagne, having decided that dull old ditchwater requires investigation. Everything should and can be 'interesting'; what is necessary is a vigilant inspection of the content to ensure that it has social purpose. It is also argued that the inculcation of 'skills' is of greatest import and transfer of training is still accepted *sotto voce* e.g. the logical thought one needs for life can be learned from mathematics. Leaving aside the inadequate correlation between first-rate mathematicians and high grade lives, what is wrong with learning it from life? If all these 'skills' are so essential in life, why are not life themes more frequently used to exercise them?

Reading offers an instance of this. The range of approaches and the acrid debate over the pros and cons of each reading mystique is quite phenomenal, so much so that reading has come to be regarded as an end rather than a means. It matters not only how children read, but what and why they read. As the coincidence of the rise in public education and popular literature suggests, reading can be a soporific and not a stimulant. We may even be preventing some people from purposive action because we give them the escapist tranquilliser of a bad book. There is no reason why reading, like writing, creativity and everything else, shouldn't be geared to the child's growing awareness of his reality.

Here therefore is a major task for the community school, both at primary and secondary level. A principal goal might be the familiarization of the child with his immediate environment, in all its moods and manners, warts and all. Schools have occasionally rejected this – sometimes on 'compensatory' grounds – preferring to cosset the children with the consolations of suburban culture, attempting (in the kindest and most well-intentioned fashion) to give the children a taste of life on the other side of the tracks. Attractive though this is, it has certain defects. In offering an alien clime for an hour or so a day, it risks socially schizophrenic children and it does nothing to help the children who must perforce remain in the neighbourhood. When this approach is aligned with the pyramidal educational system, with everyone entering for the same prizes but with only a few winning them, it adds up to a training for frustration which might possibly be one of the causes of social unrest today. One sometimes hears teachers talk of broadening the children's horizons when, in effect, they are doing no more than temporarily exchanging them. This duality of approach and content amounts to the same weakness – the consequence of forcing the academic pace is to reduce the realism of the curriculum, just as the pressing of a foreign cultural norm also dilutes the immediacy of the child's education.

Conversely, if we were to concentrate on the everyone who will be a citizen/parent as opposed to the someone who will be a college student, and if we were to concentrate on the many who are called as opposed to the few who, with their O level certificates brandished like visas, are chosen, it might be a more productive assignment. Social education – the exercise of social skills on related social materials – would take precedence and, in the visionary long term, new concepts of city life might emerge. Even in the short term one might, in A. H. Halsey's compelling phrase, 'raise the heights of their dilemmas'. Only on a thorough grounding in and understanding of the situation can one hope to develop the abilities to perceive exactly what is amiss and how it might be righted. It is not so much moving from the known to the unknown as making the known more knowable.

This does not mean a dogmatic assertion of any ideology. If anything is dogmatic, it should be the assertion of tolerance and openendedness. The teachers' role would become more one of guide in the art of choice and taste, less of mentor in prejudged standards and valuations. Many teachers would agree that studies should be locality based; in some degree it is merely the 'child centredness' beloved of the educational psychologists, while many see the commonsense point of using easily sought and convenient resources. It is this possible change of social attitude that will, if accepted, impose most strain on teachers, for traditionally the teacher has been a mainstay of the *status quo* and a guardian of society's customs and mores. It would take years of arduous and genuine soul searching for teachers to agree that openmindedness and relative value systems and extreme toleration are or should be the finest hallmarks of a free and democratic society. The teachers' conventional support of certain established planks may have to be lessened, as they endeavour to conduct an objective examination of the issues facing people today in the city centres. This might include a questioning of, say, the viability of local government procedures or the validity of social and cultural standards. If teachers are to teach children to stand on their own feet, they must expect to have their own toes trodden on occasionally.

The community-oriented curriculum has three possible subsidiary advantages beyond the prior, long term hope for a higher level of civic participation. First, it is likely that given a socially-oriented content children will do as well and probably better in traditional attainments, simply because the exercise of their reading, writing and so on will be directly geared to their experience. This answers a much-pressed criticism of social education i.e. the suggestion that 'academic' prowess suffers. Second, the child is dignified by the acceptance that education can be about him and his environs, that he is an historical character in a geographical situation with social, spiritual, technical and other problems facing him. The ceaseless wandering off to the cowsheds of rurality or the poesy of yesteryear can be a constant reminder to the child that 'education' is by implication not of his world. Third, parental involvement and support for curricular enterprises would probably be enhanced by a socially relevant curriculum, in that the parents' own experience, occupations, insights and so forth would be material evidence. The mysteries of the school would be, in part, replaced by a substance well known to the parent.

Two strong arguments against the community-oriented curriculum must also be met. One claims that a downtown curriculum for downtown schools helps create a ghetto or some kind of proletarian enclave. This puts the question in reverse. Does anyone doubt that social polarization exists and that, be the borderlines blurred, unequal circumstances have created massively unequal lifechances? If this is so, a uniform educational system might well be drawing a curtain of normalcy over the gross inequalities of life. In brief it might be fairer and more honest to tell the children the truth and help them face up to the reality constructively; it might, conceivably, be more encouraging for teachers to embark on such an enterprise rather than constantly submit themselves to immaterial standardizations. Admittedly, this is a harsh doctrine. Superficially it may appear to run counter to the grand concept of equality and opportunity, but this is not so; rather does it insist that the only chance of producing equal opportunity is by differential or discriminatory treatment. Here it meets the twin grand concept of the realization of best self; it is an attempt to allow each child to realize his most fruitful potential. Socially, it is a pretence to assume that this can be done by 'equal', that is uniform, educational treatment.

The other argument is that a downtown curriculum for downtown schools indicates a second-class sort of education, a reversion to the Victorian two-tier system of one education for the rich and one for the poor. It is argued that this teaches the child to accept his lot patiently and, by concentrating on his environment, fails to thrill him with the stirring challenge of fresh horizons, such as a lesson on the climate of New Zealand or the armour of the New Model Army. It is right to be suspicious, for it was a long uphill struggle earlier in this century to establish education for all at all levels. Indeed, this is the ideal that informs the community school approach. This approach accepts the ideal but points out that implemented as a system, it has failed to work simply because social background has proved so crucial an element in educational performance. And those who think the community-based curriculum is a recipe for resignation have totally missed the point. By stretching the children intellectually and creatively on the social issues that confront them, one hopes to produce adults provoked and challenged into a positive and constructive response.

In short, it is an outward looking attitude not an introverted one. It is intended that, from the stable base of an understanding of their own locale, children can look outwards to wider frames of reference. A mastery of the immediate situation is surely the most practical means of fitting children for adaptation to other situations. It is a question of exercising social skills in viable and immediate content. Heaven knows one would not begrudge the children reading a fascinating story of long ago and far away or travelling out for joyful days in the woodlands and pastures. But let us not beatify this as some kind of 'cultural enrichment' which will transfigure the children. The majority of EPA children will live in their present neighbourhoods or on the redevelopment estates; this is the chief likelihood for which we must educate. A coach trip to the seaside or a gambol in the fields does little to redress the present inadequacies of children's preparation for their often grim destiny. A day in the country is a welcome holiday not a social solution.

So much for the fine talk. What steps have we taken on the project to explore the possibilities of a locally-based curriculum? Frankly but predictably this is one of the slower and more laborious aspects of the project. The schools have cooperated freely and, considering what must have appeared a rather hare brained analysis, bravely. Most of the project schools have undertaken the exploration of a curricular element, attempting to assess its relevance to the modern life of the urban child, and college of education teams have assisted most energetically in these investigations. The slowness of results forthcoming is relative to the quicker turnover of, for instance, home and school activities where results are immediate and obvious, be they for good or ill. It is in the nature of curriculum development to be a lengthier process, involved as it must necessarily be with the educative evolution of the child. This is even more accentuated when one is not initially concerned with short term pay-off like reading age or writing ability, but with the child's capacity for social adaptation later in life. Further, the teacher would be right to approach wholesale reappraisal warily, knowing that the children could be the critical sufferers if things went adrift. Nor would it be reasonable to expect teachers, trained and experienced in one set of methods and approaches, suddenly to adopt a different set on the say-so of any crank who happens on the school. Put another way, the theories that project directors must perforce peddle automatically come into contest with the practical realities of the school situation and the Liverpool Project team is immensely appreciative of the kindly and encouraging fashion in which the schools have given them house-room.

Perhaps our social environment probes are the most straightforward examples with which to begin. There are five of these. Two of them examine with immense detail and care some immediate social agency such as the school itself, the church, the street or the shops. This is in part a physical examination, searching out the minutiae of fabric ostensibly well known to the children and drawing on varied media to represent it. Another investigates the cultural and literary heritage of the area, looking critically, for example, at the differing religious sects and other institutions around about or re-creating, verbally and dramatically, local life and stories. Another bases its local studies on features like street surfaces and furniture, derivation of street names and changes in building usage. An infant school utilizes the everyday festivals like Guy Fawkes Day or Pancake Tuesday as foci for its work and parents are invited in to find enjoyment and instruction in the outcome. All these explorations add up to a distinctive and vigorous investigation of many facets of the locality. The manhole covers, the Victorian lamposts and pillar boxes, the types of windows, grids, hydrants and paving stones – all these give the primary child the chance to get down to a well-founded knowledge and awareness of his environ.

Creative expression is another *modus operandi*. The group in question choose a theme, such as 'occupations', 'streets', 'money', 'transport' or 'the city'. The children apply all creative media, verbal, oral, dramatic, artistic in two and three dimensions, musical and dance, to a representation of the theme, flexing their creative muscles on matters native to them, learning to conceive of responses to immediate issues. In another school a whole range of recreational activities are aimed at offering a breadth of possible leisure opportunities for the children both now and in the future. These run from film making and gardening to fishing and ice-skating, The relevancy of animal/plant studies is raised in another school where, against the background of a well-stocked animal room, the possibilities are explored of children in highrise dwellings finding pleasure and value in small scale home experiments with bulbs or larvae.

We have two infant number projects which attempt to improve the pupil's grasp of mathematical concepts with a utilitarian base like area or money. We have done a little work with junior language kits constructed around local features like the docks, and another group have composed and gathered together a series of local folksongs. This amounts to a dozen or so miniature probes. Unfortunately, because of organizational difficulties, the language work we had planned in an infant school collapsed and left us without any direct linguistic exploration, but by and large, we had been able to begin in a minor key an across-the-board sounding of the normal curriculum.

It would be folly to pretend that in a few short months the results have been startling. It took the first year of the project to complete a reconnaissance, negotiate college linkages and fields for curricular activity and navigate our way through the early weeks of difficulties. Only by and during the second year of the project (that is, the academic session 1969–1970) was the curricular work in any way structured. Even then it was, on the whole, framed thematically and in half-termly phrases. Flexibility was maintained. These probes sometimes went on much longer than had been expected if teachers adjudged them fruitful. No attempt was made to institute formal evaluation mechanisms, not only because of the fluidity of the activity and the concentration on a strategic frame rather than tactical detail, but also because the outcomes watched for were not traditional ones. We were not primarily interested, for instance, in reading age, intelligence quotients and other attainments. We were anxious to maintain an open observation of the general reaction to these activities and our interpretation of them will be founded on the consensus of the carefully prepared reports of heads, teachers, tutors and students. As in many other aspects of the project, we are looking for hypotheses which might in the future be subjected to more puristic scrutiny.

Several teachers and others find little of value in the exercise, because (as we would agree) it is not by any means novel or because (as we would agree) it bears too little relation to the conventional school timetable. Others press, with respectable reasoning, for a blitz on language and reading, while others see the work as pleasant but diversionary. So let there be no mistaking that we do not present a united front. Nonetheless, many seem agreed that two minor outcomes are evident. The first is that through the introduction of student teams and the consequent improvement of the adult/child ratio, the children have shown some general educational betterment, measured not just in terms of the actual field investigated but more in terms of the broader social relationships established. The second is a general acceptance that, whatever else, language and communications generally have been uplifted, and given the disappearance of our one language exploration, that comes as something of a relief.

It is fairly obvious that the mounting of student teams and possibly the introduction of fresh stimuli and equipment have been the major cause of this, but we do feel encouraged to add a third minor outcome, albeit a negative sounding one. The utilization of immediate resources has not created any problems of indiscipline, of time-wasting nor, more significantly, of a decline in traditional standards. There have been isolated complaints that this kind of socially-based work robs time and energy from 'bread and butter' subjects, but all in all many teachers appear to conclude that whatever else, it doesn't make any difference. Some go beyond this healthy teaching reaction and positively affirm that locality-based work does add that extra dimension of stimulation and value for the child. We are inclined to argue, therefore, that if reappraisal content does not critically impede the conventional educational development of the child, it might as well be included. The child might as well exercise his skills on locality-based materials in the hope that, overall, social awareness and purpose might be generated. Whatever our somewhat theological faith in the community curriculum, it would on the available evidence be unfair to go further than this rather wishy-washy conclusion. We are inclined toward the opinion that we have tried out several curricular pointers that could, without let or hindrance, be profitably drafted into the normal primary school syllabus.

The general nature of the project's curriculum work may be best described by what is perhaps our most picturesque illustration. A junior school undertaking a maths project decided to simulate a moderately-sized supermarket in a large, vacant domestic science room. With the help of the Tesco company, a dozen or so other firms and the enthusiastic collections of the children, this supermarket was established, complete with genuine shelving stacked with dummy packets and products, a till, baskets, and shoals of new decimal coinage. 'Chatty Stores' is now an excellent teaching aid for the school and it splendidly demonstrates the integrated character of a well chosen centre of interest. The money studies are an obvious starting point, with role-playing, stock-taking, porterage and other adjuncts. A considerable amount of allied maths has been undertaken, chiefly based on surveys of local shopping provision and habits, simple market research, household budgeting and a host of other pointers. In turn, many of these lead to meaningful social studies. For instance, a graph showing the types of shop in the vicinity may lead to the question, why are there eight chip shops and no banks? The whole social and economic issue of shopping is open to examination and is of course of great importance in the children's lives. There are art and craft possibilities – window dressing, trading stamps and so forth – and moral educational themes like shoplifting, advertising and smoking may be pursued. One could continue taking off layer after layer of potential teaching resource, all of it geared to a relevant and significant simulation, all of it interflowing without too much 'subject' division and all of it delighting the children with its real life pleasure. 'Supermarket' could become a subject in its own right.

We have certainly examined the curriculum in breadth, if not in depth, from the standpoint of locality. One reaction is fairly common. As might be expected in the excellent primary schools where we operate, the integrational fluidity, mentioned specifically with regard to the supermarket, is pretty much a constant feature. Although one school might begin with creative expression and another with animal and plant life, the overflow into all other curricular realms has been deliciously encouraging. We receive reports of children's language benefiting from a maths project or of attractive creative work emanating from an environmental exploration. The chief approach is thematic: one creative expression approach has been based on the street; one social environment approach was based on the street. The point of entry was different but the overall product differs only in mild emphasis. This feature is impressive enough to tempt one to go the whole hog and recommend that the timetable be jettisoned in favour of community themes to be pursued as widely as possible. This may be flying a little too high at the moment. The set pattern of reading, maths, physical education, religious education and the like will not be dislodged quite so simply.

As a basis for negotiation, one might suggest the compromise of half the sessions (say two mornings and three afternoons) being devoted to social education for the junior child. One bids so high not only because of the urgent importance of such work, but because the social or communal centre of interest can embrace all other curricular forms. Beyond that, it does not embrace them merely; it enlivens them with immediacy, so that the child can master the 'skills' of reading, talking, writing, number, physique, movement, art, drama, religion and all the rest in an exercise of relevant utility. Pick your theme. Draw up, in consultation with the children, your flow diagram of the points of interest and concern that commend themselves as natural and spontaneous manifestations of the theme. Organize the work load accordingly and programme the production so that it has some pattern or notion of ensemble, so that eventually the entire group will witness and benefit from the final outcome.

The implication here is that by the age of seven or eight, if not before, the primary child is ready to examine his community thoroughly. Some teachers argue that it is too early and that it is better left to the secondary school. Granted, the secondary school should do likewise at a higher and more sophisticated level, but the irony is that this method is more easily implemented in the primary school, where happily the fits and starts of the secondary schools timetable do not incommode the regular and natural commission of project-style work. But apart from the freer and less artificial clime of the normal primary school, some people underrate the social capacity of junior children in educational priority areas. One never ceases to be amazed at their resilience and aplomb, at the mature manner with which they cope with social situations and problems that might test the emotional and intellectual stamina of many an adult. To us, some of these responsibilities thrust on small children seem appalling and occasionally teachers see the school as a respite from such tribulations and a temporary five-hour shelter from the cold blasts of reality. This can be being kind to be cruel. It would be kinder to help them withstand these circumstances and it is certain that it is rarely too early, in terms of the children's experience, to begin social enquiry of the type now suggested.

Encouragingly many teachers are persuaded of the need for a community-oriented curriculum, but two objects are paramount. One, already referred to, is the question of attitude, of whether teachers should (whatever their own especial beliefs, which need not of course remain hidden) attempt to impose and set particular value systems on children. This is highly controversial country and one could not expect teachers – or for that matter parents – to shift their traditional ground sharply or swiftly. Unluckily, it is a truism to state that we are unlikely to obtain informed, constructive and articulate social criticism if we are overcircumspect about encouraging it in schools.

The other problem is more humdrum and less fraught with philosophic and moral subtleties. It is the question of resources. Education is privately serviced, and inescapably the publishers of books and other teaching aids must sell their wares both at Land's End and John O'Groats. So much of our teaching material is thus rendered neuter, abstract and 'national'. It is this which is in part responsible for the perpetuation of content which teachers often realize is either irrelevant or divorced from the children's reality. This applies not only to history and geography but to 'readers' which so often dwell in another world amazing to behold. Teachers, therefore, quite fairly argue that it is difficult to base teaching on Liverpool 7 when the available materials deal with Francis Drake, pygmies and Janet and John. Educational theorists would reply that teachers should prepare their own resources, but teachers would remind educational theorists that forty or more children won't fend for themselves while this is being accomplished. EPA teachers devote long and arduous hours to their tasks and, while many perform miracles of creation in terms of materials, there is a limit to this. Moreover the teacher might justly add that if community-oriented studies are our idea and one we make such a song and dance about, we could at least offer some concrete examples.

This we are endeavouring to do with the production of teaching kits called *Projectors* – a generic label for a very varied assortment of bits and pieces, culled from work on the project, and put into some form of order for all the Liverpool EPA schools. Five are already published. These are *Social Environment in the Downtown School,* a packet of teacher-centred suggestions on using the immediate environment, and *Down Your Way*, a large, well illustrated workbook for junior children, leading them to examine the roads and buildings in their area more thoroughly. Then there is *Home-School Horse-Sense*, an advisory wallet arising from the parental links developed by the project but including a certain amount of advice on curricular activities related to this theme. Another is an educational game, *Streets Ahead*, designed to strengthen social awareness; it can operate at three levels – the development of buildings, shops, houses and other social institutions, the uses and issues arising from the usage of these social agencies, and the children's assessment of other pupil teams' efforts in these fields. We entertain high hopes of the enjoyment and value to be found in *Streets Ahead*. The last is *Wotever Next*, a language kit for the four to six age range, with stories and characters based on the local subculture, a gradual introduction of a graded vocabulary, advice on followup work, a puppet 'presenter' and wall illustrations. This is for use in play groups and possibly nursery and reception classes. It is hoped that in future many more materials of a community-oriented nature will be made available to schools. A couple of barriers face us – money and time. There is no need to elaborate on inadequate financing, and lack of time is an obvious handicap. In puristic terms, some of these notions of language kits and games need years of time and hundreds of pounds to resolve the snags and polish the corners. All we are claiming for these *Projectors* is that they are the kind of community-based teaching aids that a teachers' resources centre might produce for its clientele. Like practically everything else in the project, they are pilot examples of what could be accomplished rather than finished answers to the problem.

It will be a long, maybe a never ending haul. Nonetheless, there are good signs. The progressive primary school method of the controlled enquiry and discovery brand is ideally suited to the content delineated. Carried to its logical conclusion, 'discovery' could lead to the open-ended attitude to social investigation that may be necessary. The operation of the pedocentric or child-centred approach has meant a considerable amount of 'localization' of the curriculum and we on the project do feel that we have opened up the area of relevant content still further. Sometimes teachers say 'This is all very well, but you can't do it until you've dealt with the basics.' Our ambition is to make social environmental or community study one of the basics.

6. Community Education: Instruction for Inequality

M. W. Merson and R. J. Campbell

Source: *Education for Teaching*, Spring 1974, pp. 43–9.

Merson and Campbell argue that recent programmes for community education are based on a myth: that socially cohesive communities, which are capable of effective community action, exist or can easily be developed in urban areas. This myth has led community educators to abandon the goal of equality of educational opportunity, through an academic curriculum for all, in favour of a curriculum based on 'relevance' to the child in his local environment. But community education is irrelevant in terms both of access to forms of knowledge and admission to the groups that exercise political control. It prevents the inner-city child from entering the mainstream of social and political discourse, and thus becomes 'a safe instrument of state ideology'.

In the last five years, Community Education in urban areas has rapidly established itself as one of the most fashionable trends in education. The reasons for the popularity of this area of innovation are not difficult to elucidate; community education has some weighty and respectable support. The Plowden Report and Halsey's Educational Priority Area Report can both be adduced in justification and the Home Office is currently sponsoring research into the field. Above all, it has the charismatic propagandist in Eric Midwinter whose books and lectures have challenged both the relevance of the conventional curriculum and the assumed feasibility of equal educational opportunity. And yet the feasibility of community or even the concept of community itself are scarcely examined. It might be useful to subject the whole concept of community education to a critical analysis and to warn about the likely consequences of its success.

We have anxieties about the current programmes which fall into three categories and provide a useful basis for our conceptual critique. They are concerned with:

1. the myth of the community in inner city areas;
2. the limited political vision of the content of community education programmes;
3. the growth of community action and development ideologies generally.

In the first place the community educators seem to have a fairly inaccurate or optimistic idea of the nature of the social structure of inner cities. We think that there is a large element of the mythic in their perceptions. They seem to believe that there is a potentially unified cohesive community in inner cities with deep shared values and interests which provide a basis for its members to identify and gain their identity, to a large extent, from their participation in it. In short their notion of community is close to the mechanical solidarity allegedly characterising village and peasant societies. The notion is nowhere expressly elaborated, and Midwinter does describe the Liverpool E.P.A. as a 'dislocated' area, but it is more a matter of what the community is expected to become, or is potentially. If the community doesn't meaningfully exist, it simply has to be developed. We imagine that this view of the community is implicit in community education generally because it derives from Morris and the village colleges in Cambridge and now Leicestershire.

It might of course be possible to accept this notion of community as accurate when applied to Cambridgeshire and Leicestershire, and to some of those reported in Frankenberg's 'Communities in Britain'. But its translation to an urban area seems a dubious exercise. Such areas are characterised by *social* fragmentation, and possibly degeneration, cultural pluralism, groups with widely differing and potentially conflicting values, differentiation rather than identity, competition for the possession of limited basic amenities rather than cooperation in their use, to such an extent as to make it unlikely that the term community can realistically be applied to them in any sense that is accepted. Rex and Moore's Sparkbrook, for example, comprised large elements among its residents who perceived their stay in the area as short term, and for whom it was a transitional zone; there was fierce and potentially conflictful competition, often along racial lines, for access to housing, and if there was a strong socially derived identity it was in sub-committees such as the native residents of long standing, or ethnic groups, whose identity was gained and reinforced by their differences from other groups, not any common-ness of geographical residence. We should not wish to be accused of a sort of sociological determinism, in that it is possible that the social structure of these areas may become more unified, and their population more permanent and cohesive, but there is little evidence known to us that this is happening. To believe that it is, is to believe in a myth.

If we cannot say of these areas that the people form a community, what can we say of them? We can of course talk as the community educators do (though with appropriate caution), of their deprivation. But we do not think the most important thing is their material, cultural, linguistic or spiritual "deprivation". The defining characteristic of the people living in inner cities is the fact of their political oppression – their deprivation is to be seen in their lack of power and access to sources of decision over their future. The real decisions over their present and future conditions are made elsewhere, in government, production, business and commerce and in the professions. Such oppressed areas may be said to exist in response to the distribution of power and rewards in the social structure. And it is from this relationship that all their other deprivations stem. Crucially, in the context of the present discussion, decisions about the provision of housing, education and employment reside in an economic elite who exist politically, professionally, socially and usually physically, outside the area, and access to this elite, and therefore to the decision-making processes, is not in the gift of the inhabitants of the oppressed area. Again this is not to say that conditions in which all this might be different will not exist in the future, but it is not at all clear where one might look for evidence that the sort of community development implicit in such changes is in fact happening. Nor is there any evidence of any community political theory which outlines strategies for such developments in the future. Combined with our previously stated doubts about the extent to which community identity or consciousness exists in inner city areas, and given the acknowledged impotence of schooling to achieve little other than the hidden functions of the curriculum, our first attack on community education concerns the adequacy of its analysis of the political nature of the areas in which it is operating, and the unreal expectations made upon it.

Our next concern is with the actual concept of community education and the suggested content for the curriculum. This immediately raises problems of definition since the literature proposes several varieties of programme. But we can take Midwinter's Priority Education, Halsey's E.P.A. Report, and the single publication of the Schools Council Social Education Report from Nottingham University as the dominating and most clearly thought out statements. In their terms, Community Education is not simply a matter of involving parents in their children's schooling, nor enabling adults to use the school plant in the evenings. It is a much more positive and all embracing concept derived in part from Henry Morris' notion that the community itself should be educative, that the boundaries between school and community should be dismantled, and that 'education' should occur through participation in the community's activities, and through the community's control of its own education. The education system in the urban community should become "more truthfully the people's system". In some inadequately defined sense, the community would become the curriculum (i.e. its source and arbiter). Ideally this would lead to children and adults participating in community action so as to "transform and regenerate" the conditions of their present existence. And to enable this to occur the community school would concentrate upon educating children in the skills necessary for such participation, and in the awareness of the procedures and structures of the community of which they are members. Thus, in their concept of community education there is a fundamental and reciprocal relationship between community and the educative institution, the two, in ideal circumstances, collaborating to provide learning experiences relevant to life in an inner city.

A feature of community educators' ideology that requires highlighting is their position in relation to equality of opportunity in education.

In a rigorously argued section of his E.P.A. report, Halsey suggests that two previous concepts of equality are now obsolete, because they have been shown to be unattainable. These two were, in historical sequence: a) equality of access to high status education systems – crudely that children from different social backgrounds should gain admission to grammar schools/universities in equivalent proportions to their representation in society at large. b) equality of outcome, or attainment, once access has been achieved – crudely within any level or status of education, educational attainment should not appear to be differentially distributed along social class lines. For a variety of reasons, especially empirical research findings in sociology, the notion that either the concept of equality has been realised,or is likely to be, cannot be sustained. Schools do not appear to have the power, implicitly assumed in the two concepts of equality of opportunity, significantly to modify the influences of the social structure. Thus, community education should aim to provide "opportunity for equality" rather than contribute to aspirations for equality of opportunity.

Now there is considerable force in Halsey and Midwinter's argument. The conventional curriculum is clearly irrelevant to the everyday life experience of the urban child – and most other children for that matter. And, even with Plowden's "positive" discrimination in favour of E.P.A.'s, equality in either of the traditional senses is unlikely to be achieved. As Musgrove has brilliantly argued in Patterns of Power and Authority in English Education, our schools may be less noteworthy for their effectiveness in achieving the multiplicity of goals they are expressly set, than for their apparent impotence in achieving any of them. The Community Educators, therefore, were posed with the problem of the purpose of education for the children of inner city zones. It is difficult to better Halsey's exposition:

> "What assumptions could or should be made about the world into which our E.P.A. children would enter after school? Were we concerned simply to introduce a greater measure of justice into an educational system which traditionally selected the minority for higher education and upward social mobility out of the E.P.A. district, leaving the majority to be taught, mainly by a huge hidden curriculum, a sense of their own relative incompetence and impotence – a modern humane and even relatively enjoyed form of gentling the masses? Or could we assume a wide programme of social reform which would democratise local power structures and diversify local occupational opportunities so that society would look to its schools for a supply of young people educated for political and social responsibility and linked to their communities not by failure in the competition but by rich opportunities for work and life? Even short of the assumption of extra-educational

> reform, how far should we concentrate on making recognition easier for the able minority, and how far on the majority who are destined to live their lives in the E.P.A.? And if the latter, did this not mean posing an alternative curriculum realistically related to the E.P.A. environment and designed to equip the rising generation with the knowledge and skills to cope with, give power over and in the end transform the conditions of their local community?"

We have to remark in parentheses the implicit acceptance by Halsey here of the idea of "ability" as limited to the minority (who can presumably be easily identified) of children in the inner city. This is strangely out of line with his other views on intelligence, but perhaps may be made sense of in the general perspective of the assumptions behind community education. For the present we wish to draw attention to how well the paragraph condenses the rationale of community education and provokes all the important anxieties we feel about it.

Now for our concern for the actual community curriculum and its relation to any realistic notion of community politics present or future. Here again we find the problem of differences among the various proposals, but this time exaggerated by the surprising absence of anything approximating to curriculum designs, or sets of principles for curriculum planning. A general picture only can be elucidated. Firstly a good deal of the children's work is community or social action projects, though it is not restricted to community service activities such as cleaning old people's windows. It is the "exercise of social skills on related social materials". Thus a study of a shopping precinct became a basis for its recreation in the school and for parents to be invited to buy things the children had made. 'The Supermarket' became a basis for realistic maths work, the more relevant because of support from the local Tesco. And it became the stimulus for reflection upon the local planning of commercial facilities, and for consideration of moral issues such as shoplifting.

It would be unfair to report the curriculum as a host of interesting and locally relevant activities. It is also concerned to increase children's social awareness, to give them some cognitive grasp of the structure of their immediate environment. Thus the Schools Council Social Education Project proposes that children analyse their locality in a Profile of headings such as Local Problems, Authority and You, The Leaders in the Area, etc. This analysis would help the pupils identify problems and projects for local action. It is not altogether clear how much time is proposed for these kinds of activities. Midwinter suggests as a transitional step that half the school curriculum be given over to them, that the balance change from 'academic' to 'social', from the irrelevant to the relevant. Thus the reported descriptions of the pupil's work suggest an extremely fragmented set of activities or projects, whose major common feature is their alleged 'relevance' to the environment in which the pupil exists.

The inadequate specification of the concept of relevance is remarkable. In the first place it is by no means self-evident that what is relevant to learning about the realities of urban existence, is relevant in any other sense. Indeed, we suggest that in terms of access both to forms of knowledge and admission into the groups that exercise political control, the relevance of the community curriculum is probably a supreme irrelevance. For within the terms of the most extreme analysis of what the curriculum is about, community curriculum makes an absurd entry. Not only from the Hirstian position that the curriculum is (ought to be) about initiation into the distinctive forms of rationality and thus will enable the child eventually through the use of reason to be freed from what is deceptive or doubtful, but also from the current cynical sociological perspective that the curriculum is a collection of values and procedures thought essential by a socially dominant group for the initiation of their children into dominance, the socially relevant curriculum is a frightening prospect. In either perspective, the community educated child will be isolated and impotent in his curriculum. There are no claims made for the universals of rationality nor is there any recognition of the very real form of the intellectual procedures and languages that every child destined for any degree of political autonomy must acquire.

As a consequence of abandoning the goal of equal educational opportunity, we are left with an even more flagrant transgression of the principle of equality, namely the probability that Community Education will disqualify these children from entering the realms of political discourse at all. By political discourse we mean the widest sense of entering into and influencing the various channels of political expression over our lives: government, courts, councils, trade unions, professional bodies, and indeed the various associations relating to the economics of production and distribution. These channels are and still will be, dominated by those who have the universalistic education and have been appropriately recruited. How then will the generation of the community-educated, their terms of discourse bounded by the political and material oppression of their circumstances, gain voice? Who will be their spokesmen, what languages will they use to express their strategies for transformation and regeneration?

The task of education, then, is to find appropriate ways of initiating children who will otherwise be considered ineducable into forms of discourse that will enable them to resist manipulation and gain control over those channels which constrain their lives. In practical terms we must find more effective methods of achieving the same educational goals for them as are claimed for the academic child – the so-called less-able child must also be initiated into the languages of dominance. As John White so cogently argued in New Society, if a child is 'less able' in mathematics, say, then far from being allowed to give it up in favour of something else with which he can cope, he should be given more, perhaps differently oriented teaching in the discipline, so that he eventually becomes able in it. "Ability in these subjects is not a given, it is an urgent goal." This concept of ability contrasts with Halsey's reactionary and deterministic notion of the 'able minority' and presumably the less able majority, and highlights the dangerous pessimism of community education. Genuine radicalism lies in ensuring that no child shall be cut off from the mainstream of social and political discourse by the accident of inner urban residence.

In this light, community education translates, along with other community activities and projects, into a safe instrument of state ideology. It is first the myth of community and then, worse, the myth that the community can and will control its own destiny. By their actions so far, such communities (if they exist) do not seem to be constituting a very real threat to the present distribution of power in our society.

BIBLIOGRAPHY

Frankenberg, T.: *Communities in Britain*. Penguin 1965.
Halsey, A. H. (ed.): *Educational Priority*, Vol. 1. H.M.S.O. 1972.
Hirst, P. H.: "Liberal Education and the Nature of Knowledge" in Archambault, R. D. (ed.) *Philosophical Analysis and Education*. U.L.P. 1964.
Midwinter, E.: *Priority Education*, Penguin 1972.
Midwinter, E.: *Projections*. Ward Lock 1972.
Rex, J. and Moore, R.: *Race, Community and Conflict*. O.U.P. 1967.
White, J. P.: "Instruction in Obedience", *New Society*, 2nd May, 1968.
White, J. P.: "The Curriculum Mongers: Education in Reverse", *New Society*, 6th March, 1969.
Young, M. F. D. (ed.): *Knowledge and Control*, Collier-MacMillan 1971.

7. The Problem of Balance

Elliott Eisner

Source: Elliott W. Eisner, 'Persistent Dilemmas in Curriculum Decision-making', in Elliott W. Eisner (ed.), *Confronting Curriculum Reform*, (Little, Brown and Co., Boston) 1971, pp. 162–73.

How to achieve balance in the curriculum poses a persistent dilemma in curriculum decision-making. How can a curriculum reconcile two goals: to introduce children to the major fields of inquiry that form our culture and to enable them to cultivate in-depth understanding in the fields that interest them? Elliott Eisner discusses this dilemma.

A second dilemma that nags my educational soul deals with the age-old educational question of how to achieve balance in the curriculum. For decades there has been a strong desire among educators, especially at the elementary school level, to provide a curriculum having "balance". While "balance" is not a term having great precision, I generally take it to mean with respect to the school curriculum that children will have access to the major intellectual and artistic disciplines that have historically been a part of our culture. A variety of scholars – Hutchins, Bestor, Koerner, Phenix, and others – argue that the major fields of inquiry constitute a fundamental core of intellectual and artistic subject matter and that becoming educated requires an understanding and appreciation of the ideas and methods which these fields provide.[1] Phenix has argued that the way man secures meaning from experience is by interpreting his sensations within the frames of reference, or, as Phenix calls them, the realms of meaning, that constitute the disciplines. It then follows that the school curriculum, if it is to provide for the development of educated men, should introduce students to the major realms of meaning and should enable them to use the ideas and modes of inquiry that constitute these realms.

Now the ideal of providing an educational program that will prepare students to derive meaning from experience through the diverse windows that the various arts and sciences provide is surely appealing. In a way, our schools have attempted to achieve this ideal by offering to elementary, and to some degree to secondary and college students, a range of fields and then requiring that students study them. When school curricula became heavily laden with the sciences, both educators and parents became concerned that the ideal of curriculum balance was being sacrificed and that educational redress be provided. In some ways the currently emerging interest in the arts and humanities is evidence of the recognition that the school curriculum has been skewed to the sciences and to mathematics and needs, therefore, to be brought back into balance.[2]

Balance in the curriculum has been and is an idealized criterion for deciding upon curriculum content. Like the well-balanced diet, the well-balanced curriculum contributes to educational health.

Yet the goal of balance in curriculum is not without a lusty competitor. While schoolmen are concerned with balance, they also are concerned with, as Harold Benjamin called it, the cultivation of idiosyncrasy.[3] How does one ensure the cultivation of idiosyncrasy while, at the same time, requiring students to study the wide range of subject matters that make for educationally balanced men. By the cultivation of idiosyncrasy, I mean providing students with the opportunity to attend deeply and extensively to the pursuit of their own aesthetic and intellectual interests. By the cultivation of idiosyncrasy, I mean not only providing such opportunities but encouraging students to seek them out and to attend to the development of those particular talents and aptitudes that differentiate one man from another. In practical terms, such an approach might mean neglecting some areas of study completely and giving only a passing nod to others, while immersing oneself in the type of artistic or academic work that "turns one on". The committee that developed the new curriculum policy at Stanford has opted for this choice in revamping the Institution's undergraduate program. The authors of *The Study of Education at Stanford* present their rationale in this way:

> Our faculty must be in the places where knowledge is advanced and with this comes a need in our day to specialize intensively so that the frontiers of knowledge can be reached. This demand derives, we believe, not from the so-called "publish or perish" rule of academic success, but from a complex set of motivations to travel the path of discovery. For the most part it is because faculty members are interested in the unknown or the misunderstood that they have come to the University in the first place. The intense specialization that results from this characteristic of the faculty seems to militate against the demand for "general education" in the traditional sense, with its stress on a common body of knowledge and a concomitant insistence upon a highly prescriptive curriculum. "General education" courses turn out to be an unwelcome chore for both faculty and students in a setting where teaching or learning something prescribed by a committee is rightly looked upon as the bottom of the academic barrel. . . . Let the objective of curricular planning be to encourage the faculty member to teach what he likes to teach and the student to learn what seems vital to him – the intellectual history of Europe in the nineteenth century rather than the history of Western Civilization, modern consciousness rather than freshman English, organizational behavior rather than introduction to sociology – and from this common freedom may emerge a form

of general education far better suited to the characteristic of the University than to that to which we pay lip service now.[4]

It is clear in which direction the authors of *The Study of Education at Stanford* have moved. Both teachers and students should, in their view, be free to select their own areas of interest for teaching and learning. Is such an orientation to curriculum viable for American secondary schools? The advocates of this conception of curriculum content believe that the problem of securing breadth of understanding can be resolved by getting students to immerse themselves in the areas of study which are particularly interesting to them. Specialization, they hold, is not contrary to the development of broadly based intellectual interests. By understanding a particular field in depth, the student will somehow come to appreciate the wider array of intellectual tools and artistic achievements that constitute man's cultural past and which enable him to secure significant meaning from the present.

At first blush, this position has an undeniable attractiveness. An in-depth understanding of a field of study can have aesthetic as well as merely instrumental consequences. For the specialist, specialized understanding is probably the only "real" way to understand and appreciate the power and elegance of ideas. Yet, I am not convinced by the thesis that specialization breeds general understanding or that it cultivates an appreciation of the variety of ways in which meaning can be secured. I am painfully aware of my own failure to validate the claim that general appreciation emanates from specialized intellectual focus. And frankly, in general, I am not impressed with the level of intellectual catholicity that my specialized colleagues possess. Thus, the second dilemma: If attention to a wide range of problems and fields of study is necessary for the type of personal and intellectual range one wishes to develop in students, how then can one cultivate, in depth, those idiosyncratic interests and aptitudes which almost all students have?

One putative solution to this dilemma that has emerged rather recently deals with the ideal of fostering high-level cognitive processes in students. Some authorities claim that what schools need is the development of curricula that facilitate problem-solving skills, curricula which enable children to exercise those cognitive abilities that will enable them to cope effectively with problems no matter what the source or mode of presentation. The development of general inquiry skills seems to provide the answer for curricula that are now, according to these authorities, subject-bound. But to me this approach also fails to resolve the issue. Problems come in various shapes, sizes, and media. General process development, like contentless form, is something which I, at least, cannot conceive of. The problems and processes involved in painting and in writing poetry, just to take two art forms as examples, are of different orders. If they were not, poets would be painters and vice versa. Generalized process development unrelated to the characteristics and demands of the particular medium of perception and expression do not appear to me to hold promise for resolving the dilemma of curriculum balance. How can we develop educational programs that give students an appreciation of the reach of man's mind and, at the same time, enable him to savor the experience that comes from study in depth of a particular field?

NOTES

1. Robert Maynard Hutchins, *The Conflicts of Education in a Democratic Society*, New York: Harper, 1953; Arthur Bestor, *Educational Wastelands; the Retreat from Learning in Our Public Schools,* Urbana: University of Illinois Press, 1953; James D. Koerner, *The Case for Basic Education,* Boston: Little, Brown and Co., 1959; Phillip Phenix, *Realms of Meaning; A Philosophy of the Curriculum for General Education,* New York: McGraw-Hill, 1964.
2. For an example of the curriculum theorists' concern for balance see *Balance in the Curriculum*, ASCD Yearbook, 1961.
3. Harold Benjamin, *The Cultivation of Idiosyncrasy,* Cambridge: Harvard University Press, 1949.
4. *The Study of Education at Stanford: Report to the University,* Stanford: Stanford University Press, 1968.

II CURRICULUM ORGANISATION

8. Structure of the Disciplines: Meanings and Significances

Joseph J. Schwab

Source: A. W. Ford and Lawrence Pugno (eds.), *The Structure of Knowledge and the Curriculum* (Rand McNally, Chicago, 1964), pp. 6–30.

History has seen many changes in the distinctions recognised among different orders of phenomena as grounds for maintaining different bodies of knowledge and disciplines of enquiry. This does not mean to say that there are no genuine differences among phenomena. But it does mean that education must concern itself with the task of making the structure of the disciplines it teaches apparent to students, to enable them to appreciate their strengths, limitations and possible alternatives. Schwab explores three sets of problems constituting the problem of the structure of the disciplines: the organisation of the disciplines (how many there are and how they relate to each other); the substance of each discipline (their conceptual structures); and the methods of enquiry and criteria of truth for each.

We embark here on an exploration of one of the most difficult of terrains: investigation of the nature, variety, and extent of human knowledge; and the attempt to determine what that nature, variety, and extent have to tell us about teaching and learning. My share of this task is a specialized one and a preliminary one. It is simply to map that terrain.

What is meant by the structure of the disciplines? It means three things, three distinct but related sets of problems. Let us take a foretaste of all three together without discriminating them by name.

It has been widely supposed that there are indubitable grounds for recognizing basically different orders of phenomena, each requiring a different discipline for its investigation because of the differences in the character of the phenomena.

There are many different views based on such a premise. For example, many philosophers have insisted on a fundamental distinction between living phenomena and non-living, thus generating the notion that there are two fundamentally different sciences, the biological and the physio-chemical. These two sciences were supposed to differ in method, in guiding conceptions, in the kind of knowledge produced, and in degree of certainty, differing to precisely the same extent that their subject matters were supposed to differ.

Another such view is generated by a distinction between man and nature, a distinction in which nature is conceived as bound by inexorable laws while men are in some sense and in some degree free. In this view, two major areas of investigation are again discriminated: on the one hand, science, concerned with the inexorable laws that nature presumably obeys; and on the other hand, a discipline in the neighborhood of ethics and politics, which would investigate the freedom that man has and the ways in which men make their choices.

There is also a view that emphasizes the vast difference between the generality of "natural" phenomena (i.e., their predictability, the tendency of "natural" things to behave or be the same in instance after instance) and the particularity of human events (the essentially unique and non-repeating character of acts notable in the behavior of man). Again, two widely different bodies of investigation and study are generated: science on the one hand and history on the other. Science, in this view, would seek the general laws that characterize the repeating behavior of natural things, while history would seek to determine the precise, unique events that characterized each life, each era, each civilization or culture that it studied. Hence, again, there would be two basically different curriculum components, differing in method, principle, and warrantability.

There have been similar separations of other disciplines, notably mathematics and logic. Mathematics was long ago seen to differ radically from other disciplines, including the sciences, in that its subject matter appeared to have no material existence. The objects of physical or biological enquiry could be seen, touched, smelled, tasted. The objects of mathematics could not. The plane, the line, the point, unity, number, etc. existed in some way which was not material or did not exist at all. This peculiarity of mathematical objects continues to be a puzzle. No one view of the nature of mathematics has been developed which is satisfactory to all concerned, though most moderns are agreed that mathematics differs radically from the other sciences.

Logic has been set apart because of its unique relationship to other disciplines rather than because of something peculiar about its subject matter. To one degree or another, all other disciplines test the reliability of their conclusions by appealing to canons of reasoning and of evidence which are developed in the first place by the discipline of logic. Since logic is responsible for developing these canons, it cannot itself use them to check its own work. Logic thus stands as a sort of "queen of the sciences", dictating their rules but having for itself rules of some other and puzzling sort. Unlike the case of mathematics, this peculiarity of logic is no longer universally recognized. In some quarters, for example, it is held that logic does no more than formulate the methods and the canons of reasoning and of evidence which other sciences have developed, used, and bear witness to by their effectiveness. In this view, logic is not so much the queen of the sciences as their handmaiden.

Let us continue our foretaste of the problems of the structures of the disciplines by noting a peculiarity of the distinctions we have described. The peculiarity is that the differences among phenomena which appear at one period in the history of the disciplines to be radical and self-evident may at a later date disappear or become inconsequential as bases for differentiating disciplines. Take, for example, the differentiation of biology from the physical-chemical sciences. In early times and through the eighteenth century, fundamental differences between the living and non-living could not be evaded. The living thing was "self-moving"; no other object was. The living thing reproduced itself; the living thing developed, had a personal history which no non-living thing could duplicate. Then, in the middle to late nineteenth century, some of these differences ceased to be notable, others disappeared entirely from human recognition. In this altered climate, the physiologist Claude Bernard pleaded for a study of living things strictly in terms of physics and chemistry. Since then, such an approach to living things has been so fruitful that it is now safe to say that it will be only a brief time before we shall synthesize living molecules in the laboratory. In recent years a still further shift in outlook has taken place: we now hear pleas from some physicists that certain physical phenomena be treated in much the way that living things were investigated *before* Bernard.

A similar shift is visible on a smaller scale in the history of the science of mechanics. Three hundred years ago the behavior of celestial bodies (the planets and the stars) and the behavior of terrestrial bodies in motion (things rolling on the surface of the earth and things thrown or propelled through the air) appeared to be radically different. Terrestrial bodies inevitably came to rest and fell to earth; celestial bodies inevitably continued in their regular motion without stop. Then, with Newton, these differences, though still visible, became entirely unimportant.

In brief, what we see of and in things changes from epoch to epoch. Differences that once appeared to be radical are seen later to be illusory or trivial; then, at another period, some of these differences reappear in a new guise. What can account for such changes in what appears to be objectively perceived? The answer is most easily exemplified in the case of mechanics, where in our own day the once radical difference between terrestrial and celestial bodies continues to be treated as illusory.

Granted that this difference was an illusion, what made the illusion disappear? The answer is this: Newton conceived an idea called universal gravitation. In the light of this idea, it became desirable and possible to examine the motion of the celestial bodies (in Newton's case, the moon) in a new way. Specifically, it became desirable and possible to measure the changing directions and changing velocities of the moon in such a fashion that it could be described as continually falling toward earth, while, at the same time, continually moving in a straight line at an angle to its fall. Thus its continuous orbit of the earth could be understood as the resultant of these two motions. In the same way it became possible to conceive of a terrestrial missile as falling to earth and coming to rest there only because its initial velocity in a straight line was not great enough to carry it straight forward beyond the bend of the earth before its fall brought it into contact with the earth. One could then see that as the initial velocity of a missile became greater and greater, it would not only go farther before it fell to earth, but at some point the increased velocity would be so great that the fall of the missile would be compensated by the falling away of the spherical surface of the earth. Such a missile would then become a satellite of the earth precisely like the moon. In brief, a new conception dictating new studies and a new way to interpret the data exhibited the movement of celestial bodies as nothing more than an extreme case of the motions of familiar terrestrial bodies moving at lower velocities.

In general, two collections of phenomena appear to be vastly different because we have used separate and distinct bodies of conceptions in studying them and discovering knowledge about them. Each such body of conceptions dictates what data we think we should seek, what experiments to perform, and what to make of our data by way of knowledge. If widely different conceptions are used to guide enquiries on two different collections of phenomena, we end inevitably with bodies of knowledge which exhibit few similarities and many differences. It is through the limiting or distorting lenses of these bodies of knowledge that we look at things. Hence, if the lenses distort or limit in different ways, we see things as different. The differences we see disappear if, but only if, a new conception is given birth which permits the study of both collections of phenomena in one set of terms and therefore makes for unity where diversity existed before.

Before we discriminate the problems of the structure of the disciplines, let us take note of a *caveat*. It is this: the integration of previously separate bodies of knowledge by new and unifying conceptions should not blind us to the possibility that some of the differences we recognize among phenomena may be genuine; some differentiation of disciplines may be perennial. There really may be joints in nature, a forearm, then an elbow, and then an upper arm. Science, ethics, and aesthetics may indeed represent three widely variant objects of enquiry. The doctrine of the unity of science, which insists on a unification of all knowledge, is either a dogma or a hope but not a fact. There are no data from which to conclude decisively that eventually all the disciplines will become or should become one.

Now let us step back and identify in this foretaste of knowledge and knowledge-seeking the three major but related sets of problems which define the area called structure of the disciplines.

Recall first our brief review of efforts to discriminate life from non-life, science from history, and so on. These efforts illustrate the first problem of the structure of the disciplines. It is the problem of determining the membership and organization of the disciplines, of identifying the significantly different disciplines, and of locating their relations to one another.

This set of problems is illustrated by the following questions. *Is* mathematical knowledge significantly different from knowledge of physical things? If so, how are the behaviors of mathematical objects related to the behaviors of physical objects? That is, how must we account for the extraordinary usefulness of mathematics to the sciences? Is it because we impose mathematical forms on our observation of physical things, or is it because, in some mysterious way, the objects of the external world behave according to patterns that we discover through mathematical enquiry into our own intellects? Similarly, we might raise questions about practical knowledge and scientific or theoretical knowledge. Are they much the same or truly different? Is practical knowledge merely the application of science? Or does science take hold of ideal objects extrapolated from experience of things while practical knowledge must supply the bridge for return from scientific knowledge of such ideal objects to the actual and practicable? This set of problems may properly be called a problem of the structure of the disciplines, if we keep in mind that by the plural "disciplines" we refer to them collectively rather than distributively, while "structure" is singular and refers to the organization of the disciplines *inter se.*

The significance of this set of problems to education is obvious enough. To identify the disciplines that constitute contemporary knowledge and mastery of the world, is to identify the subject matter of education, the material that constitutes both its resources and its obligations. To locate the relations of these disciplines to one another is to determine what may be joined together for purposes of instruction and what should be held apart; these same relations will also weigh heavily in determining our decisions about the sequence of instruction, for it will tell us what must come before what, or what is most desirably placed first, or second, or third.

The second set of problems of the structure of the disciplines is exemplified by the tremendous role of the concept of universal gravitation in supplying us with a more nearly universal mechanics. A similar role is played by other conceptions in the attainment and formulation of all scientific knowledge. Embedded in the knowledge we have of the workings of the human body lies one or another concept of the nature of an organism, of the character of the parts of such an organism and how they relate to one another. Back to our knowledge of heredity lies a conception of particles behaving as do the terms in the expansion of a binominal to the second or higher powers. Back of our ability to make decisions in playing games lie similar conceptions. Again, the conceptions happen to be mathematical: the expansion of the binominal or a more complex mathematical structure derived by taking the expansion of the binominal to its limit. These mathematical conceptions provide us with a body of probability theory with which we play poker, determine tactics in battle, plan the production and sale of the products of our industries. Similarly, knowledge of human behavior, both individual and social, has arisen only as the men concerned with enquiry in psychology, sociology, and anthropology have developed conceptions that have enabled them to plan their researches.

In general then, enquiry has its origin in a conceptual structure, often mathematical, but not necessarily so. It is this conceptual structure through which we are able to formulate a telling question. It is through the telling question that we know what data to seek and what experiments to perform to get those data. Once the data are in hand, the same conceptual structure tells us how to interpret them, what to make of them by way of knowledge. Finally, the knowledge itself is formulated in the terms provided by the same conception. Thus we formulate and convey some of the knowledge we discover about the body in terms of organs and functions; we formulate and communicate our knowledge of atomic structure in terms of a concept of particles and waves; we formulate some of our knowledge of human personality in terms of psychic organs and their functions and other portions of it in terms of interpersonal relations.

In each science and in many arts such conceptual structures prevail. The second problem of the structure of the disciplines is to identify these structures and understand the powers and limits of the enquiries that take place under their guidance. Let us call this set of problems the problem of the *substantive* structures of each discipline.

Again, the significance of this problem of the structure of the disciplines to education is obvious enough – or at least one part of it is. For to know what structures underlie a given body of knowledge is to know what problems we shall face in imparting this knowledge. Perhaps the conceptual structure is no more complex than that involved in the discrimination of two classes of things by a single criterion, such as color or shape. In that case, we may suppose that little difficulty would be encountered in teaching this body of knowledge even to the very young. Perhaps the conceptual structure is more complex but so firmly embedded in common-sense knowledge of things that the child at some early, given age will already have encountered it and became familiar with it. In that case, we should, again, have little difficulty in imparting our knowledge, provided that we impart it at the right time in the development of the child in our culture. However, suppose the conceptual structure is both complex and largely unused in common-sense knowledge? This would be the case at the moment for the physical conception of a wave-like particle. In such a case, to locate and identify the conception is to locate and identify a difficult problem of instruction requiring much experiment and study.

A second curricular significance of the problem of the substantive structures of each discipline is less obvious. It concerns a peculiar consequence of the role of conceptual structures on our knowledge, a consequence little noted until recently. The dependence of knowledge on a conceptual structure means that any body of knowledge is likely to be of only temporary significance. For the knowledge which develops from the use of a given concept usually discloses new complexities of the subject matter which call forth new concepts. These new concepts in turn give rise to new bodies of enquiry and, therefore, to new and more complete bodies of knowledge stated in new terms. The significance of this ephemeral character of knowledge to education consists in the fact that it exhibits the desirability if not the necessity for so teaching what we teach that students understand that the knowledge we possess is not mere literal, factual truth but a kind of knowledge which is true in a more complex sense. This in turn means that we must clarify for students the role of concepts in making knowledge possible (and limiting its validity) and impart to them some idea of the particular concepts that underlie present knowledge of each subject matter, together with the reasons for the appropriateness of these concepts and some hint of their limitations.

The third problem of the structure of the disciplines we shall call the problem of the *syntactical* structure of the disciplines. This problem is hidden in the fact that if different sciences pursue knowledge of their respective subject matters by means of different conceptual frames, it is very likely that there will be major differences between one discipline and another in the way and in the extent to which it can verify its knowledge. There is, then, the problem of determining for each discipline what it does by way of discovery and proof, what criteria it uses for measuring the quality of its data, how strictly it can apply canons of evidence, and in general, of determining the route or pathway by which the discipline moves from its raw data through a longer or shorter process of interpretation to its conclusion.

Again, certain obvious consequences to education accrue from such a study. For, unless we intend to treat all knowledge as literal, true dogma, and thereby treat students as mere passive, obedient servants of our current culture, we want our students to know, concerning each body of knowledge learned, how sound, how dependable it is.

In summary then, three different sets of problems constitute the general problem of the structure of the disciplines. First there is the problem of the organization of the disciplines: how many there are; what they are; and how they relate to one another. Second, there is the problem of the substantive conceptual structures used by each discipline. Third, there is the problem of the syntax of each discipline: what its canons of evidence and proof are and how well they can be applied. Let us turn now to a brief investigation of each of these problems.

The Problems of the Organization of the Disciplines

With the problem of the organization of the disciplines we must face at once one of the inevitable complexities of this terrain, the fact that it does not and cannot supply a single, authoritative answer to the question of what disciplines there are, how many there are, and how they are related to one another. The reason for this complexity is fairly obvious. The problem of organization is a problem of classification primarily. If we classify any group of complex things, we are faced with a wide choice of bases of classification. (Even with postage stamps, we could classify by country of origin, by color, by shape or size, or by some combination of two or more of these.) Disciplines are very complex, hence the diversity and variety of available modes of classification are great. Consequently, depending on what one emphasizes about the disciplines, one or another or still a third or a fifth or a tenth classification of them is generated.

Four bases of classification of disciplines have always demanded attention: (1) their subject matter, what they aim to investigate, or work upon; (2) their practitioners, what competences and habits are required to carry on their work; (2) their methods (syntax), and modes of enquiry by which the enquirer brings himself to bear on the subject matter; (4) their ends, the kinds of knowledge or other outcomes at which they aim. Let us, then, examine a few organizations of the disciplines which use one or more of these, choosing them for the light they may throw on current curriculum problems.

The basic organization of the sciences proposed by Aristotle is worth taking a brief look at nowadays because we have tended to forget what it emphasizes. In this organization, Aristotle made most use of the end or aim of the disciplines together with the character of the materials they work on, the subject matter. Using these two as bases of classification, Aristotle distinguished three major groups of disciplines, the names of which have survived even in our current commonsense knowledge of the disciplines – though the significance assigned them has altered or been lost. The three basic divisions are the *Theoretical*, the *Practical*, and the *Productive.*

The theoretical disciplines are those whose aim is to know. For Aristotle, "to know" meant to know indubitably. Therefore, the theoretical disciplines included only those whose subject matters exhibited such inexorable regularity that they could be considered proper objects of "knowing" enquiry. Aristotle thought there were three such "knowing" or theoretical disciplines: physics, mathematics, and metaphysics. Today, though we would be very doubtful about the possibility of indubitable knowledge, we would, nevertheless, recognize a group of "theoretical" disciplines whose aim was to know and whose subject matters were such that the knowledge these disciplines sought was as nearly stable as knowledge can be. We would include the physical and biological sciences in this group. We would include substantial portions of the social sciences. We would exclude metaphysics as doubtful indeed. We would exclude mathematics, not because it is doubtful, but because we would consider it very special.

The practical disciplines, for Aristotle, included those concerned with choice, decision, and action based on deliberate decision. Precisely because its aim was to do, and therefore to alter the course of things, its subject matter had to have the property that was exactly opposite to the property required for the theoretical sciences. The subject matters of the practical sciences by necessity, must be not inexorable in their behavior, but capable of alteration, not fixed and stable but changeable.

It is exceedingly important, if we are to appreciate the bearing of this Aristotelian classification on modern problems, that we realize that "deliberate action" meant to Aristotle actions undertaken for their *own sakes* and not actions undertaken merely as the necessary preliminaries to some other end. Such actions, undertaken for their own sakes, constitute, then, what we mean by "a good life". They are the activities that stem from the expression of the best of which each man is capable. The practical sciences were (and are) therefore, ethics and politics. For us in modern times, ethics and politics would include not only each individual effort to lead and examine a deliberate life and the governing and policymaking in high places, but also the difficult and terrifying business of being parents, of being teachers *deliberately* and not as automatons, and the responsible work of administration and policymaking at all levels, together with those parts of the social sciences which contribute to such activities. I need not add that of all the things the schools might do, they do least of this. A few nursery schools, a very few teachers at the elementary level, and some few men and women at the college level give thought and time and energy toward evoking in their students the competencies and habits that lead to the making of good choices and good decisions and help the person to act in ways commensurate with his decisions. But by and large, the time, the energy, and the resources of our public schools ignore the very existence of practical disciplines in the Aristotelian sense.

The productive disciplines in the Aristotelian scheme are what the work "productive" suggests. They are the disciplines devoted to *making*: the fine arts, the applied arts, engineering. In connection with the significance of the Aristotelian productive disciplines for modern curriculum problems, let us note a principal characteristic of the entire Aristotelian organization: it emphasizes the sharp differences among the three groups of disciplines. The theoretical disciplines, devoted to knowing, concern themselves with those aspects of things which are fixed, stable, enduring. Hence, the theoretical disciplines are concerned with precisely these aspects of things which we cannot alter by making or make use of by doing. The productive disciplines are concerned with what is malleable, capable of being changed. The practical disciplines are concerned with another sort of malleability of human character, its ability to deliberate on its future and (within limits) to do as it sees fit.

We, on the other hand, have tended to fall into the habit of treating all disciplines proper to the schools as if they were theoretical. We manage to maintain this preoccupation in the case of the practical disciplines by ignoring them. In the case of the productive disciplines, we ignore them in some cases and in others resort to the trick of treating them as if they were theoretical. Music appreciation is taught as if its purpose were to recognise obvious themes of symphonies or concertos and proudly announce the opus number and the composer's name. Performing music is taught as if the aim were merely to follow the notes and obey the teacher's instructions about the score. Literature is taught as if dramas and novels were windows looking out on life, or worse, as if, as in the case of music appreciation, the object of the game were to know choice titbits about the character, the life, or the times of the author. Art is taught, like literature, as if its aims were to provide a true, a faithful photograph of life. Happily, the exceptions of these strictures are increasing. Music appreciation is more and more being taught as a mastery of those arts by which the ear and the mind creatively take in the form and content of music. Performing music is more and more being taught in such a way that the students learn the grounds by which to discover and select from alternative interpretations of the score. Poetry, literature, and drama are more and more the objects of the kind of scrutiny which permits their appreciation as works of art rather than as sources of vicarious experience. More and more teachers ~~of~~ art permit their students the freedom for creation which society has long since accorded the professional artist. Nevertheless, the theoretizing of the productive disciplines is still prevalent enough to render this warning relevant.

Let us turn to another organization of the sciences, notable in that one version of it is reborn with every undergraduate generation. This is Auguste Comte's positive hierarchy of the sciences. This scheme is based on the view that subject matter, and only subject matter, should provide the basis for classification. It takes a further view that subject matters should be ordered in terms of their subject matters; that is, Comte maintains that orders of phenomena can be discerned, each order consisting of members of the next lower order organized into more complex structures. Using this Chinese box conception of the world, Comte locates physical things as the simplest of all orders (presumably something like our modern fundamental particles). Chemicals come next, as consisting of physicals organized in a new way. Then come biologicals as still higher organizations of chemicals. Finally, at the top, come socials as organizations of biologicals. Thus the Comtian hierarchy of the sciences runs: physics, chemistry, biology, the social sciences. Then Comte adds one last factor. At the bottom of the entire structure he places another "science"—mathematics, mathematics conceived as a kind of natural logic governing the study of all the sciences above it.

Perhaps because of its simplicity and its tendency to be reborn in every generation, this particular organization of the disciplines has been one of the most tyrannical and unexamined curriculum principles in our time. It has dictated, I suspect, at least thirty-five per cent of all the sequences and orders of study of the sciences at the high school and college level in the country. The biologist tries to make his task easier by insisting that chemistry precede his subject field. In turn, the chemist demands that physics precede his. The physicist demands that mathematics precede physics. And each appeals to the Comtian hierarchy as the principal reason for his demand.

There is some justice in this view but there is injustice too. For it is quite possible to read the Comtian hierarchy the other way around. The inverted reading can, indeed, be done without departing from Comte's own principles, as Comte himself well knew. The principle in question requires that each science in the hierarchy shall be well developed before the one above it can be developed. Thus an adequate sociology must wait upon a thoroughly adequate biology; biology, in turn, cannot become complete until chemistry is complete, and so on. This *seems* to suggest that physics ought to be developed by a study simply of physical things, postponing chemistry until the study of physicals is complete; in the same way chemistry would be developed by a study of chemicals, postponing biology until the chemistry is complete. However, if we look closely at the basic Comtian principles, we realize that a complete, positive knowledge of the constituents and the organization of chemicals can be developed only if we have sought out and identified all the behaviors of which chemicals are capable. At this point arises the starting corollary that leads to an inverted reading of the Comtian hierarchy. For, clearly, if biologicals are organizations of chemicals, biologicals constitute the place in which some large array of chemical potentialities becomes real and can be seen. It follows, then, that a study of biologicals must precede any completion of chemistry; a study of socials must, in the same way, precede complete knowledge of biologicals, and so on.

The developments of science since the days of Comte most certainly bear out this reading of his hierarchy. Organic chemistry has developed only as we have studied the complex chemistry of the living organism. The behavior of the human individual has become better understood as we have studied human culture and society. The development by physicists of adequate theories of atomic structure rests upon knowledge of chemicals. Thus we see that it is just as plausible to read the Comtian hierarchy downward from sociology through biology, chemistry, and physics to mathematics, as it is to read it upward from mathematics to physics, to chemistry, to biology, and finally to social science.

We cannot, then, rest our arguments for mathematics as prerequisite to physics, physics prerequisite to chemistry, and so on, on the assumption that the upward reading of the Comtian hierarchy constitutes an unequivocal curriculum principle. Rather, we might well argue that bits and portions of each of these alleged prerequisites should be taught as the need arises during the study of the higher sciences. For example, physics might well be taught by examining the obvious behaviors of physical things up to the point where it becomes clear to student and teacher alike that further progress in the physics requires mastery of certain mathematical conceptions of operations. At this point, the class would turn to the mastery of the mathematics required by the physics under study. In the same way, the complex study of the microchemistry of the living cell would not be taught as a prerequisite to study of the organism and its larger parts and functions; rather, the visible behaviors of the organism, of its organ systems and gross organs might well come first, with the biochemical materials so placed as to be meaningful to the students as the physio-chemical basis for the behaviors already known.

The curriculum sequence of prerequisites based on the upward reading of the Comtian hierarchy (i.e., mathematics to physics to chemistry, etc.) is often referred to as the "logical order" of instruction. The fact that the Comtian hierarchy can be read plausibly in either direction requires us to realize, however, that the phrase "logical order" applied only to one of them is a special pleading. Either order is "logical". The upward order from mathematics to the social sciences we might well call the dogmatic order, i.e., the order that runs from the current explanation to that which is explained. The downward order from, say, biology to chemistry, we might call the order of enquiry, i.e., the order that runs from a display of phenomena calling for explanation to the explanation the science has developed. A curriculum choice between the order of enquiry and the dogmatic order cannot be made on subject-matter criteria alone. Rather, we must look to the capacities of our students, to knowledge of ways in which learning takes place, and to our objectives, what we hope our students will achieve, in order to make our decision.

The Problem of the Syntax of the Disciplines

If all disciplines sought only to know and if the knowledge they sought were merely the simple facts, the syntax of the disciplines would be no problem. As we have seen, the disciplines are not this simple. Many are not, in the Aristotelian sense, theoretical at all: they seek ends that are not knowledge but something else – making, the appreciation of what is made, the arts and habits of deliberation, choice, and action. Those that are theoretical seek knowledge of different kinds (commensurate to their subject matters), hence use different methods and different canons of evidence and warrantability. For example, science seeks very general or even universal knowledge, while much history seeks the most detailed and particular knowledge. Each of these objects of enquiry poses problems peculiar to itself. Hence knowledge of each of them is sought in different ways. Even within the sciences there is much variability. Biologists find it necessary or desirable to seek knowledge in bits and pieces while physicists, at the other extreme, work hard to develop broad, comprehensive theories which embrace vast ranges of subject matter. The evidence that justifies the acceptance of an isolated bit of knowledge and the evidence that justifies the acceptance of a broad, comprehensive theory are of different sorts. There is a problem, therefore, of determining for each discipline or for small groups of disciplines what pathway of enquiry they use, what they mean by verified knowledge and how they go about this verification.

To illustrate this diversity, let us take three "things" that are asserted to exist and to have certain defining properties and behaviors. Let us take, first, an automobile, second, an electron, third, a neutrino. Let the three statements read as follows:

The automobile in front of the house is black.

The electron is a particle with a small mass and a negative electrical charge.

The neutrino is a particle with neither charge nor rest mass.

All three statements, let us suppose, are "true". That they are "true" in different senses becomes plain when we consider the following points. We say that the car in front of the house is black and say it with confidence on two bases. First, we look at the car and its neighborhood and report what we see. Second, we invite a colleague to look at the car and its neighborhood; we repeat the statement that reports what we saw; our colleague nods agreement. This, then, is a very simple syntax of discovery, requiring only a naive, private experience of the objects we propose to make statements about plus a transaction between ourself, another enquirer, and the same objects.

By contrast, the syntax that leads us to assert that the electron is a particle with a small mass and negative electrical charge is far more complex. The statement most certainly does not rest on the fact that I have looked at an electron and that my colleague has also looked and nodded agreement. It cannot arise from such a syntax because the electron is not visible. It rests, rather, on a syntax that involves looking at quite different things, seeking agreement about them, and then adding two further steps. We note certain phenomena; others note the same; then we seek an *explanation* for what we have seen. For explanation we conceive the existence of a minute particle. To it, we assign precisely the mass and precisely the magnitude and kind of charge which would permit this particle – if it existed – to give rise to the phenomena we have observed. The two additional steps are hidden in the additional process of seeking explanation. First, we conceive of something that would account for the phenomena we are concerned about. However, we are not satisfied to use just any conception that will account for it. Rather, we demand that the conception fulfill a second condition: that it fit in with, be coherent with, the rest of the body of knowledge that constitutes our science. In the case of our electron we meet this condition by choosing a particular mass and a particular charge as its important properties. The choice of a particular mass ties our electron to the entire body of physical knowledge called gravitational dynamics. The assignment of a certain electrical charge ties our particle to our knowledge of electricity and its dynamical laws.

The assertion about the neutrino rests on still a third kind of syntactical structure. For not only are neutrinos invisible by definition but they have been assigned a *lack* of such properties as charge and rest mass which characterize the electron. The assigned lack of such properties means that in the ordinary course of events the behavior of neutrinos would have no detectable consequences, would give rise to no phenomena such as we observed and accounted for by positing the existence of the electron. Instead, the ground for positing the existence of the neutrino was roughly as follows: certain effects were found in a phenomenon called beta decay which appeared to be exceptions to certain of the so-called conservation laws, laws that formed part of the very foundation of the body of physical knowledge. One way to account for these beta decay phenomena would be to treat them as "disproofs" of these conservation laws. Another way would have been to treat the decay phenomena as exceptions to the conservation laws and then to dream up an ad hoc explanation for the exception. Physicists preferred, however (for reasons I shall not go into now), to keep the conservation laws intact and universal, and the only conceived alternative enabling them to retain these laws was to suppose the existence of a well-nigh undetectable particle that carried off the quantities whose disappearance would otherwise have called the conservation laws into question.

We have here, then, three different senses in which statements are said to be "true" or warranted, differences of sense not revealed by the statements themselves. The statements are all of the same form – the automobile is black, the neutrino is such and such, the electron is something else. Only the context, the structure of problem, evidence, inference, and interpretation which constitutes the syntax of discovery behind each statement, would reveal to us the different senses in which each is true.

The significance of this variety of modes of enquiry of patterns of discovery and verification, lies in this: most statements of most disciplines are like the single words of a sentence. They take their most telling meanings, not from their dictionary sense, not from their sense in isolation, but from their context, their place in the syntax. The meaning of F = MA or of free fall, of electron or neutrino, is understood properly only in the context of the enquiry that produced them.

This need for context of enquiry wherewith to make teaching and learning clear has been almost universally overlooked because of a singular failure in the subject-matter preparation of teachers. They have been permitted to assume, or indeed, have been flatly told, that "induction" or "scientific method" stands for something simple, single, and well defined. Quite the contrary is true: "induction" is not the name for some single, definite process but merely an honorific word attached by various philosophers to whatever mode of enquiry they favor. To a few philosophers, "induction" means the process of simple enumeration of a large number of instances of something or other by which we try to discern what is common among them. In this view, the outcome of "induction" is "generalization". To other philosophers, "induction" means the analysis of phenomena into unit events and the attempt to find out which events invariably precede which others. To still others, "induction" means the attempt to conceive ideas, however remote they may be from the possibility of direct verification, which will "explain", "account for", "embrace", the largest possible variety of phenomena with the greatest economy.

The Problem of the Substantive Structures of the Disciplines

Let us first redevelop the idea of substantive structures and their role in enquiry as sketched in our introduction.

The fact that we propose to investigate a given subject is to admit that we are, in large part, ignorant of it. We may have some superficial knowledge: we may have dealt with the subject matter as part of our round of practical problems; but the very fact that we propose to investigate the subject means that we mistrust our knowledge or consider it entirely inadequate. Thus, enquiry begins in virtual ignorance. Ignorance however, cannot originate an enquiry. Subjects complex enough to demand enquiry are subjects that confound us by the great variety of characteristics, qualities, behaviors, and interactions they present to our view. This richness paralyzes enquiry, for it is far too much to handle all at once and, in our ignorance, we have no way of discerning the greater from the lesser fact; we cannot discriminate the facts that are most "telling" about our subject matter from those that are trivial. In short, if data are to be collected, we must have some sort of guide to relevance and irrelevance, importance and unimportance.

This role of guide to the enquiry is played by a conception borrowed or invented by the enquirer. These conceptions constitute the substantive structures of a discipline.

Let us take, as an example of a primitive beginning of enquiry, the situation that prevailed in the study of animal behavior some sixty years ago. Our knowledge of the behavior of small aquatic animals at that time was no greater than might have been possessed by an alert, small boy who had watched the darting of fish, the play of tadpoles, and the movements of insect larvae in the ponds and streams of his farm. What, then, should we investigate about these dartings, movements, and plays? Should we ask what needs they serve? Perhaps. Yet we do not even know that needs are involved. Shall we ask what purposes the animals have in mind? We do not know whether they have purposes or not. Shall we then try to discover the patterns of these motions, the order in which they occur? The trouble with this is that when a vast number of movements are involved, we must suppose, by analogy to ourselves, that they do not all belong together. Hence the over-all order of them would be meaningless. Yet we cannot discern each coherent sub-group of motions because we do not yet know either the beginnings ("wants", "needs", "stimuli") or their terminations ("goals", "needs satisfied", "terminal response").

This frustration of enquiry was resolved by appealing to the then popular view that all things, including living things, were no more than simple machines, the pattern of which was the simple one known to nineteenth-century physics. This idea of a simple machine was applied to the study of behavior by supposing that every movement through space of an animal was a response to some single, specific, stimulating factor in the environment. It was further supposed that each such stimulated response could be one of only two possible kinds – a movement toward the stimulus or a movement away from it. Such a movement was dubbed a "tropism", "taxis"; movements toward the stimulus being called positive, those away from the stimulus, negative.

This naive and now obsolete conception removed the frustration of enquiry by giving us questions to ask. We were to determine for each organism what stimuli it responded to and whether it responded in the positive or negative sense. These identified questions in turn determined the pattern of experiment. We were to place our aquatic organism in a tank of water, make sure that all physical stimuli but one were uniform throughout the tank, let one stimulus, light, for example, be of high intensity at one end of the tank and low intensity at the other, and then note, as our important datum, which way the animal went. Then our knowledge of animal behavior was to be summed up in a catalogue of negative and positive tropisms characteristic of each species investigated.

Similar naive conceptions enabled us to begin enquiry in other complex fields. Chemistry was able to make great advances in the study of the array of substances of the world by imposing on them the notion of "element". By "element" was meant a substance of ultimate simplicity, a substance made only of itself and incapable of being changed into another such simple substance. This conception dictated the questions to be asked of matter by chemists and the patterns of experiment. The fundamental question was: into what simpler substance can this substance be decomposed? Hence the patterns of experiment were analysis and synthesis. Similar "elements" were devised to guide our earliest enquiries into human personality. We conceived of each human person as consisting of a greater or lesser quantity of each of a number of "traits". Like the chemical elements, each such "trait" (such as courage, imagination, logical reasoning, assiduity) was supposed to be simple (made of no further sub-traits) and independent of all other traits.

The substantive principles chosen to guide enquiry are controlled by two opposing criteria. One of these I shall call reliability. Reliability requires that the guiding principle be free of vagueness and ambiguity, that the referents of its terms have unequivocal location and limit, and that the measurements or manipulations of these referents can be made precisely and can be repeated with uniform results. The substantive structures cited as examples above meet this criterion as well as could be expected.

They do not, however, satisfactorily fulfill the second criterion, which I shall call validity. Note the failure in each case which illustrates the lack of adequate validity. Animal behavior is reduced to a catalogue of independent responses to independently acting stimuli. Yet our knowledge of ourselves and of higher animals makes it highly unlikely that any animal's behavior will be a repertory of separate and independent responses to stimuli. It is much more likely (we suspect) that previous responses modify later ones and that the response to two stimuli presented simultaneously will *not* be the algebraic sum of the responses to each when presented separately. The idea of simple and independent traits, which enabled us to make a start on a study of human personality, is similarly questionable. It is entirely likely that traits are not independent at all but, rather, affect one another. Further, traits may not be fixed quantities but products of experience, changing as our experience grows and changes. Indeed, it may be that a much richer and more complete understanding of human personality could be achieved by doing away entirely with a notion of traits in any form. The notion of chemical element and compound in its most primitive form we may also suspect to be highly incomplete. It supposes that the properties of a compound arise simply by juxtaposition or union of two or more elements. Yet our experience in art, architecture, and engineering tells us that it is not only the constituents of a compound which confer properties on the compound but the organization of these constituents as well.

In short, the criterion of validity asks that the data we use be not only reliable but representative. It asks that the substantive structure that points to these data as the appropriate data of enquiry reflect as much as possible of the richness and complexity of the subject matter to which it is applied.

The existence of these two criteria is important to us because they lead to two characteristics of knowledge which, in turn, have important implications for curriculum. In the first place, the play of these two criteria confer on scientific knowledge a distinctly revisionary character. In the second place, in some sciences the same interplay leads to the concurrent development of a number of bodies of knowledge of the same subject matter.

The revisionary character of scientific knowledge accrues from the continuing assessment and modification of substantive structures. As investigations proceed under the guidance of an early, naive structure, we begin to detect inconsistencies in our data and disparities between our conclusions and the behavior of our subject. These inconsistencies and disparities help us identify the invalidities in our conception. Meanwhile, the naive structure has enabled us nevertheless to gain some knowledge of our subject and to sharpen our techniques for study. Our new knowledge of the subject, our improved techniques, and our sharpened awareness of inadequacies in our substantive structures enable us to conceive new structures more complex than the old, more adequate to the richness of the subject matter. With the advent of a new structure, the knowledge contained in the older conceptions, though "right" enough in its own terms, is rendered obsolete and replaced by a new formulation which puts old facts and new ones together in more revealing ways.

While different substantive structures tend to succeed one another in physics, chemistry, and biology, other disciplines are characterized by the concurrent utilization of several sets of structures. In the recent study of human personality, for example, two bodies of knowledge competed in the market place at the same time. One body of knowledge had been developed by conceiving personality, after the analogy of the body, as consisting of physic organs. The other body of knowledge had been developed by conceiving of personalities as arising from the need of persons for one another, as developing, for better or for worse, out of the experience of self and of others. Personality, this body of knowledge held, is best described in terms of the various relations the self can establish with others.

Such a pluralism of substantive structures and of bodies of knowledge is characteristic of the social sciences generally and of many humane studies. There is more than one body of economic knowledge; different anthropologists and different sociologists tackle their problems in different terms and in different ways; different critics use widely different conceptions of the art object in the analysis and evaluation of drama, poetry, music, and painting.

The curricular significances of the revisionary character of knowledge and the plural character of knowledge are too numerous to develop fully here. Let us be satisfied with three.

In the first place, both characteristics point to the danger of a purely dogmatic, inculcative curriculum. If we dogmatically select one of several bodies of theory in a given field and dogmatically teach this as the truth about its subject matter, we shall create division and failure of communication among our citizens. Students of different school systems in different regions who are dogmatically taught different histories of crucial moments in our nation's development are an obvious case in point. It is no less divisive, however, if our future citizens are barred from sharing enjoyment of literature and the arts by having been the victims of different dogmas, or barred from understanding each other by having been inculcated with different dogmatic views of the roots of human action or the origins of culture and civilization. The alternative is to avoid indoctrination. We may, if we like, choose but one of several pluralities of bodies of knowledge. But if we do, let it be taught in such a way that the student learns what substantive structures gave rise to the chosen body of knowledge, what the strengths and limitations of these structures are, and what some of the alternative structures are which give rise to alternative bodies of knowledge.

The revisionary character of knowledge assumes curriculum significance because revisions now take place so rapidly that they will probably occur not once but several times in the lives of our students. If they have been taught their physics, chemistry, or biology dogmatically, their discovery that revision has occurred can lead only to bewilderment and disaffection. Again, the alternative is the teaching of scientific knowledge in the light of the enquiry that produced it. If students discover how one body of knowledge succeeds another, if they are aware of the substantive structures that underlie our current knowledge, if they are given a little freedom to speculate on the possible changes in structures which the future may bring, they will not only be prepared to meet future revisions with intelligence but will better understand the knowledge they are currently being taught.

9. A Project Curriculum

William H. Kilpatrick

Source: 'Introduction' by W. H. Kilpatrick to *An Experiment with a Project Curriculum*, Ellsworth Collings (Macmillan, New York, 1927), pp. xvii–xx.

Kilpatrick explains the principles behind an early attempt to implement his 'project method' in an experimental school. The curriculum is rooted firmly in pupils' active interests and is activity-based rather than subject-based. Activities arising out of pupils' interests are chosen by pupils and teachers together. Engagement in these activities necessarily involves experience relevant to wider areas of life. All learning is directly subordinated to the pursuit of these activities. The curriculum becomes a series of guided experiences that serve to progressively broaden and enrich the pupil's interests and further experience.

The ordinary school teaches a number of "subjects", such as arithmetic, spelling, or geography. Its hoped-for results may include character or citizenship, but its actual aims are the knowledge and skills included in typical school subjects. To secure these, it assigns "lessons", typically written down in books. Pupils study these and "recite" upon them. Success is technically indicated by ability to stand certain tests, and these of late years are increasingly "standardized" by a scientific procedure.

Professor Collings has worked along a very different plan. He did not teach "subjects" as these are commonly understood. The actual aims of his school were not the conventional knowledge or skills, but the bettering of the present child life of his pupils. His starting point accordingly was the actual present life of the boys and girls themselves, with all their interests and desires, good and bad. His first step forward was to help guide these children to choose the most interesting and fruitful parts of this life as the content of their school activity. Following this, his aim was twofold, first to help the boys and girls do better than they otherwise would the precise things they had chosen, and second, by means of the experience of choosing and through the experience of more effectual activity gradually to broaden the outlook of the boys and girls as to what they might further choose and then to help them better effect these new choices.

Professor Collings' philosophy was that this gradual and continuous enlarging of power and outlook, so as, however, to stay always within things that his pupils liked as boys and girls to do then and there, would promise most both for their present and for the future. His faith was that, if the school were run efficiently on this basis, the results would be evident in more wholesome attitudes towards school and toward life in general; and that these attitudes would along with the ideas and skills they were gaining work themselves out, not only at school, but also at home and in the community, and be spread at least in some measure from the children first to the other members of their own families and perhaps later to others in the community.

Four interrelated ideas constitute Professor Collings' position. *First*, in order that the school may properly discharge its function *the pupils must purpose what they do*. Parenthetically, to "wish what one does" may be miles different from merely "doing what one wishes". Here the pupils with the teacher decided after due consideration on each next "project", the teacher having final authority to refuse assent if necessary, but in fact seldom if ever using this veto power. The enterprise being so chosen, plans for executing it were similarly discussed and decided. This procedure followed out to the end constituted in the main what is here called the "project method". But the other three constituent ideas are also implied, as will be evident.

The *second* constituent idea is that *actual learning is never single.* In addition to the matter immediately in hand, there are always in simultaneous operation many concomitant learnings, chiefly perhaps the building of attitudes toward various other life interests involved in what is going on, as for example some degree of self-confidence, some sense of responsibility, a liking for or against the matter at hand, for or against the school as encouraging such, for or against the teacher for his part in it. These attendant learnings inevitably accumulating in character determine here and now the issues of current life. So understood with their immediate bearing they constituted perhaps the chief objective of the school's endeavor.

The *third* constituent idea in the position here presented is, that *all learning encouraged by the school is so encouraged because it is needed here and now in order to carry on better the enterprise now under way.* In the traditional school the activities set up by the school are precisely and intentionally subordinate to acquiring certain prior chosen subject matter. This process is here exactly reversed: the activity is first chosen, and learning and subject matter are henceforth subordinate to it. If, for example, arithmetic or history were needed for the better doing of an enterprise under way, the children learned then and there exactly what was so needed for that specific purpose. The felt pertinence of this to the purpose at hand would by well-known psychologic principles make its learning easier. It is necessary to emphasize here that to Professor Collings this procedure was no "back door" or "left-handed" method for "putting over" the conventional subject matter. In comparison with his real aim of growth in and through better and better living here and now for his boys and girls, he literally did not care whether they got the conventional subject matter of the schools. If they needed it, it would be called for and learned. If it were not called for, it was not needed. If it will later be needed, learn it then. His contrasts of comparative learnings in the matter of formal subject matter as herein presented were in fact undertaken, and are here introduced at the wish of his advisers. The reader who wishes properly to orientate himself as he takes up his book must accept at the full this statement regarding Professor Collings' attitude, however great a strain it may give one's customary habits of thought.

The *fourth* and final constituent of Professor Collings' position is that *the curriculum is a series of guided experiences so related that what is learned in one serves to elevate and enrich the subsequent stream of experience.* These experiences are guided by the teacher in the light of the three consituent ideas already discussed and of the principle of "activity leading to further activity", namely, that other things being equal, those activities are to be preferred which promise most in their leadings to further like fruitful activities. For the practical execution of such a curriculum theory four lines of activities were simultaneously carried on in the daily work of the experimental school, each of course being broadly interpreted: story telling, construction, play, and excursions. It was felt that if these four typical aspects of life be daily represented in the child's experience and if each single enterprise-experience chosen for execution be made to yield its reasonably rich return, then the future both immediate and remote is better cared for than on any other basis of selection. The emphasis here of course is on what Professor Dewey calls the "continuous reconstruction of experience". The principle of "activity leading to further activity", it may be pointed out, takes adequate care of the moral and social bearing of proposed activities. The curriculum then was continuously made "on the spot" by the joint action of pupils and teacher, present interest and foreseen possibilities, jointly judged, being the deciding factors. The fundamental thesis was that a curriculum so made would best care for all four constituent ideas here considered and so would mean most of the living of the children, – for their present living because it would best call forth their present active powers, for their future living because promising most *for* their present experience it accordingly promises most *from* their present experience.

10. Curriculum Integration

Richard Pring

Source: London Institute of Education Bulletin, Spring 1970, pp. 4–8. Reprinted by permission in R. Hooper (ed.), *The Curriculum: Content, Design and Development* (Oliver and Boyd, Edinburgh, 1972), pp. 265–72.

Curriculum integration is fashionable – integrated day, interdisciplinary enquiry are 'in' words. Pring argues that any recommendation for curriculum integration implies some underlying theory of knowledge and that too many educationists are using the word as though the value of integration was self-evident. The value is not self-evident and integrated programmes require critical examination. The intergrationalist must be ready to defend himself against those who wish to retain the subject-centred curriculum on the basis of the theory of knowledge put forward by Hirst. Pring puts forward a number of theoretical positions which could justify curriculum integration and concludes by noting that curriculum integration is a much more complex notion than is often realised.

There is no doubt that integration is an 'in' word. Plowden and Newsom recommend it; junior schools have their 'integrated day'; 'interdisciplinary enquiry' features in many secondary schools; colleges prepare junior/secondary students for interdisciplinary learning situations; the Schools Council publishes examples of good 'integrated approaches'; and there is talk of the 'seamless cloak of knowledge', the 'unity of learning', or 'a single view of the world and of life', all of which, so we are told, can be reflected adequately only in an integrated curriculum.

Integration is also a 'pro'-word. It is contrasted with the *fragmentation* of the curriculum which typifies the *traditional* school, with subject *barriers*, the *compartmentalization* or *pigeon-holing* of knowledge, with specialization and *irrelevance* to life as a whole. Rather it is connected with the *natural* enquiry of children which does not respect subject divisions.

To be both an 'in' word and a 'pro' word has its dangers. Educational theory is rife with such words: 'growth', 'needs of the child', 'creativity', and so on. They play a significant part in much educational argument, are often accepted uncritically, and have an emotive meaning that dares anyone to challenge the educational aims which they embody. (Who for example would be against children growing, developing their personalities, fulfilling their needs, or even creating?) 'Integration' is quickly becoming such a word. Who would object to knowledge or personality or life being 'integrated'? Unity, integration, wholeness seem to have a fascination and value of their own. But what do they mean? 'Integration' as such is an empty word. There must be integration of something and one cannot really understand or appreciate what is meant by curriculum integration until one has clarified what it is that is being integrated. Yet to clarify this is by no means easy. It raises important questions in epistemology and ethics. Failure to see these questions, let alone to attempt an answer to them, renders a lot of writing on curriculum integration superficial in its argument and confusing in its practical recommendations. What I would wish to argue at much greater length is that any particular recommendation for curriculum integration implies some underlying theory of knowledge or of value or of learning, and that to explain what one means by integration necessarily involves one in such theoretical considerations. Because of the failure of so many educationists to understand this, the word integration is bandied about as though its meaning were clear, and recommendations for curriculum integration are made as though its value were self-evident. Here however I can only indicate why its meaning is not clear, why its value is not self-evident, and why therefore there is a need for a much closer analytic and critical examination of 'integrated' programmes if education is not to be sacrificed to yet more conceptual muddle and practical confusion.

Curriculum integration is frequently contrasted with the 'compartmentalization' of knowledge which, apparently, is characteristic of the 'traditional' syllabus. A subject-based curriculum is said to limit enquiry, set up barriers, and confine study to a limited range of information. Often these barriers are seen to be arbitrary or simply conventional, and the integration of subjects is seen as a necessary if there is to be a 'truer', more comprehensive picture of reality. For, so it is argued, the division of knowledge into distinct subject division is artificial and does not reflect correctly the essential unity of reality and of our ordinary way of understanding and judging. It is foreign to the natural and spontaneous (words that frequently crop up in this context) method of enquiry. What is important for the school to do is to encourage 'enquiry' (and enquiry knows no limits) and for this purpose to provide a 'rich' and 'stimulating' environment.

At this stage however it is necessary for the 'integrationalist' to pause awhile and to examine a little more closely the case put forward by those who wish to retain a curriculum that is largely subject based, for the 'specialists' would argue that the distinctions between subjects are not arbitrary at all and that to blur or ignore these distinctions is to debase any claim to knowledge. To pursue this argument further would raise questions in the theory of knowledge that can be dealt with, in the limits of this paper, only in the most superficial way. But some attempt must be made to pinpoint where the issues lie.

Understanding (and education would seem to be about the development of the understanding) lies in the formation of conceptual schemes that consist in the organization, discrimination, and interpretation of experience so that it can be expressed and communicated symbolically. The development of meaning is the development of this symbolic organization characterized by certain general concepts and modes of inference and by certain accepted canons of verification and enquiry. Outside these unifying principles of experience there can be no meaning. No enquiry can take place except within a particular system of thought, and this involves recognizing the implicit rules of procedure built into the acceptance of this system rather than another. In a way it does not make sense to talk of children simply making an enquiry. It must be an enquiry of a certain sort. As soon as one 'enquires', one is involved in the use of symbols which already dictate, as it were, what moves are correct or at least permissible. Any enquiry must involve the meanings revealed at different levels within one or other of the disciplines. This is a logical point – it follows from what one *means* by mind, rational behaviour, and hence enquiry. The subjects on the curriculum, so this argument goes, are there because among other things they initiate the pupil into the different modes of understanding that are characterized by distinct organizing concepts, principles of verification, and logical connexions. Far from being merely conventional or arbitrary, they represent in their distinct disciplines of thought what it is to think, to know and to enquire.[1]

I am not wanting to defend this thesis against the advocates of curriculum integration. I wish merely to say that it is with such a thesis they must deal if they are to suggest that subject divisions are merely conventional or arbitrary. They must argue either that such is a false theory of knowledge or that it is not a complete account of knowledge and that the recognition of autonomous disciplines needs to be supplemented by some form of integration within the curriculum.

Where the second line of argument is adopted, there can be distinguished quite different theoretical reasons for proposing curriculum integration, although in practice the reasons are rarely made clear. Firstly, integration might be argued for as follows. No proposition or argument of any enquiry is, admittedly, without a logical structure which can be identified as such and which determines to some extent the role it can play in the enquiry. One knows that a given proposition is, say, an empirical claim to truth within a certain conceptual structure and that the test of truth or falsity of this kind of proposition is such and such. One knows that a particular argument implies certain criteria of validity and one can compare this argument with the norms assumed by it. Nonetheless many problems including those of considerable personal importance cannot be raised, let alone answered, within any one cognitive structure. Different sorts of enquiry have to be brought to bear upon a particular problem. Sex education, or giving adequate answers to practical questions raised about sexual behaviour, is an obvious example. No one discipline can claim a monopoly of the sorts of consideration relevant to the determination of practical principles. In many areas of understanding, especially where practical decisions have to be made, the integration of distinct disciplines of thought is essential yet cannot logically be given within any one discipline. The putting together of the distinctive enquiries represented by the disciplines is itself an educational task that should have a place within the curriculum. In other words, one might recognize the autonomy of different bodies of knowledge while at the same time recognizing the problems inherent in their synthesis. And one might make provision in the curriculum for this synthesizing element by concentrating, for at least part of the time, on areas of thought and decision-making where such an integration is indispensable. One would, as it were, learn to integrate by integrating (just as one learns to teach by teaching).[2]

A second line of reasoning for some degree of curriculum integration might be summarized as follows. The disciplines represent the *worked out* structures of knowledge, the systematic organization of experience, the particular conceptual schemes which determine how one classifies, individuates, and proceeds with yet further enquiry. The disciplines therefore constitute in the most complete and developed form the logical structure of knowledge. They do not however reflect the pupil's level and mode of understanding, nor do they indicate the process whereby the pupil might attain these structures of knowledge. For, on this line of argument, the finished product, tidied up into the logical neatness of distinct disciplines, does not contain within it the way in which it should be presented. All too often, we are told, the subject matter is presented in its completed and worked out form, and not in the manner through which it was worked out.[3] On the other hand, if the student were allowed to pursue his own interests and to satisfy his own curiosity, he would raise questions which would gradually be refined into the precise systematization characteristic of the different disciplines of thought. The 'natural' curiosity of the pupil, his 'spontaneous' enquiry, would lead to the gradual differentiation of a conceptual structure that typified the worked out modes of understanding. Although the end product might be the different forms of knowledge, the educational process towards this goal would be an integrated activity, focused upon or united in the current interest or enquiry of the pupil.

Of course it may be argued that there are no distinct disciplines of thought, characterized by different modes of enquiry. Rather is all enquiry a matter of solving problems – one is in a sort of forked-road situation. First, one is puzzled how one might proceed. Secondly, as much relevant data as possible is gathered. Thirdly, a principle of procedure is tentatively formulated in the light of this data. Finally, this is put to the test and applied in practice. Either one's problem is solved or the principle is rejected, or at least reformulated. In any case there is always the same pattern to any enquiry and the resulting knowledge is essentially that of tentative hypothesis constantly tested and reformulated. The differentiation of knowledge into distinct modes characterized by different processes of enquiry and verification is dismissed. Enquiry is basically of the same pattern, though the resulting structures of understanding might be distinguished by their respective organizing concepts (as physics is distinguished from chemistry). But the method is the same, and if encouraged and pursued will provide the integrating factor in all the classroom activities.

Sometimes of course the pupil does not appear to be 'spontaneously' or 'naturally' curious. In such cases the pupil needs to be 'stimulated'. Interdisciplinary enquiry sometimes begins with a key lesson in which the pupil is given a battery of 'stimuli' in order to 'spark him off'. Ideas are scattered freely, possible lines of enquiry suggested, problems presented, questions asked. Themes of topics might be provided and these, if suggestive enough, will make good 'starters'. Having started, the pupil is free to travel in whatever direction he likes provided that in travelling he is raising questions that open his enquiring mind to yet new experiences and fresh connexions of ideas. Themes or starters in this sense are not intended to control or set limits to the enquiry, only to trigger it off.

A further sort of reason underlying some proposals for curriculum integration arises more from ethical than from epistemological or learning theory. To the question 'What is the aim of education?' an answer might be given in terms of the needs of the child or those of society. Such an answer does not raise the epistemological issues that I have been considering. Whatever its nature, knowledge is said to be of value in so far as it meets the needs of the pupil or is of social utility. The 'needs' of the pupils are listed (different books give different lists) and these become the unifying factors in determining the balance of the curriculum. Themes like 'Man and his environment' are subdivided into smaller themes such as 'Family', 'Home', 'Leisure', 'Work'. To study material within the ambit of such themes will, it is claimed, enlighten the pupil in matters relevant to his immediate needs. Often such a programme of enquiry will be called social studies in which history, geography, literature, religious knowledge, and other subjects are integrated within the particular theme and are thereby directed to shed light on the needs of the pupil.[4]

It has been the purpose of this brief article not so much to justify or to criticize the different proposals for curriculum integration, but rather to indicate some of the different theoretical considerations which at different times underlie them. Curriculum integration is frequently pursued without any analysis of the nature of knowledge and therefore without any clear cognitive objectives. However, where there is such an analysis and where areas of autonomous studies are respected, integration may still remain an objective for curriculum planners for the quite different reasons that I have given and that I summarize here. Firstly, it is claimed, a mastery of the different disciplines is not all there is to knowledge; there is a further educative task of integrating the disciplines in so far as these are brought to bear upon a problem which cannot be fitted into the limits of any one discipline. Secondly, the curiosity and free enquiry of the pupil might be seen as the integrating factor and the final systematization of knowledge, manifest in the different disciplines, would be said to develop from such an enquiry. Thirdly it is held by some that the method of enquiry itself is unitary and that there is no theoretical justification for the proliferation of modes of understanding upon which the fragmentation of the syllabus is based. Fourthly, it is argued that the value of knowledge depends on the degree to which it satisfied the 'needs' of the individual or of society; 'needs' give direction and purpose, and thereby an integrating thread to the educational process. Fifthly, certain concepts such as 'power' and 'communications' are complex in meaning, are central to our thinking in the different disciplines of thought, need close scrutiny in themselves, and thereby offer fresh ways of entering into different areas of knowledge.

I have sought briefly to identify quite different reasons which might underlie proposals for curriculum integration. Not to recognize these distinctions which raise fundamental questions of epistemology and value is a source of confusion in practice. Let me in conclusion show how this can occur. It is a frequent practice in interdisciplinary enquiry to suggest (or impose) a theme which, instead of the traditional subject, will be the focus of study. But in the light of the distinctions that I have made in this article the theme might function in quite different ways. Firstly, it might in some way delineate an area in which practical decisions have to be made and which must therefore be a focal point of interdisciplinary thinking (e.g. sex, war, authority, etc.). Secondly, it might be the name for a complex of information which is thought relevant to the needs of the pupil or of society. Thirdly, it might through an association of ideas be a starting off point for enquiry. Fourthly, it might itself suggest a certain structured body of knowledge that needs to be mastered but which transcends the subject boundaries, and here one often hears talk of 'exploring a concept' (e.g. 'power'). Not to have clarified beforehand the function of the theme or concept may lead to a very confusing situation. It may be used simultaneously both to trigger off a line of enquiry and to set limits to the enquiry – and these are quite different functions, often in practice incompatible with each other.

Depending, too, on the particular conception of curriculum integration that one has, are such matters as the role of the teacher, the pattern of the school timetable, the use of resources, and so on. Current writing on the 'integrated day' suggests the need for a 'rich and stimulating environment'. Resources are rather like pep pills – stimulating, maintaining, and extending the pupil's interest. On the other hand where the centre of integration is an area which *ought* to be explored by the pupil or which is judged relevant to his human needs and concerns, the 'bank' of resources should be developed with these quite different reasons in mind. Items are chosen because of the lead they give along a pre-conceived line of enquiry rather than for the interest they arouse.

Curriculum integration is a much more complex notion than is often realized, not only in its conception but also in its effect upon teaching roles, use of time, organization of the school and the classroom, and so on. There is no opportunity here to enter into this in detail. Suffice to give some indication of this complexity and of the need to look much more closely at the deeper issues that lie beneath it.

NOTES

1. Reference might be made to Professor P. H. Hirst's article 'Liberal education and the nature of knowledge' (from *Philosophical analysis and education* edited by Archambault) where similar, though not identical points about what it means to know or to understand are made and developed at considerable length. Reference should be made also to Professor Hirst's contribution to *Proceedings of the Philosophy of Education Society* 1966, 'Language and thought'. A much more extensive account of the development of meaning and the structuring of experience in language is, of course, to be found in P. H. Phenix, *Realms of meaning* (McGraw-Hill, 1964).
2. Pring, R. A. 'Philosophy of education and educational practice' (*Proceedings of the Philosophy of Education Society*, 1970) especially pp. 66–68, where this point is developed at much greater length, with special reference to the study of education.
3. See Dewey, J., *Democracy and education,* chap. 14.
4. See Vincent Rogers's *Social studies in education* for examples of 'broad organizing concepts' that will supposedly provide integrating links. Unfortunately the study of 'man both as an individual and as a member of a host of groups; with man both changing and adjusting to his environment' is so broad that it includes everything and gives few clues for integration.

11. The Fourfold Curriculum

Charity James

Source: Charity James, *Young Lives at Stake: a Reappraisal of Secondary Schools* (Collins, 1968), pp. 125–32.

Charity James explains the four elements of a secondary-school curriculum developed at the Goldsmith's College Curriculum Laboratory. These provide for interdisciplinary as well as discipline-based studies, and for group work as well as individual study related to each pupil's needs and interests. The fourfold curriculum is an attempt to show how comprehensive education can provide for active and personal engagement with the environment.

The study I have made of the modes of our engagement with the environment may have seemed very general and far removed from the planning of a school's working day, but the implications are practical and demand radical re-thinking of everyday practice. The kinds of questions and answers that I move on to in this section are less general and are more open to change and development. I would not suggest that the Fourfold Curriculum is any final answer to our requirements of school, but it seems to me at the moment to be the most sensible way of meeting them.

If we look at the implications of what has gone before, certain requirements clearly emerge, fundamental to curriculum planning:

1. The school environment must be sufficiently diversified to allow different children to arrive at different points by different routes and at different times; this is what is involved in caring for individual well-being, and in thinking big about talent, and it is one way in which development through the acknowledgement of a child's relative strengths will be made possible.

It follows that any tight fitting of children into courses, and any idea that late or eccentric developers can never catch up, never belong, because they have missed certain fixed requirements, are unacceptable. Despite all difficulties the aim must be to accommodate the school to the needs of all.

2. Since curriculum is seen in terms of the quality of the engagement with the environment, the emphasis has moved from learning subject-matter to becoming at home with a subject-discipline. This is a fundamental point which I shall discuss in detail later. For the moment it is enough to say that there needs to be experience both of inter-disciplinary and intra-disciplinary studies, but that integration of subject-matter by teachers has no particular merit.

3. If motivation is to be intrinsic, bases of intrinsic motivation need to be identified. I see these as:

(*a*) Partaking in active engagement with the environment in ways to which students can make a personal contribution.

Answering other people's questions and working to other people's design have their place in the context of exploratory and creative study requires them. Within that context they may be extremely valuable, as are for instance assignments and programmes designed to help individuals or clusters to acquire skills or concepts that they need. Writ small, this occurs in IDE/M; writ large it is the function of a whole cell of the Fourfold Curriculum, the "remedial" section.

(*b*) Not only the manner but the matter of the engagement being seen by the child to have relevance to his *concerns*; and this means not merely a relevance to passing fancies that he can enjoy and leave, although this is important, but relevance to matters that have his long-term respect and commitment.

(*c*) The tasks which any student undertakes being appropriate to his level of achievement now. This aspect of motivation is sometimes ignored, but the feedback to him is fundamental: he must have sufficient challenge, but he must also have sufficient experience of success. Only teachers in close touch with pupils can know what success each individual requires, but we can expect that greater support is needed by those whose performance is not high than by the gifted. Teachers sometimes suppose that in a situation permitting more exploratory and creative work than is usual today their skill in diagnosing and guiding pupils will not be called on. On the contrary, to ensure that he maintains the dynamic that comes from work intrinsically interesting to him and at the same time to ensure that the level of challenge is just right for him and to assign the right work at the right moment, an appropriate programme, for instance when he most needs this, demands a high degree of professionalism.

4. Not only will active enquiry, making, and dialogue be the foundation of the curriculum, but the areas of investigation agreed on will have to have a certain amplitude of scale, especially as students grow into mid-adolescence. There is a place for precision in any work, but minutiae have to be justified by being essential to some larger system. Hence much of the skill of the teacher will lie in guiding the young to tasks which serve their purpose but at an appropriate level of competence.

It is to meet these kinds of requirements that I have formulated the proposal of a Fourfold Curriculum.

The elements in the Fourfold Curriculum, which are of course to be seen as four cells of activity, not four quarters, are these:

1. Interdisciplinary Studies: IDE (Interdisciplinary Enquiry) and IDM (Interdisciplinary Making)
2. Autonomous Studies (intra-disciplinary studies)
3. Remedial Education or "Clinic" (education related to special

needs)

4. Special-interest Studies or "Orbital Studies"

1. Interdisciplinary Studies

In introducing IDE in 1965 I wrote:

> We stand for a policy unique in English education. The essence of our work is the belief that if people are to live well in a creative, flexible society the human gift of enquiry and exploration must be fostered throughout school and later life, and that it is the special feature of a democratic society that all its aspects are open to investigation by all its members. Our first pillar is therefore ENQUIRY, enquiry which is active in process and often leads to action. Secondly we believe that once one starts to enquire into and attempt to solve fundamental problems, the barriers between subjects, which seem formidable when they are dividing up a fixed body of knowledge, seem less relevant, and the work necessarily becomes INTERDISCIPLINARY: we have to use a variety of disciplines in formulating the problem, creating hypotheses as to its solution, working on and communicating our findings. It is no accident that in the knowledge explosion it is in the areas between subjects that the great advances are being made, and it does no service to learners at any level to suggest that subject boundaries are important when they cease to be convenient. On the other hand it does them no service either to suggest that the great disciplines which the human mind has created are trivial; on the contrary, as pupils move out of childhood and are co-opted into the adult world they need the chance to become aware of some of the key concepts, the great general ideas that have emerged in these disciplines and to understand, by using them, the theoretical structures which embody these ideas. Our concern can therefore be identified as being with INTERDISCIPLINARY ENQUIRY IN THE SECONDARY SCHOOL, which we shorten into IDE.[1]

I would now add the concept of INTERDISCIPLINARY MAKING, and I am hesitant of using the phrase 'interdisciplinary studies' lest these shall be supposed to be integrated teacher-directed studies, where teachers plan an integrated course by combining subject-matter. It is safer therefore to refer to this section as IDE/M. In IDE/M, clusters of children with "the provocative assistance of focus-groups of teachers"[2] that is to say interdisciplinary groups of teachers, concern themselves with important areas of investigation or undertake creative enterprises of a scale which call on a number of disciplines.

2. Autonomous Studies

Edwin Mason has outlined the other cells of the curriculum so succinctly that I welcome the opportunity to quote him:

> *Autonomous Studies*, in subjects which demand linear treatment, which are not "coming through" in interdisciplinary enquiry, and which are nevertheless deemed necessary at the time. All subjects are likely to be appropriate for autonomous study at some time: the case is not that some subjects are appropriate for IDE and others not. It is rather that in all areas attention to the discipline of a subject will be called for some time, and in some subjects this kind of attention may need to be regular and persistent, so that it will need to be time-tabled. Autonomous studies need not be conducted in classes and should be heuristically and creatively taught, within the framework of the discipline. Here again clustering is individual or paired work on programmes (anything from job-cards to "structured programmed learning"[3] with sophisticated machinery). Expressive arts need also at times to be autonomous, enjoyed for their own sake and not bent to the ends of a given enquiry.

Autonomous studies in this sense are of course not to be confused with the independent study by individuals, which can take place at any time.

The composition of this group of autonomous studies will vary a good deal from one school to another, since it would be against the ethos of the collaborative school to demand inter-disciplinary teaching of a teacher who did not approve of it. Thus already in some schools mathematics is at the heart of IDE (although not confined to it), whereas at others the mathematicians prefer to do all their work independently, and this is accepted. As a rule teachers emerge who do not at first wish to engage in the experiments of the first focus-groups but who rapidly recognize the increased involvement, the developing powers of observation, and other valuable characteristics of pupils undertaking IDE/M, which carry over to their autonomous studies; and these teachers are ready then to work in interdisciplinary studies. On the other hand schools working in IDE/M are still in the earliest stages, and we may well come to a time, therefore, when new and more theoretical bases can be evolved for distinguishing autonomous from interdisciplinary studies, and achieve a greatly increased flexibility as children pass from one to the other. In the end autonomous studies may melt into the Remedial and Special Interests sections, in so far as they cannot be accommodated in IDE/M. For the moment their autonomy is vital.

It is important, too, to recognize that there is a danger that IDE/M, if it were diminished into an element in the administrative routine of a mechanical school, would soon be used to steam roller individuality, and would thereby immediately lose its collaborative, creative exploratory character.

3. Remedial Education

"It is never too late" should be the rallying cry of the collaborative school, and the remedial section or *clinic* is the organizational expression of this faith.

> Every adolescent needs to receive expert specific remedial help with any learning or skill technique which is holding him back from achieving an immediate, subjectively-important learning-objective. (This does apply to all: it matters as much to the "bright" thirteen-year-old inventor of a hovercraft as it does to the "dull" fifteen-year-old who cannot read his instruction-manual for servicing an engine, and we assert that "remedial education" must be thought of in the same way for all students); . . . .
> Hence the remedial element is designed specifically to give rapid and massive support where specific weaknesses are identified as blocking progress either in IDE or in autonomous studies. This again may be offered in groups of any size; but it is here that the most expert possible diagnosis of individual constellations of difficulties is needed, and quite individual support is most likely to be profitable. The setting of children in "rag-bag groups" of the "generally weak" is damaging to them and defeats its own ends; so it is here that the development of a greatly varied store of individual remedial programmes is an urgent task for schools to undertake, as well as for research-institutes and publishers.[4]

Some "remedial work" is best done by using members of staff as peripatetic teachers, some by students going to teachers in their specialist accommodation, but much of it will best be accomplished by a school having an extremely well-indexed supply of programmes, concept loops, and so on, which should be seen as appropriate for meeting the needs of small groups and of individuals rather than as a medium for mass instruction.

4. Special-Interest Studies

The fourth cell is devoted to:

> *Special-interest Studies*: time in which the young can follow as deeply as they wish strong personal interest, individually or in any kind of group which helps them. . . . This should not be organized as a forced-choice from a variety of possible interests envisaged by the

staff, but entirely open. Many special interests may prove ephemeral, but they have none the less value for that.

In proposing this Special-interest cell I was introducing into the Fourfold Curriculum an element which had been an integral part of the work of another colleague, Leslie Smith, as headmaster of an East London school – his concept of "orbit":

> Examples of orbital arrangements include remedial language, remedial mathematics, advanced engineering, extra lathe practice, office practice, certain aspects of commercial studies, advanced art, stagecraft for purposes of school productions, life-saving and advanced swimming, various aspects of athletic training and games coaching, various outdoor pursuits like canoeing, construction work on school projects, individual and group project work of all kinds, field work, motor vehicle maintenance, advanced joinery, television and radio maintenance, community services and dozens more besides . . . . The organization of the orbital scheme is complicated, but possible. Teachers are placed outside the normal time-tabled programme – in orbit – with powers to extract children from their normal lessons provided the pupils concerned are likely to benefit from such orbital activity. Sometimes, it is possible to place a teacher in orbit on two or three sessions each week – a lot depends on staffing ratios – so that a number of children can follow a course for, say, six weeks or a term.

The Fourfold Curriculum provides a diverse environment in which very different children can find what they need. It is in my view the direction in which comprehensive schools must move if they are to provide comprehensive education for diverse children without divisiveness.

NOTES

1. A. E. Mason and C. M. James, eds., *The Raising of the School Leaving Age:* Report of the Second Pilot Course for Experienced Teachers (1966), p. 2.
2. A. E. Mason, ed., *New Roles for the Learner*. Report of the Fifth Pilot Course for Experienced Teachers (1967), p. 32.
3. For an outline of "Structural Programming" as devised by the centre for Structural Communication, see Anthony Hodgson, "A Communication Technique for the Future", *IDEAS*, No. 7.
4. A. E. Mason, Fifth Report, pp. 32–3. For proposals for the free use of this "clinic" in the later years of schooling see C. M. James, "The Raising of the School Leaving Age and the Fourfold Curriculum", *IDEAS*, No. 4, 1967.

III APPROACHES TO CURRICULUM PLANNING

12. The Nature and Structure of Curriculum Objectives
P. H. Hirst

Source: P. H. Hirst, 'Curriculum Objectives', in *Knowledge and the Curriculum* (Routledge and Kegan Paul Ltd., London, 1975).

Clear and logically accurate statements of objectives are necessary for curriculum planning. For Hirst, the fundamental objectives of education are cognitive in character. What is needed for effective curriculum planning, therefore, is an understanding of what is involved in the acquisition of knowledge. Hirst's contention is that knowledge is in fact differentiated into seven or eight distinctive 'forms'. Behavioural objectives will not universally suffice for curriculum planning since, though some objectives are logically behavioural, other more basic objectives in education are essentially covert. In those cases, 'behaviours' could only be evidence for, rather than constituents of, the achievement of a rational mind.

If curriculum planning is a matter of planning means to specified ends, and an educational curriculum therefore serves educational ends, the clearer we are about those ends and their nature the more adequate the planning can be. Something has already been said about their character in discussing the logic of curriculum planning, but further elucidation is called for if even the most general problems we face in contemporary planning are to be rationally approached. Not long ago educationists talked about 'aims' rather than 'objectives' and this shift to a more technical term alone indicates a growing awareness that more detailed description of the achievements we are after is desirable. If what it is we want to achieve is first indicated in expressions of great generality, these need to be unpacked into much more specific terms or little positive guidance is provided for educational practice. To be of value we must eventually analyse these ends down to particular achievements we wish pupils to reach, detailed enough for us to be able to judge how to promote these and not other achievements with which they could be confused, and detailed enough for us to be able to judge when pupils have and have not reached them. By curriculum objectives, I shall mean the achievements we want, specified to this degree. In common parlance and educational debate, both 'aims' and 'objectives' can have varying degrees of specificity and nothing is gained by attempting to legislate particular uses for these terms. Indeed, it seems to me necessary on different occasions to discuss educational ends at different levels depending on the character of the issues at stake. When we get down to the job of drawing up curricula for implementation in school, however, the greater the degree of specificity the better, and in speaking of curriculum objectives I shall have in mind as tight a description of what is to be learnt as is available.

There is however one way of characterising educational ends which is unsatisfactory not merely because it is general, but because it can be used to evade the detailed specification of what is being aimed at and even to suggest that specification is unnecessary or undesirable. It has begun to be extremely common to speak of the curriculum as being concerned with promoting pupils' 'growth', satisfying their 'needs' or following their 'interests'. These terms are global in their intentions, and their content is totally unspecified. 'Growth' and 'need' can be used as educational objectives because they presuppose a set of in-built norms, in-built standards, and so indicate, however vaguely, something that is thought to be desirable. But talking about the pursuit of growth and the satisfaction of needs must not blind us to the need to formulate in detail what objectives constitute growth and what precisely it is that pupils need. The notion of growth itself, once taken out of its biological context, contains no clear indications as to what is to be aimed at. Take Dewey's old example: is pursuing burglary, and developing a high art in this, 'growth'? Well, obviously in an educational sense, no. But why not exactly? What developments, what objectives, do constitute growth? The term itself picks out no clear answer; we have to determine quite independently what content it shall have. If one turns to a term like 'needs', then one can certainly talk about basic needs which people may have of a biological or a psychological kind. But do these really spell out curriculum objectives for us? In what sense do children need arithmetic or need to solve practical problems? In what sense do they need to understand the science taught to them? Only in a highly conventionalised social sense. The norm or value that makes us think of these as needs is a social norm, not a 'natural' one. Saying what children need is only a cloaked way of saying what we judge they ought to have. Let us then remove the cloak and its suggestions that in nature alone we can find what children ought to have in terms of their growth and their needs. And let us accept the fact that we must plan and specify ourselves which educational objectives we are after.

The idea that educational objectives can be spelt out in terms of interests can, I think, also be analysed away. The interests of children – if one takes the felt interests that they have – will never, in many cases, produce the educational objectives we want. What is more important is the frequent assumption that interests, like needs, are naturally given and are not the product of social factors. But interests can be created, and it is surely a basic function of education to create interests in what is worthwhile. Once more we must realise that a global term cannot be the source of specific educational objectives. It just hides the fact that people are writing in their own judgments as to what objectives should be chosen. Such terms cannot give us specific educational objectives which can function as aims in the educational enterprise at a working level, for to be meaningful they all presuppose a particular content of the very kind we are seeking.[1]

But what does the demand for the detailed specification of objectives involve? What categories are we to use? What is the nature of these objectives and what inter-relations do they have?

B. S. Bloom and his colleagues have in recent years produced two instalments of a now celebrated classification of objectives.[2] They divide the area into three domains: the cognitive, the affective, and the psychomotor. In the cognitive domain they list first such objectives as a knowledge of specifics – meaning by this, a knowledge of particular items of information, of terminology, of conventions, of classifications, of methodologies, of principles and generalisations, of theories. They then classify intellectual abilities and skills, dividing these into such groups as the abilities and skills connected with comprehension, translation, application, the analysis and breaking down into elements of communications that we receive, synthesising communications and evaluating them.

In the same way there is an attempt to classify objectives in the affective domain. First there are objectives connected with attending to phenomena, from awareness to controlled selection. There follow groupings of dispositions to respond, from mere acquiescence to enjoyment. Similarly in matters of valuing, organizing and the formation of a whole complex of values.

This attempt at setting out a framework of categories in which we can clearly distinguish educational objectives has enormous value. To begin with, it brings out the tremendous diversity of the kinds of objectives we are after in education. We are not simply after people learning facts, not simply after their learning skills, not simply after their learning values or attitudes or habits. We are after all these things and more, and within any of these categories, with very diverse skills, attitudes and dispositions. Certainly to list objectives in these categories, provided we formulate them in great detail, is an extremely important exercise if only as an antidote to our concentrating on the usual limited range of objectives of which we are most directly conscious when we think about school work. But the classification is also concerned with specifying objectives in terms of intended changes in the behaviour of students. Set out in these terms, it is then possible to see whether or not students do in fact achieve these objectives intended as a result of the education they receive.

But in spite of these advantages, the taxonomy is limited in its value. Though it can help us in listing objectives, it provokes rather than answers questions about the nature and structure of objectives. What is involved in knowing facts, solving problems, applying knowledge and so on? Even in general terms what kinds of achievements are they and how does one achievement relate to another? What for instance is involved in teaching a child a simple fact, such as that in 1973 Heath was Prime Minister? If a child is to understand this fact, this item of knowledge, then to begin with he must understand what a Prime Minister is. He must also be able to identify Edward Heath. What is more, if he is to learn this as a fact he must know that it is true, and he must have some idea of what difference it makes that Edward Heath and not someone else was the Prime Minister. I would suggest therefore that it is quite impossible to learn facts, to know them as facts, without acquiring the basic concepts and the criteria for truth involved. Now that is to suggest that the notion of a fact is not a logically primitive educational objective. It presupposes certain other more fundamental objectives so that without the pursuit of these, possibly in the same context, one cannot teach facts. One might, of course, teach words, but that is not the point. In commenting on this I have given the beginning of a simple analysis of what is meant by a fact. We usually think of facts, in our everyday context, as just lying about the world, somehow being registered by us as on sensitive plates. But of course the facts are always what we know to be the case, and, without certain concepts, we would fail to be aware of certain facts, even about a room in which we may be sitting. The notion of a fact needs therefore to be spelt out with great care if we are to know what is involved in teaching facts. And one can go further, of course. I have said that one cannot have facts without concepts. But what is a concept? Is this a logically primitive element?

Or take another range of objectives altogether. What is an intellectual skill, for example adding up in arithmetic, being able to count? What is the ability to deduce that we wish children to acquire? Unless we know what we mean by deduction, or by counting, it seems to me that we may be using methods in our education which are not seriously, in a considered way, directed to the objectives. Deduction is a very good example here. Is to deduce something to have a piece of mental machinery ticking over in a certain way? Is a person who can deduce from A and B that C is the case, somebody who has got a piece of psychological machinery 'tuned' to work effectively? Is the person who cannot deduce one who suffers from having a 'rusty' piece of machinery instead? We usually think of deduction as a psychological process, but is it a sequence of events in the mind? Are there any actual psychological processes which are in fact necessary to deducing? The prime example of deduction is perhaps a mathematical theorem, so how do mathematicians work out theorems? Do they go down a ladder of reasoning, working strictly in a given order? Generally speaking, no mathematician does that. Frequently he starts from the bottom and works backwards, he shoots up a blind alley in the middle and fails to get anywhere, or thinks of a useful analogy. What the sequence of his thought is does not in fact matter, for his processes of thought are not the deduction; the deduction is the pattern of the end achievement that he establishes. To teach children to deduce is not to teach them to think along particular psychological channels, it is to teach them, whatever channels or psychological processes they use, to produce certain patterns of statements in the end. If one sees deducing as achieving certain public performances rather than as achieving an inner sequence of thought, one's objectives in this enterprise are of a quite different nature.

Or again, take something like the ability to solve problems. What is meant by this phrase? Obviously one begins by asking what problems: moral problems, scientific problems, mathematical problems? Clearly these are very different in nature. Can we assume that the ability to solve mathematical problems is the same as the ability to solve problems in morals? What is more, even to understand a scientific problem, as distinct from a moral problem, presupposes a great deal of scientific knowledge. It is only when one has done a lot of science that one can recognise scientific problems for what they are. And similarly, it is only when one has done a great deal of thinking about moral matters that one recognises moral problems as different in kind from those of science, needing to be solved in a quite different manner. The notion, therefore, of developing an ability to solve problems is radically suspect in a way that cannot be revealed simply by a classification of objectives. And further, one can only pursue the solving of particular types of problems if at the same time one is prepared to teach a very great deal of fact, a very large number of principles, of criteria and tests for truth. All of these must be employed in recognising a problem for what it is, let alone solving it. One cannot therefore pursue the end of a problem-solving for one type of problem in isolation from pursuing other objectives; and one cannot, in pursuing the ability to solve scientific problems, assume one is thereby pursuing the ability to solve moral problems or historical problems as well. There are many terms of this sort for objectives, but listing them without a grasp of their character helps little.

From what has been said, curriculum planning seems to lack some overall structure within which possible objectives can be seen in their logical relationships to each other and this would not seem likely to be forthcoming unless we can get clear at least the general character of objectives. One doctrinaire answer to all questions about their nature has troubled work in this area for many years and it is perhaps as well to comment on it right away. Under the influence of behaviourist psychology, it has repeatedly been said that all significant objectives are changes of behaviour. In its extreme forms this thesis claims either that a statement of an objective is a statement of the observable behavioural changes that are being sought, or that the behavioural changes such an objective implies are all that is relevant in curriculum planning. From this point of view, to pursue the development of a pupil's understanding and appreciation of a poem is to pursue his responding in certain ways to particular stimuli. To teach a child a certain fact is to teach him a new pattern of speech and action. To this account, there are many objections. One immediate objection is that one can doubt if it is in fact possible to specify the pattern of speech and action that goes with knowledge of a fact. Is not that infinitely variable, depending entirely on the circumstances? More fundamentally important, however, this view either legislates a meaning for such terms as say 'understanding' and 'appreciation' which is simply false, or it confuses understanding and appreciation with observable evidence for them. Achieving understanding does not necessarily result in a person's doing or saying anything of any kind, no matter what the stimuli. And to achieve certain outward and visible signs as the objectives in one's teaching is all too frequently consistent with failing to achieve the state of mind desired.

Most of the central objectives we are interested in in education are not themselves reducible to observable states, and to imagine they are, whatever the basis of that claim, is to lose the heart of the business. What is certainly true is that the observable correlates are the only evidence we have that objectives which label states of mind have been achieved, but states of mind should never be confused with the evidence for them. That this is the case can be most obviously seen if we consider states such as that of being in pain. To be in pain is certainly not to be equated with emitting shrieks and groans and to change a person's behaviour so that he makes no such noises does not itself modify his state of mind at all. Confusing what Wittgenstein called the criteria for a state of mind with that state is simply to succumb to a logical confusion.

What we need in curriculum planning is as specific and detailed a characterisation of objectives as possible, using as logically simple terms as are available. But these terms must reflect the proper character of the objectives and not distort them. States of mind are not analysable into observable states without committing category mistakes of some consequence. Of course we do want to know the observable criteria for the states of mind we are after. Not so that these can be aimed at in themselves, however, but so that we are able to assess responsibly when the objectives have been achieved. Assessment and evaluation rely on observable evidence, but these evidences are not the object of the teaching enterprise.

If objectives are not all behavioural in this doctrinaire sense, though certainly some may be of this character, can we give a more accurate account of the general nature of at least the central objectives? From a cursory survey of the objectives mentioned by Bloom and from what has already been said, it would seem that they are above all developments of a person and primarily developments of the characteristics of a rational mind. This is not to say that education is concerned only with intellectual development, as if, for example, emotional development was to be ignored, and knowledge and belief taken to be the only manifestations of mind. Nor is it even to say that education is concerned only with mental development in its widest sense. Rather it is to say that all those forms of development with which education is concerned are related to the pupil's progress in rational understanding. This means that physical education, for instance, is pursued in accordance with a rational appraisal of the place and value of physical activities in human life which we wish the pupil to acquire, that the activities themselves are viewed as those of a developing rational being, not merely an animal, and that they therefore constitute part of the life of a rational person. But to characterise the objectives of education in relation to the development of rationality, is certainly to put at the very centre of what is pursued those forms of knowledge and belief in which we make sense of our experience. It is necessarily by means of knowledge, if not by knowledge alone, that fancy gives place to a recognition of fact, that irrational wishes give place to reasonable wants, and that emotional reactions give place to justifiable actions. Thus, although all the possible or justifiable objectives of education are not themselves explicitly developments of mind, it is, I suggest, by their connection with such specific developments that other objectives have their place and their justification in education at all. In seeking to clarify further the nature and structure of objectives I shall therefore confine myself to considering what is involved in the achievements of those most central objectives of all, the acquisition of knowledge and rational beliefs, without which the development of rationality in any wider sense is logically impossible.

What then is involved in the acquisition of knowledge? Certainly it involves learning many different concepts, using these in a growing awareness of facts, truths and norms of many kinds, mastering many logical operations and principles, applying the criteria of different types of judgment and so on. What an exhaustive list of elements would be, I would not like to say, but what matters for my purpose at the moment is not a complete classification of them in independent categories, so much as a recognition of the kind of achievements that these are. They are, in fact, neither more nor less than the achievements basic to the development of mind itself.

Unfortunately our concept of mind is so persistently bedevilled by myths, largely of an empiricist nature, that we all too easily misconceive entirely what is going on in learning to understand and in acquiring knowledge. We have an almost ineradicable conviction that the mind is to be thought of as a room or box into which, via the senses, ideas or images come as ready-made copies of objects or events or facts in the external world. Further, these ideas come into the mind as quite distinct elements of awareness, rather as furniture might be put into a room. The ideas are there in the room, but they are in no sense essentially part of the room. In addition we tend to regard the mind as a kind of machine, designed to carry out certain processes of rational thought on the ideas which the senses convey, thereby building new ideas from what is given, by processes of abstraction, deduction and the like. Thus there is produced new furniture to be housed and stored, within the mind, ready for use when required. Some of us have less effective machinery than others when it comes to reasoning, and practice and exercise are needed to get the best out of what each of us is given. But essentially the processes of rational thought are regarded as natural activities of the mind. On this kind of picture, the acquiring of knowledge and understanding as the objective of education, involves two major tasks: furnishing the mind with the right ideas, and getting the machine working properly.

Now there are many reasons why this kind of account of mind must be totally rejected, three of which are particularly relevant here. First the account does not begin to do justice to what we know about the development of understanding, even at the level of sense-perception. What we see or understand about any situation is not a simple given. It is dependent on those concepts and categories, those basic units of intelligibility, which the mind brings to the situation. The possibility of discriminating elements in our experience at all necessitates having concepts. To see things is not just to register things for what they are, it is for them to be picked out or articulated in our consciousness. Only by the use of certain concepts is the mind able to discriminate. What the development of understanding involves is, in fact, a progressive differentiation of our experience through the acquisition of new concepts under which it is intelligible. The mind is therefore not a passive recipient of ideas which bring understanding from the external world. It is rather that we achieve understanding through the use of categorial and conceptual apparatus. Having such an apparatus of concepts is a necessary part of what it means to have a mind. Thus the development of a mind involves the achievement of an array of concepts and on this all intelligibility depends. The provision of experience in itself is quite inadequate for developing even the simplest body of concepts, and without these nothing more complex can possibly be achieved.[3]

In the second place, the view I am criticising regards knowledge as something which the mind may or may not possess. Knowledge is not in any sense constitutive of mind. To acquire new knowledge is simply as it were to acquire different furniture or new furniture for a room. To have scientific knowledge as distinct from historical knowledge, is for the furniture to be of one kind rather than another. For the mind itself, nothing turns on this, the room itself remains unchanged; it simply lacks the other type of furniture. In essence minds do not differ in any way by having different knowledge. The real differences between minds are simply in what is naturally given. To acquire one form of knowledge rather than another in no way affects the fundamental characteristics of the mind. Yet surely this will not do. To be without any knowledge at all is to be without mind in any significant sense. Nor is it just that the mind needs some content to work on, as if otherwise its characteristics could not be expressed. The acquisition of knowledge is itself a development of mind and new knowledge means a new development of mind in some sense. Knowledge is not a free-floating possession. It is characteristic of minds themselves. Thus to fail to acquire knowledge of a certain fundamental kind, is to fail to achieve rational mind in that significant respect. Not all knowledge is of equal importance in the development of rationality, of course, yet the fundamental relationship between knowledge and the development of mind is of central educational significance. Nor must we regard knowledge as unrelated to the development of other aspects of mind, an outlook encouraged by the view I am opposing. It is in large measure by acquiring new knowledge that we begin to reconceive our activities and that we come to feel differently about them.

In the third place we must, as I suggested earlier when discussing the nature of deduction, reject the notion that the mind naturally carries out certain mental activities according to the canons of valid reasoning, as if logical principles were laws of psychological functioning. The question of the development of the rational mind is surely not a question of the strengthening or habitualising of certain patterns of mental functioning. It is rather a question of developing a recognition that one's beliefs and one's arguments, the outcomes of thought, must satisfy important public tests. Tests of rationality are tests to be applied to the *achievements* of one's thought as formulated in propositions, not tests for thought processes themselves. To say one has reasoned something out is not to describe a particular sequence of mental occurrences, it is to say that one has achieved in the end a relationship between propositions which satisfies the public criteria necessary for giving reasons. What is more, these standards that define the achievements of reason, are certainly not natural possessions of mind. They have to be learnt, usually by dint of considerable hard work. The development of rationality is, therefore, not dependent on the exercising of particular mental processes, but it is dependent on one's coming to recognise that there are tests of validity for one's arguments and tests of truth for one's beliefs.

But if the fundamental objectives of education are developments of the rational mind, what formal relationships are there between the various objectives, the concepts, facts, norms, principles, and so on? In spite of an immediate tendency to think of these items of knowledge as detached and isolated from each other, a little reflection quickly suggests this is not the case. It is because the concepts are used in a particular way that any proposition is meaningful. The concepts on which our knowledge is built form distinctive networks of relationships. If we transgress the rules of the relationships which the concepts meaningfully permit, we necessarily produce nonsense. If we talk about magnetic fields being angry, actions being coloured, beauty having weight, or stones being right or wrong we have simply produced conceptual confusions. But not only do we convey meaning by the use of networks of interrelated concepts, meaningful propositions are judged true or false, valid or invalid, by criteria appropriate to the types of propositions. A moral judgment is not validated in the same way as a mathematical theorem, nor a historical explanation in the same way as a theological proposition. There are thus within knowledge a number of distinct types of rational judgment. From considerations of this kind it can be seen that the acquisition of knowledge in any area involves the mastery of an interrelated group of concepts, of operations with these, of particular criteria of truth or validity associated with these concepts, as well as more general criteria of reasoning common to all areas of knowledge. Indeed, the objectives of education we have been considering are closely related together as elements of distinguishable cognitive structures, each unique in crucial respects.

Looked at this way, the development of mind has been marked by the progressive differentiation in human consciousness of some seven or eight distinguishable cognitive structures, each of which involves the making of a distinctive form of reasoned judgment and is, therefore, a unique expression of man's rationality. This is to say that all knowledge and understanding is logically locatable within a number of domains, within, I suggest, mathematics, the physical sciences, knowledge of persons, literature and the fine arts, morals, religion and philosophy. These would seem to me to be the logically distinct areas, though this division might well be disputed. It is not, of course, that these forms of knowledge are totally separate from each other. That is not what I am saying. Manifestly there are overlaps in the concepts used in the different forms, and there are overlaps in the patterns of valid reasoning. But in respect of the distinctive rational judgments concerned, each structure involves elements which are irreducible to any of the others, singly or in combination. Moral judgments and scientific judgments are different in logical character, needing distinct forms of justification, and that in spite of the fact that these may at times use some of the same concepts and some of the same criteria for reasoning. The objectives with which education is most centrally concerned are thus not isolated ends but elements within integrated developing structures of understanding. Certainly all the concepts, truths, norms, principles, criteria, all the developments of mind we are interested in, have their appropriate place in relation to these structures, and even those elements which are common to different areas have significance only within these structures.[4]

If what I have said is valid, then the domain of knowledge can be seen to have important structural features, and nothing could be further from the truth than to suggest that that domain is an unintelligible chaos. Knowledge has not disintegrated, it has become more clearly differentiated. It is not even that the traditional medieval map of knowledge has become totally unacceptable, for many of the logical distinctions there made are perfectly valid.[5] It is simply that the picture is more complicated than was once the case, or thought to be the case, and that the development of knowledge necessitates some new lines in the picture. We may no longer have a hierarchy of knowledge based on realist metaphysics, but we are not without the important logical distinctions that make it possible for us to see some intelligible pattern of knowledge. We may no longer have a clear grasp of the unity of knowledge, as if it all formed, in the end, one coherent network of harmonious elements. Yet unifying theories are part of the pursuit of the sub-divisions within the areas I have mentioned and there is every reason to hope that we can become much clearer on the relationships between the logically distinct forms that I have distinguished.

Yet what then of the modern transgressions of the old frontiers? Is it not the case that besides the progressive differentiation of, say, the sciences or historical studies, there are new disciplines or forms of knowledge emerging? Maybe this is so. I see no *a priori* reason whatever why new forms of knowledge should not arise. But there is, I think, little positive reason to think that this is in fact what is happening. What there are in abundance now, are new interdisciplinary areas of study in which different forms of knowledge are focused on some particular interest, and because of the relations between the forms, what is understood in each discipline is thereby deepened. Such new areas of study do not constitute new areas on a map of knowledge based on the logical distinctions I have mentioned. They are essentially composite, second-order constructions, not to be confused with the primary forms of knowledge which I have distinguished on logical grounds. In terms of these primary forms of knowledge, the new areas seem to be exhaustively analysable.

From the preceding paragraphs it is no doubt apparent that to my mind understanding the nature of curriculum objectives is first and foremost a matter of understanding what is involved in the acquisition of knowledge. Other objectives would seem to be intelligible in character only in relation to the acquisition of knowledge. The forms of character development and skills that are frequently sought, for instance, are what they are in part because of the cognitive elements they necessarily involve. Having a critical attitude, or a preparedness to accept social change, is dependent on possessing much relevant knowledge without reference to which neither quality of mind can be adequately described or acquired. It would seem likely then that our analysis of the nature of educational objectives will in general reveal their being tied to and dependent on cognitive objectives and that their over-all structure of logical interrelations will show them to rest on the logical structure of knowledge.

It is a logical mapping of objectives that curriculum planning needs, not a categorisation of them that fails to display their logical relations. Only with this is it plain just what has to be learnt, what must necessarily be grasped, in achieving any particular objective we may care to select.

The elucidation of this logical structure is a vast philosophical undertaking and one indeed which in different ways philosophers have always been engaged on. Its difficulties are immense and the agreed conclusions modest. At present curriculum planning must work with the very partial and scattered achievements of epistemology and philosophy of mind using these where appropriate. The significance of philosophical considerations of this nature should not however be underestimated, for they can constitute powerful arguments in determining educational practice. That this is so can be seen from certain implications of the two main philosophical claims that have been voiced earlier.

If the acquisition of knowledge is the logically basic form of the development of a rational mind, and if the domain of knowledge consists of a limited number of different autonomous forms, the importance within the curriculum of the pursuit of knowledge is seen to be considerable and the significance of restricting the curriculum to certain areas of knowledge carries inescapable results for the pupils. On the first of these points, a curriculum which underplays objectives of a cognitive nature is limiting the pupils' development not only in those cognitive respects but in all other ways that presuppose those cognitive achievements. It seems to me to follow that we must firmly reject the anti-intellectualism of certain contemporary movements in education. No matter what the ability of the child may be, the heart of all this development as a rational being is, I am saying, intellectual, and we must never lose sight of these ends on which so much else, nearly everything else, depends. This means that we must get away completely from the idea that linguistic and abstract forms of thought are not for some people. If one is to develop any degree of understanding in any area of knowledge, then it is logically necessary to master the use of the appropriate symbolism. Mastery of that symbolism is not an extra to understanding but the very medium in which these forms of understanding can be acquired. I am, of course, here including the symbolism of music and the fine arts. The use of symbolism is basic to the development of mind, each area of understanding necessarily demanding a grasp of the appropriate symbols. We must therefore get away from what can be called a retreat into the arts and practical activities, as being more suitable for the less intellectually able. There is a central place in education for the arts and the practical, and that goes for all pupils. But the educational significance of these is limited, and any retreat from the demands of the many forms of language that are so central to human development is to set barriers to that development for many children.

How we can best teach such abstract, intellectual elements to the majority of pupils, let alone the less able, is not obvious. There are ways of easing the difficulties. But there are good ways of doing this and bad ways, and we need to distinguish between them. It is all too easy, with the best intentions in the world, to cease to teach such elements to the less able pupil in any significant sense at all. By not really bothering whether or not they have got hold of the concepts and can use them, by being content with memorised statements, by allowing pure repetition of operations, by omitting anything which demands even the briefest unrehearsed argument or justification, we simply evade all the problems and totally fail to develop any significant understanding. However we accommodate ourselves to the less able, it must not be by losing essential concepts, by losing genuine operations with them, by being uncritical of invalid reasoning, and so on. The necessary elements of knowledge are necessary elements and we cannot evade the implications of that simple tautology, try as we may. Yet there are things we can do. We can reduce the complexities by seeing that the conceptual relations we include are those absolutely essential for our purpose. Every unnecessary element that might befog an explanation can be omitted. We can cut down the extent of sustained argument by carefully analysing the stages that are demanded. We can use every opportunity to emphasise the central core of what is being done, rather than go in for extension and exploration of the ideas and their more complex applications. At least this is how we can set about things in the first place, and in our best teaching we do this already.

But if the cognitive objectives of the curriculum are important, the range of such objectives must not be forgotten. If the concepts and logical structure of one form of knowledge are necessarily valueless as vehicles for knowledge and understanding in another domain, to narrow the range of a child's curriculum to exclude certain forms is to leave the pupil unhelped in certain whole dimensions of thought and mental development. The business of 'subject-mindedness', paraded so outrageously in the Crowther Report as a natural phenomenon,[6] is not to be wondered at if knowledge is fundamentally differentiated. For our 'specialisation' we necessarily must pay the price.

Philosophical claims can at times provide powerful arguments in curriculum planning. And whether we like it or not our planning reflects certain philosophical beliefs. The question is simply how justifiable these are. The philosophical claims voiced here are to say the least debatable, but their significance surely is not. What we need above all in curriculum planning is a much more profound grasp of the nature of the objectives of the exercise and their logical interrelations. If we can get the ends clearer maybe we can plan more effective means.

NOTES

1. For a fuller discussion of the role of 'growth', 'needs' and 'interests' in educational planning, see R. F. Dearden, *The Philosophy of Primary Education,* Routledge & Kegan Paul, 1968.
2. B. S. Bloom, *et al., Taxonomy of Educational Objectives,* McKay Co., Inc., New York, 1956.
3. R. S. Peters, *Ethics and Education*, Allen & Unwin, 1966, ch. 2; also W. Kneale, *On Having a Mind,* Cambridge University Press, 1962.
4. For a further discussion of the distinctions between different forms of knowledge see Chapter 3, 'Liberal education and the nature of knowledge'. See also S. Elam (ed.), *Education and the Structure of Knowledge*, Rand McNally, Chicago, 1964.
5. J. Maritain, *The Degrees of Knowledge,* Geoffrey Bles, 1959, Pt I.
6. *'15 to 18' a Report of the Central Advisory Council for Education,* vol. I, ch. 25, HMSO, 1959. See also A.D.C. Peterson, 'The myth of subjectmindedness', *Universities Quarterly,* June 1960.

13. Writing General Objectives and Writing Specific Objectives

I. K. Davies

Source: I. K. Davies, *Objectives in Teaching and Learning: a Perspective* (McGraw Hill, London, Forthcoming), Chapters 6 and 7.

Davies discusses the process of choice in objective-formation. The process of choice involves an appreciative exploration of the educational possibilities of particular situations. Dewey's characteristic emphasis on relevance, flexibility and action is compared with a view of objectives as hypotheses. By contrast, Tyler's prescription for objectives in terms of behaviour and content with its attendant techniques is discussed. In view of the fact that the second extract is self-descriptive in adopting an approach through specific objectives, no more need be said by way of introduction than the author offers under the heading Focus.

Writing General Objectives

Focus
"How Do You Write General Objectives?"

Goals of the chapter. After carefully reading and studying this chapter, you will be able to:

1. Choose between the right sets of objectives.
2. Design and write general objectives appropriate to each of the following THREE formats:
   a. Aims (having the properties suggested by John Dewey).
   b. Hypotheses.
   c. Goals (having the properties suggested by Ralph Tyler).
3. Describe the use of the graphic two-dimensional chart specifying content and behaviour.

Hypotheses. After reading this chapter, the author assumes that you will:

1. Be aware of, and value, the importance of general objectives in development; teaching and learning.
2. Incorporate the procedures, whenever appropriate, into the organization of your development and teaching skills, so that they become characteristic of your professional style.

> To understand a complex thing you must
> take it apart systematically.
>
> Hans Selye

One of the most critical decisions a developer or teacher can make involves deciding upon the objectives of a learning situation. Not only will the decision give *direction* to what has to be achieved, but it will also define or delineate the *goal* to be accomplished. An objective implies direction and goal, cause and effect, process and product. A total perspective is involved, as the dictionary points out, to action, thought and feeling. The decision not only has implications in terms of what is prescribed for learning, but it also has implications in terms of content, teaching methods, resources, environment and evaluation procedures required. Such an important decision, therefore, needs to be taken seriously.

The seriousness of the decision is further highlighted when it is remembered that objectives are rarely conceived in isolation. Education does not entail the achievement of just one objective, myriads of *sets* of objectives are involved. Even in the relatively simple context of a single lesson, multiple rather than single objectives are usually involved, all of which must be related and inter-related, harmonized and balanced, into a total viable yet rich learning experience. To talk of objectives as though the problem simply entails identifying the "one right objective" is not misleading, but is mischievous as well as possibly harmful. Objectives need to be viewed within a total design or plan, rather than a list of rather isolated goals to be checked off one by one.

Design of any kind involves sensitivity and craftsmanship, labour and discipline, spirit and matter. Good teaching, too, involves rather more than assembling the right parts in the right order, just as art involves something more than painting by numbers. Paolo Soleri, the Italian philosopher-poet, argues that "Performance is to creation what structure is to form. When one performs, one produces. When one creates, one becomes." So it is with teaching. To argue, as are some curriculum developers, that it is expecting too much of harassed teachers to generate their own objectives possibly misunderstands the whole spirit of teaching and education. Imposing objectives on teachers, or requiring teachers to draw objectives from some sort of central agency can be too easy a solution for it not to be open to wide abuses.

It can be argued that teachers need to have some opportunity to write at least some of their own objectives, and they ought to feel a sufficient sense of the importance of the task to find the time to do it – even at the expense of other activities. Setting up the right priorities, knowing when and where to apply their effort, gearing effort to results, usually depend upon choosing just the right sets of objectives. Whilst teachers, like artists, are generally interested in each other's work, the creative process requires that participants listen to the workings of their own inspiration rather than necessarily taking over other people's ideas wholesale. However, the issue of teacher autonomy is too big and too important an issue to be debated adequately here. The issue involves much more than objectives.

Choosing Just the Right Sets of Objectives

Choosing just the right sets of objectives, as teachers and developers know only too well, is much more difficult than it appears. What so often appears to be obvious after the event is rarely obvious before it. What is commonsense from one perspective may not be commonsense from another. Choice involves exploring alternative sets of objectives, deliberately and conscientiously, and then deciding which set is likely to be more appropriate to the situation, the learning task and the children at one particular moment in time. Objectives which are appropriate today almost certainly will not be so appropriate tomorrow. Yet strangely enough, this deliberate act of choosing between alternative sets of possible objectives is not one that has been highlighted in the literature. It is almost as if there is an implicit assumption that, providing you have carried out the *right* type of analysis beforehand, the appropriate objective will come readily to mind.

One of the main advantages of writing objectives, however, comes from the *process* of choosing between alternatives. Writing objectives which contain as little inbuilt ambiguity as is possible helps curriculum developers, teachers and evaluators more easily compare and contrast alternative ways of proceeding. Some alternatives will obviously be trivial or irrelevant, and can be dismissed out of hand. Others require deeper consideration before a better choice can be determined. But the important thing is that the process is alive and dynamic, involving a conscious exploration of various advantages and disadvantages before a final selection is made. If the objectives chosen are cold, mechanistic and trivial, then something is wrong with the process that has been followed, as well as with the objectives selected.

Choosing just the right sets of objectives from a group of possible alternatives involves a deliberate exploration of the educational possibilities of the situation. It involves inquiring into the potential of that situation. Whilst choice suggests some form of limitation, it also implies that a wide range of conflicting possibilities have been determined and critically examined before a selection is made. Objectives, far from being peripheral to the art *of* teaching, are central to the exploring, questioning, inquiring, and searching activities of good craftsmanship *in* teaching. Unless a teacher considers alternatives, his or her mind will be closed to the range of competing possibilities which every situation offers.

But how is the better choice to be made? Sometimes objectives are chosen on the basis of expediency, because they are the most convenient, easiest, or least controversial. Sometimes objectives are just accepted, with little or no attempt made to explore alternatives and conscientiously choose between them. Sometimes objectives are imposed upon a situation from outside, for political or personal reasons. The right set of objectives, however, are usually chosen as a result of a process which begins with opinions or untested hypotheses. These must then be deliberately explored and verified by inquiry.

Logically, the best way of choosing between competing sets of alternatives might appear to involve starting out with the "facts". Beginning with the "facts", however, is impossible unless one knows which "facts" are relevant and which are irrelevant. As Peter Drucker remarked in 1966:

> To get the facts first is impossible. There are no facts unless one has a criteria of relevance. Events by themselves are not facts. . . but people do not start out with a search for facts. They start out with an opinion. . . to ask them to search for the facts first is even undesirable. They will simply do what everyone is far too prone to do anyhow; look for the facts that fit the conclusion that they have already reached. And no one has ever failed to find the facts he is looking for. The good statistician knows this and distrusts all figures – he either knows the fellow who found them or he does not know him; in either case he is suspicious.

Deliberately starting out with conflicting opinions, so that one has conscientiously to choose between competing alternatives, is a far better way of choosing just the right sets of objectives for the situation with which one is faced.

Whilst people talk about starting out with the facts when they choose between alternatives, they almost always start out with opinions. There is nothing wrong with this approach. In fact, it is probably the most reasonable way of beginning. For teachers not to have opinions after a number of years spent in training and in teaching would be odd, if not puzzling. It would suggest that they had gained little or no benefit from the opportunities to which they had been exposed. Opinions – or more accurately untested hypotheses – are as good a starting point in teaching as they are in science, for we know what to do with hypotheses.

You don't argue with hypotheses, you test them against reality. What facts support which hypothesis? What facts support which sets of objectives? Once the facts have been collected, to support the different hypotheses you have made about each alternative set of objectives, the right choice can usually be made and subsequently verified in the classroom. Teachers soon find out how good their decisions have been, or how inappropriate or inadequate they are.

Stating Objectives in a General Form

There are many ways of writing objectives, but no one format has yet been shown to be better than any other. Yet most people in the objectives movement, both in this country and in America, still seem to argue that objectives must be written in the most explicit, behavioural form possible, otherwise the labour involved is in vain. This line of reasoning, however, seems to ignore the fact that empirical evidence, as we have seen, presently shows no advantage for one type of format over any other. All formats seem to work equally well, and sometimes equally badly. The position taken in this book, therefore, is that until a clear advantage is demonstrated, commonsense suggests that the format chosen should be suitable and appropriate to the situation which it serves. A conscious choice must be made between formats, and the selection subsequently verified in the learning situation. In this way, the means of stating an objective should become more appropriate to the ends which the objective ultimately represents. Function does seem to follow form.

In some situations, it may not be educationally advantageous to transform broad, general and somewhat vague aims into precise, unambiguous, specific objectives. Myron Atkin, for instance, argues that it can unnecessarily restrict the teaching-learning possibilities of a situation. Objectives which are too explicit can limit the range of exploration, and teachers can be kept away, or warned off, potentially productive tangents. Curriculum developers, he feels, should start with *general objectives*, and then refine the programme through a series of successive approximations. In almost every learning situation skills have to be mastered and concepts learned. It is as important to ensure that goals are worthwhile, as it is to ensure that they are clearly articulated. There is no guarantee that what we can most easily define in explicit terms necessarily represents the most telling educational activity.

Dewey-like Aims

John Dewey in his book *Democracy and education*, written in 1916, spends a chapter considering "aims in education". He reminds us that aims belong *within* rather than *without* the educational process, before he goes on to draw a distinction between results and ends. Ends, he points out, are terminations, they represent the completion of something that has gone before. Results, on the other hand, are never completed, never fulfilled. They represent a stage achieved in some continuous activity. Aims, he feels, possess both of these properties, but in different ways.

An aim is a foreseen end, yet it relates always to results. For this reason, care must be taken to ensure that aims are written so as to express and emphasize the property of intrinsic continuity. Aims should not be written in simple serial order, in which one thing comes before another. Dewey points out that:

> To talk about an educational aim when approximately each act of a pupil is dictated by the teacher, when only the order in the sequence of his acts is that which comes from the assignment of lessons and the giving of directions by another, is to talk nonsense. It is equally fatal to an aim to permit capricious or discontinuous

> action in the name of spontaneous self-expression. An aim implies an orderly and ordered activity, one in which the order consists in the progress and completing of a process. Given an activity having a time span and cumulative growth within the time succession, an aim means foresight in advance of the end of possible termination.

Aims, of course, can only be written for those learning situations that permit the end results to be identified beforehand. It is not possible to write and aim for a situation whose results cannot be foreseen.

An aim as "a foreseen end gives direction to the activity", influencing the steps that are to be taken to ensure that it is achieved. For this reason, the aims as a foreseen end depends upon careful observation, in order to determine what it is likely to assist, and what is likely to hinder, teachers and learners realizing this end. Its achievement also depends upon appropriate sequencing, as well as upon selecting the better of the alternatives available. Unless deliberate choices are made, Dewey argues, it is not possible to compare relative value and desirability. Observation, sequencing and choice are important as part of the continuing process of predicting the end result. Since Dewey feels that "acting with an aim is one with acting intelligently", it is essential that the prediction which the aim represents is well founded.

John Dewey goes on to establish the criteria for what he believes to be a good aim. In identifying and writing aims in education care must be taken, he feels, to ensure that:

(a) *The aim is relevant to the situation.* There is no point in assuming "ends lying outside our activities; ends foreign to the concrete make up of the situation; ends which issue from some outside source."

(b) *The aim is flexible and capable of being changed.* Aims are "tentative sketches", in which "the act of striving to realize it tests its worth". If an aim is useful, nothing more is necessary. If it is not useful, then it must be rewritten or scrapped. This is why aims that are externally imposed can be unhelpful. Their very rigidity is at odds with the flexibility that an aim implies.

(c) *The aim should encourage a freeing of activities.* An aim does not represent the process of *doing* something, it represents only the end-in-view. It does not directly dictate activities, but frees them so that the end is reached. Nothing static, nothing fixed, nothing frozen is intended as far as activities are concerned.

Dewey also refers to an aim as an "end-in-view", emphasizing the process rather than the target itself. He points out that if one conceives of an aim as a fixed end, then "activity is a mere unavoidable means to something else". To think of activity as unimportant in itself is to misjudge the very essence of the teaching-learning process.

An aim, then, is a means of action, an acceptance of responsibility. It is only of value in so far as it is helpful in choosing between alternatives, and subsequently guiding teaching, learning and evaluation. But as Dewey points out, it is important to remind ourselves that education has no aims of its own, only people have aims – this is why aims and objectives tend to be so diverse and varied. There is nothing abstract or God-given about them. They are merely "suggestions" as to what is worthwhile and important, liberating and freeing. In driving home these points, Dewey stresses that defining and writing aims must be based upon the intrinsic needs and activities of the children themselves. All too often people tend to forget "existing powers, and find the aim in some remote accomplishment or responsibility" often related to what is important to adults. There is a tendency to settle on "aims which are so uniform as to neglect the specific powers and requirements of an individual, forgetting that all learning is something which happens to an individual at a given time and place".

Aims should be written in such a way that it is possible to translate them into specific learning environments and activities. Unless they guide teaching and learning, they are worthless, if not possible barriers to action. Dewey warns teachers to be on their guard against "ends that are alleged to be general and ultimate"; all too often this means abstract and remote. This "throws us back, once more, upon teaching and learning as mere means of getting ready for an end disconnected from the means". It ignores the fact that education is supposed to be worthwhile on its own account.

The nearest thing that Dewey comes to in giving an example of an aim for a specific learning situation occurs in the preface to his book. There he defines his aim for *Democracy and Education* as:

> an endeavour to *detect* and *state* the ideas implied in a democratic society and to *apply* these ideas to the problem of the enterprise of education. (italics added)

The advice that he gives, however, about the nature of aims, the criteria of good aims, and the warnings that he raises are as valid today as they were almost half a century ago. Acting with an aim, or an end-in-view, is still one with acting intelligently, but only if the aim is relevant, flexible and freeing rather than imposed, fixed and constricting.

Hypotheses as guides

John Dewey also made a perceptive distinction between "thinking" and "thought". Thinking, he says, is an active, vital, dynamic process, full of natural excitement and wonder involving the constant testing of hypotheses. Thought, on the other hand, is the end of the process, both its fruit and its termination – unless, of course, thought gives rise to another chain of thinking. Much of what is represented by aims and objectives is thought, the results of other people's challenges and struggles. Not surprisingly, much of the excitement has been lost, the thinking eliminated, and learners asked to store and value other people's harvests.

A related distinction has also been made by Gilbert Ryle in *The concept of mind.* In an attempt to debunk the widely-held belief that knowledge is fundamentally verbal or symbolic, Ryle distinguishes between knowing *how* and knowing *that*. The former emphasized procedures or processes, whilst the latter emphasized facts or products. Whilst both of these concepts are obviously related to each other, they can be viewed as somewhat independent in many teaching-learning situations. Knowing that there is a relationship between temperature and pressure does not necessarily imply that you also possess the necessary process skills to determine what the relationship actually is. Furthermore, knowing *that* something is so (e.g. that King Charles I lost his head in 1649) can be evaluated as either true or false, whereas knowing *how* to do something (i.e. how to teach) cannot be evaluated in such clear-cut terms. Operations or skills are normally accomplished to a greater or lesser degree. In drawing this distinction between two forms of knowing, John Hartland Swann, in a critical review, points out that Professor Ryle may inadvertently have demonstrated that all knowledge is essentially of the performance or knowing *how* variety. In other words, knowing *that* the Battle of Hastings was fought in 1066 is nothing more than knowing *how* to answer such questions as "When was the Battle of Hastings fought?" Or to put it another way, having verbal knowledge of one kind or another means that you know *how* to "perform" in certain ways and at certain times.

Gilbert Ryle, in the same work, then goes on to draw another distinction of importance to teachers. He points out that it is analytically useful to distinguish between "task" words and "achievement" or success words. Task words express *activities* like listing, defining, describing and writing; achievement words signify *events* like prove, find, discover – all of which suggest actual success or attainment. Thus, teaching can be thought of as a task word, and learning as the parallel achievement word.* We can say of a task that it is performed well, even skilfully, or perhaps ineptly, if not ineffectively. Teaching, for instance, can be successful or unsuccessful, but it is contradictory to claim that someone has learned unsuccessfully. Thus, teaching and learning. Recognizing that learning does not necessarily result from teaching, even successful teaching, is significant from the point of view of objectives. All that we can do is to hypothesize that the activities normally associated with good teaching (such as defining, classifying, explaining, inferring, comparing, contrasting, valuing, encouraging, criticising, praising, accepting etc.) will lead to learning in the direction desired.

Hypotheses serve an orientating and alerting function, as do objectives

*Unlike the word 'training' which is a task word, 'education' has both task and achievement overtones.

in general. They represent an eye for focussing on a thinking rather than a thought situation, under circumstances calling for the development of knowing *how* rather than knowing *that* skills. From a broad hypothesis, a set of specific hypotheses can be deduced, just as a set of specific objectives can be deduced from a more general objective or aim. Just as objectives direct thought, so hypotheses direct thinking. Whilst objectives can be evaluated, hypotheses can be tested. Objectives serve as guides to explicit and replicative learning; hypotheses can serve as guides to tacit and interpretive learning.

Fig. 1 summarizes the set of procedures around which the Schools Council Humanities Curriculum project was designed. Procedures were used rather than objectives. It is hypothesized that teachers following these procedures will be able to exercise a neutral role in classroom discussions on the value issues involved. There is some evidence, however, that this hypothesis was, in fact, misguided (see *Towards Judgement,* edited by D. Namengson). As so often happens expectations in this bold project sometimes exceeded reality in this regard.

Hypotheses are nothing more than calculated guesses, suggested answers to a problem. For instance, in a recent "O" level geography examination, children were asked to explain "Why Perth aerodrome is located in area 155285? Why there are embankments along the River Earn? Why routes converge at Perth?" The children were expected to answer these questions from studying the Ordnance Survey map extract. Obviously, careful study of the map will suggest possible explanations. For instance, the airport is located on the only large area of level land, the land is above the flood plains, and has ready access to Perth etc. But these are hypotheses, the location of the airport may have been the result of chance ownership of land. There is no way of knowing this from the map. To ask children to examine an accompanying map, and then explain why something is so, is to ask the wrong question. They should have been asked to tender hypotheses, possible explanations. As Hugh Prudden of Yeovil School recently remarked in the *Times Educational Supplement,* "examiners must use more and not fewer words to convey their fragile ideas to the minds" of children.

Hypotheses have an obvious place in science, in experimental work for instance, but their role in the humanities is at least as central. In the humanities there is rarely a ready explanation, only an interpretative "educated" guess. Statistics, photographs and tables invite hypotheses, but so do poems, plays, music and paintings. Sensitive appreciation, problem-solving, inquiry and discovery all depend upon well-identified, clearly written, and appropriate hypotheses; rather than upon specific objectives.

But how are hypotheses to be written when they are to preface a learning situation? Since they represent, like aims, an "ends-in-view", they must be clearly deduced from the problem statement. Hypotheses should clearly flow from the question that is being asked. Postulated relationships

Pattern of procedures for teachers wishing to know *how* to use the Schools Council Humanities Curriculum Project materials, whilst still maintaining a strictly neutral role in the classroom discussion:

1) The fundamental educational values of rationality, imagination, sensitivity, readiness to listen to the views of others, and so forth, must be built into the principles of procedure in the classroom.

2) The pattern of teaching must renounce the authority of the teacher as an "expert" capable of solving value issues since this authority cannot be justified either epistemologically or politically. In short, the teacher must aspire to be neutral.

3) The teaching strategy must maintain the procedural authority of the teacher in the classroom, but contain it within rules which can be justified in terms of the need for discipline and rigour in attaining understanding.

4) The strategy must be such as to satisfy parents and pupils that every possible effort is being made to avoid the use of the teacher's authority position to indoctrinate his own views.

5) The procedure must enable pupils to understand divergence and hence must depend upon a group working together through discussion and shared activities. In such a group opinions should be respected, and minority opinions should be protected from ridicule or from social pressure.

6) In sensitive issues, thought must be given to preserving privacy and protecting students, e.g. illegitimate children, children from broken homes, children of prostitutes, should be borne in mind when discussing the family or relations between the sexes.

7) Above all, the aim should be understanding. This implies that one should not force pupils towards opinions or premature commitments which harden into prejudice. Nor should one see particular virtue in a change of view. The object is that the pupil should come to understand the nature and implications of his point of view, and grow to adult responsibility by adopting it in his own person and assuming accountability for it. Whether or not the pupil changes his point of view is not significant for the attainment of understanding.

Figure 1. Pattern of teaching procedures envisaged in the Schools Council Humanities Curriculum Project. (Reproduced from Stenhouse, L, (1969). "Handling Controversial Issues in The Classroom", *Education Canada,* 9, 4.

should be clear and self-evident, and hypotheses clean-cut and specific. Above all they should be capable of being tested. To put it much too simply, hypotheses should be stated in a form which indicates what is expected to happen or to be. They should only be used, of course, when there is a basis for prediction. Two procedures are available: either one can pose a question and then ask the learners to suggest hypotheses (and possibly test them), or else one can pose the hypotheses, and ask the learners to test them themselves. The latter case has been used at the beginning of each of the chapters in the book. In either case, posing the question and asking for hypotheses or offering hypotheses for verification serves an orientating and alerting function.

An example of the sort of thing that can be done might involve one of Galileo's classic experiments. Rather than tell children that Galileo found that such and such was so, a teacher might decide that children would benefit more if they could experience something of Galileo's thinking for themselves. The objective, as far as the children are concerned, might be "discover a satisfactory explanation for motion by testing the following three hypotheses:

Hypothesis 1. The velocity with which bodies fall is proportional to the weight of the body.

Hypothesis 2. Velocity is proportional to the distance through which the body travels.

Hypothesis 3. Velocity is proportional to the length of the time taken during which the body falls."

Each of these hypotheses, of course, is a possible solution to the same question, and the goal is to determine which answer offers the most satisfactory explanation. Similarly, hypotheses can be constructed for climatic statistics, interpretations of a poem, and the character of Enobarbus in Shakespeare's *Anthony and Cleopatra.*

Tyler like general objectives

As was pointed out in an earlier chapter, Ralph Tyler outlined a method of stating objectives in 1949 which has stood the test of time. Empirically it appears to be at least as effective as the method subsequently suggested by Robert Mager in 1962. In his book *Basic principles of curriculum and instruction*, Professor Tyler points out that it is desirable to state objectives in a form which makes them "most helpful in selecting learning experiences and in guiding learning". He then goes on to argue that teachers, however, commonly write objectives in one of three ways, all of which have serious limitations.

One of the most common ways is to state objectives in terms of what *a teacher is going to do*, e.g. to outline the form of a sonnet, to introduce the idea of magnetism, to argue for proportional representation etc. But this format overlooks the fact that education is about learning, not teaching, and there is no way of judging whether these activities are either necessary or even appropriate. Activities like these are not the ultimate ends of a learning experience and so are not really objectives. They do not provide a satisfactory guide to teaching, learning nor evaluation.

Another commonly-used method of stating objectives is *to list the content* of a lesson or course, as is usually done in books. This is either achieved by stating the *topics* to be covered (e.g. the origin of theories; confirmation and discrepancies; simple laws of science; credibility, truth and "inner perfection" of scientific theories; engineering and science; predictions and projections; science and society), or the objectives are given in the form of a list of slogans or generalizations (e.g. that education begins in the home; that education is growth; that environment influences character; that education involves balance and harmony; that teachers should be educated men and women; that leisure is activity for its own sake; that democracy requires leaders; that we must be clear what we are educated for). The sets of objectives used here, incidentally, are the complete listings for real courses currently being taught in a well-known college. Such lists, however, are unsatisfactory as objectives for there is no indication as to what the learners are expected to do with each of the elements in the list. Of the two examples, the list of generalizations is certainly the more suggestive, but there is still no real guidance of what is expected.

A third way in which objectives are sometimes stated involves a list of *generalized patterns of behaviour*, but without any indication of the context in which the behaviour applies. Examples of objectives in this form would include the following which P. L. Dressel and L. B. Mayhew might have suggested for a project in critical thinking: (1) to identify central issues; (2) to recognize underlying assumptions; (3) to evaluate evidence or authority (which includes to recognize stereotypes and clichés, to recognize bias and emotional factors, to distinguish between verifiable and unverifiable dates, to distinguish between relevant and non-relevant, to distinguish between essential and incidental, to recognize the adequacy of data, to determine whether the facts support the data); and (4) finally to draw unwarranted conclusions. Objectives such as these do indicate what changes are expected in the students as a result of undergoing the suggested course, but the specification is still unsatisfactory since there is no clear indication of either the content or the context involved. It is not enough to talk about developing skills in critical thinking, without referring to what kind of critical thinking you have in mind, under what circumstances, and under what conditions. Much more guidance is necessary.

Professor Tyler then argues that the most useful way of defining an objective is to express it in such a way that TWO pieces of information are included. The two dimensions that he recognizes are:

(a) *Behaviour:* "the kind of behaviour to be developed in the student", and

(b) *Content:* "the content or area of life in which the behaviour is to operate."

Behaviour by itself can be misleading, for the description can be far too general e.g. Think critically about what? What is meant by critical thinking? etc. Content by itself can also be misleading, for it is important to know what the learners are supposed to do with the content that they have acquired e.g. What do you do with Newton's law of motion? What am I supposed to do with this information about a sonnet?

An objective, therefore, should contain two elements. Subject matter should not become an end in itself, but neither should abilities and skills. Both dimensions require content, if they are to take on meaning. Jerome Bruner made the point rather nicely in his book *Toward a theory of instruction*, when he wrote that:

> There is a dilemma in describing a course of study. One must begin by setting forth the intellectual substance of what is to be taught, else there can be no sense of what challenges and shapes the curiosity of the student. Yet the moment one succumbs to the temptation to "get across" the subject, at that moment the ingredient of pedagogy is in jeopardy. For it is only in a trivial sense that one gives a course to "get something across", merely to impart information. There are better means to that end than teaching. Unless the learner also masters himself, disciplines his taste, deepens his view of the world, the "something" that is got across is hardly worth the effort of transmission.
>
> The more elementary a course and the younger its students, the more serious must be its pedagogical aim of forming the intellectual powers of those it serves. It is as important that a good mathematics course be justified by the intellectual discipline it provides or the honesty it promotes as by the mathematics it transmits. Indeed, neither can be accomplished without the other.

Intellectual substance or content, as well as intellectual powers or behaviour, must be defined. Figure 2 gives an example of a blueprint or set of objectives for the first block on "The nature of educational research" in the Open University third level course on "Methods of educational enquiry". The other blocks deal with research design, data collection, data analysis, experiment in educational research, and evaluation and assessment of educational research.

A further example of this type of format is to be found in Professor Tyler's own book *Basic principles of curriculum design and instruction,* where he used an interesting variation of the technique. First he describes the rationale, or logical basis, on which the book is written. Then he outlines his own aim as author, i.e. to explain *one* rationale "for viewing, analyzing and interpreting the curriculum and instructional program of an educational institution". Having laid the groundwork for his intentions, he goes on to state the objectives of the book:

(a) *Behaviour.* To encourage the student "to *examine* other rationales and to *develop* his own conception of the elements and relationships."
(b) *Content* "involved in an effective curriculum" for an educational institution.

Professor Tyler then focusses on the objectives of each chapter by asking a diagnostic type question, before warning readers that he is offering a set of procedures rather than a pat solution.

A further illustration of this method of writing objectives will be found in Figure 3, which outlines not only the general objectives of a course on French literature, but also the related activities and methods of education, and in Eugene Smith and Ralph Tyler's book *Appraising and recording student progress,* written in 1942, which also contains a wealth of examples of educational objectives operationalized in the form of content area and overt learner behaviour. Tyler often asserts that educational objectives can be most usefully clarified by sample or prototype exercises. Such exercises help refine and operationalize the objective, and are rather reminiscent of the technique used by Walter Guiler in his book "*Objectives and activities in arithmetic*".

Having so clearly set up the two-dimensional aspects of educational objectives, Ralph Tyler then goes on to recommend a graphic two-dimensional chart, rather similar to that put forward by Werret Charters in 1924 who used "ideals" and "activities" to categorize the two dimensions. The chart gives further precision, indicates in a compact form the total objectives of the programme or course, and records relationships and inter-relationships between each of the behaviours and items of content. Such a two-dimensional portrait has immediate meaning as a guide to teachers, learners and evaluators. An example, for a course in educational research, is illustrated in Figure 4. The vertical axis lists content, and the horizontal axis behaviour. If necessary, much more detailed charts can, of course, be constructed.

With this recommendation, Professor Tyler goes beyond the disadvantages implicit in a straightforward list of objectives. The chart indicates a network of the knowledge apparently involved, and readily emphasized that the course objectives aim at something much more complex than the simple acquisition of information. An "X" at the intersection of a vertical and horizontal column indicates that the behavioural aspect applies to that particular content area. If there is no "X", then no relationship is perceived or the relationship, if it does exist, is considered immaterial to the purposes of the course. This charting of techniques has been widely used in curriculum development and evaluation, including the Schools Council who have pointed out its usefulness in examining. See Figure 5 where an attempt is made to suggest how a simple matrix may help also with the construction of a written examination question paper. Similar matrices have been used for A-level physics tests at the Institute of Educational Technology in the University of Surrey. Figure 4 has a different function to Figure 5; the former is used in planning and the latter in testing. It is highly recommended as a very practical method for weaving objectives into a coherent and consistent whole.

Before we leave this discussion of Professor Tyler's format for writing objectives, a number of points should be considered regarding the degree of generality and specificity necessary. Tyler suggests that broadly speaking "more general objectives are desirable rather than less general objectives". He suggests, however, that it is helpful to differentiate different types of behaviour quite sharply, i.e. clearly distinguish between specific facts and concepts, concepts and principles, criteria and methodology, non-quantitative and quantitative, identification of problems and identification of assumptions etc. Each different type of behaviour, he feels, has quite different characteristics and requirements. In terms of content, it is desirable to have enough categories to distinguish the important from the unimportant, and the appropriate from the inappropriate. His final advice is to suggest that, as a general rule, 10 to 30 content categories, and 7 to 15 behavioural categories, are to be preferred for a year's work in a subject.

Conclusion

There are many situations in education, as distinct perhaps from a great deal of training, where it is NOT necessary to go beyond a general statement of aim or objective. Whilst clarity is always a commendable goal, too great a degree of specificity may limit educational opportunities. Some objectives should intentionally be left vague, otherwise limits are placed upon inquiry and exploration. At other times, a much greater degree of explicitness is necessary, since the detail helps to ensure that a particular level of adequacy is accomplished. Whilst specific objectives specify, as unambiguously as possible, the particular skills and knowledge that a child is to acquire, general objectives are concerned with both the quality of the experience as well as its end result. General objectives tend to be more expressive, evocative and thematic than specific objectives, and, therefore, possibly less predictive.

By the time you have completed this block you should be able to:

Section 1 (Introduction)

1 Realize that research can make a positive contribution to thinking about educational problems.

2 Recognize the limitations of personal experience as a guide to decisions about education problems.

3 Recognize that consensus is rare without objective evidence.

4 Be aware of the impossibility of obtaining from research studies complete solutions to practical problems.

Section 2 (Scientific Approaches)

5 Appreciate the way in which evidence may be drawn from a variety of sources.

6 Be aware of differences in opinion as to the extent to which scientific approaches are applicable to educational research.

7 Distinguish between nomothetic and idiographic methods and understand their relevance to educational inquiry.

Section 3 (Experimental Surveys)

8 Be aware of the general purpose of course as a whole.

9 Distinguish among, and understand the advantages and disadvantages of, case studies, descriptive surveys, explanatory surveys and experiments.

10 Understand a number of technical terms, such as *causality* and *concomitant variation; dependent* and *independent variables; control; experimental* and *matched groups;* and *pre-* and *post-tests.*

11 Recognize that exploratory studies have value in paving the way for more definitive investigations.

Section 4 (Strategies and Constraints)

12 Understand in general terms what is involved in the stages generally identified in doing educational research.

13 Appreciate how practical constraints may influence both the design and the conduct of research studies.

Section 5 (Choosing Research Topics)

14 Know a little about the various institutions concerned with educational research.

15 Understand how to set about looking for a research topic to investigate.

16 Be aware of a variety of problems which might be worth investigating.

17 Appreciate that even small scale studies may be beneficial, at least to the person carrying out the study.

Figure 2. A set of general objectives for an Open University block on "The nature of educational research". (Reproduced from Entwistel, N.J. (1973). *The nature of educational research. Educational Studies: A third level course. Methods of educational inquiry E341, Block 1.* Bletchley, Open University.)

OBJECTIVES	CORRESPONDENCE ACTIVITIES	CORRESPONDENCE EVALUATION
A. Skills		
The students will: 1. gain a historical perspective, appreciating the originality of a writer in relation to his time as well as the enduring qualities in writing,	read and discuss texts which were important when they were produced as well as those which have stood the test of time	(a) During the course by means of: continuous assessment of essays, exposés and quality of oral contribution in tutorial groups, on the basis of acquired knowledge, sensitivity and ability to order ideas.
2. learn to write well in both English and French, showing logical organization, richness of vocabulary, appropriateness of vocabulary, richness of grammatical structure and variety in type of sentence pattern,	discussion in small groups, comparing merits of writers (tutor circulating)	(b) In final papers, essay-type questions demanding ability to organize ideas, integrate knowledge and personal reactions, to write fluently and intelligently under controlled conditions without recourse to dictionaries or reference books. A searching oral examination is given, requiring fluency in French and ability to discuss literary works and other matters of an intellectual nature. Written language proficiency is tested (at the moment) by means of a 3-hour Eng./Fr. trans., a 3-hour Fr./Eng. trans. and a 3-hour essay (on a literary, abstract philosophical or moral topic).
3. learn to recognize differences between discursive and dramatic writing and to use both styles	write additional scenes for plays, adapt short stories into plays	
B. Knowledge		
The students will: 1. become familiar with philosophical, aesthetic and moral views of major French writers from the Middle Ages to the present day, 2. gain a knowledge of social background and history,	background reading	
3. study authors exemplifying varieties of form and subject matter and widely contrasting styles, e.g.: 16 cent. Rabelais, Ronsard,	Comparison of writers in discussion, write on problems of moral philosophy in terms of theories and views expressed, comment on good qualities in	(a) Sessional examination at end of 1st year in 4 study areas (e.g. philosophy, 17th-cent. tragedy, 19th-cent. novel, translation Eng./Fr., Fr./Eng.)

cont. . .

continued . . .

OBJECTIVES	CORRESPONDENCE ACTIVITIES	CORRESPONDENCE EVALUATION
Montaigne, Du Bellay, etc., 17th cent. Racine, Molière, Corneille, La Rochefoucauld, Descartes, Pascal, etc. 18th Cent. Voltaire, Rousseau, Diderot, Montesquieu, Marivaux, etc., 19th cent. Chateaubriand, Constant, Mme de Staël, Hugo, Balzac, Baudelaire, Stendhal, Flaubert, Zola, Leconte de Lisle, Mallarmé, etc., 20th cent. Gide, Proust, Céline, Sartre, Beckett, Robbe-Grillet, Ionesco, etc.	common, etc. In 3rd year: write in their different styles. Attend lectures aimed at: (i) inspiring enthusiasm for the subj., (ii) illuminating difficult authors' works, (iii) giving specialist guidance on bibliographies, (iv) synthesizing information available in books and periodicals, (v) giving information not available in print.	(b) A final series of 8 3-hour papers covering history of French language and literature from the Middle Ages to the present day, Essay-type questions.
C. Aesthetic appreciation		
The students will:		
1. learn to appreciate form and style in terms of intensity of experience conveyed, economy and concentration of style, power and impact,	discussion in small groups comparing merits of writers	
2. learn to distinguish and define those qualities which make writing memorable,	in 3rd year, writing in different styles	
3. study rhetorical style, e.g. incantatory power, auditive pleasure and persuasiveness (as in Bossuet's sermons and De Gaulle's speeches).		

Figure 3. General objectives in teaching French literature. (Reproduced from Beard, R. (1970). *Teaching and learning in higher education.* London: Penguin.)

Content-aspect of the objectives	Behavioural aspect of the objectives					
	Knows terms	Knows procedures	Uses concept	Sees discrimination	Applies principle	Values idea
A. BACKGROUND						
Methods of knowledge acquisition		X			X	X
Concepts in scientific inquiry			X	X		X
Nature of observation						
Sources of reference materials		X				
B. STAGES IN INQUIRY						
Identifying a problem	X	X		X		
Analyzing a problem	X	X		X		
Solving a problem	X	X		X		
Evaluating a solution	X	X		X		
C. TYPES OF INQUIRY						
Theoretical	X		X	X		X
Historical	X		X	X	X	X
Descriptive	X		X	X		X
Experimental	X		X	X	X	X
D. TECHNIQUES						
Tools for inquiry	X	X				
Analyzing data	X	X				
Making decisions	X	X				
Writing report	X	X			X	
Evaluating report	X	X				
Points about publication	X	X				

Figure 4. Illustration of the use of a two-dimensional chart for stating objectives for a course in educational research.

A. Stage I 'General Statement'

Subject: Geography

"The purpose of the written paper in geography is to evaluate the candidate's knowledge of an appropriate range of facts and definitions in geography; his skill in constructing and using maps and other tools of the geography. Such knowledge, understanding and skill to be evaluated by the written paper to be confined to areas of the candidate's immediate experience, his study of specific geographical areas, human activities, and environmental changes both physical and human, as well as to his appreciation of the interrelationship of men throughout the world."

B. Stage 2 'Written Paper "Job Card" or "Table of Specifications" '

Content	Behaviour					Total
	Know-ledge of facts, etc.	Under-standing of concepts	Applica-tion of concepts	Skills	Relevant Imaginative Insight	
British Isles	4	4	6	2	4	20
World Geography	4	4	6	2	4	20
Special Regions	4	4	4	4	4	20
World Issues	8	4	2	2	4	20
Local Geographical Experience	4	3	3	6	4	20
Total	24	19	21	16	20	100

Figure 5. A framework for constructing an examination paper in geography. (Reproduced from Schools Council (1964). *The Certificate of Secondary Education: an introduction to some techniques of examining.* London: HMSO.)

Suggestions for Further Reading

Schools Council (1964). *The certificate of secondary education: an introduction to some techniques of examining.* Bulletin No. 3, HMSO: London.

John Dewey (1916). *Democracy and Education.* New York: Macmillan, pages 117 to 129.

James Freeman, H. J. Butcher and T. Christie (1971). *Creativity: a selected review of research.* London: Society for Research into Higher Education, pages 41 to 59.

Ralph Tyler (1964). "Some persistent questions on the defining of objectives." In C. M. Lindvall (ed.). *Defining educational objectives.* Pittsburgh: University of Pittsburgh Press, pages 77 to 83.

A. N. Whitehead (1932). *The aims of education.* London: Williams & Horgate, pages 1 to 23.

BIBLIOGRAPHY

Atkin, M. J. (1968). Behavioural objectives in curriculum design: a cautionary note. *The Science Teacher,* 35, 8, 27–30.

Bruner, J. S. (1966). *Toward a theory of instruction.* New York: Macmillan.

Dewey, J. (1916). *Democracy and education.* New York: Macmillan.

Dressell, P. L. & Mayhew, L. B. (1954). *Critical thinking in social science: a handbook of suggestions for evaluation and teaching.* Dubuque, Iowa: Brown.

Drucker, P. F. (1966). *The effective executive.* New York: Harper & Row.

Guiler, W. S. (1926). *Objectives and activities in arithmetic.* Chicago: Rand McNally.

Hamengson, D. (1973) (ed.). *Towards judgement. CARE Occasional Publication No. 1.* Norwich: University of East Anglia.

Hartland-Swann J. (1956). The logical studies of 'knowing that', *Analysis,* 16, 111–115.

Writing Specific Objectives

Focus

"And How Do You Write Specific Objectives?"

Specific objectives of the chapter. After carefully reading and studying this chapter, it is envisaged that:

1. Given a specific teaching-learning situation, you will be able to identify orally, appropriate action-verbs *not* open to multiple interpretations, which stress what a learner is expected to be able to do in order to demonstrate mastery of the task. No reference should be made to lists of action-verbs.

2. Given a particular teaching-learning situation for which specific objectives are appropriate, you will identify in writing, objectives designed according to the formats of:

   a. Dr. Robert Mager (using all *three* of his suggested components in the construction of the objectives), and

b. Dr. Robert Gagné and Dr. Leslie Briggs (using all *five* of their behavioural components in the construction of the objectives).

This task is to be accomplished without reference to technical reference material on the writing of objectives, and in a manner which fulfils the criteria laid down by originators of the format.

Hypotheses. After reading this chapter, the author assumes that you will:

1. Be aware of, and value, the importance of specific objectives in development, teaching and learning.
2. Incorporate the procedures, whenever appropriate, into the organization of your development and teaching skills, so that they become characteristic of your professional style.

> His thought is not to give flame first and then smoke, but from smoke to let light break out.
>
> Horace

In 1927, Percy Bridgman, in his book *The logic of modern physics,* pointed out the importance of defining terms. Rather than use synonyms for the term to be defined, Bridgman suggested that a useful alternative would be to describe the properties that would be used in its measurement. This suggestion was quickly taken up by educators and psychologists in their pursuit for a scientific basis for their disciplines – a pursuit that so characterized the early years of the century. The idea of using what became known as "point-at-able and measurable behaviours" particularly intrigued members of the fast-emerging schools of behaviourism and testing. This operational approach to definition, with its emphasis on clear, unambiguous statements, was the neutral forerunner of what was later to be referred to as "behavioural objectives" and later still as "performance objectives".

One of the charges often made against "behavioural objectives" is that they tend to use what Charity James, in her book *Young lives at stake,* calls "the language of assembly-line processing of products, not of patient observation of students. The setting is one of selecting objectives for a unit of work and then planning experience. The underlying image is of the factory rather than the consulting-room or the school". The language used in many specific-type objectives too often tends to reflect the concerns of applied science in the early years of the century, as well as the process of operationalization derived from the problems of definition and measurement in the physical sciences.

But there is another characteristic that Mrs. James does not mention, which some teachers find equally disturbing. This is the concept of "the one best way", which seems to be implied in the "behavioural objectives" approach. Not only does there appear to be an implicit belief that everything *must* begin with objectives, but it is also made fairly obvious that there is also a best way of writing them. For this reason, enormous detail and guidance – including quite detailed check-lists – are usually provided, so as to make sure that "the resulting objectives are as meaningful as possible".

Action-verb Emphasis

In operationalizing objectives, great stress is usually laid on the form of the verb used. Clarity, specificity and explicitness, it is argued, depend to a very large measure on this one element. Finding just the right verb, it has been said, is "getting down to the action". Benjamin Bloom, Thomas Hastings and George Madaus, writing in their encyclopaedic *Handbook on formative and summative evaluation of student learning,* state that to:

> define objectives so that they are not open to multiple interpretations involves translating the verbs that are open to inference into action verbs that entail direct observation and, when appropriate, specifying the criteria to be used interpreting adverbs. The overt behaviour or the procedure for observing it must be described so that all who read the description can agree whether or not a given student's performance or product testifies to the presence of the objective in question.
>
> Thus, while "understands", "appreciates", "learns", and the like are perfectly good words and can be used in an initial general statement of an objective, they should be further clarified by the use of active or operational verbs not open to misinterpretation.

They then go on to suggest that good "point-at-able" verbs include: to state, to recognize, to distinguish, to match, to put, to evaluate, to predict, to volunteer, to use, to punctuate, to compute, to select, to take, to name, to list etc.

From the point of view of clarifying alone, action verbs certainly do have a great deal to commend them. Perhaps one of the more lasting benefits of the movement for specific objectives has been that it has made teachers aware of, and sensitive to, the weaknesses of some of the language that is often employed in statements of aim and goal. Certainly the verb "to understand" has become almost a rallying call for defence or attack in educational circles.

If an objective is to communicate, ambiguity or vagueness should be avoided wherever possible. Some words commonly used in writing objectives are fuzzy and open to many interpretations. Others are more precise and tell you what to expect. A list of such words is included in Figure 6. Research, however, by S. L. Deno and J. R. Jenkins shows that verbs do not divide so cleanly into action verbs (like "to list") and state verbs (like "to understand"). Nearly half of the 100 verbs they used in the experiment fell somewhere in the middle, between ambiguity and

WORDS OPEN TO MANY INTERPRETATIONS	WORDS OPEN TO FEWER INTERPRETATIONS
to know	to write
to understand	to recite
to *really* understand	to identify
to appreciate	to differentiate
to *fully* appreciate	to solve
to grasp the significance of	to construct
to enjoy	to list
to believe	to compare
to have faith in	to contrast

Figure 6. Words open to many, and to fewer, interpretations. (Reproduced from Mager, R. F. (1962). *Preparing instructional objectives*, Belmont, California: Fearon).

unambiguity. Even more worrying was the lack of agreement among the teachers taking part in the investigation as to which verbs were ambiguous and which were not. Despite the care that may be taken in choosing just the right action verb, some ambiguity still seems likely to remain.

The important point about the stress that is laid on using action verbs, is that it does place the emphasis on what the learner is going to *do*. This is the reason for rejecting verbs like "to understand" and accepting verbs like "to identify". Robert Mager, in his book *Preparing instructional objectives,* points out that "Until you describe what the learner will be DOING when demonstrating that he 'understands' or 'appreciates' you have described very little at all. Thus, the statement which communicates best will be one which describes the terminal behaviour of the learner well enough to preclude misinterpretation." Unless action verbs are employed, Dr. Mager argues that the situation is likely to be loaded in favour of a certain degree of fuzziness or uncertainty.

Using action verbs also has an additional advantage in teaching. Their relative precision and clarity make it somewhat easier to sequence objectives in a more logical manner. For instance, objectives which include action verbs like "define", "list", "state", "name", and "calculate" might occupy a different place in a teaching sequence (perhaps at the beginning) than objectives which include verbs like "recognize", "distinguish", "compare", and "explain". These, in their turn, might be in a different part of the teaching sequence than objectives which include verbs like "judge", "evaluate", "support", "defend", "criticize" etc., all of which might be located at the end of a teaching situation. In other words, there is a hierarchy within action verbs that is relevant and useful to both classroom planning and practice.

But whatever view is taken of the emphasis on action verbs, the important point to remember is that from the broadest perspective, it represents nothing more than a move towards increased clarity. The behaviouristic trappings may or may not be offensive, but the emphasis on good communication in teaching should be displeasing to no one.

Stating Objectives in a Specific Form

A number of formats have been suggested for writing highly specific objectives, although the formats are called different names like "behavioural objectives", "instruction objectives" and more recently "performance objectives". Although the schemes differ in detail, they do tend to emphasize the same sort of things since they are more detailed versions of the original Tyler model. At their heart lies the process of operationalization, the effect of which has been to take Ralph Tyler's two components and define them rather more rigorously and in rather greater detail.

General Objectives plus Action Verb

One format that the author has found useful on occasions capitalizes on some of the features of both general and specific objectives. The precision of general objectives, of course, can always be enhanced by an appropriate use of just the right action verbs. But there is another variation possible, in which action verbs can be used as appendages to the general objective, adding a particular direction to what might otherwise have been construed as a rather general aim.

For instance, the general aim which reads "The purpose of this lesson is to help you understand Ohm's Law" can be made more explicit by operationalizing the state verb "to understand". This can be achieved by adding "You will be asked to *'define', verify* and *identify* applications."[1] Another example of this technique would be "Prepare half a page of notes on longitude and latitude; ensure that you *define* and *distinguish* between them". The question might be asked, of course, why you don't write a specific objective anyway. But this overlooks the point that you may really want students to *understand* Ohm's Law. Appending the action verbs in this way, at the end of the general type objective, serves as an alerting function for some of the emphases that you want the children to note.

Mager-style Objectives

Dr. Robert Mager, in his book *Preparing instruction objectives*, argues that an "objective describes a desired outcome of the course." It will tell what a learner will be able to do after a learning experience. He feels that "When clearly defined goals are lacking, it is impossible to evaluate a course or program efficiently, and there is no sound basis for selecting appropriate materials, content, or instructional methods." A further advantage is that clearly defined objectives permit a learner to evaluate his own progress, and organize his own efforts in such a way as to increase the probability of success.

In discussing the characteristics of a good objective, Dr. Mager identifies three components:

(a) *Behaviour.* "First, identify the terminal behaviour by name; you can specify the kind of behaviour that will be accepted as evidence that the learner has achieved the objective."

(b) *Conditions.* "Second, try to define the desired behaviour further by describing the important conditions under which the behaviour will be expected to occur."

(c) *Standards.* "Third, specify the criteria of acceptable performance by describing how well the learner must perform to be considered acceptable."

The first component, which identifies the actual behaviour desired includes both of Ralph Tyler's two dimensions. Implicit in "terminal behaviour" is both the kind of behaviour you want a learner to be able to do at the completion of the learning task, as well as the content of area of life in which the behaviour is to be found operating.

Dr. Mager points out that these three components are identified for the sake of guidance; he does not intend to suggest that every objective must include all three. Once an objective successfully communicates a teacher's intentions, there is no longer any point in including excess detail. Indeed, Mager suggests that you can quickly tell whether an objective is sufficient by asking "Can another competent person select successful learners in terms of the objective so that you, the objective writer, agree with the selections?" If the answer is "Yes", then the objective has been clearly identified and defined.

In describing the *behaviour component* of an objective, it is important to identify, in very clear terms, exactly what the learner is expected to *do* when demonstrating competence. Using an appropriate action verb is obviously a central core around which a behaviour statement can be built. Behaviour can take many forms, from producing a product (e.g. an essay, a speech, or a painting etc.) to engaging in an active process (e.g. enquiring, making, engaging in a dialogue etc.). At the same time, care must be taken to ensure that the behaviour that is being asked for and defined is a rewarding and enriching one. There is little point in correctly defining behaviour that leads to what Charity James calls "apathy, passivity and oblivion". The behaviour component of an objective should certainly emphasize what the learner will be doing, but it should also be written in such a way that what is being done is rewarding and full of meaning.

Once the behaviour component has been defined, the conditions component and the standards component can be built around it. For instance, the behaviour statement "will distinguish between 'revolution' and 'rotation' in the earth-sun relationship" is an incomplete objective. There is no indication as to what limitation if any, will be placed upon the child, nor any suggestion as to how success or failure to accomplish the task will be recognized. Further information is still required to make the objective as complete as possible. Will the learner be supplied with a working model, so that the distinction can be drawn more easily by "modelling" rotation and revolution? The distinction is much more difficult to draw in words. Will the learner be allowed to use a reference book or notes, or must the operation be performed entirely from memory without error? These are the sort of questions that still need to be answered.

The *conditions component* of an objective is the next step in the jigsaw of constructing a specific objective. It normally consists of a fairly precise statement of the conditions or limitations (the "givens" as they are sometimes referred to) that will be placed upon the pupil when demonstrating achievement. Generally speaking, the conditions are dictated by the learning task itself, but sometimes they are imposed on the task so as to make it more difficult or challenging! In any case, children need to be put in the picture. Despite this rather obvious point, children are still sometimes asked in examinations to describe how they would use logarithmic tables and slide rules to solve a given problem, when they have only been used to using them. School children who have been taught to use atlases in geography are still examined without them. So it is with dictionaries, books of tables and formulae, reference materials etc.

Five different types of conditions are usually involved when objectives are being framed. First, there is the range of problems that a student must learn to solve. Should a learner be required to solve all the problems of a given general type, or only a limited range of specific problems? For instance, when you want children to be able to solve algebraic equations, what type of equations do you have in mind? All of them, or just simultaneous and quadratic equations? Next, do you wish to limit the range of methods for arriving at a solution? Algebraic equations and geometrical theorems, for instance, can be solved and proved in a number of ways. Are all of these acceptable, or is one method mandatory?

Other limitations can involve the equipment, reference materials and clothing the learner may or perhaps must use. Environmental conditions, too, sometimes need to be defined. Can the problem be answered at home, in the library, classroom or laboratory? On paper or verbally? Finally, some conditions involve special physical demands. Squatting, lying down or kneeling can increase the difficulty of a task, and the time taken to accomplish it, because of the discomfort involved.

The final element of an objective is the *standards component.* This defines the standards of performance the learner must meet when mastery or accomplishment is demonstrated. Three types of standard are normally involved. The first concerns the number, proportion or percentage of problems that the learner must be able to work through successfully. Do students have to get them all right, or just some of them? In which case which, if any, must be correctly answered, and which involve some discretion? Next, the tolerances within which learners will have to work need to be considered. For example, do the learners have to get the answer correct to the 5th decimal place, or just in round figures? Finally, are there certain time standards to be met? Presumably an essay should be completed by a particular time, and an experiment carried out within a certain time span etc.

Once the three parts of the objective have been designed, they can be fitted together rather like a jigsaw. Figure 7 gives an example of the sort of process that is involved in writing objectives in the Mager format. But it should also be borne in mind that objectives also need to be fitted together to make a set, and set of objectives fitted together to make a course or a programme. All this demands a feeling for the total design, as a complete educational experience, rather than just thinking of objectives in isolation.

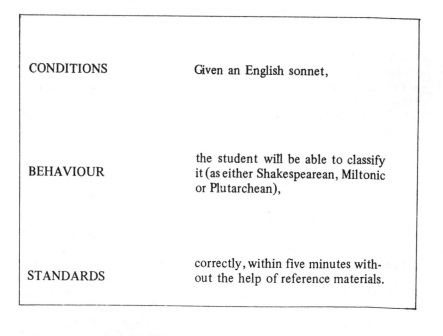

CONDITIONS	Given an English sonnet,
BEHAVIOUR	the student will be able to classify it (as either Shakespearean, Miltonic or Plutarchean),
STANDARDS	correctly, within five minutes without the help of reference materials.

Figure 7. The three parts of an objective using the R. F. Mager format.

There is no requirement, of course, for objectives to be written as a single sentence. There are many ways of breaking up an interminable objective so as to improve its clarity and intelligibility. Yet strangely enough there seems to be a commonly held belief that only one sentence is permitted. The only danger with longer objectives is that it is easier to fall into the error of confusing and so combining several objectives into one.

Parenthetical asides can also be added to an objective, whenever they seem to be necessary for clarity or other reasons. Indeed, they can increase the precision of what is being asked for, as in the example "be able to name the parts (i.e. skeletal and muscular) of the human body system". A series of objectives, for illustrative purposes will be found in Figure 8.

Gagné-style Objectives

In the same year that Robert Mager published his scheme for writing objectives, Robert Miller – who at that time was working with IBM – published a format for objectives that has had a great deal of influence in both educational and training circles. Although Dr. Miller was particularly interested in the analysis of complex physical skills, his scheme has been useful for both cognitive and psycho-motor tasks. Robert Gagné, summarizing the work of Mager and Miller in *The conditions of learning*, came to the conclusion that objectives should preferably be conceived as consisting of four components.

This approach gives yet further precision to Robert Mager's format. First, Dr. Gagné identifies the conditions ("Given two numerals connected by the sign +"), then the behaviour ("states") the object to be acted upon ("in writing"), and finally the characteristics of the performance that indicate its correctness ("the correct name of the number which is the sum of the two"). This very detailed approach reflects Dr. Gagné's stimulus-response frame of reference, with its emphasis on a molecular rather than a molar perspective. However, this is not to be taken as a criticism, for Dr. Gagné's work has had a profound influence upon science teaching and the development of curriculum materials.

Not surprisingly, Robert Gagné places great emphasis upon the importance of defining an objective in the most explicit terms possible. In a recent book, *Principles of instructional design,* written with his colleague Dr. Leslie Briggs, he puts forward a detailed scheme for achieving greater precision. Gagné and Briggs suggest that it is useful to try and identify the general course purposes or goals in terms of what they refer to as "expected current outcomes". In other words, like Robert Mager, they are insistent upon the importance of defining what the learner will be doing at the end of the course, but they add the thought that aims which are too distant in terms of time should be

1. Model
(*Condition*) Given a reproduction of David's "*The oath of the Horatic*", (*behaviour*) the student will outline six reasons that may be used to substantiate the argument that this painting represented a new type of revolutionary classicism in art. (*Standards*) Reference should be made to composition, action, expression and accessories in the reasons.

2. Examples
Given the details of the climatic statistics (monthly temperature, rainfall and humidity) for ten cities, the student will correctly identify in writing the name of the type of climate associated with each set of statistics. At least three reasons must be given substantiating the reasoning behind each of the ten decisions. The lower limit of acceptable performance will be 8 correct identifications out of 10 within a time period of thirty minutes.

Given a human skeleton, the student will correctly identify orally the names of all the bones in the left hand and the right leg below the knee. There will be no penalty for guessing. The task should be completed in thirty minutes, without the aid of reference material.

Given a copy of Antonia Fraser's biography of *Cromwell: the lord protector,* the student will read the book and write a ten-page essay relating the material in Part One: The Government of Himself, dealing with the years from 1599 to 1642, to the events in *either* Part Three or Part Four. The task is to be completed by the 22nd August. The material in the essay should seek to justify John Milton's remark that Cromwell "first acquired the government of himself, and over himself acquired the most signal victories, so that on the first day he took the field against the external enemy, he was a veteran in arms, consummately practised in the toils and exigencies of war."

The student will orally define the terms: electric charge, electrical current, electromotive force, resistance and potential difference. These five concepts should then be used to explain the principle of Ohm's Law.

The student will construct a simple network containing up to ten events, from a narrative describing the activities, without error or reference materials, and within a period of time not exceeding thirty minutes.

Figure 8. A series of examples written according to the format for objectives suggested by R. F. Mager.

avoided. Many of the examples that they give for course purposes are very reminiscent of the flavour of Dr. Ralph Tyler's general objectives, e.g. "understands the principle of commutativity in multiplication" and "reads with enjoyment short stories with simple plots".

Dr. Gagné and Dr. Briggs feel that, although these statements are eminently reasonable, communicative and practical, they are not models of precision. In order to operationalize them further, they make a distinction between what they call *"action verbs"* and *"learned capabilities"*. The former are an example of Ryle's task words discussed (above), and the latter are an example of his achievement words. Gagné and Briggs argue that action verbs are not the most important verbs in the objective. This role is reserved for the verb that describes the learned capability, since the action verb "writing", for instance, may not identify the actual skill that has to be acquired.

Figure 9 gives a series of examples of the range of verbs that are typically used to describe human capabilities: discriminates, identifies, classifies, demonstrates, generates, originates, states, executes and chooses. Both Robert Gagné and Leslie Briggs argue that only these verbs make the skill really distinctive.

For instance, in an objective involving learners "testing a hypothesis", the capability might centre around the verb "discriminates". In an objective involving "learning a poem", the capability centres around the verb "states". Five verbs for human capabilities involving intellectual skills are suggested, not because they "feel wedded to them as words (some surely have approximate synonyms), but because we consider that there are *five necessary distinctions to be made."* Using these five words as verbs for intellectual skills has the desirable effect of preserving these distinctions. Trying to achieve a better "literary" style for statements of objectives can easily lead to nothing better than the introduction of added confusion where there should be as little as possible.

Having made the distinction between action verbs and learned human capabilities, their design capitalizes upon the role of these two verbs. Basically an objective in this format consists of five components (the verbs are asterisked).

*(a) *Action.* This involves the behaviour as described by an action verb.

(b) *Object.* This involves what has to be produced or processed.

(c) *Situation.* This is the situation which faces the learner when he or she is asked to do something.

(d) *Tools and other constraints.* The question here is "How must the performance be carried out?"

(e) *Capability to be learned.* This represents the kind of performance the learner is expected to demonstrate.

An example of the kind of objective format that Gagné and Briggs are suggesting is "Given a received letter inquiring about the shipping of an

1. *Verbs denoting the action to be performed (Task verbs)*
The right choice of an action verb is very important, ambiguity should be avoided. For this reason, verbs like writing, solving, listing are preferable to more ambiguous verbs like knowing, understanding and appreciating.

2. *Verbs denoting the capability to be learned (Achievement verbs)*
The choice of this verb has greater implications for curriculum development and teaching. Whilst the choice of action verbs is unlimited, the verb denoting the learned capability should be chosen, according to Dr. Gagné, from the following schema:

A. *Verbs for capabilities involving intellectual skills:*
- (a) Procedural task: *"demonstrates"*
  e.g. demonstrates by developing the photograph
- (b) Discrimination task: *"discriminates"*
  e.g. discriminates between latitude and longitude
- (c) Conceptual task: *"identifies", "classifies"*
  e.g. identifies an example of refraction
  e.g. classifies different sculptures
- (d) Problem-solving task: *"generates"*
  e.g. generates a solution

B. *Verbs for capabilities involving non-intellectual tasks:*
- (a) Cognitive strategies: *"originates"*
  e.g. originates a sonnet
- (b) Information skills: *"states"*
  e.g. states Ohm's Law
- (c) Motor skills: *"executes"*
  e.g. executes a swallow dive
- (d) Attitudes: *"chooses"*
  e.g. chooses to value an idea

3. *The role of the two verbs in an objective – an example*
Given twelve sonnets, *identifies* (learned capability denoting a conceptual task) the sestet by *underlining* (action verb defining the specific performance required) the appropriate lines in each case.

Figure 9. The two verb components of a well written objective. (Partly based upon information in Chapter 5 of Gagné, R. M. & Briggs, I. J. (1974). *Principles of instructional design.* New York: Holt, Rinehart & Winston.)

1. *Model*
(*Situation*) Given a reproduction of David's *"The oath of the Horatii"*, (*capability*) the student generates (*object*) six reasons (*action*) that may be used to substantiate the argument that this painting represented a new type of revolutionary classicism in art. (*Constraint*) Reference should be made to composition, action, expression and accessories in the reasons.

2. *Examples*
Given a list of ten complex sentences, identify the clauses, classifying them as adjectival or adverbial according to the definition previously given, without reference materials or other help.

Given a Norstedt science kit, the student demonstrates the relationship between potential difference, resistance and current by setting up a practical situation that enables the relationship to be observed and data collected.

Given a car radiator and told to fill it with an appropriate amount of antifreeze for a British winter, the student identifies the amount of antifreeze required for temperatures not below −10°C, using a hydrometer and antifreeze calculating chart, and executes the task to an accuracy of within one-eighth of a pint.

Given the responsibility of writing specific objectives for a new course in political science, the student-teacher identifies the aims, goals and specific objectives from the information given, and states these in list form using the format suggested by Dr. Robert Gagné whenever appropriate.

Figure 10. A series of examples written according to the format for objectives suggested by R. M. Gagné.

order *(situation)*, generates *(learned capability)* a letter in reply *(object)* by typing *(action)* using an electric IBM Selectric typewriter, making one carbon of a one page letter *(tools and other constraints)*." The form of the objective can be changed by substituting the learned capability "generate" which implies a problem solving process, with the capability "executes", which implies merely copy typing. Other examples of objectives using this format will be found in Figure 10.

When objectives are written in this manner they reveal something of the "fine-grained nature of the instructional process". The classes of objectives that they describe constitute, as they point out, a taxonomy, which is as useful in the preparation of tests for evaluation purposes, as it is for designing teaching sequences. Although the amount of detail is great, compared to some of the formats reviewed in the previous chapter, there are circumstances that call for this amount of information.

A great deal depends upon how critical the task is, the amount of precision that is necessary, the difficulties that are typically associated with mastering the task, and the nature of the achievement itself.

Conclusion

In this chapter, we have reviewed just a few of the many formats available to teachers wishing to write specific type objectives. Some of the alternatives are obviously more suitable for some situations than for others. Some developers and teachers will prefer one scheme, and others another. There is, however, a basic rule of thumb which can help in the selection of an appropriate format. Starting from the perspective of the most specific and detailed objective that it is possible to write, choose the most general level possible. The important thing is not to write a more detailed objective than the situation requires. There has been too great a tendency to consider that all curriculum development and teaching should, without exception, be based upon the most detailed objectives it is possible to write. This is wasteful. In the majority of situations, Tyler-type objectives are probably sufficient particularly when it is remembered that highly detailed and specific objectives may take a long time to identify and define. Whenever possible, the expense and time involved in writing the more detailed objectives should be reserved for those occasions when the benefits are likely to be greatest.

Suggestions for Further Reading

Ruth Beard, F. G. Healey, & P. J. Holloway (1970). *Objectives in higher education.* London: Society for Research into Higher Education, pages 1 to 55.

Ruth Beard (1970). *Teaching and learning in higher education.* London: Penguin, pages 61 to 90.

Ivor K. Davies (1972). *The management of learning.* London: McGraw-Hill, pages 71 to 85.

Robert Mager (1962). *Preparing instructional objectives.* Belmont, California.

L. F. Ennever and Bill Harlen (1969). *With objectives in mind. Schools Council 5/13 Project.* London: Macdonald Education.

BIBLIOGRAPHY

Bloom, B. S., Hastings, J. T. & Madaus, G. F. (1971). *Handbook on formative and summative Evaluation of Student Learning.* New York: McGraw-Hill.

Bridgman, P. (1927). *The logic of modern physics.* New York: Macmillan.

Deno, S. L. & Jenkins, J. R. (1969). On the behaviourality of behavioural

objectives. *Psychology in the Schools,* 6, pages 18–24.
Gagné, R. M. (1970). *The conditions of learning.* New York: Holt, Rinehart & Winston (2/e).
Gagné, R. M. & Briggs, L. J. (1974). *Principles of instructional design.* New York: Holt, Rinehart & Winston.
James, C. (1968). *Young lives at stake.* London: William Collins.
Mager, R. F. (1962). *Preparing instructional objectives.* Belmont, California Fearon.
Miller, R. B. (1962). "Task description and analysis." In R. M. Gagné (ed.), *Psychological principles in system development.* New York: Holt, Rinehart & Winston.

14. Mastery Learning and its Implications for Curriculum Development

B. S. Bloom

Source: E. W. Eisner (ed.), *Confronting Curriculum Reform* (Little, Brown, Boston, 1971), Sections I–IV.

Bloom argues that objectives have to be determined which are realistic in terms of individual students' achievements. The emphasis is upon the success of a programme conceived of as the sum of the successes of students' learning. The purpose of evaluation, on this account is not to discriminate among students but rather to ensure that course designs are such as to permit maximum efficiency in learning.

I. Introduction

Each teacher begins a new term – or course – with the expectation that about a third of his students will adequately learn what he has to teach. He expects about a third of his students to fail or to just "get by". Finally, he expects another third to learn a good deal of what he has to teach, but not enough to be regarded as "good students". This set of expectations, supported by school policies and practices in grading, becomes transmitted to the students through the grading procedures and through the methods and materials of instruction. This system creates a self-fulfilling prophecy such that the final sorting of students through the grading process becomes approximately equivalent to the original expectations.

This set of expectations, which fixes the academic goals of teachers and students, is the most wasteful and destructive aspect of the present educational system. It reduces the aspirations of both teachers and students. It reduces motivation for learning in students, and it systematically destroys the ego and self-concept of a sizeable group of the students who are legally required to attend school for ten to twelve years under conditions which are frustrating and humiliating year after year. The cost of this system in reducing opportunities for further learning and in alienating youth from both school and society is so great that no society can tolerate it for long.

Most students (perhaps over 90 per cent) can master what we have to teach them and it is the task of instruction to find the means which will enable our students to master the subject under consideration. A basic task is to determine what we mean by mastery of the subject and to search for the methods and materials which will enable the largest proportion of our students to attain such mastery.

Background. Some societies can utilize only a small number of highly educated persons in the economy and can provide the economic support for only a small proportion of the students to complete secondary or higher education. Under such conditions much of the effort of the schools and the external examining system is to find ways of rejecting the majority of students at various points in the educational system and to discover the talented few who are to be given advanced educational opportunities. Such societies invest a great deal more in the prediction and selection of talent than in the development of such talent.

The complexities of the skills required by the work force in the United States and in other highly developed nations means that we can no longer operate on the assumption that completion of secondary and advanced education is for the few. The increasing evidence (Schultz, 1963; Bowman, 1966) that investment in the education of humans pays off at a greater rate than does capital investment suggests that we cannot return to an economy of scarcity of educational opportunity.

Whatever might have been the case previously, highly developed nations must seek to find ways to increase the proportion of the age group that can successfully complete both secondary and higher education. The problem is no longer one of finding the few who can succeed. The basic problem is determining how the largest proportion of the age group can learn effectively those skills and subject matter regarded as essential for their own development in a complex society.

However, given another set of philosophic and psychological presuppositions, we may express our concern for the intellectual and personality consequences of lack of clear success in the learning tasks of the school. Increasingly, learning throughout life (continuing learning) will be necessary for the largest proportion of the work force. If school learning is regarded as frustrating and even impossible by a sizeable proportion of students, then little can be done at later levels to kindle a genuine interest in further learning. School learning must be successful and rewarding as one basis for ensuring that learning can continue throughout one's life as needed.

Even more important in modern society is the malaise about values. As the secular society becomes more and more central, the values remaining for the individual have to do with hedonism, interpersonal relations, self-development, and ideas. If the schools frustrate the students in the latter two areas, only the first two are available to the individual. Whatever the case may be for each of these values, the schools must strive to assure all students of successful learning experiences in the realm of ideas and self-development.

There is little question that the schools now do provide successful learning experiences for some students – perhaps as high as one-third of the students. If the schools are to provide successful and satisfying learning experiences for at least 90 per cent of the students, major changes must take place in the attitudes of students, teachers, and administrators; changes must also take place in teaching strategies and in the role of evaluation.

The Normal Curve. As educators we have for so long used the normal curve in grading students that we have come to believe in it. Achievement measures are designed to detect differences among our learners – even if the differences are trivial in terms of the subject matter. We then distribute our grades in a normal fashion. In any group of students we expect to have some small per cent receive A grades. We are surprised when the percentage differs greatly from about 10 per cent. We are also prepared to fail an equal proportion of students. Quite frequently this failure is determined by the rank order of the students in the group rather than by their failure to grasp the essential ideas of the course. Thus, we have become accustomed to classifying students into about five categories of level of performance and to assigning grades in some relative fashion. It matters not that the failures of one year performed at about the same level as the C students of another year. Nor does it matter that the A students of one school do about as well as the F students of another school.

Having become "conditioned" to the normal distribution, we set grade policies in these terms and are horrified when some teacher attempts to recommend a very different distribution of grades. But even more important, we find ways of convincing students that they can only do C work or D work by our grading system and even by our system of quiz and progress testing. Finally, we proceed in our teaching as though only the minority of our students should be able to learn what we have to teach.

There is nothing sacred about the normal curve. It is the distribution most appropriate to chance and random activity. Education is a purposeful activity and we seek to have the students learn what we have to teach. If we are effective in our instruction the distribution of achievement should be very different from the normal curve. In fact, we may even insist that our educational efforts have been *unsuccessful* to the extent to which our distribution of achievement approximates the normal distribution.

"Individual differences" in learners is a fact that can be demonstrated in many ways. That students vary in many ways can never be forgotten. That these variations must be reflected in learning standards and achievement criteria is a reflection of our policies and practices rather than the necessities of the case. The basic task in education is to find strategies which will take individual differences into consideration but which will do so in such a way as to promote the fullest development of the individual.

II. The Variables for Mastery Learning Strategies

A learning strategy for mastery may be derived from the work of Carroll (1963), supported by the ideas of Morrison (1926), Bruner (1966),

Skinner (1954), Suppes (1966), Goodlad and Anderson (1959), and Glaser (1968). In presenting these ideas we will refer to some of the research findings which bear on them. However, our main concern here is with the major variables in a model of school learning and the ways in which these variables may be utilized in a strategy for mastery learning.

Put in its briefest form, the model proposed by Carroll (1963) makes it clear that if the students are normally distributed with respect to *aptitude* for some subject (mathematics, science, literature, history, etc.) and all the students are provided with exactly the *same instruction* (same in terms of amount of instruction, quality of instruction, and time available for learning) the end result will be a normal distribution on an appropriate measure of achievement. Furthermore, the relation between aptitude and achievement will be relatively high (correlations of +.70 or higher are to be expected if the aptitude and achievement measures are valid and reliable). Conversely, if the students are normally distributed with respect to aptitude, but the kind and quality of instruction and the amount of time available for learning are made appropriate to the characteristics and needs of *each* student, the majority of students may be expected to achieve mastery of the subject. And, the relation between aptitude and achievement should approach zero. It is this basic set of ideas we wish to develop in the following material.

A. Aptitude for Particular Kinds of Learning.

Teachers have come to recognize that individuals do differ in their aptitudes for particular kinds of learning and over the years test makers have developed a large number of aptitude tests to measure these differences. In study after study it has been found that aptitude tests are relatively good predictors of achievement criteria (achievement tests or teacher judgments). Thus, a good set of mathematics aptitude tests given at the beginning of the year will correlate as high as +.70 with the mathematics achievement tests given at the end of the course in algebra, or some other mathematics subject.

The use of aptitude tests for predictive purposes and the high correlations between such tests and achievement criteria have led many of us to the view that high levels of achievement are possible only for the most able students. From this, it is an easy step to some notion of a causal connection between aptitude and achievement. The simplest notion of causality is that the students with high levels of aptitude can learn the complex ideas of the subject while the students with low levels of aptitude can learn only the simplest ideas of the subject.

Quite in contrast to this is Carroll's (1963) view that *aptitude is the amount of time required by the learner to attain mastery of a learning task.* Implicit in this formulation is the assumption that, given enough time, all students can conceivably attain mastery of a learning task. If Carroll is right, then learning mastery is theoretically available to all, if we can find the means for helping each student. This formulation of Carroll's has the most fundamental implications for education.

One type of support for this view is to be found in the grade norms for many standardized achievement tests. These norms demonstrate that selected criterion scores achieved by the top students at one grade level are achieved by the majority of students at a later grade level. Further support is available in studies where students can learn at their own rate. These studies show that although most students eventually reach mastery on each learning task, some students achieve mastery much sooner than other students (Glaser, 1968; Atkinson, 1967).

Can all students learn a subject equally well? That is, can all students master a learning task at a high level of complexity? From a study of aptitude distributions in relation to student performance, we have become convinced that there are differences between the extreme students and the remainder of the population. At the top of the aptitude distribution (1 to 5 per cent) are likely to be some students who have a special talent for the subject. Such students are able to learn and to use the subject with greater fluency than other students. The student with special aptitudes for music or foreign languages can learn these subjects in ways not available to most other students. Whether this is a matter of native endowment or the effect of previous training is not clear, although this must vary from subject to subject. It is likely that some individuals are born with sensory organs better attuned to sounds (music, language, etc.) than are others and that these constitutional characteristics give them special advantages in learning such subjects over others. For other subjects, special training, particular interests, etc., may develop these high-level aptitudes.

At the other extreme of the aptitude distribution, there are individuals with special disabilities for particular learning. The tone-deaf individual will have great difficulty in learning music; the color-blind individual will have special problems in learning art; the individual who thinks in concrete forms will have special problems in learning highly abstract conceptual systems such as philosophy. Again, it is believed these may constitute less than 5 per cent of the distribution, but this will vary with the subject and the aptitudes.

In between are approximately 90 per cent of the individuals where the writer believes, as does Carroll, that aptitudes are predictive of the rate of learning rather than the level (or complexity) of learning that is possible. Thus, we are expressing the view that, given sufficient time (and appropriate types of help), 95 per cent of students – the top 5 per cent plus the next 90 per cent – can learn a subject up to a high level of mastery. We are convinced that the grade of A as an index of mastery of a subject can, under appropriate conditions, be achieved by up to 95 per cent of the students in a class.

It is assumed that it will take some students more effort, time, and help to achieve this level than it will other students. For some students the effort and help required may make it prohibitive. Thus, to learn high school algebra to a point of mastery may require a year or more for some students but only a fraction of a year for other students. Whether mastery learning is worth this great effort for the students who may need the longer time is highly questionable. One basic problem for a mastery learning strategy is to find ways of reducing the amount of time required by the slower students to a point where it is no longer a prohibitively long and difficult task for these less able students.

It is not assumed that aptitude for particular learning tasks is completely stable. There is evidence (Bloom, 1964; Hunt, 1961) that the aptitude for particular learning tasks may be modified by appropriate environmental conditions or learning experiences in the school and the home. The major task of educational programs concerned with learning to learn and general education should be to produce positive changes in the students' basic aptitudes. It is likely that these aptitudes can be most markedly affected during the early years in the home and during the elementary years of school. Undoubtedly, however, some changes can take place at later points in the individual's career.

However, even if marked changes are not made in the individual's aptitudes it is highly probable that more effective learning conditions can reduce the amount of time required to learn a subject to mastery for all students and especially for the students with lower aptitudes. It is this problem which must be directly attacked by strategies for mastery learning.

B. Quality of Instruction

The schools have usually proceeded on the assumption that there is a standard classroom situation for all students. Typically, this has been expressed in the teacher-student ratio of one to thirty, with group instruction as the central means of teaching. There is the expectation that each teacher will teach the subject in much the same way as other teachers. This standardization is further emphasized by textbook adoption which specifies the instructional material to be provided each class. Closely related to this is the extensive research over the past fifty years which seeks to find the one instructional method, material, or curriculum program that is best for all students.

Thus, over the years, researchers have fallen into the "educational trap" of specifying quality of instruction in terms of good and poor teachers, teaching, instructional materials, curriculum – all in terms of group results. They persist in asking such questions as: Who is the best teacher for the group? What is the best method of instruction for the group? What is the best instructional material for the group?

One may start with the very different assumption that individual students may need very different types and qualities of instruction to achieve mastery. That is, the same content and objectives of instruction may be learned by different students as the result of very different types of instruction. Carroll (1963) defines the *quality of instruction in terms of the degree to which the presentation, explanation, and ordering of elements of the task to be learned approach the optimum for a given learner.*

Much research is needed to determine how individual differences in learners can be related to variations in the quality of instruction. There is evidence that some students can learn quite well through independent learning efforts while others need highly structured teaching-learning situations (Congreve, 1965). It seems reasonable to expect that some students will need more concrete illustrations and explanations than will others; some students may need more examples to get an idea than do others; some students may need more approval and reinforcement than others; and some students may need to have several repetitions of the explanation while others may be able to get it the first time.

We believe that if every student had a very good tutor, most of them would be able to learn a particular subject to a high degree. It is the good tutor who attempts to find the qualities of instruction (and motivation) best suited to a given learner. And, there is some evidence (Dave, 1963) that middle-class parents do attempt to tutor their children when they believe that the quality of instruction in school is inadequate in a particular subject. In an unpublished study, the writer found that one-third of the students in an algebra course in a middle-class school were receiving as much tutorial instruction in the home in algebra as they were receiving group instruction in the school. These students received relatively high grades for the algebra course. For these students, the relationship between their mathematics aptitude scores at the beginning of the year and their achievement in algebra at the end of the year was almost zero. In contrast, for the students who received no additional instruction other than the regular classroom instruction, the relationship between their mathematics aptitude scores and their algebra achievement scores was very high (+.90). While this type of research needs to be replicated, it is evident in this small study that the home tutoring help was providing the quality of instruction needed by these students to learn the algebra – that is, the instruction was adapted to the needs of the individual learners.

The main point to be stressed is that the quality of instruction is to be considered in terms of its effects on individual learners rather than on random groups of learners. One hopes that the research of the future may lead to the definition of the qualities and kinds of instruction needed by various types of learners. Such research may suggest more effective group instruction since it is unlikely that the schools will be able to provide instruction for each learner separately.

C. Ability to Understand Instruction

In most courses at the high school and college level there is a single teacher and a single set of instructional materials. If the student has facility in understanding the teacher's communications about the learning and the instructional material (usually a textbook), he has little difficulty in learning the subject. If he has difficulty in understanding the teacher's instruction and/or the instructional material, he is likely to have great difficulty in learning the subject. *The ability to understand instruction may be defined as the ability of the learner to understand the nature of the task he is to learn and the procedures he is to follow in the learning of the task.*

Here is a point at which the students' abilities interact with the instructional materials and the instructor's abilities in teaching. For the student in our highly verbal schools it is likely that this ability to understand instruction is primarily determined by verbal ability and reading comprehension. These two measures of language ability are significantly related to achievement in the majority of subjects and they are highly related (+.50 to +.60) to grade-point averages at the high school or college level. What this suggests is that verbal ability (independent of specific aptitudes for each subject) determines some general ability to learn from teachers and instructional materials.

While it is possible to alter an individual's verbal ability by appropriate training, there are limits to the amount of change that can be produced. Most change in verbal ability can be produced at the pre-school and elementary school levels, with less and less change being likely as the student gets older (Bloom, 1964). However, vocabulary and reading ability may be improved to some extent at all age levels, even though there is diminishing utility to this approach with increasing age. Improvements in verbal abilities should result in improvements in the individual's ability to understand instruction.

The greatest immediate payoff in dealing with the ability to understand instruction is likely to come from modifications in instruction in order to meet the needs of individual students. There is no doubt that some teachers do attempt to modify their instruction to fit a given group of students. Many teachers center their instruction at the middle group of their students, others at the top or bottom group. These choices are, however, only reflections of the teacher's habits and attitudes; they are by no means determinants of what it is *possible* for a teacher to do. Given help and various types of aids, individual teachers can find ways of modifying their instruction to fit the differing needs of their students.

Group-study procedures should be available to students as they need it. In our own experience we have found that small groups of students (two or three students) meeting regularly to go over points of difficulty in the learning process were most effective, especially when the students could cooperate and help each other without any danger of giving each other special advantages in a competitive situation. Where learning can be turned into a cooperative process with everyone likely to gain from the process, small-group learning procedures can be very effective.

Tutorial help (one to one relations between teacher and learner) represents the most costly type of help and should be used only where alternative procedures are not effective. However, this type of help should be available to students as they need it, especially where individuals have particular difficulties that can't be corrected in other ways. The tutor, ideally, should be someone other than the teacher, since he should bring a fresh way of viewing the idea or the process. The tutor must be skillful in detecting the points of difficulty in the student's learning and should help him in such a way as to free the student from continued dependence on him.

Throughout the use of alternative methods of instruction and instructional material, the essential point to be borne in mind is that these are attempts to improve the *quality of instruction* in relation to the ability of each student to *understand the instruction.* As feedback methods inform the teachers of particular errors and difficulties the majority of students are having, it is to be expected that the regular group instruction could be modified so as to correct these difficulties. As particular students are helped individually, the goal should be not only to help the student over particular learning difficulties but also to enable him to become more independent in his learning and to help him identify the alternative ways by which he can comprehend new ideas.

D. Perseverance

Carroll defines perseverance as *the time the learner is willing to spend in learning.* Obviously, if a student needs to spend a certain amount of time to master a particular task, and he spends less than this amount in active learning, he is not likely to learn the task to the level of mastery. Carroll attempts to differentiate between spending time on learning and the amount of time the student is actively engaged in learning.

There is no doubt that students vary in the amount of perseverance they bring to a specific learning task. However, students appear to approach different learning tasks with different amounts of perseverance. The student who gives up quickly in his efforts to learn an academic subject may persevere an unusually long time in learning how to repair an automobile or in learning to play a musical instrument. It would appear to us that as a student finds the effort rewarding, he is likely to spend more time on a particular learning task. If, on the other hand, the student is frustrated in his learning, he must – in self-defence – reduce the amount of time he devotes to the learning. While the frustration level of students may vary, we believe that all students must sooner or later give up a task if it is too painful for them.

While efforts may be made to increase the amount of perseverance in students, it is likely the manipulation of the instruction and learning materials may be more effective in helping students master a given learning task, in spite of their present level of perseverance. Frequency of reward and evidence of success in learning can increase the student's perseverance in a learning situation. As students attain mastery of a given task, they are likely to increase their perseverance for a related learning task.

Research at Chicago is showing that the demands for perseverance may be sharply reduced if students are provided with the instructional resources most appropriate for them. Frequent feedback accompanied by specific help in instruction and material as needed can reduce the time (and perseverance) required. Improvement in the quality of instruction or of the explanations and illustrations may reduce the amount of perseverance necessary for a given learning task.

There seems to be little reason to make learning so difficult that only a small proportion of the students can persevere to mastery. Endurance and unusual perseverance may be appropriate for long distance running; they are not great virtues in their own right. The emphasis should be on learning, not on vague ideas of discipline and endurance.

E. Time Allowed for Learning

Throughout the world schools are organized to give group instruction, with definite periods of time allocated for particular learning tasks. A course in history at the secondary level may be planned for an academic year of instruction, another course may be planned for a semester, while the amount of instructional time allocated for a subject like arithmetic at the fifth grade may be fixed. Whatever the amount of time allowed by the school and the curriculum for particular subjects or learning tasks, it is likely to be too much for some students and not enough for others.

For Carroll, the time spent on learning is the key to mastery. His basic assumption is that aptitude determines the rate of learning and that most, if not all students can achieve mastery if they devote the amount of time needed to the learning. This implies not only that the student must spend the amount of time he needs on the learning task but also that he be *allowed* enough time for the learning to take place.

There seems to be little doubt that students with high levels of aptitude are likely to be more efficient in their learning and to require less time for learning than students with lower levels of aptitude. Whether most students can be helped to become highly efficient learners in general is a problem for future research.

The amount of time students need for a particular kind of learning has not been studied directly. One indication of the time needed comes from studies of the amount of time students spend on homework. In reviewing the amount of time spent by 13-year-old students on mathematics homework in the International Study of Educational Achievement (Husen, 1967), we find that if we omit the extreme 5 per cent of the subjects, the ratio is roughly six to one. That is, some students spend six times as much time on mathematics homework as do others. Other studies of student use of time suggest that this is roughly the order of magnitude to be expected.

If instruction and student use of time become more effective, it is likely that most students will need less time to learn the subject to mastery and the ratio of time required for the slower and the faster learners may be reduced from about six to one to perhaps three to one.

We are convinced that it is not the sheer amount of time spent in learning – either in school or out of school – that accounts for the level of learning. Each student should be allowed the time he needs to learn a subject. And, the time he needs to learn the subject is likely to be affected by the student's aptitudes, his verbal ability, the quality of instruction he receives in class, and the quality of the help he receives out of class. The task of a strategy for mastery learning is to find ways of altering the time individual students need for learning as well as to find ways of providing whatever time is needed by each student. Thus, a strategy for mastery learning must find some way of solving the instructional problems as well as the school organizational problems, including that of time.

III. Why Mastery Learning?

The curriculum maker in the past did not have to contend with the many problems raised by mastery learning. He attempted to devise what he believed to be an effective curriculum for the teaching of selected subjects and he was quite prepared to accept a high rate of failure or at least a sizeable proportion of students who just got by with some low minimum of learning. However, when one faces the possibility that "all" should be able to learn, curriculum making is confronted with the problem of why all should learn any specific subject. What is so important that all should learn?

Parents (and even curriculum makers) have no difficulty in accepting mastery learning as important when physical survival is at stake. A parent teaching his child to cross the road safely, or to avoid dangerous situations such as fire, poison, use of dangerous tools, machinery, and equipment, etc., is not content with partial learning. He will spend the necessary time, use the reinforcement he believes appropriate, and evaluate the child's behavior in the situation until he is fully assured that the child has mastered the learning. One could cite many examples of mastery learning in the home, industry, and even in military training where the instructor insists that all learners reach an acceptable level of mastery before instruction ceases. These examples are usually seen as so important for the physical survival of the individual learner that the teacher (or parent) takes it for granted that less than mastery of the learning task is unacceptable.

More recently we have begun to realize the relation between economic survival (at least a decent standard of life) and the development of certain abilities, skills, interests, and aptitudes. Some of these may be learned on the job while others may be prerequisites to employment in satisfactory occupations. As we come to recognize the minimal language skills, cognitive abilities, and affective characteristics necessary for economic survival, the curriculum maker must become preoccupied with the means by which mastery of these behaviors can be developed in all or almost all students.

In a complex society such as ours there are a variety of citizenship skills, understandings, interests, and attitudes that may be necessary for the individual to lead a satisfying life and for the nation to survive as a democratic and open society. Such kinds of behavior become more difficult to define and to set standards for, but they too require at least minimal levels of mastery.

While I have by no means exhausted the consideration of the types of behavior or subjects for which mastery learning may provide survival benefits in a complex society, there is another type of criteria for justification of mastery in learning. In addition to the overt and substantive curriculum with which the curriculum makers and teachers are preoccupied, there is a latent or covert curriculum which may be equally important from the viewpoint of the learner. The learner comes to view himself as adequate or inadequate in terms of his effectiveness in learning what the school or curriculum expects of him. Whether the learning task be important or trivial, the learner judges his own adequacy as a human in terms of his effectiveness relative to other learners. He is judged by teachers, examinations, and his own peers on the basis of his success – or lack of it – in the learning tasks set by the school and the curriculum. These judgments which are communicated to him in the classroom and the school are further reinforced by his parents. For the student to consistently get low grades or perform poorly in school is to become frustrated and to develop a negative self-concept. On the other hand, to consistently do well in school over a number of years is likely to lead to the development of a feeling of adequacy and a positive self-image. Mastery learning, then, helps to provide the individual with the basis for positive ego development and a sense of adequacy. Thus, one may justify mastery learning in terms of its opening up of interests in further learning and its developing of a positive attitude toward school and school learning, as well as of a healthy self-concept. There is evidence that mental health is promoted by success in school learning, whereas repeated failure or lack of success in school learning is a source of anxiety and, over a period of time, a source of infection with respect to mental illness.

All of this is to suggest that mastery learning notions are relatively easy to comprehend and accept where the survival and well-being of the individual in the society are at issue. It is where the schools and the curriculum makers are not really convinced of the importance of what they have to teach that they have difficulty in deciding on standards to be reached and that they become satisfied if a few of the learners really do learn what is being taught.

In the past, a small proportion of "successful" learners were identified for further learning. In a society where all the learners are expected to complete ten to twelve years of learning, where as high as 50 to 60 per cent of the learners are expected to secure some form of higher education, and where almost all individuals are expected to continue learning throughout life, obviously we can no longer be satisfied when only some small proportion of learners adequately learn what the schools have to teach. Increasingly, curriculum makers and teachers are going to be judged in terms of the proportion of the learners who have "mastered" the learning tasks of the school as well as the proportion of students who develop a positive self-concept through their interaction with the school environment.

IV. Where is Mastery Learning Most Appropriate?

In our experience so far, mastery learning has been relatively easy to achieve in school subjects with a minimum of prerequisites. For example, first-year algebra has a minimum of specific prerequisites and therefore a one-year course with appropriate feedback and corrective techniques has been especially successful in bringing the large majority of students up to a given standard of mastery. Similarly, secondary school courses in biology and chemistry have been relatively successful from the viewpoint of mastery learning. College courses in statistics, introductory psychology, biology, and even philosophy have also been effective from this viewpoint.

Although we do not have information about mastery strategies in many subject areas, we doubt the likelihood that a seventh- or eighth-grade arithmetic course could reach acceptable levels of mastery learning with a heterogeneous group of learners, because such courses depend heavily on the mastery of earlier concepts and skills in the arithmetic program from grades one to six. Likewise, we believe it easier to secure mastery learning in a first course in a second language than in a course in the mother tongue because of the greater heterogeneity of the students in the prerequisite skills and abilities at the beginning of the course in the mother tongue.

Thus, we are arguing that relatively quick demonstrations of effective mastery learning may be achieved in courses where a large portion of the learners have the minimal prerequisite learning at the time of entrance to the course or where the subject demands relatively little in the way of specific prerequisite learning.

We are convinced that it would be possible to organize an entire curriculum over many years (e.g., grades one to six, nine to twelve, etc.) where students could achieve mastery learning each year as they progressed through the curriculum. And, we suggest that developmental and research efforts be instituted to bring about such results, because mastery learning at these critical ages and grades could make for more effective learning throughout the student's educational career. And, even more important is the likelihood that early mastery learning could have long-term consequences on the individual's self-concept and mental health.

In spite of these considerations of where mastery learning is easier or more difficult to produce, there are more fundamental considerations of where mastery learning is appropriate or inappropriate. Clearly, not all school subjects need strive for mastery learning, and perhaps not all students should strive for mastery learning in all subjects.

It would seem to us that subjects which are *required, sequential, closed,* and which emphasize *convergent thinking* should, insofar as possible, employ mastery learning strategies. Perhaps we can explain these points briefly.

If a subject is *required* of the learners, then someone has regarded it as important for the learners or for the society, and better or more adequate learning of such a subject is to be preferred to a lesser level of learning. If a subject is required we believe that the learner should be given every opportunity to succeed in it and, conversely, the learner's failure in a required subject should be seen as a defect in the curriculum and/or the instruction. We believe that a high rate of failure (or a low level of learning) in a required subject needlessly inflicts a negative self-concept on a group of learners who have no choice about being in the learning situation or course. Since about two-thirds of the K through 12 curriculum in the United States is required, we are expressing the view that at least this portion of the curriculum should employ mastery learning strategies.

An even better case can be made for mastery learning in *sequential* subjects. If learning of some set of school subjects (arithmetic, language, arts, mathematics, etc.) is sequential in the sense that the second course builds on – and requires – the first course (and the third course builds on the first two courses, etc.), then the student should be assured of successful progress through the sequence, insofar as this is possible. This, of course, places a very heavy burden on the first course, since inadequate learning in this course almost assures inadequate learning in each of the subsequent courses in the sequence. Mastery learning thus requires a greater concern on the part of the curriculum maker about sequence and more careful consideration of what is truly sequential in learning and why. In the first criterion (that of required courses), we believe that it is in some ways *immoral* to permit inadequacies in the curriculum or instruction "to fail" students where they have no choice about what learning tasks they are to do. For our second criterion, we believe that it is *inefficient* to permit inadequacies in the curriculum or instruction to produce low levels of learning in a sequential arrangement of learning tasks where adequate levels of learning in the earlier part of a sequence make it highly probable that the students will be able to learn the later parts of the sequence to relatively high levels of adequacy.

By *closed* subjects we mean subjects where there is a finite set of ideas and behaviors to be learned about which there is considerable agreement among curriculum makers and teachers. A closed subject is also one which is unlikely to change much over a decade or more. For example, arithmetic and mathematics may be regarded as relatively closed subjects. Even though there may be much change in the methods of teaching these subjects, their content and behaviors do not change fundamentally. History, many science courses, second-language courses, and, to a lesser extent, mother tongue courses may also be regarded as closed subjects. Here the argument for mastery learning stems from the relative ease with which mastery learning standards can be developed, the general consensus about what learning is important for the students to acquire, and the great likelihood that once mastery learning strategies have been adequately developed for one generation or group of learners they can be employed for subsequent cycles of learners and teachers.

Finally, we believe that courses which emphasize *convergent thinking,* that is, thinking for which there are "right answers", "good solutions", and "appropriate thought processes" should employ mastery learning strategies. The argument here again stems from the ease with which mastery learning standards can be derived and the availability of considerable consensus not only about the *products* of thinking (and learning) but also about the *processes* of thinking that should be developed. Here again, subjects like mathematics, history, much of language arts, and second-language courses are believed to be appropriate for mastery learning since convergent thinking appears to be the major behavior which is emphasized in such courses.

Space and time considerations suggest that I leave it to the reader to determine whether or not arguments for mastery learning are less compelling for elective courses, for non-sequential learning tasks, for "open" subjects, and for courses that emphasize divergent thinking and creativity. While I believe that mastery learning strategies could – and should – be employed in such courses, I do admit that it is more difficult to determine standards and criteria and I suspect it is more difficult to develop appropriate mastery learning strategies for such courses and for the students in them.

Perhaps another way of looking at the same problem is to point out that highly centralized curriculum development efforts are usually invested in subjects which are required, sequential, closed, and which emphasize convergent thinking. While teachers clearly do have considerable influence on the effectiveness of learning in such subjects, it is the curriculum maker who must bear the burden of demonstrating what can and should be learned by the students. And, it is the curriculum maker who must find the strategies which will ensure that the largest proportion of students will learn adequately if the curriculum and its materials and methods are used properly. It is the curriculum maker who must develop in-service training programs to insure that teacher inadequacy or misunderstanding is not responsible for the failure of the curriculum or the students. And, we assert here that it is the curriculum maker who must develop the variety of alternative learning materials required for mastery learning as well as the measurement materials needed to support a given strategy for mastery learning.

BIBLIOGRAPHY

R. C. Atkinson, "Computerized Instruction and the Learning Process". Technical Report No. 122, Stanford, California: Institute for Mathematical Studies in the Social Sciences, 1967.

B. S. Bloom (ed.), *Taxonomy of Educational Objectives: Handbook I, Cognitive Domain,* New York: David McKay and Co., 1956.

B. S. Bloom, *Stability and Change in Human Characteristics,* New York: John Wiley and Sons, 1964.

M. J. Bowman, "The New Economics of Education", *International Journal of Educational Sciences,* Vol. 1, 1966, 29–46.

Jerome Bruner, *Toward a Theory of Instruction,* Cambridge: Harvard University Press, 1966.

John Carroll, "A Model of School Learning", *Teachers College Record,* Vol. 64, 1963, 723–33.

W. J. Congreve, "Independent Learning", *North Central Association Quarterly,* Vol. 40, 1965, 222–28.

R. H. Dave, "The identification and measurement of environmental process variables that are related to educational achievement", unpublished Ph.D. dissertation, University of Chicago, 1963.

Robert M. Gagnè, *The Conditions of Learning,* New York: Holt, Rinehart and Winston, 1965.

R. Glaser, "Adapting the Elementary School Curriculum to Individual Performance", *Proceedings* of the 1967 Invitational Conference on Testing Problems, Princeton, N.J.: Educational Testing Service, 1968.

J. I. Goodlad, and R. H. Anderson, *The Non-Graded Elementary School,* New York: Harcourt, Brace and World, 1959.

J. McV. Hunt, *Intelligence and Experience,* New York: Ronald Press Co., 1961.

T. Husén (ed.), *International Study of Educational Achievement in Mathematics: A Comparison of Twelve Countries. Volumes I and II.* New York: John Wiley and Sons, 1967.

H. C. Morrison, *The Practice of Teaching in the Secondary School,* Chicago:

University of Chicago Press, 1926.

T. W. Schultz, *The Economic Value of Education*, New York: Columbia University Press, 1963.

Michael Scriven, "The Methodology of Evaluation", in R. Stake (ed.), *Perspectives of Curriculum Evaluation,* Chicago: Rand McNally & Co., 1967.

B. F. Skinner, "The Science of Learning and the Art of Teaching", *Harvard Educational Review,* Vol. 24, 1954, 86–97.

P. Suppes, "The Uses of Computers in Education", *Scientific American,* Vol. 215, 1966, 206–21.

15. Instructional and Expressive Objectives

E. W. Eisner

Source: E. W. Eisner, *AERA Monograph Series on Curriculum Evaluation,* No. 3.

The way in which educational objectives should be formulated is a subject of a vigorous professional debate. Eisner distinguishes two different sorts of objectives.

It seems to me appropriate to differentiate between two types of educational objectives which can be formulated in curriculum planning. The first type is familiar to most readers and is called an *instructional objective;* the second I have called an *expressive objective.*

Instructional objectives are objectives which specify unambiguously the particular behavior (skill, item of knowledge, and so forth) the student is to acquire after having completed one or more learning activities. These objectives fit the scheme or criteria identified earlier. They are usually drawn from cultural products such as the disciplines and are laid out in intervals of time appropriate for the children who are to acquire them.

Instructional objectives are used in a predictive model of curriculum development. A predictive model is one in which objectives are formulated and activities selected which are predicted to be useful in enabling children to attain the specific behavior embodied in the objective. In this model, evaluation is aimed at determining the extent to which the objective has been achieved. If the objective has not been achieved, various courses of action may follow. The objective may be changed. The instructional method may be altered. The content of the curriculum may be revised.

With an instructional objective the teacher as well as the children (if they are told what the objective is) are likely to focus upon the attainment of a specific array of behaviors. The teacher in the instructional context knows what to look for as an indicator of achievement since the objective unambiguously defines the behavior. Insofar as the children are at similar stages of development and insofar as the curriculum and the instruction are effective, the outcomes of the learning activity will be homogeneous in character. The effective curriculum, when it is aimed at instructional objectives, will develop forms of behavior whose characteristics are known beforehand and, as likely as not, will be common across students – if not at the identical point in time, at some point during the school program.

The use of instructional objectives has a variety of educational ramifications. In preparing reading material in the social studies, for example, study questions at the beginning of a chapter can be used as cues to guide the student's attention to certain concepts or generalizations which the teacher intends to help the student learn. In the development of certain motor skills the teacher may provide examples of such skills and thus show the student what he is supposed to be able to do upon terminating the program. With the use of instructional objectives clarity of terminal behavior is crucial since it serves as a standard against which to appraise the effectiveness of the curriculum. *In an effective curriculum using instructional objectives the terminal behavior of the student and the objectives are isomorphic.*

Expressive objectives differ considerably from instructional objectives. An expressive objective does not specify the behavior the student is to acquire after having engaged in one or more learning activities. An expressive objective describes an educational encounter: It identifies a situation in which children are to work, a problem with which they are to cope, a task in which they are to engage; but it does not specify what from that encounter, situation, problem, or task they are to learn. An expressive objective provides both the teacher and the student with an invitation to explore, defer, or focus on issues that are of peculiar interest or import to the inquirer. An expressive objective is evocative rather than prescriptive.

The expressive objective is intended to serve as a theme around which skills and understandings learned earlier can be brought to bear, but through which those skills and understandings can be expanded, elaborated, and made idiosyncratic. With an expressive objective what is desired is not homogeneity of response among students but diversity. In the expressive context the teacher hopes to provide a situation in which meanings become personalized and in which children produce products, both theoretical and qualitative, that are as diverse as themselves. Consequently the evaluative task in this situation is not one of applying a common standard to the products produced but one of reflecting upon what has been produced in order to reveal its uniqueness and significance. In the expressive context, the product is likely to be as much of a surprise to the maker as it is for the teacher who encounters it.

Statements of expressive objectives might read:

1) To interpret the meaning of *Paradise Lost,*

2) To examine and appraise the significance of *The Old Man and the Sea,*

3) To develop a three-dimensional form through the use of wire and wood,

4) To visit the zoo and discuss what was of interest there.

What should be noted about such objectives is that they do not specify what the student is to be able to do after he engages in an educational activity; rather they identify the type of encounter he is to have. From this encounter both teacher and student acquire data useful for evaluation. In this context the mode of evaluation is similar to aesthetic criticism; that is, the critic appraises a product, examines its qualities and import, but does not direct the artist toward the painting of a specific type of picture. The critic's subject-matter is the work done – he does not prescribe a blueprint of its construction.

Now I happen to believe that expressive objectives are the type that teachers most frequently use. Given the range and the diversity of children it is more useful to identify potentially fruitful encounters than to specify instructional objectives.

Although I believe that the use of expressive objectives is generally more common than the use of instructional objectives, in certain subject areas curriculum specialists have tended to emphasize one rather than the other. In mathematics, for example, much greater attention historically has been given to the instructional objective than in the visual arts where the dominant emphasis has been on the expressive.

I believe that the most sophisticated modes of intellectual work – those, for example, undertaken in the studio, the research laboratory, and the graduate seminar – most frequently employ expressive rather than instructional objectives. In the doctoral seminar, for example, a theme will be identified around which both teacher and students can interact in an effort to cope more adequately with the problems related to the theme. In such situations educational outcomes are appraised after they emerge; specific learnings are seldom formulated in terms of instructional objectives. The dialogue unfolds and is followed as well as led. In such situations the skills and understandings developed are used as instruments for inquiring more deeply into the significant or puzzling. Occasionally such problems require the invention of new intellectual tools, thus inducing the creative act and the creative contribution. Once devised or fashioned these new tools become candidates for instructional attention.

Since these two types of objectives – instructional and expressive – require different kinds of curriculum activities and evaluation procedures, they each must occupy a distinctive place in curriculum theory and development. Instructional objectives embody the codes and the skills that culture has to provide and which make inquiry possible. Expressive objectives designate those circumstances in which the codes and the skills acquired in instructional contexts can be used and elaborated; through their expansion and reconstruction culture remains vital. Both types of objectives and the learning activities they imply constitute, to modify Whitehead's phrase, "the rhythm of curriculum". That is, instructional objectives emphasize the acquisition of the known; while expressive objectives its elaboration, modification, and, at times, the production of the utterly new.

Curriculum can be developed with an eye toward the alternating of such objectives. We can, I believe, study curriculum to determine the extent to which instructional and expressive educational objectives are employed, and we can raise questions about the types of relationships between them which are most productive for various types of students, for various types of learning, and for various subject matters.

16. Behavioural Objectives: A Critical Review

M. Macdonald-Ross

Source: M. Macdonald-Ross, *Instructional Science 2* (Amsterdam Elsevier Scientific Publishing Co., 1973), pp. 1–52, abridged.

Macdonald-Ross discusses a wide range of difficulties inherent in the use of behavioural objectives. He concludes that most of the claims for behavioural objectives seem to be weakened or negated. However, behavioural objectives have provided a framework for some, if limited, progress in curriculum-design techniques. The limitations are outcomes of the conceptual basis of the behavioural approach; for example, its reliance upon a defective model of learning and the assumption that lists can represent the structure of knowledge.

The Case Against Behavioural Objectives

> Any of the objections given by teachers to instructional objectives seem to be predicated upon inadequate conceptions of education, curriculum, or instruction (L. Tyler, 1969).

In the writings of the advocates of behavioural objectives one often senses a certain lack of patience with those who do not entirely concur with their dogma. Opposition from educators is often interpreted as symptomatic of laziness, ignorance, self-interest or general incompetence. Of course, this will be true of some individuals. But it is worth considering another interpretation, i.e. perhaps teachers sense that at the very basis of the dogma lie certain crucial difficulties – difficulties so fundamental that they cannot be entirely eradicated no matter what effort is applied, difficulties that arise from the very conceptual framework upon which the behavioural objective/systematic approach is constructed.

The central message of this paper is that such difficulties do exist, they are real and cannot be avoided. The purpose is to document and analyse these difficulties in such a way that their implications are clear and cannot be easily evaded. Most of the examples have been developed from my experience using the systematic approach at the Open University and elsewhere, though some have appeared in the literature previously in one form or another.

1. Where do Objectives Come From?

The first and most natural question for teachers to ask after hearing about the behavioural objective dogma is, Where do objectives come from, and how are they derived? This immediately uncovers the serious and deep-seated problem of *origins*, which has never been solved by advocates of the systematic approach, though various unsatisfactory attempts have been made.

a. Avoiding the Issue

Quite a few people have discovered to their surprise that some leading advocates go out of their way to avoid this problem altogether, as Mager (1962) did in his preface:

> This book is NOT about the philosophy of education, nor is it about *who* should select objectives, nor is it about *which* objectives should be selected.

Now, an author is perfectly entitled to limit his area of discussion if he so wishes. But the problem does not go away, and Mager's subsequent books have not brought the solution much closer.

Gilbert's (1962) attempt to construct a technology of education, which he called "mathetics", also foundered on the same rock. He says of mathetics that "its techniques do not extend with any authority to the problems of human value" (and what, then, is education supposed to be about?), and goes on to explain:

> The responsibility of those who design the teaching materials does not extend to determining the constituents of mastery; technical knowledge of the learning process does not supply special wisdom about what *should* be taught. The matheticist, ***as a technical person,*** has no alternative but to assume that the repertories of synthetic behaviour prescribed by the public school authorities represent the best available account of the public's educational objectives.

This evasion amounts to a truncation of the process of planning – chopping off the normative and strategic levels, and concentrating on operational issues. The adoption of a "technical person" disclaimer would only be appropriate if there existed fairly widespread and detailed agreement about the desired nature of education. Otherwise, the technical person would be avoiding the most important issues, and perhaps applying his energies in a quite misconceived direction. Does a widespread agreement exist about what constitutes a relevant and worthwhile education these days? There is plenty of evidence that it does not – not among teachers, certainly not among students, and probably not in the public at large (who often complain, and maybe justifiably, at the products of our educational system). A whole body of literature has now arisen to articulate this discontent, sufficient one would imagine to demolish naive faith in the "public school authorities" (Goodman, 1962; Holt, 1964; Illich, 1971; Kozol, 1967; Neill, 1962; Postman and Weingartner, 1969; Reimer, 1971).

There is one possible defence of Gilbert's position, namely the defence provided by the behavioural therapist Bandura (1969, see Chapter 2, "Value issues and objectives"). He makes the avoidance of normative judgment by the therapist a virtue, as follows:

> "Behavioural objectives are frequently (left) unspecified in order to avoid acknowledging the value judgments and social influences involved in the modification of behaviour." And again ". . . the choice of behavioural objectives is rightfully the *client's*."

This style of argument may be translated into educational terms rather like this: a teacher is entitled to teach (or "shape the behaviour of") a student *if and only if* that student agrees to the list of behavioural objectives that represent the goals of the transaction. This is, at first sight, quite a good defence; for a start it eliminates many of the deschooling critics mentioned earlier, since they, too, believe the "client" should exert a controlling influence. Alas, the defence is not completely adequate. though it has much to commend it. The key weakness lies in the differences between the educational enterprise and the enterprise of behaviour modification. For instance, if I compulsively wash my hands several hundred times a day, or if I have a morbid fear of cats, then I will probably be only too keen to agree that such behaviours should be "extinguished". No problems of morals would seem to arise, and even if they did only two people would need to agree – myself and my therapist.

But many factors would militate against such a simple procedure in education. Some (many?) students genuinely do not know what they wish to learn and expect the teacher to provide guidance and leadership. Even if a student *agrees* that he wishes to learn, say, chemistry, then he is bound to be ignorant of the *meaning* of the terminal goals (whereas the patient knows only too well what compulsions or phobias mean). And then, the detailed goals may be independent of both the teacher and the learner, in the sense of Popper's (1972), "third world" of objective knowledge. It would not be possible for a student to agree to learn chemistry and at the same time not agree to learn about chemical reactions. That is part of chemistry whether he likes it or not. Finally we should note that teacher and learner are not alone in this transaction; many others have a right and a duty to influence the nature of education, just as they assist its execution (even if only by paying taxes). So no *simple* contractual situation exists, though the needs and wishes of the student might well be allowed to exert more influence than they do at present.

If Bandura's defence is not sufficient, then the problem of origins must be faced. We need to know, in some detail, how objectives can be derived. What would a solution to this problem look like? Minimally, objectives must be *justified* (by considerations at the strategic and normative levels) and explicitly-stated selection *procedures* must be provided. To their credit, most experts have paid attention to methods of deriving objectives; we shall now see whether their prescriptions are satisfactory. Two schools of thought have emerged. One set of authorities attempts to provide explicit rules for converting observable human action into behavioural objectives. These, the "hardliners", tend to minimise or deny the distinctions between knowledge and skills and consequently between education and training. The other group, the "softliners", acknowledges the distinction between education and training, and concentrates on trying to justify the objectives.

This latter group usually presents no explicit rules for moving from the normative to the operational level, thus leaving much to individual hunch or intuition. As a consequence of their positions, the hardliners stress the feedforward role of the systematic approach, whereas the softliners emphasise the need for cycling and successive adjustment. Each of these prescriptions will now be examined.

b. The Hardliners

The basis of the hardliners' case was laid during and after the Second World War, when great advances were made in the theory and practice of military and industrial training. The strongest set of procedures (task analysis) owes its origin to R. B. Miller, working on the problems of the American Air Force. Like other armed forces, the AAF found itself able to develop new equipment faster than trained personnel. The object of Miller's (1962) research was to find how to reduce the lag (sometimes amounting to several years) between the introduction of new equipment and the availability of trained personnel to operate and maintain it. Though the details of Miller's scheme will not be presented here (since it is really geared to man-machine systems training), the first of his "major classes of training decisions" is worth noting, namely: *What are the criterion performance requirements?* This shows how the results of task analysis lead naturally to a behavioural specification of objectives.

The criteria for man-machine systems can be deduced before they are operational from the predicted machine and system performance characteristics. But more usually, task analysis descriptions are taken from actual observations of experienced workers or "master performers". The most extreme formulation of this idea was contained in Seymour's (1968) skills analysis:

> Starting from the detailed breakdown provided by work study, the skills analyst proceeds to identify and to record in detail each movement made by an experienced worker . . .

There might seem to be no insuperable obstacle to deriving behavioural objectives if the intention is to train people to do things. What else, it may be asked, should be the criterion of a skill except the ability to perform? Actually, this kind of specification of training by the exhaustive description of behaviours has quite severe limitations, even in the industrial training context for which it was created. Jobs change and new jobs arise (in which case there is no "experienced worker" available); and the list of behaviours exhibited by a master performer may be so long that a training program designed to cover them all would be most costly. The critical incident technique of Flanagan (1954) is an attempt to face this problem by identifying those performances which are *most critical* for the job; and in the last resort the objectives of training must contribute significantly to the objectives of the whole organisation (Odiorne, 1970). Unfortunately the problem of relevance is even less tractable in the field of education.

Another typical problem of industrial training occurs when personnel need to think and use their own initiative rather than follow set procedures. The mere mention of the word "think" is enough to make a training analyst shiver, yet its use seems inescapable. For example, the United Kingdom Atomic Energy Authority (UKAEA) have a whole training film devoted to the necessity of thinking. Apparently technicians using high energy electrical equipment are taught the acronym SIDET, meaning.

1. Switch off
2. Isolate
3. Dump
4. Earth

and THINK

Why should thinking be necessary if the procedure is adequate? In short, because all sorts of alarming accidents may occur if the procedure is followed blindly. Thinking about the principles underlying the procedure of earthing is the surest (and most economical) safeguard against unforeseen occurrences.

But still, it may be conceded that task analysis is a valuable tool for training analysts.[1] Is it possible to transfer the technique, using it as a strong procedure for deriving *educational* objectives? This is what the hardliners propose.

For this purpose it is necessary to deny that any real distinction exists between education and training, so that the technique which worked for training would automatically work for education. Duncan (1972), for instance, talks about avoiding "the arbitrary distinction between skill and knowledge". But this is a pretty uncomfortable stand to adopt, as I have said elsewhere:

> The distinction between knowledge and skills is actually quite valuable, as a little reflection will show. We can ask about an idea (expressed, for example, as a statement): is it true or false? how did we come to know it? how can it be justified? And we can then note that knowledge consists of meaningful ideas linked together to form a coherent view of the world (notice that you can say "skills" but not "knowledges"). The notions of truth and coherence aren't directly applicable to skills; they are the identifying features of knowledge. On the other hand, skills are usually useful and are performed to given standards. They become refined, repeatable, routinised, predictable and eventually may come to be performed subconsciously. In any event, it is easy to find types of educational experience which have nothing to do with skills – learning for learning's sake, for instance. The distinction between knowledge and skills is deeply embedded in our ordinary language for the excellent reason that it is meaningful and functionally necessary. To have a skill is to have the ability to execute useful tasks to publicly agreed standards of performance. This clearly implies that a task analysis procedure might be effective for skills but inadequate for general education (Macdonald-Ross, 1972c).[2]

If this type of argument is accepted then the hardline approach must fail, for it does not show what extra must be added to task analysis to make it suitable for education. Look at it this way: where observable actions really are an end in themselves, and are supported by minimal knowledge or understanding, then task analysis procedures are appropriate. But to specify the objectives for a course on economics by going along to observe a "master performer" would be quite fruitless unless you were also willing to take seriously the huge network of knowledge and understanding that lay behind his actions. And these are the very notions that were initially supposed to be rejected.

The merit of the task analysis approach is to draw attention to the performatory aspects of education. Students do have to pass exams, and will be expected to operate in the outside world.

The question is, how should these performances be related to the objectives? One prescription is that given by Evans who comments on the difficulty of constructing good objectives ("nobody in the world but Bob Mager and myself knows how to write behavioural objectives and sometimes I wonder about Mager"), and suggests that test items could usefully do service in place of objectives. This makes a good deal of sense; students often do take tests and examinations to be the real objectives of a course, and with some justification. But it would take rather a lot of test items to specify a whole course – too many for easy comprehension. And where, pray, do the test items come from?

The hardline case thus seems to fail. It is not sufficient to use observations of action (whether of action at work, or during examinations) for a prescription of educational objectives, if one takes the meaning of the word "education" at all seriously. This is a blow to the hopes of a straightforward no-nonsense prescriptive approach to education.

c. The Softliners

In contrast, softliners fully accept that educational objectives need to be derived in a way which does justice to the difference between education and training. This makes their approach safer, though this gain is achieved at the price of being less explicit than the hardliners about the mechanism of derivation. Typical of this school are the works of R. W. Tyler and Popham (Tyler, 1950; Popham and Baker, 1970a, b – see especially diagram on page 96 of the latter). Tyler's suggestion, which Popham endorses, is that objectives are derived from three major sources of data – the *learner*, the *society* and the *subject-matter*. Most people would have to think hard to imagine any *other* sources – but *how* should the derivation be made? No answer is given, except that the philosophy of education and the psychology of learning should act as filters. Now the notion that philosophy and psychology can be used to turn "tentative general objectives" into "precise instructional objectives" is frankly hilarious – one cannot believe the authors are seriously suggesting this as an operational procedure. All the critical decisions seem to be left to the intuition and common sense of the teacher, a strange position for a systematic approach to be in. And the situation is not much improved by providing behavioural objective banks – on what basis should the teacher make his selection?

How should the softline approach be rated? This depends on what claims are initially made for the systematic approach. If it is supposed to provide successful, predictive solutions to the problems of education, then it is not sufficient to provide weak rules for deriving objectives that leave so much to the intuition of the individual. On the other hand, if the systematic approach is seen as a fairly weak crutch, better than nothing but not leading to powerful prescriptions, then perhaps the softline approach does all that is required. But it is not my impression that the advocates of behavioural objectives wish to be driven into such a corner; that is their dilemma. Weak versions of the systematic approach cannot support such ambitious and demanding schemes as, for instance, payment by results or mastery learning. More important, it is not clear whether weak procedures can deliver the goods: that is, whether the outcomes of education can be brought in line with the initial aims. And that, surely, was the purpose of the whole enterprise.

2. Design

Now assume that the list of behaviours is *agreed*. If the dogma is correct then such a list should show how the learning situation should be designed (strongly prescriptive), or at any rate be extremely helpful in the design process (a weaker formulation). That is, from the list of behaviours can be derived, by a rigorously logical procedure, both the strategy and the tactics of the many educational experiences which are to be presented to the student. This ambition, very prominent in the writings of Gagné for instance, runs into some serious snags.

a. Voyages of Exploration. We sometimes find it useful at the Open University to distinguish between those course units which represent a voyage of exploration by the author, and those which are simply a mechanical repetition of a task often performed before. On the one hand the author struggles with ideas he may never have fully worked out before, let alone taught. Or he tries to present familiar ideas in an entirely new light. In the second case he will have run such courses many times before, set and marked examinations on the course, written papers and text books, and so on.

Now it is a sad fact that on voyages of exploration people most need guidance, and are least likely to get it. Only while actually creating and running the course will the author solve his conceptual problems. In a very real sense he does not really know where he is going until he gets there. That doesn't mean he lacks purpose, but it does make the detailed prespecification of goals rather pointless. In exploratory situations authors are (rightly) reluctant to close their options too early, and if browbeaten into writing behavioural objectives will face the uncomfortable option of having their creative choices constrained, or else constantly changing the objectives. In the latter case, of course, the hope of using the objectives prescriptively fades.

In contrast, it is rather easier for an author to produce and use behavioural objectives for courses whose conceptual problems he has already faced and solved. In general, he has worked out a reasonably effective teaching procedure for getting students through the kinds of tests or examinations he wishes to set. But this amounts to saying that the objectives are descriptive rather than prescriptive, or at any rate, that they have only a marginal influence on the design process.

b. The Anti-Planner. The kind of teacher who is often criticized by systematic theorists is the one who lays great stress on flexibility and the need to adapt to take advantage of the opportunities that occur in the classroom. This is a classic stance for an anti-planner (see Churchman, 1968b) and is so often encountered that it deserves mention here. Popham responds, quite reasonably, by saying that adaptation should take place within the context of planned objectives. This would be adequate, if it did not lead to another problem: if the teacher has just a short list of aims, he can remember them, but they are rather general; whereas if he has a fully specified list of behavioural objectives they are too unwieldy to use in a classroom. This is the level of specificity problem, discussed later.

Should teachers consult their protocol of behaviours before deciding how to adapt? Is there a procedure which works and can be suggested as a response to the anti-planner?

c. Instructional Sequence. Is there one best sequence for all students, or one optimal pathway through the subject-matter? It used to be thought by linear programmed learning enthusiasts, that the answer to this question ought to be yes. The reasoning was that whatever terminal behaviour required could be shaped by applying an appropriate schedule of reinforcement. And the word "schedule" entails the notion of sequence.

The relationship between goals was investigated by Gagné (1965) who concluded that the psychological organisation of knowledge could be represented as a hierarchy of principles. This has the consequence of strongly constraining the order in which principles may be learnt, since "the learning of higher-level principles was dependent on the mastery of prerequisite lower-level principles in a highly predictable fashion."

But it is possible to mount a radical attack on the notion of such strongly constrained options on the instructional sequence. Strangely enough, Mager (1961) himself showed how this might be done. Over ten years ago he carried out experiments on learner-controlled sequencing. In the first of these experiments students were given neither teaching material nor objectives but simply allowed access to instructors who would answer any question on the subject of electronics. The questions asked and the sequences followed were noted. It was found that the students' chosen sequences varied greatly one from another, and what is more, bore little relationship to sequences in formal courses designed by experts.

In subsequent experiments students were given a 24-page statement of objectives and access to instructors (Mager and McCann, 1962). In this case sequences varied *and* the learning time was 65% shorter than the length of the formal course. These results are supported and extended by recent experiments conducted by Pask to explore his notion of human learning as a form of information processing (Pask, 1972a,b; Pask and Scott, 1972). The realisation of the huge variety of pathways available to a learner is quite discomforting for believers in the systematic approach, and none have so far offered to explain how it may be encompassed in their scheme. Perhaps it is no surprise that a traditional course (badly constructed as so many are) should prove inefficient, but the variety of successful alternative pathways chosen by students is difficult to explain on the presuppositions outlined earlier. Apparently, no matter how well objectives are specified initially, major design problems remain which cannot be solved inside the conceptual framework of the systematic approach. If true, this is a serious objection. All the old problems of teaching return, perhaps ameliorated somewhat by the initial specification of objectives.

It may well be possible to cope with these problems under an alternative conceptual framework – a framework which takes account of the structure of knowledge, views the interaction between teacher and student as a defined type of conversational dialogue, and which admits (indeed insists) on the meaningfulness of knowledge, understanding and explanation. But to present this scheme in full would require an article at least as long again as the present.

d. Subject-Matter Differences. One of the prime claims of the systematic approach is to apply to all subjects at whatever level they may be taught. This presupposes that behavioural goals are appropriate for all subjects, a claim that has brought most complaints from the humanities and the arts (Eisner, 1967a,b, 1969; Stenhouse, 1971).

The typical argument runs like this: Arts subjects are concerned, not to reach goals once and for all, but to develop standards of judgment, taste and criticism. Often these aims stay the same year after year, but the student is expected to become even more effective in their application. If this amounts to saying that process is more important than content, then the argument may apply to all subject areas. For example, a scientist might well believe that the process of scientific problem-solving is more significant than the particular results of the process. Such "manner of behaving" objectives are dealt with later under "attacks on goal-directed models of education". Typically, it is possible to apply standards after the event, but extraordinarily difficult to predict correct behaviour in advance – that is, to use the feedforward mode.

Now, a lot depends on whether the behavioural advocate regards his list of objectives as *just instances* of acceptable behaviour or whether he regards the process skills as *nothing but* the list of objectives. The first position is weak but safe – weak because he gives no rules for generating further instances and safe because he avoids "nothing-buttery". The second position is strong but vulnerable – strong because if the student can exhibit these behaviours then he must (by definition) be well-educated, and vulnerable since there are so many correct behaviours that can mask misunderstanding.

The second style of attack is to point to the occasions where a personal response to a work of art is required. Since both the observer and the work of art are, in some senses, unique individuals, if the student is expected to exhibit predictable behaviour, a self-defeating situation arises. But if the objectives just say "principles of critical judgment should be applied," is this not just the kind of "imprecise" formulation that was supposed to be eschewed? Similar considerations hold for creative activities where the systematic advocate is reduced to such spineless formulations as noting whether or not a response had been made previously (as if that was what was meant by creativity).

Another argument points to the paradox involved in the use of ordinary language for encoding objectives relating to other art forms. Although language can be used to *refer* to the meaning of non-linguistic arts, the reference can never convey the same meaning as the original:

> . . . the notion that any kind of commentary will even explain any kind of poetry is of course vulgar. Even if there is a hidden meaning, the poem which contains no more than what an explanation of that meaning can translate should have been written in the form of the explanation in the first place (Northrop Frye, 1947).

And doubly so for the visual and musical arts. It is difficult to know whether this fundamentally prevents the use of behavioural objectives in such subject areas. Probably it does not, though one is bound to notice that the systematic approach has rarely been successful in the fine arts.

This section has raised several difficulties whose significance is difficult to judge. First, humanities were held to be exceptions because they entailed "manner of behaving" or process objectives. Though it is clear that most subject-matters could make such a claim, it was agreed that such objectives were difficult to use in prescriptive mode. The second and third points claimed that responses to works of art were of necessity individual, and in any event non-linguistic objectives could not be adequately coded in linguistic form. It is difficult to gauge the weight of these objections. There is little in the behavioural objectives literature on these matters, and not much practical experience of applying the method to these subjects.

It seems possible to have objectives relating to standards for judgment that can be applied *after the event.* Such objectives are of little use for prescriptive design purposes, though they could be invaluable if one cycles a number of times round the same system. This allows the weaker (cyclical) formulation some scope; even so a lot depends on the extent to which presuppositions underpinning the judgmental process can be made public – an exceedingly difficult task.

3. Problems of Evaluation

According to the theory, objectives determine the test items. Test constructors who justify items on any other grounds suffer the stinging rebuke of "arranging the target after the shot has been fired". This shows quite clearly how the advocates of behavioural objectives see the systematic approach as (in theory) a feedforward process, though in practice they are forced to adopt a cyclical design procedure.

Now, the claim that behavioural objectives provide the only objective basis for evaluation must be taken seriously, for if true it would quite alter the traditional theory and practice of educational assessment. It might be difficult to justify those systems where the pattern of marks approximates a normal distribution. Instead, criterion-based tests would put the emphasis on absolute standards and mastery learning. Many would regard such a shift of emphasis as beneficial. Also, the need for complicated and tortuous discussions about content validity or construct validity (Cronbach, 1971) would be by-passed, for by definition such matters would be settled in advance by the selection of objectives. This would be a great and welcome simplification – if it were possible.

Unfortunately it turns out that objectives do not in practice, and cannot even in principle, determine by themselves the validity of test items. Three principle reasons are adduced to support this opinion: first, that the significance of a test item depends in part upon the nature of the learning experiences the student has been engaged in. Second, that objectives are inherently ambiguous, and so, typically, various items can be written for each objective. Third, it seems impossible in principle even to relate objectives and test results in a simple fashion whenever the student's behaviour change may be assigned to causes outside the learning situation. Finally, attempts to reduce ambiguity by specifying objectives even more finely run up against the level of specificity problem. These issues will now be discussed in detail.

a. Interactions Within the Learning System. Seemingly excellent objectives and test items depend in part for their validity upon the integrity of the teaching process. Obviously, students can be "crammed" for exams, thus turning the items into measures of role learning. So objectives cannot by themselves determine the validity of test items *unless* the objectives also specify in detail the nature of the designed learning situation. And we have just seen that objectives leave a lot to be desired as prescriptors of design, so that defence is not available. How close *should* test items be to the examples given by the teacher? No one has *ever* solved this problem (except intuitively), and it seems the solution is not brought much closer by adopting behavioural objectives.

b. Interactions Outside the Learning System. Consider the evaluation of complex or long-term aims. Imagine a management education course lasting a month whose aim is to improve the performance of the managers when they return to their operational positions. Now some of the component goals can be evaluated at the end of the month; but no evaluation which did not consider the managers' performances on the job would be regarded as complete. Let's suppose that it is possible (having regard to his span of discretion) to assess the manager once a year. So a year later, assuming a management by objective system has been installed (and that has snags, too), we get the first measure of the manager's improved performance. Suppose he improves by *X%*. What does this mean? Can we assign the improvement to the course? Or has he got insights from other sources? Or perhaps his environment has ameliorated? How would the systematic paradigm help to disentangle these factors? At any rate it's clear that no protocol of behaviours could be *sufficient* for a full evaluation in these circumstances.

Similar considerations apply to many complex, long-term aims in schools, for instance high-level effective and cognitive objectives. Months or years may elapse before students' behaviour changes appreciably, by which time other factors will be candidates for responsibility. Popham (and Baker, 1970a) says, sensibly enough, that difficulty in measuring such elusive attributes as "a scientific attitude" should not discourage a teacher's efforts to get at them. Quite right; but in the first place this admits that theoretical constructs are valuable (more of this later), and in the second place it does damage the claim of behavioural objectives as *prescriptive* (it amounts to saying that you only know when an instance of behaviour is an example of scientific attitude after the event).

c. Ambiguity of Behavioural Objectives. If objectives did unambiguously specify observable actions, then of course they would specify the test items. But unless the objectives are actually identical (synonymous) with the test items, some degree of ambiguity must and does remain. In brief, it is easy to "fix" tests, and if the learning situation is "fixed" as well, then any performance criteria can be guaranteed in advance. It has been common knowledge among programmed learning experts for some time that the pass rate for a program can be improved by the simple strategy of revising the test items. This is a good deal cheaper than revising the program, and not easily detected since both sets of test items can be seen to relate to the same set of behavioural objectives. So when administrators install 90-90 criteria, accountability and payment by results, you can guess how crafty teachers will react.

If indeed verbs did divide cleanly into verbs of state (to know, to understand, etc.) and verbs of action (to cut, to cover, etc.) then naturally a great reduction in ambiguity would be achieved by using only verbs of action, as Mager advocated. We have already gladly conceded that "to know how a car engine works" is an imprecise formulation, and have no intention of retreating from that position. But, alas, not all cases are so clear-cut. Actually, most verbs do not fit comfortably in either category, for reasons that only a sophisticated linguistic analysis would reveal. An interesting experiment by Deno and Jenkins (1969) showed just how difficult it is for people to decide whether a verb describes an observable behaviour or not. Eleven teachers were asked to place verbs on a five-point scale from one (clearly observable action, e.g. to bite) to five (clearly unobservable states, e.g. to believe). Table I shows their results.

Notice that nearly half the verbs are placed between 2.0 and 4.0. This group contained many of the verbs teachers value and use most frequently (Why is that? Interesting question). Many of these verbs also had large variances, indicating lack of agreement among the teachers. The prize example is "to solve" at 4.2 – a verb Mager lists as "open to fewer interpretations"! Of course, the meaning of *any* word, verb or not, is essentially ambiguous. Not infinitely flexible, just ambiguous. The ambiguity can be resolved by taking the semantic and syntactic context into account; but sometimes a great deal of content is necessary, more than is provided by even a well-specified behavioural objective.

All this militates against any simple-minded classification of objectives into dichotomous observable/non-observable categories, and ensures that some essential ambiguity remains with any objective. Even if tests were not deliberately fixed, the problem would remain.

d. Ambiguity of Test Items. Philosophers often make the distinction between behaviours (movements or muscle twitches) and actions (which must meet various *criteria*). This is what MacMillan and McClellan (1968) allude to when they say:

> But the curious thing about the acceptable objectives is that they do not give descriptions of behaviour, but rather specify criteria of correctness of *results* of behaviour . . . the behavioural objectives, then, are not behavioural.

That this is not just a matter of terminology is shown by this example (from Evans, 1960):

> Objective: to solve quadratic equations. Test: solve $X^2 + 5x + 6 = 0$.
>
> The equation can be solved by factoring or by completing the square or by using the quadratic formula. But we have not said which method should be used, and it may be (for all one knows) a matter of educational consequence. To that extent the test item is ambiguous, as indeed is the objective, as indeed is any description of an action which can be performed in various ways. This relates to an earlier comment about making right responses for wrong reasons.

e. Level of Specificity. The natural defence to the ambiguity of objectives and test items is to suggest that objectives should be specified ever more finely. This defence does not hold water; indeed it raises one of the most critical defects of behavioural objectives – the absence of suitable rules for deciding at which level of specificity objectives should be pitched.

The level of specificity problem is the most cruel dilemma faced by the advocate of behavioural objectives. It runs like this: If you have only a few general objectives they are easy to remember and handle, but too vague and ambiguous. But if you try to eliminate ambiguity by splitting down the objectives and qualifying the conditions of performance, then the list becomes impossibly long.

TABLE I Rank-Order Distribution of Means and Variances for 99 Verb Ratings (Deno and Jenkins, 1969).

Terms	Means	Variances	Terms	Means	Variances
to cover with a card	1.0	0.0	*to add	3.0	1.3
to lever press	1.0	0.0	*to supply	3.0	1.3
to line-draw	1.0	0.0	*to demonstrate	3.1	0.8
to mark	1.0	0.0	*to regroup	3.1	1.0
to point to	1.0	0.0	*to multiply	3.1	1.2
to cross out	1.1	0.3	*to round off	3.1	1.4
to underline	1.1	0.3	*to group	3.2	0.5
to walk	1.1	0.3	*to complete	3.2	0.9
*to circle	1.2	0.3	*to respond to	3.3	0.6
to repeat orally	1.2	0.3	*to average	3.3	1.1
*to count orally	1.2	0.7	to summarize	3.3	1.1
*to say	1.2	0.7	to inquire	3.5	0.8
*to write	1.3	0.4	to utilize	3.5	1.0
*to put on	1.4	0.4	*to borrow	3.5	0.4
*to read orally	1.5	0.4	to acknowledge	3.5	1.1
*to shade	1.5	0.8	*to find	3.6	1.6
to number	1.5	0.4	*to identify	3.8	0.8
*to name	1.5	0.8	to see	3.8	2.3
*to fill in	1.6	0.9	*to convert	3.9	1.3
to label	1.7	1.1	to distinguish	4.1	0.8
*to state	1.7	1.4	*to solve	4.2	0.9
*to remove	1.9	0.6	*to apply	4.2	1.1
*to place	1.9	0.9	to develop	4.3	0.4
to tell what	1.9	1.1	*to test	4.3	0.4
*to draw	2.0	0.9	*to determine	4.3	0.6
*to identify in writing	2.1	1.4	to generate	4.3	0.7
*to check	2.2	1.2	*to create	4.3	1.1
*to construct	2.2	1.2	to discriminate	4.5	0.6
*to match	2.3	0.7	*to recognize	4.5	0.4
*to take away	2.3	1.1	to discover	4.7	0.2
*to make	2.4	0.9	to become competent	4.7	0.3
*to arrange	2.5	0.6	to infer	4.7	0.3
to finish	2.5	0.6	to like	4.7	0.3
*to read	2.5	0.8	to analyze	4.8	0.1
*to play	2.5	1.7	to be curious	4.8	0.1
*to locate	2.6	0.6	to conclude	4.8	0.1
*to connect	2.6	1.1	*to deduce	4.8	0.1
*to give	2.6	1.3	to feel	4.8	0.1
*to reject	2.7	1.1	to concentrate	4.8	0.3
*to select	2.7	1.4	to perceive	4.8	0.3

TABLE I (continued)

*to change	2.9	0.9	to learn	4.8	0.3
*to use	2.9	1.1	to appreciate	4.9	0.0
*to subtract	2.9	1.3	to be aware	4.9	0.0
*to perform	3.0	1.8	to know	4.9	0.0
*to total	3.0	1.8	to wonder	4.9	0.0
*to divide	3.0	0.8	to realize fully	5.0	0.0
*to order	3.0	0.9	to understand	5.0	0.0
*to measure	3.0	1.1			

*Denotes verbs extracted from the objectives of a "behaviouristic" curriculum.

Here are two examples, taken from a text on behavioural objectives, which show how the advocates of the systematic approach have no rules for deciding the level of specificity:

> Objective: the student should *apply* the principle that plants are dependent on animals and animals are dependent upon plants and both are dependent on the environment.
>
> 1. The fish in which tank would survive the longest? Why?
> 2. In what tank would the plants survive the longest? Why?
> 3. If you were going to alter tank 1 what would you do and why?
>
> (Sund and Picard, 1972. A diagram of the three tanks accompanies the test items.)

This objective is so general that an almost *infinite* number of items could be legitimately generated. There is no sense in which such objectives can be said to prescribe the test items, but you wouldn't need many to cover a whole biology course.

> Objective: The student should *explain* why the retrograde motion of Mars occurs.
> Item: The diagram below shows the movement of the planet Mars. How would you explain why it appears to move the way it does? (Sund and Picard, 1972).

Now this objective is quite specific and only a limited number of test items could validly follow. (Note though, that it is not so clear what kind of behaviour is going to count as an explanation.) But the cost of moving even to this level of specificity is quite serious: if all the objectives in a physics course were at this level they would run into thousands and fill a small book. This is no exaggeration, incidentally. In a review of a recent book on objectives in educational psychology (Stones and Anderson, 1972) I estimated that if the authors had followed Mager's rules strictly they would need to produce 10,000 objectives – a volume of 150,000 words, at least, probably more. At this juncture it is worth remembering Eisner's (1969) comment:

> In retrospect it is not difficult to understand why this (the objectives) movement in curriculum collapsed under its own weight in the 1930s. Teachers could not manage fifty highly specified objects, let alone hundreds.

Every time behavioural objectives have been constructed on a large scale this problem of specificity has proved quite fearsomely difficult. No satisfactory rules have emerged though prominent advocates have long been aware of the need (for instance, both Gagné and Mager worked on Project Plan). Suggestions have ranged from extreme specificity [replacing objectives by test items (Evans, 1960)] to the generality of Tyler's (1954, 1960) objectives. Perhaps the problem is insoluble in principle.

4. Objectives as Instruments of Communication

Objectives can certainly be useful instruments whereby a teacher can show his colleagues and students what he expects the outcome of learning to be. But there are certain limits to this communication, limits which are rarely discussed in the literature.

Earlier we saw how objectives can be used to assist co-ordination between members of a design team or curriculum reform group. Each person must know where his contribution lies, and what he can safely rely on others to do. The chief limitation is, of course, the extent to which different people will make different interpretations of the same objective.

Objectives are, as we have seen, always capable of being interpreted in various ways, even of being misinterpreted. This is because they are ambiguous. To some extent, it is not practicable (even if it were possible) to eliminate all possible misunderstanding by ever finer specification. There is a limit to the extent to which any human can understand the intention of another no matter what, though in practice and in certain circumstances the risk of serious error can be minimised.

So it would be foolish to suppose that agreement on a list of objectives constitutes a general understanding of intent. Several other heuristics are necessary to reduce the possibility of misunderstanding, of which the most powerful makes use of the insight that every person's world-view is unique to the extent to which his unrevealed *presuppositions* are unique. So, as a minimal procedure, designers can attempt to explain their presuppositions to each other, thus revealing how some objectives rather than others are chosen. Such presuppositions contain, as it were, routines for interpreting objectives so as to reduce their ambiguity.

Objectives are also supposed to be a vital kind of "advance organiser" for the student's learning. Students should be given objectives so they can appreciate the nature of the goal they are working towards. And the experiments where students are given just goal statements and allowed to organise their own learning show that this claim has some validity (Mager and McCann, 1962). But our experience at the Open University has shown the limitations of this idea. Teachers understand what objectives mean because they have already attained the goal. They have been there, experienced the terminal behaviour if you wish, and this personal experience gives the words meaning for them. But the student does not have this experience.

This dilemma is seen quite forcibly whenever a subject has a vocabulary of technical terms (and many subjects in higher or technical education do). If the objectives are written using the technical terms, then the list can be kept reasonably manageable, and ambiguities kept to a minimum. Such objectives are useless for the student who doesn't know what the terms mean, though they might be helpful during revision to direct his attention to the crucial parts of the course. But if the technical terms are described in ordinary language the list becomes impossibly unwieldy, virtually as long as the teaching material itself. Objectives are a useful but deficient tool of communication. They need to be supplemented by the teacher revealing his *presuppositions* and his reasons for believing the education to be *relevant*. In such a discussion the student should gain some interpretive routines which will help him make sense of the objectives.

So behavioural objectives are not a foolproof system of communication. More realistically they are useful, but rather weak, needing to be buttressed by extensive in-depth discussions between the concerned parties.

5. Other Objections

a. Triviality. The complaint is often heard that the most trivial aims are the easiest to operationalise. This much, everyone agrees on. Advocates usually try to turn this to their advantage by pointing out that trivial objectives can be weeded out as being unworthy of educational effort. (This is the response Popham gives; see later.) But this assumes that the problems of operationalising "worthwhile" aims has been solved, else what shall we do if none of the objectives are worthwhile? We should have nothing left. Thus, this complaint (of triviality) is real, but may be subsumed under the broader problem of origins. It is also strongly connected with the question of operationalism, discussed below.

b. Attacks on Goal-Directed Models of Education. Sometimes behavioural objectives have come under fire from those who wish to make a radical assault on the central notion of goal-directed behaviour as a suitable model for education. For instance, Vickers (1968) says "most human regulatory behaviour is norm-seeking, and as such, cannot be resolved into goal-seeking." Oakeshott (1962) puts it elegantly like this:

> It is asked: why travel if there is no prefigured and final destination? But it may be replied: why suppose that the analogy of a journey towards a prefigured destination is relevant? It is clearly irrelevant in science, in art, in poetry, and in human life in general, none of which have prefigured final destinations and none of which are (on that account) considered to be "pointless" activities . . . To describe the enterprise as "keeping afloat and on an even keel" is to assign it an office neither to be overrated nor despised.

This line of argument, which enjoys quite a vogue amongst philosophers of education, is a more general case of one of the difficulties raised above under "Subject-Matter Differences". It is puzzling to know what would count as an adequate answer to this objection, but there is one defence that might be tried. Cyberneticians usually distinguish between two kinds of goal-directed systems; the ones which cease functioning once a specific goal is reached (for instance, once an insect lays its eggs the ovipositor is retracted, and the whole system is then out of action), and the ones which continually act so as to keep some parameter within set limits (for example, a thermostat). It is possible to imagine objectives so worded that they would count as members of the second (regulative) class of goal-directed systems. But, as discussed previously, this type of regulation occurs after the event, and its value in prescription is limited.

c. Costs of Feedback (Cyclical) Design Systems. The costs of designing systems which do not initially work well can be quite considerable. For example, at the Open University our courses are designed to last basically for four years. If the initial design is unsatisfactory then thousands of students may suffer, and considerable sums of money spent in remedying defects. There are times when one *does* want to get design as near right as possible the first time round. So the retreat from the ambitious, but untenable, feedforward prescriptive mode to the less demanding cyclical mode is a significant, and at times costly, retreat.

d. Lists do not Adequately Represent the Structure of Knowledge. Many of the surface difficulties experienced by those trying to apply the systematic approach are caused by deep underlying problems which are rarely if ever articulated. One of these deep issues concerns the structure of knowledge. Since knowledge or understanding presupposes a coherence amongst ideas – a fitting together or interlocking of parts to form a meaningful whole – it is difficult to see why advocates of the systematic approach are so addicted to list structures. For behavioural objectives *are* presented in lists, lists which virtually demolish any structure that might once have existed.

Some lists reveal structure when surrounded by well-specified interpretive routines (e.g. computer programs). But lists of behavioural objectives are more like heaps – they show little of the complex manner in which ideas are interrelated, and so have no higher-level structure. This is important in itself, and must be taken seriously as soon as it is realised that some of the intransigent problems raised earlier are primarily due to this lack of structure. For example, it has been shown how there exist no procedures for justifying the inclusion or exclusion of a given objective unless (a) it relates to an obviously necessary task, or (b) hunch or intuition is resorted to. This arises from the absence of a way of representing the whole structure so that the interrelation of parts can be seen in manipulable terms.

Once more, apologies must be made for arbitrarily truncating the discussion. Pask and I have raised this topic before, and will do so again (Macdonald-Ross, 1972a, b; Pask, 1972a, b).

e. Model of Teacher-Learner Interaction. It is actually true, but not easy to explain, that the use of behavioural objectives implies a poverty-stricken model of student-teacher interaction. This point was made by Pask and Lewis (private communication) when they analysed the systemic implications of various curriculum schemes. The following Table II contrasts the main features of a behaviour-shaping curriculum with the theoretical approach favoured by Pask, Lewis and myself (which envisages the teacher and learner as general learning systems and the interaction as "conversational learning").

Since it would take a paper at least as long again as the present one to explore fully all the ideas contained in Table II, we must be content to realise that the existence (even by implication) of the primitive behaviour-shaping model sets limits to what can be achieved by a behavioural objectives approach.

f. Operationalism. The notion of behavioural objectives is strongly related to the philosophical position of *operationalism.* This is an embarrassing relationship, to say the least, for it is now clear that operationalism suffers from some severe defects and is generally regarded by philosophers of science to be in a mortally wounded condition. At first sight, however, it does seem an attractive proposition, as shown in this extract from Bridgeman's (1927) original account:

> To find the length of an object, we have to perform certain physical operations. The concept of length is therefore fixed when the operations by which the length is measured are fixed: that is, the concept of length involves as much as and nothing more than the set of operations by which length is determined. In general, we mean by any concept nothing more than a set of operations; the

TABLE II Contrast of Behaviour-Shaping With Conversational Learning Models*

	Behaviour Shaping	Conversational learning
View of teacher:	Simple regulator	General learning system
View of student:	Simple adaptive machine	General learning system
View of subject-matter:	List of target behaviours and list of reinforcements	Knowledge or entailment structure and associated descriptions and tasks
Communication restrictions (form of transactions allowed):	Stimuli (which or whether questions) and assertions (cues, prompts)	Assertions; problems (including how and why questions) with explanations as solutions
	Schedules of reinforcing events Responses (answers to which or whether questions)	Goal or subgoal statements; evaluative statements; pupil's selection of strategy and description of this state; teacher's instructions about how to learn, etc.

* meaning of technical terms regrettably beyond scope of present paper.

concept is synonymous with the corresponding set of operations.

Such a prescription appears to free the scientist from the need to deal with "occult qualities" (theoretical constructs, in this context knowing, understanding, etc.). But closer examination reveals critical problems. For instance, what exactly counts as an operation? What happens to the concepts when we are not performing operations? What happens if we cannot physically perform operations or if we have not yet learnt how to perform them? Do we wish to say, in these circumstances, that no kind of scientific discourse is possible? Hempel (1958) says:

> Scientific systematisation is ultimately aimed at establishing explanatory and predictive order among the bewilderingly complex "data" of our experience, the phenomena that can be "directly observed" by us. It is a remarkable fact, therefore, that the greatest advances in scientific systematisation have not been accomplished by means of laws referring explicitly to *observables,* i.e. to things and events which are ascertainable by direct observation, but rather by means of laws that speak of various *hypothetical* or *theoretical entities*, i.e. presumptive objects, events, and attributes which cannot be perceived or otherwise directly observed by us.

Now it is sufficient for present purposes to realise what implications follow from the demand that terms such as "know" and "understand" should always be fully reinterpreted as lists of observable actions. These implications have never been faced by the protagonists of behavioural objectives. As Cronbach (1971) wrote recently:

> The writers on curriculum and evaluation who insist that objectives must be "defined in terms of behaviour" are taking an ultra operationalist position, though they have not offered a scholarly philosophical analysis of the issue. A person who insists on "behavioural" objectives is denying the appropriateness and usefulness of constructs (=theoretical terms). The educator who states objectives in terms of constructs (e.g. self-confidence, scientific attitude, a habit of suiting one's writing style to one's purpose) regards observables as indicators from which the presence of the characteristics described by the construct can be inferred. But he will not for example *substitute* "volunteers ideas and answers in class" for "self-confidence". From the construct point of view behaviour such as this is an indicator of confidence but not a definer. Indeed no list of specific responses-to-situations, however lengthy, can define the construct, since the construct is intended to apply to situations that will arise in the future and cannot be specified now.

This short discussion of operationalism shows how some of the problems encountered in the behavioural objective domain are extensions of the basic problems faced by operationalism. For instance, it explains why trivial aims are easiest to state in behavioural terms: they are always close to their empirical basis, whereas long-term or complex higher-level aims may be quite abstract or far removed from empirical indicators. Again, we can now see why lists of objectives get so long and are so tedious to prepare, for it is possible to operationalise a theoretical concept in almost limitless detail. The decisions about levels of specificity and the meaning of key terms are also problems to operationalism and in the context of behavioural objectives.

6. Summary of Objections

These are the objections that have been raised to behavioural objectives. In some cases the items are interconnected, and it is possible to slice the pie in various fashions. But this would not greatly alter the points that have been made:

1. No consistent view exists as to the origin of objectives.
2. In the educational domain no well-defined prescriptions are available for deriving objectives.

3. Defining objectives before the event conflicts with voyages of exploration.
4. Advocates do not show how teachers can use objectives to guide unpredicted classroom events.
5. There are an extremely large number of paths through any body of knowledge, thus reducing the effectiveness of objectives in design.
6. In some disciplines criteria can only be applied after the event.
7. Objectives do *not* prescribe the validity of test items.
8. Objectives are inherently ambiguous.
9. The level of specificity problem has never been solved.
10. Objectives do not communicate intent unambiguously, especially to students.
11. Trivial objectives *are* the easiest to operationalise, and this *is* a problem.
12. The relevance of goal-referenced models of education can be questioned.
13. Weak prescriptions lead to cycling. This can be costly.
14. Lists of behaviours do not adequately represent the structure of knowledge.
15. The use of behavioural objectives implies a poverty-stricken model of student-teacher interaction.
16. The behavioural objective scheme suffers from many of the weaknesses of any operationalist dogma.

The most important items, in this author's opinion, are 1, 2, 7, 9, and 13 to 16 inclusive. The difficulty of writing objectives, often mentioned in the literature, has not been listed here. It seems most likely to arise from some combination of the above list of intractable problems. Many of the more detailed objections can be traced back to the three really fundamental problems: 14, 15 and 16. Such problems are hardly soluble within the conceptual framework of behavioural objectives and the systematic approach. This opinion contrasts sharply with the view of advocates of the systematic approach who, though admitting problems, believe they are soluble simply by applying more effort in the same direction.

A Reassessment of Popham's Defence

> Yet, as a partisan in the controversy (about behavioural objectives) I would prefer unanimous support of the position to which I subscribe. You see, the other people are wrong . . . Moreover, their particular form of sin . . . will probably harm more people than the most exotic forms of pornography. (Popham, 1968)

Under the magnificent title of "Probing the Validity of Arguments Against Behavioural Goals", Dr. James Popham presented in 1967 his own response to "most of the arguments used to resist the implementation of precise instructional objectives". It is now necessary to re-examine this defence. The necessity arises because Popham's defence is so widely regarded by systematic advocates as a complete answer to criticisms of behavioural objectives; it is often quoted, and has been reprinted at least three times since the original conference (originally presented at conferences in California in 1967 and Chicago in 1968; reprinted in Popham *et al.*, 1969; Kibler *et al.*, 1970; and Davis and Hartley, 1972). There is only one way to approach this task – which is to take each objection and rebuttal one by one and examine them, making use of the framework established earlier in this paper.

Reason one: Trivial learner behaviours are the easiest to operationalise, hence the really important outcomes of education will be underemphasised.

This has already been discussed above (Part III, Section 5a). We there noted that Popham's response (that trivial objectives can be weeded out once revealed) is true, but not sufficient since it ducks the huge problems of origins and operationalism (which have also been discussed above).

So we are bound to conclude that the problem of triviality is still a problem. Presumably this objection should have been phrased thus: "What are your (explicit) procedures for generating worthwhile objectives?" Since Popham's procedures are safe but weak, as discussed above under origins, it is not clear that he could answer such a question adequately.

Reason two: prespecification of explicit goals prevents the teacher from taking advantage of instructional opportunities unexpectedly occurring in the classroom.

This we have also briefly discussed (Part III, Section 2b). Popham's response (that "serendipity in the classroom . . . should always be justified in terms of its contribution to the learner's attainment of worthwhile objectives") is perfectly reasonable, but again does not raise the underlying problem, which is, how can teachers do it? This is the level of specificity problem in yet another guise, for if the teacher has a set of very detailed objectives he surely cannot use them in real-time action, but if "the lesson plan is written at a level of generality upon which the teacher can function" (Popham and Baker, 1970a) then few of the benefits of precise objectives will be reaped. You can't have it both ways.

Reason three: Besides pupil behaviour changes, there are other types of educational outcomes which are important, such as changes in parental attitudes, the professional staff, community values, etc.

This objection comes as something of a surprise, since it is so weak and so obviously asking for the treatment which it deservedly gets from Dr. Popham (". . . the school's primary responsibility is to its pupils").

This is the first of the straw men. (By using the term "straw men" I do not wish to imply that Dr. Popham invented the objection. But some objections are so lame that their reproduction in a professional paper and subsequent destruction give the behavioural objective schema a reputation which it hardly deserves.)

Reason four: Measurability implies behaviour which can be objectively, mechanistically measured, hence there must be something dehumanizing about the approach.

It's difficult to know how to respond to an objection which itself is so full of confusions. Measurement is not the same as observation; what is said to be "implied" is not actually implied; what does "something dehumanizing" mean? – and so on. I suppose what lies behind this muddle is a concern with the validity of evaluation procedures based on behavioural objectives. If this *is* the case then we have already seen what a considerable problem this presents (Part III, Section 3). Popham's excellent example (of how human judges can accurately score springboard divers) shows that valid assessment of complex behaviours can be obtained, but does not show how this may generally be achieved by a systematic procedure.

Reason five: It is somehow undemocratic to plan in advance precisely how the learner should behave after instruction.

This is the old chestnut raised by Arnstine (1964) about programmed learning. The rebuttal (described by Popham as "a brilliant refutation") came from Komisar and McClellan (1965) who said that instruction is by its very nature undemocratic, and to pretend that classrooms are democratic places would be untruthful. This is a good start, but more could be said. For instance, the use of "democracy" in this context is rather odd; it is not clear that this concept can rightfully be used, or if it is used then what, exactly, would count as being "democratic"? Perhaps we are really talking about the need for *justification*, which is part of the problem of origins. If so, then the problem is a good deal more deep-seated than the question of where control resides in a classroom.

Reason six: That isn't really the way teaching is; teachers rarely specify their goals in terms of measurable learner behaviours; so let's set realistic expectations of teachers.

This invertebrate specimen is the second straw man. It gets the treatment it deserves (maybe teachers do not, but they ought to).

Reason seven: In certain subject areas, e.g. fine arts and humanities, it is more difficult to identify measurable pupil behaviours.

This has already been discussed (Part III, Section 2d) as an objection whose validity is difficult to assess. Popham rightly says that arts and humanities teachers do have standards, and do make judgments. He advises them to put their evaluative criteria "on the line", good advice, but not absolutely sufficient. Behavioural objectives are supposed to be prescriptive (before the event) tools, and when criteria of judgment are applied, say, to works of art, they are applied *after the event*. (Because you know a good painting when you see one does not mean you can predict all the good paintings that might ever be created, nor even need you be able to specify how to create a good painting.) So in these cases the prescriptive benefits of objectives are weakened.

Reason eight: While loose general statements of objectives may appear worthwhile to an outsider, if most educational goals were stated precisely, they would be revealed as generally innocuous.

This is the third straw man. In such circumstances (where worthless education is the rule) the explicit nature of objectives is of positive benefit – so it is perverse to raise this as an objection, as Popham shows in no uncertain fashion – "We must abandon the ploy of 'obfuscation by generality' and make clear exactly what we are doing."

Reason nine: Measurability implies accountability; teachers might be judged on their ability to produce results in learners rather than on the many bases now used as indices of competence.

Should teachers be accountable for securing behaviour changes? Popham believes they should be, and goes on to say that a teacher "should not be judged on the particular instruction *means* he uses to bring about desirable *ends*." This response is no surprise, for advocates are prone to claim for the systematic approach that it lays an objective basis for accountability. But all systems of accountability depend on (1) agreement as to what ends are desirable, and (2) valid and reliable methods of evaluation. And we have already seen that the problems of origins and evaluation are quite intractable inside the world-view of the systematic approach. It is *this* which causes opposition to accountability, not love of incompetence or "mysticism".

Reason ten: It is far more difficult to generate such precise objectives than to talk about objectives in our customarily vague terms.

Interestingly, Popham says this is "a very significant objection to the development of precise goals." This may not be entirely unconnected with the idea of a behavioural objectives bank, one of which he organises, and which allow teachers to select objectives and so short-cut the hard work of specification. However, the question arises as to whether difficulty in generating objectives is due to psychological factors (i.e. teachers are incompetent, or, only a few of us are skilled in writing objectives) or due to basic logical deficiencies embedded deep inside the systematic approach. In other words, it is no surprise people find it difficult to write objectives *if* there are no rules for generating them, for deciding their specificity, for deciding how their attainment may be assessed, and so on. In these circumstances one might begin to suspect anyone who *did* find objectives easy to generate. Now suppose (by magic, as it were) there were a complete bank of objectives, numbering tens of millions. On what criteria should teachers select?

Reason eleven: In evaluating the worth of instructional schemes it is often the unanticipated results which are really important, but prespecified goals may make the evaluator inattentive to the unforseen.

This objection contains the assumption that the prespecified goals are not the most important ones. We are supposed to have been protected from this sort of thing by the prespecification of design, and undoubtedly a "hardliner" would have responded by advising you to improve your task analysis. Popham (following the "softliner" strategy, as you will remember) cannot give this rebuke, and is bound to admit tacitly that such an occurrence is possible. The advice given ("keep your eyes open") is both weak (as he acknowledges) and an admission of failure.

Of Popham's eleven objections, three are straw men which provide him with targets which are altogether too easy. The other eight contain indications of serious, deeper problems though these are not precisely articulated. In virtually every case Dr. Popham has chosen to give a superficially convincing answer to the surface problem, but has neither uncovered nor answered the deeper issues.

Conclusions

Most of the claims made for behavioural objectives need to be weakened or even negated as a result of the criticisms raised. There appear to be no reliable and explicit principles for generating relevant objectives: the various suggestions made fall short in one respect or another. There are no clear rules even for deciding on the specificity of objectives. And once objectives have been specified they do not prescribe the choice of instructional means, nor ensure the content validity of test items. These objections were tried out on one of the best-known defences of behavioural objectives. The fair conclusion to draw from this analysis is that the defence was not sufficient. This means that the case against behavioural objectives must be taken seriously.

The original ambition of the systematic approach was to make education more effective and to bring the outcomes of learning in line with the intentions of the educator. This ambition is now in some danger of falling short of its goal. The strong feedforward version of the systematic approach rested heavily on behavioural objectives laying the foundation for explicit, adequate and well-justified procedures which would work when applied by anyone who understood them. This position is now undermined; the prescriptive approach fails – unless in practice it is buttressed by unspecified and unformulated intuitive skills imported *ad hoc* to support the design system. This reliance on intuitive skills was just what the "hardliners" hoped to avoid.

The cyclical versions of the systematic approach are still viable, though weakened. Advocates of this approach never did expect objectives to be sufficient for prescriptive purposes. They are willing to settle for a final internal coherence reached after repeated trial and revision. A sensible attitude, adopted by many successful consultants when operating in the field. But this approach has costs attached, for example the cost of cycling, that is, of not getting the design right the first time around. Successes are certainly recorded by people working within the cyclical framework. But –are the successes due to the procedures of the systematic approach, or are they due to the unformulated personal skills of the consultant, teacher or design group?

This article has *not* argued that behavioural objectives are worthless, nor is it doubted that the systematic approach represents an advance on purely intuitive methods of curriculum design. The criticisms of traditional methods were entirely justified – no one wishes to put the clock back. But the application of behavioural objectives and the systematic approach needs to be tempered with an understanding of its inherent deficiencies. The chief function of this paper has been to identify these deficiencies so that they may be allowed for in some way.

The question arises, Can these defects be repaired, or are there limits which the systematic approach can never transcend? Insofar as they admit any such defects, advocates of behavioural objectives have always believed they could be overcome by experience and hard work. My view is quite different. I think that behavioural objectives will never achieve all that their supporters hope, for they are limited by the very presuppositions on which they are based. The defects of operationalism, the poverty-stricken model of learning and the assumption that lists can represent the structure of knowledge: these are embedded deep inside the behavioural objective schema, and cannot be transcended.

Behavioural objectives provide a framework which has led to some progress in the design of educational systems. The conceptual framework which provided the basis also sets certain absolute limitations. If we are close to those limitations then improvements are likely to be of marginal importance. In my opinion a new and potentially more fruitful conceptualisation is needed; meanwhile the strengths and weaknesses of the behavioural objectives paradigm can at least be seen in sharper focus.

NOTES

1. See Ammerman and Melching (1966) and Chapanis (1959) for further references on task analysis and methods of direct observation.
2. The fact that the right answer can be given for the wrong reason is a further argument for retaining concepts such as knowledge and understanding.

REFERENCES

Alexander, C. (1964). *Notes on the Synthesis of Form.* Cambridge: Harvard University Press.

Ammerman, H. L. and Melching, W. H. (1966). "The Derivation, Analysis and Classification of Instructional Objectives", *Technical Report 66 4, Task INGO.* HumRRO, George Washington University.

Ansoff, H. I. (1965). *Corporate Strategy.* New York: MacGraw-Hill.

Arnstine, D. G. (1964). "The language and values of programmed instruction, Part 2", *The Educational Forum.*

Bandura, A. (1969). *Principles of Behaviour Modification.* New York: Holt, Rinehart and Winston.

Bishop, L. K. (1970). *Individualising Instructional Systems.* New York: Harper Row.

Block, J. H., ed. (1971). *Mastery Learning.* New York: Holt, Rinehart and Winston.

Bobitt, F. (1924). *How to Make a Curriculum.* Boston: Houghton Mifflin.

Braybrooke, D. and Lindblom, C. E. (1963). *A Strategy of Decision.* Glencoe, III.: Free Press.

Bridgeman, P. W. (1927). *The Logic of Modern Physics.* London: Macmillan.

Butler, Lord R. A. (1971). *The Art of the Possible.* London: Hamish Hamilton.

Chapanis, A. (1959). *Research Techniques in Human Engineering.* Baltimore: Johns Hopkins Press.

Charters, W. W. and Waples, D. (1929). *The Commonwealth Teacher-Training Study.* Chicago: Chicago University Press.

Churchman, C. W. (1968a). *Challenge to Reason.* New York: McGraw-Hill.

Churchman, C. W. (1968b). *The Systems Approach.* New York: Dell.

Cronbach, L. J. (1971). "Test Validation", in Thorndike, R. L., ed., *Educational Measurement.* American Council on Education.

Dale, E. (1967). "Historical Setting of Programmed Instruction", in Lange, P. ed., *Programmed Instruction.* Washington D. C.: National Society for the Study of Education.

Davies, I. K. (1971). *The Management of Learning.* New York: McGraw-Hill.

Davies, I. K. and Hartley, J. (1972). *Contributions to an Educational Technology.* London: Butterworths.

Deno, S. L. and Jenkins, J. R. (1969). "On the behaviourality of behavioural objectives", *Psychology of the Schools,* 6, 18–24.

Duncan, K. (1972). "Strategies for Analysis of the Task", in Hartley, J., ed., *Strategies for Programmed Instruction: An Educational Technology.* London: Butterworths.

Eisner, E. W. (1967a). "Educational objectives: help or hindrance?" *School Review* 75, 250–60.

Eisner, E. W. (1967b). "A response to my critics", *School Review* 75, 227–82.

Eisner, E. W. (1969). "Instructional and Expressive Educational Objectives: Their Formulation and use in Curriculum", in Popham *et al., Instructional Objectives,* AERA Monograph No. 3. Chicago: Rand McNally.

Esbensen, T. (1968). *Working with Individualised Instruction.* Palo Alto, Calif.: Fearon.

Evans, J. (1968). "Behavioural Objectives are no Damn Good", in *Technology and*

Innovation in Education. New York: Praeger.

Flanagan, J. C. (1954). "The critical incident techniques", *Psychol. Bull.*, 51, 327–58.

Gagné, R. (1965). *The Conditions of Learning.* New York: Holt, Rinehart and Winston.

Gagné, R. (1967). "Curriculum Research and the Promotion of Learning", in *Perspectives of Curriculum Evaluation.* AERA Monograph I. Chicago: Rand McNally.

Gilbert, T. F. (1962). "Mathetics: the Technology of Education." Reprinted in *RECALL Supplement No. 1* (Longmac, 1969).

Goodman, P. (1962). *Compulsory Miseducation.* New York: Horizon Press.

Hauenstein, A. D. (1972). *Curriculum Planning for Behavioural Development.* Worthington, Ohio: Charles Jones.

Hartley, J. ed. (1972). *Strategies for Programmed Instruction: an Educational Technology.* London: Butterworths.

Hempel, C. G. (1965). "The Theoretician's Dilemma: A Study in the Logic of Theory Construction," in Hempel, C. G., *Aspects of Scientific Explanation.* Glencoe, III.: Free Press.

Holt, J. (1964). *How Children Fail.* London: Pitman.

Howes, V. M. (1970). *Individualisation of Instruction.* London: Macmillan.

Illich, I. D. (1971). *Deschooling Society.* New York: Harper and Row.

Kahn, H. (1962). *Thinking about the Unthinkable.* New York: Horizon Press.

Kahn, H. (1972). *The Prospects for Mankind.* Hudson Institute Report 111-1648/4-D.

Kemp, J. E. (1971). *Instructional Design.* Palo Alto, Calif.: Fearon.

Kibler, R. J., Barker, L. L. and Miles, D. T. (1970). *Behavioural Objectives and Instruction.* Rockleigh, N. J.: Allyn and Bacon.

Komisar, O. B. and McClellan, J. E. (1965). "Professor Arnstine and Programmed Instruction," *The Educational Forum.*

Kozol, J. (1967). *Death at an Early Age.* Boston: Houghton Mifflin.

Lewis, B. N. and Cook, J. A. (1969). "Toward a theory of telling," *Int. J. Man-Machine Studies* 1, 129–76.

McAshan, H. H. (1970). *Writing Behavioural Objectives.* New York: Harper and Row.

Macdonald-Ross, M. (1970). "Introductory Notes on Objectives, Assessment and Activities," *IET working paper No. 2,* The Open University, Bletchley, England.

Macdonald-Ross, M. (1972a). "Behavioural Objectives and the Structure of Knowledge," in Austwick, K. and Harris, N. D. C., eds., *Aspects of Educational Technology VI.* London: Pitmans.

Macdonald-Ross, M. (1972b). "The Problem of Representing Knowledge." Paper presented to Structural Learning Conference, Philadelphia (copies available from author).

Macdonald-Ross, M. (1972c). Review of Hartley, ed., "Strategies for Programmed Instruction: an Educational Technology," (Butterworths, 1972), in *Brit. J. Educational Technology,* 3:3, 246–49.

Macmillan, C. J. B. and McClellan, J. E. (1968). "Can and Should Means-Ends Reasoning be Used in Teaching?" in Macmillans and Nelson, eds., *Concepts of Teaching: Philosophical Essays.* Chicago: Rand McNally.

Mager, R. F. (1961). "On the sequencing of instructional content," *Psychological Reports* IX, 504–13.

Mager, R. F. (1962). *Preparing Instructional Objectives.* Palo Alto, Calif.: Fearon.

Mager, R. F. (1968). *Developing Attitude toward Learning.* Palo Alto, Calif.: Fearon.

Mager, R. F. (1972). *Goal Analysis.* Palo Alto, Calif.: Fearon.

Mager, R. F. and McCann, J. (1962). *Learner-Controlled Instruction.* Varian Associates.

Mager, R. F. and Beach, K. M. (1967). *Developing Vocational Instruction.* Palo Alto, Calif.: Fearon.

Mager, R. F. and Pipe, P. (1970). *Analysing Performance Problems.* Palo Alto, Calif.: Fearon.

Miller, R. B. (1962): "Analysis and Specification of Behaviour for Training," in Glaser, R., Ed., *Training Research and Education.* Science edition, John Wiley: New York.

Neill, A. S. (1962). *Summerhill.* London: Gollancz.

Noar, G. (1972). *Individualised Instruction: Every Child a Winner.* New York: Wiley.

Oakeshott, M. (1962). "Political Education," in Oakeshott, M., *Rationalism in Politics.* London: Methuen.

Odiorne, G. S. (1965). *Management by Objectives.* London: Pitman.

Odiorne, G. S. (1970). *Training by Objectives.* London: Macmillan.

Ozbekhan, H. (1969). "Toward a General Theory of Planning," in Jantsch, E., ed., *Perspectives of Planning,* OECD.

Ozbekhan, H. (1971). "Planning and Human Action," in Weiss, P., ed., *Hierarchically Organised Systems in Theory and Practice.* New York: Hafner.

Pask, G. (1972a). "A Fresh Look at Cognition and the Individual," *Int. J. Man-Machine Studies 4,* 211–16.

Pask, G. (1972b). "CASTE: A System for Exhibiting Learning Strategies and Regulating Uncertainty," *Int. J. Man-Machine Studies,* in press.

Pask, G. and Scott, B. C. E. (1972). "Learning Strategies and Individual Competence," *Int. J. Man-Machine Studies 4,* 217–53.

Popham, J. W. and Baker, E. L. (1970a). *Systematic Instruction.* Englewood Cliffs N. J.: Prentice-Hall.

Popham, W. J. and Baker, E. L. (1970b). *Establishing Instructional Goals.* Englewood Cliffs, N.J.: Prentice-Hall.

Popham, W. J., Eisner, E. W., Sullivan, H. J. and Tyler, L. L. (1969). *Instructional Objectives.* AERA Monographs on curriculum evaluation No. 3. Chicago: Rand McNally.

Popper, Sir K. R. (1945). *The Open Society and its Enemies, Vol. I. Plato, Vol. II Hegel and Marx,* London: Routledge and Kegan Paul.

Popper, Sir K. R. (1957). *The Poverty of Historicism.* London: Routledge and Kegan Paul.

Popper, Sir K. R. (1972). "Epistemology Without a Knowing Subject," in *Objective Knowledge.* Oxford: Oxford University Press.

Postman, N. and Weingartner, C. (1969). *Teaching as a Subversive Activity.* Delacorte.

Quade, E. S., ed. (1967). *Analysis for Military Decisions.* Chicago: Rand McNally.

Rapoport, A. (1964). *Strategy and Conscience.* New York: Harper and Row.

Reimer, E. (1971). *School is Dead.* Harmondsworth: Penguin.

Ross, A. (1968). *Directives and Norms.* London: Routledge and Kegan Paul.

Ryle, G. (1949). *The Concept of Mind.* London: Hutchinson.

Seymour, W. D. (1968). *Skills Analysis Training.* London: Pitman.

Stenhouse, L. (1971). "Some Limitations of the use of Objectives in Curriculum Research and Planning," *Paedagogica Europaea.*

Stones, E. and Anderson, D. (1972). *Educational Objectives and the Teaching of Educational Psychology.* London: Methuen.

Sund, R. S. and Picard, A. J. (1972). *Behavioural Objectives and Evaluational Measures: Science and Mathematics.* Columbus, Ohio: Merrill.

Tyler, L. L. (1969). "A Case History: Formulation of Objectives from a Psychoanalytic Framework," in Popham, W. J. *et al., Instructional Objectives.* AFRA Monograph No. 3. Chicago: Rand McNally.

Tyler, R. W. (1950). *Basic Principles of Curriculum and Instruction.* Chicago: University Press.

Tyler, R. W. (1964). "Some Persistent Questions on the Defining of Objectives," in Lindvall, C. M. ed., *Defining Educational Objectives.* Pittsburgh: University Press.

Vargas, J. S. (1972). *Writing Worthwhile Behavioural Objectives.* New York:

Harper and Row.
Vickers, Sir G. (1959). *The Undirected Society.* Toronto: University of Toronto Press.
Vickers, Sir G. (1965). *The Art of Judgment.* London: Chapman and Hall.
Vickers, Sir G. (1967). *Towards a Sociology of Management.* London: Chapman and Hall.
Vickers, Sir G. (1968). *Value Systems and Social Process.* London: Tavistock.
Vickers, Sir G. (1970). *Freedom in a Rocking Boat.* Harmondsworth: Penguin.
Weisgerber, R. A., ed. (1971a). *Developmental Efforts in Individualised Learning.* Peacock.
Weisgerber, R. A., ed. (1971b). *Perspectives in Individualised Learning.* Peacock.
Von Wright, G. H. (1963). *Norm and Action.* London: Routledge and Kegan Paul.

IV CURRICULUM EVALUATION

17. The Concept of Curriculum Evaluation

J.P. White

Source: J.P. White, *Journal of Curriculum Studies*, vol.3, No.2 (November 1971), pp.101-12.

There is no one single process of evaluation. White distinguishes empirical *evaluation, which is concerned with the efficiency of curricula towards stated ends and may be summative or formative in character, and* non-empirical *evaluation, in which curricular objectives are themselves evaluated. Non-empirical objectives need not be arbitrary and subjective, for objectives themselves ultimately have to be argued for. A further form of evaluation concerns itself with the internal logic and consistency of curriculum plans. Objectives are necessary to evaluation. Objectives which* are *behavioural are to be distinguished from objectives for which behaviour is evidence. Finally, evaluators may concern themselves with effects of given curricula, though such evaluation could never be sufficient as an account of a curriculum. For that purpose, all forms of evaluation have a part to play.*

"Curriculum evaluation" is a term used more and more in educational discussion. New curricula are being developed on every hand. These curricula have to be "evaluated". "Curriculum evaluators" are being appointed to current research projects. It is important, in the early days of a new large-scale educational venture such as the present curriculum reform movement, to make sure that the conceptual framework within which it is being undertaken is as clear as may be. This paper is a rough-hewn attempt at clarifying the concept of curriculum evaluation.

How does one find out what curriculum evaluation is? One way would be to go to a book like D. K. Wheeler's on *Curriculum Process*, for instance, and see what he has to say in his chapter on the topic.[1] Here it seems that evaluation is a phase in the process of constructing and reconstructing curricula. Its purpose is to see whether curriculum objectives are being, or have been, achieved[2]—so that modifications in them can be made if necessary. Evaluating is here, then, a part of *making* a curriculum.

But the word "evaluation" may have other meanings, besides this semi-technical one. The people who work for "Which?" are, I suppose, evaluating products. What they are doing is seeing if they are worth while buying, seeing how good they are in comparison with others. Evaluating something is assessing its value—or, to leave Latin altogether for Anglo-Saxon—it is seeing whether it is any *good*. Now things can be good in many different ways: people and actions may be morally good; paintings and poems can be aesthetically good; a knife or a car can be instrumentally good, i.e. as an efficient means to an end–and so forth. When we evaluate something, therefore, we can assess its worth from many points of view; a painting, for instance, can be evaluated financially–as a possible good investment–or aesthetically–as a possible candidate for a National Gallery.

Like anything else, a new curriculum can be evaluated in all sorts of ways. Some of these we can clearly leave out of the picture. A dictator might evaluate a history curriculum as better than its rivals as a means of inculcating obedience to the Party. A mercenary educational publisher might see a curriculum as likely to catch on and as a good means of increasing his profits. I take it we can eliminate points of view like these. For I assume that when educationists evaluate new curricula they are assessing their value largely from an educational point of view, rather than from a political or a financial one. I say "*largely* from an educational point of view", because there do seem to be situations when non-educational evaluations are required. If, for instance, curriculum A is being compared with curriculum B to see which is the better, and if there is no difference between A and B in the time in which children tend to complete either, or the degree to which they remember what they have learnt, etc., but curriculum A requires materials five times as costly as those in B, then, all in all, B may be said to be a better buy than A. Again one might compare *this* sort of curriculum-evaluation with a "Which?" report on, say, record-players. The prime consideration in buying a record-player is whether it does its job well–i.e. if it faithfully produces the sounds on the record; but a very important subsidiary consideration is how much it costs. Curriculum evaluation, similarly, must have educational criteria largely in mind, but cost and perhaps other factors cannot be omitted.

It might be worth following this analogy with "Which?" evaluations a little further. Just as private individuals want to know the overall best buy in record-players or hair-driers, so teachers, teacher-trainers, inspectors, etc., want to know what is the overall best buy in methods and curricula. Warburton and Southgate's recently published evaluation of I.T.A. as against traditional orthography is precisely the sort of thing required.[3] Of course, Warburton and Southgate were concerned with a reading scheme rather than with a new curriculum. *Their* evaluation problems were complex enough. No doubt comparisons between whole curricula will be even more complicated. But they will have to be made if the recent upsurge of interest in developing new curricula is not to be fruitless: we cannot just assume that "new" means "better".

The kind of evaluation I have just been describing–where one curriculum is compared with another against certain criteria–economy in time or money, etc., is largely empirical. It is not the only kind of empirical evaluation. There is also that described earlier by Wheeler, whose purpose is to see whether a curriculum under construction is achieving its objectives—to see, for instance, whether one designed in theory to teach such and such concepts to eleven-year-olds succeeds in practice in engaging with their interests and abilities and is not, say, too abstract or boring. Evaluation of the latter sort is sometimes called "formative" or "on-going"; it is a part of *making* a curriculum, not of putting it through a Which?-type test. The latter is an example of what is sometimes called "summative" or "final evaluation". Problems arise about where one draws the line between "formative" and "summative" evaluation—and perhaps there is no hard-and-fast line to draw. But all I want to stress here is that these both proceed by empirical observation.

I bring them together in this way to distinguish them from other forms of evaluation which are *not empirical*. Both the empirical types mentioned presuppose that the curriculum under investigation has clear objectives and that criteria can be laid down in terms of pupil behaviour for when these objectives have been attained. But suppose that curriculum A has been evaluated both in a Wheeler-type way and in a Which?-type way and has turned out to be more economical in time and money etc., than curricula B and C. Would this show that it was a good buy? Not necessarily. For nothing has been said yet to show that its *objectives* are any good. One curriculum may be better than another in getting children to learn off all the "capes and bays" of Europe. It may be good instrumentally as a means to this objective, but whether it is good *educationally*—i.e. whether its objectives are worth while—is another matter. We are back with the extreme generality and many-sidedness of the word "Good"—and in reaching this point, we see that the term "curriculum evaluation" can be taken in quite another sense, where now it is the objectives themselves which are being evaluated, to see if they are educationally any good.

How does one do this? What methods can the curriculum evaluator use? Wheeler has little doubt that these are empirical. He writes (p. 284): "The answer to the question 'What, in our rapidly-changing society, is of most worth to children and youth?' is still too often given in terms of 'philosophical' orientation and traditional practice. As more becomes known about human growth and social interaction, objectives must more and more be derived from facts, principles and theories which relate to these areas. Behaviour, learning process, social and individual needs, all give rise to theoretical models . . ." As often, it is not always clear quite what Wheeler has in mind in this passage, but it is at least clear that he thinks that further research in the human sciences, in psychology and sociology, will provide the criteria of curricular worthwhileness that we are looking for. But how can empirical research alone determine what should be taught? No empirical fact can alone justify a conclusion that something is right or ought to be done (in this case, that the objectives of curriculum x are educationally all right). For how do you pass from an empirical statement, about something which is the case (and contains no value-term) to a statement which *does* contain a "right" or an "ought"? There is just no argument here: it simply cannot be done.

This fact is often obscured, as in Wheeler's case, by a reference to "social" or "individual needs". This appeal to needs is a favourite among curriculum-makers: children must learn such and such because they have a need to earn a living, to develop a sense of responsibility, etc.– or because society needs an adaptable labour force etc. etc. There is no logical objection to defending objectives by reference to needs, as long as it is clear that individual needs cannot be discovered by psychology, or social needs by sociology. Needs are not observable features of individuals or of societies. The term "need" is necessarily value-laden. To say that a hungry man needs food is not only to say that without food he will die: it is also to imply that dying would be a bad thing, that he ought to keep alive. If we say that society needs an adaptable labour force, this is to assume that whatever this adaptable labour force is needed for–e.g. high productivity or a higher standard of living–is a good thing. So while we may agree with Wheeler that curriculum objectives may be justified by reference to needs, this is not to accept his belief that everything can now be left to empirical science; for we are still left with value statements which themselves have to be justified.[4]

Statements about individual and social needs are easily translatable into statements about what is good for individuals or societies, or, if you like, about what is in their interests. We are now clearly in the realm of values. And at this point some curriculum theorists see the red light. Wheeler, again, for instance. Contradicting rather what he says elsewhere, he writes that "this (evaluation) process itself, because it involves value-judgments, must necessarily be more subjective than objective" (p. 273). Value-judgments, it seems, are largely subjective matters. If so, it is understandable that some curriculum theorists tend to shy away from evaluating objectives. For any evaluation–in terms, say, of whether the stated objectives are in the pupils' or society's interests–will necessarily reflect the evaluator's own subjective beliefs about these interests; and what right has any man to impose his personal preferences in this way, especially when the social consequences of such imposition might be so immense?

While this stance is admirable in its liberalism, one should not overlook its unfortunate consequences. For curriculum objectives themselves imply value-judgments–that it is *good*, from some point of view or other, for children to learn such and such. But if all value-judgments are subjective, the curriculum objectives must simply express *someone's* personal preferences, whether those of the development team themselves, or, if already existing objectives are being used, those of others who have managed to influence curricula in their own preferred directions. *Someone* is going to have to decide what things shall be taught; and if there can be no independent, objective evaluation of such decisions, it seems that it will be the strongest pressure groups which will do this.

This is an unwelcome conclusion, but it seems the only one open. We cannot hope to find the objectivity we are looking for by making the evaluation of objectives empirical; and given that such evaluation is value-laden, it seems to be necessarily subjective and therefore not worth doing. Laissez-faire seems the only alternative. If a pressure group is strong enough to get the Schools Council to promote a new curriculum to teach Spanish from the age of six or housecraft for less able thirteen-year-old girls, so be it: we can only pray that, *per impossibile*, some Invisible Hand will regulate what happens for the pupils' and the common good.

But there is no reason for such despair. There is no reason to assume *a priori* that any evaluation of curricular objectives must reflect mere personal preferences. The general proposition on which this despair rests—that all value judgments are subjective, i.e. cannot, in the last analysis, be rationally defended—itself must be argued for: it cannot just be assumed to be true. To look into all the arguments pro and con would be a long job, and something I could not do here. But it is important, once again, to stress the great *variety* of kinds of value-judgment that can be made.[5] Whether one can say objectively whether something is a good knife is one question; whether Guinness is (truly) good for you is another; and whether one can determine on rational grounds the Good Life for Man is a third. Each type of goodness—and there are many more than these—must be separately examined.

Mention of the Good Life for Man raises a further point. I would be prepared to argue that value judgments in this area are to a large extent subjective. Different individuals may have very different ideals of life: in saying that I prefer a life of comfort to a life of action or contemplation, I am expressing a personal preference: I am sceptical about how far individual ideals can be objectively rated, as better or worse. Now a curriculum theorist holding a similar view *might* conclude that value-judgments about curricular objectives are likewise subjective, on the following argument. Any curriculum ought to be at least in the interests of the child; but if one cannot say objectively—i.e. on the basis of reasons that any rational man would accept—what sort of life a child should lead when he grows up, how can one say what it is in his interests to learn at school? But a reply to this argument is that subjectivity about what life a person ought to lead does not entail subjectivity about what he ought to learn at school. Indeed, the clearer it becomes that we *cannot* predetermine the Good Life for others, the clearer it seems to become that we ought to ensure that by the time he grows up a child can understand the nature of all the different activities which *might*—or might not—form a part of the Good Life, as he sees it, so that he is in a position to decide himself what life to lead. This, as I have argued elsewhere[6], would give one a good reason for insisting on the compulsory inclusion in every child's curriculum of those activities—mathematics, physics, the arts etc.—which, unlike playing football, or cooking, or speaking French, cannot be understood at all from the outside, i.e. without actually engaging in them. Being a subjectivist about the Good Life is thus compatible with being a rather tough-minded supporter of the compulsory teaching of the "disciplines": indeed, one position leads pretty directly to the other. Subjectivism in this area does *not* imply, as some appear to think, leaving the child as free as possible to decide what things he wants to learn.

Whatever the rights and wrongs of these particular arguments, my main point here is that in assessing curricular objectives, one should not just *assume* that objectivity will be impossible. One must simply work through the arguments presented for the objectives, see if they are valid, and press for further arguments to support the premisses on which they rest. It is only when people begin to discuss the rationale for curriculum objectives, only when they begin to press the argument back to more fundamental values and assumptions, that we shall be able to judge how objective or subjective the issues are. It is remarkable how little of this *fundamental* questioning there has been in the recent movement for curriculum reform. Should less able children learn a foreign language? Should anyone be made to learn one? Is one purpose of R.E. to promote moral development? To what extent is "integration" of curriculum-areas a good thing? Should so-called "Newsom" children be given a non-academic curriculum? Are there any grounds for assuming that the things one child has learnt by the time he leaves school should be any different from what any other school-leaver has learnt? Etc., etc. Curriculum developers may well discuss such questions in private; but there has been very little public debate on them, at least at a more than superficial level. There should be more. Only then could one see how far *good* reasons can be given for different curriculum proposals. I am willing to bet that the area in which rational, objective assessment is possible is larger than is sometimes believed. (This is assuming that the participants to the discussion are not trammelled by a vested interest, e.g. in a particular subject, but are prepared to question the value of their own discipline (or whatever) in a serious attempt to work out what the content of education should be.)

I have mentioned so far a number of different sorts of curriculum evaluation: two empirical sorts–the on-going check on objectives and the summative comparison of one curriculum with another; and one non-empirical sort, the evaluation of objectives in terms of their educational value. All these forms of evaluation presuppose one thing in common: that the curriculum under investigation has clear objectives. If it has not, then it makes no sense either to ask whether they are being attained (or are attained, e.g. more quickly than by another curriculum) or to ask whether they are educationally respectable.

All this indicates that there is room for another–another non-empirical –form of evaluation. This will review the internal logic of the new curriculum, presumably at a quite early stage in the development project. The questions asked will be: has the curriculum got clear, behaviourally-testable objectives? If so, is the curriculum internally organized, in its different parts, in such a way that it is likely to achieve these objectives? As already indicated, this latter question is partly empirical: one cannot tell simply from a blueprint whether children will learn through it. But it is not wholly empirical: an historian could tell without experiment, just by reference, that a curriculum which consisted, say, in rote-learning certain historical names and dates could never succeed in its objective of getting children to understand different historical interpretations of the causes of the Russian Revolution. There is room, therefore, for experts in a discipline to assess whether the material and the order in which it is presented are prima facie likely to promote the objectives.

What, now, of the other job just mentioned, of assessing whether or not the objectives themselves are clear? This is clearly a task of major importance. It is especially important, I would suggest, as far as many of the Schools Council's curriculum schemes are concerned. This applies particularly to some of the schemes produced for the Young School Leaver. Working Paper No. 11, "Society and the Young School Leaver", is one example. I have described elsewhere[7] how difficult it is to see just what it is aiming at; that one moment it looks like a newfangled means to promote the oldfangled end of producing an obedient and contented proletariat and the next it seems like a rather muddled attempt to get some sociology on to the curriculum. It would not be difficult to take other such curricula to pieces in this way, the one entitled *An Approach through Religious Education*, for instance.[8] I am aware that these are only working papers, not fully elaborated curricula. Perhaps it is unfair to make these charges when one is very much on the sidelines; but it does seem, at least to this outside observer, that some of the Schools Council's projects could well be improved in the clarity with which they explain what they are about. This is not unconnected with the earlier points I made, about the need to evaluate the objectives of particular curricula in the light of reflection on more general educational values. The Schools Council, as far as I am aware, has done very little fundamental thinking on what the curriculum as a whole should be like: if anything, it tended, in its early days, to take over a rather traditional framework of assumptions, dating back, through the Newsom Report, to the elementary tradition of prewar times.[9] It is not surprising, if fundamental value-issues are not thought through, that the objectives of specific curricula are so often blurred or woolly. Let us hope that things will not always be like this.

One reason why the objectives of many of the Young School Leaver projects are not clear is that it is uncertain quite who the Young School Leaver is. When I first looked at these schemes, I imagined they were short-term solutions to the problem of educating those fourteen or fifteen year-old children of low ability who are anxious to leave school as soon as possible. But it seems from the Foreword to Working Paper No. 14 that they are to be the bases of "relevant and useful five year courses for pupils leaving school at sixteen". The Young School Leaver is thus identified,

I take it, at eleven, not in his last year or so. It is crucially important to be clear who the Young School Leaver is meant to be. If he is the pupil in his last year or so, there is a short-term problem of knowing what to do with him. (Whether solutions to the problem should become *institutionalized* is another matter. It would be disastrous if last year curricula of this sort came to structure the whole of secondary education.) If he is being selected at *eleven*, however, to follow curricula designed on the assumption that he will *not* be staying on beyond sixteen, this is just as educationally indefensible as the old elementary system: it is closing doors for the child, not opening them, shunting him off along the downhill track. I suggest that this ambiguity in the expression "Young School Leaver" helps to account for the obscurity of purpose of several of these schemes.

The general point I wish to make here is that curricula, if they are to be evaluated in any way, must have clear objectives. *A fortiori*, they must have objectives. It might seem that this is a truism. But apparently it is not: some would wish to question it. Charity James, for instance, argues explicitly in her book *Young Lives at Stake* against planning curricula in terms of objectives.[10] Her main argument is that Bloom's "Taxonomy", which she considers the "subtlest enterprise in this field", is not very helpful and so, by implication, if this will not do, what will? But this is a poor argument. The "Taxonomy" is an attempt to classify possible *sorts* of objectives, in a highly abstract, subject-neutral fashion. How could a mere classification possibly help one to select which objectives to go for in a new chemistry of history curriculum? If objectives cannot be derived from empirical investigation, neither can they be derived from a logical classification of objectives. But the fact that Bloom's "Taxonomy" cannot be used for this purpose does not show that planning in terms of objectives is useless. How else, indeed, could one plan?

Charity James is not alone in her opposition to objectives. She keeps company in this with Lawrence Stenhouse. He wrote in a recent description of his Humanities Project in *Education Canada*.

> "The main interest of our design is the absence of behavioural objectives from the conceptualization and planning of our curriculum. Any sophisticated worker is bound to be aware of the limitations of a design directed towards specified terminal student behaviour. Objectives are merely a simplifying device to help us choose from the range of hypotheses we could put forward about the effects of a curriculum innovation in a school or system."[11]

This passage, in its apparent conflation of "objective" with "behavioural objective", provokes a question of relevance not only to the Humanities Project but to curriculum development in general: are all curriculum objectives behavioural? To answer it, let us look more closely at the phrase "behavioural objectives". This could mean one of two things: (i) objectives which themselves *consist in* pupils' behaving in certain ways; (ii) objectives whose attainment is *tested by* observing pupils behaving in certain ways. It is important to make this distinction. The objective of an elocution course may be to make one speak in such and such ways. Here the objective is "behavioural" in both senses, (i) and (ii). Not only this: but the particular behaviour aimed at is also the behaviour observed in testing. This need not always be the case. One objective of a course in clear thinking, for instance, may be to get students to test the validity of arguments which people put to them. The objective here is likewise "behavioural" in sense (i), but the behaviour here—the pupils' reflection on the validity of arguments—is not *observable*, as in the elocution case. On the other hand, any *testing* of whether this objective has been reached will necessarily go by what the pupil can be *observed* to do—e.g. his verbal or written accounts of fallacies. The clear-thinking course has thus a "behavioural objective" in both senses, (i) and (ii), just like the elocution course; unlike the latter, however, the behaviour referred to in (i) differs from the behaviour in (ii). It would be wrong, however, to think that if a curriculum has "behavioural objectives" in sense (ii), it must also have them in sense (i), either observably or non-observably. The objective of a course in poetry appreciation may be to get pupils to come to respond aesthetically to certain poems. It is doubtful how far aesthetic responses to works of art should be called forms of "behaviour". Behaviour is something active, intention guided. This is equally true of observable behaviour, like walking down the street, as of unobservable, like solving a mathematics problem in one's head. But aesthetic response is, like other emotional reactions, a *passive* rather than an active phenomenon. If so, the objective in question is not "behavioural" in sense (i). Neither are other likely curriculum objectives. Knowing that such and such is the case may well be a curriculum objective; but a person who knows something is not necessarily *doing* anything. But a curriculum can lack "behavioural objectives" in sense (i), but have them in sense (ii). Aesthetic response may not be a form of behaviour, but whether someone has learnt to respond aesthetically in the way required can only be tested by what he can be observed to say or write, etc. The same is true of knowing.

Need a new curriculum have "behavioural objectives"? It depends on the sense of the term. Objectives need not be "behavioural" in sense (i), as we have seen. But it does not follow that there should be no "behavioural objectives" in sense (ii). On the contrary. Any new curriculum must be aiming at changing pupils (not necessarily changing their *behaviour*) in some ways. Whether or not it succeeds in this aim can only be discovered by observing pupils' behaviour, to see, e.g., whether they have acquired such and such items of knowledge, capacities, responses, etc. Any curriculum should have objectives; though these need only be "behavioural" in sense (ii).

It is thus easy to see how someone might come to believe that new curricula need not be planned in terms of objectives. The germ of truth in one's premisses might be that objectives need not be "behavioural" in sense (i). From this it would be easy to slide to the–false–proposition that they need not be "behavioural" in sense (ii). If one then assumed that all objectives were behavioural, one could quickly end up holding that curricula need not have objectives of any sort. It would be unfortunate if this conclusion–however it was arrived at–became widely accepted in curriculum development circles: for, as stated earlier, a curriculum without (behaviourally testable) objectives cannot be evaluated in any of the ways discussed so far.

I have described a number of different forms of curriculum evaluation, and it might be thought that the few examples we have seen to date of evaluation projects in this country would fit under one of these rubrics or another. But several of the projects described in J. D. Williams's article on evaluation in H. J. Butcher's book on *Educational Research*[12] do not fit. Clare Burstall's evaluation of French teaching in primary schools studies the *effects* of such teaching on other areas of learning, e.g. on pupils' attainment in English and arithmetic. Williams's own study of modern mathematics tests the hypothesis that learning modern mathematics at an early age will raise performance on intelligence tests. Both of these, then, examine certain *effects* of a new curriculum–which is a different form of evaluation from those mentioned.

It also raises new difficulties. By what criteria does one select the possible effects one wants to study, given that there are innumerable such effects? Why select performance in intelligence, English tests etc. in evaluating new French and mathematics curricula? Some reason must be given for this beyond the obvious fact that it is relatively easy to do empirical research of this sort. The same goes for projects examining the effects of a curriculum on changes in children's attitudes or motivation, where these are not part of the curriculum's original objectives. What is from a research point of view a manageable study is not, for that reason alone, a useful one.

This is not necessarily to exclude all evaluation of effects. Some may be very valuable: one would have to look into a project's rationale to see this. But it is clear, at least, that it is *not enough* to evaluate a curriculum by its effects, however useful this evaluation is. This brings me back to the main point which I wish to underline in this paper, and with which I shall end. There is no single "process" of curriculum evaluation: there are many different forms of it. All (or most) of them can and should play a part in assessing whether or not a new curriculum is any good, whether or not it is worth teachers' while adopting it. This, I take it, is the ultimate point of all curriculum evaluation. A curriculum has not been positively evaluated in this full sense until it has been shown to have clear objectives and appropriate means to achieve them; to have objectives which have been proved against all comers to be educationally respectable; to connect with the abilities of those pupils for whom it is designed; and to be more efficient than rivals in the field. Only then can it get its tick. There is a distinct danger that if one keeps the term "evaluation" only for a particular *kind* of evaluation, e.g. for Wheeler's on-going, feedback evaluation, or for evaluation of effects, the result may be confusion. People may confuse the broader with the restricted sense. It may then seem that as long as a curriculum has been evaluated (in one of the restricted senses) it has been shown to be worth adopting. But this simply is not so. Whether it is any good or not can only be seen when *all* the different kinds of evaluation just described have been carried out.

For many of the distinctions I have drawn in this paper I am indebted to Michael Scriven's recent article on "The Methodology of Evaluation".[13] And I would like to conclude by emphasizing, with Scriven, the importance and the complexity of curriculum evaluation. If all the different roles described are to be filled by the same person, he will have to be equipped not only with skills of empirical research, and a knowledge of relevant aspects of the economics of education, of costing, for instance, but also with a knowledge of the subject matter to be taught and some experience of teaching it. A philosophical training would also be useful, though not perhaps a *sine qua non*, for assessing the overall clarity of curriculum objectives and the arguments for or against their educational value. Also, if all these roles are to be filled by one person, he will be both—as an "on-going" evaluator—a part of the development team, and, in his other roles, an independent judge of its activities, the guardian of teachers' and pupils' interests, the man who sees that public money tied up in these schemes is well spent. It seems too much to expect one person to carry all these roles. How far is there a case for a division of labour here—into, say, (*a*) on-going evaluators (*b*) non-empirical evaluators of the clarity and worthwhileness of objectives and (*c*) summative evaluators on the "Which?" model?

Notes

1 D. K. Wheeler, *Curriculum Process* (University of London Press, 1967) Ch. 10, cf. also Ch. 2.
2 This definition of evaluation is common in recent discussions of the subject. See, e.g., J. F. Kerr, *Changing the Curriculum* (University of London Press, 1968) p. 21.
3 F. W. Warburton and Vera Southgate, *ITA: an Independent Evaluation* (John Murray & W. R. Chambers, 1969).
4 For a further "need" see ' "Need" in Education', *British Journal of Educational Studies*, November 1966.
5 G. H. von Wright, *The Varieties of Goodness*, (London, Kegan Paul, 1963).
6 "Learn as you Will", *New Society*, 4.12.67.
7 "Instruction in Obedience", *New Society*, 2.5.68.
8 "Humanities for the Young School Leaver. An approach through Religious Education", (Schools Council, 1969). Cf. also "An approach through History", (Schools Council, 1969).

9 Cf. my 'The Curriculum Mongers', *New Society*, 6.3.69.
10 C. James, *Young Lives at Stake* (London, Collins, 1968).
11 L. Stenhouse, "Handling Controversial Issues in the Classroom" in *Education Canada*, December, 1969.
12 H. J. Butcher, *Educational Research in Britain*, (University of London Press, 1968).
13 M. Scriven, 'The Methodology of Evaluation', in A.E.R.A. Monographs No. 1, *Perspectives of Curriculum Evaluation* (Chicago, Rand McNally, 1967).

18. Course Improvement Through Evaluation

L.J. Cronbach

Source: L.J. Cronbach, *Teachers College Record*, vol. 64 (1963). pp. 672-83.

There are important distinctions to be made in considering the relationship between curriculum evaluation and decision-taking. Decisions about individuals and administrative decisions rely on evaluation data. Cronbach argues, however, that evaluation is also a fundamental part of curriculum development. The greatest service of evaluation is to identify aspects of a course where revision is necessary. Evaluation, therefore, needs to be formative and ongoing in this context. Measurement procedures will necessarily vary with the purposes for which they are adopted. For course improvement, the direct comparison of one course with another should not be allowed to dominate evaluation. Rather the deployment of a wide battery of techniques is necessary to describe and assess the outcomes of courses.

The national interest in improving education has generated several highly important projects to improve curricula, particularly at the secondary-school level. In conferences of directors of "course content improvement" programs sponsored by the National Science Foundation, questions about evaluation are frequently raised.[1] Those who inquire about evaluation have motives, ranging from sheer scientific curiosity about class-room events to a desire to assure a sponsor that money has been well spent. While the curriculum developers sincerely wish to use the skills of evaluation specialists, I am not certain that they have a clear picture of what evaluation can do and should try to do. And, on the other hand, I am becoming convinced that some techniques and habits of thought of the evaluation specialist are ill suited to current curriculum studies. To serve these studies, what philosophy and methods of evaluation are required? And particularly, how must we depart from the familiar doctrines and rituals of the testing game?

Programmatic Decisions

To draw attention to its full range of functions, we may define "evaluation" broadly as the *collection and use of information to make decisions about an educational program*. The program may be a set of instructional materials distributed nationally, the instructional activities of a single school, or the educational experiences of a single pupil. Many types of decisions are to be made, and many varieties of information are useful. It becomes immediately apparent that evaluation is a diversified activity and that no one set of principles will suffice for all situations. But measurement specialists have so concentrated upon one process–the preparation of pencil-and-paper achievement tests for assigning scores to individual pupils–that the principles pertinent to that process have somehow become enshrined as *the* principles of evaluation. "Tests," we are told, "should fit the content of the curriculum." Also, "only those evaluation procedures should be used that yield reliable scores." These and other hallowed principles are not entirely appropriate to evaluation for course improvement. Before proceeding to support this contention, I wish to distinguish among purposes of evaluation and to relate them to historical developments in testing and curriculum making.

We may separate three types of decisions for which evaluation is used:

1. Course improvement: deciding what instructional materials and methods are satisfactory and where change is needed.
2. Decisions about individuals: identifying the needs of the pupil for the sake of planning his instruction, judging pupil merit for purposes of selection and grouping, acquainting the pupil with his own progress and deficiencies.
3. Administrative regulation: judging how good the school system is, how good individual teachers are, etc.

Course improvement is set apart by its broad temporal and geographical reference; it involves the modification of recurrently used materials and methods. Developing a standard exercise to overcome a misunderstanding would be course improvement, but deciding whether a certain pupil should work through that exercise would be an individual decision. Administrative regulation likewise is local in effect, whereas an improvement in a course is likely to be pertinent wherever the course is offered.

It was for the sake of course improvement that systematic evaluation was first introduced. When that famous muck-raker Joseph Rice gave the same spelling test in a number of American schools, and so gave the first impetus to the educational testing movement, he was interested in evaluating a curriculum. Crusading against the extended spelling drills that then loomed large in the school schedule–"the spelling grind"–Rice collected evidence of their worthlessness so as to provoke curriculum revision. As the testing movement developed, however, it took on a different function.

The Turning Tides

The greatest expansion of systematic achievement testing occurred in the 1920s. At that time, the content of any course was taken pretty much as established and beyond criticism save for small shifts of topical emphasis. At the administrator's direction, standard tests covering the curriculum were given to assess the efficiency of the teacher or the school system.

Such administrative testing fell into disfavor when used injudiciously and heavyhandedly in the 1920s and 1930s. Administrators and accrediting agencies fell back upon descriptive features of the school program in judging adequacy. Instead of collecting direct evidence of educational impact, they judged schools in terms of size of budget, student-staff ratio, square feet of laboratory space, and the number of advanced credits accumulated by the teacher. This tide, it appears, is about to turn. On many university campuses, administrators wanting to know more about their product are installing "operations research offices." Testing directed toward quality control seems likely to increase in the lower schools as well, as is most forcefully indicated by the statewide testing recently ordered by the California legislature.

After 1930 or thereabouts, tests were given almost exclusively for judgments about individuals—to select students for advanced training, to assign marks within a class, and to diagnose individual competences and deficiencies. For any such decisions, one wants precise and valid comparisons of one individual with other individuals or with a standard. Much of test theory and test technology has been concerned with making measurements precise. Important though precision is for most decisions about individuals, I shall argue that in evaluating courses we need not struggle to obtain precise scores for individuals.

While measurers have been well content with the devices used to make scores precise, they have been less complacent about validity. Prior to 1935, the pupil was examined mostly on factual knowledge and mastery of fundamental skills. Tyler's research and writings of that period developed awareness that higher mental processes are not evoked by simple factual tests, and that instruction that promotes factual knowledge may not promote—indeed, may interfere with— other more important educational outcomes. Tyler, Lindquist, and their students demonstrated that tests can be designed to measure such general educational outcomes as ability to comprehend scientific method. Whereas a student can prepare for a factual test only through a course of study that includes the facts tested, many different courses of study may promote the same *general* understandings and attitudes. In evaluating today's new curricula, it will clearly be important to appraise the student's general educational growth, which curriculum developers say is more important than mastery of the specific lessons presented. Note, for example, that the Biological Sciences Curriculum Study offers three courses with substantially different "subject matter" as alternative routes to much the same educational ends.

Although some instruments capable of measuring general outcomes were prepared during the 1930s, they were never very widely employed. The prevailing philosophy of the curriculum, particularly among "progressives," called for developing a program to fit local requirements, capitalizing on the capacities and experiences of local pupils. The faith of the 1920s in a "standard" curriculum was replaced by a faith that the best learning would result from teacher-pupil planning in each classroom. Since each teacher or each class could choose different content and even different objectives, this philosophy left little place for standard testing.

Tests as Training

Many evaluation specialists came to see test development as a strategy for training the teacher in service, so that the process of test making came to be valued more than the test—or the test data—that resulted. The following remarks by Bloom (*2*) are representative of a whole school of thought:[2]

> The criterion for determining the quality of a school and its educational functions would be the extent to which it achieves the objectives it has set for itself. . . . Our experiences suggest that unless the school has translated the objectives into specific and operational definitions, little is likely to be done about the objectives. They remain pious hopes and platitudes. . . . Participation of the teaching staff in selecting as well as constructing evaluation instruments has resulted in improved instruments on one hand and, on the other hand, it has resulted in clarifying the objectives of instruction and in making them real and meaningful to teachers. . . . When teachers have actively participated in defining objectives and in selecting or constructing evaluation instruments, they return to the learning problems with great vigor and remarkable creativity. . . . Teachers who have become committed to a set of educational objectives which they thoroughly understand respond by developing a variety of learning experiences which are as diverse and as complex as the situation requires.

Thus, "evaluation" becomes a local and beneficial teacher-training activity. The benefit is attributed to thinking about what data to collect. Little is said about the actual use of test results: one has the impression that when test-making ends, the test itself is forgotten. Certainly, there is little enthusiasm for refining tests so that they can be used in other schools, for to do so would be to rob those teachers of the benefits of working out their own objectives and instruments.

Bloom and Tyler describe both curriculum making and evaluation as integral parts of classroom instruction, which is necessarily decentralized. This outlook is far from that of "course improvement." The current national curriculum studies assume that curriculum making can be centralized. They prepare materials to be used in much the same way by teachers everywhere. It is assumed that having experts draft materials, and revising these after tryout, produces better instructional activities than the local teacher would be likely to devise. In this context, it seems wholly appropriate to have most tests prepared by a central staff and to have results returned to that staff to guide further course improvement.

When evaluation is carried out in the service of course improvement, the chief aim is to ascertain what effects the course has—that is, what changes it produces in pupils. This is not to inquire merely whether the course is effective or ineffective. Outcomes of instruction are multidimensional, and a satisfactory investigation will map out the effects of the course along these dimensions separately. To agglomerate many types of post-course performance into a single score is a mistake, because failure to achieve one objective is masked by success in another direction. Moreover, since a composite score embodies (and usually conceals) judgments about the importance of the various outcomes, only a report that treats the outcomes separately can be useful to educators who have different value hierarchies.

The greatest service evaluation can perform is to identify aspects of the course where revision is desirable. Those responsible for developing a course would like to present evidence that their course is effective. They are intrigued by the idea of having an "independent testing agency" render a judgment on their product. But to call in the evaluator only upon the completion of course development, to confirm what has been done, is to offer him a menial role and to make meager use of his services. To be influential in course improvement, evidence must become available midway in curriculum development, not in the home stretch, when the developer is naturally reluctant to tear open a supposedly finished body of materials and techniques. Evaluation, used to improve the course while it is still fluid, contributes more to improvement of education than evaluation used to appraise a product already placed on the market.

Effects and Effectiveness

Insofar as possible, evaluation should be used to understand how the course produces its effects and what parameters influence its effectiveness. It is important to learn, for example, that the outcome of programmed instruction depends very much upon the attitude of the teacher; indeed, this may be more important than to learn that on the average such instruction produces slightly better or worse results than conventional instruction.

Hopefully, evaluation studies will go beyond reporting on this or that course and help us to understand educational learning. Such insight will, in the end, contribute to the development of all courses rather than just the course under test. In certain of the new curricula, there are data to suggest that aptitude measures correlate much less with end-of-course achievement than they do with achievement on early units. This finding is not well confirmed, but it is highly significant if true. If it is true for the new curricula and only for them, it has one implication; if the same effect appears in traditional courses, it means something else. Either way, it provides food for thought for teachers, counselors, and theorists. Evaluation studies should generate knowledge about the nature of the abilities that constitute educational goals. Twenty years after the Eight-Year Study of the Progressive Education Association, its testing techniques are in good repute, but we still know very little about what these instruments measure. Consider "Application of Principles in Science." Is this in any sense a unitary ability? Or has the able student only mastered certain principles one by one? Is the ability demonstrated on a test of this sort more prognostic of any latter achievement than is factual knowledge? Such questions ought to receive substantial attention, although to the makers of any one course they are of only peripheral interest.

The aim to compare one course with another should not dominate plans for evaluation. To be sure, decision makers have to choose between courses, and any evaluation report will be interpreted in part comparatively. But formally designed experiments, pitting one course against another, are rarely definitive enough to justify their cost. Differences between average test scores resulting from different courses are usually small relative to the wide differences among and within classes taking the same course. At best, an experiment never does more than compare the present version of one course with the present version of another. A major effort to bring the losing contender nearer to perfection would be very likely to reverse the verdict of the experiment.

Any failure to equate the classes taking the competing courses will jeopardize the interpretation of an experiment—and such failures are almost inevitable. In testing a drug, we know that valid results cannot be obtained without a double-blind control in which the doses for half the subjects are inert placebos; the placebo and the drug look alike, so that neither doctor nor patient knows who is receiving medication. Without this control, the results are useless even when the state of the patient is checked by completely objective indices. In an educational experiment, it is difficult to keep pupils unaware that they are an experimental group. And it is quite impossible to neutralize the biases of the teacher as those of the doctor are neutralized in the double-blind design. It is thus never certain whether any observed advantage is attributable to the educational innovation as such, or to the greater energy that teachers and students put forth when a method is fresh and "experimental." Some have contended that any course, even the most excellent, loses much of its potency as soon as success enthrones it as "the traditional method."

Weakness of Comparisons

Since group comparisons give equivocal results, I believe that a formal study should be designed primarily to determine the post-course performance of a well-described group with respect to many important objectives and side effects. Ours is a problem like that of the engineer examining a new automobile. He can set himself the task of defining its performance characteristics and its dependability. It would be merely distracting to put his question in the form, "Is this car better or worse than the competing brand?" Moreover, in an experiment where the treatments compared differ in a dozen respects, no understanding is gained from the fact that the experiment shows a numerical advantage in favor of the new course. No one knows which of the ingredients is responsible for the advantage. More analytic experiments are much more useful than field trials applying markedly dissimilar treatments to different groups. Small-scale, well controlled studies can profitably be used to compare alternative versions of the same course; in such a study, the differences between treatments are few enough and well enough defined that the results have explanatory value.

The three purposes—course improvement, decisions about individuals, and administrative regulation—call for measurement procedures having somewhat different qualities. When a test will be used to make an administrative judgment on the individual teacher, it is necessary to measure thoroughly and with conspicuous fairness; such testing, if it is to cover more than one outcome, becomes extremely time consuming. In judging a course, however, one can make satisfactory interpretations from data collected on a sampling basis, with no pretense of measuring thoroughly the accomplishments of any one class. A similar point is to be made about testing for decisions about individuals. A test of individuals must be conspicuously fair and extensive enough to provide a dependable score for each person. But if the performance will not influence the fate of the individual, we can ask him to perform tasks for which the course has not directly prepared him, and we can use techniques that would be prohibitively expensive if applied in a manner thorough enough to measure each person reliably.

Evaluation is too often visualized as the administration of a formal test, an hour or so in duration, at the close of a course. But there are many other methods for examining pupil performance, and pupil attainment is not the only basis for appraising a course.

It is quite appropriate to ask scholars whether the statements made in the course are consistent with the best contemporary knowledge. This is a sound and even a necessary procedure. One may go on to evaluate the pedagogy of the new course by soliciting opinions, but here there is considerable hazard. If the opinions are based on some preconception about teaching method, the findings will be controversial and very probably misleading. There are no theories of pedagogy so well established that one can say, without tryout, what will prove educative.

Systematic Observation

One can accept the need for a pragmatic test of the curriculum and still employ opinions as a source of evidence. During the tryout stages of curriculum making, one relies heavily on the teachers' reports of pupil accomplishment—"Here they had trouble"; "This they found dull"; "Here they needed only half as many exercises as were provided," etc. This is behaviour observation even though unsystematic, and it is of great value. The reason for shifting to systematic observation is that this is more impartial, more public, and sometimes more penetrating. While I bow to the historian or mathematician as a judge of the technical soundness of course content, I do not agree that the experienced history or mathematics teacher who tries out a course gives the best possible judgment on its effectiveness. Scholars have too often deluded themselves about their effectiveness as teachers–particularly, have they too often accepted parroting of words as evidence of insight–for their unaided judgment to be trusted. Systematic observation is costly, and introduces some delay between the moment of teaching and the feedback of results. Hence, systematic observation will never be the curriculum developer's sole source of evidence. Systematic data collection becomes profitable in the intermediate stages of curriculum development, after the more obvious bugs in early drafts have been dealt with.

The approaches to evaluation include process studies, proficiency measures, attitude measures, and follow-up studies. A process study is concerned with events taking place in the classroom, proficiency and attitude measures with changes observed in pupils, and follow-up studies with the later careers of those who participated in the course.

The follow-up study comes closest to observing ultimate educational contributions, but the completion of such a study is so far removed in time from the initial instruction that it is of minor value in improving the course or explaining its effects. The follow-up study differs strikingly from the other types of evaluation study in one respect. I have already expressed the view that evaluation should be primarily concerned with the effects of the course under study rather than with comparisons of courses. That is to say, I would emphasize departures of attained results from the ideal, differences in apparent effectiveness of different parts of the course, and differences from item to item; all these suggest places where the course could be strengthened. But this view cannot be applied to the follow-up study, which appraises effects of the course as a whole and which has very little meaning unless outcomes can be compared with some sort of base rate. Suppose we find that 65 per cent of the boys graduating from an experimental curriculum enroll as scientific and technical majors in college. We cannot judge whether this is a high or low figure save by comparing it with the rate among boys who have not had the course. In a follow-up study, it is necessary to obtain data on a control group equated at least crudely to the experimental cases on the obvious demographic variables.

Despite the fact that such groups are hard to equate and that follow-up data do not tell much about how to improve the course, such studies should have a place in research on the new curricula, whose national samples provide unusual opportunity for follow-up that can shed light on important questions. One obvious type of follow-up study traces the student's success in a college course founded upon the high-school course.

One may examine the student's grades or ask him what topics in the college course he found himself poorly prepared for. It is hoped that some of the new science and mathematics courses will arouse greater interest than usual among girls; whether this hope is well founded can be checked by finding out what majors and what electives these ex-students pursue in college. Career choices likewise merit attention. Some proponents of the new curricula would like to see a greater flow of talent into basic science as distinct from technology, whereas others would regard this as potentially disastrous; but no one would regard facts about this flow as lacking significance.

Measuring Meanings

Attitudes are prominent among the outcomes with which course developers are concerned. Attitudes are meanings or beliefs, not mere expressions of approval or disapproval. One's attitude toward science includes ideas about the matters on which a scientist can be an authority, about the benefits to be obtained from moon shots and studies of monkey mothers, and about depletion of natural resources. Equally important is the match between self-concept and concept of the field: What roles does science offer to a person like me? Would I want to marry a scientist? And so on. Each learning activity also contributes to attitudes that reach far beyond any one subject, such as the pupil's sense of his own competence and desire to learn.

Attitudes can be measured in many ways; the choices revealed in follow-up studies, for example, are pertinent evidence. But measurement usually takes the form of direct or indirect questioning. Interviews, questionnaires, and the like are quite valuable when not trusted blindly. Certainly, we should take seriously any *un*desirable opinion expressed by a substantial proportion of the graduates of a course (*e.g.*, the belief that the scientist speaks with peculiar authority on political and ethical questions, or the belief that mathematics is a finished subject rather than a field for current investigation).

Attitude questionnaires have been much criticized because they are subject to distortion, especially where the student hopes to gain by being less than frank. Particularly if the questions are asked in a context far removed from the experimental course, the returns are likely to be trustworthy. Thus, a general questionnaire administered through homerooms (or required English courses) may include questions about liking for various subjects and activities; these same questions administered by the mathematics teacher would give much less trustworthy data on attitude toward mathematics. While students may give reports more favorable than their true beliefs, this distortion is not likely to be greater one year than another, or greater among students who take an experimental course than among those who do not. In group averages, many distortions balance out. But questionnaires insufficiently valid for individual testing can be used in evaluating curricula, both because the student has little motive to distort and because the evaluator is comparing averages rather than individuals.

Process and Proficiency

For measuring proficiency, techniques are likewise varied. Standardized tests are useful. But for course evaluation it makes sense to assign *different* questions to different students. Giving each student in a population of 500 the same test of 50 questions will provide far less information to the course developer than drawing for each student 50 questions from a pool of, say, 700. The latter plan determines the mean success of about 75 representative students on every one of the 700 items; the former reports on only 50 items (*5*). Essay tests and open-ended questions, generally too expensive to use for routine evaluation, can profitably be employed to appraise certain abilities. One can go further and observe individuals or groups as they attack a research problem in the laboratory or work through some other complex problem. Since it is necessary to test only a representative sample of pupils, costs are not a serious consideration as in routine testing. Additional aspects of proficiency testing will be considered below.

Process measures have especial value in showing how a course can be improved because they examine what happens during instruction. In the development of programmed instructional materials, for example, records are collected showing how many pupils miss each item presented; any piling up of errors implies a need for better explanation or a more gradual approach to a difficult topic. Immediately after showing a teaching film, one can interview students, perhaps asking them to describe a still photograph taken from the film. Misleading presentations, ideas given insufficient emphasis, and matters left unclear will be identified by such methods. Similar interviews can disclose what pupils take away from a laboratory activity or a discussion. A process study may turn attention to what the teacher does in the classroom. In those curricula that allow choice of topics, for example, it is worthwhile to find out which topics are chosen and how much time is allotted to each. A log of class activities (preferably recorded by a pupil rather than the teacher) will show which of the techniques suggested in a summer institute are actually adopted and which form "part of the new course" only in the developer's fantasies.

I have indicated that I consider item data to be more important than test scores. The total score may give confidence in a curriculum or give rise to discouragement, but it tells very little about how to produce further improvement. And, as Ferris (*4*) has noted, such scores are quite likely to be mis- or overinterpreted. The score on a single item, or on a problem that demands several responses in succession, is more likely than the test score to suggest how to alter the presentation. When we accept item scores as useful, we need no longer think of evaluation as a one-shot, end-of-year operation. Proficiency can be measured at any moment, with particular interest attaching to those items most related to the recent lessons. Other items calling for general abilities can profitably be administered repeatedly during the course (perhaps to different random samples of pupils) so that we can begin to learn when and from what experiences change in these abilities comes.

In course evaluation, we need not be much concerned about making measuring instruments fit the curriculum. However startling this declaration may seem, and however contrary to the principles of evaluation for other purposes, this must be our position if we want to know what changes a course produces in the pupil. An ideal evaluation would include measures of all the types of proficiency that might reasonably be desired in the area in question, not just the selected outcomes to which this curriculum directs substantial attention. If you wish only to know how well a curriculum is achieving *its* objectives, you fit the test to the curriculum; but if you wish to know how well the curriculum is serving the national interest, you measure all outcomes that might be worth striving for. One of the new mathematics courses may disavow any attempt to teach numerical trigonometry, and indeed, might discard nearly all computational work. It is still perfectly reasonable to ask how well graduates of the course can compute and can solve right triangles. Even if the course developers went so far as to contend that computational skill is no proper objective of secondary instruction, they will encounter educators and laymen who do not share their view. If it can be shown that students who come through the new course are fairly proficient in computation despite the lack of direct teaching, the doubters will be reassured. If not, the evidence makes clear how much is being sacrificed. Similarly, when the biologists offer alternative courses emphasizing microbiology and ecology, it is fair to ask how well the graduate of one course can understand issues treated in the other. Ideal evaluation in mathematics will collect evidence on all the abilities toward which a mathematics course might reasonably aim; likewise in biology, English, or any other subject.

Ferris states that the ACS Chemistry Test, however well constructed, is inadequate for evaluating the new CBA and CHEM programs because it does not cover their objectives. One can agree with this without regarding the ACS test as inappropriate to use with these courses. It is important that this test not stand *alone*, as the sole evaluation device. It will tell us something worth knowing, namely, just how much "conventional" knowledge the new curriculum does or does not provide. The curriculum developers deliberately planned to sacrifice some of the conventional attainments and have nothing to fear from this measurement, competently interpreted (particularly if data are examined item by item).

Security, Content, Terms

The demand that tests be closely matched to the aims of a course reflects awareness that examinations of the usual sort "determine what is taught." If questions are known in advance, students give more attention to learning their answers than to learning other aspects of the course. This is not necessarily detrimental. Wherever it is critically important to master certain content, the knowledge that it will be tested produces a desirable concentration of effort. On the other hand, learning the answer to a set question is by no means the same as acquiring understanding of whatever topic that question represents. There is, therefore, a possible advantage in using "secure" tests for course evaluation. Security is achieved only at a price: One must prepare new tests each year and consequently cannot make before-and-after comparisons with the same items. One would hope that the use of different items with different students, and the fact that there is less incentive to coach when no judgment is to be passed on the pupils and the teachers, would make security a less critical problem.

The distinction between factual tests and tests of higher mental processes, as elaborated for example in the *Taxonomy of Educational Objectives*, is of some value in planning tests, although classifying items as measures of knowledge, application, original problem solving, etc., is difficult and often impossible. Whether a given response represents rote recall or reasoning depends upon how the pupil has been taught, not solely upon the question asked. One may, for example, describe a biological environment and ask for predictions regarding the effect of a certain intervention. Students who have never dealt with ecological data will succeed or fail according to their general ability to reason about complex events; those who have studied ecological biology will be more likely to succeed, reasoning from specific principles; and those who have lived in such an ecology or read about it may answer successfully on the basis of memory. We rarely, therefore, will want to test whether a student "knows" or "does not know" certain material. Knowledge is a matter of degree. Two persons may be acquainted with the same facts or principles, but one will be more expert in his understanding, better able to cope with inconsistent data, irrelevant sources of confusion, and apparent exceptions to the principle. To measure intellectual competence is to measure depth, connectedness, and applicability of knowledge.

Too often, test questions are course-specific, stated in such a way that only the person who has been specifically taught to understand what is being asked for can answer the question. Such questions can usually be identified by their use of conventions. Some conventions are commonplace, and we can assume that all the pupils we test will know them. But a biology test that describes a metabolic process with the aid of the $\rightleftharpoons$ symbol presents difficulties for students who can think through the scientific question about equilibrium but are unfamiliar with the symbol. A trigonometry problem that requires use of a trigonometric table is unreasonable, unless we want to test familiarity with the conventional names of functions. The same problem in numerical trigonometry can be cast in a form clear to the average pupil *entering* high school; if necessary, the tables of functions can be presented along with a comprehensible explanation. So stated, the problem becomes course-independent. It is fair to ask whether graduates of the experimental course can solve such problems, not previously encountered, whereas it is pointless to ask whether they can answer questions whose language is strange to them. To be sure, knowledge of certain terminology is a significant objective of instruction, but for course evaluation, testing of terminology should very likely be separated from testing of other understandings. To appraise understanding of processes and relations, the fair question is one comprehensible to a pupil who has not taken the course. This is not to say that he should know the answer or the procedure to follow in attaining the answer, but he should understand what he is being asked. Such course-independent questions can be used as standard instruments to investigate any instructional program.

Pupils who have not studied a topic will usually be less facile than those who have studied it. Graduates of my hypothetical mathematics course will take longer to solve trigonometry problems than will those who have studied trig. But speed and power should not be confused; in intellectual studies, power is almost always of greater importance. If the course equips the pupil to deal correctly, even though haltingly, with a topic not studied, we can expect him to develop facility later when that topic comes before him frequently.

Two Types of Transfer

The chief objective in many of the new curricula seems to be to develop aptitude for mastering new materials in the field. A biology course cannot cover all valuable biological content, but it may reasonably aspire to equip the pupil to understand descriptions of unfamiliar organisms, to comprehend a new theory and the reasoning behind it, and to plan an experiment to test a new hypothesis. This is transfer of learning. It has been insufficiently recognized that there are two types of transfer. The two types shade into one another, being arranged on a continuum of immediacy of effect; we can label the more immediate pole *applicational transfer*, and speak of slower-acting effects as *gains in aptitude* (*3*).

Nearly all educational research on transfer has tested immediate performance on a partly new task. We teach pupils to solve equations in x, and include in the test equations stated in a or z. We teach the principles of ecological balance by referring to forests, and as a transfer test, ask what effect pollution will have on the population of a lake. We describe an experiment not presented in the text, and ask the student to discuss possible interpretations and needed controls. Any of these tests can be administered in a short time. But the more significant type of transfer may be the increased ability to learn in a particular field. There is very likely a considerable difference between the ability to draw conclusions from a neatly finished experiment, and the ability to tease insight out of the disorderly and inconsistent observations that come with continuous laboratory work on a problem. The student who masters a good biology course may become better able to comprehend certain types of theory and data, so that he gains more from a subsequent year of study in ethnology; we do not measure this gain by testing his understanding of short passages in ethnology. There has rarely been an appraisal of ability to work through a problem situation or a complex body of knowledge over a period of days or months. Despite the practical difficulties that attend an attempt to measure the effect of a course on a person's subsequent learning, such "learning to learn" is so important that a serious effort should be made to detect such effects and to understand how they may be fostered.

The techniques of programmed instruction may be adapted to appraise learning ability. One may, for example, test the student's rate of mastery of a self-contained, programed unit on the physics of heat or some other topic not studied. If the program is truly self-contained, every student can master it, but the one with greater scientific comprehension will hopefully make fewer errors and progress faster. The program can be prepared in several logically complete versions, ranging from one with very small "steps" to one with minimal internal redundancy, on the hypothesis that the better educated student could cope with the less redundant program. Moreover, he might prefer its greater elegance.

Toward Deeper Understanding

Old habits of thought and long established techniques are poor guides to the evaluation required for course improvement. Traditionally, educational measurement has been chiefly concerned with producing fair and precise scores for comparing individuals. Educational experimentation has been concerned with comparing score averages of competing courses. But course evaluation calls for description of outcomes. This description should be made on the broadest possible scale, even at the sacrifice of superficial fairness and precision.

Course evaluation should ascertain what changes a course produces and should identify aspects of the course that need revision. The outcomes observed should include general outcomes ranging far beyond the content of the curriculum itself–attitudes, career choices, general understandings and intellectual powers, and aptitude for further learning in the field. Analysis of performance or single items or types of problems is more informative than analysis of composite scores. It is not necessary or desirable to give the same test to all pupils; rather, as many questions as possible should be given, each to a different, moderate sized sample of pupils. Costly techniques, such as interviews and essay tests, can profitably be applied to samples of pupils, whereas testing everyone would be out of the question.

Asking the right questions about educational outcomes can do much to improve educational effectiveness. Even if the right data are collected, however, evaluation will have contributed too little if it only places a seal of approval on certain courses and casts others into disfavor. Evaluation is a fundamental part of curriculum development, not an appendage. Its job is to collect facts the course developer can and will use to do a better job, and facts from which a deeper understanding of the educational process will emerge.

Notes

1 My comments on these questions, and on certain more significant questions that *should* have been raised, have been greatly clarified by the reactions of several of these directors and of my colleagues in evaluation to a draft of this paper. J. Thomas Hastings and Robert Heath have been especially helpful. What I voice, however, are my personal views, deliberately more provocative than "authoritative."–LJC

2 See also Tyler, R.W. (1951).

References

1 Bloom, B. S. (Ed.) *Taxonomy of educational objectives*, New York: Longmans, Green, 1956.

2 Bloom, B. S. Quality control in education. *Tomorrow's teaching*. Oklahoma City: Frontiers of Science Foundation, 1961. Pp. 54-61.

3 Ferguson, G. A. On learning and human ability. *Canadian J. Psychol.*, 1954, 8, 95-112.

4 Ferris, F. L., Jr. Testing in the new curriculums: Numerology, tyranny, or common sense? *School Rev.*, 1962, 70, 112-131.

5 Lord, F. M. Estimating norms by item-sampling. *Educ. psychol. Measms.*, 1962, 22, 259-268.

6 Tyler, R. W. The functions of measurement in improving instruction. In E. F. Lindquist (Ed.), *Educational measurement.* Washington, D.C.: Amer. Council Educ., 1951. Pp. 47-67.

19. Evaluating Innovations in Teaching

M. Parlett

Source: M. Parlett, Research Unit on Intellectual Development, Edinburgh (unpublished paper, 1970), 11 pp.

Innovation raises complex institutional consequences. Here, two types of evaluation are distinguished. The 'agricultural-botany' paradigm regards evaluation as lying within the province of testing, seeks quantitative data and stresses objectivity, reliability and the neutrality of the evaluator. It relies heavily upon an objectives-based approach to curriculum design. However, in practice it is difficult to sustain this typical approach: the evaluator becomes remote from the developing concern of teachers. By contrast, the 'social-anthropology' paradigm seeks a wider information base. The evaluator is more involved in day-to-day working of the curriculum and attempts to illuminate issues that emerge in the course of study. The methodological problems in such an approach have much in common with anthropology, psychiatry and related disciplines.

The Nature of Innovations

In this paper, the phrase 'innovations in teaching' includes what others might regard as 'evolutionary changes', 'experiments', and 'applications of educational technology'. It embraces the large scale and the small. By large scale is meant those that embody totally new curricula, or radically changed course structures. For instance, at the Massachusetts Institute of Technology there are currently two different experiments with teaching freshmen. In each, students work entirely under their own steam, instructors and tutors serving as consultants, and lecturing by request. In Britain, changes of this magnitude – though common at primary level and increasingly so at secondary level – have yet to appear in higher education.

On the medium scale there are substitutions of 'cook-book' laboratory courses by others based on projects; or the teaching of subjects in a 'concentrated' or 'intensive' form,[1] such as has been tried in the Department of Architecture, Heriot Watt University. Small-scale innovations may include introducing a programmed text to replace part of a lecture course; using videotaped feedback in the learning of interpersonal skills; printing of lecture notes; and providing tapes and film loops for private viewing.

Clearly there are enormous differences between wholesale re-writings of curricula and the adoption, in a single course, of certain audio-visual aids. However, there is one characteristic they share: their introduction is a more complicated affair than is often acknowledged. Changing one component of an interrelated system affects other components; revising one part of the curriculum necessitates further changes; purchase of tape recorders for one purpose means they are now available for others. For the innovator, too, all is not straightforward. For instance, there are unforeseen difficulties, trivial in themselves, but which can throw neat plans off course: e.g. technicians leave, equipment fails.

Making such observations is not to dredge up difficulties for the sake of it. The intention is to offset the spurious impression of ordered change, the picture often presented to outsiders. Whatever prospectus-like constructions are erected *post hoc*, the reality, we know, tends to be murky. Usually, the proponents of a new scheme have to fight for its adoption. There are questions of territory and deployment of resources that fan old rivalries between or within departments. Compromises are sought. Plans, however carefully laid, need revision in the press of teaching.

This distinction, only slightly caricatured here, between the immaculate ideal and the rumpled reality, between the tidy and the untidy, is one that needs to be aired; especially when it comes to considering how innovations are to be evaluated. In the course of this paper two very different types of evaluation will be considered in detail. In contrasting them, the tidy/untidy distinction will be central.

Evaluation as Testing – the 'Agricultural Botany Paradigm'

One of the common professional grumbles of someone asked to do an evaluation is that frequently he is approached too late in the day. A proper evaluation requires that the experiment or project is structured, from the start, with the design requirements of the evaluator in mind. Only in this way can a thorough-going study be launched. Carefully matched samples must be picked and controls established; and the variables selected for which data will be gathered. The evaluator is likely to require the scheme's organisers to define their objectives, either from scratch or using objectives taken from pre-existing lists (e.g. Bloom's).[2,3]

The next stage is to select or construct appropriate objective tests. Pre-testing, item analysis, checks on reliability, and also, perhaps, the piloting of questionnaires and attitude inventories, can then all follow. Next comes the administering of the tests. This completed, the evaluator disappears from the field to analyse his data, and reappears some months or years later bearing his report.

Clearly this over-simplifies the evaluator's task, and glosses over the considerable technical and statistical problems that he must surmount. What is unambiguous, though, is that evaluation is regarded as lying within the province of testing. Tests are used to yield quantitative data from which statistical inferences can be drawn. The evaluator's credibility lies in the objectivity and reliability of his test materials; in the sophistication and rigour of his data handling and statistical techniques; and in the neutrality of his enquiry.

This description of evaluation procedures would not be complete without first specifying what would be its most supreme creation, its *ne plus ultra*. It would take the following form: large, finely balanced samples are formed into experimental and control groups; they are tested before the pedagogical 'treatment' is applied; and tested again afterwards; 'before and after' and 'between samples' comparisons can then be drawn.

If few educational evaluation studies even approach this ideal, it is not for want of trying. If they fall short of it, it is due to circumstances beyond the evaluator's control; and he voices his regrets.

Of the parent model two points can be made. The first is that it is pervasive and influential in evaluation thinking, and warrants being regarded as paradigmatic, in Kuhn's[4] sense. Second, as a model, it bears marked resemblance to research in another discipline altogether, that of agricultural botany. Plant dimensions and attainment measures are different enough; so, of course, are the precise experimental skills required. But there are distinct similarities too: for instance, the notion of testing for beneficial effects; the preoccupation with controlling or eliminating as many random variables as possible; and the power that statistical requirements exert on the design of enquiries. These seem common to both the testing of plant chemicals and the testing of educational innovations. When one realises that the early history of parametric statistics – the lynch-pin of much evaluative testing, as of psychometrics – is written in the annals of agricultural botany, the connection becomes explicit.

A Paradigm for Plants, not People

In the first section we noted a distinction between the 'tidy' and the 'untidy': between a conception of teaching innovations as neatly planned and executed like clockwork; and another, more realistic, in which due place is given to inevitable haphazard elements. The view of evaluation stemming from the agricultural botany paradigm is uncompromisingly 'tidy'. The rest of this paper will be concerned with pointing to certain defects of this approach; and with suggesting an alternative 'untidy' way of evaluating, based on a different paradigm.

The chief deficiency of a testing type of evaluation is that the restrictions and pre-structuring required for it are so formidable, that the more one thinks about it, the more its total impracticability becomes apparent. Where are the large-scale innovations, with samples of hundreds of students? The universities and colleges, or even departments, who are willing and able to co-operate in some joint experimental venture? The vice-chancellors and heads of departments, who are prepared to countenance dividing students into experimentals and controls?

If, to put it bluntly, the agricultural botany paradigm gives rise to research which it is impossible to do properly in practice, it is surprising that the choice of paradigm itself is not subject to more critical review. On the contrary, it is retained, and often strongly defended. Most educational research derives from it.

If choosing a paradigm was of no great moment, a matter simply of personal preference, it would be wrong to interfere. But adherence to a paradigm has wide implications. It offers to its followers intellectual security, and a framework for common purpose. But it can also become a dogma that stifles free enquiry; dictating within a research area what it is proper to do and what it is not.[5] Perhaps the agricultural botany paradigm survives in the evaluation field not because of inherent strengths, but because its deficiencies in this area are never faced.

This is best demonstrated with a specific example. In recent years it has become fashionable to construct lists of formalised teaching objectives, defined by practising teachers. These can then be used as criteria of teaching success. It's impossible, the argument goes, to weigh advantages and disadvantages of different modes of teaching without such criteria. These should not be externally defined; they should be the teachers' own criteria. Hence the simple device of asking them what, precisely, they are trying to do. Of all possible variables, only very few can be studied. Fixing on objectives seems the most sensible choice. (Throughout this paper, the use of the term 'objectives' will be confined, in order to avoid confusion, to these highly specific statements of aims, made by teachers.)

Plausible though the argument is, difficulties soon appear. First, it is rare indeed for teachers even to approach agreement on objectives. Second, language is imprecise, so that objectives are either so generalised and diffuse as to be interpretable in numerous ways; or alternatively, expressed so specifically that literally hundreds must be listed. For example, take: 'Acquisition of Laboratory Skills'. As it stands, it is too broad; yet if one splits it up, the list of sub-objectives becomes unwieldy. Third, getting an instructor to state his objectives requires his being highly articulate – which he may not be naturally – often about something he comprehends intuitively as sensible, but which he thinks would sound banal: like 'getting a feel for hunches'. Finally there is the discomforting fact that actions speak louder than statements of intent.

Those who are asked to cite their objectives often point out these difficulties to the evaluator, who is anyway finding the compiling of the list a tricky exercise. Professor Merton Kahne, at the Massachusetts Institute of Technology, studied a large electrical engineering class, in a department noted for its interest in teaching methods. Twenty staff members took part concurrently in the course, teaching different sections of students. He writes:[6]

> In one part of the research I attempted to generate a listing of course objectives. After talking with the staff individually on many occasions and even taking notes, I still found myself uncertain of what I was being told. For a group of people who were usually extremely lucid in communications, I found my notes nearly useless in drawing

> up the list. At any rate, I constructed a list which best captured what I thought had been described to me and submitted it for criticism. Its semantic obscurity and, in some instances, triviality and inutility, was carefully pointed out. I offered another try, after taking almost verbatim notes. These were re-submitted but not acted upon until I urged action. Now my original statements were unwittingly paraphrased as being closer to the core of the objectives, and the list was regarded as clearer but unfortunately, if one were to try to create even a primitive rank ordering in importance, this would be wrong because many of the objectives were practically equivalent in importance and more importantly they were important along different dimensions, i.e. in different ways. Besides any quantitative results would probably more reflect differences in semantic interpretation than anything else! Even direct quotes from the syllabus, written by staff members, were rejected as inappropriate. Finally I wrote a letter to all the staff outlining my difficulties and eliciting their help in constructing the list (in writing); slightly over one half responded.

Kahne was not working within the context of the agricultural botany paradigm. His listing of objectives comprised only a small part of his study, and certainly was not intended as the basis of criteria for judging teaching effectiveness.

But supposing the listing of objectives had been so intended, what could he have done? What do evaluators do when they come up against such wilful unpredictability? Well, if they waver momentarily in their resolve, the paradigm is there, as steady as a rock, to reassure them. First, the investigator's concern is with aggregate not individual data. Second, obviously one expects deviations from the mean. Third, it is undoubtedly a difficult, and sometimes soul-searching business imposing quantitative order upon a jumble of human disorder; but the effort is worthwhile, for despite its limitations, the value of an objective approach is self-evident. The natural tendency, then, is to make the best of it; to take and use the best available list of objectives as a sort of lowest common denominator; or to hammer away discussing them till some verbal formula is devised that everyone appears to agree upon. One can sense from Kahne's experience the futility of such expediencies.

This discussion about the use of objectives has underlined the acute difficulties in applying the paradigm in question. By imposing its own pattern and assumptions, the paradigm forces people to oversimplify, almost to the point of rendering the data meaningless. Conceived originally with massive samples and good controls in mind, it is nevertheless regarded as the model to be striven for, even if numbers are small; even if research situations are idiosyncratic in the extreme; even if random and uncontrollable factors intrude to a marked degree. Because it presents itself as objective, reliable, quantitative, and value-free, all – apparently – is forgiven.

Seeking an Alternative

In considering alternative strategies it may be salutary to ask why innovations are evaluated in the first place. Often a programme's financial sponsors, or a college committee, demand it. Sometimes one wonders whether all that is wanted at the end is a weighty-looking report. One evaluator, known to the writer, was told that whatever else went into his report he should definitely include plenty of tables, graphs, and statistics.

If an evaluation study has been commissioned and an outside investigator brought in (the form of the paper, for simplicity's sake, assumes this arrangement) then presumably, if they are serious, those who have commissioned it want to discover how well the innovation works and whether its short- and long-term effects are 'beneficial'. Some will consider the only criterion that matters is whether students get better exam results. It is assumed, however, that 'benefits' are being defined in less backwoodsmanish fashion, and that a range of changes is envisaged, embracing attitudes and interests as well as learning and various cognitive skills. But it is highly probable that these expectations will be couched in general terms if verbalised at all, and will be far from constituting a comprehensive rationale in the shape of a detailed list of objectives.

Given the absence of such a rationale, the pre-specifying of variables or problems to be researched – theoretically tidy though it may be – is grossly unrealistic. More useful, if also less tidy, would be the development of evaluation studies which permitted post-specification of problem areas. Beforehand no one has more than a hazy idea of the way in which a new scheme will develop. Even with prior experience to draw on, there are still unpredictable elements relating to individual teachers and classes and their inter-reactions together. Thus, for instance, teachers encountering particularly bored classes may deliberately make major tactical changes in order to spark, at all costs, some signs of interest.

The notion of post-specifying an evaluation's problems and variables is one that has implications both numerous and profound. Whatever its pros and cons, it is undoubtedly a mode of asking questions, more natural to non-specialists, than specifying them all in advance. This is shown in the following example, which is imaginary, but based on experience.

Suppose a new curriculum is evaluated. It involves, say, adopting a programmed text, but only by half the course. Others work from text books and lectures. The evaluator, on the basis of a set of objectives, has constructed objective tests and administered these to both groups. He aims to provide a definitive answer to the question: 'which method is best?' At the beginning of the next term, he is invited to speak to the departmental staff about his study.

Those that were directly involved listen politely as the evaluator operating within the customary paradigm, describes the tests, controls, and statistics. He reminds them, in the course of his talk, that his study employed criteria – in the form of detailed objectives – that they had themselves defined. It is all the more interesting then, that the discussion afterwards reveals that little of his presentations has resonated with their own concerns. For the teaching staff – in the light of their experience – now view with faint embarrassment the wordy objectives they had been required to give at the beginning. But they do have numerous questions on their minds. Why, in one group, did attendance fall off? What did the bright students do with themselves when they had romped through the programmed text in half the allotted time? Why was one group's comprehension of a particularly central concept so manifestly inferior to that of the other group? What were the differences between students who liked and disliked working with the programmed text?

Such questions as these, arising out of the teachers' experience with the new course, are not the ones the evaluator has set himself to answer. Confronted with them he is likely to be unnerved. If he answers at all, he has truthfully to point out that they are merely his opinions, 'off the record', and not based on actual data. Or he can attempt to parry the question, rephrasing it to permit quotation of a test result he does have. To the proverbial visitor from Mars his position may appear untenable. But he can defend it, for his own peace of mind as well as for others', in two ways. He rebuts any suggestion that he is 'an expert who can be consulted'; and he continually re-emphasises the necessarily circumscribed nature of his study.

It is hardly surprising, then, that he soon becomes regarded as someone who is 'outside'. Maybe he can test the innovation's overall effects. But he seems unable and unwilling either to disentangle causes of behavioural and social phenomena witnessed in the classroom; or to take a constructive part in discussion concerning future teaching; or even to explain the reasons for differences or effects he finds by testing.

The effect of this withdrawal from the world of teaching itself, with its busy and uncertain practicalities, is devastating. Evaluation studies come to be regarded as only of academic interest, not relevant to teaching as such, and dull and pretentious to boot. They can be safely consigned to journals for educational research and educational psychology, long regarded by most practising teachers and a lot of social scientists, as repositories of irrelevant turgidity and pretentious pedantry. To change this state of affairs needs a radical shift, indeed of paradigmatic dimensions.

Evaluation as Interpretation – the 'Social Anthropology Paradigm'

If the post-specifying of problem areas makes an evaluation study more illuminating and helpful, then the evaluator aiming to do such a study has to acquire a special kind of knowledge. Compared with the type of evaluation discussed above, his information base has to be far wider; and if he is to contribute effectively to discussions about the innovation, he must know far more about its day-to-day workings. Indeed, he has to know a good deal more than his interrogators if he is to survive their cross-examination and avoid the label of 'someone who tells us what we know already'.

If he is going to know about individual courses so thoroughly, clearly he cannot choose to work with huge samples, a handful of variables and elaborate tests. Instead he must conduct a smaller-scale study, but be prepared to range across a wide range of variables, collecting what data he can, as best as he can. This, of course, dramatically flouts the assumptions of the agricultural botany paradigm: it turns it on its head.

But there are precedents elsewhere: for instance in social anthropological field work. Here the investigator literally lives with the community he is studying. His investigation is extremely far-ranging; he collects data with a variety of techniques: e.g. observations, films, conversations and study of written records. His aim is to understand and portray the cultural setting he is in. He works by building up an overall picture, model, or schema that is constantly modified and expanded, as he acquires new information. He seeks to comprehend relationships: e.g. between beliefs and practices, and between organisational patterns and customary responses of individuals. The end product of his research is not a set of 'findings', as such, nor an undigested assembly of facts and figures, but an interpretation of a highly complex system. It is based on a mass of data which he has distilled, and from which he has drawn his extensive citations of evidence.

To speak of an evaluation stemming from a social anthropology paradigm is not to propose, of course, that the evaluator proceed exactly as if he were an anthropologist on location. The paradigm only provides a general framework, or research philosophy. The chief connection with social anthropology is the emphasis on interpreting; on building up explanatory models of particular systems; on discovering patterns of coherence and interconnectedness that usually go unnoticed.

It is important to emphasise that social anthropologists do not, of course, go into the field with their minds a complete blank. Nor will the evaluator who adopts the social anthropology paradigm do so. Being able to cope efficiently with questions posed after the event does not preclude pre-specifying others in advance. But, not unlike the teacher – whose aims, as we have seen, naturally tend to be couched in general and even conflicting terms – the suggested new-style evaluator, like his social anthropologist mentor, is likely to have framed only general research concerns, in chapter heading terms; and nothing like the orderly research design of his counterpart in the other paradigm.

Thus, in the writer's own evaluation work,[1,7] his general aim, in evaluating an innovation, is to find out the effects it has; on pupils' learning, concentration and studying habits, on the development of their interest and involvement in the subject, on their style of working, on their self-confidence and creative independence.

Such a study takes the investigator into many quarters. He will look at the background, origin, and departmental politics of the project. He will be closely involved with the students: their short- and long-term goals; their habits of study; their common conceptual difficulties; their perceptions of the subject, the instructor, and the value of the innovation; their 'hidden curriculum'[8] and shared languages, spoken and unspoken. He will also communicate extensively with the staff: their aims, expectations, and disappointments; their private and public assessments of students' progress; their switches in direction and emphasis as the course proceeds; and their detailed opinions – at successive stages – of the innovation or scheme in question.

An evaluation study of this type uses many different techniques: chiefly interviews, conversations, questionnaires and unobtrusive observation; but also, occasionally, timetables or diaries, perusal of examination scripts, personality tests, and check lists of activities. These are employed, in a variety of ways, to answer questions that emerge in the course of the study. Thus, why did attendance drop at a certain point? Why did the instructor decide to extend a deadline? Why did many students find the examination more punishing than usual? Why did the programmed text lose its allure?

Research of this type tends to be accused of ignoring methodology. This should not be the case; the research problems are formidable, and an evaluator disregards them at his peril. However, he can draw some grains of comfort, for similar difficulties in varied ways, face others: not only anthropologists, but also psychiatrists, management consultants, sociologists basing their research on ethnomethodology[9] or on symbolic interactionism,[10,11] and indeed teachers themselves.

Two chief problems are as follows. First, there is a welter of data; it requires brutal editing and selectivity, and the end result, the interpretation, is a personal one. How can gross bias be other than inevitable? (a) The best answer is to have multiple observers throughout. This is not usually possible, but open-ended material should customarily be coded by someone outside. (b) All major conclusions should be cross-checked, with information drawn from several sources and with separate techniques. (c) Investigators must learn, like Darwin did, to note down – before they forget it – negative evidence that does not fit, and also voluntarily to submit their 'case' to frequent critical exposure. (d) Careful demarcation of established fact and cheerful speculation is required in reporting the work. Evidence should be quoted in a way that others can judge its quality. (e) There should be no pig-headed reaction against quantitative data. Whenever information can be easily and sensibly quantified, it should be.

Second, in a study such as this, the behaviour of the evaluator himself is of paramount importance. He seeks a high level of co-operation. He cannot compel individuals to talk to him; he has to win their confidence. He asks personal questions, and listens to private opinions in conditions of confidentiality. He wants to be accepted informally by different groups, who may only have a formal relationship to one another. He is observing certain individuals at crucial times of their lives; e.g. students on the borderline of being asked to leave, and instructors deeply involved in teaching in a way they never have before. He is in danger of being perceived as 'a tool of the administration' or as 'a focus of unrest', or both at the same time. Finally, of course, there is no doubt that his mere presence will have profound effects on the progress of the innovation.

There are no clear formulae, only general guidelines to assist the evaluator in facing such daunting issues. He is placed in an acutely responsible position, requiring professional standards equivalent in many ways to those of a psychiatrist. Obviously he needs tact and sensitivity; he must respect individuals' absolute right to privacy and non-participation; he must be thoroughly honest about his political position if it becomes relevant (which it rarely does). Such research as this, as in other fields, is open to abuse: the evaluator could be a thorough nuisance; or worse, a snooper or cold manipulator. Such individuals should not receive a second assignment. If his presence as an evaluator inevitably has effects, they should at least be beneficial ones.

The two methodological issues so briefly raised both follow from the intensive, participatory nature of the research. To avoid them, rather than facing them, would entail pursuing the study from a position 'outside'. It is exactly a disinclination to do this that is central to the social anthropology paradigm.

The type of study proposed here is, perhaps, so different that a new word is necessary. 'Evaluation' suggests decisions made by an impartial authority, concerning the relative 'values' of alternatives. Educators should not be allowed to duck and transfer their responsibility for making policy in such a way. Investigators should not make decisions; but instead should help policy-makers to do so, by throwing light on the implications of different policies, by challenging stereo-typed thinking, and by communicating their specialised knowledge and insight.

Innovations change crucial dimensions in instruction: for instance, the presentation and organisation of content; and implicit and explicit systems of reward. These will affect what it is that is learned. Decisions between alternatives, therefore, are extremely complicated; and can benefit from the information and analysis that is generated in the type of study described here. Moreover, it is only by connecting research and teaching together in this way, that we can hope to achieve even an approximate understanding of our immediate and long-term educational goals. Research should not stem from objectives: objectives should stem from research.

I am grateful to David Bloor, David Edge, Liam Hudson and Brian Torode for their comments on a draft of this paper.

Notes

1 Parlett, M. R. and King, J. G., *Research in Higher Education Monograph* 'Concentrated Study' (in preparation).
2 Bloom, B. S. (ed.), *Taxonomy of Educational Objectives. Handbook I: Cognitive Domain*, D. McKay and Co. Inc., 1954.
3 Bloom, B. S. (ed.), *Taxonomy of Educational Objectives. Handbook II: Affective Domain*, D. McKay and Co. Inc., 1956.
4 Kuhn, T. S., *The Structure of Scientific Revolutions*, University of Chicago Press, 1962.
5 Hudson, L., *Bulletin of the British Psychological Society*, 'The Choice of Hercules' (in press).
6 Kahne, M. J., *Medical Trial Technique Quarterly*, 'Psychiatrist Observer in the Classroom', *15*, 1969.
7 Parlett, M. R., *Nature*, 'Undergraduate Teaching Observed', *223*, 5211, 1969.
8 Snyder, B. R., *The Hidden Curriculum*, Knopf, 1970.
9 Garfinkel, H., *Studies in Ethnomethodology*, Prentice-Hall, 1967.
10 Blumer, H., *American Journal of Sociology*, 'Sociological implications of the thought of George Herbert Mead', *71*, 1966.
11 Mead, G. H., *Mind, Self and Society*, University of Chicago Press, 1934.

20. Science 5–13 Project

W. Harlen

Source: W. Harlen, *Evaluation in Curriculum Development: Twelve Case Studies*, (Macmillan for Schools Council, London, 1973), pp. 16-35.

An account by an evaluator of her role in one project. In the Science 5–13 Project, the evaluator had a formative role. As a member of the project team itself, rather than an outsider, she was able to help in the writing of objectives that were behavioural and therefore measurable. She also took on the key role of preparation of teachers, particularly in explaining that evaluation was concerned with the utility of the materials rather than with testing children or teachers. When the evaluator is a member of the project team there are advantages in terms of understanding and communication to balance some disadvantages in terms of loss of objectivity through commitment. Four aspects of the evaluation plan are identified and the battery of techniques used described and assessed.

This project, sponsored jointly by the Schools Council, the Nuffield Foundation and the Scottish Education Department, was set up in 1967 at the University of Bristol School of Education to consolidate and extend the work of its predecessor, the Nuffield Junior Science Project. Initially intended to run for three years and later extended for a further two, it concerns children throughout the age range 5–13.

The terms of reference for the project included 'the identification and development, at appropriate levels, of topics or areas of science related to a framework of concepts appropriate to the ages of the pupils. The aim of the development [was] to assist teachers to help children, through discovery methods, to gain experience and understanding of the environment and to develop their powers of thinking effectively about it' (Table 0.1). The project was also to take account of the needs of children with varied knowledge of science, to advise colleges of education on the science content of curriculum courses and to maintain close liaison with other related projects.

A search through the literature for 'a framework of concepts appropriate to the ages of the pupils' revealed that it did not exist. The attempt to create such a framework, although an unreliable guide in itself, proved a useful starting point from which to consider the project objectives. It was relatively easy to state the broad aims in general terms, but breaking these down into more specific statements expressed in behavioural terms occupied a large part of the team's time, and particularly that of the evaluator, during the first year of the project and at intervals throughout its life. That the statement of objectives eventually took the form it did and was included in the project's material for teachers (see, for instance, *With Objectives in Mind*, Macdonald Educational, 1972, pp. 59-65) was due to two circumstances in particular. One was the presence of an evaluator as a team member; the other was the reaction of various groups of teachers who were consulted about the objectives whilst these were being drafted. The teachers' immediate response was to request a copy of the objectives and start using it as a guide for their work in the classroom; it was realized that part of the help the project could give was in supplying teachers with clear objectives for their children. So the statement of objectives, initially drawn up as a necessary step to clarify the minds and guide the writing of team members, became an important part of the project material.

The objectives, 150 or so statements, were grouped according to stages of children's intellectual development; the concept of stages was for convenience in accommodating the changes in modes of thought of children in the age range 5–13. Three stages were chosen; they had the same properties as those of Piaget, whose ideas and findings were widely used, but the boundaries and definitions of these stages were such as to be more useful in the context of school organization:

stage 1: the transition from intuitive to concrete operational thinking and the early phases of concrete operational thinking;

stage 2: the later phases of concrete operational thinking;

stage 3: the transition from concrete operational to formal operational thinking.

Project Material

Material has been written for teachers in the form of units, each concerning one topic area for science activities. A unit is intended to guide the teacher on activities suitable for children at one or another stage of development, to suggest objectives he might keep in mind for the children during the activities, and to provide suitable background information which the teacher himself may lack and not be able to find easily in a suitable form. The introductory book, *With Objectives in Mind*, gives a general explanation of the project's philosophy and includes the list of objectives.

The units each take a selection of objectives from this list[1] and show how these objectives could be achieved by children if they are working in a particular subject area or with particular material. They suggest activities relating to a study of the unit's content area, through which it is possible for children to achieve specified objectives. They do not provide a course, but are rather seen as illustrations which will help teachers to provide children with experiences to suit their individual requirements and preferences.

The four units which were the subject of the evaluation plan described here are:

Table 3.1 Organization of the Science 5–13 Project

	MAIN TEAM		EVALUATION		SCHOOLS INVOLVED		LEAs INVOLVED *(England & Wales)*	
	Staff	Budget*	Staff	Budget*	With trials	Associated informally	With trials	Indirectly
August 1967	3		½		–		–	
1968	4		½		–		–	
1969	5		½		130		12	
1970	5	£141,000 approx.	1	£20,000 approx.	90	111	19	141
1971	5½		1		2[illegible]0		19	
1972 extension	1½		1		–		12	
1973	1		1		–		–	

History	*Aims*	*Scope*	*Activities*	*Materials*
Set up a year after the Nuffield Junior Science Project ended, with the intention of building further on the ideas of that project and taking note of other work in primary science.	To help teachers in that part of their work concerned with educating children through science. To advise colleges of education on the science content of curriculum courses; to study how to increase primary school teachers' knowledge of science.	For teachers in any primary school and any kind of secondary or middle school in which children up to the age of 13 are educated. For teachers of children with a wide variety of ability and environment.	The development of materials to guide teachers in the provision of suitable science activities for their children and the supply of background information for the teachers. Helping with courses for teachers in local centres and running large national courses about twice a year. Disseminating the project's ideas to schools and colleges through lectures, visits, newsletters.	Units for teachers on various topics, e.g. time, metals, trees, coloured things. Some consist of a book of classroom activities and a separate book of background information. Others consist of one book which includes background information. A book introducing the project's ideas, giving its objectives in detail and generally supporting the units. Material suitable for teachers to use with children reaching the stage of formal thinking, in upper junior and lower secondary classes.

*The division between main team and evaluation is only approximate, since evaluation was not costed spearately. The total grant of £161,000 was provided by the Schools Council, the Nuffield Foundation, the Scottish Education Department and the Plastics Institute.

Working with Wood, stages 1 and 2
Metals, stages 1 and 2
Time, stages 1 and 2
Trees, stages 1 and 2

All except *Trees* comprised two books–one relating to classroom activities and one of background information for teachers. They were to be given the trials in junior schools or junior departments of primary schools with children aged seven to eleven. Before describing these trials, it seems important to clarify the role of the evaluator in the project and describe her activities during development of the unit material.

The Evaluator's Role

The purpose of the evaluator's work on the Science 5–13 Project was to assist in the development of the project's ideas and material. The form of assistance was different from that given by the other members of the team, since the evaluator was not directly involved with researching and writing the units, but rather with clarifying the objectives of the project's material and providing information as to how well it was achieving its intended purposes. The roles of the writers and the evaluators were therefore distinct and yet intimately interconnected. Evaluation was an integral part of the project's development from the start, but was separated from other functions of the project by being the sole responsibility of one person.

There are advantages and disadvantages to this close relationship between evaluator and other team members but on the whole the advantages, which centre round ease of communication, outweigh the disadvantages, which arise from loss of objectivity on the part of the evaluator. It is no doubt important for the evaluation of material to be in the hands of someone who is not emotionally or intellectually committed to it. Such commitment is bound to follow in anyone who has wrestled with the problems of developing and writing material, and clearly the person thus committed cannot stand back from the material, look at it objectively and gather evidence about it impartially. It is not a fault in the writer, but a result of his necessary involvement in his work, that what he produces is more likely to be improved if it is evaluated by another person. But this is only if the other person is sufficiently well informed about the purpose, content and context of the work to enable him to gather useful evidence. The uncommitted evaluator is faced with the problem of communication: if he tries to remain impartial and objective, he may end up also ignorant of many things which he should understand to do his job properly. It is no easy matter for an evaluator who is not close to the project team to understand the aims of their work sufficiently to plan a valid and useful evaluation. This is particularly so in the case of on-going or formative evaluation, but also true to some extent in the case of final or summative evaluation. When the evaluator is a team member, the communication problem is reduced but at the risk of too much involvement in the development of material. So there are drawbacks to both situations, which cannot be avoided but only minimized by being fully aware of them and consciously taking appropriate steps.

In this project the evaluator took no part in writing the units but kept in close contact with the material at all stages of its production. Fig. 1 shows the parallel development of unit material and evaluation material. The unit, beginning as a skeleton, was first read by the evaluator in its pre-draft form, at which point it was possible to develop the first ideas about suitable evaluation material. After small-scale informal classroom trials and discussion amongst the writing members of the team, the pre-draft material was revised. The ensuing draft form had a wider circulation to people whose comments were invited, and was tried out by more teachers. These later classroom trials, called pre-pilot trials, were used to provide examples of children's work and give further immediate feedback for revision. They were also used by the evaluator as pilot trials for test material.

Of the instruments which might be used in the evaluation, the tests for children were the most elaborate and took the greatest time to produce, so these were the first to be given attention. The first draft of some possible test items was discussed with the unit's author before any test production was begun. These discussions were of considerable benefit to both participants, being part of the close communication which was established in this project. Each found value in seeing how the other had interpreted the unit's objectives and, without necessarily changing any ideas or opinions, appreciated another point of view. The chief reason for discussing the test items at this early stage was to ensure as far as possible that the items would detect the kind of behavioural change which the unit's author intended to promote, that they were acceptable in terms of their content, and that they covered adequately any aspects of the unit which the author particularly wished to be explored. To do this involved digging deeply into the meaning of the objectives, analysing situations in which achievement could be promoted or could show itself, considering the expected degree of achievement, and so on. Such exchanges, early on, before ideas had become too firmly rooted, caused both writer and evaluator to think more carefully about the purpose and effectiveness of what they were producing.

Arrangements for Trials

The project inherited the arrangements for trials set up by its predecessor, Nuffield Junior Science Project; this limitation must be remembered in considering the descriptions which follow. The trials were to be conducted in schools in 12 LEAs in England and Wales and in 4 counties in Scotland. Although there were disadvantages to having the pilot areas pre-selected, the advantage was that within these areas it would be easy to find classes

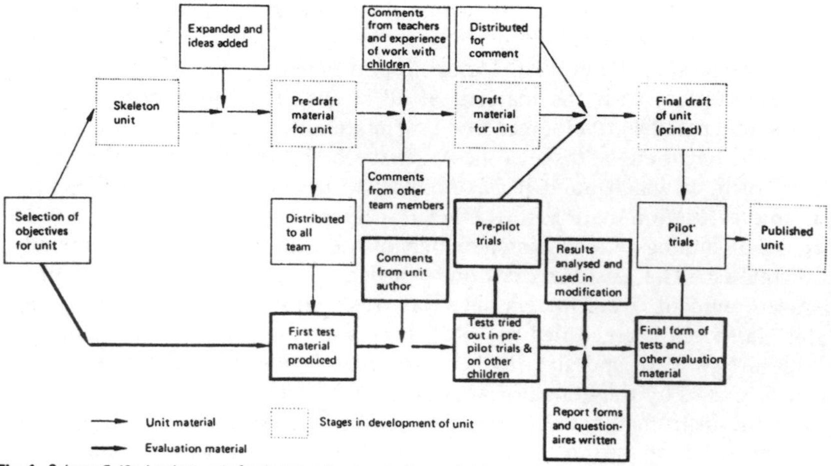

Fig. 1 Science 5–13: development of unit material and evaluation material

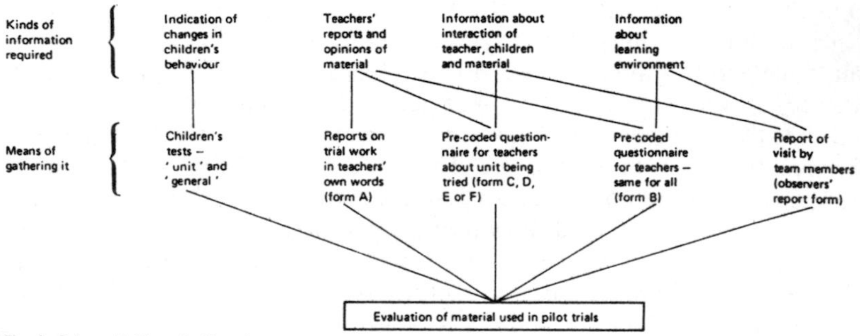

Fig. 2 Science 5–13: evaluation plan

which already had experience of active methods of learning–derived in part from the previous project–and in which it might be hoped that learning through discovery was already going on. These were the kind of classes wanted for the trials, so that the value and effect of the materials could be without the interfering consequences of introducing a new way of working. Obviously it is necessary to reduce the number of uncontrolled variables in the trial situation, so the introduction of the material should be accompanied by as few other changes as possible.

The project laid considerable emphasis on thorough preparation of teachers for taking part in the trials. This was necessary to overcome the anxiety and suspicion which the word 'evaluation' evokes in many teachers. To most the word is taken to be synonymous with 'testing' and in primary schools generally, particularly the more progressive ones, there is an understandable dislike of testing. The project evaluator consciously tried to improve the attitude towards evaluation held by teachers taking part in the trials, and felt that the efforts in this direction met with considerable success. Through lectures, courses and discussions it was possible to explain the reason for the evaluation and the plan devised for it. Experience showed that when teachers realized that the evaluation was essential to the development of the material, that it was concerned with this material and not with assessing their children or themselves, and that they had a valuable part to play in it, then they were prepared to co-operate and not prejudge the work. The teachers became genuine partners in the project's attempt to help them.

Guidelines for the Evaluation

Five guiding principles were drawn out of experience and deliberation during the first year and a half of the project.

(*a*) An evaluator must be prepared to spend a great deal of time and effort to find out exactly what it is that the project aims to do through the material it is producing. This means breaking down such statements of aim as 'helping teachers to help children learn science' until these can be expressed as identifiable behaviours; only then can the achievement of the aim be evaluated. Such analysis is essential, exhausting and apparently unproductive but unless it is done thoroughly everything which follows is insecurely based.

(*b*) Evaluation must be concerned with children's behaviours; the material being evaluated is an agent of change in this behaviour. Since behaviour is very complex, the problem must be looked at from all angles, different kinds of instruments used, both subjective assessments and objective methods of testing employed if appropriate, and evidence gathered about changes in attitudes as well as in cognitive abilities.

(*c*) It is most important to find or develop techniques of evaluation which are appropriate to the behaviours being investigated but which interfere as little as possible with these behaviours and the activities in which they are made evident. The evaluation techniques should be enjoyable, if possible, but in any case as easy and straightforward to use as can be. A project's material is invariably intended to be stimulating and interesting for both teachers and pupils, and if this positive, enthusiastic response is found, the evaluation must do nothing to diminish it.

(*d*) There is an obligation to think ahead very carefully about the probable results of using any evaluation instrument, to consider how usable the collection of certain information may be and whether the amount of data it would yield could be handled in the time available: this may save wasted effort on the part of the evaluator and all those who provide the information. It is as important not to over-collect as not to under-collect information. Assembling data about behaviour always involves other people, whose time and efforts must be respected. It falls to the evaluator to consider carefully what questions need to be asked, to ask only 'real' questions–those whose answers are honestly needed and can be used.

(*e*) Finally, the project will benefit greatly if teachers are really involved in evaluating the material. It helps both the evaluation and the teachers if they are not merely required to fill in forms, send them back, and hear no more until the next set of questions arrives. Meetings arranged to discuss questions on the forms can encourage better observation and reporting on the part of the teachers when they appreciate the purpose of the questions, and better questioning on the part of the evaluator, who realizes how teachers have struggled with inadequate questionnaires. Where possible, the teachers should carry out the direct testing of children, since this reduces the interference with normal work caused by the arrival of an outside administrator.

Formation of the Evaluation Plan–a Four-Sided Attack

These guidelines were applied to the material being evaluated and the situation in which the trials would take place, in order to choose what kinds of information should be gathered. Any data would have to be readily gathered and rapidly interpreted, be the most relevant, interfere as little as possible with the progress of the trial work, and be such as could combine with other data to produce as complete a description of the trial work as possible. Of course there had to be a compromise, for it would have been an advantage to gather all possible relevant information, exploring many aspects of the learning situation, but this would undoubtedly have caused too much interference. So the compromise was that there should be an attempt to gather evidence about four main aspects. The choice of these four followed from the nature of the project.

The ultimate aim of the project's material was to change the children's behaviours, as expressed in the objectives. Therefore it was necessary to investigate whether or not any of the expected changes had taken place. Yet the material only affected the children indirectly, through the teachers for whom it was written. There were two important links in the chain from the project's material to the children: from the material and the teachers and from the teachers and children. If the material was not adequately communicated to the teachers, then no matter how successful the project's ideas might be in theory, they would fail to produce any results in practice. If the teachers understood the material but the material was not effective in helping children learn, then again there would be no practical results. To have any chance of estimating cause and effect relationships, both these links had to be investigated. Finally, the learning environment was thought to be very relevant to the effect of the material, and included the social as well as the physical environment, both within and outside the school.

These, then, were the four aspects to be investigated: changes in children's behaviours, teachers' reports and opinions of the material, the interaction of teachers, children and material, and the learning environment. The techniques chosen for each investigation are indicated in Fig. 2 and described below.

Changes in Children's Behaviours

Since interest was in the changes in behaviour and not in any particular level of attainment or in differences between individuals, a 'before' and 'after' pattern of testing was planned. Since the trial work might have no connexion with any changes observed in this way, a control group of children had to be tested in the same manner as the group undertaking the trial work. The control group made it possible to estimate what part of the trial group's behaviour changes was the result of experiences connected with the trial material, and what part was due to the combined effect of test sophistication, maturation and other experiences.

The control group would only serve this function adequately if it matched the trial group as fully as possible. Complete matching on a large scale is impossible, so in this case differences between classes in the two groups were randomized. The mechanism for this was as follows. Pairs of classes were suggested for participation in the trials, the classes in each pair being as similar as possible in respect of the children's age range, type and size of school, characteristics of the neighbourhood and teacher's experience. These classes were then assigned randomly to either the control or trial group, so that no systematic bias was introduced.

The form which the test items should take was decided in the light of previous work by the evaluator which had dealt with the problem of measuring young children's achievement in science. This work led to the development of a method in which the test items were introduced by a film sequence showing a demonstration, a situation or some objects, which posed the problem the children were to solve. The answers were recorded by the children in booklets by ticking one of the alternative responses given. This form of test was preferred to the conventional pencil and paper type because it drastically reduces the dependence on verbal ability and enables the presentation of the problems to be as real as possible. Since the objectives of science teaching are concerned with how a child will act or deal with practical problems, the most obvious way to find out whether he has or has not developed a concept or idea is to present him with a real situation, so chosen that he cannot deal with it successfully unless he has developed the concept or grasped the idea. However, since this would require individual administration, it was completely impracticable in the present case. The most attractive alternative, which would avoid the disadvantages of the pencil and paper form of test, was to use moving film. Although film is a two-dimensional medium, the movement of objects and apparatus provide the necessary cues for their real nature and form to be appreciated. The most practical kind of projector was chosen–one suitable for use in daylight, and with an integral rear projection screen, for convenience. This projector has the added advantage of resemblance to a television set, so children are already familiar with it as a source of information.

The test items were so written as to detect the various kinds of behaviour described in the project's objectives. Only a fraction of these objectives relate to 'knowledge'; by far the majority deal with the many other kinds of behaviour involved in learning. The old idea that only knowledge can be tested has been largely dispelled, but it still remains true that knowledge is the easiest to test by conventional means. Fortunately, the film medium is a good one for presenting items which are not testing merely for knowledge. The film can, for instance, present a problem where solution calls for ability to identify and manipulate variables, in a way which is much clearer than a verbal description would be. It can also introduce problems which test understanding of such things as sorting, grouping and classification. It can provide data in an easily grasped form and be used for items in which all information is provided and the question demands reasoning or explanations. The use of film is not, of course, restricted to cognitive abilities–in fact it may well have greater relative value for testing behaviours in the affective domain.

The test items contained situations or problems so designed that the children's responses would show whether they had achieved a particular objective. Where possible, care was taken to avoid using problems described or suggested in the units, because the criterion of success in this part of the evaluation was the achievement of objectives, not how thoroughly the problems in the units had been studied. To have based the items directly on problems selected from unit activities would not only have implied that those activities were more worthy of attention than others, but would have indicated that the teachers were expected to follow the unit in a way which the project never intended. As has already been said, the units are not a course, therefore a test based on a course could have no relevance.

A separate test was thus required for each unit; four 'unit' tests were produced, each consisting of thirty-four items. But in addition there were objectives common to all units–objectives chosen to guide the approach to active learning in science which pervaded all the project's material. A 'general' test was devised to assess the achievement of these general objectives. The items in it tested application and transfer to other problems to an even greater degree than the unit test items. For example, in one item the film shows two equal-sized pieces of paper, one plain writing paper and the other newspaper. They are picked up and a strip is cut from each; the strip of newspaper is wider than the plain paper but they are the same length. These strips are then attached to separate bulldog clips hanging from a frame. Similar clips are put on the bottom of the strips and weights hung from them as the first part of the sequence ends. At this point the commentator administering the test asks the children to record in their booklets whether or not they think this is a fair test of which kind of paper is the stronger. The film sequence then continues: two more strips of paper are seen hung side by side on the frame. This time they are of equal width as well as equal length, and again weights are being hung from them as the sequence ends. The children are then asked to record in their booklet their judgement of this test of the paper, by ticking 'Fair' or 'Not fair' in the second part of the question. The objective under test here is 'awareness that more than one variable may be involved in a particular change' (stage I).

The general test was in two parts: the first dealt with the general cognitive objectives, and the second with the objectives of the affective domain. In the latter an attempt was made to measure children's liking for certain activities, both in science and in other areas of work. The children were asked to state their liking for the various activities in terms of a three-point scale presented visually to them. In the introduction to this part of the test, the film sequence showed two children eating ice cream. The children taking the test were asked to imagine themselves doing this and say how much they liked doing it. It was imagined that almost all would like this 'very much', so a personal standard for liking something 'very much' was established. The second sequence showed children polishing shoes, which provided a standard for liking something 'not very much'. After this the sequences showed other activities; in each case the children were invited to imagine themselves doing the same things and to note how much they liked it–'very much', 'a little' or 'not very much'. The point of filming these activities rather than simply giving the children a list was that titles such as 'looking after animals' or 'gardening' could be interpreted in many different ways by different children, whereas the film shows a definite activity. All the children can thus respond to the same situation, not to their own idea of what the activities involve.

The general test and one of the unit tests were given to each child in both the trial group and the control group at the beginning and end of the trial period. The same test was used on both occasions; the limited advantages of using two parallel forms of the test were not considered to justify the extra expense and time involved in producing them. The tests were administered in most cases by the class teacher, who was supplied with a suggested film commentary as well as the film loops and children's booklets. The teacher also marked the tests, using the mark scheme and score sheets provided. As the marking was objective throughout, re-marking by the project was not thought necessary.

A disproportionate amount of attention has been given here to the children's tests because they were of a novel kind. However, it must be stressed that the tests were but one of four types of evidence which contributed to the evaluation, and were not considered to be any more important than the others. There is plenty of experience to show that evidence of behaviour changes by itself is of little consequence for evaluation of curricular change. It is only of value if the conditions under which such changes did or did not take place are also known.

Teachers' Reports and Opinions

These were collected formally by questionnaire and informally at meetings and during visits of team members and others to the classrooms. Three forms, to be completed by all the trial class teachers, were distributed at the start of the trials:

form A mainly blank paper on which teachers were invited to write an account of the relevant activities of the children during the trial period;

form B a questionnaire, mostly pre-coded, asking for information about the class, school, relevant biographical data about the teachers, details of the test administrations, and opinions about the project's introductory book, *With Objectives in Mind;*

form C D, E, or F (one of these according to which unit was being tried by the teacher); another pre-coded questionnaire asking for information, observations and opinions about the unit.

In planning these forms, an attempt was made to arrange the questions in the order in which things might be encountered. This was to encourage teachers to record their impressions at frequent intervals rather than leaving all the recording to the end of the trial period, when they might have forgotten certain points which occurred to them weeks before.

Interaction of Teachers, Children and Material

Because of the difficulty of arranging the prolonged observations and records in the classroom which are needed if interaction is to be analysed on a formal basis, this work was done only by informal observation. A team member visited each trial class whilst work was in progress. After the visit the team member filled in a form, recording what had been observed about such things as the class organization, the use being made of the material, the attitude of the teacher to the project's ideas, the teacher-pupil relationship, etc. There were also some questions on the teachers' report forms designed to indicate how the material was used and how the children reacted.

The Learning Environment

Information about this was gathered from the teachers and from the visiting team members. Questions which required factual answers and did not depend on making a decision or a value judgement were included in the teachers' report form B. The other questions were included in the observers' report form. This was not because teachers were thought to be incapable of making judgements of the kind required, but because they were not in a position to do so. For example, a teacher might consider the children's working space was 'adequate' if she had always been used to teaching in very poor and cramped conditions, but for the purposes of the evaluation the judgement needed to be made on standards which are more widely applicable. The team member, visiting many schools in many parts of the country, was able to make a more useful judgement of such things as the adequacy of space within and outside the classroom, and its adequacy not only in quantity but also in quality, and of the use which was being made of it.

Organization of the Trials

Numbers Taking Part

There were four units ready for trials starting in September 1969

TABLE 2 Basis of sample for evaluation of one unit (provided jointly by three pilot areas)

Age range	Type of school	No. of classes Experimental	Control
Younger (7-9)	Rural	3	3
Older (9-11)	Rural	3	3
Younger (7-9)	Urban, prosperous catchment area	3	3
Older (9-11)	Urban, prosperous catchment area	3	3
Younger (7-9)	Urban, disadvantaged catchment area	3	3
Older (9-11)	Urban, depressed catchment area	3	3

these were allocated to the twelve pilot areas so that each area tried only one unit. Thus three areas were concerned with the evaluation of each unit except in the case of *Time*, which was also given trials in Scotland. In each English or Welsh area six classes helped evaluate the unit and six control classes were involved in the testing. Scotland had eight trial and eight control classes. Thus the number of classes trying out a unit was eighteen for *Metals*, *Working with Wood* and *Trees*, and twenty-six for *Time* (a total of eighty).

Duration of Trials

The pre-trial testing took place in the first half of the autumn term 1969; trial work was begun in any trial class as soon as the tests had been completed in that class. By the end of the spring term 1970, the trial work and post-trial testing was completed for *Metals*, *Working with Wood* and *Time*. The working time of the trials was one full term, spread over two terms. To give *Trees* a proper trial, the work was spread over a full year so that all the seasonal changes could be included in the trial period.

Table

TABLE 3 Programme for trials

	Sep–Oct 1969	Nov–Dec 1969 Jan–Feb 1970	Mar–Apr 1970
Trial classes	All take both unit and general tests	Children's activities guided by teacher using trial unit	All take both unit and general tests
Control classes	All take both unit and general tests	Children's activities continued as previously	All take both unit and general tests

Report on the Trials

The trials were completed as planned with a loss by the end of only three experimental classes out of the eighty constituting the original sample. This very low rate of drop-out probably resulted from careful selection and preparation of classes in the first place, and from the fact that teachers were supplied with necessary materials or means to purchase them, and visits were paid to the classes during the trials. Much of the credit for this must go to the local organizers; these were local inspectors, advisers or teachers who undertook the distribution of materials and were responsible for liaison with the project team. Team members also played an important part in the trials by visiting the classes and attending local meetings of trial teachers. The observers' report forms completed by the team members after their visits were found to be of great value, and without the information they contained it would not have been possible to interpret the teachers' questionnaire responses as usefully as was in fact done.

Administering the tests to the children took longer in many cases than was anticipated. The reasons for this were chiefly lack of experience with the use of film loops on the part of many teachers, the failure of some loops to run, due to being inefficiently put into the cassettes, and the malfunctioning of many of the projectors. These technical problems tried the patience of many teachers, and of the evaluator (who tried to put things right as quickly as they went wrong) almost to the limit. Teachers were asked to report on the testing and a few expressed their feelings clearly:

> Whilst the method of testing might appear very attractive in theory, in practice I found it to be unreliable, time-consuming and a great tax on one's patience. The children seemed to enjoy the films and generally found the method of answering easy to understand. Nevertheless . . . they found the constant interruptions very tiresome.

However, the problems were overcome and it was encouraging to find that, despite the trouble, teachers saw the point of the work:

> I cannot see how this administration could be made easier, but a section in the unit on *Time* explaining how twenty-four hours in a day could be extended to about thirty hours would have been useful! To be serious, it meant extra work but we felt it worth while!

Analysis of Results

Class mean scores, rather than scores of individuals, were the basis for statistical analysis of the children's test results; the sample size was thus quite small, being the number of classes and not the number of children involved. The mean scores were derived from the scores of children who completed both tests on both occasions. In the case of three unit tests, the difference between post-test scores for trial and control was statistically significant (at the 0.05 level). For each of these three units an analysis of variance showed that variance attributable to difference between trial and control classes was negligible for the pre-trial test scores but highly significant (beyond the 0.001 level) for the post-trial test scores. The results for the fourth unit were complicated by considerable initial difference between the trial and control scores, but they showed the same trend—a greater rate of increase in the trial group as compared with the control.

Satisfying though these overall test results were, they had little consequence for rewriting. To give some indication of which parts of the unit were most effective in terms of the children's performance, the scores for different groups of items in the tests were calculated separately. Change in score on the groups of items relating to each of the objectives represented in the tests were compared, trial with control. This gave some guidance as to the relative effectiveness of the parts of the units relating to these objectives. Such a procedure could only suggest hypotheses, and other information was examined for evidence to support or reject them.

Alongside this analysis of children's test results, data from the various questionnaires and report forms were used in two main ways: information, suggestions and comments of teachers which could not be coded were extracted and collated; the rest was coded and transferred to IBM cards along with other information about the classes. The coded information–about 300 items for each class–was analysed by computer, using a program for classifying qualitative data by cluster analysis. This greatly helped the treatment of questionnaire responses, which would otherwise have been very clumsy, since on almost every question there is a range of opinion and mere totals of replies in one category or another convey little more than that some like one thing and some like another. It is much more helpful to know whether a certain reply to one question tends to occur with a certain reply to another, whether there are patterns in the responses and, if so, what conditions are associated with particular patterns. The cluster analysis program sets the computer to search through the lists of code numbers to find those numbers which occur together in the lists more frequently than would be expected to happen by chance. It collects together a group of numbers which each have a value of observed coincidence greater than the expected coincidence with other numbers in the list. Several groups of numbers are found in this way, many of which overlap to a large extent. With the help of a further part of the computer program it is possible to identify the two most useful groups–those where the coincidence between the numbers is greatest in opposite directions. These two groups form the opposite ends of a dimension, and when the numbers in them are decoded, it is quite easy to see which, in the terms of the project, is the 'positive' end and which is the 'negative' end.

This program was used separately on five different sets of information, one for each unit and one for all classes combined. The latter included all the information which was not specific to any unit, i.e. from teachers' form B, from the observers' report form and from the children's test results. Here are some of the items in the positive group found in the analysis of combined class results:

(*a*) The children's test score on attitude to science activities increased during the trial.

(*b*) The class had previously been working through active discovery methods.

(*c*) The desks or tables in the classroom were arranged in irregular groups.

(*d*) The class timetable was fully integrated.

(*e*) At most times of the day the children worked individually or in groups at their own tasks.

(*f*) The children regularly worked outside the classroom.

(*g*) The children formed their own groups for working.

(*h*) Science activities were carried on by different groups at different times, as chosen by the children.

(*i*) The children could work on their own ploys.

(*j*) The teacher had warmly approved the project's ideas on first being introduced to them.

(*k*) The teacher appreciated very well the meaning of objectives.

(*l*) The teacher used a discovery approach in most areas of the curriculum.

(*m*) The teacher had made some use of the project's statement of objectives apart from using it in connexion with the trial work.

And in the negative group:

(*a*) The class had previously been used to working through formal methods.

(*b*) The children's activities were very largely directed by the teacher.

(*c*) The desks or tables in the classroom were arranged in regular groups or rows.

(*d*) The children worked as a whole class at most times of the day.

(*e*) Science activities were organized so that all groups always worked at the same time.

(*f*) Science activities were organized so that all the children worked on much the same problem.

(*g*) The teacher allocated the children to groups for science activities.

(*h*) Science activities had not been included in the children's work before the trials.

(*i*) The teacher had a poor appreciation of what objectives are.

(*j*) The teacher used a discovery approach hardly at all.

(*k*) The teacher thought that evaluation of whether or not objectives had been achieved was unnecessary.

Interpretation and use in Rewriting

An internal report for each unit gave the results of the cluster analysis and an interpretation of the statistical analysis of the children's test results. In addition to the data constituting the positive and negative groups, the weightings of other responses or items of information were used to indicate the degree to which each was associated with the positive or negative group. A bonus from this process was the light it shed on the value of collecting different kinds of information and on the usefulness of various questionnaire items; had this been done at the pre-pilot stage, more efficient questionnaires could have been written for use in the trials.

In general it was found that the items of information in or closely associated with the positive groups expressed success and satisfaction with the material, whilst the reverse was true for the negative groups. By treating the negative group responses as reasons for dissatisfaction, points requiring attention in rewriting were identified. For instance, nearly all the negative groups contained the item 'teacher wanted help with class management and group work organization, which was not supplied by the unit'. This was evidently a cause of dissatisfaction which could be met during the revision by writing in suggestions to provide the help needed. Usually it was possible to find ways of correcting the cause of dissatisfaction without upsetting those who were satisfied with it; in this case, it was unlikely that including help with class organization would upset those who had been able to use the units successfully without it.

A good example of how the results of evaluation were used is provided by the unit *Working with Wood*. The material in this unit was completely reorganized in response to the discovery that teachers felt the topic was too narrow to suit the wide-ranging exploration which is appropriate in the junior years. The suggested investigations concerning wood were consequently re-written to fit into a wider context, and more trouble was taken to explain how they could lead to and support other classroom activities. In doing this, much more practical help with classroom management was brought in.

The cluster analysis results also cast more light on teachers' written comments and suggestions. By looking to see which of teachers' questionnaire responses were in the positive and negative groups it was possible to estimate to what extent a teacher making any particular comment was one who was satisfied and able to make use of the unit or one who was dissatisfied and not helped much by the unit. The comments had much greater value when examined in this way than if they were treated as all coming from the same background of opinion.

Whilst the computer sorted out the information, it did not, of course, make judgements. Criteria for rewriting still had to be decided by discussion amongst the team. For whom were the units being written? For teachers at one end of the dimension or the other, or those in between? Was it possible to cater for people at all points along the dimension? These were the questions which still had to be answered after the computer had done its work.

Unanswered Questions

The evaluation results did not provide answers to several questions which seemed very important at the time of rewriting but which had not existed at the time of the trials. The interval of time between the beginning of the trials and the revision of the units was eighteen months—at least six months longer than necessary, on account of delays caused by constant failure of the computer to complete the five long analyses. During this time the writers in the team had produced two further sets of units, and in doing so had made use of their subjective impressions of the way the trials described here were progressing. Changes were thus made in the writing style and form of guidance given in the new units because the team had absorbed some of the evaluation results before they were fully analysed, but also, probably more so, because ideas had developed in the intervening time. So when the first set of units came to be revised, questions to which the writers most wanted answers were:

Are the new ways of writing preferable to the old?
Which is the more acceptable form of guidance?
Shall we rewrite the first units in the style of the latest ones?
Should an index to objectives be included?

The evaluation could not supply answers–the index of objectives, for instance, was brought up several months after the trials of the first units had ended! In these trials teachers each tried only one unit and could not compare one with another even on the same set, let alone make comparisons with units still unwritten at the time of the trials. Many liked what they tried, but might have been less easily satisfied had alternatives been known. The plans for later trials were drawn up so as to enable comparative judgements to be made–another example of the way the results proved formative in refining evaluation items rather than the material.

It would seem that one of the main problems confronting anyone attempting formative evaluation is to define the areas to be investigated, i.e. formulate the objectives of the evaluation. But the main obstacle to achieving what the evaluator sets out to do is that these objectives will be constantly changing with the inevitable development of the project team's ideas. Formative evaluation could only be completely 'successful' if the writers' ideas stood still–hardly a characteristic of a lively and creative team. Maybe the measure of a good team of writers is the failure of its formative evaluation!

Publisher for the project: Macdonald Educational.

Note

1 The first units to be produced were written according to this pattern. The evaluation showed that this pattern had serious disadvantages; in revising the first units and writing later ones, the activities were directed towards a wider range of objectives.

V CASE STUDY—MAN: A COURSE OF STUDY

21. The Importance of Structure

Jerome S. Bruner

Source: J. Bruner, *The Process of Education* (Vintage Books, Random House, New York, 1960.

MACOS approaches the question 'What makes man human?' through an exploration of five key subjects or 'humanizing forces', namely tool making, language, social organisation, child rearing and man's drive to explain and represent his world. The aim of providing intellectually honest starting points for younger children's enquiry was taken seriously, and to that end leading scholars in the relevant fields were enlisted. Here Bruner elaborates his views on the structure of subject-matter, arguing that curricula should be organised around the fundamental concepts and relationships giving mere information meaning. Bruner makes four claims for the importance of structure: (1) Understanding fundamentals makes a subject more comprehensible; (2) Organising knowledge in terms of principles and ideas aids memory; (3) Mastery of general principles is the basis for transfer of training; (4) Emphasis on fundamentals reduces the gap between 'elementary' and 'advanced' knowledge in a field. This concept of 'structure' is heavily influential on the MACOS course design.

It is interesting that around the turn of the last century the conception of the learning process as depicted by psychology gradually shifted away from an emphasis upon the production of general understanding to an emphasis on the acquisition of specific skills. The study of "transfer" provides the type case – the problem of the gain in mastery of other activities that one achieves from having mastered a particular learning task. Whereas the earlier emphasis had led to research studies on the transfer of formal discipline – the value obtained from the training of such "faculties" as analysis, judgment, memory, and so forth – later work tended to explore the transfer of identical elements or specific skills. In consequence, there was relatively little work by American psychologists during the first four decades of this century on the manner in which the student could be trained to grasp the underlying structure of significance of complex knowledge. Virtually all of the evidence of the last two decades on the nature of learning and transfer has indicated that, while the original theory of formal discipline was poorly stated in terms of the training of faculties, it is indeed a fact that massive general transfer can be achieved by appropriate learning, even to the degree that learning properly under optimum conditions leads one to "learn how to learn". These studies have stimulated a renewed interest in complex learning of a kind that one finds in schools, learning designed to produce general understanding of the structure of a subject matter. Interest in curricular problems at large has, in consequence, been rekindled among psychologists concerned with the learning process.

A word is needed at this point to explain in fuller detail what is meant by the *structure* of a subject, for we shall have occasion to return to this idea often in later pages. Three simple examples – from biology, from mathematics, and from the learning of language – help to make the idea clearer. Take first a set of observations on an inchworm crossing a sheet of graph paper mounted on a board. The board is horizontal; the animal moves in a straight line. We tilt the board so that the inclined plane or upward grade is 30°. We observe that the animal does not go straight up, but travels at an angle of 45° from the line of maximum climb. We now tilt the board to 60°. At what angle does the animal travel with respect to the line of maximum climb? Now, say, he travels along a line 75° off the straight-up line. From these two measures, we may infer that inchworms "prefer" to travel uphill, if uphill they must go, along an incline of 15°. We have discovered a tropism, as it is called, indeed a geotropism. It is not an isolated fact. We can go on to show that among simple organisms, such phenomena – regulation of locomotion according to a fixed or built-in standard – are the rule. There is a preferred level of illumination toward which lower organisms orient, a preferred level of salinity, of temperature, and so on. Once a student grasps this basic relation between external stimulation and locomotor action, he is well on his way toward being able to handle a good deal of seemingly new but, in fact, highly related information. The swarming of locusts where temperature determines the swarm density in which locusts are forced to travel, the species maintenance of insects at different altitudes on the side of a mountain where crossbreeding is prevented by a tendency of each species to travel in its preferred oxygen zone, and many other phenomena in biology can be understood in the light of tropisms. Grasping the structure of a subject is understanding it in a way that permits many other things to be related to it meaningfully. To learn structure, in short, is to learn how things are related.

Much more briefly, to take an example from mathematics, algebra is a way of arranging knowns and unknowns in equations so that the unknowns are made knowable. The three fundamentals involved in working with these equations are commutation, distribution, and association. Once a student grasps the ideas embodied by these three fundamentals, he is in a position to recognize wherein "new" equations to be solved are not new at all, but variants on a familiar theme. Whether the student knows the formal names of these operations is less important for transfer than whether he is able to use them.

The often unconscious nature of learning structures is perhaps best illustrated in learning one's native language. Having grasped the subtle structure of a sentence, the child very rapidly learns to generate many other sentences based on this model though different in content from the original sentence learned. And having mastered the rules for transforming sentences without altering their meaning – "The dog bit the man" and "The man was bitten by the dog" – the child is able to vary his sentences much more widely. Yet, while young children are able to *use* the structural rules of English, they are certainly not able to say what the rules are.

The scientists constructing curricula in physics and mathematics have been highly mindful of the problem of teaching the structure of their subjects, and it may be that their early successes have been due to this emphasis. Their emphasis upon structure has stimulated students of the learning process. The reader will find the emphasis reflected many times in the pages that follow.

The first object of any act of learning, over and beyond the pleasure it may give, is that it should serve us in the future. Learning should not only take us somewhere; it should allow us later to go further more easily. There are two ways in which learning serves the future. One is through its specific applicability to tasks that are highly similar to those we originally learned to perform. Psychologists refer to this phenomenon as specific transfer of training; perhaps it should be called the extension of habits or associations. Its utility appears to be limited in the main to what we usually speak of as skills. Having learned how to hammer nails, we are better able later to learn how to hammer tacks or chip wood. Learning in school undoubtedly creates skills of a kind that transfer to activities encountered later, either in school or after. A second way in which earlier learning renders later performance more efficient is through what is conveniently called nonspecific transfer or, more accurately, the transfer of principles and attitudes. In essence, it consists of learning initially not a skill but a general idea, which can then be used as a basis for recognizing subsequent problems as special cases of the idea originally mastered. This type of transfer is at the heart of the educational process – the continual broadening and deepening of knowledge in terms of basic and general ideas.

The continuity of learning that is produced by the second type of transfer, transfer of principles, is dependent upon mastery of the structure of the subject matter, as structure was described in the preceding chapter. That is to say, in order for a person to be able to recognize the applicability or inapplicability of an idea to a new situation and to broaden his learning thereby, he must have clearly in mind the general nature of the phenomenon with which he is dealing. The more fundamental or basic is the idea he has learned, almost by definition, the greater will be its breadth of applicability to new problems. Indeed, this is almost a tautology, for what is meant by "fundamental" in this sense is precisely that an idea has wide as well as powerful applicability. It is simple enough to proclaim, of course, that school curricula and methods of teaching should be geared to the teaching of fundamental ideas in whatever subject is being taught. But as soon as one makes such a statement a host of problems arise, many of which can be solved only with the aid of considerably more research. We turn to some of these now.

The first and most obvious problem is how to construct curricula that can be taught by ordinary teachers to ordinary students and that at the same time reflect clearly the basic underlying principles of various fields of inquiry. The problem is twofold: first, how to have the basic subjects rewritten and their teaching materials revamped in such a way that the pervading and powerful ideas and attitudes relating to them are given a central role; second, how to match the levels of these materials to the capacities of students of different abilities at different grades in school.

The experience of the past several years has taught at least one important lesson about the design of a curriculum that is true to the underlying structure of its subject matter. It is that the best minds in any particular discipline must be put to work on the task. The decision as to what should be taught in American history to elementary school children or what should be taught in arithmetic is a decision that can best be reached with the aid of those with a high degree of vision and competence in each of these fields. To decide that the elementary ideas of algebra depend upon the fundamentals of the commutative, distributive, and associative laws, one must be a mathematician in a position to appreciate and understand the fundamentals of mathematics. Whether schoolchildren require an understanding of Frederick Jackson Turner's ideas about the role of the frontier in American history before they can sort out the facts and trends of American history – this again is a decision that requires the help of the scholar who has a deep understanding of the American past. Only by the use of our best minds in devising curricula will we bring the fruits of scholarship and wisdom to the student just beginning his studies.

The question will be raised, "How enlist the aid of our most able scholars and scientists in designing curricula for primary and secondary schools?" The answer has already been given, at least in part. The School Mathematics Study Group, the University of Illinois mathematics projects, the Physical Science Study Committee, and the Biological Sciences Curriculum Study have indeed been enlisting the aid of eminent men in their various fields, doing so by means of summer projects, supplemented in part by year-long leaves of absence for certain key people involved. They have been aided in these projects by outstanding elementary and secondary school teachers and, for special purposes, by professional writers, film makers, designers, and others required in such a complex enterprise.

There is at least one major matter that is left unsettled even by a large-scale revision of curricula in the direction indicated. Mastery of the fundamental ideas of a field involves not only the grasping of general principles, but also the development of an attitude toward learning and inquiry, toward guessing and hunches, toward the possibility of solving problems on one's own. Just as a physicist has certain attitudes about the ultimate orderliness of nature and a conviction that order can be discovered, so a young physics student needs some working version of these attitudes if he is to organize his learning in such a way as to make what he learns usable and meaningful in his thinking. To instill such attitudes by teaching requires something more than the mere presentation of fundamental ideas. Just what it takes to bring off such teaching is something on which a great deal of research is needed, but it would seem that an important ingredient is a sense of excitement about discovery – discovery of regularities of previously unrecognized relations and similarities between ideas, with a resulting sense of self-confidence in one's abilities. Various people who have worked on curricula in science and mathematics have urged that it is possible to present the fundamental structure of a discipline in such a way as to preserve some of the exciting sequences that lead a student to discover for himself.

It is particularly the Committee on School Mathematics and the Arithmetic Project of the University of Illinois that have emphasized the importance of discovery as an aid to teaching. They have been active in devising methods that permit a student to discover for himself the generalization that lies behind a particular mathematical operation, and they contrast this approach with the "method of assertion and proof" in which the generalization is first stated by the teacher and the class asked to proceed through the proof. It has also been pointed out by the Illinois group that the method of discovery would be too time-consuming for presenting all of what a student must cover in mathematics. The proper balance between the two is anything but plain, and research is in progress to elucidate the matter, though more is needed. Is the inductive approach a better technique for teaching principles? Does it have a desirable effect on attitudes?

That the method of discovery need not be limited to such highly formalized subjects as mathematics and physics is illustrated by some experimentation on social studies carried out by the Harvard Cognition Project. A sixth-grade class, having been through a conventional unit on the social and economic geography of the South-eastern states, was introduced to the North Central region by being asked to locate the major cities of the area on a map containing physical features and natural resources, but no place names. The resulting class discussion very rapidly produced a variety of plausible theories concerning the requirements of a city – a water transportation theory that placed Chicago at the junction of the three lakes, a mineral resources theory that placed it near the Mesabi range, a food-supply theory that put a great city on the rich soil of Iowa, and so on. The level of interest as well as the level of conceptual sophistication was far above that of control classes. Most striking, however, was the attitude of children to whom, for the first time, the location of a city appeared as a problem, and one to which an answer could be discovered by taking thought. Not only was there pleasure and excitement in the pursuit of a question, but in the end the discovery was worth making, at least for urban children for whom the phenomenon of the city was something that had before been taken for granted.

How do we tailor fundamental knowledge to the interests and capacities of children? This is a theme we shall return to later, and only a word need be said about it here. It requires a combination of deep understanding and patient honesty to present physical or any other phenomena in a way that is simultaneously exciting, correct, and rewardingly comprehensible. In examining certain teaching materials in physics, for example, we have found much patient honesty in presentation that has come to naught because the authors did not have a deep enough understanding of the subject they were presenting.

A good case in point is to be found in the usual attempt to explain the nature of tides. Ask the majority of high school students to explain tides and they will speak of the gravitational pull of the moon on the surface of the earth and how it pulls the water on the moon's side into a bulge. Ask them now why there is also a bulge of less magnitude on the side of the earth opposite to the moon, and they will almost always be without a satisfactory answer. Or ask them where the maximum bulge of the incoming tide is with respect to the relative position of the earth and moon, and the answer will usually be that it is at the point on the earth's surface nearest to the moon. If the student knows there is a lag in the tidal crest, he will usually not know why. The failure in both cases comes from an inadequate picture of how gravity acts upon a free-moving elastic body, and a failure to connect the idea of inertia with the idea of gravitational action. In short, the tides are explained without a share of the excitement that can come from understanding Newton's great discovery of universal gravitation and its mode of action. Correct and illuminating explanations are no more difficult and often easier to grasp than ones that are partly correct and therefore too complicated and too restricted. It is the consensus of virtually all the men and women who have been working on curriculum projects that making material interesting is in no way incompatible with presenting it soundly; indeed, a correct general explanation is often the most interesting of all. Inherent in the preceding discussions are at least four general claims that can be made for teaching the fundamental structure of a subject, claims in need of detailed study.

The first is that understanding fundamentals makes a subject more comprehensible. This is true not only in physics and mathematics, where we have principally illustrated the point, but equally in the social studies and literature. Once one has grasped the fundamental idea that a nation must trade in order to live, then such a presumably special phenomenon as the Triangular Trade of the American colonies becomes altogether simpler to understand as something more than commerce in molasses, sugar cane, rum, and slaves in an atmosphere of violation of British trade regulations. The high school student reading *Moby Dick* can only understand more deeply if he can be led to understand that Melville's novel is, among other things, a study of the theme of evil and the plight of those pursuing this "killing whale". And if the student is led further to understand that there are a relatively limited number of human plights about which novels are written, he understands literature the better for it.

The second point relates to human memory. Perhaps the most basic thing that can be said about human memory, after a century of intensive research, is that unless detail is placed into a structured pattern, it is rapidly forgotten. Detailed material is conserved in memory by the use of simplified ways of representing it. These simplified representations have what may be called a "regenerative" character. A good example of this regenerative property of long-term memory can be found in science. A scientist does not try to remember the distances traversed by falling bodies in different gravitational fields over different periods of time. What he carries in memory instead is a formula that permits him with varying degrees of accuracy to regenerate the details on which the more easily remembered formula is based. So he commits to memory the formula $s = \frac{1}{2} gt^2$ and not a handbook of distances, times, and gravitational constants. Similarly, one does not remember exactly what Marlow, the commentator in *Lord Jim*, said about the chief protagonist's plight, but, rather, simply that he was the dispassionate onlooker, the man who tried to understand without judging what had led Lord Jim into the straits in which he found himself. We remember a formula, a vivid detail that carries the meaning of an event, an average that stands for a range of events, a caricature or picture that preserves an essence – all of them techniques of condensation and representation. What learning general or fundamental principles does is to ensure that memory loss will not mean total loss, that what remains will permit us to reconstruct the details when needed. A good theory is the vehicle not only for understanding a phenomenon now but also for remembering it tomorrow.

Third, an understanding of fundamental principles and ideas, as noted earlier, appears to be the main road to adequate "transfer of training". To understand something as a specific instance of a more general case – which is what understanding a more fundamental principle or structure means – is to have learned not only a specific thing but also a model for understanding other things like it that one may encounter. If a student could grasp in its most human sense the weariness of Europe at the close of the Hundred Years' War and how it created the conditions for a workable but not ideologically absolute Treaty of Westphalia, he might be better able to think about the ideological struggle of East and West – though the parallel is anything but exact. A carefully wrought understanding should also permit him to recognize the limits of the generalization as well. The idea of "principles" and "concepts" as a basis for transfer is hardly new. It is much in need of more research of a specific kind that would provide detailed knowledge of how best to proceed in the teaching of different subjects in different grades.

The fourth claim for emphasis on structure and principles in teaching is that by constantly reexamining material taught in elementary and secondary schools for its fundamental character, one is able to narrow the gap between "advanced" knowledge and "elementary" knowledge. Part of the difficulty now found in the progression from primary school through high school to college is that material learned earlier is either out of date or misleading by virtue of its lagging too far behind developments in a field. This gap can be reduced by the kind of emphasis set forth in the preceding discussion.

Consider now some specific problems that received considerable discussion at Woods Hole. One of them has to do with the troubled topic of "general science". There are certain recurrent ideas that appear in virtually all branches of science. If in one subject one has learned them well and generally, that achievement should make the task of learning them again in different form elsewhere in science much easier. Various teachers and scientists have raised the question whether these basic ideas should not be "isolated", so to speak, and taught more explicitly in a manner that frees them from specific areas of science. The type of idea can be easily illustrated: categorization and its uses, the unit of measure and its development, the indirectness of information in science and the need for operational definition of ideas, and so forth. With respect to the last, for example, we do not *see* pressure or the chemical bond directly but infer it indirectly from a set of measures. So too body temperature. So too sadness in another person. Can these and similar ideas be presented effectively and with a variety of concrete illustrations in the early grades in order to give the child a better basis for understanding their specific representation in various special disciplines later? Is it wise to teach such "general science" as an introduction to disciplinary sciences in the later grades? How should they be taught and what could we reasonably expect by way of easier learning later? Much research is needed on this promising topic – research not only on the usefulness of such an approach, but also on the kinds of general scientific ideas that might be taught.

Indeed, it may well be that there are certain general attitudes or approaches toward science or literature that can be taught in the earlier grades that would have considerable relevance for later learning. The attitude that things are connected and not isolated is a case in point. One can indeed imagine kindergarten games designed to make children more actively alert to how things affect or are connected with each other – a kind of introduction to the idea of multiple determination of events in the physical and the social world. Any working scientist is usually able to say something about the ways of thinking or attitudes that are a part of his craft. Historians have written rather extensively on this subject as far as their field is concerned. Literary men have even evolved a genre of writing about the forms of sensibility that make for literary taste and vigor. In mathematics, this subject has a formal name, "heuristic", to describe the approach one takes to solving problems. One may well argue, as it was argued at Woods Hole by men in widely differing disciplines, that it might be wise to assess what attitudes or heuristic devices are most pervasive and useful, and that an effort should be made to teach children a rudimentary version of them that might be further refined as they progress through school. Again, the reader will sense that the argument for such an approach is premised on the assumption that there is a continuity between what a scholar does on the forefront of his discipline and what a child does in approaching it for the first time. This is not to say that the task is a simple one, only that it is worthy of careful consideration and research.

Perhaps the chief arguments put forward in opposition to the idea of such efforts at teaching general principles and general attitudes are, first, that it is better to approach the general through the specific and, second, that working attitudes should be kept implicit rather than being made explicit. For example, one of the principal organizing concepts in biology is the persistent question, "What function does this thing serve?" – a question premised on the assumption that everything one finds in an organism serves some function or it probably would not have survived. Other general ideas are related to this question. The student who makes progress in biology learns to ask the question more and more subtly, to relate more and more things to it. At the next step he asks what function a particular structure or process serves in the light of what is required in the total functioning of an organism. Measuring and categorizing are carried out in the service of the general idea of function. Then beyond that he may organize his knowledge in terms of a still more comprehensive notion of function, turning to cellular structure or to phylogenetic comparison. It may well be that the style of thought of a particular discipline is necessary as a background for learning the working meaning of general concepts, in which case a general introduction to the meaning of "function" might be less effective than teaching it in the context of biology.

As for "attitude" teaching or even the teaching of heuristic in mathematics, the argument runs that if the learner becomes too aware of his own attitudes or approach, he may become mechanical or trick-oriented in his work. No evidence exists on the point, and research is needed before any effort is made to teach in this way. Work is now going on at Illinois on training children to be more effective in asking questions about physical phenomena, but much more information is needed before the issue is clear.

One hears often the distinction between "doing" and "understanding". It is distinction applied to the case, for example, of a student who presumably understands a mathematical idea but does not know how to use it in computation. While the distinction is probably a false one – since how can one know what a student understands save by seeing what he does – it points to an interesting difference in emphasis in teaching and in learning. Thus one finds in some of the classic books on the psychology of problem solving (such as Max Wertheimer's *Productive Thinking*) a sharp line drawn between "rote drill" and "understanding". In point of fact, drill need not be rote and, alas, emphasis on understanding may lead the student to a certain verbal glibness. It has been the experience of members of the School Mathematics Study Group that computational practice may be a necessary step toward understanding conceptual ideas in mathematics. Similarly one may try to give the high school student a sense of styles by having him read contrasting authors, yet final insight into style may come only when the student himself tries his hand at writing in different styles. Indeed, it is the underlying premise of laboratory exercises that doing something helps one understand it. There is a certain wisdom in the quip made by a psychologist at Woods Hole: "How do I know what I think until I feel what I do?" In any case, the distinction is not a very helpful one. What is more to the point is to ask what methods of exercise in any given field are most likely to give the student a sense of intelligent mastery over the material. What are the most fruitful computational exercises that one can use in various branches of mathematics? Does the effort to write in the style of Henry James give one an especially good insight into that author's style? Perhaps a good start toward understanding such matters would be to study the methods used by successful teachers. It would be surprising if the information compiled failed to suggest a host of worthwhile laboratory studies on techniques of teaching – or, indeed, on techniques of imparting complex information generally.

A word is needed, finally, on examinations. It is obvious that an examination can be bad in the sense of emphasizing trivial aspects of a subject. Such examinations can encourage teaching in a disconnected fashion and learning by rote. What is often overlooked, however, is that examinations can also be allies in the battle to improve curricula and teaching. Whether an examination is of the "objective" type involving multiple choices or of the essay type, it can be devised so as to emphasize an understanding of the broad principles of a subject. Indeed, even when one examines on detailed knowledge, it can be done in such a way as to require an understanding by the student of the connectedness between specific facts. There is a concerted effort now under way among national testing organizations like the Educational Testing Service to construct examinations that will emphasize an understanding of fundamental principles. Such efforts can be of great help. Additional help might be given to local school systems by making available to them manuals that describe the variety of ways in which examinations can be constructed. The searching examination is not easy to make, and a thoughtful manual on the subject would be welcome.

To recapitulate, the main theme of this chapter has been that the curriculum of a subject should be determined by the most fundamental understanding that can be achieved of the underlying principles that give structure to the subject. Teaching specific topics or skills without making clear their context in the broader fundamental structure of a field of knowledge is uneconomical in several deep senses. In the first place, such teaching makes it exceedingly difficult for the student to generalize from what he has learned to what he will encounter later. In the second place, learning that has fallen short of a grasp of general principles has little reward in terms of intellectual excitement. The best way to create interest in a subject is to render it worth knowing, which means to make the knowledge gained usable in one's thinking beyond the situation in which the learning has occurred. Third, knowledge one has acquired without sufficient structure to tie it together is knowledge that is likely to be forgotten. An unconnected set of facts has a pitiably short half-life in memory. Organizing facts in terms of principles and ideas from which they may be inferred is the only known way of reducing the quick rate of loss of human memory.

Designing curricula in a way that reflects the basic structure of a field of knowledge requires the most fundamental understanding of that field. It is a task that cannot be carried out without the active participation of the ablest scholars and scientists. The experience of the past several years has shown that such scholars and scientists, working in conjunction with experienced teachers and students of child development, can prepare curricula of the sort we have been considering. Much more effort in the actual preparation of curriculum materials, in teacher training, and in supporting research will be necessary if improvements in our educational practices are to be of an order that will meet the challenges of the scientific and social revolution through which we are now living.

There are many problems of how to teach general principles in a way that will be both effective and interesting, and several of the key issues have been passed in review. What is abundantly clear is that much work remains to be done by way of examining currently effective practices, fashioning curricula that may be tried out on an experimental basis, and carrying out the kinds of research that can give support and guidance to the general effort at improving teaching.

22. Man: A Course of Study – A Critique

R.M. Jones

Source: *Fantasy and Feeling in Education*, Richard M. Jones, (Penguin, Harmondsworth, 1972), pp.76-85, 184-8. ©New York University, 1968.

Here Bruner's original conception for 'Man: a course of study' is criticised for its over-emphasis on cognitive skills and curriculum materials and its under-emphasis on emotional skills and pedagogy. Jones illustrates how, in classroom use, the course can inhibit children's expression of the vivid emotional responses that the materials evoke. He also illustrates how guidance in teaching can correct this. This critique stems from the conviction that the study of man is necessarily isomorphic with the development of the child's inner life. A teacher understanding the subject-matter of social studies should therefore be able to engage children's intuitive and imaginative powers in directly relevant ways.

> Children, like adults, need reassurance that it is all right to entertain and express highly subjective ideas, to treat a task as a problem where you *invent* an answer rather than *finding* one out there in the book or on the blackboard. With children in elementary school, there is often a need to devise emotionally vivid, special games, story-making episodes, or construction projects to re-establish in the child's mind his right not only to have his own private ideas but to express them in the public setting of a classroom.

But these are not this writer's words. They are Bruner's.[1] He had been speaking of how to stimulate thought in the setting of a school, and had concluded that this is best done by teachers who offer tasks which represent problems to be solved, rather than solutions to be memorized. He goes on to note that the progressive movement's emphasis on personalized knowledge had led to the banalities about the friendly postman, etc., and he suggests that there is more merit in children's discoveries of 'kinship and likeness in what at first seemed bizarre, exotic, and even a little repellent'. He concludes with an illustration:

> It has to do with Alexei who, with his father's help, devises a snare and catches a gull. There is a scene in which he stones the gull to death. Our children watched, horror struck. One girl, Kathy, blurted out, 'He's not even human, doing that to the seagull.' The class was silent. Then another girl, Jennine, said quietly: 'He's got to grow up to be a hunter. His mother was smiling when he was doing that.' And then an extended discussion about how people have to do

> things to learn and even do things to learn how to feel appropriately. 'What would you do if you had to live there? Would you be as smart about getting along as they are with what they've got?' said one boy, going back to the accusation that Alexei was inhuman to stone the bird.

Well said, but while the illustration speaks to the pedagogical power of emotionally vivid *stimuli* (in this instance a very authentic film), it offers nothing to teachers in the way of guidance as to how they are to bring the children into controlled and productive ways of responding to their responses to these stimuli. The teacher is thus led to conclude that she has but to show the film in order to bring about the kind of discussion described.

I cannot refrain from saying that I speak with some authority on these points, since it was I who devised the lesson which supplied my friend with his illustration. And two very accomplished teachers, Mr David Martin and Mrs Linda Braun, who made it work with the children. Therefore, claiming whatever squatter's rights may apply here, I will give the illustration its full context.

The youngsters were, once again, in pursuit of understanding the Netsilik. As reported:

> In the films, a single nuclear family, Zachary, Marta and their four year old Alexei, is followed through the year–spring sealing, summer fishing at the stone weir, fall caribou hunting, early winter fishing through the ice, winter at the big ceremonial igloo. The children report that at first the three members of the family look weird and uncouth. In time, they look normal, and eventually, as when Marta finds sticks around which to wrap her braids, the girls speak of how pretty she is. That much is superficial – or so it seems.

'But consider a second episode,' says Bruner, and uses the illustration quoted above. A good deal had transpired between the superficial and the profound in this class. In fact, the children had been growing increasingly restive and unreachable as they were shown the films of spring sealing, summer fishing at the stone weir, and fall caribou hunting. Moreover, they had begun to develop attitudes towards the Netsilik which were the opposite of those the course was designed to instil. The Netsilik were coming to be seen alternately as savages with no hearts (and therefore too disagreeable to comprehend) and just one more distant society of which it can be said that 'they have their customs, and we have ours' (thus, too trivial to comprehend). In other words, instead of cultivating deepened awareness of the humanizing forces at work in all human societies, we were dangerously close to teaching generalized attitudes of prejudice and apathy. Mr Martin sought out a consultant to talk over what might be done to remedy the situation.

Was this behaviour typical of the children? 'No, they were "Newton children".' What, then, did he sense the trouble to be? 'The films!' . . . 'The kids have had a daily diet of blood and cruelty, and the eating of fish eyes. I think they just want to holler "Ouch".' Why not let them? 'I'm not sure I know how. . . . Besides, they're supposed to be thinking of Arctic ecology, and the advantages of social organization, division of labour, and so forth.'

That very morning Mr Martin had shown the film of the fall caribou hunt. It superbly depicts the advantages that accrue to the Netsilik as a consequence of social organization and division of labour in hunting the much needed caribou. The film opens with scenes of one group of hunters decoying two caribou into the water, where caribou are at great disadvantage. Further out at bay two other hunters are waiting in their kayaks. Under these circumstances the caribou are clearly no match for the hunters. The hunters, just as obviously, do not press their luck. They do press the feelings of the viewer, however. If ever there was an unfair contest it is this! With red blood, drooping heads, and begging brown eyes to accentuate whatever experiences with unfair contests the viewer may be bringing to these scenes. Clearly, a couple of caribou must inevitably give themselves over to a couple of socially organized *homo sapiens* capable of dividing their labours! [. . .]

The children, as their teacher well knew, had every cause to be 'restive'. But why 'unreachable'? What did Mr Martin think? 'I think they need to vent some steam before they can appreciate the points about social organization and division of labour.' Why not let them, then? 'How?'

We should first appreciate Mr Martin's style of conducting a class. He is always very calmly on the move. Within any span of five minutes, every child has tangibly felt his presence – the brush of a trouser leg, the tap of a finger, a palm on shoulder, or, when necessary, the firm grip of his eyes. All very soothing to the children. It says to them: there is little danger in this class of anyone getting out of control, so you can think as you wish. In this atmosphere the first signs of boisterousness in response to the films had merely required 'None of that!', and emotional control held sway. This was inhibitory control, however, and Mr Martin was now concerned that it was being carried too far. How to help the children to replace their *inhibitory* emotional skills with *regulative* emotional skills?

The following plan was devised: a short lesson on language would first be given in which the children would distinguish 'instruction' messages. The teacher would then confront the children with a mock dilemma: someone had put it to him the day before that the Netsilik were, in fact, not human beings at all, but some other species! How would the class instruct him to answer that person? Then, assuming the children to be on the side of Netsilik humanness, they would be given an opportunity to share the feelings they had until now inhibited in respect to some of the more repellent aspects of Netsilik behaviour. The children would then be given an opportunity to *use* these feelings by trying to empathize with Alexei in what was known to be the most repellent scene in the Netsilik footage: the stoning of the seagull. Finally, they would be shown a film of Netsilik children at more familiar kinds of play, and asked to contrast it with the seagull sequence.

Mr Martin had one major obstacle to overcome before proceeding with the plan. To a man, his supporting staff of evaluators and researchers were opposed to it: the seagull sequence *was* inhuman and should be excluded from the curriculum. It would 'push the kids too far'; the films they had seen already were 'a bit much'; this one would surely convince them the Netsilik were not human! One lady threatened not to attend the class if Mr Martin persisted in this 'abusive' plan.

The children's responses are worth reporting in detail (after the lesson on 'instruction' and 'feeling' messages):

TEACHER: Why is it good to be able to send 'instruction' messages?
STUDENT: For planning.
S: The future.
S: The world wouldn't be right – parents wouldn't be able to tell children what to do.
S: For driving, like: 'Slow down here' etc.
T: Why is it good to be able to express feelings?
S: If you're mad at someone you have it out with them.
S: It's nice to say when you're happy.
S: It feels good for *you* to say when you're mad.
S: Maybe you want to kill someone for playing badly in a game. If you say so, you're less likely to act violently.
T: Yesterday someone came up to me and said that these Netsilik were not human beings at all. I wasn't sure what to say to him. Can you tell me what to say?
[*A chorus of excitedly waving hands*]
S: They look like us.
S: They have the same bone structure.
S: They don't look like animals.
S: You could test their temperature to see if it's the same.
S: They have spears.
S: They build homes.
S: They make clothes.
S: They use their brains. Animals have instincts.
S: They speak a language without using other parts of their bodies.
S: They can be killed . . . by a walrus.
T: Now I want you to write in your notebooks some things you've seen the Netsilik do that you found difficult to understand, or that *you* could never do.

Examples

'Clean a fish and get so bloody.'
'Eat seal raw.'
'Eat blood.'
'Eat eyes.'
'Why the Netsilik don't multiply more.'
'How can they be so heartless?'
'Cut a seal open.'
'How could they eat fish? I know I would never eat a fish eye, or drink blood soup, or eat seal meat raw, or skin the seal the way they do. I would help skin one, but I would never do one myself.' 'Spear caribou, when they can't fight back.'

T: Now we're going to see two films of Netsilik children playing. The second one will be familiar to you, the kinds of play you engage in. The first film will be difficult to understand. So I want you to pay close attention in the first film to how the boy is *feeling* and how his mother is *feeling.*

From notebooks:

'I think the boy felt happy because in the film he seemed so happy when he killed it.'

'I don't think the boy had any trouble killing the bird because he wants to be like his father, so he had to kill the bird. The mother was very happy and proud because she saw that her son would not have any problem in killing something to eat. The way she smiled at him, as if she were saying "Good work, son".'

'I thought the boy had no feelings because he let the bird suffer. I think if he was going to be killed, they should kill him with a knife. I think the mother felt sorry because she was looking kind of sad when the boy was killing the bird.'

'I think the boy was happy because it was sort of like a game to him and he was smiling as though it was fun. I thought the mother was glad they had the bird because she picked up the boy and swung him around and she acted as though she needed the food.' 'I think the mother was happy for the son the way she kissed him.' 'He felt proud of himself because he was killing the bird. She felt proud of her son because he was killing the bird and would soon be a fine hunter.'

'I think the boy felt glad that he could really be like his father to kill a bird and then a seal. The mother, I think, felt proud of her little boy and that he was doing a good job of killing him.'

'The boy felt happy and proud because that was probably the first he had killed. The mother was kind of sad to see the bird being crucified and struggling.'

'I think the boy enjoyed killing the bird because he didn't cry about it and he looked happy. I think he liked playing with the legs because they were like toys. The mother was happy because she had some food for the family She hugged her son when he brought her the bird. I felt sorry for the bird because it was suffering, but happy for the boy.'

'He must have felt very happy because that might have been the first animal he caught, and the way the mother hugged the boy showed she must have been proud of him for the good work he did. I felt like I was standing on my head. I felt awful because I was sad for the bird.'

After the second film, a discussion followed:

JERRY: I killed a bird once myself.
BILLY: Yeah, I was with him and it took us quite a while but we finally did it.
EMILY: I felt awful sorry for the bird in the film.
ELAINE: But we kill animals too, for meat, and nobody seems to mind.
RICHARD: Yeah, how about slaughter houses and all those cows?
PAT: The Eskimo children seem to be loving children in the second film, especially the girl holding the dog.
RICHARD: They were playing house in that film.
AUDREY: The first film showed a boy practising to be a hunter, but the second one showed some children just playing.
EMILY: In the first film it seemed to me the boy was being sort of mean, but in the second film they were being very nice.
JERRY: Don't forget they have to kill to live, though.
JOHN: Yeah, and in the second film they're not having to kill anything.
JEAN: We are all civilized in different ways.
ELLEN: Yes, but some of you kids are looking at these Eskimos from the way *you* see things, and not the way *they* see them.

It was in the course of this discussion that Kathy and Jennine engaged in the interchange cited earlier.

Let us take another example. Bruner begins his description of 'Man: a course of study' with these inviting phrases:

> . . . It is only in a trivial sense that one gives a course to 'get something across', merely to impart information. There are better means to that end than teaching. Unless the learner also masters himself, disciplines his tastes, deepens his views of the world, the something that is got across is hardly worth the effort of transmission.[2]

There follows, eloquently, a description of the content of the course, and of the materials that will carry this content. As to pedagogy, we hear of the powers of the contrast case, the benefits of 'informed guessing', the values of student participation and the advantages of stimulating 'self-consciousness about thinking'. A generation of teachers has come to call the aggregate of these the 'self-discovery method' – wherein one can sometimes observe the self, discovering, all right, but rarely the discovering of self.

What must the teacher conclude who was initially led to expect guidance in teaching the course in such ways as would help the student 'master himself, discipline his tastes, and deepen his views of the world'? Either that Bruner said it and she didn't get it, and so it must be beyond her. Or that since he refers exclusively to the *cognitive* self, to *rational* tastes, and to *intellectual* views of the world, he must mean that the emotional and evaluative aspects of these processes will somehow take care of themselves. Thus, the counter-reformational suggestion: do as always, only more so.

For calling Bruner on this way he has of sometimes leading teachers up the more heady reaches of familiar paths, John Holt got called a romancer of 'no-think thinking'; Gordon Allport, who once called Bruner a rationalist, was let off more easily – his being presumed to be a case of preoccupation with an 'appearance'. With some trepidation, therefore, I shall contend that Bruner's impact on teachers has been that of a rationalist.

His over-emphasis on cognitive skills and curricular materials, and his corresponding under-emphasis on emotional skills and pedagogy have been generally illustrated in the fore-going accounts. [. . .] I should like to bring attention to two other general imbalances in his writings on education. The first pertains to a preoccupation with that aggregate of human motives which have been variously termed 'autonomous', 'aggressive', 'agentic', etc., to the seeming exclusion of another aggregate of human motives which various of our colleagues have termed 'homonomous', 'libidinal', 'communal', etc. The second imbalance pertains to a preoccupation with the processes of 'concept attainment', or discovery; to the seeming exclusion of the processes of concept formation', or invention.

Neither form of exclusivism reflects deliberate choice. Doubtless they reflect the shape of one man's curiosity. As such, they would merit the respect of silence, were it not that the sweep of Bruner's pen sometimes conjures other shapes.

Intrinsic motivation is a more durable aid to learning than extrinsic motivation, says Bruner. Teachers should therefore wean the child whenever possible from a system of extrinsic rewards and punishments to a system of self-reward. In itself, this point is very well taken. Also emphasized is that Man's use of mind is dependent upon his ability to develop and use tools, instruments and technologies. The main emphasis in education should therefore be placed upon skills – 'skills in handling in seeing and imagining, and in symbolic operations, particularly as these relate to the technologies that have made them so powerful in their human expression'.[3]

These points are also, in themselves, well taken. In presenting 'Man: a course of study' he has it that technology, social organization, language, education and cosmology are the five great humanizing forces in that they amplify the human animal's powers and enable him to extend dominion over his environment:

> Man gains better technical control of his world through modern science than he does through mythic explanation; but in science and in myth, the same component processes or logical operations provide the base. It is in this sense that we try to make clear that man is equally human whether he uses a stone axe or a steel one, explains eclipses by astronomy or by spirits, murders with a gun or by the use of magic.[4]

Again, very well taken.

But one looks in vain for the needed counterpoints. Teachers and children mean more to each other than can be expressed by reference to reward systems – self – or otherwise. Man's use of mind is certainly amplified by his tools and technologies, but so is his use of heart. People make myths and scientific theories, not only the better to explain their lives, but also the better to share them.

There has been criticism that the materials of 'Man: a course of study' have, during the course of their various stages of development and production, come to place a disproportionate emphasis on technology at the expense of the other fundamental humanizing agents; language, social organization, cosmology and education. Perhaps this criticism is merited. I do sometimes sense the influence of a monocular interpretation of the Washburn thesis in these materials. Perhaps, too, a certain technological drift is inherent in producing curricular materials in the first place, since they are themselves tools. At best, however, this criticism misses the point. It is true that a teacher who has not made an intellectual home of her own for these subjects may end up teaching a course on seal hunting, warthog catching, harpoon making, or whatever the materials, taken alone, may suggest, rather than a course on man. Give the same teacher cross-cultural materials on child-rearing practices, comparative mythology, or the design features of communication systems, however, and she will still not teach a course on man, but, more than likely, a series of disjointed lessons about 'children from other lands', 'science and superstition', and 'the amazing bee'.

On the other hand, let us take a teacher who is herself in the process of mastering the subject of cultural evolution, its continuities and discontinuities with organic and inorganic evolution – a teacher on whom it has perhaps dawned that the single most illustrative case in point of her subject is the manifest presence of she and the children at the apex of seven billion years of ordered change on this planet, engaged in the transmitting and inheriting of what it may be all about. It would be inconceivable to such a teacher that a unit on Eskimo seal hunting might be used as anything but another avenue to the study of psychosocial adaptation in its full and fulfilling complexities, such as how human technology amplifies and redefines the human arm, leg, or sense organs; how the environment itself is thus amplified and redefined as regards its life-giving possibilities. Rather, one would expect to find this teacher formulating lessons in terms of such heuristics as: what kind of an animal is it that fashions an arm that flies like a bird, pierces like a fang, and holds onto its prey like a snake? (See Zachary stalk, decoy and harpoon his seal.) Is it not an animal that fulfils its dreams? And what kind of an animal is it that submits the conduct of its life to imagined versions of prey which nature, in four billion years, never produced? Is it not an animal that dreams some of its fulfilments? And what kind of an animal could so act like its prey as to seem to be one? And so on. Is it not a play-acting animal? What other tools and rules does this 'arm' presume, enable, require? What are the ways that this animal *must* relate and what are some ways that it *may* relate, to others of its kind, as a function of its capacity to develop such 'arms'? What are the problems it solves and what are the problems it poses? What are the choices it gives? What are the choices it takes away? And what are some corresponding thoughts about certain contemporary 'arms': the one that reaches to Pelly Bay in the overhead projector, or from the principal's office on the PA system, or to the moon from Cape Kennedy, or to hell from Omaha?

Such a teacher will also not be embarrassed to entertain whatever the children may choose to believe, or to make believe, that this is all about.

We come now to the point of relevance about 'relevance'. It was Elting Morison, the former director of EDC's[5] social studies programmes, who once said to a group of teachers that they should find ways of 'constantly bringing the children to the engagement of intuitive and imaginative powers which reach beyond the data'. By 'data' he meant the social studies materials being produced by [EDC]. I hope I have been sufficiently persuasive in previous chapters to remind Mr Morison that the intuitive and imaginative powers of schoolchildren reside in their emotion-toned inner lives. And that, by overseeing the construction of a curriculum which is necessarily isomorphic with the development of these inner lives, he has made it likely that teachers who understand both their subject matter and their pupils will probably succeed in following his directives.

What does it mean, that the study of man is necessarily isomorphic with the development of children's inner lives? One thing it means is that we cannot employ such an outline of the human life cycle as was detailed in chapter 6* without commensurately highlighting the three nuclear distinctions of our species: prolonged maturation [. . .]; symbolization [. . .] and socialization [. . .]. There is in the social studies and humanities, in other words, a built-in economy which can find the teacher implicitly exercising her comprehension of children while explicitly seeking to comprehend the subject matter, and implicitly exercising her comprehension of the subject matter while explicitly seeking to comprehend the children.

Another dimension of isomorphism was implied when it was said that children can best discover this particular subject for themselves by discovering themselves in this particular subject. There is more than rhetorical value in this statement. Rather, it follows quite literally from the fact that man's prolonged and singularly sequenced maturation *is* one of the three nuclear conditions to which psychosocial evolution can be traced. Thus no lesson in a course of study on man can be optimally taught without some consideration of its relevance to human childhood. For example, should we want to teach grade schoolers the basic differences between human languages and other systems of animal communication we would have to find a way to make the design features of 'arbitrariness' (reference to events in ways that are independent of the events themselves) and 'productivity' (transformation of events in ways that go beyond direct experience of the events) interesting and meaningful to them. The ablest of teachers, equipped with the cleverest of materials, have found these objectives to be out of reach, because they drew illustrations and analogies from the referential field of linguistics alone. The children first needed to objectify more familiar experiences of arbitrariness and productivity, in order to assimilate the highly abstract linguistic connotations of these concepts.

Now, while admittedly the question of the origins of human language is a highly speculative one, and likely to remain so, it is surely not coincidental that the design features of arbitrariness and productivity became fundamental to the communication system of a large-brained animal that spends a large portion of its life span in a state of dependence on its progenitors, and whose survival is therefore contingent on its ability to adapt both to the 'arbitrariness' of its protectors and to the 'productivity' of its central nervous system. Thus, exercises, lessons and activities which sought to help the children to objectify and to articulate their homely experiences with parental restraints and with their own worlds of make-believe would be of prime relevance *in the hands of a teacher who understood the subject matter.* Such exercises, lessons and activities, so far from being more diversionary indulgences of children's narcissistic whims, as they are sometimes accused of being, might, on the contrary, provide just that angle of pedagogic leverage without which instruction in such abstract matters must be seen as too far for children to fetch [. . .].

Admittedly, these auxiliary exercises would derive their special interest value from their proximity to the special interests of children. But that is precisely the point to be emphasized: it happens in this particular course of study – man – that what happens to be especially interesting to the children also happens to be especially honest in respect to the subject.

In other courses of study appeals to narcissism may be diversionary in effect. In *this* course of study, however, such appeals are exactly indicated not only as means of motivating the children but as crucial curricular objectives in their own right.

Notes

1 BRUNER, J.S. (1965), 'The growth of mind', *Amer. Psychol.*, vol. 20, pp.1007-17.
2 BRUNER, J.S. (1966), *Toward a Theory of Instruction*, Harvard University Press, p.73.
3 BRUNER (1966), p.34.
4 ibid., p.88.
5 Education Development Center, Cambridge, Mass.

23. Curiosity, Competence, Community

Janet P. Hanley, Dean K. Whitla, Eunice Moss and Arlene S. Walter

Source: *Curiosity, Competence, Community – Man: a course of study, an evaluation: a summary of the original two-volume edition,* Janet P. Hanley, Dean K. Whitla, Eunice W. Moss and Arlene S. Walter (Education Development Center, 1969, 1970), pp.8-15, 33-49.

The MACOS evaluation program was guided by the evaluators' understanding of the humanistic aims and framework of the course itself. In the first of these extracts from the summary of their report they explain the rationale and diversified methodology of the evaluation program. In the second they draw their main conclusions as to how far MACOS can be judged a success in its own terms.

During the process of evaluating *Man: A Course of Study*, we frequently encountered from educators and researchers questions as to behavioral goals. The course has not been framed within the confines of a behavioral psychology, nor have its developers thought specifically in behaviorist terms as they prepared and tested it. Rather, the course was developed within a humanistic framework, by way of its emphasis upon the anthropological, biological and ethnographic. Its organizing question, "What makes man human?" has always been asked in the broadest possible sense, and its framers, from Bruner on, have emphasized the resonance of the question within the material.

We did attempt to review various lessons of the course in terms of specified inputs and expected outcomes, but disenchantment with this method was quick. It was indeed possible to pinpoint and specify behavior for each individual lesson, but the course as presented within such an outline lost its special power and charm. It lost its essential quality: the inclusive coherence of several powerful organizing ideas. By their specificity and attachment to a given lesson, the defined behaviors undermined what the developers expected to be the culminating objective of a theme as it recurred throughout the course. We were, in fact, reminded of William James's judgement many years ago on his own field of psychology when he declared it "a nasty little subject – all one cares to know lies outside." This was a good part of the problem. From another perspective, one working party member who had helped to create the materials of the course said:

> We hope that the theme of learning gives youngsters a way of considering the effect of learning on their own lives and the importance

of learning to the human species. The formal way in which these behavioral goals are stated leaves little room for the importance of individual a-ha's: those moments when a child gets an idea that helps him order his experience in a new way. We can't predict what causes this to happen in any one classroom, but we know that it does. For example, as I once did (one of the) exercises with a class, one child became fascinated with the idea that what she was learning was shaping her life, would influence her life as an adult. She began looking at what she was doing with this perspective, using the experience of other children to contrast with her own.

The global nature of the course does not mean that we cannot assess outcomes in the classroom. The goals are accessible to research and provoked us to reach beyond traditional methods for measuring learning, to more innovative and reflective ways of evaluation. The questions below have given focus to this assessment:

1. Does *Man: A Course of Study* help students learn to understand themselves and others in ways they were incapable of before, and are they able to use this new knowledge in and out of the classroom?
2. Do students gain a more accurate knowledge of specific topics by using these materials?

   Are they better at using evidence (including evidence from all types of media, not only written) and observing natural and social phenomena?

   Can they go beyond specifics to some organizing conjectures about human behavior?
3. Is there a consistent style of pedagogy embedded in *Man: A Course of Study* that is identifiable by and appropriate for different types of students?

   Are the pedagogy and approach of the materials different from those of traditional social studies?

   If so, how does this pedagogy affect learning and class activities?
4. Do teachers' styles change in the course of teaching these materials?
5. How do the socio-economic and ability variables affect the teaching and learning of this material?

   Is the course most effective with highly verbal students, or does it work as well for students with poorer reading and writing skills?

   Does a unit function as well in the inner city as in well-to-do suburban systems?

   Are there special motivational values for disadvantaged youngsters in various media?

We have looked on the evaluation process in the most global sense as extension of a human need: to know where one has been to understand where one is going; to see what was in order to see what is. Both students and teachers need ways of summarizing and reflecting upon what has been learned if mastery and growth are to be recognized and consolidated. But we have found that youngsters have seldom been asked to participate in the considerations affecting the process of their own education, though educators expect such curricula as the social studies to provide children with resources for making decisions affecting their private and public lives. Much of this evaluation, then, is centered on youngsters' perceptions and critical insights; by eliciting from them their own ideas about the materials, we hoped also to strengthen the student's ability to use ethnographic sources of evidence, to progress in skills of hypothesizing, analyzing and synthesizing, and to become an active participant in the classroom. A piece of curriculum cannot be evaluated realistically without understanding its impact and functioning from the student's point of view. In the past, evaluation has been focused too much on teacher assessments with only achievement test scores speaking for the students.

Jerome Bruner's *Toward a Theory of Instruction* has set down valuable guidelines for those with temerity enough to venture into the area of comprehensive evaluation. His emphasis on the "intelligence" function of evaluation, and on the importance of understanding the teacher who is teaching and the student who is learning, were vital components of our work. In addition, his point of view on the morality of the profession underscored the need to evaluate in an exploratory, thoughtful, yet disciplined manner:

> The aims of the educational enterprise . . . center upon the problem of assisting the development of human beings so that they can use their potential powers to achieve a good life and make an effective contribution to their society. When one loses sight of that objective, both education and its evaluation become technical and sterile. The task of understanding how human beings, in fact, can be assisted in their learning and development is the central task of a theory of instruction, and techniques of evaluation derive from it in the same way that the practice of medicine derives from the medical sciences.[1]

Methodology

We have used the *interview* method to understand what children make of the course, and how intimately they use the materials; *classroom environment checklists* [. . .] to understand how, both as individuals and as groups, they view the course materials and the work they do in class; and *tests* to judge the consistency with which a body of information was conveyed to groups of children. We have no fondness for test-giving, or test-taking per se, and have minimized these elements in this evaluation. Written pre-tests and post-tests at the beginning and end of each of the two *Man: A Course of*

Study sections have served mainly as group measures to provide a standard against which we can compare how children from different settings and grade levels are able to deal with the materials.

A personal response has been sought from teachers. Here again, the *interview* has proved a flexible technique; *observing* in the classroom has given us an understanding of the course-in-action on a daily basis, and has permitted an evaluation of changes in teacher style that may be attributable to the course.

The range of these methods has provided a validity that excelled that of any one technique. When several different techniques resulted in corroborating information, we began to feel confidence in the findings. Essentially, we have used both clinical and quantitative assessment. In addition, we have experimented with ways of measuring objective and subjective behavior, and in experimenting, have found that the devices themselves affect the students, for our interviews and checklists seem to provide youngsters with a methodology in itself – an approach to evaluating situations such as the classroom and their own responses to a course of study.

The Clinical Method. During the teaching of the course, we interviewed periodically a sample of city and suburban students who represented all ability levels. These interviews were conducted using semistructured open-ended leading questions. Students were interviewed either individually or in small groups by trained interviewers, and the interviews were recorded. When interviews were analyzed from transcriptions, they provided not only rich illumination of the more objective data, but causal explanations for the objective performance.

The Quantitative Method. Completed by all students involved in the field test, checklists gathered information on classroom environment, student involvement and participation, success of presentation of materials through various media, reading and homework, students' assessment of their own attitudes and learning styles. Results of these checklists were tabulated according to demographic sub-groups and were subjected to factor analytic techniques. In addition, the responses to open-ended questions at the end of the checklist helped us interpret the limited-choice questions.

Pre-tests and Post-tests. These tests, based on objective essay and scale formats, stressed many attributes of student learning: reading skills, use of evidence and ability to generalize, vocabulary, graphing and mapping, interpretation of visual materials, attitudes and personal preferences.

Classroom and Teacher Training Evaluation

Studying the classroom from the students' perspective, we soon learned that we had to focus also on a critical variable in the educational process: the classroom teacher. The first year's assessments of the teacher's role were culled from the students' point of view. For the last two years of field testing, we added an extensive series of classroom and seminar observations and teacher interviews to supplement the first findings and to determine the effect of the teacher training program. Through classroom observations especially, we wanted to learn more about the interaction of curriculum, methods, students and teachers.

We sought the teacher's reactions to the curriculum materials, classroom style, student response, and the workshop experience. Teachers were asked to define their roles and to give their views of the functioning of a unit. Coupled with this intensive material, the additional information from observers' reports of classrooms and workshops permitted us to evaluate more directly the relationship between teacher characteristics and student characteristics, with our curriculum materials as the catalyst.

Perspective of the Evaluators

The tests and checklists were constructed by evaluation staff members working closely with the course developers. As we developed and carried through the evaluation program, we confronted the issue of bias, of contamination of our findings caused by long and close exposure to the EDC philosophy and to *Man: A Course of Study.* This close relationship could result in distorted findings. Keeping this caveat in mind, we realized that no evaluation can be, or should be, value-free. Everyone has assumptions about education and its best goals. To work freely and well in a situation, the evaluators must feel sympathy for the intentions of the curriculum project – in this case, creating the inquiring, interactive classroom focused around issues of man's humanness. Our task was to learn how, and to what degree if any, the curriculum achieved its purpose, and at the same time to shed more light on the process of learning.

Does the Course Succeed on its own Terms?

Reciprocity and Diversity

The fundamental learning style of *Man: A Course of Study* is the emphasis on reciprocal learning. The course lessons mirror closely the process by which it was constructed – not by single individuals working independently of one another, but through a group process (the working party) where approaches and ideas were exchanged and debated by scholars, teachers, artists, and researchers. Translated into classroom terms, this means that the responsibility for formulating a position is shifted from "authority" centers – texts, teachers, lectures, didactic films – to student resourcefulness in integrating information from data sources. Ideally, the teacher is central not as a source of "answers" but as the catalyst of events, as a model of one who explores and questions human behavior and who is visible and available to students in a mutually concerned search for understanding. Films, field research, information and concept booklets, student and teacher inputs serve as these data sources. The suggested activities raise questions and pose problems, but the materials are intended as the triggering mechanisms for student-generated questions.

If the desired outcome of social studies in the schools is a totally consistent and common body of information, then the methods of this course are not the appropriate ones. If, however, the educator believes that knowledge about behavior is not definitive, not circumscribed, but open-ended and subject to a range of educated response, then this course makes that responsiveness possible.

> Reciprocity ... requires recognition of one critically important matter: you cannot have both reciprocity and the demand that everyone learn the same thing or be "completely" well rounded in the same way all the time. If reciprocally operative groups are to give support to learning by stimulating each person to join his efforts to a group, then we shall need tolerance for the specialized roles that develop – the critic, the innovator, the second helper, the cautionary. For it is from the cultivation of these interlocking roles that the participants get the sense of operating reciprocally in a group.[2]

Juxtaposed against the diversity of expected outcome is the *given* nature of the materials. Both students and teachers comment frequently on the "packaged" aspect of the basic data sources. This input could be viewed as the structured or programmed attribute of the course; students and teachers are presented with a sequence of activities and a set of materials such that there is no need, unless desired, to search out further material or to decide upon basic pedagogic strategy.

Is there a contradiction inherent in this situation of packaged materials and open-ended expectations? Not in operation, for the core materials are not intended to function as the boundaries of the course or as pieces of a jig-saw puzzle. They are more like paints in an artist's palette; how they are selected and used depends upon the talents and predispositions of the painter (with a corresponding range of results).

Social Learning

It is evident from the evaluation that *Man: A Course of Study* has been especially successful in meeting its goals for social learning, as critical as the more content-oriented goals. The idea of a community of learning, of people actively engaged in exploring and sharing ideas together, was preceived by the majority of children and teachers as a reality and a pleasure, adding a new dimension to the life of the classroom.

We observed, and deduced from objective data, a range of teacher styles running from the very open to the quite traditional, but we found that on the whole, teachers seemed to utilize the general methods suggested in the teacher manuals, and to notice as a result children's increased confidence in expressing ideas, new attention to each other, and ability to communicate effectively in discussion situations. In terms of social learning, this is a notable accomplishment. It appears that the combination of curriculum materials and pedagogical suggestions worked to produce a high degree of environmental consistency in classrooms across the country. More variety of activities and materials, more small group work and open discussion and teacher mediation and guidance, rather than dominance and authoritativeness, were the norms rather than the exceptions [. . .] The "approach" rather than "avoidance" attitude is encouraged by the structuring of *Man: A Course of Study* lessons, and the kinds of questions raised by the course content. A child in the center city put it this way:

> I think when we went in small groups for discussion and we gave up our own thought (was best). That's all we knew about it – our thoughts. And then when the other children brought up their thoughts, we learned more.

Social learning of this type is not didactic, not second hand; it is experiential learning that comes from doing, from participating in the classroom – what we could describe as real-life learning of socially interactive skills.

This emphasis on what might be called, after Bruner, the reciprocally operative group, reflects one way of considering the learning process, one method of arranging classroom happenings and children's time in school. It emphasizes social process and consensual task completion, in that children do the same things at the same time. Thus interactive learning can be contrasted with another style of more independent or individualized instruction, where the child works more on his own, on projects or research of special interest without the continuous flow of interaction in a class.

While we do not have research evidence to shed light on learning gains, student satisfaction in learning, or attitude development attributable to the latter method (were *Man: A Course of Study* materials utilized in this way), it seems reasonable to suggest that the interactive mode may be a particularly felicitous mode for upper elementary age youngsters, where task orientation and working with peers are known to be pertinent concerns of youngsters at that stage of personal development. [. . .]

Problems of Conceptual Mastery

We found many instances, both in tests and interviews, where there appear to be special problems for children in mastering the larger conceptual issues of the course. Youngsters have considerable difficulty in grasping the uniquely human quality of language, in correctly identifying innate versus learned behaviors in humans and other animals, and in dealing with the topic of natural selection.

The problems demonstrated in answering test questions in these areas were illustrated in interview material. For example, many youngsters were not able to make conceptual distinctions between behavior controlled by innate urges of animal species – the internal drives that are beyond control or understanding by the animal – and behavior governed by man's symbol system for organizing experience and creating rules of life.

Some of the problem seems to be explainable in terms of children's level of cognitive development and the accompanying need for a great wealth of good, graspable examples. Children of this age utilize in their thinking one-to-one correspondences; generalizations seem to be rather accidental rewards drawn out of a series of examples. Teachers also find *Man: A Course of Study* content new and very difficult, which further contributes to conceptual problems of children. Research into long-term use would help to determine if teachers master the course over time.

Knowing that children schooled in the suburban settings of the interviewed field sample had a history of learning with pedagogy more like *Man: A Course of Study* methods than had children in the center city, we do not find it surprising that on the whole suburban youngsters showed more ability to elaborate an idea in conversation, to deal with conceptual themes fluently and to show a somewhat more highly developed level of formal relational thinking in their interviews. In fact, in light of the comparative observations made in city control classes indicating the lack of emphasis on opinion-giving, drawing conclusions from evidence, or hypothetical or reflective thinking, it is encouraging that center city fifth graders, in the course of one year, could show growth in the communicative, reflective ways that seem to occur.

Inquiry

While the interviews show, and checklist findings indicate, children's use of inquiring attitude, hypothesizing and observing during the study of this course, it is difficult in verbal evaluations to judge how well they understand that these are approaches to problems. At this age, they are not self-conscious about the methods they are using. They do use these methods but the majority have not translated the "doing" into an articulated system that they can express. The observation exercises now part of the course were introduced specifically to make explicit within the context of the child's own family, school and neighborhood, methods for data gathering and analysis.

Ethnocentrism

Since one of the learning goals of the course is "to awaken in children an awareness of the fact that what we regard as acceptable behavior is a product of our culture," the issue of ethnocentrism is important to an evaluation of the Netsilik unit.

The interview materials demonstrated that children do make links between some Netsilik ways and our own, for example, between feelings for family and friends and their way of relating to one another, and such as we express them. Where basic similarities in human behavior have been grasped, children demonstrate verbally that the unit is having positive effect in creating a sense of the family of man.

Do children go beyond the easy correlation of similarity, however, and begin to understand and sometimes enjoy the *diversity* of human behavior? To this question, we have less clear signs of growth. There is evidence that at the functional level bridging occurs. By that we mean that the instrumental problem-solving behavior of the Netsilik elicits most favorable reaction from children as an expression of a culture different from their own, not highly technological, but very inventive. Netsilik solutions to hunting and survival needs are considered clever and functional by youngsters.

The diversities that elicit *emotional responses* do not so easily build to positive attitudes: the issues of infanticide and senilicide, the killing point of the hunt, the skinning of animals, and the treat of the caribou eye. For example, one scene in a film showing the food treat of the fish eye, was universally mentioned by the children who saw it as the most difficult scene to stomach, in a literal sense. There is rational understanding of such behavior, but it is not really seen as "acceptable" – its visceral impact is too disturbing. Even the physical appearance of the Netsilik – sallow and less groomed than our own prevailing adult standards dictate – evokes comment about the poor, sad looking Netsilik without much consideration of differing standards.

The Netsilik belief system, expressed in terms of magic and spirits, seems to skirt some middle ground of feeling and draws out both sympathetic and distancing responses. The distancing reactions could be attributed to several factors. Children are learning the myths and beliefs of their own culture, and the magical and shamanistic system of the Eskimo is in some conflict with our scientific interpretations of the world. Eskimo beliefs, because they do carry out a "magical" view, are ridiculed by some youngsters who have themselves barely emerged from the "magical" interpretations of early childhood. When they do not take a position of cultural relativism, they take an "adult" stand of scientism: we have science instead of magic, we now know the answers. This is always put forth in the form of a rather easy, top of the head kind of comment. A class case study also documents that in some cases children never come to understand that myths are not literal interpretations of reality; in these cases, the teacher seems especially responsible for such misinterpretation.

However, despite some misunderstanding or skepticism and relegating of magical beliefs to a more "primitive" way of dealing with experience, many children do grasp the importance of a belief system for organizing and understanding daily life. On a word list exercise in the interviews where they select from several options the two words most important to the Netsilik in their daily lives, almost without exception children select "beliefs," and with good reasons. One concise insight was this: "If you believe in something, you're not afraid." The sympathetic, even empathetic responses of some children seem to derive from emotional kinship, from delight in the imaginary, the make-believe, and the intuitively true. They feel drawn to the imaginative and perceptive qualities of the Netsilik songs and stories. It seems appropriate to emphasize these in the course. In addition, most of the Netsilik myths contain acutely realistic insights into human feelings and behavior that strike resonant chords in children. Sharing, guilt, appeasing the powers that be, all contain elements of human psychology that ring true.

It is important to note that children begin to value diverse expressions of humanness not through rational understanding of technology, social organization or cultural symbols, but through encounters with personalities and their stories, either shown on films or told through records and written material, where basic psychological dimensions are illuminated through examples specific to Netsilik culture and beliefs. Telling stories is as old as man, and clearly the impact of "Stories of Beginning Times," "Songs and Stories of the Netsilik Eskimos," and of other personal expressions can be felt in the remarks youngsters formulated that show a good deal of sympathetic understanding.

Relevance

It is often difficult for center city children to develop a sense of agency, of power to shape their existence, as they cope with the complex multiverse of experience that surrounds them. There are different avenues of approach in education that can be taken toward helping them develop this sense of control. In social studies, these avenues amount to a decision between teaching surface or external craftiness (specific ways to function in the daily world) and teaching models for organizing experience, aiming for long-term, internalized understanding. The kinds of topics viewed as relevant under the first rubric would be dealings with police, shopping in the supermarket, how to get a specific job, etc.

The consideration of these topics can be fruitful school pursuits. But is it enough? Does it not relegate these children to the dead-end status of third-rate minds, never being challenged to develop and use models for organizing experience? Jean Piaget has stressed that the mind is developed through use. To believe that more general and inter-disciplinary education is not relevant to the center city child is to relegate a whole group of citizens to an inferior status and create a society that cannot be changed.

What are the alternatives? *Man: A Course of Study* appears to have demonstrated one viable way – examining the most basic survival mechanisms of living creatures, with a view to contrasting and comparing behavior of different species, including and emphasizing man. Are these questions that children consider worth inquiring into? At what points do children touch base with their own lives and concerns? The issue of relevance has been a legitimate and important one among educators, particularly as it pertains to children in the center city. Considering that these children are as much, if not more, concerned with basic dimensions of survival than are children in suburban situations, *Man: A Course of Study* has taken as its concerns: family and social relationships; issues of dominance and protectiveness; roles of males and females; what makes a good parent; the meaning of dependency; how a group survives. It is hard to think of a set of issues more closely reflecting the psychological needs of center city children. Throughout the evaluation of the course, these dimensions have shown consistent power to motivate children to want to learn and to generate reflective thinking. Their interests range from the salmon to the Netsilik, but always with a personal reflection that shows the links of course materials to the child's life.

> What I liked about the salmon, they made me most curious. At first I wondered, why do you want to swim up this stream, this certain stream to lay the eggs? And . . . he does not know he's going to die after he reaches this point. This made me like him more. And I liked his struggle, he struggled very hard to go upstream. And sometimes they'd make it and sometimes they'd fail.

Interviews reveal a growing sense of the inter-dependence of creatures, and indicate a budding model for considering human needs, involving cooperation, nurturance, protection, and the sharing of responsibilities. It is hard to deny the relevance of these issues. Further, the intimacy with which materials are put together to show the time, energy, and methods a person brings to the study of a field – made strong impressions on youngsters:

> This man – Niko Tinbergen, I think it is – he made this big study on gulls. Thirty years he spent listening to the gulls.

Teachers noted that the "model" experiences coupled with the opportunity to carry on experimentation and observation on their own, helped children to understand why persistence and long-term effort can be necessary to achieve goals and find out the meanings in experience.

There is another dimension to relevance, in terms of personal competence and human curiosity: learning is relevant if it makes people feel more able, more in control of situations, and possessed of more understanding about fundamental issues of behavior. Along this dimension of mastery, children express, as the course progresses, many ways in which its materials and classroom exercises contribute to competence and understanding, in which student-initiated learning is taking over from external imposition of ideas.

> Before the teacher used to always give us the answers. Now we have to find it out for ourselves in the book. [Is that harder or easier?] Easier. [Why?] Sometimes you never have questions to ask, but when you do, you write them down, then look at the film, and then you know the answer. By figuring out answers yourself, you learn more . . . when the teacher tells you all the answers, you don't hardly know because you forget. [. . .]

Teachers recognized this element of relevance in the scope of discussion opened up by the course. Students were using their learning outside of school, in home situations where, even in television viewing, they felt an area of expertise, a competence, that delighted them and gave them pleasure in learning. This *is* personal relevance of a high power.

> Kids love to discuss things. And if the teacher can come up with the right questions or the right answers at the right time, it's tremendous. You find the discussion going all over the place. I mean, you start out with the herring gulls and territories, and you end up talking about territories all over the world. You talk about salmon laying six thousand eggs and you end up talking about population explosions in China. You talk about why animals fight with one another, and you end up talking about the war in Vietnam.

[. . .] As another child put it: "We can grow up now." This self-reflection on the ways one learns, on how one generates ideas by observation, question-posing and careful recording of information is a truly. relevant skill. It is the scientific method made operational for organizing the experiences of daily life, in that it gives children workable procedure, and the opportunity to employ it over time.

Children have expressed in their own words many examples of *Man: A Course of Study* materials dealing with ideas close to the cutting edge of their own experience. Their overriding concern appears to be the area of relationships; for example, the child's relationship with its parents, friends' relationships with each other, a female's relationship with a male. [. . .]

One of the problems, of course, is that later school work does not always provide continuing opportunities for using these methods. When children return to traditional classrooms, or to situations where the quality of curriculum materials is far different from *Man: A Course of Study*, the half-life of this experience may not be long. We have done very little follow-up work, and what we did undertake shows that most youngsters did not address a newly posed problem with the methods they had learned in *Man: A Course of Study*. We need further follow-up research, but one anticipates disappointments, particularly for children who return to a school career dominated by more traditional styles of learning, to which they must either adapt or opt out.

Notes

1 *Toward a Theory of Instruction*, 166-7.
2 *Toward a Theory of Instruction*, 126-7.

VI CASE STUDY – TEACHER EDUCATION

24. The Balance of Studies in Colleges of Education

J. B. Browne

and

Commentary

M. Skilbeck

Source: J.B. Browne and M. Skilbeck, *Towards a Policy for the Education of Teachers* (Butterworth, London, 1968).

Colleges of education have both 'vocational' and 'educative' objectives. These need not be contradictory and in a concurrent course they are pursued in parallel. The relationship between practical experience and theoretical studies and the desirable contents of these areas are discussed. There is, in Browne's view, a place for a continued study of school subjects, though what is learned is of secondary importance to the manner of learning. Skilbeck points to the key concept of 'balance of studies' in its relation to holistic interpretations of the term 'curriculum'. These ideas must be related, too, to the needs of individual students, for it is the wholeness of students' individual experience that is of importance. Skilbeck enters a further element into the scales, that of 'enculturation'. This is important since teachers are in significant ways products of the college culture and because they are themselves, potentially, instruments of cultural change on a wider scale. Courses should therefore reflect a commitment to self-conscious and deliberate analyses of social change.

The Balance of Studies in Colleges of Education

The colleges are in origin and intention vocational institutions. Students are selected, partly at least, on their supposed suitability for teaching; they are assumed to have chosen the teaching profession as their future career, and are even asked to make a choice before coming to college of the age range that they want to teach. The Certificate of Education is not recognized as a qualification for any other calling. Though the 'pledge' has disappeared enquiries are made if the finished product does not reach the schools.

The colleges are also concerned as institutions of higher education with the personal education of their students beyond the school level. Students should go from them not only better informed but able to respond to an intellectual challenge, with experiences that have enlarged their understanding and sympathy, and with some sense of the community, its problems and its promise.

There is no necessary clash between these two objectives, and indeed the persistence of the colleges in advocating a concurrent course shows that it is widely believed, not only that there is no dichotomy here, but that there are positive merits in pursuing the two aims at one time. In 1961 the A.T.C.D.E. in its evidence to the Robbins Committee said—'The combination of academic and professional education is a distinctive feature of the colleges which we are most anxious to preserve. They are concerned with the education of students as persons and as teachers, each reinforcing the other'. This point of view was accepted by the Robbins Committee which decided against setting up Liberal Arts Colleges. The concurrent character of the course was also picked out by the Newsom Committee as being most likely to fit teachers to cope with the average and below average children in the secondary school.

The thinking behind these pronouncements and supporting the concurrent course centred round the following ideas: that some students felt more able to pursue their own education with persistence and success if they had some definite vocation in view; that for those concerned particularly with the education of primary and lower secondary children and also with those of lesser ability it was important to have in mind their problems and needs as early as possible and not have to make the adjustment from academic subject-based standards in one year at the end of a specialist course. On the other hand it was recognized that too narrow a concentration on a future vocation would not produce a fully educated and mature teacher, so that some studies should be pursued for the personal education of the future teacher. The nature of education would be the subject of exploration theoretically and practically, while the subject, in another sense, was himself being educated.

This paper proposes to accept the concept of a concurrent course but to raise questions about the balance of studies in colleges and in particular about the relationship between theory and practice and between professional and personal education, in Education and its related disciplines and in the academic subject fields. It is not proposed to arrive at any conclusions about the exact proportion of the different elements in the course but to discuss their relationship and their relevance to the aims of the institution.

One false distinction should be cleared out of the way at the beginning. The idea that main academic studies contribute to a student's personal development while Education does not, is as false as the opposite view that the study of a subject discipline has no effect on a student's teaching unless he is teaching that subject to older pupils. There may be cases where these propositions are true, but they arise where a very narrow view is taken in each field.

It will be argued that all sides of a student's course should and can contribute to his professional education, and that his professional understanding as it grows will affect his personal development. The distinction lies rather between those parts of the course in which theory and practice are immediately seen to be connected and where the link is constantly forged, and those where more mature reflection and some withdrawal from the scene of action to understand a discipline is required.

The Concurrent Courses–Usual Pattern of Studies

As is well known the usual pattern of studies in colleges of education consists of:

(1) Education–child development; the psychology of childhood; the history, sociology and philosophy of education in some degree. General approach to the curriculum.

(2) Curriculum or professional studies. Approach to and material of the curriculum of different age range–infant, junior or secondary or a combination of these.

(3) Practice of teaching–in this may be included school visits and the many kinds of study practice that have been attempted lately.

(4) Main subject study. One, two or three main subjects may be studied at various levels. Although these may be the subjects that the students are going to teach at secondary level, the main purpose of the studies is the further education of the student.

Except for some differences in nomenclature this is the scheme proposed by the McNair Report. Although there is variety of emphasis and approach, perhaps it is rather surprising that the pattern throughout the country should be so uniform.

Recent Changes

Since the beginning of the three year course in 1960, and more particularly, since the idea of a future degree course was first considered, emphasis has been laid on the raising of the academic standards within the colleges. The achievement of this has been made possible by improvement in the intellectual level of candidates and by better facilities in the colleges, for example, the provision of libraries which, although not of University level as yet, as they should be, are incomparably better than they were ten years ago.

This change has shown itself in the study of the academic subjects where specialist staff, many of them with recent higher degree studies to their credit, have stiffened and enlivened the approach to the subject disciplines. Changes have also taken place in the Education course so that it is less usual to find it treated as a blanket term and taught by one tutor to a group of students throughout the course. It is more usual to find some disciplined study of psychology, sociology and in some cases an approach to philosophy related to educational problems; it is becoming customary to offer to students at some point in the course a series of options through which they can deepen their understanding of certain parts of the material.

Who are the Critics and What do they Say?

The usual pattern of the course and especially the recent developments described above have met with criticism from several sides.

(1) Head teachers claim that students are concentrating on academic work to the exclusion of learning how to become skilled and knowledgeable practitioners. Practising teachers have always tended to discount the effects of specialized academic study, but their criticism today springs from rather a different point of view. The schools are experiencing a profound period of change both of the organizational pattern and the curriculum. They are heavily under pressure and feel that the new recruits to the profession are not made aware enough of the changes that are taking place or ready to cope. Dissatisfaction may in reality spring from the fact that the recruits, vastly greater in numbers than the established teachers, may not stay in the same school or even in the profession for long enough to gain the experience that would enable them to make a reasonable contribution.

(2) Students are apt to follow the line of experienced teachers, especially after a period in school, for they are often deeply influenced by their future colleagues. Their reaction to the idea of concurrence, especially at times of great pressure, is that they cannot do so many things at once, and that their time tables are still overcrowded. They would like more time to investigate matters for themselves and seek more direct relevance in their studies to their future career. Not all are prepared to make the effort required to overcome superficiality by hard individual study, and some forget that their main teaching career may lie far ahead, so that genuine understanding rather than immediate competence is the main goal. In studies that closely link theory with practice they are at their best.

(3) Some of the members of college staffs are critical too; sometimes self-critical. Procedures are revised fairly frequently but perhaps not fundamentally. Staff critics tend to fall into two camps—those who regret the pastoral care lavished on students as persons and indeed as future teachers in more leisurely days, and those who want more concentration on subject study. According to the first view, emphasis on disciplines, whether in main subject courses or in Education, has led to less coherence of training than previously. Remedies may be sought in the introduction of inter-disciplinary studies or in the conception of Education as an all-embracing whole out of which all the students' practical and theoretical studies shall develop. Those who want more leisure to study the subject disciplines are critical of the multitude of things the student is still asked to do and complain of superficiality of treatment and lack of time for individual study.

In searching for any new or revised balance of studies, one will have to bear these criticisms in mind, but also take into account the likely developments in education in the next fifty years, and what educational research has to tell us about the effectiveness of courses and ways of learning. The role of the teacher in the society of the future will also be of importance.

In so far as we can look into the future and see what kind of world and school situation we are training for, it seems that readiness to accept and participate in change is one important feature, and if this is not to have devastating effects, sympathetic awareness of personal and group tensions must be a characteristic of the teacher. School will probably be much less of a closed shop than it is at present, and the teacher will be aware of what goes on in the world of work and will have to join forces with other agencies of social change, communication or welfare. Education will increasingly make use of technology and the teacher will have to learn to evaluate and use its resources and act as a leader in teams some of whose members will have other skills or play more limited roles (Lynch and Preen 1967).

The colleges of education have perhaps not gone far astray in the elements that they have put into the course. Students must be prepared in practice as well as in theory to cope with the actual curriculum of the schools; they must understand to some extent the background sciences that affect children's education whether they relate to the individual, the group or to the community and they must begin to discuss questions as to where they are going and what they are aiming at. In these crucial years of late adolescence or young adulthood, when they are given this time for study which is denied to some of their contemporaries, they must pursue their own education. What is not so certain is whether we have tried to pursue these ends through the right media or with the best balance between the parts.

The main difficulty of making the whole course centre directly round professional training, or arise out of education, as some would put it (although admittedly these are not quite the same proposition), is that the student has not much experience to build on and in the studies that he undertakes on this side he will have to start from scratch, so that it may be difficult to reach any depth. There are those who, to get over the first problem, would plunge the student, after a nodding acquaintance with the college, into a period of apprenticeship in school. But apprenticeship has not been found to bring understanding in the past, and can be interpreted as a form of 'learning from Nelly'. Even if he is fortunate enough to learn from a skilled practitioner the danger is that he is learning about yesterday's practice rather than looking forward to tomorrow. Moreover, the student coming straight from the Sixth Form seems either to want a period of being a student, living away from home for preference, or of earning a living in some other capacity, rather than being plunged back into a school of whatever type. One does not get very far by involving the young student in all the details of classroom practice without constant evaluation of what he is doing.

Types of Practical Experience

Students will need to get practical experience early in their course, but it should be with children and young people and those in charge of them in playgroups, clinics, youth clubs, residential camps and the world of work as well as in schools. As far as possible it should touch different ages, classes, races and environments. Observation must take place at first hand, but for more exact and repeatable viewing and analysis, film and television will be in normal use. Practising teachers must be called in more than at present to take part in advising and supervising students, but they must help them to evaluate their experience according to principles of education agreed between themselves and the college.

Opportunities should be found for students to discuss with teachers the apparatus used in the classroom and how it has been found to work, and also to consult with social workers as to how they view the growing child and his family. Thus they will see themselves from the beginning as belonging to one among many agencies. The first periods of observation should be short, of a week or a fortnight in duration, linked to theoretical work, and followed by individual visits of all kinds. However, from perhaps the first long vacation, it might be possible to employ the students as helpers or auxiliaries attached to a team of teachers with a salary of some kind, at the beginning or end of the school year or on other occasions according to the organization of the college. Employment of students would help to make them feel independent and might enable more teachers to be released for extended vacation courses. Practical experience before the end of the course should have included observation of children and teachers, experience in places where there are children and young people other than in schools, study practice with a particular end in view such as the teaching of a small group of backward children, working with a team of teachers with pupils grouped in different ways and finally a trial period with greater responsibility, of approximately a term in length in the third year of the course. It should be assessed on a pass/fail basis and the college should keep in touch with the new teacher and his employers in the probationary year that follows qualification.

Education–The Child in Society

Side by side with this practical experience the theoretical study of education should begin. It is not intended to sketch out an education course here, but it should be concerned in the first place with the norms of a child's development, how he reads, learns, feels as an individual and as a member of the group. This part will be followed up by the student in individual child studies. Learning theories and the study of concept formation will be linked not only with work in school, but with the study of the curriculum. The structure and culture of the groups to which the child belongs, the family, the neighbourhood, the social class, and the groups within the school, which have been found to affect children's learning so profoundly will also be a subject for study by all students. The role of the adult, including the teacher, in the world of childhood will be considered, with inevitable attention being given to such ideas as authority, freedom, discipline, over which the student may still be in conflict or lately have emerged from it. Students will deepen their understanding by studying practical problems which yet have psychological and sociological content such as backwardness, the education of immigrant pupils, the structure of a class or some form of special education. They will look at some of these questions in time and space for historical and comparative study can throw a new light on present issues in our own country, and student-teachers should be neither insular nor naive in their expectations. All that they do should be authentic and relevant to the understanding of the children they will teach, though it should not be narrowly related to any particular age range. It is important that lectures given to Education students should make use of modern techniques of presentation, but the lecture and tutorial programme should never be so heavy that it does not leave time to read books and journals and to become conversant with what has been recently discovered on the subject of growing up and learning in our society. Moreover students must be able to express themselves on these subjects in speech and in writing for they will no doubt have to expound and defend their views in the future. These details are given because it is necessary to make it clear that the basis for further psychological, sociological and philosophical study of education should be laid, but in the three year course an individual student will only have time to explore one of these disciplines in a way thorough enough to affect his thinking.

The Curriculum and its Communication

Perhaps this is the side of the work that should have progressed most, but which has not been revised in any radical enough way in the colleges. The difficulty has been that it has seemed necessary both to train for the schools as they are and as they may be in the future. It is absolutely essential to tackle the matter now in this period of rapid change in the field, especially as the main teaching career of many women students may be far in the future, following a period spent in raising a family. Some experience in the changing curriculum will be acquired in the schools, and, as they are set up, in the teachers' centres where it is hoped both students and tutors will have an opportunity of working. It will, however, be the province of selected Education lecturers and selected subject specialists working together to review the theoretical structure of the curriculum, connect it with learning theories and the study of children's concepts and arrange a series of classes and workshops in which the students will participate. There are many ways in which these studies may be grouped, but they should not be watertight compartments. One might analyze them, for instance, according to the type of activity, e.g. creative, discovery, etc., or according to the subject matter grouped in certain constellations e.g. language, environment, or according to the sources of material and inspiration and methods of learning. (See chart.)

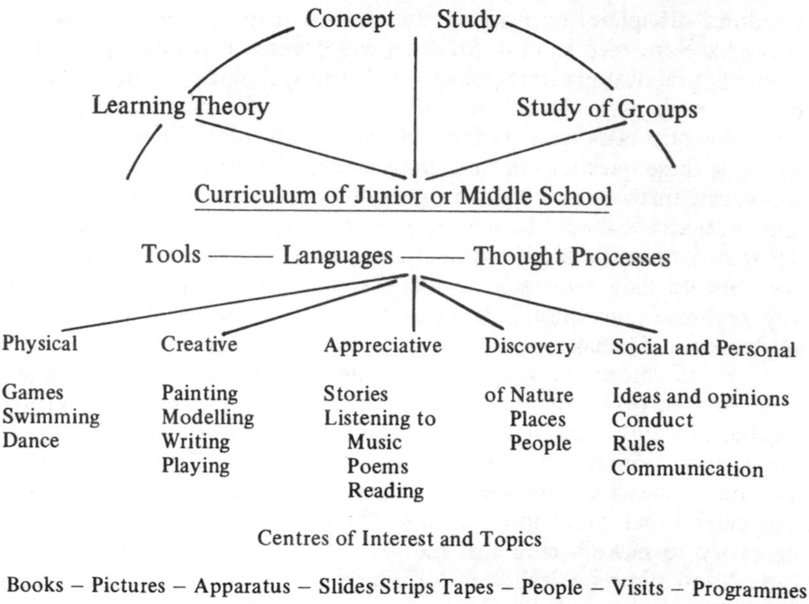

Students would have some experience and examine and prepare material from all these fields but choose one or two for further study in latter part of course.

It is difficult to generalize when one is speaking of such a wide range of studies but certain principles seem clear. In the first place students must be made familiar with at least some of the apparatus and material coming from so many sources in the present day, *and must learn to evaluate it.* If they do not make a start in learning how to do this in college they are going to be passive recipients of kits and packages all their days. They will be helped in evaluation if they can look at the material both from the point of view of the specialist in education and from that of the subject specialist. Secondly they must have experience themselves of working on the material in the same way that children will be expected to work, that is, with appropriate technological aids, and in different kinds of groupings. Thirdly, they must be prepared to throw the material of the curriculum into novel combinations and study the principles involved in integrated or inter-disciplinary studies and traditional subject study at different ages. New methods of study will require new and careful methods of assessment of what is learned. It is difficult to say how wide a field each individual student should be expected to cover and this should be to some extent at least tailored to his own needs and the type of school in which he intends to teach.

In the latter part of this course he might pick one or two fields for further study, for example, children's language, in relation to general linguistic theories, and differences of social class. This type of study would be a suitable subsidiary subject where the Main subject was in one of the academic fields. The curriculum field has been considered in some detail because it is one which is developing very rapidly, and in which the personal and vocational education of the student can come together and draw on the skills of both Education and subject tutor. He should be encouraged to regard himself as an agent for change preparing to assist practitioners who are engaged in the processes of innovation and discovery. Professional studies of this type are geared closely to a student's future career, but it is often in considering material and methods suitable for children, provided that he is an active participant and not a passive recipient of information, that his sense of personal responsibility and involvement grows.

It will be necessary to develop the buildings of the colleges on this side so that students can work in curriculum laboratories and Resources centres where all modern resources for learning are available. The study should be challenging and is certainly time consuming. Is it adequate in scope to make up the whole course with the studies in Education described previously?

Main Courses

A student is a young adult and cannot educate himself wholly through task-centred education. The object of main subject studies is often said to be the personal education of the student, but if this end is to be brought about, attention must be paid to *how the subject is learned* rather than to *what is learned*, as is too often the emphasis still in the colleges. The discipline should, too, be practised as well as given critical examination. By this is meant that a student of History should write some short critical study using original sources, and the student of Literature attempt some creative as well as critical and appreciative work. Creative work is already a main feature of college courses in Drama and Art and Crafts; here perhaps it is critical appreciation and the cultivation of aesthetic judgment that is often lacking. Only by looking deeply at the process of learning as he undertakes it himself at a level suitable to a student can he understand what education is about and acquire the standards by which to judge his professional work.

It has been argued that the same ends can be achieved through the study of disciplines relevant to Education (Price 1966), and it is certainly not my contention that these cannot provide the stimulus usually attributed to the 'school' subjects. Indeed, it is one of the arguments of this paper that the distinction in studies pursued in Colleges of Education should not lie between Education and the subject disciplines, but between the practice or task-linked part of the curriculum, and those studies which back it up and concentrate not on the task but on the fields of human learning.

For most students coming straight from school a deeper level of understanding seems to be reached by continuing at least one of the studies that has been taken in the Sixth form, or for which they have already developed some taste or talent, such as Music or Drama. There seems particular value in the future teacher pursuing one of the Arts or Sciences as an object, at the same time as he explores one of the studies related to the process of Education; it is this combination that seems most fruitful for the best students. Moreover, it is only in progressing reasonably far in the commonly accepted forms of higher education that the future teacher can hope to hold his own as a student and scholar—though this is not of course an argument against the social sciences. Finally, the main subject fields are, at whatever level, highly relevant to professional work and are hardly likely to be replaced as organizations of human learning, although their boundaries and methods are always changing.

The choices offered should be wide and we should be prepared to recognize new combinations and unorthodox approaches. Grouped courses such as European, American, Commonwealth and Environmental studies should be encouraged, provided that these groupings are not only for information, that they allow some concentration on the processes of learning and can be studied at student level. Probably one of the greatest needs is for Scientific studies for those who have not taken science in the Sixth form, which should aim at getting over the essence of scientific ways of thought. It has been argued (Bramwell 1965) that groupings of subject disciplines or faculty organization should take the place of separate subjects. There may be advantages in this at staff level, but for the student who wishes to concentrate on one subject there is plenty of 'width' elsewhere in the course.

One must make the proviso, not always easy to carry out, that the individual subjects must be taught in an imaginative way and their links with other subjects brought out.

It is already fairly common to allow one of the disciplines related to Education such as Sociology or Social Psychology, to be chosen as a main subject, and further experiments on these lines should be encouraged. Care obviously has to be taken that there is no overlap in the course. Such concentration would probably help the mature student, and there is no question of building on school experience here. It is this type of student who might also benefit from being allowed to let his main subject study grow out of curriculum courses, for most mature students begin with more experience of children, and their curriculum work more rapidly reaches a better level.

Arrangements should be made from time to time for students and tutors from different disciplines, including Education, to come together to study a topic of common interest where the different approaches can be seen and understood. The same object might be achieved by offering to all students at some point a theme to follow up such as 'Issues of our Time'. They might usefully plan it for themselves for each succeeding year. It could consist of lectures followed by discussion or the presentation of drama or a 'happening', or hinge around a T.V. programme. It might also be fruitful to draw together students from different institutions for some such purpose. If sufficient attention is paid to planning these inter-disciplinary activities they might well contain some of 'the peak learning experiences' that have been found to be of such importance to students. It is difficult to conceive of the whole time table being organized along these lines, especially in a large college where it seems essential to define courses and allow various choices.

It is impossible to legislate about the exact proportions of these different sections, but time could be saved by being certain that tutors are not dealing with similar material at the same level, e.g. the study of the practical uses of audio-visual aids and the theory of communication should be connected but rationalized so as not to be repeated by subject, curriculum and Education course tutor. It is also probably best not to tackle all sections at the same time, as that is to carry the principle of concurrence to extremes. For example, while there is concentration on practical work in school and curriculum courses, the theoretical parts of Education and main subjects could be given a rest. Thus the course could be divided into half terms in which groups of students would study not more than two of the following elements:

(1) *Curriculum Studies and Observation/Visits/Study Practice:*

(2) *Main Subject(s)* including any inter-disciplinary study:

(3) *Education* or *Related Disciplines.*

Block practices in school could be arranged in terms or half terms. There should be more of (1) in the earlier part of the course with (2) and (3) predominating later when block practice is taken.

What I have arrived at is a belief that the different elements in the course are valid, but that they might be arranged in different proportions and with different weightings for individual students. Courses should be tailored to individual capacity as well as to the age range to be taught, although the latter will always be an important factor. It ought not to be beyond the wit of man, nor of tutors, to devise some equivalence which could be understood by student and employer, for after all we are speaking of an initial qualification. It might, on the other hand, be preferable to have a basic qualification plus either an immediate degree course, or an agreed level of study which should allow the pursuit of a degree at some later date without the necessity for interim 'improvement'. Certainly, initial qualification should be connected not only with the studies of the probationary year but with regular compulsory renewals. These should be progressive in quality for those who are able to progress. For returners, the Open University as well as more regularly arranged summer courses should be available.

It has been found by those studying the effect of college education on students that often it is less than is expected by the staff, but that a powerful environment can make for significant growth. This may arise less from any carefully planned balance of studies than from an insistence on certain approaches throughout the college. Some such approaches would be, in my opinion, the encouragement of initiative and individual effort at every turn, the exploration through all subjects of the balance between tradition and change, and the practice of respect and concern for persons of whatever age, class, religion and race. If we cannot do something to accomplish this with the present structure of colleges then the structure must be changed, for the future of education depends on it.

References

BRAMWELL, R. D. (1965) 'Grouped Main Subjects', *Education for Teaching* **68**, November.

LYNCH, J. and PREEN, D. W. (1967) 'The Flexible College', *Education for Teaching* **74**, May.

PRICE, G. (1966) 'Education as a Main Course', *Education for Teaching* **70**.

Commentary

The concept of a 'balance of studies' is of central importance in a theory of general education, and the general education of teachers is what Miss Browne's paper is about. Unfortunately, 'balance', like many other concepts to which educators commonly give approval, is both vague and complex. Not surprisingly, Miss Browne has elected to concentrate her discussion on general questions of curriculum provision and reconstruction in the colleges rather than on an elucidation of the concept. We are left to infer that curriculum 'balance' is what the best of our colleges have now achieved or are in the process of achieving

While what is best about the current achievements of colleges is not analyzed with any finality, it is clear that Miss Browne intends us to connect in our minds the ideas of 'balance' and of 'wholeness'. A balanced college curriculum, whatever else it may be, is according to this view an organized, or even an integrated whole, a moving pattern of parts—theoretical, practical, professional, personal, academic, applied—whose full significance is realized only insofar as they are seen to inter-penetrate and to support each other.

The idea of the wholeness of the college curriculum has a history which has never been carefully probed, and this is not the place or the time to probe it. However, it may not be either fanciful or irrelevant to suggest that there is significance in the very close relationships existing between many colleges of education and primary schools, where curriculum integration continues to be the dominating ideal. The mission-like, heavily ideological atmosphere of Christian humanitarianism, or of militant feminism in which many colleges had their beginnings has left its mark, too, in the continuing disposition to make running attacks on the philistines outside the portals. Again, the small size of most colleges until very recently made it a relatively easy matter for them to establish a unique identity, frequently the product of a charismatic principal and the myths and legends surrounding her. All of this, and much more besides, may help to explain why the idea of wholeness and ideological unity of studies maintains its strength in the colleges while in most other institutions of higher learning it is little more than subject-matter for nostalgic reverie, tinged by faint memories of Cardinal Newman's *The Idea of a University* or of A. D. Lindsay and what used to be described more or less affectionately as the Keele 'experiment'.

Except for a small handful of the newer foundations, it is hard to imagine a vice-chancellor or a binary-sector principal taking very seriously the notion that there is or could be a definable, concrete set of relationships between all of the major elements of the curriculum of his institution. We have become resigned to a much more limited view of balance, as either an uneasy truce between factions and sections, or as a workable educational procedure within a single department or at most, faculty. Admittedly, there is a significant difference of scope between a single professional school, i.e. a college of education, and the multiplicity of professional schools that comprise a university, and it may well be that if and when colleges of education become multi-professional schools, the enthusiasm that teacher-trainers now display in discussing the total college programme will be replaced by something which, in institutional terms, is much narrower and more circumscribed.

My first main observation, then, on the trend of thought Miss Browne's paper displays is that 'balance of studies' is equated with wholeness or integrity of studies, that this in turn figures as a key concept in a view of liberal, or general education that she is advancing, and that she is treating the college as a single, coherent entity, an institution with a character and style of its own. This is a view of teacher education that is strongly rooted in the distinctive traditions of the colleges, and it is, we may surmise, a view of the fitness of things that the college presents to its students in a wide variety of ways. There may thus be a reciprocal relationship between the strong feeling for integration in primary schools and the pattern of studies pursued by the colleges.

I do not wish so much to challenge this holistic view as to suggest that with the quantitative expansion and diversification of the modern college, with the increasing pressure for specialization in all subjects, and with the emergence of what is perhaps a more pragmatic and opportunistic generation of college teachers and students, such a view is likely to be seen increasingly as a rationalization of a traditional, entrenched interest, what Mannheim refers to as an ideology. That this is more my *interpretation* of events and less my *judgment* of an educational theory, will emerge later in this commentary, when I enter a plea for a further holistic set of ideals– again in Mannheim's parlance, when I put forward a utopian position of my own.[1]

One criticism I do wish to make of the conception of balance of studies as the meaningful interrelationships of parts of the total college programme, rests on a distinction between institutional provision and individual need. This distinction Miss Browne makes but she does not I think in her proposals consider its implications. An institution may to the satisfaction of its hierarchy produce a total curriculum which attempts to balance the various legitimate claims of the college departments and of teacher training as a generalized abstraction: professional and personal, theoretical and practical studies. Thus a visitor may be shown a college timetable and course outlines which appear both to recognize and to harmonize a variety of legitimate interests, and reasons may be forthcoming for the great mass of time inequalities as between the constituent subjects and activities. However, the idea of a balanced curriculum remains an abstraction until it is related to the specific needs of all the students in the college. In making these relationships we may find that what student X needs is not a miniature, concrete version of the balance of studies which the total programme expresses, but much more of this and much less of that. Another way of putting this point is that a basic curriculum task facing nay educational institution is to individualize learning. Given that student needs differ very significantly, what we may agree is the college balance of studies will be likely to be at any one time unsuitable for some students. I suggest that there is a considerable danger in practice of obscuring the problem of individual student differences in need and learning styles under the general college banner of a balance of studies. There are problems here about the relationship of the common elements of a general education programme to individual need that have been scarcely touched upon.

I should like now to discuss just a few of the more specific points that Miss Browne's paper gives rise to. The first of these takes the form of an extrapolation of her initial analysis of the twin objectives of the colleges, and of her later brief references to the teacher's role as that of a change agent. Miss Browne lists two objectives for the colleges, vocational preparation and personal development. To these I would like to add a third by taking some of the constituents of these two objectives and giving them a more definite identity under the title of 'socialization' or 'enculturation'. I make this suggestion because it more easily enables me to ask a question that it is both proper and important to put at the present time: the question is, what, from a national, or a social, or a cultural standpoint, is *the vocation* of teaching, and for what kind of national, social, cultural life are we proposing to educate our student teachers as *persons*?

I grant that by joining together 'national', 'social', and 'cultural' I am connecting into a single concept ideas which require a lot of detailed discussion. I do this not to forestall such discussion but to emphasize what students of the literature of English education can hardly fail to note, that the larger social and cultural purposes of any form of education, especially early education, are commonly taken for granted, or examined very briefly. It may be a mark of a very mature and wise culture that so much should be implicit and so little of the social purpose of education made explicit; on the other hand, it may be that neither educationists nor social and political theorists have paid sufficient attention to the relationship of formal educational agencies to society in an emerging democracy. I will give just two examples of this:

(1) The failure of the Plowden Committee to set the discussion of educational policy for primary schools in a cultural context, relying instead on a tacit understanding about the future directions of culture in this country and confining disagreements over directions and purpose to a few minor firecrackers in the appendices.

(2) The celebrated document from the Secretary of State proclaiming the national reconstruction of secondary education, circular 10/65, which must rank as one of the flimsiest bases ever for an educational change of the most far-reaching social importance. There has been no national inquiry into the social purposes of the secondary school, yet social arguments underlie the case for the comprehensive school; there has not even been, since the report of the Bryce Commission in 1895, a single national report on the whole of secondary education, let alone an inquiry into the relationships between the parts of the system.

For teacher education, the point which might be emphasized in discussion is the one Miss Browne makes in a couple of places, where she refers to the teacher as a potential agent of social change. If it is a sensitive appreciation of what teachers can and might do in society to describe them as change agents,[2] then in a democracy where questions about the future of culture are open for the most searching discussion and disagreement, it is obviously important to debate the kinds of changes that teachers are expected to make in the culture. It is at this juncture that tacit understandings, implicit beliefs, the conventional wisdom, the bottomside of the iceberg, and so forth, need to be disclosed to inquiry. This inquiry will in part take the form of an ideological debate, and here I return to my earlier point about ideologies and utopias. The significant questions to raise in discussing the teacher's role as change agent are questions about the quality and direction of change, and in answering or attempting to answer these questions we are bound to express our ideological and value preferences. It is to my mind honest and realistic to accept that as educators we are not morally or culturally neutral, but that we have a position or positions to advance; and to accept also that as members of a democratic community we have a responsibility in developing our educational policies to enter into an active dialogue with the promulgators of national policy goals.[3]

An urgent task, then, faces the college of education curriculum maker. This task is to find ways whereby the large and heterogeneous staffs of the colleges can enter into effective discourse with each other over ideological issues. Also, they need to develop a sensitivity to the concepts of national, social, and cultural objectives.[4] The curriculum of the college will, in turn, express in vital and concrete ways not only the ideas about vocational expertise and personal development that Miss Browne has discussed, but also views about culture and culture change, and the teachers and the schools as culture change agents. While I have not thought out in any detail the likely practical outcomes of this culture-orientation, the following courses suggest themselves:

(1) Synoptic studies of the theory of culture;

(2) Analytic and interpretive studies in the theory of social change;

(3) Empirical, comparative studies of contemporary and historical social change processes including change barriers;

(4) Interpretive and applicative studies in the social psychology of change;

(5) Personal and case study analysis of change mechanisms.

I have tried by inadequate adjectival qualifications to suggest that these studies should not be carried out in a spirit of simple detachment and non-involvement. I do not believe that Miss Browne in her paper wished to suggest that the concept of 'balance of studies' implies neutrality in respect of various forms of action–such a view could hardly be held consistently in a professional school. There may, however, be a temptation to read into reconciliation, balance, harmony and integration of interests a sense of neutrality as between the various claims. The kinds of courses I have just proposed are courses that arise out of and express positions of commitment, not of neutrality.[5]

The position of self-conscious, deliberate commitment that I am proposing has of course its own peculiar difficulties and limitations. The concept of education is a concept of rational thought and conduct, of free-ranging inquiry, and of active concern for the growth and strengthening of these attributes in all people and throughout the world.[6] But this is not to say that, in the name of rational argument, there will not continue to be extreme differences of viewpoint. For an institution like a college both to encourage the formation and expression of a culturally committed position and at the same time to seek, as it must, a single, coherent general policy is to ask for what seems like the impossible. I could elaborate this point by referring to deficiencies in the machinery of consultation, discussion, and decision-taking which needs a much more drastic overhaul than what the Weaver Report has given rise to, but there is no room for such a discussion in the present context.

There are three further ideas Miss Browne examines which I would like to comment on:

(1) Individual learning programmes;

(2) 'learning from Nelly';

(3) Preparing teachers as curriculum developers.

I have already argued that there is a danger that by focusing on the total balance of studies we may obscure the needs of individual students. What many students need may well be a very different weighting and pacing of studies than the overall college timetable provides for. The problem of individualizing learning in many colleges is, I believe, exacerbated by excessive and competitive timetabling. To teach anyone the concepts of freedom, responsibility and free inquiry has seemed to philosophers from Aristotle onwards to mean giving them experience of free and responsible actions and of the conduct of inquiry. While it may be logically possible to teach for freedom by unfree methods[7] there is an underlying absurdity in the idea which some college tutors have still failed to see. A college timetable which, if you will forgive the physiological metaphors, emphasizes an alternation of compulsory eyeball contact and pastoral hand-holding throughout the day must be to some extent self-defeating. As an immediate target, we might aim for the following (except possibly in the sciences).

(1) The timetabling of not more than 50 per cent of a working day of seven or eight hours;

(2) The calculation of a study week on a budget that provides three hours of independent study time for every hour of class or tutorial time;

(3) The adoption of a study assignment system, including programmed learning materials;

(4) The introduction of elective courses, chosen under tutorial guidance and given as much prominence and importance in the student's programme as compulsory subjects;

(5) The direct involvement of students in planning their own courses of study through college academic committees and less formally in individual courses;

(6) The abandonment of the educationally absurd arrangement of 'main subject' and 'education' days and its replacement by more rhythmic alternation between less rigidly separated courses.

These changes would, in some colleges at least, be startling enough in their impact. A more drastic change would be to take a little more seriously the proposal that Miss Browne perhaps too hastily dismisses as 'learning from Nelly'. If Nelly in fact knows what she is about, and if what she is about is worthwhile, to learn from her may be a good thing. Since Miss Browne has suggested that far more use could be made of experienced, practising teachers in the training of student teachers, she is herself accepting that Nelly has much to offer. But is Nelly's offer only satisfactory if she is having her hand held by the college tutor? I am left wondering just why a modified apprenticeship system which would make far more effective use of selected school teachers as trainers than is at present the case should not be very seriously considered. There are three issues here; first, the kind of work experience that is most valuable for trainee teachers; second, the phasing of that work-experience in relation to more analytic and interpretive studies; and, third, the locus of supervisory authority in teaching practice. I have some specific suggestions to make on these points but instead of attempting to argue them out I will present, as a possible theme for discussion, a 'learning from Nelly' scheme. It is as follows:

(1) Students move into college from school for one year.

(2) They work for three years on a sandwich basis (work-college at six monthly intervals) in a variety of placements, gaining work experience relevant to their teaching roles in the light of their previous home and school experiences, but not just as classroom teachers.

(3) They serve as probationers for two years under the joint but light supervision of college and school.

(4) They return as part-time (evening) students to college or university for subsequent specialized training.

The last point I wish to raise takes the form of an interpretation of Miss Browne's careful appraisal of the tasks facing colleges in preparing students as curriculum developers. Notwithstanding the massive engagement of the Schools Council in curriculum development work, there is in the British system, which confers such opportunities and responsibilities on the teacher and the school, a profound need to train teachers as curriculum planners.[8] For teachers, curriculum development work can be divided analytically into two main forms of activity. First, there is in every school subject or grouping of subject matter a structure of ideas, comprising both fundamental general concepts, and processes or models of inquiry. Miss Browne rightly stresses the importance of inquiry methods in teaching subject matter. Second, there faces every curriculum development worker a set of tasks which may be summarized altogether too briefly as: studying the situation, and making, implementing, and evaluating curricula.[9]

Traditionally, subject-matter teaching in schools and colleges has stressed the informational aspect of subjects; or, where skills are concerned, replications of established procedures have been stressed to the detriment of either conceptual or what I will call inquiry-model understanding. As a practical task, college departments might be asked to produce sets of operational objectives for their courses, and to show how their assessment procedures test the achievement in practice of these objectives. To involve students in this task would be both valuable experience for them and a positive step in removing the barriers that still separate the initiated expert from the student.

The procedural task of curriculum making has also been allowed to suffer neglect or distortion. Student teachers emerging from college, as Miss Browne points out, are criticized for a lack of expertise in teaching. That many of them still come from the colleges never having operationally planned a term's work in a subject or subject area provides legitimate grounds for this criticism. From the scarcity of literature on the subject, it may not be unfair to conclude that curriculum planning in English education is yet another 'implicit area' about which it is still slightly vulgar to ask pointed questions. But with the activity of some forty Schools Council projects on curriculum development we will not for long lack models. It is hoped that those responsible for the curricula of the colleges of education will show in their response to these and other challenges that willingness to adapt and innovate that characterizes the effective change agent.

Notes and References

1 MANNHEIM, K. (1936) *Ideology and Utopia*, Ch. 2. London: Routledge and Kegan Paul.

2. A summary statement of the argument for this ascription of role is that since it is impossible for the schools to transmit the whole of culture they select from and in various ways refine the available reservoirs of cultural experience. At the minimum, this process of selective reinforcement of certain elements and tendencies in culture will, if successful, make the culture of the future somewhat different from the culture of the past. Empirically it has never been shown just what effects schooling has on culture, even on quite limited elements such as political attitudes, but the logical refutation of the transmission-without-change thesis might be a

good basis on which to conduct such research. A further point is that communication, an indispensable feature of the teaching-learning process, involves a flow of ideas from one context, that of the teacher's thinking, to another, that of the pupil, and back again. In this exchange, the meanings of ideas change. Education is thus itself a culture change process not a culture reproductive process, whether one adopts a radical or a conservative stance towards the culture of one's own times. The significant questions, then, concern the quality and direction of change. See Plato's *Republic*, still the basic text of the culture change theory; also, COLEMAN, J. S. (ed.) (1965) *Educational and Political Development*, Princeton: N.J., Princeton University Press; DEWEY, J. (May 1939) 'Education and Social Change', *The Social Frontier*; FOSTER, P. (1965) *Education and Social Change in Ghana*, London: Routledge & Kegan Paul; KAZAMIAS, A. M. and B. G. MASSIALAS (1965) *Tradition and Change in Education*, Chs. 8 and 9; New Jersey: Prentice-Hall; KRAFT, I. (April 1967) 'A new man in the kibbutz?' *Teachers College Record* **68**, 7; MANNHEIM, K. (1951) *Freedom, Power and Democratic Planning*, Ch. 10, London: Routledge & Kegan Paul; RUSSELL, B. (1932) *Education and the Social Order*, London: George Allen and Unwin; WHITEHEAD, A. N. (1933) *Adventures of Ideas*, Harmondsworth, Middlesex: Penguin Books, 1948.

3 For a philosophical assessment of the uses and limitations of ideological thinking, see CORBETT, P. (1965) *Ideologies*, London: Hutchinson; for a literary treatment, MANN, THOMAS. *The Magic Mountain*; on the history of the concept, see LICHTHEIM, G. (1965) 'The Concept of Ideology'. *History and Theory* **IV**, 164-195.

4 For a striking example of contemporary educational thinking expressed as a response to national objectives, see INDIAN EDUCATION COMMISSION: *Education and National Development* (1966), New Delhi, especially Ch. 1.

5 Literature relevant to discussion of such an approach includes: CASSIRER, E. *Philosophy of Symbolic Forms*; BENNIS, W. G., K. D. BENNE and R. CHIN (eds.) (1961) *The Planning of Change*, Readings in the Applied Behavioral Sciences, New York; Holt, Rinehart & Winston; ETZIONI, A. and E. (eds.) *Social Change*: Sources, Patterns and Consequences, New York; LIPPITT, R. J. WATSON, and B. WESTLEY (1958) *The Dynamics of Planned Change*, New York: Harcourt, Brace & World; MILES, M. (ed.) (1964) *Innovation in Education*, New York: Teachers College, Columbia University.

6 DEWEY, J. *Democracy and Education*, New York: Macmillan; PETERS, R. S. (ed.) (1967) *The Concept of Education*, London: Routledge & Kegan Paul.

7 HARDIE, C. D. (1942) *Truth and Fallacy in Educational Theory*, especially the discussion of Dewey's views on democratic practices in schools, Cambridge: Cambridge University Press.

8 For a quick summary, see CORBETT, ANNE (1968) 'Reforming the School Curriculum', *New Society*. January 25.

9 For the first of these approaches, see BROUDY, H., B. O. SMITH and W. BURNETT (1964) *Democracy and Excellence in American Secondary Education*, Chicago: Rand McNally; BRUNER, J. (1966) *Toward a Theory of Instruction*, Cambridge, Mass.: Harvard University Press; ELAM, S. (ed.) (1964) *Education and the Structure of Knowledge*, Chicago: Rand McNally; PHENIX, P. (1964) *Realms of Meaning*, New York, McGraw-Hill.

For the second, see BLOOM, B. *et al.* (1956) *Taxonomy of Educational Objectives I Cognitive Domain*, New York: David McKay Co.; HERRICK, V. E. (edited by McDonald, Anderson and May) (1965) *Strategies of Curriculum Development*, Colombus, Ohio: Chas. C. Merril Books; KERR, J. F. (1967). *The Problem of Curriculum Reform*, University of Leicester Press; KRATHWOHL, D. R. *et al.* (1964) *Taxonomy of Educational Objectives II Affective Domain*, New York: David McKay Co.; KRUG, E. A. (1957) *Curriculum Planning*, New

York: Harper; TAYLOR, P. H. (1967) *Purpose and Structure in the Curriculum*, University of Birmingham Press; WHEELER, D. K. (1967) *Curriculum Process*, London: University of London Press; TABA, H. (1962) *Curriculum Development*, New York: Harcourt, Brace & World.

25. The Objectives and Structure of the College Curriculum
P. Renshaw

Source: J.W. Tibble (ed.), *The Future of Teacher Training* (Routledge & Kegan Paul, London, 1971).

Colleges of education have a purpose unique to themselves. That purpose combines 'academic' and 'professional' education. Academic study has traditionally been conceived of as contributing to the personal development of the student, but the breadth of the concept 'personal development', which has the idea of rational autonomy at its heart, means that a wide variety of experience must contribute to its development. A version of the college curriculum is presented which conceives academic and professional studies as an integral whole.

The Function of a College Education

In this chapter the argument will be limited to a discussion of the principles that underlie the structure of the concurrent certificate course in colleges of education. My main thesis is that the college of education, by virtue of its dual concern with academic and professional studies, has a distinctive role to perform. Each institution within tertiary education needs to be viewed as an entity with its own unique function and educational autonomy within a unitary national system. The main purpose of a university, for instance, is to cultivate a spirit of critical enquiry and to develop in students the desire to pursue knowledge for its intrinsic value. A university is concerned with the life of the intellect and with building up a community of scholars and students engaged in the task of seeking truth. Colleges of technology and polytechnics, on the other hand, are multivocational institutions, which encompass a great variety of professional education and training.

But the college of education, as constituted at present, has a unique character resulting from its dual function in the education and training of students for the sole profession of teaching. Although one of its objectives is to develop those qualities of mind associated with a university education, both staff and students are bound by a distinctive professional commitment. In a college of education those academic studies designed for the education of students as persons may be pursued for their intrinsic value, but because of the nature of the institution these studies may be structured to have professional significance. Instead of the dichotomy that tends to exist between academic and professional studies, there should be a very close relationship between the education and training of the student. But this raises several pertinent questions. What do we understand by academic and professional study in a college of education? Furthermore, in what ways can a college curriculum be structured to emphasize the interrelationships between academic and professional studies, thus helping to forge the link between theory and practice?

Academic Study in a College of Education

In colleges academic study has been traditionally associated with the main subject, its central concern being the 'personal development' of the student.[1] When the revised course for the Teacher's Certificate was introduced in 1949 the main subject was conceived 'primarily for its value in the personal development of the student, and not necessarily having any direct connection with his teaching work'.[2] Its professional relevance was recognized for secondary specialist teachers in 1963,[3] but it has continued to have very little professional significance for the primary student-teacher.

This conception of the main subject has led to some unfortunate results. In many cases courses have been modelled on the traditional pattern of the university honours school, thus investing the main subject with a status that has tended to separate academic and professional studies. But why must the idea of academic study be limited to the main subject? Furthermore, in a teacher education curriculum might it not be more appropriate to view academic study as an integral part of professional study? In which case, perhaps the idea of 'personal development' might embrace both types of study and not be limited to the main subject. Let us examine these questions in greater detail.

First, what do we understand by the concept 'person'? This is, of course, an enormous philosophical problem, but I would suggest that central to the idea of a person is man's capacity to reflect on himself as a person and to grasp the relationship between himself and the world. In other words, a person is a centre of consciousness whose awareness gradually develops into a deeper understanding of the different modes of thought and feeling that constitute the basis of our civilization. The notion 'personal development' partly implies that man's simplistic view of the world is refined and widened as he builds up elaborate conceptual structures and learns to make more sophisticated discriminations in his experience. As his understanding is transformed he develops certain qualities of mind, values and beliefs as to what is worthwhile, and he learns to evaluate his actions according to rational principles. A stage is reached when he can formulate intentions, make responsible choices and use reason in acting and judging. This quest for reasons and justifications gradually 'frees' a person from external authority, and the central concern becomes the search for truth and the development of a personal autonomy based on reason.

But, although rational autonomy is central to a student's personal development, other qualities are also important if he is to gain the balanced personality and the breadth of maturity so necessary for teaching. For instance, emotional stability, self-control, personal insight, the ability to establish interpersonal relationships, and sensitivity towards other people's interests and feelings—all form part of the development of a person, but they will hardly be acquired through the study of one main subject, or even through a range of subjects. In order to develop such qualities, not only a variety of teaching experiences with children is needed, but also the college itself should create an 'open' atmosphere and present a wide range of liberalizing experiences aimed at maturing the students as people, broadening their outlook and giving them a realistic understanding of the world outside teaching.

The central point in this argument is that the concept 'personal development' embraces a range of qualities that cannot be realized through the academic study of a main subject alone. Some, in fact, could not be developed through the curriculum at all, as they are more likely to be the result of social and emotional experiences outside college or within the student-staff community.

Undoubtedly, the objective systematic study of an area of knowledge pursued in depth for intrinsic reasons can contribute to the personal development of the student. Such study should enable a person to reflect critically on the logic and nature of his discipline, to master the appropriate validation procedures and to view its distinctive characteristics in relation to other forms of understanding. This submission of the mind to the rigorous canons of a form of thought not only brings a student to the point of asking fundamental questions concerning the value, standards, methods, assumptions and scope of the activity, but it also enables him to build up a personal commitment to the discipline so that it becomes significant to him. This care and respect for a form of thought can contribute to both the mastery of the subject and to the development of personal knowledge within that discipline. Academic study, then, can give students the opportunity to develop such qualities of mind as rationality, autonomy, judgment, imagination, critical and logical thought, but these qualities can be understood only in relation to a specific area of knowledge.[4] Aesthetic judgment, for instance, is logically distinct from moral or mathematical judgment. Imagination in history is different in kind from imagination in literature or biology. Since no discipline can develop these qualities *in general*, the experiences gained from studying one main subject can contribute only to a small part of a student's personal development. In other words, if a student is 'to realize himself as a person' he needs to submit himself to a far wider range of experiences than can be provided by the academic study of one main subject. In fact, the idea of 'academic study' need not be confined to one subject; whilst the notion 'personal development' embraces a variety of experiences which include both academic and professional study, thereby cutting across all aspects of the college curriculum, as well as extending outside it.

This view can be substantiated if we examine what is entailed in 'learning how to teach'. Essentially, teaching is an ability which involves developing a critical skill in order to give an intelligent performance. This skill is guided by a body of theoretical knowledge, rules and principles, which needs to be acquired through academic study. But building up technical competence through training and critical practice is also a disciplined activity, in which a student learns how to make independent judgments, to formulate intentions and to make rational choices. In other words, rational autonomy, which is a central feature of 'personal development', can be achieved not only through reading a main subject, but also through the academic study of education and in the practical activity of teaching. Further, moreover, good teaching requires the ability to gain a relationship with children based on respect for each child as a person and on impartiality. Any constraints imposed on children must be capable of rational justification. In fact, the very concept 'teaching' implies respecting a pupil's judgment, welcoming critical discussion and being prepared to offer rational explanations. These qualities, attitudes and values associated with good teaching must be considered essential to the personal development of the student, but they are acquired through the study of educational theory partnered by school experience. This example of 'learning how to teach' should help to demonstrate the absurdity of limiting the idea of 'personal development' to the study of a main subject.

The concept 'personal development', then, embraces both academic and professional study, and includes those experiences gained from extra-curricular activities and the life of the institution in general. The notion of 'academic study' is limited in its scope, but not so narrow as to be identified solely with the main subject. For instance, it also has a significant role in the theoretical study of education and in certain elements of the curriculum courses. Furthermore, as the college of education has a professional objective, all academic study ought to be conceived within a professional frame of reference; it ought not to be pursued for intrinsic reasons alone.[5]

Professional Study in a College of Education

Essentially, the idea of 'professional study' implies a partnership between a body of theoretical knowledge and the practical skills which are needed for achieving competence in a particular profession. The development of these critical skills, acquired through training, must be informed by theoretical knowledge gained through academic study, otherwise a student is unlikely to build up the authority, autonomy and breadth of understanding which are so fundamental to the making of responsible professional judgments. Professional study is not limited to the development of technical competence in a narrow, specific task, for the partnership between theoretical and practical knowledge is central to the idea of initiating students into a profession, rather than training them for a trade or occupation. Therefore a balance between theory and practice needs to be maintained in professional study but, as much of the theoretical knowledge must be acquired through academic study, there also needs to be a close relationship between academic and professional studies.

In a college of education, with its dual function of educating and training students for a profession, certain conflicts and tensions are likely to arise in the process of achieving this balance. For instance, study for its intrinsic value as opposed to that with an instrumental end; theoretical as distinct from practical activity; differences in understanding between schools and colleges, as well as between subject and education departments. Individual lecturers and students will also be involved in a constant inner dialogue between academic and professional commitments. Nevertheless, a sharp dichotomy need not arise if a close link be established between academic and professional studies. This should be feasible if it is understood that academic study need not stand in isolation, but is in fact an integral part of professional study.

Let me illustrate this central point of the argument with reference to the main subject, educational theory and the curriculum courses in colleges.

(a) *Main subject*

If students are to engage in academic study without sacrificing the idea of professional relevance, I would suggest that the main course contain four interrelated elements–the nature of the discipline; the place of the subject in education; the psychological aspects of learning the subject; and the subject matter for schools and teaching methods. Perhaps it ought to be pointed out that the criterion of 'professional relevance' in this context must not be interpreted solely in relation to the immediate practical needs of the classroom, for it can have a much wider connotation. Viewing the term in its broader sense, I would maintain that the interaction between academic and professional studies ought to be central to the main course, with the intention that disciplined theoretical study will impinge on educational practice. The sort of programme envisaged would necessitate joint planning and some team-teaching, thereby establishing strong lines of communication between subject and education departments, and between schools and colleges. Each component will be examined now in greater detail.

The academic study of the nature of the discipline would form the central core of the main course, thus providing the very necessary conceptual foundations prior to the examination of the more directly professional aspects of teaching the subject. What does such study entail? If a student is to learn to formulate concepts and to communicate in a discipline, knowledge of the basic facts, definitions, terms and symbols within the particular form of thought is essential.[6] In history, for example, knowledge of specific dates, events, persons, places and sources of information is necessary for the beginning of historical thinking. However, knowledge must not remain at this inert level, for a thorough grasp of the discipline can be achieved only by building up an understanding of the central concepts and fundamental ideas of the particular mode of thought.[7] Such concepts as causality, time, development and revolution in history, or form, rhythm, style and balance in aesthetics enable us to structure our experience in an economical and connected way.[8] This emphasis on economy of experience is important because if certain basic concepts and principles represent the main characteristics of a discipline, a sound knowledge of these ideas is more valuable than the learning of a large number of specific items of information. In other words, the understanding need not be gained from an encyclopaedic body of content, for the academic study may be concentrated on a few paradigm cases selected to exemplify the main features of the discipline. From these particular examples generalization may be drawn to show the range of understanding within the area of knowledge. This approach to a subject would also try to demonstrate that each mode of thought contains its own distinctive conceptual structure which binds it into a whole and defines its boundaries of enquiry. Furthermore, considerable emphasis would be placed on learning how to use the appropriate technical procedures for evaluating the truth of facts, principles and statements within the discipline.[9] In history, for instance, students would learn how historians collect evidence and how they use it to reconstruct and to interpret the unique events of the past. Through the handling of primary sources students would learn how to validate historical evidence, judge conflicting interpretations, detect bias and distinguish truth. This sort of academic study is not only of logical significance, but its professional relevance can be demonstrated. For example, the subject matter studied can be selected to illustrate the main features and procedural skills of the discipline, as well as having relevance to the learning and teaching of history in schools. In addition, emphasis can be placed on making explicit the conceptual inter-connections between areas of knowledge, thus building up a student's perspective, which is not only of intrinsic value but also essential for successful interdisciplinary work with children.

Although the critical examination of the nature of the discipline would form the centre of the main course, the other three components would enable the students especially to focus their academic study within a professional frame of reference. For instance, it is of central concern to explore the justification for including the area of knowledge in the school curriculum. What is the place of the subject in education? What are the principles underpinning the teaching of the subject in schools? This particular area of the main course needs to be related to a range of wider questions concerning educational justifications and curriculum objectives.

It could be argued that the logical and psychological aspects of learning and teaching are at the core of the work in a college, and thus the third component in the main course ought to be devoted to the psychological features that influence the learning of the particular subject. This must not be divorced from the education course, which needs to examine such relevant areas as human development, concept formation, the learning of different types of content, motivational factors in learning, educational technology, and evaluation procedures and testing. It is vital that these psychological principles be applied to the learning of the particular subject being studied.

In the fourth component of the main course, the theoretical aspects of learning and teaching the subject need to be related more directly to educational practice. For instance, students must have a grasp of the criteria that can be used for determining the selection of subject-matter, so that they have a realistic idea of the content appropriate for children at the different stages of their development. Finally, they need to build up a capital of practical knowledge including the teaching methods, classroom activities and audio-visual material that enable children to learn the facts, concepts, skills and procedures of the particular discipline.

(b) *Educational theory*

The aim of educational theory is to initiate students into those areas of knowledge which contribute to the formulation of principles that guide the solving of practical educational problems. Throughout this chapter it has been assumed that education can be studied academically, but the validity of this contention depends on the status and nature of educational theory. Until comparatively recently there has been a tendency to conceive of education as an autonomous unitary discipline.[10] But it is more logical to view it as a 'focus or meeting-place of disciplines',[11] or a 'practical theory',[12] which draws on a number of distinct areas of knowledge that contribute towards the making of practical judgments as to what ought to be done in educational practice. It is logically impossible for the contributory disciplines to be subsumed under a general unitary mode of understanding, because each area contains its own concepts, truth criteria and validation procedures. For instance, sociology and psychology use empirical evidence and statistical techniques to describe and explain certain states of affairs. Philosophy, on the other hand, is concerned with questions of meaning, patterns of argument and criteria of justification.

This differentiated approach has enabled the study of education, through its distinctive disciplines, to be truly academic. The formulation of rational principles must be achieved through the objective systematic study of the contributory disciplines. At some stage of the education course these must be pursued for intrinsic reasons; the emphasis must be on impartial academic enquiry, with its high concern for cognitive content, search for truth and the mastery of procedural skills. This sort of study must play an important part in the personal education of the student, but its professional significance must not be overlooked. The content must be selected not only to exemplify the main features of philosophy, psychology and so on, but also for its professional relevance.

The aim of philosophy of education during initial training, for example, is not to cultivate miniature philosophers, whose commitment to the discipline makes them blind to the realities of teaching in the classroom. What philosophy can do is to give students the conceptual apparatus with which to reflect critically and clearly on the nature of their job. By examining the use of language and the meaning of educational concepts, and through raising fundamental questions, seeking justifications, and challenging the basis of assumptions and value-judgments, a student-teacher can begin to build up an important dimension of his professional life.

The theoretical study of education, then, must be allied to a growing knowledge of children and schools. It must inform the teacher's professional judgments and actions, and provide him with a sufficient range of concepts and skills with which to evaluate the new ideas and research findings of educational innovation.

(c) *Curriculum courses*

Curriculum courses form the third area in which academic study can play a significant role in the professional education of the student. At present most students, from infant to junior/secondary, are exposed to a multiplicity of curriculum courses which act as an introduction to the basic content of a range of subjects, as well as giving insight into how to teach them. Many of these courses are of a factual nature, whilst others concentrate on teaching methodology; in many cases they are criticized as being superficial and intellectually undemanding, which is probably inevitable in the time available. This raises the fundamental question about the purpose and function of a curriculum course, and whether there is a need for subject lecturers, education tutors and teachers to work together more closely in order to draw out the logical and psychological aspects of teaching and learning a subject.

I would suggest that if academic and professional studies be conceived as an integral whole, the structure of a curriculum course might comprise three distinct and yet interrelated elements: conceptual, factual content and methodological. The conceptual aspect would emphasize fundamental ideas and principles, as it would focus on the nature of the particular activity and the justification for teaching it. The content would be selected to illustrate some of the salient features of the discipline, thus enabling students to move with confidence within a subject without having to digest an amorphous mass of inert information. The methodological element would concentrate on the procedural skills of the discipline, allied to the practical knowledge of how to teach. Thus a combination of the conceptual and factual elements acquired through academic study would contribute to the personal education of the student, whilst all three components would be examined within a professional context thereby satisfying the criterion of relevance. Central to such a course is the recognition of the need to draw out the conceptual and practical relationships between educational theory, subjects and practice, because I would maintain that it is this knowledge of concepts, principles, structures, validation procedures and the ability to grasp interconnections that form the essence of 'professionalism'.

But although this section has tried to demonstrate that academic study in a college of education may be conceived as an integral part of professional study, this is not to neglect the more practical dimension of an initial training programme. Professional study must also aim at building up a high level of technical expertise, but these skills required for teaching must be gained through training and practical experience. If teaching be characterized as a critical skill or 'intelligent capacity',[13] rather than a mere habit, the professional training of teachers must be concerned with both theoretical and practical knowledge, which entails the intelligent application of rules. The idea of an intelligent action suggests that a person is thinking in a purposive way; not only is his action related to an end but the appropriate means are being employed to achieve the end. An intelligently executed operation also involves judgment and understanding, thus enabling the person to give a critical performance. This means that when a person is being trained, he must learn how to apply the relevant rules and principles using critical judgment. Such judgment is built up through intelligent critical practice, when one performance is modified by previous performances.

In the process of learning how to teach, some valuable technical knowledge can justifiably be passed on at college prior to practice; for instance, certain general rules of procedure, management techniques and possible plans of action. Nevertheless, Ryle makes the significant point that 'we learn *how* by practice, schooled indeed by criticism and example, but often quite unaided by any lessons in the theory'.[14] This implies that formal explanations of the principles of teaching are likely to have far less effect on students than periods of critical practice accompanied by theoretical advice from college staff and teachers in a practical context. Informed and guided school experience is central to the development of the practical knowledge required in teaching, but both the judgment and style implicit in good teaching may be best acquired by students in continuous contact with a competent performer. There is much to be said for the adoption of a 'teacher-tutor' system in schools, because as a student needs to identify himself with some model, it is preferable that the exemplar be an expert, so that there is less chance of reverting to some unsatisfactory earlier model.[15] In such a system the essential interaction between the theoretical and practical knowledge could be drawn out by the teacher as well as by the college tutor. The supervisory role of the teacher-tutor would have to be made explicit, and he would need to be specially trained to assist in the planning of student programmes, to guide students in the evaluation of their work and to help them develop the ability to make informed practical judgments in different teaching situations. Not only would students benefit from such a scheme, but it would also enable a closer relationship between schools and colleges to be established, and encourage teachers to reflect critically on both the nature of their task and on the rationale underlying the many practical and theoretical activities that take place in a classroom.

This closer link between schools and colleges must assume central importance in the future, not only in the course of initial training but also during the probationary year and subsequent in-service training. At present, as Professor Perry demonstrates,[16] there is a tendency for some schools to *retrain* probationary teachers along lines which conflict with the principles underlying initial training; in fact, there is a gulf in communication between the different sectors engaged in the training of teachers. Perry crystallizes the difference between initial training and school retraining when he states that 'whereas the initial system attempts to cultivate a self-critical appraisal of teaching, the school retraining ... regards teaching as a static and routine situation for which permanent solutions in terms of teaching method are applicable'.[17] If this state of affairs is to improve, initial training, probationary year and in-service training must be viewed as a continuum based on a body of rationally determined and agreed principles. This is essential if we are to achieve a cohesive knowledge-based profession. Implicit in this idea of professionalism is the need for teachers to gain the authority, autonomy and breadth of understanding which will enable them to make informed professional judgments. This strengthens the case for student-teachers to receive a general education which must be gained through academic study conceived within a professional frame of reference.

The Objectives of the College of Education Curriculum

In the light of the preceding analysis of academic and professional studies are we any nearer to formulating the general principles that might guide the planning of a college curriculum? Can we make explicit a set of objectives that are both logically consistent and that reflect the growing professional, technological and social demands confronting the teacher in schools? I would suggest that the following objectives are central to any teacher education programme, but in order to be effective guides for action they would have to be reformulated in more specific operational terms and then applied to the relevant components of the college curriculum.

(a) To develop, through academic study, an understanding of those areas of knowledge which have professional significance. Such study would involve:

(i) Grasping the central facts, concepts and principles of the particular disciplines that the student intends to teach.

(ii) Understanding the specific organization or distinctive structure of key concepts within each area of knowledge.

(iii) Learning how to use the different methods of enquiry and verification procedures within each form of thought.

(iv) Gaining a broad perspective through grasping the conceptual interconnections between different modes of understanding.

(v) Developing such qualities of mind as logical and critical thought, creative imagination, judgment, rationality and autonomy in relation to each area of knowledge.

(b) To develop, through academic study, an understanding of educational theory which will inform professional judgments and actions. In this area of the curriculum the emphasis would be on:

(i) The formulation of rational principles acquired through the objective study of the contributory disciplines.

(ii) The examination of the principles underlying curriculum planning and evaluation in schools.

(iii) Understanding the factors that affect the development of children.

(iv) Acquiring a sensitive awareness of the dynamic relationship between school and society.

(v) Building up hte knowledge and attitudes that will enable students to understand the demands and pressures arising from our advanced industrial and pluralistic society.

(vi) Gaining an understanding of the diffuse nature of the teacher's role.

(vii) Developing an occupational consciousness by sharpening the student's political, economic and sociological insights.

(viii) Fostering a flexibility of mind and a constructive, critical attitude towards educational innovation, which will enable students to evaluate the changing conception of teaching and research findings in the light of rational criteria.

(c) To develop, through training and practical experience, the technical skills necessary for the achievement of professional competence in teaching. This area of activity would stress:

(i) The acquisition of a range of skills focused on teaching methods, appropriate learning experiences and motivation in the classroom, management and organizational expertise, evaluation procedures and record keeping.

(ii) The development of the student's critical skill, judgment and powers of reflection, thus giving him the ability to modify his performances in the light of growing experience.

(d) To develop, through academic and professional study, a knowledge of the relationship between the logical and psychological aspects of learning and teaching at the different stages of children's development.

In conclusion, I would stress that the overall aim of a college curriculum is to produce teachers who, by virtue of their education and training, are sensitive, self-confident, self-critical and adaptable persons with the ability to work as a link in a complex differentiated teaching force. If this aim were realized, perhaps we could achieve a knowledge-based profession, thus raising the academic and professional standards of the teacher, which would enhance his status in society and benefit future generations of children.

References

1 Ministry of Education (1957), *The Training of Teachers*, Pamphlet No. 34, London, H.M.S.O., p. 6.

2 University of London Institute of Education (1951-2), *Regulations and Syllabuses for the Teacher's Certificate*, pp. 7-8, para. 8.

3 University of London Institute of Education (1963-4), *Regulations and Syllabuses for the Teacher's Certificate*, p. 10, para. 8.

4 Hirst, P. H. (1965), 'Liberal education and the nature of knowledge' in Archambault, R. D., ed., *Philosophical Analysis and Education*, Routledge & Kegan Paul, pp. 116-21.

5 Higginbotham, P. J. (1969), 'The concepts of professional and academic studies in relation to courses in institutes of higher education (particularly colleges of education)' in *British Journal of Educational Studies*, Vol. XVII, No. I, February, p. 57.

6 Bloom, B. S. (1965), *Taxonomy of Educational Objectives*, Vol. I, 'Cognitive domain', New York, D. McKay, p. 62.

7 Bruner, J. S. (1960), *The Process of Education*, Cambridge, Harvard University Press, p. 23.

8 Bruner, J. S. (1962), *On Knowing*, Cambridge, Harvard University Press, p. 120.

9 Bloom, B. S., ed., *ibid.*, pp. 72-3.

10 Taylor, W. (1964), 'The organization of educational studies', in *Education for Teaching*, No. 65, November, p. 29.

11 Peters, R. S., 'Comments on a discipline of education', in Walton, J. and Kuethe, J. L. (1963), eds., *The Discipline of Education*, Wisconsin Press, p. 17.

12 Hirst, P. H. (1966), 'Educational theory', in Tibble, J. W., ed., *The Study of Education*, Routledge & Kegan Paul, pp. 47-57.

13 Ryle, G. (1963), *The Concept of Mind*, Peregrine, p. 42.

14 Ryle, G., *ibid.*, p. 41.

15 For instance see:

Baker, J. R. (1967), 'A teacher co-tutor scheme', in *Education for Teaching*, No. 73, pp. 25-30.

Caspari, I. E., and Eggleston, J. (1965), 'A new approach to supervision of teaching practice', in *Education for Teaching*, No. 68, November, pp. 42-52.

Hollins, T. H. B. (1969), *Another Look at Teacher Training*, Leeds University Press, pp. 18-19.

Taylor, W. (1969), *Society and the Education of Teachers*, Faber, pp. 163-4.

Tibble, J. W. (1966), 'Practical work training in the education of teachers', in *Education for Teaching*, No. 70, May, pp. 49-54.

16 Perry, L. R. (1969), 'Training', in *Education for Teaching*, No. 79, p. 6.

17 Ibid., p. 8.

26. Some Case Studies of Teacher Preparation

G. Brown

Source: *British Journal of Teacher Education*, vol. I, No. I, January 1975.

Course design in teacher education has evolved on particular assumptions about the relationship between the elements of college courses (including teaching practice) on the one hand and teaching performance in the classroom on the other. Brown presents some empirical evidence relating the two new techniques of microteaching and interaction analysis to teaching performance.

Teacher Performance and Teaching Education

The training of teachers was institutionalized in Britain in or about 1798. By 1815 a pattern of concurrent training and school experience had been established as the mode of training for elementary school teachers (Dent, 1971). Later in the century education as a field of study emerged (Tibble, 1967), and later still university departments of education were developed to train graduates for elementary, and eventually secondary schools (Tuck, 1973).

Arguments about the merits of concurrent and consecutive courses of teacher preparation and of the study of education itself have persisted (Ross, 1973) but until recently school experience has been assumed to be the only way to develop teaching skills. The McNair report (1944) had recommended college-based as well as school-based practice and some colleges continued to use demonstration lessons up to the nineteen-fifties. But for the majority of students, college was where you learnt about education and schools were where you learnt about teaching. It was not until the early nineteen-sixties that any new methods of training emerged. Two of these, microteaching and interaction analysis have become accepted features of many courses in the United States (Ward, 1970; Flanders, 1970), Australia (Turney, 1973) and developing countries (UNESCO, 1972). In Britain, the Universities of Stirling and Ulster have pioneered and researched these new modes of training.

Microteaching

Of these methods microteaching is the more widely used. It may be described as a scaled down teaching encounter in which a student teaches a small group of pupils for up to fifteen minutes. The proceedings are usually videorecorded and supervisors and students discuss the playback. The student then may teach the lesson again to another group of pupils and again discuss it. Each cycle of microteaching may be devoted to a particular skill or cluster of skills such as *explaining, questioning* or gaining *pupil participation*. Usually the initial and final cycles are devoted to global teaching. The earlier forms of microteaching focused almost exclusively upon performance, the newer programmes such as the one at Ulster (Brown, 1975) are based upon a model of teaching and it gives training in planning, performance and the perception of teaching. Classes of ten pupils are now used and the videorecord shows both teachers and pupils.

The present Ulster programme grew out of some of the research reported in this paper and from discussions with tutors, teachers, students and pupils. Rating schedules were adapted and developed for use in the programme. The items of three of these, the Stanford Teacher Competence Appraisal Guide (STCAG) (Allen & Ryan, 1969), the Lesson Appraisal Guide (LAG) and the pupil rating form are given in Figure 1.

Interaction Analysis

The other widely used new approach, interaction analysis, may be described as the systematic observation of teachers and pupils in teaching situations. There are now well over a hundred systems in existence (Simon & Boyer, 1970; Rosenshine & Furst, 1973).

The most widely used system was developed by Flanders (1970) and it is generally known as FIAC. It has ten basic categories. Teacher-pupil verbal exchanges are categorized every third second. Matrices of successive pairs of categorizations and various ratios such as *teacher talk: pupil talk* may be computed. The basic categories are also given in Figure 1.

Both FIAC and rating schedules were used in the case studies reported here. Rating schedules were used to *evaluate* changes in teaching performance and FIAC to *describe* changes in performance. FIAC was also used as a method of training in some of the microteaching experiments.

Despite the new developments reported here and the long history of teacher preparation, there has been a surprising neglect of the central question: To what extent does training change a student's teaching performance? In fact most research in teacher education has been concerned with selection (for example, Lovell, 1951; Butterworth, 1968) and prediction (Warburton, Butcher & Forest, 1963; Cortis, 1968). This research appears to have grown out of a concern to improve the quality of entrants to teacher preparation courses rather than to improve the quality of teacher preparation. This paper grew out of a concern for the latter. It describes studies carried out at Ulster which explore some of the historically based assumptions about teacher preparation. At the outset, it is stressed that the findings are illuminating rather than generalizable, exploratory rather than definitive. The paper does not review the field of teacher education although it does give guidelines for further enquiry (for example, Taylor,

Rating schedules

STCAG (7 point scales)

1 Clarity of aims
2 Appropriateness of aims
3 Organization of lesson
4 Selection of content
5 Selection of materials
6 Beginning the lesson
7 Clarity of presentation
8 Pacing the lesson
9 Pupil participation and attention
10 Ending the lesson

LAG (7 point scales)

1 Gaining pupil's attention
2 Explanation and narration
3 Giving directions
4 Asking and adapting questions
5 Recognizing difficulties of understanding
6 Voice and speech habits
7 Non-verbal cues
8 Encouraging appropriate responses
9 Holding pupils' attention
10 Gaining pupil participation
11 Pupil control
12 Use of aids
13 Allocation of time for pupil learning
14 Lesson planning and structure

Pupil ratings (5 point scales)

1 Understanding of lesson
2 Teacher's organization
3 Interest of lesson
4 Did the lesson pass quickly?
5 Teacher friendliness
6 Teacher liveliness
7 Teacher helpfulness
8 Enjoyment of talking with teacher
9 Enjoyment of lesson activities
10 How much did the teacher talk?
11 Did you like the lesson?

FIAC (categorized every third second)

1 Accepts feeling
2 Praises
3 Uses pupils' ideas
4 Asks questions
5 Lectures
6 Gives directions
7 Criticizes, justifies authority
8 Pupil response
9 Pupil initiated response
10 Silence or confusion

RYAN'S X_0, Y_0, Z_0 scales (7 point scales)

X_0 Responsible, businesslike, systematic *v.* Unplanned, slipshod
Y_0 Warm, understanding, friendly *v.* Aloof, egocentric, restricted
Z_0 Stimulating, imaginative, enthusiastic *v.* Dull, boring, unimaginative

FIGURE 1.

1969; Stones & Morris, 1972*a*; and Lomax, 1973) and blueprints for action (for example, Smith, 1969; Brown, 1975). It does not attempt an exegesis of the nature of teaching (see Hirst, 1971) nor recite a litany on teacher effectiveness (see Tittle & Handle, 1970). Instead it focuses on some studies of training and teaching performance.

Case 1. Teaching Performance and the Study of Education

It is usually assumed that the study of education changes attitudes and the classroom performance of teachers. However the evidence suggests that attitude change during three-year teacher preparation courses is more a consequence of teaching experience than the study of the subject 'Education' (Morrison & McIntyre, 1967; McIntyre & Morrison, 1967). Correlation between teaching practice assessments and marks gained in theory of education papers are usually significant but low (Warburton *et al.*, 1963; Cortis, 1968). Such studies merely tell us that students who do well in written examinations also tend to do well in practical examinations and vice versa, and there is little direct evidence on the effects of studying education (Collins, 1964).

In an attempt to obtain some evidence about the effect of the study of education on teaching the performance of students who had studied education was compared with those who had not. The subjects were two groups of eight second-year female under-graduates. One group had studied English and education for three semesters, the other had studied English only. Neither group had any teaching experience. All the students were of a similar age and academic performance.

The students were asked to prepare and teach fifteen-minute lessons to one of two groups of five nine-year-old pupils who had experienced micro-teaching for half a day per week for a semester. The pupils rated the students' performance on the pupil rating guide immediately after the lesson and the students rated their own performances before and after viewing a videorecording of the lessons. Two independent observers also rated the videotaped lessons in counterbalanced order. They were not aware that some students had studied education and some had not.

An analysis was made of the various ratings and the FIAC categories of the two groups of students. No statistically significant differences were detected between the self-ratings of the two groups either before or after viewing their videorecordings. Similarly, no significant differences were detected between the pupils' ratings of the two groups or the ratings of the independent observers. The only differences in the FIAC categories were in the relatively rare categories of 1 (accepts feeling) and 7 (criticizes). There was, however, considerable variation in the ratings of all students and the mean ratings of the students taking education were higher than those of the other group. Thus the initial variations in ratings of teaching performance may be swamping the effect of the study of education. Nevertheless the trend of the mean was in favour of the education students, which suggests that replication with increased sample sizes might yield interesting and significant results. In addition it is possible that English, which is concerned in large measure with human relationships, is more akin to education than other subjects and other comparisons with a wider range of university subjects is recommended.

The case for the study of education *per se* obviously does not solely rest upon its effects on initial teaching performance. Nonetheless, it is salutary that its effect seemed so marginal. Before dismissing it as a chance event, teacher educators should repeat the experiment in their own institutions and consider the implications of their results.

Case 2. Teaching Performance and School Experience

In Case 1 the differential effects of the study of education and an academic subject on teaching performance were reported. The second considers the effect of school experience on teaching performance and examines the efficacy of concurrent and consecutive methods of training. There is little direct evidence on either of these two questions. One study by Wragg (1973) found that the teaching styles of 100 postgraduate certificate students changed after one term in school according to lesson analyses made using an interaction category system. Another by Brown & Duggan (1971) found that over a period of six years concurrent degree students obtained more As and Ds on teaching practice. They also found that head teachers' and tutors' ratings of cooperativeness favoured the concurrently trained group.

The questions asked in this study were: Does school experience affect teaching performance? and Do concurrent training and consecutive training differ in their effects on teaching performance? The subjects in the study comprised eighteen PGCE students, twenty-seven final (fourth) year concurrent degree students and thirty-two third-year concurrent degree students. All the students took the same range of units in specialist subjects. The students' teaching performance was assessed by supervisors and teacher-tutors at the beginning and end of school experience on the Lesson Appraisal Guide. The students were familiar with the Guide and it may be reasonably assumed that it gave them a set of objectives in their teaching. Their performance during the last two weeks of the practice was assessed globally on a 15 point scale and on the modified form of Ryan's X_0, Y_0, and Z_0 scales (Ryan, 1960) by the supervisors who observed them on at least three separate occasions.

Analysis of the data found that change scores by supervisors and teacher-tutors were very highly statistically significant with the exception of one item. This was the supervisors' rating of the allocation of time for pupil learning. Thus as far as supervisors and teacher-tutors were concerned, all the students improved substantially throughout school experience. The answer to the first question would seem to be, then, that there is a difference in student performance following school experience, unless the difference in scores is entirely due to rater expectations of improvement.

A comparison of the PGCE and final year post-primary students (concurrent) sheds some light on the second question (see Table 1). The final mark favoured the concurrent degree students and so did their ratings on the Ryan scales and the global assessment. The pattern of teacher-tutors' ratings is less clear but it should be remembered that they only see students working in their schools. Correlations between supervisors and teacher-tutors, however, were highly significant (Table 2).

These results do not give definitive answers to the questions. Teacher-tutors saw students only in their own schools and supervisors saw students in several schools. Teacher-tutors in secondary schools were predominantly graduates and they marginally preferred the intending teachers labelled 'graduates'. Supervisors preferred concurrent students who had been initiated into education over a period of three to four years. These students are more likely to have acquired, or at least to manifest, their supervisors' notions of 'good' teaching. Interestingly enough supervisors and primary school teachers involved in this study seem to have common notions of good teaching. On the other hand subject-based specialists in post-primary schools had different ideas of good teaching and good teachers.

Clearly this study is only a straw in the wind and very many questions about the effect of different approaches to teaching practice are still to be answered. However the results give no support at all to the James report's predilection for consecutive training. Perhaps we should devote more attention to fostering shared notions of good teaching and improving *both* modes of training.

One additional factor in the present study seems of interest. The PGCE students had five weeks more teaching practice than the concurrent students. However, the latter had eight sessions of microteaching. In view of the fact that the concurrent students did better on the whole than the consecutive ones the possibility that microteaching helped student development more effectively than additional teaching practice cannot be ruled out.

In order to test this possibility, correlations between microteaching performance and teaching practice score were run. Correlations between microteaching score and teaching practice mark were significant even after a period of 12 months. To investigate the effects of microteaching on performance in school, a multiple stepwise regression equation was computed based on supervisors' scores throughout microteaching and the final score in teaching practice. This equation enabled comparisons to be made between the final score in teaching experience and the different elements in the microteaching programme. The multiple R (0.65) was highly significant ($P = < 0.01$). The best single predictors of teaching practice performance were the microteaching elements concerned with learning the

Table 1 PGCE *v.* Concurrent courses

	Mean Scores				
	PGCE	*4th year secondary*	*4th year primary*	*3rd year secondary*	*3rd year primary*
Teaching practice marks (15 point scale)	7.47	9.13*	9.83**	9.43**	10.33**
Supervisor's ratings					
Initial LAG†	51.67	60.33	50.10	50.40	69.15**
Final LAG†	60.12	67.67	70.40	57.60	74.85**
X_0 (businesslike *v.* slipshod)†	4.74	5.33	5.50	4.50	5.86*
Y_0 (warm, friendly *v.* aloof, egocentric)	4.58	5.33	5.08	5.10	5.79*
Z_0 (imaginative *v.* unimaginative)††	4.47	5.00	4.67	4.00	5.79**
Total of X_0, Y_0, Z_0††	13.84	15.80	15.08	13.60	17.43**
Global rating (15 point scale)††	7.58	9.67*	9.58	8.00	10.57**
Teacher's ratings					
Initial LAG	67.50	64.14	69.70	70.27	75.93
Final LAG†	77.33	69.21	79.20	77.73	85.07
X_0 (businesslike *v.* slipshod)†	6.06	5.21	6.10	5.42	6.36
Y_0 (warm, friendly *v.* aloof, egocentric)	5.94	5.43	6.00	5.75	6.71
Z_0 (imaginative *v.* unimaginative)††	5.59	4.79	5.90	5.08	6.43
Total of X_0, Y_0, Z_0††	17.53	15.43	18.00	16.25	19.50
Global rating (15 point scale)	9.94	9.07	10.40	8.58	11.50

* = 0.05 significant difference from PGCE group; ** = 0.01 significant difference from PGCE group.

† = *F* ratio significant at 0.05 level; †† = *F* ratio significant at 0.01 level.

Table 2 Supervisor-teacher correlations

Initial rating on Lesson Appraisal Guide	0.44**
Final rating	0.29*
X_0	0.24
Y_0	0.45**
Z_0	0.47**
Total X_0 Y_0 Z_0	0.43**
Global 15 point scale	0.50**

n = 54 cases

* = 0.05; ** = 0.01 significance levels.

skill of fostering pupil participation and with welding the various microteaching skills together at the end of training. The last cycle of microteaching was one of the poorest predictors. This result may be explained in this study by the fact that the last cycle took place immediately after a vacation, since rest pauses boost skill performance. The regression equation yielded 14 predicted teaching practice marks within one mark of the actual ones and 20 cases within two of the actual scores. These results suggest that microteaching does have an effect upon subsequent teaching in schools.

Case 3. Microteaching and Teaching Performance

The results of the previous experiment suggested that five weeks additional school experience in a PGCE programme was no better than eight sessions of microteaching in a concurrent programme. Obviously one cannot legitimately conclude from this that microteaching is better than school experience. School experience as a mode of training is fraught with difficulties (Stones & Morris, 1972*b*). A student teacher has to get his pupils to learn whilst he learns to teach. He has to master planning, organization and control techniques. to learn the meanings of various verbal and nonverbal signals given by his pupils and to anticipate their moves and difficulties. At the same time in schools a student learns, almost unavoidably, about interpersonal relationships in the staff room and the social organization of the school. Students may spend several weeks in classrooms yet they may be helped by a supervisor perhaps only once per week and even less frequently by the class teacher (Shipman, 1965, 1966; Cope, 1971). The students are unlikely to be given objectives for learning to teach. They have to rely largely upon their own intuitions about a lesson and, of course, they cannot see themselves teach, nor study at leisure their pupils' responses.

In contrast, microteaching with videotape gives the students opportunities for practice and feedback under controlled conditions. They can learn to plan, perform and observe their pupils and they receive guidance and support from their supervisors and their peers every time they teach. Their practice teaching is distributed rather than massed, their tasks are clearly specified and the feedback they receive is related to a record of their own performance and not someone else's assertions about it.

One would therefore, on *a priori* grounds, expect microteaching to be more efficient than school experience during the *initial* stages of learning to teach. The work of Kallenbach & Gall (1969), Allen & Fortune (1966), Berliner (1969) and Borg (1970) show that different microteaching programmes with videotaped feedback do yield changes in teaching. In the study reported below teaching performance ratings and FIAC measures of the students' first and last microteaching experience were compared. At the same time it was decided to explore the nature of teaching as a

Table 3 Mean microteaching scores (STCAG)

	Microteaching cycle							
	1	2	3	4	5	6	7	8
Group 1 (n = 27)								
Self-rating Mn	48.15	43.22	42.93	47.44	61.89**	53.33	58.74**	62.93**
Supervisor's rating Mn	52.33	52.15	50.26	52.92	65.96**	57.74	58.85	62.44**
Group 2 (n = 16)								
Self-rating Mn	55.58	44.56**	45.69**	54.25	61.32**	S	52.25	54.69**
Supervisor's rating Mn	56.00	47.94	44.81	53.90	70.75**	S	61.00	68.69**
Independent Mn	58	–	–	–	–	–	–	63.69**

All scores expressed as percentages.

Probability levels * = 0.05; ** = 0.01. Asterisks refer to significant differences from cycle 1.

Observers rated first and last lessons only.

S = university strike during cycle 6.

set of social skills.

Argyle (1970) has persuasively argued that teaching is a set of social skills and social skills are closely analogous to psycho-motor skills. If this is true it follows that practice with feedback should change performance and the pattern of scores obtained in microteaching should not be dissimilar from skill learning curves. In order to examine this view empirically the pattern of microteaching scores was analysed.

Table 3 sets out the main results for two groups of students. The scores were derived from the rating schedules. The students' self-ratings, supervisors' ratings and independent observers' ratings all yielded significant changes. Trend analysis confirmed these findings. Group 2's results were incomplete because of a strike in the university (one of the many hazards of long-term experiments). Analyses of individual items of the independent observers' rating schedules yielded significant differences on clarity of presentation and the beginning and ending of lessons.

Supervisors, independent observers and the students themselves considered that teaching performance had improved through microteaching experience. This does not of course prove the point. To do that one would need to randomly assign large numbers of students to a control and experimental group and compare their pre and post scores. This was not possible in the undergraduate programme.

The pattern of scores in both experimental surveys shows that there was a relatively high score in the first microteaching cycle followed by a

Table 4 Training in FIAC: Main change scores

	Mean change scores		
	FIAC trained group	*Control group*	*Overall*
Evaluation of standard lesson on STCAG	−14.0	−5.0	−9.5**
Performance ratings on STCAG†			
Self†	20.13	−1.9	9.10**
Supervisor	14.73	11.63	12.69**
Independent observer	8.00	3.38	5.69**
FIAC variables			
1. Accepts feelings†	3.94	1.22	2.58
2. Praises	−1.26	−2.86	−2.06
3. Uses pupils' ideas††	0.68	4.99	2.83**
4. Asks questions	−8.04	−11.03	−9.54**
5. Lectures	0.0	0.54	2.28
6. Gives directions	8.41	5.53	6.07**
7. Criticizes, justifies authority	0.39	0.04	0.52
8. Pupil response†	−12.42	−23.89	−18.15**
9. Pupil initiated response	8.49	12.78	10.64**
10. Silence	2.00	8.33	5.17**

* = 0.05, ** = 0.01 levels of significance.
† = 0.05, †† = 0.01 levels of significance of F ratios for differences between FIAC and control group.
Overall mean change scores tested using correlated t.

decline and a gradual rise to the fifth week followed by a decline towards the end of the term and then a sharp rise after the rest pause of four weeks. The pattern is certainly not dissimilar to that of a skill curve. It is based upon supervisors' and students' self-assessments so expectations may have partly influenced the results. None the less, expectations are unlikely accurately to mirror skill learning curves, so one can tentatively conclude that the pattern of scores gives some support to the view that teaching is a set of social skills which is learnt.

Case 4. Interaction analysis training, feedback and teaching performance

Some experiments on interaction analysis and school experience carried out at Temple University and elsewhere (see Amidon & Hough, 1967) indicated that training in FIAC improved teaching performance. This puzzled the present writer, for FIAC training is a form of discrimination training which is therefore more likely to change perceptions of teaching rather than performance. In order to investigate the question two studies were carried out. The first was based upon training in FIAC and the other upon feedback derived from FIAC category counts.

The sample of the first study comprised sixteen students. They rated a lesson by an unknown student on the Stanford Teacher Competence Appraisal Guide at the beginning and end of the microteaching semester. Half of the students were then given six hours' training in FIAC. At the end of their training their Scott (1955) inter observer reliability coefficients were all above 0.7, indicating close agreement on ratings. The remaining eight students were shown and discussed the same videotaped lessons which the FIAC group used for training. None of the students' own lessons were used and they all agreed (with relief) not to read any works on interaction analysis during the semester. Supervisors' and independent observers' pre and post ratings were also available. The supervisors knew nothing about FIAC and did not know which student had had FIAC training.

Table 4 sets out the main results. Both groups changed significantly their evaluation of the specimen lesson after their experience of microteaching but the changes in the FIAC trained group were significantly different from the control group's changes. On rating their own lessons the FIAC group considered that they had improved, although it must be recognized that this may be partly because they had invested six hours' intensive training in interaction analysis. Supervisors' and independent observers' ratings were not significantly different for the two groups but they both increased significantly their rating scores for both groups between pre and post ratings. The point must be reiterated, however, that there may be wide variations in teaching abilities that mask some of the effects of training.

Examination of the FIAC change scores found significant differences on categories 1, 3 and 8. The greatest changes were by the control group not the experimental group. Thus one may tentatively conclude the training in FIAC sharpened perceptions of teaching performance but did not improve the perceivers' own performance. As Tuckman, McCall & Hyman (1969) suggest of their experiment 'it appears that previous work with this system has produced changes based on something other than just teaching the system of interaction analysis to students' (p. 617).

In the second study nineteen graduate students who were involved in four microteaching sessions were split into two groups. One group received feedback of the FIAC categories related to their teaching immediately after a fifteen minute microteaching session and the categories were used in supervisory discussions. The other group received no FIAC feedback in the supervisory sessions following microteaching. As before all the students rated a standard videotaped lesson using the STCAG at the beginning and end of the three weeks of microteaching. They also rated two of their own microlessons, one as a pre test and one as a post test on the STCAG.

Table 5 Feedback from FIAC: Main change scores

	Mean change scores		
	FIAC feedback group	*Control group*	*Overall*
Evaluation of standard lesson on STCAG	0.18	−4.57	2.19
Performance ratings			
Self (STCAG)	8.64	3.63	6.13*
Peer (STCAG)†	9.91	3.50	6.70**
Supervisor (STCAG)	11.91	5.13	8.52*
Independent observer (LAG)[1]	12.18	2.33	7.26*
Independent observer (X_0, Y_0, Z_0 scales)†	2.64	0.00	1.32
FIAC variables			
1. Accepts feeling	−0.37	−1.30	−0.84
2. Praises	2.01	0.87	1.44**
3. Uses pupils' ideas††	3.19	−1.01	1.00
4. Asks questions	3.74	3.03	3.39
5. Lectures	−9.87	−2.89	−6.40
6. Gives directions	−3.45	0.67	−1.39
7. Criticizes, justifies authority†	0.20	−0.53	−0.16
8. Pupil response	5.85	6.68	6.26
9. Pupil initiated response	−1.80	−6.59	−5.27
10. Silence	−11.67	1.12	−5.27

* = 0.05, ** = 0.01 levels of significance.
[1] = 0.1, † = 0.05, †† = 0.01 levels of significance of *F* ratios.
Overall mean change tested using correlated *t*

Ratings of the pre and post test lessons were also obtained from the students' peers, from supervisors and from independent observers. Table 5 sets out the main results.

In this study there were no significant changes in the experimental and control groups' perceptions of the standard lesson. Peer supervisor and independent observer ratings yielded a significant difference in favour of the group receiving FIAC feedback. The FIAC group also significantly increased their use of pupils' ideas, and there were fewer silences during their teaching. They slightly increased their use of criticism whereas the control group's use of criticism declined. Taken together the two studies revealed that training in FIAC is associated with changes in perceptions of teaching and only marginally with changes in performance, whereas feedback from FIAC is associated with changed performance but only marginally with changed perception. The overall results of the studies give further support to the view that microteaching with videotape feedback changes students' teaching performance.

However we must bear in mind that neither the samples nor the time devoted to microteaching in the two studies were identical. One should therefore be cautious in generalizing the results to other students and other courses.

Summary and conclusions

The experiments described in this paper are the modest fruit of one experimenter's labour. They are by no means vigorous, statistically pure experiments of high generalizability. None the less the results do suggest the following conclusions:

Teaching is a *learnt* activity not simply a function of personality. Training in teaching skills does change and improve performance. Microteaching appears to be an efficient method of training. Feedback from interaction analysis changes performance but not perceptions of teaching, and training in interaction analysis changes perceptions of teaching but only marginally affects performance. The academic study of education *per se* appears to have no more (or less) effect than the study of English Literature in the first teaching performance of students. Concurrent students are rated more favourably by their supervisors than consecutive (PGCE) trained students but the latter are marginally favoured by teacher-tutors.

All of the above studies require further replication and exploration. They are presented here in the hope that other researchers and course designers will improve upon them and in so doing improve their programmes of teacher preparation.

References

ALLEN, D. W. & FORTUNE, J. C. (1966) An analysis in microteaching: New procedures in teacher education in *Microteaching: A Description* (California: Stanford University School of Education).

ALLEN, D. W. & RYAN, K. A. (1969) *Microteaching* (New York: Addison-Wesley).

AMIDON, E. J. & HOUGH, J. B. (eds) (1967) *Interaction Analysis: Theory Research and Applications* (New York: Addison-Wesley).

ARGYLE, M. (1970) *Social Interaction* (Methuen).

BERLINER, D. C. (1969) *Microteaching and the Technical Skills Approach to Teacher Training,* Technical Report No. 8 (California: Stanford University).

BORG, W. R., KELLEY, M. L., LANGER, P. & GALL, M. D. (1970) *The Minicourse: A Microteaching Approach to Teacher Education* (New York: Collier-Macmillan).

BROWN, G. A. (1975) *Microteaching: Programme of Teaching Skills* (Methuen, in the Press).

BROWN, G. N. & DUGGAN, E. P. (1967) A comparison of concurrent and postgraduate courses in education in the University of Keele Department of Education 1965-70. Mimeo.

BUTTERWORTH, A. B. (1968) Some predictors of the final teaching marks of students in a college of education. M.Ed. dissertation, University of Manchester.

COLLINS, M. (1964) Untrained and trained graduate teachers: A comparison of their experiences during the probationary year. *Brit. J. Educ. Psychol.* **34**, 75-84.

COPE, E. (1971) *School Experience in Teacher Education* (University of Bristol School of Education).

CORTIS, G. A. (1968) Predicting student performance in colleges of education. *Brit. J. Educ. Psychol.* **38**, 115-22.

DENT, H. C. (1971) An historical perspective, in S. Hewett (ed.) *The Training of Teachers: A Factual Survey* (University of London Press). See also chapters by Tibble and Logan.

FLANDERS, N. A. (1970) *Analysing Teaching Behaviour* (New York: Addison-Wesley).

HIRST, P. H. (1971) What is teaching? *J. Curriculum Studies*, **3**, 5-18.

KALLENBACH, W. W. & GALL, M. D. (1969) Microteaching versus conventional methods in training elementary intern teachers. *J. Educ. Res.* **63**, 136-41.

LOMAX, D. (ed.) (1973) *The Education of Teachers in Britain* (New York and Chichester: J. Wiley).

LOVELL, K. (1951) An investigation into factors underlying teaching ability in primary and secondary schools with a view to improving the methods of selecting potential teachers. M.A. thesis, University of London.

McINTYRE, D. & MORRISON, A. (1967) The educational opinions of teachers in training. *Brit. J. Soc. Clin. Psychol.* **6**, 32-7.

McNAIR (Chmn) (1944) *Teachers and Youth Leaders* (HMSO).

MORRISON, A. & McINTYRE, D. (1967) Changes in opinion about education during the first year of teaching. *Brit. J. Clin. Psychol.* **6**, 161-3.

ROSENSHINE, B. & FURST, N. (1973) The use of direct observation to study teaching, in R. W. Travers (ed.) *Second Handbook of Research on Teaching* (Chicago: Rand McNally).

ROSS, A. M. (1973) The development of teacher education in colleges of education in D. Lomax (ed.) *The Education of Teachers in Britain* (J. Wiley).

RYAN, D. G. (1960) *The Characteristics of Teachers* (Washington, D. C: American Council of Education).

SCOTT, W. A. (1955) Reliability of content analysis: The case of nominal coding. *Public Op. Qtly* **19**, 321-5.

SHIPMAN, M. D. (1965) Personal and social influences on the work of a teacher training college. Ph.D. thesis, University of London.

SHIPMAN, M. D. (1966) The assessment of teaching practice. *Educ. for Teaching,* **70** (May), 28-31.

SIMON, A. & BOYER, G. E. (eds) (1967, 2nd ed. 1970) *Mirrors for Behaviour: An Anthology of Classroom Observation Instruments* (Philadelphia: Research for Better Schools).

SMITH, B. O. (1969) *Teachers for the Real World* (American Association of Colleges for Teacher Education).

STONES, E. & MORRIS, S. (1972*a*) *Teaching Practice, Problems and Perspectives* (Methuen).

STONES, E. & MORRIS, S. (1972*b*) The assessment of practical teaching. *Educ. Research* **14**, 111-14.

TAYLOR, W. (1969) Towards a policy for the education of teachers. Colston Papers **20**, (London: Butterworth).

TIBBLE, J. W. (ed.) (1967) *The Study of Education* (Routledge & Kegan Paul).

TITTLE, C. J. & HANDLE, C. (1970) Research on practical experience in teacher education: A selected annotated bibliography, Report No. 70-12 (Office of Institutional Research and Program Evaluation, City University, New York).

TUCK, J. P. (1973) From day training college to university department of education, in D. E. Lomax (ed.), *The Education of Teachers in Britain* (J. Wiley).

TUCKMAN, B. W., McCALL, K. M. & HYMAN, R. T. (1969) The modification of teacher behaviour: Effects of dissonance and coded feedback. *Amer. Ed. Rsch. Jnl* **6**, 607-19.

TURNEY, C. (1973) *Microteaching, Research Theory and Development* (Sydney University Press).

UNESCO (1972) Selected project reports on new methods and techniques in teacher training (Division of Methods and Materials, UNESCO, Paris).

WARBURTON, F. W., BUTCHER, H. J. and FORREST, G. M. (1963) Predictory student performance in a university department of education. *Brit. J. Educ. Psychol.* **33**, 68-79.

WARD, B. E. (1970) A survey of microteaching in secondary education programmes of all N.C.A.T.E. accredited colleges and universities, Memo. No. 70 (Stanford Center for Research and Development in Teaching).

WRAGG, E. C. (1973) A study of student teachers in the classroom, in G. Chanan (ed.), *Towards a Science of Teaching* (NFER).

INDEX